Book **G**

Specific Skill Series

Working Within Words

Richard A. Boning

Fifth Edition

MW00774918

SRA/McGraw-Hill
Columbus, Ohio

SRA/McGraw-Hill

*A Division of The **McGraw·Hill** Companies*

Printed in the United States of America.

Send all inquiries to:
  SRA/McGraw-Hill
  8787 Orion Place
  Columbus, OH 43240-4027

ISBN 0-02-687927-1

  6 7 IPC 02 01

PURPOSE:
WORKING WITHIN WORDS helps pupils put sounds and other word elements to work to determine word meaning. Many units in WORKING WITHIN WORDS develop understandings about sound-symbol (phonic) associations. Other units treat letter combinations, syllabication, roots and affixes, accent patterns, compound words, longer words, and spelling changes caused by adding endings.

FOR WHOM:
The skill of WORKING WITHIN WORDS is developed through a series of books spanning ten levels (Picture, Preparatory, A, B, C, D, E, F, G, H). The Picture Level is for pupils who have not acquired a basic sight vocabulary. The Preparatory Level is for pupils who have a basic sight vocabulary but are not yet ready for the first-grade-level book. Books A through H are appropriate for pupils who can read on levels one through eight, respectively. **The use of the *Specific Skill Series Placement Test* is recommended to determine the appropriate level.**

THE NEW EDITION:
The fifth edition of the *Specific Skill Series* maintains the quality and focus that has distinguished this program for more than 25 years. A key element central to the program's success has been the unique nature of the reading selections. Nonfiction pieces about current topics have been designed to stimulate the interest of students, motivating them to use the comprehension strategies they have learned to further their reading. To keep this important aspect of the program intact, a percentage of the reading selections have been replaced in order to ensure the continued relevance of the subject material.

In addition, a significant percentage of the artwork in the program has been replaced to give the books a contemporary look. The cover photographs are designed to appeal to readers of all ages.

SESSIONS:
Short practice sessions are the most effective. It is desirable to have a practice session every day or every other day, using a few units each session.

SCORING:
Pupils should record their answers on the reproducible worksheets. The worksheets make scoring easier and provide uniform records of the pupils' work. Using work-sheets also avoids consuming the exercise books.

To the Teacher

It is important for pupils to know how well they are doing. For this reason, units should be scored as soon as they have been completed. Then a discussion can be held in which pupils justify their choices. (The Integrated Language Activities, many of which are open-ended, do not lend themselves to an objective score; thus there are no answer keys for these pages.)

GENERAL INFORMATION ON *WORKING WITHIN WORDS*:

The units are of two types: concept builders and functional exercises. The concept units focus the reader's attention on common patterns and parts of words. Each generalization is built step-by-step on the structure of previously formed concepts. The functional exercises either follow the concept units or are contained within them. They provide the reader with many immediate and repeated experiences with words involving particular patterns or principles. Sentence settings are typical for the pupils' level; often the choices offered are new words.

As WORKING WITHIN WORDS progresses through different word elements there is constant reinforcement. The more elementary booklets focus on phonic elements such as consonant sounds, consonant substitutions, blends, phonograms, and vowel sounds. As the level of difficulty increases, the emphasis shifts to syllabication, prefixes, suffixes, and roots.

A unit-by-unit list of concepts developed in this book is found on page 64.

INSTRUCTIONS:

Minimal direction is required. Pupils' attention must be drawn to the answer choices. In the concept units only two or three answer choices are offered. In the units that provide application of understandings, four to nine answer choices are offered, providing more experiences with words of a particular pattern. In units which offer an *F* choice, the *F* stands for NONE. This means that none of the choices makes sense in that particular setting.

RELATED MATERIALS:

Specific Skill Series Placement Tests, which enable the teacher to place pupils at their appropriate levels in each skill, are available for the Elementary (Pre-1–6) and Midway (4–8) grade levels.

About This Book

In written words, letters stand for sounds. A reader **decodes** a word the way a spy decodes a secret message. If you know the sounds that letters stand for, you can begin to unlock the secret message of a word.

Knowing the sounds of a word is only a beginning. Just as a secret message may have many parts, a word may have more than one part, too. In order to read and understand a word, you need to understand the parts of the word.

Word parts can be added to words to make new words with new meanings. For example, if you *like* someone, you find that person *likable*. Someone else, however, may *dislike* that same person. How did the suffix *able* and the prefix *dis* change the meaning of *like*? How would the prefix *un* change the word *likable*?

Some words are related to each other in both meaning and spelling because they have a common *root*. A *root* is often not a word by itself, but it is part of many different words. The root *vis*, for example, comes from a Latin word that means "to see." These words are all formed from one common root: *vision*, *visual*, *invisible*. How are their meanings related?

In this book, you will study many words. You will learn to recognize the parts of words and patterns in words. Then you will use what you have learned. As you unlock the meanings of the words in this book, you will be practicing the skills of a master decoder!

1. There is a common root in _____.

   (A) vapor   (B) intermission   (C) divisor
   vault   miniature   dividend

2. There is a common root in _____.

   (A) dominate   (B) individualist   (C) misjudge
   dormitory   division   juvenile

3. There is a common root in _____.

   (A) jovial   (B) triumphant   (C) divider
   violet   turpentine   divisive

4. So far all the correct answers have the root _____.

   (A) dyn   (B) div   (C) domin

5. How many of the following words have the same root?

   divide   dizzy   divisible
   donation   doubtless   individually

   (A) two   (B) three   (C) four

6. The word that means **to separate into parts** is _____.

   (A) divisive   (B) divide   (C) individually

7. The word that means **a single person, animal,** or **thing** is _____.

   (A) divider   (B) dividend   (C) individual

8. The word that means **separable** is _____.

   (A) individualist   (B) divisible   (C) divine

9. The word that means **the legal ending of a marriage** is _____.

   (A) dividing   (B) divisor   (C) divorce

10. From these examples, we can tell that the root **div** means _____.

    (A) divine   (B) separate   (C) death

1. There is a common root in ———.

    (A) sedate
       sentiment

    (B) versatile
       conversation

    (C) paramount
       philosopher

2. There is a common root in ———.

    (A) revert
       convert

    (B) quantity
       radiant

    (C) redundant
       calculable

3. There is a common root in ———.

    (A) correspond
       character

    (B) charade
       sclerosis

    (C) anniversary
       universal

4. So far all the correct answers have the roots ———.

    (A) vers/vert

    (B) duc/duct

    (C) tens/tend/tent

5. How many of the following words have the same root?

    introvert
    subvert
    (A) four

    convert
    villain
    (B) five

    vitamin
    vertically
    (C) six

6. The word that means **to turn upside down** is ———.

    (A) versatile

    (B) invert

    (C) advertisement

7. The word that means **to turn away or turn aside** is ———.

    (A) anniversary

    (B) vertical

    (C) avert

8. The word that means **to change one's religion, party, or belief to another** is
   ———.

    (A) convert

    (B) universal

    (C) university

9. The word that means **able to be turned opposite or backward** is ———.

    (A) subvert

    (B) reversible

    (C) diversify

10. From these examples, we can tell that the roots **vers** and **vert** mean ———.

    (A) turn

    (B) feel/be aware of

    (C) believe/trust

1. There is a common root in _____.

   (A) obese   (B) sentiment   (C) tragic
       pudgy   sentinel   chastise

2. There is a common root in _____.

   (A) flabby   (B) affect   (C) insensible
       obscure   alter   nonsense

3. There is a common root in _____.

   (A) petite   (B) resentment   (C) vacillate
       buxom   sentry   vertical

4. So far all the correct answers have the roots _____.

   (A) sens/sent   (B) vert/vers   (C) viv/vit/vict

5. How many of the following words have the same root?

   insensate   senseless   sense
   supersensory   sensitive   sensory
   (A) four   (B) five   (C) six

6. The word that means **easily affected or influenced** is _____.

   (A) resentment   (B) sentry   (C) sensitive

7. The word that means **an attitude** or **tender feeling** is _____.

   (A) sentence   (B) sentiment   (C) nonsense

8. The word that means **one whose job it is to be aware, alert, and on guard** is _____.

   (A) senseless   (B) sentinel   (C) resent

9. The word that means **to make unaware or less sensitive in feeling** is _____.

   (A) dissent   (B) desensitize   (C) supersensory

10. From these examples, we can tell that the roots **sens** and **sent** mean _____.

   (A) test/prove   (B) feel/be aware of   (C) equal

1. There is a common root in _____.

    (A) arbitrate
       aquarium

    (B) magnetic
       proponent

    (C) activate
       reaction

2. There is a common root in _____.

    (A) gentility
       melancholy

    (B) actor
       enact

    (C) harmonica
       melodious

3. There is a common root in _____.

    (A) stupendous
       stratosphere

    (B) activism
       activator

    (C) petunia
       preposition

4. So far all the correct answers have the root _____.

    (A) val

    (B) tele

    (C) act

5. How many of the following words have the same root?

    actual   react   enact
    activate   actor   transact

    (A) four

    (B) five

    (C) six

6. The word that means **the process or state of doing** is _____.

    (A) reactionary

    (B) react

    (C) action

7. The word that means **a person who acts in stage plays** is _____.

    (A) transact

    (B) actor

    (C) enact

8. The word that means **to act as the result of some influence or event** is _____.

    (A) react

    (B) actual

    (C) transaction

9. The word that means **to manage or carry on business** is _____.

    (A) actress

    (B) actualize

    (C) transact

10. From these examples, we can tell that the root **act** means _____.

    (A) not

    (B) large

    (C) do

1. There is a common root in _____.

   (A) thermostat   (B) verdict   (C) comfort
       barricade   circumstance   forte

2. There is a common root in _____.

   (A) fortress   (B) annual   (C) marines
       fortify   dungeon   induct

3. There is a common root in _____.

   (A) proverb   (B) convert   (C) fortitude
       merchant   endeavor   fortification

4. So far all the correct answers have the root _____.

   (A) fort   (B) centr   (C) norm

5. How many of the following words have the same root?

   camouflage   comfort   fortitude
   frankfurter   fortify   comfortable

   (A) four   (B) five   (C) six

6. The word that means **that in which one excels** is _____.

   (A) fortitude   (B) forte   (C) fortis

7. The word that means **to soothe or console** is _____.

   (A) comfort   (B) fortis   (C) fortification

8. The word that means **to strengthen** is _____.

   (A) fortunately   (B) comfortable   (C) fortify

9. The word that means **moral strength** or **endurance** is _____.

   (A) comfort   (B) fortitude   (C) fortress

10. From these examples, we can tell that the root **fort** means _____.

    (A) four   (B) strong   (C) fight

UNIT 6
Root Concepts and Practice—sid, sed, ses

1. There is a common root in _____.

   (A) routine   (B) session   (C) terminal
       rummage   obsess   minnow

2. There is a common root in _____.

   (A) sheath   (B) obstruct   (C) resident
       shampoo   stroll   subside

3. There is a common root in _____.

   (A) scripture   (B) sedentary   (C) testament
       sergeant   sedate   temporary

4. So far all the correct answers have the root(s) _____.

   (A) sid/sed/sess   (B) tempor   (C) sub

5. How many of the following words have the same roots?

   residential   obsession   subsiding
   session   sedation   sedentary

   (A) four   (B) five   (C) six

6. The word that means **a sitting or a meeting of a court council or legislature** is
   _____.

   (A) session   (B) sedation   (C) residential

7. The word that means **to become less active** or **settle down** is _____.

   (A) residency   (B) sedate   (C) subside

8. The word that means **any matter that settles to the bottom of a liquid** is _____.

   (A) sediment   (B) obsessed   (C) residence

9. The word that means **a person living in a place permanently** is _____.

   (A) sedentary   (B) sedimentary   (C) resident

10. From these examples, we can tell that the roots **sid, sed,** and **sess** mean _____.

    (A) sit/settle   (B) old/tired   (C) fight

11

1. There is a common root in _____.

   (A) **exorbitant**
      flagrant
   (B) **masquerade**
      duplicity
   (C) **progress**
      transgress

2. There is a common root in _____.

   (A) **hierarchy**
      phonogram
   (B) **aggressive**
      regressive
   (C) **conveyor**
      rejuvenate

3. There is a common root in _____.

   (A) **ponderous**
      picturesque
   (B) **gradual**
      grade
   (C) **capillary**
      botanical

4. So far all the correct answers have the roots _____.

   (A) **gress/grad**
   (B) **gnos/gnom**
   (C) **mit(t)/mis(s)**

5. How many of the following words have the same roots?

   egress
   transgress
   (A) **four**
   aggressive
   ingress
   (B) **five**
   congress
   digress
   (C) **six**

6. The word that means **to step beyond or over a limit or boundary** is _____.

   (A) **progress**
   (B) **transgress**
   (C) **congress**

7. The word that means **step, move, or go backward** is _____.

   (A) **ingress**
   (B) **egress**
   (C) **regress**

8. The word that means **changing little by little or step by step** is _____.

   (A) **gradual**
   (B) **graduate**
   (C) **grade**

9. The word that means **to wander** or **to step away from the main topic or purpose** is _____.

   (A) **retrogression**
   (B) **progressive**
   (C) **digress**

10. From these examples, we can tell that the roots **gress** and **grad** mean _____.

   (A) **take/seize**
   (B) **step**
   (C) **hear**

UNIT 8
Root Concepts and Practice—ven

1. There is a common root in ———.
   (A) narrative   (B) eventual   (C) seminary
       capture   convention   integrity

2. There is a common root in ———.
   (A) intervene   (B) parentage   (C) sinuous
       convenient   pitiful   technology

3. There is a common root in ———.
   (A) abstinence   (B) vehement   (C) advent
       abundant   veterinary   prevent

4. So far all the correct answers have the root(s) ———.
   (A) scrib/script   (B) vag   (C) ven

5. How many of the following words have the same root?
   convene   circumvent   invention
   adventure   eventual   convention
   (A) four   (B) five   (C) six

6. The word that means **a meeting** or **a gathering** is ———.
   (A) advent   (B) convention   (C) convenient

7. The word that means **a building that houses women who live together and devote their lives to religion** is ———.
   (A) prevent   (B) advent   (C) convent

8. The word that means **happening at some indefinite future time** is ———.
   (A) convene   (B) circumvent   (C) eventual

9. The word that means **to come between** is ———.
   (A) intervene   (B) invention   (C) supervene

10. From these examples, we can tell that the root **ven** means ———.
    (A) water   (B) lead   (C) come

1. There is a common root in _____.

   (A) peculiar
   centennial

   (B) conduction
   educt

   (C) sinister
   ceremonious

2. There is a common root in _____.

   (A) memorial
   cordial

   (B) supervisor
   correspondence

   (C) educate
   reduction

3. There is a common root in _____.

   (A) glandular
   gallantry

   (B) introduce
   reduce

   (C) voluminous
   voucher

4. So far all the correct answers have the roots _____.

   (A) duc/duct

   (B) stu/stit/sest

   (C) viv/vit/vict

5. How many of the following words have the same root?

   conduct
   induction

   viaduct
   deduct

   aqueduct
   introduction

   (A) four

   (B) five

   (C) six

6. The word that means **to kidnap** or **lead away by force** is _____.

   (A) abduct

   (B) conduct

   (C) deduce

7. The word that means **that which is taken away or subtracted** is _____.

   (A) reproduction

   (B) deduction

   (C) aqueduct

8. The word that means **to make acquainted** or **to make known** is _____.

   (A) viaduct

   (B) reduction

   (C) introduce

9. The word that means **to direct or transmit heat or electricity** is _____.

   (A) reproduce

   (B) conduct

   (C) reduce

10. From these examples, we can tell that the roots **duc** and **duct** mean _____.

    (A) lead

    (B) say/tell

    (C) write

UNIT 10
Root Concepts and Practice—mov, mot, mob

1. There is a common root in _____.

   (A) facetious moderator   (B) minuet dilemma   (C) motion motive

2. There is a common root in _____.

   (A) movement remove   (B) realist sacred   (C) anthracite agitation

3. There is a common root in _____.

   (A) repulsive skeptical   (B) dazzle mezzanine   (C) mobile mobilize

4. So far all the correct answers have the root(s) _____.

   (A) cred   (B) mov/mot/mob   (C) mort

5. How many of the following words have the same root?

   | motor | demote | motion |
   | portage | promote | mortal |

   (A) four   (B) five   (C) six

6. The word that means **a vehicle that carries its own engine and is used for travel on streets and highways** is _____.

   (A) mobile   (B) automobile   (C) demote

7. The word that means **a machine that turns electric power into motion** is _____.

   (A) motor   (B) mobility   (C) mover

8. The word that means **a moving picture** is _____.

   (A) promote   (B) mobilize   (C) movie

9. The word that means **to move or reduce to a lower rank** is _____.

   (A) demote   (B) motion   (C) movable

10. From these examples, we can tell that the roots **mov, mot,** and **mob** mean _____.

    (A) stop   (B) bend   (C) move

1. There is a common root in _____.

   (A) fugitive   (B) reflex   (C) seize
          inferior   circumflex   sentry

2. There is a common root in _____.

   (A) foyer   (B) reflector   (C) liable
          fossil   inflection   lynch

3. There is a common root in _____.

   (A) integrate   (B) furlough   (C) deflect
          granite   frankfurter   reflection

4. So far all the correct answers have the roots _____.

   (A) fac/fic   (B) flect/flex   (C) ject/jac

5. How many of the following words have the same roots?

   flexible   flexure   flexagon
   hibernate   deflection   reflect

   (A) four   (B) six   (C) five

6. The word that means **can be bent without breaking** is _____.

   (A) flexible   (B) deflect   (C) flexor

7. The word that means **to turn back** or **throw back** is _____.

   (A) flexible   (B) reflect   (C) circumflex

8. The word that means **a change in the tone or pitch of the voice** is _____.

   (A) flexibility   (B) reflection   (C) inflection

9. The word that means **any thing, surface, or device that throws back light, heat, or sound** is _____.

   (A) reflector   (B) flexuous   (C) inflexible

10. From these examples, we can tell that the roots **flect** and **flex** mean _____.

    (A) bend   (B) fight   (C) light

1. There is a common root in _____ .

    (A) tedious
       telescope

    (B) emphasis
       encounter

    (C) technician
       technique

2. There is a common root in _____ .

    (A) temporary
       tenement

    (B) technology
       technologize

    (C) choir
       chisel

3. There is a common root in _____ .

    (A) technicality
       technocracy

    (B) eclipse
       ebony

    (C) tarpaulin
       tangerine

4. So far all the correct answers have the root _____ .

    (A) terr

    (B) tech

    (C) surg

5. How many of the following words have the same root?

    technologist
    pyrotechnics

    technographic
    thermostat

    technically
    technocrat

    (A) four

    (B) five

    (C) six

6. The word that means **the skill of a composing artist, such as a musician, painter, sculptor, or poet**, is _____ .

    (A) technocrat

    (B) technique

    (C) technicality

7. The word that means **the science of the mechanical and industrial arts** is _____ .

    (A) technology

    (B) technolithic

    (C) technologist

8. The word that means **an expert in the details of a subject or skill, especially a mechanical one**, is _____ .

    (A) technician

    (B) technicalize

    (C) technograph

9. The word that means **having to do with the special facts of a science or art** is _____ .

    (A) pyrotechnic

    (B) technical

    (C) technocracy

10. From these examples, we can tell that the root **tech** means _____ .

    (A) people

    (B) art/skill

    (C) write

Word roots are word parts that form the base of many words. They are the main part of a word to which prefixes and suffixes are added. Like prefixes and suffixes, word roots have meanings of their own. Most word roots come from Latin and Greek. Look for a familiar word root when you see an unfamiliar word. If you know the meaning of the root, you just may be able to figure out the meaning of the word.

A. Exercising Your Skill

Have you ever watched young children with a pile of building blocks? They stack one upon another until the pile falls over. Then they do it again. Sometimes, after stacking three or four perhaps, they will look at their tower, and with a whoop or a squeal of laughter, they will knock the tower over. That, to them, is power.

Word roots and prefixes and suffixes are building blocks. We can put them together to build words. If we put the wrong ones together, the words fall apart—they mean nothing. But putting these blocks together in the right way builds us thousands of words. That is power, too.

Look at the columns of prefixes, word roots, and suffixes below. How many words can you build by combining them? On your paper, write the three columns of word parts. Draw lines from one column to another to show the parts that can be combined. Then list the words you made. You may be able to build some words by combining a word root with both a prefix and suffix, such as *reduction*. If you are not sure whether a certain combination is really a word, check the dictionary.

prefixes	word roots	suffixes
	vers/vert	
re	act	able/ible
con	flect/flex	ment
im/in	duc	tion/ion
	ven	

B. Expanding Your Skill

How did you do? Compare the list you made with your classmates' lists. Can you discover new words using these prefixes, word roots, and suffixes? Brainstorm with your classmates and add more prefixes and suffixes to your list. How many word blocks can you stack together and still build a word? What is the longest word you can build?

C. Exploring Language

Stories of all kinds are built of words and sentences. Stringing, or stacking, them together so they make sense is not always easy. You may not know what to say next or quite how to say it. That is when you bring in the tools that can help you. For example, if you get stuck trying to think of the right word, you can use a dictionary or a thesaurus for help.

Copy the paragraph below. The writer became stuck five times trying to come up with the right word. Use the word roots given as clues in the spaces, and write words that fit.

Hal turned over in bed. He felt a strange _(sens)_. But what? He _(grad)_ sat up and climbed out of bed. Then he _(gress)_ slowly to the window. As he raised the shade, a blinding brightness shone in on him. Hal _(act)_ by quickly _(vert)_ his eyes.

Sometimes you need help with a sentence rather than a single word. You are not sure what idea you want to express next. If you are writing a story like the one above, "what if" questions can be very good tools for getting your ideas flowing. Right now you are stuck with Hal standing at the window, feeling a little uneasy about the day. What happens next? Here is a "what if" question to get you started:

What if the brightness was not from the sun?

Write two more questions. Finish the story by answering the questions.

D. Expressing Yourself

Choose one of these activities.

1. Reports in newspapers are built around questions. The first paragraph in a news report answers all or most of the questions Who? What? Where? When? Why? How? Rewrite your story about Hal. Write it as a news report, giving only facts about what happened to Hal.

2. Write the opening paragraph of a story. In your paragraph, use five words whose roots you have learned in this book. When your paragraph is finished, copy it over, this time drawing blank lines in place of the five words. Below each blank line, write the root of the missing word. Now ask a classmate to read your paragraph and fill in the missing words. Did your classmate write the words that you had in mind? If not, do the new words fit just as well? How do they change the story?

3. Work with two or three classmates to "build" a story. Take turns supplying sentences. If someone gets "stuck" on his or her turn, the others can help by asking "what if" questions.

19

1. There is a common root in _____.

   (A) leisurely   (B) assimilate   (C) evacuate
        licentious   dissimilar   executor

2. There is a common root in _____.

   (A) simultaneous   (B) delegate   (C) testimony
        simulate   decadence   tremendous

3. There is a common root in _____.

   (A) pliable   (B) catalyst   (C) assembly
        pulsate   canopy   resemble

4. So far all the correct answers have the roots _____.

   (A) simil/simul/sembl   (B) plic/plex/ply   (C) fac/fic/fect

5. How many of the following words have the same root?

dissimilar	simile	sardonic
similitude	slaughter	similar

   (A) four   (B) five   (C) six

6. The word that means **an exact copy** is _____.

   (A) facsimile   (B) assembly   (C) semblance

7. The word that means **to imitate, act like,** or **look like** is _____.

   (A) simile   (B) simultaneous   (C) simulate

8. The word that means **to look like** or **to be like** is _____.

   (A) disassemble   (B) assimilate   (C) resemble

9. The word that means **unlike** or **different** is _____.

   (A) dissimilar   (B) similar   (C) resemblance

10. From these examples, we can tell that the roots **simil, simul,** and **semble** mean _____.

    (A) together/like   (B) move/yield   (C) shut/close

1. There is a common root in _____.

   (A) perfection   (B) sentimental   (C) fragile
      lecherous   sergeant   fragment

2. There is a common root in _____.

   (A) invalid   (B) fracture   (C) rampant
      rehearse   fraction   repulsion

3. There is a common root in _____.

   (A) faction   (B) transcribe   (C) fractious
      predicate   manual   fractional

4. So far all the correct answers have the roots _____.

   (A) fract/frag   (B) vid/vis   (C) pend/pens

5. How many of the following words have the same root?

fraction	frame	fantastic
fracture	fractional	fractious
(A) four	(B) five	(C) six

6. The word that means **a part broken off** is _____.

   (A) fragmentize   (B) fragile   (C) fragment

7. The word that means **easily broken** is _____.

   (A) fraction   (B) fractus   (C) fragile

8. The word that means **a part or portion of a whole** is _____.

   (A) fraction   (B) fracture   (C) fractious

9. The word that means **the breaking of a bone or cartilage** is _____.

   (A) fracture   (B) fraction   (C) fragile

10. From these examples, we can tell that the roots **fract** and **frag** mean _____.

    (A) stop   (B) break   (C) foot

1. There is a common root in _____.
   - (A) intrigue
     principal
   - (B) magnify
     magnitude
   - (C) salariat
     sonata

2. There is a common root in _____.
   - (A) maximum
     maximize
   - (B) manuscript
     licit
   - (C) adjacent
     mandate

3. There is a common root in _____.
   - (A) magnum
     magnificent
   - (B) glamorize
     captivate
   - (C) turmoil
     tutorial

4. So far all the correct answers have the roots _____.
   - (A) dent/dont
   - (B) magn/maxim
   - (C) vers/vert

5. How many of the following words have the same root?
   spectrum   magnify   magnum
   magnitude   mangle   magnificent
   - (A) four
   - (B) five
   - (C) six

6. The word that means **to increase the apparent size of** is _____.
   - (A) magnanimous
   - (B) magnify
   - (C) magnitude

7. The word that means **to increase to the greatest possible amount or degree** is _____.
   - (A) magnitude
   - (B) maximize
   - (C) magnificent

8. The word that means **great** or **grand** is _____.
   - (A) maximum
   - (B) magnetron
   - (C) magnificent

9. The word that means **great size** or **extent** is _____.
   - (A) magnitude
   - (B) magnum
   - (C) magnification

10. From these examples, we can tell that the roots **magn** and **maxim** mean _____.
    - (A) strong
    - (B) great/large
    - (C) small

UNIT 16
Root Concepts and Practice—vid, vis

1. There is a common root in _____.

   (A) perfection   (B) evident   (C) unison
          entertain   video   vestment

2. There is a common root in _____.

   (A) permanent   (B) visit   (C) willowy
          omission   vista   wrangle

3. There is a common root in _____.

   (A) invisible   (B) winterize   (C) prevent
          television   zoology   punctual

4. So far all the correct answers have the roots _____.

   (A) duc/duct   (B) vid/vis   (C) polis/polit

5. How many of the following words have the same root?

visualize	invisible	vocabulary
television	revise	vista

   (A) four   (B) five   (C) six

6. The word that means **clear to see** is _____.

   (A) indivisible   (B) evident   (C) visitation

7. The word that means **to picture in one's mind** is _____.

   (A) television   (B) provide   (C) visualize

8. The word that means **to go or come to see** is _____.

   (A) video   (B) revise   (C) visit

9. The word that means **unable to be seen** is _____.

   (A) vista   (B) provision   (C) invisible

10. From these examples, we can tell that the roots **vid** and **vis** mean _____.

    (A) hear   (B) see/look   (C) turn

UNIT 17
Root Concepts and Practice—puls, pel

1. There is a common root in _____.
   - (A) modernism
     panhandle
   - (B) expel
     propel
   - (C) zombie
     roustabout

2. There is a common root in _____.
   - (A) compulsion
     repulsion
   - (B) rampant
     sanction
   - (C) omnibus
     metrical

3. There is a common root in _____.
   - (A) snobbish
     solitary
   - (B) repel
     impel
   - (C) hormone
     foray

4. So far all the correct answers have the roots _____.
   - (A) voc/voke
   - (B) vers/vert
   - (C) puls/pel

5. How many of the following words have the same root?

repellent	dispel	invert
expel	propeller	membrane
(A) four	(B) five	(C) six

6. The word that means **to drive out** or **put out forcefully** is _____.
   - (A) dispel
   - (B) expel
   - (C) repellent

7. The word that means **to bring about by force** is _____.
   - (A) expulsion
   - (B) impulsion
   - (C) compel

8. The word that means **a device consisting of rotating blades for driving boats and airplanes forward** is _____.
   - (A) compulsion
   - (B) propeller
   - (C) repulsion

9. The word that means **to drive back** is _____.
   - (A) repulse
   - (B) propulsion
   - (C) propellant

10. From these examples, we can tell that the roots **puls** and **pel** mean _____.
    - (A) stand
    - (B) drive/push
    - (C) carry

1. There is a common root in ———.

    (A) ascribe   (B) photogenic   (C) manual

        spectacles   photography   social

2. There is a common root in ———.

    (A) spectrum   (B) postscript   (C) phosphorescent

        mandate   dismiss   phosphor

3. There is a common root in ———.

    (A) photosynthesis   (B) capacity   (C) overhaul

        photocopy   factual   parable

4. So far all the correct answers have the roots ———.

    (A) vers/vert   (B) spec/spic   (C) phot/phos

5. How many of the following words have the same root?

    photocell   photographer   facsimile

    photocopy   photographic   captor

    (A) four   (B) five   (C) six

6. The word that means **a picture made with a camera containing a film or glass plate which is sensitive to light** is ———.

    (A) photogenic   (B) photograph   (C) phosphor

7. The word that means **an abnormal or extreme fear or intolerance of light** is

    ———.

    (A) photocell   (B) photograph   (C) photophobia

8. The word that means **a person who takes photographs** is ———.

    (A) photosynthesis   (B) photographer   (C) photomural

9. The word that means **a particular element that is luminous in the dark** is

    ———.

    (A) phosphorus   (B) photogenic   (C) photocopy

10. From these examples, we can tell that the roots **phot** and **phos** mean ———.

    (A) write   (B) come   (C) light

1. There is a common root in _____.

   (A) receptacle
      reconnect
   (B) collaborate
      controversy
   (C) object
      rejection

2. There is a common root in _____.

   (A) projectile
      subject
   (B) program
      predacious
   (C) cavalier
      buttress

3. There is a common root in _____.

   (A) shallop
      shamrock
   (B) rejection
      dejection
   (C) lickerish
      appease

4. So far all the correct answers have the root(s) _____.

   (A) jur/jus
   (B) fac/fic/fect
   (C) ject

5. How many of the following words have the same root?

   eject   interject   injection
   trajectory   quintuplet   restrict
   (A) three   (B) four   (C) five

6. The word that means **a body or missile thrown forth by force** is _____.

   (A) object   (B) projectile   (C) inject

7. The word that means **to throw out** or **to expel** is _____.

   (A) subject   (B) eject   (C) dejected

8. The word that means **to discard** or **to throw away as worthless** is _____.

   (A) objection   (B) deject   (C) reject

9. The word that means **the apparatus that throws or projects images on a screen** is _____.

   (A) projector   (B) rejection   (C) subjection

10. From these examples, we can tell that the root **ject** means _____.

    (A) take/seize (B) foot   (C) throw

UNIT 20
Root Concepts and Practice—tract

1. There is a common root in _____.
   - (A) retract
     distract
   - (B) twister
     tyranny
   - (C) spectator
     tyrant

2. There is a common root in _____.
   - (A) attractive
     subtraction
   - (B) entertain
     exquisite
   - (C) obstinate
     elegance

3. There is a common root in _____.
   - (A) anticipate
     vicinity
   - (B) extracted
     detractor
   - (C) latent
     indemnity

4. So far all the correct answers have the root(s) _____.
   - (A) ped
   - (B) graph/gram
   - (C) tract

5. How many of the following words have the same root?
   tractable   abstract   contractual
   distract   victim   vomit
   - (A) three
   - (B) four
   - (C) five

6. The word that means **to draw or take away one's attention** is _____.
   - (A) tractor
   - (B) subtract
   - (C) distract

7. The word that means **to draw one's muscles together** is _____.
   - (A) protractor
   - (B) contract
   - (C) abstract

8. The word that means **to draw out or take out a tooth** is _____.
   - (A) attraction
   - (B) extract
   - (C) traction

9. The word that means **to withdraw one's statement** is _____.
   - (A) attract
   - (B) detract
   - (C) retract

10. From these examples, we can tell that the root **tract** means _____.
   - (A) draw/drag
   - (B) throw
   - (C) law

1. Think of what **comfort, fortify, fortress** mean. The root **fort** means _____.

   (A) four   (B) strong   (C) fight

2. Think of what **event, intervene, advent** mean. The root **ven** means _____.

   (A) voice/call   (B) break/burst   (C) come

3. Think of what **magnificent, maximum, magnify** mean. The roots **magn** and **maxim** mean _____.

   (A) turn   (B) small   (C) great/large

4. Think of what **propel, dispel, repulse** mean. The roots **puls** and **pel** mean _____.

   (A) drive/push   (B) death   (C) city

5. Think of what **reflex, deflect, reflection** mean. The roots **flect** and **flex** mean _____.

   (A) light   (B) need   (C) bend

6. Think of what **photograph, phosphorus, photocopy** mean. The roots **phot** and **phos** mean _____.

   (A) light   (B) heavy   (C) old

7. Think of what **extract, traction, contract** mean. The root **tract** means _____.

   (A) have/hold   (B) carry   (C) draw/drag

8. Think of what **technician, technology, technologist** mean. The root **tech** means _____.

   (A) know   (B) write   (C) art/skill

9. Think of what **avert, reverse, diversify** mean. The roots **vers** and **vert** mean _____.

   (A) believe/trust (B) turn   (C) death

10. Think of what **divisible, individually, divorce** mean. The root **div** means _____.

    (A) separate   (B) person   (C) divine

1. Think of what **session, resident, sedate** mean. The roots **sid, sed,** and **sess** mean _____.

   (A) sit/settle   (B) place/home   (C) stop

2. Think of what **sense, sensitive, sentinel** mean. The roots **sens** and **sent** mean _____.

   (A) write   (B) voice/call   (C) feel/be aware of

3. Think of what **fraction, fragile, fracture** mean. The roots **fract** and **frag** mean _____.

   (A) break   (B) stop   (C) foot

4. Think of what **visible, video, visualize** mean. The roots **vid** and **vis** mean _____.

   (A) write   (B) look/see   (C) carry

5. Think of what **reject, project, eject** mean. The root **ject** means _____.

   (A) look/see   (B) throw   (C) tell/say

6. Think of what **progress, regress, gradual** mean. The roots **gress** and **grad** mean _____.

   (A) step   (B) believe/trust   (C) look/see

7. Think of what **motion, mobile, movement** mean. The roots **mot, mob,** and **mov** mean _____.

   (A) stop   (B) move   (C) see

8. Think of what **activate, react, enact** mean. The root **act** means _____.

   (A) not   (B) do   (C) large

9. Think of what **deduction, conductor, introduce** mean. The roots **duc** and **duct** mean _____.

   (A) call/voice   (B) lead   (C) turn

10. Think of what **semblance, simultaneous, similar** mean. The roots **simil, simul,** and **sembl** mean _____.

    (A) write   (B) together/like   (C) have/hold

1. Some prefixes have more than one meaning. The prefix **under** can mean **beneath, below,** or **of a lower position or rank. Underground** means _____ the ground.

   (A) beneath   (B) above   (C) over

2. The word that means **an official of a government department ranking just below the official who is at the head** is _____.

   (A) underscore   (B) underside   (C) undersecretary

3. The word that means **bushes, shrubs, and small trees growing under larger trees in woods or forests** is _____.

   (A) underbrush   (B) underglaze   (C) underlie

4. The word that means **a person who can act as a substitute for an actor, actress, or any other regular performer** is _____.

   (A) underfoot   (B) understudy   (C) underclothing

5. From these examples, we can tell that the prefix _____ can mean **beneath, below,** or **of a lower position or rank.**

   (A) over   (B) under   (C) uni

6. The prefix **under** can also mean **not enough** or **below normal. Underestimate** means **to estimate at** _____ **a value, amount, rate.**

   (A) never   (B) too much   (C) too little

7. The word that means **not to stress enough** is _____.

   (A) understrength   (B) underemphasize   (C) underfeed

8. The word that means **to supply insufficiently or inadequately** is _____.

   (A) underutilize   (B) underdevelop   (C) undersupply

9. The word that means **poorly or insufficiently educated** is _____.

   (A) underexposed   (B) underact   (C) undereducated

10. From these examples, we can tell that the prefix _____ can also mean **not enough** or **below normal.**

    (A) under   (B) ultra   (C) un

1. Some prefixes have more than one meaning. The prefix **be** can mean **make** or cause to be. **Belittle** means to ———— **to seem less important.**

   (A) find   (B) cause   (C) think

2. The word that means **to make calm** is ————.

   (A) bestow   (B) befoul   (C) becalm

3. The word that means **to make numb** is ————.

   (A) befuddle   (B) benumb   (C) belabor

4. The word that means **to make wet and dirty** is ————.

   (A) bedraggle   (B) bewilder   (C) before

5. From these examples, we can tell that the prefix ———— means **make** or **cause to be.**

   (A) bi   (B) be   (C) bio

6. The prefix **be** can also mean **thoroughly** or **all around. Bespatter** means **to spatter** ————.

   (A) all over   (B) under   (C) in

7. The word that means **to smear all over** is ————.

   (A) besmirch   (B) bescreen   (C) besmear

8. The word that means **to use brilliancy and splendor to confuse** is ————.

   (A) becloud   (B) bedazzle   (C) bedabble

9. The word that means **to adorn with jewels** is ————.

   (A) besiege   (B) bejewel   (C) becloud

10. From these examples, we can tell that the prefix ———— can also mean **thoroughly** or **all over.**

    (A) be   (B) bi   (C) by

Many of the words we use have their roots in the Latin and Greek languages. Learning to recognize these roots, and learning what they mean, helps us figure out the meaning of words we do not know. Suppose you are not familiar with the word *infraction*, but you know that *fract* means "break." If you come across this sentence: "Keith, your late arrival is an infraction of the rules." You would probably understand that Keith is in trouble. Knowing the word root and seeing how the word is used in a sentence often gives you enough information to figure out the meaning of the word.

A. Exercising Your Skill

Does your life seem filled with rules? Cross streets only at corners; don't eat a snack right before dinner; don't run in the hallway. Most of the time we might agree that rules have their place. After all, imagine what would happen if everyone in school ran in the hallways at once!

How do rules relate to word roots? The meanings of words are rules of a kind. They are something we agree on. What would happen if everyone had different meanings for words? It might be worse than everyone running in the hallway at the same time.

As you know, a root contains the heart of the word's meaning. Read the word roots in the box. On your paper, write each root next to the correct meaning shown below. Then write as many words as you can think of that contain that root. Think about the meanings of the words you write. Think about how they relate to the meaning of the root.

fract/frag	ject	tract	vid/vis

break	see, look	throw	drive, push
————	————	————	————
————	————	————	————
————	————	————	————

B. Expanding Your Skill

How did you do? Discuss with your classmates the words you wrote. Are there other words you can add to your list? Do you "see" the meaning of the root in each of your words? Use a dictionary to find other words you can add to your list.

C. Exploring Language

The roots *magn* and *maxima* are from Latin and mean "great" or "large." We see these roots in the words *magnitude, magnificent,* and *maximum.* We can also see the root in the word *maxim.* A maxim is a saying that people have passed along for generations which seems to contain great wisdom or truth. Sometimes people use maxims as rules for behavior. For example, follow the advice in this maxim: Early to bed and early to rise, makes one healthy, wealthy, and wise.

Read the maxims below. Look at the underlined word or words in each. On your paper, write the root from Part A that has the same meaning as the underlined word or words. Then rewrite the maxim in your own words, using one word that contains that root.

Example: Don't <u>throw out</u> dirty water until you get fresh.
Don't <u>eject</u> dirty water until you get fresh.

<u>Look</u> before you leap.
It is easier to <u>push</u> down than to build up.
Sticks and stones will <u>break</u> my bones, but names will never hurt me.

What other maxims do you know? Write them on your paper.

D. Expressing Yourself

Choose one of these activities.

1. If you look in a thesaurus, you'll find that *adage*, *proverb*, *saying*, and *cliché* are all synonyms for *maxim*. But they do have their differences. What are the differences? Find out how a dictionary defines each one. Write down the definitions, and for each synonym make up a sentence that shows an example.

2. Jokes sometimes have maxims as punch lines, often in the form of a pun. For example, here's a joke based on the maxim "Haste makes waste."

    Q: What did the cook say to the chef when the chef's pie crust came out undercooked and sticky?
    A: "Haste makes paste!"

    Try your hand at writing a joke based on a common figure of speech.

3. Make up a maxim about some bit of wisdom of your own. Make your maxim brief and catchy, so that people will remember it. You might want to use rhyming words. You might also want to talk about something specific that stands for something general. For example, "Look before you leap" really means "Don't do anything without thinking about the consequences"—but "Look before you leap" is a much catchier way to say it.

33

1. Some prefixes have more than one meaning. The prefix **out** can mean **outside, outward, away,** or **forth. Outburst** means **the act of bursting** _____.

   (A) in   (B) clear   (C) forth

2. The word that means **the part of the baseball field beyond the diamond or infield** is _____.

   (A) outfield   (B) outflood   (C) outrun

3. The word that means **a person or animal cast out from home and friends** is _____.

   (A) outstream   (B) outcast   (C) outsize

4. The word that means **out in the open air** is _____.

   (A) outpupil   (B) outsmart   (C) outdoors

5. From these examples, we can tell that the prefix _____ can mean **outside, outward, away** or **forth.**

   (A) oct   (B) out   (C) in

6. The prefix **out** can also mean **more than** or **better than. Outlive** means **to live** _____.

   (A) longer than   (B) sooner than   (C) near

7. The word that means **to play better than** is _____.

   (A) outworn   (B) outlabor   (C) outplay

8. The word that means **to spend more** is _____.

   (A) outdrink   (B) outspend   (C) outwear

9. The word that means **to sing better than** is _____.

   (A) outplan   (B) outsing   (C) outwork

10. From these examples, we can tell that the prefix _____ can also mean **more than** or **better than.**

    (A) out   (B) ortho   (C) on

1. Some prefixes have more than one meaning. The prefix **by** can mean **near, close,** or **aside**. Bypass means **to set** _____ or **ignore**.

   (A) **together**   (B) **all**   (C) **aside**

2. The word that means **a person nearby but not involved** is _____ .

   (A) **bystander**   (B) **byway**   (C) **byline**

3. The word that means **a pathway not often used** is _____ .

   (A) **byway**   (B) **bygone**   (C) **bypast**

4. The word that means **a path alongside** is _____ .

   (A) **bypath**   (B) **byplay**   (C) **bygone**

5. From these examples, we can tell that the prefix _____ can mean **near, close,** or **aside.**

   (A) **bene**   (B) **bio**   (C) **by**

6. The prefix **by** can also mean **of less importance, secondary,** or **minor. Bylaw** means a _____ **law or rule not of prime importance.**

   (A) **historical**   (B) **new**   (C) **secondary**

7. The word that means **a secondary name** is _____ .

   (A) **by-election**   (B) **byname**   (C) **byword**

8. The word that means **something of value produced in making the main product** is _____ .

   (A) **bylaw**   (B) **by-product**   (C) **byline**

9. The word that means **a secondary street off a main road** is _____ .

   (A) **byword**   (B) **bystreet**   (C) **bylaw**

10. From these examples, we can tell that the prefix _____ can also mean **less important** or **secondary.**

   (A) **by**   (B) **bi**   (C) **bio**

1. The prefixes **bi** and **twi** mean **two. Binomial,** for example, means **having or using** _____ **names.**

    (A) **bright**
    (B) **several**
    (C) **two**

2. The word that means **two times** is _____.

    (A) **bicentennial**
    (B) **twice**
    (C) **bicycle**

3. The word that means **happening once every two months** or **twice in one month** is _____.

    (A) **bimonthly**
    (B) **twin**
    (C) **bicuspid**

4. The word that means **happening two times in a year** is _____.

    (A) **twilight**
    (B) **biannual**
    (C) **twine**

5. From these examples, we can tell that the prefixes _____ mean **two.**

    (A) **by/bibli**
    (B) **bi/twi**
    (C) **bene/bio**

6. The prefixes **tri** and **ter** mean **three, threefold, having three parts,** or **occurring once every third. Trisect,** for example, means **to divide into** _____ **parts.**

    (A) **many**
    (B) **three**
    (C) **two**

7. The word that means **of the third order, rank, or formation** is _____.

    (A) **tertiary**
    (B) **trivial**
    (C) **trimonthly**

8. The word that means **a small light vehicle having three wheels** is _____.

    (A) **triplex**
    (B) **tricycle**
    (C) **terchloride**

9. The word that means **a three-legged support or stand for a camera, transit, or other instrument** is _____.

    (A) **tripod**
    (B) **triplet**
    (C) **triennial**

10. From these examples, we can tell that the prefixes _____ mean **three, threefold, having three parts,** or **occurring once every third.**

    (A) **tele/tetra**
    (B) **tri/ter**
    (C) **trans/twi**

1. The prefix **auto** means **self. Automatic,** for example, means **moving or acting by** _____.

   (A) itself   (B) time   (C) force

2. The word that means **self-moving vehicle** is _____.

   (A) autograph   (B) automobile   (C) automation

3. The word that means **story of a person's life written by that person** is _____.

   (A) automation   (B) autobiography (C) autodidact

4. The word that means **a self-operated machine in a restaurant** is _____.

   (A) automat   (B) autocratic   (C) autocracy

5. From these examples, we can tell that the prefix _____ means **self.**

   (A) auto   (B) aster   (C) ambi

6. The prefix **tele** means **distant** or **over a distance. Telephone,** for example, means **an instrument for transmitting speech or sound by electricity from a** _____.

   (A) radio   (B) book   (C) distance

7. The word that means **an instrument for making far-away objects look larger and nearer** is _____.

   (A) telephonist   (B) telepath   (C) telescope

8. The word that means **to send a message from a distance by wire or radio** is _____.

   (A) telemetry   (B) telegraph   (C) teleguide

9. A word that means **the communication of one mind with another by means other than the five senses** is _____.

   (A) telescopic   (B) telephoto   (C) telepathy

10. From these examples, we can tell that the prefix _____ means **distant** or **over a distance.**

   (A) tetra   (B) ter   (C) tele

1. The prefix **down** means **in a lower place or condition. Downfall,** for example, means **to bring** _____ or **overthrow.**

   (A) over   (B) through   (C) down

2. The word that means **a heavy rain** is _____.

   (A) downpour   (B) downswing   (C) downcast

3. The word that means **a downward current as of air** is _____.

   (A) downfold   (B) downbound   (C) downdraft

4. The word that means **in low spirits** is _____.

   (A) downstroke   (B) downgrade   (C) downhearted

5. From these examples, we can tell that the prefix _____ means **in a lower place or condition.**

   (A) di   (B) du   (C) down

6. The prefix **with** means **away, back, against,** or **with. Withdraw,** for example, means to **draw** _____.

   (A) some   (B) up   (C) back

7. The word that means **to refuse to give** or **to restrain** is _____.

   (A) withdrew   (B) withdrawn   (C) withhold

8. The word that means **to stand up against** is _____.

   (A) withstand   (B) within   (C) withdrawal

9. The word that means **with no** or **not having** is _____.

   (A) withstood   (B) withheld   (C) without

10. From these examples, we can tell that the prefix _____ means **away, back, against,** or **with.**

    (A) with   (B) vice   (C) infra

UNIT 30
Prefix Concepts and Practice—multi, uni

1. The prefix **multi** means **many. Multilingual,** for example, means **knowing** or **using** _____ **languages.**

   (A) one (B) many (C) foreign

2. The word that means **having many different shapes or kinds** is _____.

   (A) multiform (B) multicolor (C) multiengine

3. The word that means **using a combination of various media, such as tapes, film, phonograph records, and slides to entertain, teach, and communicate** is _____.

   (A) multicolor (B) multilane (C) multimedia

4. The word that means **a great many of** is _____.

   (A) multiplicand (B) multilevel (C) multitude

5. From these examples, we can tell that the prefix _____ means **many.**

   (A) multi (B) milli (C) mid

6. The prefix **uni** means **one. Unite,** for example, means **to join together** or **to make** _____.

   (A) different (B) various (C) one

7. The word that means **the whole of existing or created things regarded collectively** is _____.

   (A) unify (B) universe (C) union

8. The word that means **always the same** is _____.

   (A) uniform (B) unicycle (C) university

9. The word that means **being the only one of its kind** is _____.

   (A) unilateral (B) unique (C) unicorn

10. From these examples, we can tell that the prefix _____ means **one.**

    (A) under (B) uni (C) un

1. The prefix **con** means **with** or **together. Connect,** for example, means **to fasten or join** _____.

   (A) together   (B) tightly   (C) everything

2. The word that means **a formal meeting or assembly** is _____.

   (A) concur   (B) confirm   (C) congress

3. The word that means **to act in accordance with laws or rules** is _____.

   (A) concentric   (B) conform   (C) concourse

4. The word that means **to talk things over together** is _____.

   (A) confederation   (B) consult   (C) confine

5. From these examples, we can tell that the prefix _____ means **with** or **together.**

   (A) con   (B) counter   (C) crypto

6. The prefix **com** also means **with** or **together. Compress,** for example, means **to squeeze** _____.

   (A) together   (B) under   (C) over

7. The word that means **having more than one part** is _____.

   (A) comparison   (B) compound   (C) compassion

8. The word that means **to find out how persons or things are alike and how they are different** is _____.

   (A) composition   (B) compare   (C) compartment

9. The word that means **to make hard to understand** is _____.

   (A) complexion   (B) complete   (C) complicate

10. From these examples, we can tell that the prefix _____ also means **with** or **together.**

    (A) com   (B) contra   (C) cis

UNIT 32
Prefix Concepts and Practice—on, off

1. The prefix **on** means **on. Onscreen,** for example, means **seen** _____ the motion-picture or television screen.

   (A) over   (B) off   (C) on

2. The word that means **approaching** or **advancing** is _____.

   (A) onflow   (B) onside   (C) oncoming

3. The word that means **a person who watches without taking part** is _____.

   (A) onset   (B) onrush   (C) onlooker

4. The word that means **continuous** or **uninterrupted** is _____.

   (A) onlooking   (B) ongoing   (C) onshore

5. From these examples we can tell that the prefix _____ means **on.**

   (A) on   (B) off   (C) omni

6. The prefix **off** means **from. Offstage,** for example, means **away** _____ the part of the stage that the audience can see.

   (A) over   (B) near   (C) from

7. The word that means **off** or **away from the shore** is _____.

   (A) offset   (B) offshore   (C) offcenter

8. The word that means **what is born from** or **grows out of something** is _____.

   (A) offspring   (B) offcast   (C) offprint

9. The word that means **a shoot from the main stem of a plant** is _____.

   (A) off-track   (B) offcut   (C) offshoot

10. From these examples, we can tell that the prefix _____ means **from.**

    (A) off   (B) over   (C) omni

UNIT 33
Prefix Review

1. Think of what **automation, autocratic, automat** mean. The prefix **auto** means
   _____.

   (A) hate   (B) machine   (C) self

2. Think of what **withhold, withstand, withstood** mean. The prefix **with** means
   away, back, _____ or **with.**

   (A) near   (B) against   (C) far

3. Think of what **unify, uniform, union** mean. The prefix **uni** means _____.

   (A) not   (B) self   (C) one

4. Think of what **offcast, offprint, offshore** mean. The prefix **off** means _____.

   (A) through   (B) from   (C) new

5. Think of what **telescope, telegraph, telephoto** mean. The prefix **tele** means **at or
   over a** _____.

   (A) distance   (B) call   (C) see

6. Think of what **downpour, downgrade, downstroke** mean. The prefix **down** means
   in a _____ **place or condition.**

   (A) lower   (B) new   (C) unhealthy

7. Think of what **multicolor, multiply, multitude** mean. The prefix **multi** means
   _____.

   (A) number   (B) different   (C) many

8. Think of what **congress, conform, convene** mean. The prefix **con** means _____.

   (A) with/together   (B) many   (C) group

9. Think of what **compassion, complete, compound** mean. The prefix **com** also
   means _____.

   (A) against   (B) element   (C) with/together

10. Think of what **onshore, onflow, onrush** mean. The prefix **on** means _____.

   (A) on   (B) after   (C) going

1. Think of what **underscore, undersecretary, underfoot** mean. The prefix **under** can mean **beneath, below,** or **of a** _____ **position or rank.**

   (A) high   (B) lower   (C) near

2. Think of what **underfeed, underdeveloped, underact** mean. The prefix **under** can also mean _____ or **below normal.**

   (A) small   (B) needless   (C) not enough

3. Think of what **bestow, befuddle, benumb** mean. The prefix **be** can mean **make** or _____.

   (A) cause to be   (B) build   (C) destroy

4. Think of what **bespatter, bedazzle, bejewel** mean. The prefix **be** can also mean _____ or **all around.**

   (A) huge   (B) all over/thoroughly   (C) small

5. Think of what **outfield, outgoing, outcast** mean. The prefix **out** can mean **outside, outward,** _____ or **forth.**

   (A) with   (B) in   (C) away

6. Think of what **outweigh, outscore, outdo** mean. The prefix **out** can also mean **more than** or _____.

   (A) near   (B) throw   (C) better than

7. Think of what **bystander, bygone, bypass** mean. The prefix **by** can mean **near, close,** or _____.

   (A) aside   (B) go   (C) high

8. Think of what **by-product, by-election, bystreet** mean. The prefix **by** can also mean **of less importance, secondary,** or _____.

   (A) size   (B) minor   (C) major

9. Think of what **bicentennial, twin, biannual** mean. The prefixes **bi** and **twi** mean _____.

   (A) two   (B) through   (C) year

10. Think of what **trimonthly, tripod, tertiary** mean. The prefixes **tri** and **ter** mean **three, threefold, having three parts,** or **occurring once every** _____.

    (A) third   (B) month   (C) time

UNIT 35
Suffix Concepts and Practice

1. The suffixes **ic** and **ical** can mean **of, like, pertaining to,** or **connected with.** **Historical** means **of or connected with history as a science. Heroic** means _____ a hero or a hero's deeds.

   (A) by   (B) like   (C) knowing

2. Choose the word that means **pertaining to numbers.**

   (A) volcanic   (B) numerical   (C) angelic

3. The suffixes **ic** and **ical** can also indicate a noun or an adjective. **Public** means _____ **the people as a whole** or **for the people as a whole. Musical** means **having the nature of music** or a theatrical production.

   (A) of or belonging to   (B) near   (C) free from

4. Choose the word that means **being in the first class or highest rank.**

   (A) classic   (B) graphic   (C) statistical

5. The suffix **gram** can mean **a record** or **something written. Program** means a **record of acts, speeches, etc., that make up an entertainment or ceremony. Telegram** means a _____ **message that was transmitted by telegraph.**

   (A) written   (B) spoken   (C) quick

6. Choose the word that means **a written chart or graph explaining or illustrating ideas, statistics, etc.**

   (A) monogram   (B) cablegram   (C) diagram

7. The suffix **gram** can also mean **a small weight used in the metric system. Kilogram** means **a weight equaling one thousand grams. Milligram** means a _____ **measuring one thousandth of a gram.**

   (A) length   (B) weight   (C) time

8. Choose the word that means **a weight equal to 10 grams.**

   (A) centigram   (B) decagram   (C) hectogram

9. The suffixes **orium** and **arium** mean **place for** or **place where. Aquarium** means **place where live water animals and water plants are kept. Auditorium** means a _____ **speeches, concerts, etc.**

   (A) need for   (B) place for   (C) idea of

10. Choose the word that means **a place for growing roses.**

    (A) solarium   (B) conservatorium   (C) rosarium

1. The suffix **let** can mean **small** or **little. Wavelet** means **a little wave. Booklet** means a _____ **book.**

   (A) interesting   **(B) small**   **(C) large**

2. Choose the word that means **a small island.**

   (A) owlet   **(B) leaflet**   **(C) islet**

3. The suffix **let** can also mean **a thing worn as a band or ornament on some part of the body. Anklet** means **anything worn around the ankle as a fetter, ornament, or support. Bracelet** means **an ornamental** _____ **or chain worn about the wrist.**

   (A) song   **(B) color**   **(C) band**

4. Choose the word that means **a curl of hair worn as an ornament on the head.**

   (A) ringlet   **(B) wristlet**   **(C) armlet**

5. The suffixes **able, ible,** and **ble** can mean **being able to be** or **having. Credible** means **worthy of belief. Readable** means _____ **to be read.**

   (A) able   **(B) one**   **(C) desire**

6. Choose the word that means **fit to eat.**

   (A) soluble   **(B) lovable**   **(C) eatable**

7. The suffixes **able, ible,** and **ble** can also mean **tending to** or **inclined to. Terrible** means **causing terror or fear. Perishable** means _____ **to spoil or decay.**

   (A) knowing   **(B) tending**   **(C) liking**

8. Choose the word that means **lasting** or **existing a long time.**

   (A) voluble   **(B) durable**   **(C) changeable**

9. The suffix **ity** means **the state or condition indicated by the stem. Verbosity** means **the state of using or containing too many words. Grandiosity** means **the** _____ **or condition having grandeur.**

   (A) state   **(B) movement**   **(C) people**

10. Choose the word that means **the condition of being eager to know.**

    (A) generosity   **(B) curiosity**   **(C) animosity**

1. The suffix **ship** has several meanings. The suffix **ship** can mean **a type of ship.** **Warship** means **a ship for or of war. Steamship** means a _____ that is driven by steam power.

   (A) ship   (B) fight   (C) night

2. Choose the word that means **a ship that is lighter than air and can be steered.**

   (A) airship   (B) flagship   (C) battleship

3. The suffix **ship** can also mean **art or skill. Penmanship** means **the art of handwriting. Horsemanship** means the _____ of riding a horse.

   (A) place   (B) skill   (C) movement

4. Choose the word that means **the skill of leading.**

   (A) craftsmanship   (B) marksmanship   (C) leadership

5. The suffix **ship** can mean **a state or condition indicating the relationship specified by the stem. Cousinship** means **the condition of being cousins. Friendship** means the _____ existing between friends.

   (A) state   (B) enemy   (C) ideas

6. Choose the word that means **the state or condition of being the proprietor, or owner, of a business establishment.**

   (A) authorship   (B) proprietorship   (C) partnership

7. The suffix **ship** can mean **office, occupation, rank,** or **position. Authorship** means **the occupation of author. Clerkship** means the _____ clerk.

   (A) reason for   (B) name of   (C) position of

8. Choose the word that means **the rank of lord.**

   (A) lordship   (B) governorship   (C) chancellorship

9. The suffix **ship** can mean **action, process,** or **that which is formed by or made of. Township** means **a part of a country having certain powers of local government. Worship** means the _____ giving religious homage to.

   (A) time of   (B) process of   (C) why

10. Choose the word that means **the action of censoring.**

   (A) censorship   (B) courtship   (C) membership

UNIT 38
Suffix Concepts and Practice

1. The suffix **ary** can mean **connected with that indicated by the stem. Honorary** means **something connected with or given as an honor. Legendary** means _____ **with legend or tradition.**

   (A) read   (B) designed   (C) connected

2. Choose the word that means **connected with custom, usage, or habit.**

   (A) customary   (B) secondary   (C) elementary

3. The suffix **ary** can mean **a place for. Library** means **a place for keeping books. Sanctuary** means _____ **refuge or protection.**

   (A) always   (B) never   (C) a place for

4. Choose the word that means **a place for treating the infirmed or ill.**

   (A) apiary   (B) infirmary   (C) aviary

5. The suffix **ary** can also mean **one who** or **that which. Dictionary** means **that book which lists words in a language, alphabetically, and with definitions, etc. Missionary** means _____ **is sent out by a religious organization to preach, teach, etc., as to a foreign country.**

   (A) one who   (B) that   (C) some

6. Choose the word that means **something which is said in admiration, respect, or flattery.**

   (A) complimentary   (B) complementary   (C) secretary

7. The suffixes **arian** and **cian** mean **one who. Physician** means **one who practices medicine. Vegetarian** means _____ **advocates a diet of only vegetables, fruits, grains, and nuts.**

   (A) speaks   (B) ties   (C) one who

8. Choose the word that means **one who is in charge of a collection of books.**

   (A) librarian   (B) mathematician   (C) grammarian

9. The suffix **bound** means **held fast** or **on the way to. Eastbound** means **on the way to the east. Stormbound** means _____ **fast in a storm.**

   (A) eat   (B) held   (C) run

10. Choose the word that means **on the way northward.**

    (A) northbound   (B) snowbound   (C) southbound

Prefixes are word parts that are added at the beginning of a root word. Prefixes help us expand our language and say things more exactly. Some prefixes are spelled the same as words and may mean the same or nearly the same as words. For example, the prefix *under* is spelled the same and means the same as the word *under*.

A. Exercising Your Skill

Synonyms are words that have the same or nearly the same meaning. Antonyms are words that are opposite in meaning. Look at the prefixes below. Each is spelled the same as a word and can have the same or nearly the same meaning as that word. Two of the prefixes—*off* and *on*—are antonyms. Now look at the words in the box. On your paper, combine the words in the box with one or more of the prefixes. Can you think of other words that contain these prefixes? Draw lines to connect any two words that are antonyms.

out	by	off	on
outcome	bystander	offside	onlooker

	side	shore	stage	rush	hand
come/coming	standing/stander		spring	center	look/looker

What other words can you think of that contain these prefixes? Check a dictionary to be sure your words are listed.

B. Expanding Your Skill

How did you do? Did you combine any of the words in the box with more than one prefix? Do not be afraid to try. You can always check the dictionary—and while you are checking, look for more words that begin with these prefixes. How many pairs of antonyms did you find? Make a list.

C. Exploring Language

Come and *go*, like *up* and *down*, are among the first antonym pairs we learn. Although *come* and *go* are antonyms, the words *oncoming* and *ongoing* are not. Their meanings are different, but not opposite. *Oncoming* means "approaching"; *ongoing* means "continuing."

What things seem to continue in your life with little or no change? Do you have an ongoing problem getting your math homework done? Does your softball team have an ongoing battle with the team from the next town? In your family, are there any jokes and family stories that come up again and again? Here's an ongoing family joke that one seventh grader told about:

> When I was small, I was afraid of bears and didn't want to walk past a certain tree because I thought a bear lived there. Since then, every time I walk past that tree with someone in my family, I get asked, "How are the bears?" The joke used to make me mad, but now I just smile and say, "The bears are fine."

Write about an ongoing joke or story in your family. How did it get started? Does it automatically get told whenever the key word or place (like the bear tree) comes up? Do the members of your family react in different ways? Why? Tell about the joke or story so that people outside of your family will understand what it is all about. Use as many words with prefixes in your composition as you can.

D. Expressing Yourself

Choose one of these activities.

1. The words *onshore* and *offshore* can refer to two types of winds that occur near oceans and other large bodies of water. Whether the wind is onshore or offshore is important to people living in such areas because it makes a big difference in their weather. What is the largest body of water near your area? Find out how this body of water and the winds that blow over it affect your weather. Write a brief report.

2. In a play, the stage directions—upstage, downstage, onstage, offstage, and so on—are almost as important as the dialogue. Work with one or two classmates to turn a simple story (perhaps a myth, legend, or children's story) into a play. Pay particular attention to writing the stage directions.

1. The suffixes **ory** and **atory** can mean **place for** or **place where. Depository** is a **place where anything is stored for safekeeping. Laboratory** is a _____ **scientific work is done.**

   (A) **place where**   (B) **country**   (C) **time**

2. Choose the word that means **a building or group of buildings where things are manufactured.**

   (A) **conservatory**   (B) **factory**   (C) **lavatory**

3. The suffixes **ory** and **atory** can mean **having to do with** or **quality. Explanatory** means **helping to make clear. Illusory** means _____ **to do with an illusion.**

   (A) **having**   (B) **playing**   (C) **painting**

4. Choose the word that means **serving to prepare.**

   (A) **preparatory**   (B) **migratory**   (C) **compulsory**

5. The suffixes **ancy** and **ency** mean **state** or **condition. Competency** means **the condition of being able. Vacancy** means the _____ **being vacant.**

   (A) **feeling**   (B) **climate**   (C) **state of**

6. Choose the word that means **the rate of occurrence.**

   (A) **brilliancy**   (B) **frequency**   (C) **dependency**

7. The suffix **ern** means **direction. Eastern** means **toward, from, of, or in the east. Western** means _____, **from, of, or in the west.**

   (A) **under**   (B) **toward**   (C) **beyond**

8. Choose the word that means **toward, from, of, or in the south.**

   (A) **southern**   (B) **northern**   (C) **northeastern**

9. The suffixes **graph** and **graphy** mean **something written** or **a record. Biography** means **a record of someone's life. Paragraph** means **a subdivision of a** _____ **chapter or letter.**

   (A) **old**   (B) **new**   (C) **written**

10. Choose the word that means **a record of images of objects upon a photosensitive surface by the chemical action of light.**

    (A) **geography**   (B) **photograph**   (C) **autograph**

1. The suffix **dom** can mean **state of. Boredom** means **a state of weariness caused by dullness. Freedom** means the _____ or condition of being free.

   (A) number   (B) state   (C) idea

2. Choose the word that means **knowledge and good judgment based on experience.**

   (A) serfdom   (B) wisdom   (C) martyrdom

3. The suffix **dom** can also mean **region, realm,** or **domain. Kingdom** means a **country that is governed by a king or queen. Dukedom** means the _____ ruled by a duke.

   (A) time   (B) lands   (C) money

4. Choose the word that means **the position or domain of officials.**

   (A) officialdom   (B) earldom   (C) heirdom

5. The suffixes **logue** and **log** mean **written or spoken discourse. Dialogue** means a **written passage, or passages, in a play or story. Epilog** means a _____ or **closing commentary added to a play or novel.**

   (A) liking   (B) thought   (C) speech

6. Choose the word that means **a speech by one speaker.**

   (A) duologue   (B) catalog   (C) monologue

7. The suffix **sphere** means **ball, like a ball in shape,** or **an enveloping global mass. Ionosphere** means **the atmosphere which envelops the earth. Bathysphere** is a _____, **watertight observation chamber lowered by cables into sea depths.**

   (A) ball-shaped   (B) square   (C) high

8. Choose the word that means **the gaseous envelope surrounding the earth.**

   (A) hydrosphere   (B) chromosphere   (C) atmosphere

9. The suffixes **ably, ibly,** and **bly** mean **in the manner indicated by the stem. Favorably** means **in a favorable manner. Responsibly** means **in an accountable**

   _____.

   (A) look   (B) idea   (C) manner

10. Choose the word that means **in a manner worthy of notice or remark.**

    (A) remarkably   (B) probably   (C) solubly

1. Think of what **boredom, wisdom, freedom** mean. The suffix **dom** can mean
   _____ .

   (A) desire for   (B) state of   (C) often

2. Think of what **kingdom, earldom, dukedom** mean. The suffix **dom** can also mean
   _____ , **realm**, or **domain**.

   (A) person   (B) region   (C) rights

3. Think of what **credible, readable, soluble** mean. The suffixes **able, ible,** and **ble**
   mean _____ or **having**.

   (A) need   (B) going   (C) able to be

4. Think of what **terrible, perishable, voluble** mean. The suffixes **able, ible,** and **ble**
   can also mean **tending to** or _____ .

   (A) completely   (B) very   (C) inclined to

5. Think of what **curiosity, generosity, verbosity** mean. The suffix **osity** means
   _____ **indicated by the stem**.

   (A) state or condition   (B) knowing   (C) many

6. Think of what **historical, heroic, numerical** mean. The suffixes **ic** and **ical** can
   mean **of, pertaining to,** or _____ .

   (A) against   (B) connected with   (C) all

7. Think of what **public, musical, graphic** mean. The suffixes **ic** and **ical** can also
   indicate **a** _____ or **an adjective**.

   (A) sound   (B) place   (C) noun

8. Think of what **program, telegram, diagram** mean. The suffix **gram** can mean **a**
   _____ , or **something written**.

   (A) record   (B) instrument   (C) kind

9. Think of what **kilogram, milligram, decagram** mean. The suffix **gram** can also
   mean **a small** _____ **used in the metric system**.

   (A) device   (B) weight   (C) sound

10. Think of what **aquarium, auditorium, solarium** mean. The suffixes **orium** and
    arium mean _____ **for or where**.

    (A) place   (B) service   (C) ordinarily

1. Think of what **honorary, secondary, customary** mean. The suffix **ary** can mean
_____.

   (A) move   (B) connected with   (C) many

2. Think of what **secretary, missionary, complimentary** mean. The suffix **ary** can
mean **that which,** or _____.

   (A) in   (B) from   (C) one who

3. Think of what **library, aviary, infirmary** mean. The suffix **ary** can also mean
_____.

   (A) a place for   (B) very   (C) small

4. Think of what **physician, librarian, vegetarian** mean. The suffixes **arian** and **cian**
mean _____.

   (A) near   (B) one who   (C) study

5. Think of what **eastern, western, southern** mean. The suffix **ern** means _____.

   (A) old   (B) past   (C) direction

6. Think of what **flagship, battleship, airship** mean. The suffix **ship** can mean a
_____.

   (A) showing   (B) fear   (C) type of ship

7. Think of what **penmanship, leadership, craftsmanship** mean. The suffix **ship** can
mean _____.

   (A) partly   (B) art/skill   (C) building

8. Think of what **partnership, cousinship, friendship** mean. The suffix **ship** can
mean _____ indicating the relationship specified by the stem.

   (A) state/condition   (B) like/love   (C) person

9. Think of what **governorship, lordship, clerkship** mean. The suffix **ship** can mean
office, occupation, rank, or _____.

   (A) need   (B) feeling   (C) position

10. Think of what **censorship, courtship, worship** mean. The suffix **ship** can also
mean **action,** _____, **that which is formed by, or made of.**

   (A) kind   (B) process   (C) truth

UNIT 43
Suffix Review

1. Think of what **snowbound, northbound, eastbound** mean. The suffix **bound** means **held fast** or _____ .

   (A) **on the way to**   (B) **motion**   (C) **hit**

2. Think of what **depository, lavatory, conservatory** mean. The suffixes **ory** and **atory** can mean _____ **for or where.**

   (A) **place**   (B) **keep**   (C) **show**

3. Think of what **explanatory, illusory, preparatory** mean. The suffixes **ory** and **atory** can also mean **having to do with** or _____ .

   (A) **need**   (B) **quality**   (C) **see**

4. Think of what **biography, photograph, paragraph** mean. The suffixes **graph** and **graphy** mean **something** _____ , or **a record.**

   (A) **known**   (B) **right**   (C) **written**

5. Think of what **brilliancy, frequency, competency** mean. The suffixes **ancy** and **ency** mean _____ .

   (A) **state/condition**   (B) **through**   (C) **idea**

6. Think of what **ionosphere, atmosphere, chromosphere** mean. The suffix **sphere** means _____ .

   (A) **spin**   (B) **ball/ball-shaped**   (C) **air**

7. Think of what **leaflet, booklet, wavelet** mean. The suffix **let** can mean _____ .

   (A) **page**   (B) **small/little**   (C) **tight**

8. Think of what **wristlet, anklet, bracelet** mean. The suffix **let** can also mean **a** _____ **as a band or ornament on some part of the body.**

   (A) **point**   (B) **instrument**   (C) **thing worn**

9. Think of what **dialogue, epilog, catalog** mean. The suffixes **logue** and **log** mean _____ **or spoken discourse.**

   (A) **written**   (B) **known**   (C) **difficult**

10. Think of what **favorably, responsibly, solubly** mean. The suffixes **ably, ibly,** and **bly** mean _____ **indicated by the stem.**

    (A) **in the manner**   (B) **time**   (C) **type**

UNIT 44
Decoding Review

1. Think of what **telegram, monogram, program** mean. The suffix **gram** can mean **a** _____ or **something written.**

   (A) fountain   (B) kind   (C) record

2. Think of what **kilogram, centigram, milligram** mean. The suffix **gram** can also mean **a small** _____ **used in the metric system.**

   (A) device   (B) sound   (C) weight

3. Think of what **sentiment, sentinel, sensitive** mean. The roots **sens** and **sent** mean _____.

   (A) write   (B) feel/be aware of   (C) voice/call

4. Think of what **befuddle, belabor, bestow** mean. The prefix **be** can mean **make** or _____.

   (A) build   (B) cause to be   (C) divide

5. Think of what **besmear, bejewel, bedazzle** mean. The prefix **be** can also mean _____ or **all around.**

   (A) enchanting   (B) near   (C) thoroughly

6. Think of what **sequence, second, consecutive** mean. The roots **sequ** and **sec** mean _____.

   (A) before   (B) three   (C) follow

7. Think of what **technology, technique, technician** mean. The root **tech** means _____.

   (A) art/skill   (B) need   (C) write

8. Think of what **biography, geography, photograph** mean. The suffixes **graph** and **graphy** mean **something** _____ or **a record.**

   (A) right   (B) written   (C) known

9. Think of what **eastern, western, northern** mean. The suffix **ern** means _____.

   (A) direction   (B) old   (C) past

10. Think of what **invisible, visualize, video** mean. The roots **vid** and **vis** mean _____.

    (A) look/see   (B) carry   (C) write

1. Think of what **factory, conservatory, depository** mean. The suffixes **ory** and **atory** can mean **place for** or _____.

   (A) keep   (B) go for   (C) place where

2. Think of what **explanatory, migratory, illusory** mean. The suffixes **ory** and **atory** can also mean **having to do with** or _____.

   (A) need   (B) quality   (C) see

3. Think of what **autobiography, automat, autocratic** mean. The prefix **auto** means
   _____.

   (A) self   (B) claim   (C) machine

4. Think of what **extract, distract, contract** mean. The root **tract** means _____.

   (A) draw/drag   (B) have/hold   (C) carry

5. Think of what **monologue, catalog, epilog** mean. The suffixes **logue** and **log** mean _____ or **spoken discourse.**

   (A) known   (B) written   (C) phase

6. Think of what **withstood, within, withstand** mean. The prefix **with** means **away, back,** _____ or **with.**

   (A) near   (B) against   (C) far

7. Think of what **generosity, curiosity, animosity** mean. The suffix **osity** means _____ **indicated by the stem.**

   (A) state or condition   (B) opinion   (C) knowing

8. Think of what **uniform, unify, universe** mean. The prefix **uni** means _____.

   (A) several   (B) self   (C) one

9. Think of what **atmosphere, ionosphere, hydrosphere** mean. The suffix **sphere** means _____.

   (A) air   (B) ball/ball-shaped   (C) spin

10. Think of what **fraction, fragment, fracture** mean. The roots **fract** and **frag** mean
    _____.

    (A) break   (B) stop   (C) foot

1. Think of what **telescope, telephone, telegram** mean. The prefix **tele** means
   ———.

   (A) see   (B) call   (C) distance

2. Think of what **compel, propel, repulse** mean. The roots **puls** and **pel** mean
   ———.

   (A) city   (B) drive/push   (C) death

3. Think of what **leaflet, owlet, booklet** mean. The suffix **let** can mean ———.
   (A) small/little   (B) page   (C) tight

4. Think of what **anklet, bracelet, ringlet** mean. The suffix **let** can also mean **a**
   ——— **as a band or ornament on some part of the body.**
   (A) thing worn   (B) point   (C) instrument

5. Think of what **intervene, eventual, advent** mean. The root **ven** means ———.
   (A) break/burst   (B) voice/call   (C) come

6. Think of what **complicate, compound, complete** mean. The prefix **com** means
   ———.

   (A) element   (B) with/together   (C) against

7. Think of what **magnificent, maximum, magnitude** mean. The roots **magn** and
   maxim mean ———.
   (A) great/large   (B) turn   (C) small

8. Think of what **physician, librarian, grammarian** mean. The suffixes **arian** and
   cian mean ———.
   (A) study   (B) one who   (C) near

9. Think of what **brilliancy, competency, vacancy** mean. The suffixes **ancy** and **ency**
   mean ———.
   (A) through   (B) idea   (C) state/condition

10. Think of what **triplex, tripod, tertiary** mean. The prefixes **tri** and **ter** mean **three,**
    threefold, having three parts, or **occurring once every** ———.
    (A) third   (B) time   (C) month

1. Think of what **individually, divisor, divisible** mean. The root **div** means _____.

   (A) separate   (B) person   (C) divine

2. Think of what **honorary, elementary, customary** mean. The suffix **ary** can mean _____.

   (A) connected with   (B) move   (C) many

3. Think of what **secretary, missionary, dictionary** mean. The suffix **ary** can mean **that which** or _____.

   (A) in   (B) one who   (C) from

4. Think of what **library, sanctuary, infirmary** mean. The suffix **ary** can also mean _____.

   (A) a place for   (B) very   (C) small

5. Think of what **outfield, outjet, outcast** mean. The prefix **out** can mean **outside, outward**, _____, or **forth.**

   (A) away   (B) with   (C) in

6. Think of what **outscore, outsing, outweigh** mean. The prefix **out** can also mean **more than** or _____.

   (A) near   (B) better than   (C) throw

7. Think of what **reflex, inflection, deflect** mean. The roots **flect** and **flex** mean _____.

   (A) light   (B) need   (C) bend

8. Think of what **bicentennial, twin, bimonthly** mean. The prefixes **bi** and **twi** mean _____.

   (A) through   (B) year   (C) two

9. Think of what **snowbound, northbound, southbound** mean. The suffix **bound** means **held fast** or _____.

   (A) hit   (B) on the way to   (C) motion

10. Think of what **photographic, phosphorus, photocopy** mean. The roots **phot** and **phos** mean _____.

    (A) old   (B) light   (C) heavy

UNIT 48
Decoding Review

1. Think of what **bystander, byway, bypast** mean. The prefix **by** can mean **near, close,** or _____.

   (A) come   (B) aside   (C) high

2. Think of what **by-product, by-election, bystreet** mean. The prefix **by** can also mean **of less importance, secondary,** or _____.

   (A) minor   (B) three   (C) figure

3. Think of what **reproduction, conductor, introduce** mean. The roots **duc** and **duct** mean _____.

   (A) lead   (B) turn   (C) call/voice

4. Think of what **comfort, fortitude, fortress** mean. The root **fort** means _____.

   (A) four   (B) fight   (C) strong

5. Think of what **underscore, undersecretary, underground** mean. The prefix **under** can mean **beneath, below,** or **of a** _____ **position or rank.**

   (A) lower   (B) high   (C) farther

6. Think of what **underfeed, underdeveloped, undersupply** mean. The prefix **under** can also mean _____ or **below normal.**

   (A) not enough   (B) small   (C) encircle

7. Think of what **semblance, simultaneous, dissimilar** mean. The roots **simil, simul,** and **sembl** mean _____.

   (A) have/hold   (B) write   (C) together/like

8. Think of what **martyrdom, wisdom, freedom** mean. The suffix **dom** can mean

   _____.

   (A) often   (B) state of   (C) desire for

9. Think of what **kingdom, officialdom, dukedom** mean. The suffix **dom** can also mean _____, **realm,** or **domain.**

   (A) region   (B) person   (C) rights

10. Think of what **multimedia, multiply, multitude** mean. The prefix **multi** means

    _____.

    (A) number   (B) many   (C) different

1. Think of what **motion, mobility, movement** mean. The roots **mot, mob,** and **mov** mean _____.

   (A) stop   (B) gross   (C) move

2. Think of what **offshoot, offprint, offshore** mean. The prefix **off** means _____.

   (A) through   (B) from   (C) new

3. Think of what **credible, lovable, soluble** mean. The suffixes **able, ible,** and **ble** mean _____ or **having.**

   (A) going   (B) need   (C) able to be

4. Think of what **terrible, durable, voluble** mean. The suffixes **able, ible,** and **ble** can also mean **tending to** or _____.

   (A) inclined to   (B) completely   (C) very

5. Think of what **progress, regress, graduate** mean. The roots **gress** and **grad** mean _____.

   (A) believe/trust   (B) step   (C) look/see

6. Think of what **aquarium, auditorium, rosarium** mean. The suffixes **orium** and **arium** mean _____ **for** or **where.**

   (A) ordinarily   (B) place   (C) service

7. Think of what **historical, heroic, volcanic** mean. The suffixes **ic** and **ical** can mean **of, like, pertaining to,** or _____.

   (A) against   (B) all   (C) connected with

8. Think of what **public, musical, statistical** mean. The suffixes **ic** and **ical** can also indicate **a** _____ or **an adjective.**

   (A) noun   (B) place   (C) verb

9. Think of **convert, reverse, diversity.** The roots **vers** and **vert** mean _____.

   (A) believe/trust   (B) turn   (C) death

10. Think of what **probably, responsibly, solubly** mean. The suffixes **ably, ibly,** and **bly** mean _____ **indicated by the stem.**

    (A) in the manner   (B) time   (C) type

UNIT 50
Decoding Review

1. Think of what **congress, conform, confederation** mean. The prefix **con** means _____ .

   (A) **number**   (B) **with/together**   (C) **many**

2. Think of what **subside, sedate, session** mean. The roots **sid, sed,** and **sess** mean _____ .

   (A) **place/home**   (B) **stop**   (C) sit/settle

3. Think of what **flagship, battleship, steamship** mean. The suffix **ship** can mean a _____ .

   (A) **building**   (B) **type of ship**   (C) **showing**

4. Think of what **penmanship, leadership, horsemanship** mean. The suffix **ship** can mean _____ .

   (A) **art/skill**   (B) **partly**   (C) **spectator**

5. Think of what **proprietorship, cousinship, friendship** mean. The suffix **ship** can mean _____ **indicating the relationship specified by the stem.**

   (A) **like/love**   (B) **state/condition**   (C) **explorer**

6. Think of what **chancellorship, lordship, clerkship** mean. The suffix **ship** can mean **office, occupation, rank,** or _____ .

   (A) **feeling**   (B) **necessary**   (C) **position**

7. Think of what **censorship, courtship, hardship** mean. The suffix **ship** can also mean **action,** _____ , or **that which is formed by or made of.**

   (A) **kind**   (B) **process**   (C) **truth**

8. Think of what **reject, interject, eject** mean. The root **ject** means _____ .

   (A) **look/see**   (B) **tell/say**   (C) **throw**

9. Think of what **downpour, downgrade, downdraft** mean. The prefix **down** means **in a** _____ **place or condition**.

   (A) **lower**   (B) **new**   (C) **unhealthy**

10. Think of what **activator, react, enact** mean. The root **act** means _____ .

    (A) **not**   (B) **do**   (C) **large**

Suffixes are word parts that are added at the end of words. Suffixes have meanings of their own, and they change the meaning of the words they are attached to. Many suffixes have the same, or nearly the same, meaning. The suffixes *dom, orium, arium, ary, ory,* and *atory,* for instance, can all mean "place."

A. Exercising Your Skill

There is an old saying, "a place for everything and everything in its place." The names for some places are familiar: *bedroom, doghouse, kitchen, garden.* Can you imagine not knowing what those words mean? But what about *apiary* and *solarium*? They are both place names, but they aren't ones we use often. Although they are less familiar, they do have something in common with *bedroom* and *doghouse*: The words are made up of parts. However, while *bedroom* and *doghouse* are made up of two whole words, *apiary* and *solarium* are made up of a word root and a suffix. Knowing the meaning of word roots and suffixes can help you figure out the meaning of words you do not know. *Apiary* and *solarium* contain two different suffixes that mean "place": *ary* and *arium*. An apiary is a place where bees are kept; a solarium is a place (room) where sunlight gathers. As the old saying goes, there is a place for everything.

Look at the word web below. Each main branch contains a suffix that means "place." Make a similar web on your paper. Then add two or more sub-branches to each suffix showing words that end in that suffix. (The word *factory* has already been added as a sub-branch.)

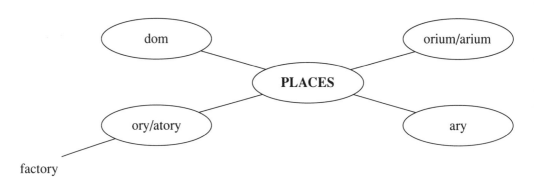

B. Expanding Your Skill

How did you do putting those places in their place?

Compare your web with the webs your classmates made. Can you learn any new words? Try finding some new place words in a dictionary or other reference book. Add them to your word web.

See if you can answer these questions: What is the difference between an oceanarium and an aquarium? between a solarium and a conservatory?

C. Exploring Language

Do you know what an emporium is? If you think that it is some sort of place, you're right. Is an emporium a place for emperors? No, it is a marketplace or a large store that sells a wide variety of merchandise. The root of the word *emporium* comes from the ancient Greek word *emporos*, which means "merchant."

What might you find in an emporium? What kinds of sellers would be there? From where might shipments of goods come? What wonderful goods might you see?

Describe an emporium you have visited or make one up. If you make one up, include in it anything you want, even unusual livestock such as penguins or chimpanzees; make it a marvelous marketplace, a bizarre bazaar. What words containing suffixes can you use in your description? Underline the ones you use.

D. Expressing Yourself

Choose one of these activities.

1. What happens to pencils when they disappear? Where do all those socks go that get lost in the laundry? Is there a place where things go when they disappear? Using suffixes that you know, invent names for four or five places where lost objects go—for example, a pencilory, a sockdom.

2. Study a map of your state and locate its wildlife sanctuaries. Find out something about them. Why are sanctuaries so named? What animals and plants do they protect? What kinds of nature programs do they have? If you can visit a sanctuary, make a list of what you see.

3. An auditorium is a place for an audience to hear (and see) performances. In a good auditorium, you can hear well no matter where you sit or stand. That is what *acoustics* is all about; it is the study of sound and how it is transmitted and received. A good auditorium should have good acoustics. How do architects and engineers design a room with good acoustics? Do some research in the library and write a brief report.

4. Some of the world's most important discoveries have been made in laboratories. A laboratory is a scientist's work place. Modern laboratories usually have all kinds of interesting equipment that allows scientists to examine matter or to create new matter, and to gather information that would otherwise be beyond our reach.

   What discovery would you like to make in a laboratory? Write one scene of a science-fiction story in which such a discovery takes place. Make sure that your reader can picture the laboratory and any equipment that the scientist uses.

CONCEPTS DEVELOPED

Book G

Specific Skill Series

Following Directions

Richard A. Boning

Fifth Edition

SRA/McGraw-Hill
Columbus, Ohio

Cover, Back Cover, ZEFA/Germany/The Stock Market

SRA/McGraw-Hill

A Division of The **McGraw·Hill** *Companies*

Printed in the United States of America.

Send all inquiries to:
    SRA/McGraw-Hill
    8787 Orion Place
    Columbus, OH 43240-4027

ISBN 0-02-687937-9

    5 6 IPC 02 01

To the Teacher

PURPOSE:
FOLLOWING DIRECTIONS is designed to develop skill in reading, understanding, and following instructions and directions. Proficiency in this basic skill is essential for success in every school subject and in nonacademic activities as well.

FOR WHOM:
The skill of FOLLOWING DIRECTIONS is developed through a series of books spanning ten levels (Picture, Preparatory, A, B, C, D, E, F, G, H). The Picture Level is for pupils who have not acquired a basic sight vocabulary. The Preparatory Level is for pupils who have a basic sight vocabulary but are not yet ready for the first-grade-level book. Books A through H are appropriate for pupils who can read on levels one through eight, respectively. **The use of the *Specific Skill Series Placement Test* is recommended to determine the appropriate level.**

THE NEW EDITION:
The fifth edition of the *Specific Skill Series* maintains the quality and focus that has distinguished this program for more than 25 years. A key element central to the program's success has been the unique nature of the reading selections. Nonfiction pieces about current topics have been designed to stimulate the interest of students, motivating them to use the comprehension strategies they have learned to further their reading. To keep this important aspect of the program intact, a percentage of the reading selections have been replaced in order to ensure the continued relevance of the subject material.

In addition, a significant percentage of the artwork in the program has been replaced to give the books a contemporary look. The cover photographs are designed to appeal to readers of all ages.

SESSIONS:
Short practice sessions are the most effective. It is desirable to have a practice session every day or every other day, using a few units each session.

SCORING:
Pupils should record their answers on the reproducible worksheets. The worksheets make scoring easier and provide uniform records of the pupils' work. Using worksheets also avoids consuming the exercise books.

To the Teacher

It is important for pupils to know how well they are doing. For this reason, units should be scored as soon as they have been completed. Then a discussion can be held in which pupils justify their choices. (The Integrated Language Activities, many of which are open-ended, do not lend themselves to an objective score; thus there are no answer keys for these pages.)

GENERAL INFORMATION ON *FOLLOWING DIRECTIONS*:

FOLLOWING DIRECTIONS focuses attention on four types of directions. The *testing and drilling* directions are like those in most textbooks and workbooks. Mastery of this type, so vital to school success, is stressed throughout FOLLOWING DIRECTIONS. The second type of direction is found in science books and involves *experimenting*. Such material requires the reader to find an answer to a problem or provides the reader with an example of practical application of a principle.

The third type of direction, *assembling*, deals with parts or ingredients and the order and way in which they are put together. Here the purpose is to make or create, rather than to solve a problem or demonstrate a principle.

Directions which tell how to do something are *performing* directions. They accent the steps in learning to do something new. The focus is on the performance rather than on the product.

SUGGESTED STEPS:

On levels A-H, pupils read the information above the first line. Then they answer the questions *below* this line. (Pupils are *not* to respond in writing to information *above* the first line; they are only to study it. Pupils should not write or mark anything in this book.) On the Picture Level, pupils tell if a picture correctly follows the directions. On the Preparatory Level, pupils tell which picture out of two correctly follows the directions.

Additional information on using FOLLOWING DIRECTIONS with pupils will be found in the **Specific Skill Series Teacher's Manual**.

RELATED MATERIALS:

Specific Skill Series Placement Tests, which enable the teacher to place pupils at their appropriate levels in each skill, are available for the Elementary (Pre-1–6) and Midway (4–8) grade levels.

About This Book

Following directions is like trying to find your way in a strange place by using a road map. If you follow the directions correctly, you will get where you want to go. If you do not understand the directions, or if you make mistakes in following them, you will become lost.

Reading directions is different from reading a story or an article. When you read directions, you should read slowly and carefully. You should reread anything you do not understand and find out the meanings of any special terms that are used. When you are following directions, you need to follow them in the right order. Direction words, such as *top*, *bottom*, *right*, and *left*, are especially important.

In this book, you will read four different kinds of directions. You will read directions that are like the directions you often find on tests and in workbooks. You will read directions that tell you how to conduct experiments and directions for putting things together. You will also read directions for doing things, such as playing a game.

After you read each set of directions, you will answer questions about the directions. One question is about the purpose of the directions. Others are about details in the directions. Read each set of directions carefully so that you can answer the questions about them.

DIRECTIONS: Many plants have uses that may not be that familiar to us. Among such plants are onions, carrots, beets, spinach, blueberries, marigolds, goldenrod, and hickory and black-walnut hulls. This experiment focuses on beets. Chop or grind beets into small pieces. Put the chopped beets into an enamel or a glass pan with just enough water to cover. Soak the beets overnight and then bring them to a boil, cooking slowly for one hour. Add just enough water to replace that which evaporates. Too much water will make a weak color. Remove the mixture from the heat, and strain it through a clean cloth into a glass or china bowl to remove any plant fibers. Pour the dye back into the saucepan. Add a small piece of white cloth (cotton, silk, or wool). Boil the dye again for fifteen minutes and stir it with a stick. Remove the cloth from the dye and let it dry.

1. These directions were written to show you how to—

    (A) **grow and harvest beets**   (B) **slice vegetables**

    (C) **bring water to a boil**   (D) **make and use a beet dye**

2. The more water, the—

    (A) **weaker the color**   (B) **better the soup**

    (C) **stronger the color**   (D) **more time required**

3. To get rid of plant fibers—

    (A) **scoop out with a spoon**   (B) **chop with a knife**

    (C) **allow time to dissolve**   (D) **strain through a cloth**

4. Remember to boil—

    (A) **overnight**   (B) **just once**

    (C) **for two hours**   (D) **twice**

DIRECTIONS: When using a metal file, always remember to bear down on the forward stroke only. On the return stroke, lift the file clear of the surface to avoid dulling the instrument's teeth. Only when working on very soft metals is it advisable to drag the file's teeth slightly on the return stroke. This helps clear out metal pieces from between the teeth. It is best to bear down just hard enough to keep the file cutting at all times. Too little pressure uses only the tips of the teeth; too much pressure can chip the teeth. Move the file in straight lines across the surface. Use a vise to grip the work so that your hands are free to hold the file. Protect your hands by equipping the file with a handle. Buy a wooden handle and install it by inserting the pointed end of the file into the handle hole.

1. These directions show you how to—
   - (A) work with a hammer
   - (B) use a file
   - (C) polish a file
   - (D) oil a vise

2. When using a file,—
   - (A) always bear down on the return stroke
   - (B) move it in a circle
   - (C) remove the handle
   - (D) press down on the forward stroke

3. When working on soft metals, you can—
   - (A) remove the handle
   - (B) clear metal pieces from the teeth
   - (C) bear down very hard on the return stroke
   - (D) file in circles

4. Protect your hands by—
   - (A) dulling the teeth
   - (B) dragging the teeth on the backstroke
   - (C) using a vise
   - (D) installing a handle

DIRECTIONS: First find a large glass jar with a mouth wide enough for your fist to fit inside. Wash the jar out well. Then pour about an inch of water in the bottom. Make a sheet of rubber by slicing up a large balloon. Place this rubber over the mouth of the jar. Put a weight on top to hold the rubber in place. Make some chalk dust by rubbing a piece of chalk on a hard surface. Collect all the dust. Remove the rubber cover from the jar after ten minutes. Place the chalk dust into the jar and quickly replace the rubber. Keep the rubber in place with some elastic. Push your fist against the rubber and into the jar. This will compress and warm the air. Remove your fist and watch the air condense around the dust, forming a cloud!

1. These directions will help you to—

   (A) save chalk dust

   (B) make your own cloud

   (C) strengthen your fist

   (D) make rain fall from a cloud

2. Before placing the rubber over the jar mouth,—

   (A) make some chalk dust

   (B) put some water in the jar

   (C) test it with your fist

   (D) shake the jar well

3. Place the chalk dust into the jar after the rubber cover has—

   (A) been on for ten minutes

   (B) just been sliced up

   (C) been off for ten minutes

   (D) been coated with the dust

4. The cloud is formed—

   (A) after you remove your fist

   (B) before the dust is in the jar

   (C) outside the jar

   (D) before you remove your fist

DIRECTIONS: First take a raw egg from your refrigerator. Place the egg in a strainer. Put the kitchen strainer and the egg on a table while you light a candle. Put the candle in a holder and wave the egg in the strainer over the flame. The egg will blacken (from the black carbon of the flame). You can wash the black off the strainer when the experiment is over. When the egg is completely black, take it from the strainer and place it in a glass pot or wide-mouthed jar filled with water. Remove the carbon from your hand. Now look at the egg. It appears to have become silver! Actually, the carbon covering does not get wet in the pot; it holds a thin film of air next to the egg. The air acts like a mirror!

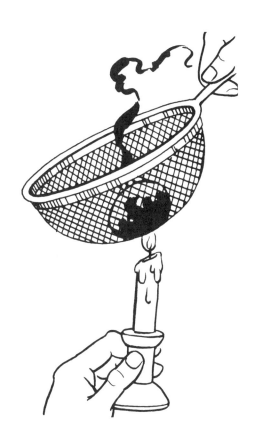

1. This experiment teaches you how to—

   (A) boil an egg
   (C) paint an egg

   (B) perform an optical illusion
   (D) make an egg disappear

2. This experiment should be performed with—

   (A) a hard-boiled egg
   (C) a raw egg

   (B) an egg painted black
   (D) a spoiled egg

3. The egg becomes black when—

   (A) it is put in the strainer
   (C) it is put in the pot of water

   (B) it is passed through the flame
   (D) you expose it to air

4. The egg appears silver in the water because the—

   (A) air film acts as a mirror
   (C) carbon washes off

   (B) carbon becomes polished
   (D) carbon gets wet

DIRECTIONS: You will need a supply of liquid soap, a large bowl, an eggbeater, a soft scrub brush, two buckets of clean water, and a few clean cloths. To begin with, use a vacuum cleaner to thoroughly clean both sides of the rug. If you do the work indoors, also clean the floor beneath the carpet. Then place some of the liquid soap in the bowl and beat it to a stiff lather. Apply this with the brush to a section of the rug not over two feet square. Wipe off the lather with a wet cloth and dry it with another cloth. After the rug is cleaned, hang it outside to dry. Support the carpet on chair backs that are standing in the shade. When the rug is dry, brush the nap in one direction.

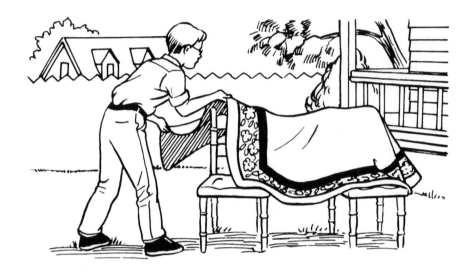

---

1. This article teaches you how to—

    (A) cut up your rug   (B) clean a floor

    (C) shampoo your rug   (D) beat a rug

2. Before beating the liquid soap,—

    (A) brush the nap of the rug   (B) hang the rug outside

    (C) wipe the rug with a wet cloth   (D) vacuum the carpet

3. The liquid soap should be brushed on—

    (A) the entire rug at once   (B) with a wet cloth

    (C) with a vacuum cleaner   (D) two square feet of the rug at one time

4. After the carpet is dry,—

    (A) rub it with a wet cloth   (B) rub in some liquid soap

    (C) brush the nap in one direction   (D) clean it with a vacuum

DIRECTIONS: First make the copying fluid. Mix four parts of water to one part turpentine. Add to this solution a piece of soap about the size of an eraser. Shake the mixture well, making sure that the soap is dissolved. The soap is important to the solution as it forms an emulsion which keeps the turpentine and water from separating. Now that the fluid is ready, find the newspaper picture you'd like to copy. Wet the picture with the copying fluid. Then place a blank piece of paper on top of the newspaper and rub with the bowl of a spoon (or with any handy flat object). Lift the top piece of paper after a few moments. You'll see that the turpentine dissolved enough of the ink so that an impression was left on the paper.

1. This article teaches you how to—

   (A) print a newspaper
   (C) ink a newspaper

   (B) make turpentine
   (D) transfer a newspaper picture

2. To make the copying fluid, mix one part turpentine to—

   (A) four parts water
   (C) four parts soap

   (B) one part water
   (D) two parts soap

3. After the soap is dissolved in the fluid,—

   (A) wet the picture with the fluid
   (C) stir it with a spoon

   (B) add some ink
   (D) wet a blank piece of paper

4. An impression is left on the blank paper because the—

   (A) paper was wet
   (C) newspaper is black

   (B) soap copied the newsprint
   (D) turpentine dissolved some ink

DIRECTIONS: Before you begin to scale the fish, make sure that you have a double thickness of newspaper under it. A scaling knife is preferable, or use any knife that is heavy, short, and not too sharp. Run the knife at a right angle from the fish. Work from the tail toward the head. Once the fish is scaled, cut through the head. Start the cut right behind the gills. You won't need to cut through the backbone. You can snap the head off rather easily. Next, the fins that remain should be cut off. If the entrails don't come out when the head is snapped off, you may have to remove them by cutting lengthwise on the underside. Lastly, split the fish open, scrape it, wash it, and dry it.

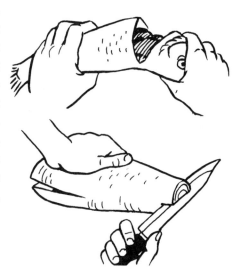

1. The article tells the way to—
   - (A) cook a fish properly
   - (B) catch a fish
   - (C) clean a fish
   - (D) make a messy job

2. Remember to scale the fish—
   - (A) with a very sharp knife
   - (B) from the tail to the head
   - (C) after you cut off the head
   - (D) before you do anything else

3. Keep in mind that the head—
   - (A) isn't touched
   - (B) is tough
   - (C) can be snapped off
   - (D) tastes best

4. The entrails sometimes come out—
   - (A) when the head is snapped off
   - (B) when the fish is washed
   - (C) upon scaling the fish
   - (D) when the fins are cut off

DIRECTIONS: Blow up a balloon. Cover the surface with several layers of newspaper strips soaked in paste or liquid starch. Use strips one or two inches wide. Three layers should be enough. You can create the figure you wish by building up the outer layer accordingly. Allow the shell to dry overnight. Stick a pin through the layers into the balloon. Now cover the shell with crepe paper or paint. Cut an opening in the top of the back and insert candies through the opening. Fasten a cord around the figure and hang it from the ceiling. Now you are ready for a piñata party. Blindfold youngsters and have them take turns at trying to break the piñata. When they succeed, they will be surprised by a shower of candy!

1. The object of this article is to show you how to—

    (A) **break a piñata**
    (B) **make a shower of candies**
    (C) **have a piñata party**
    (D) **work with newspapers**

2. The balloon should first be—

    (A) **covered with strips of newspaper**
    (B) **painted**
    (C) **attached to the ceiling**
    (D) **punctured**

3. The shell should dry overnight—

    (A) **before you build up the figure**
    (B) **after the outer layer has been built up**
    (C) **after you cut the opening**
    (D) **after you have inserted the candy**

4. The pinhole should be made—

    (A) **before the shell dries**
    (B) **after the shell dries**
    (C) **after the opening is cut**
    (D) **after the children are blindfolded**

DIRECTIONS: First combine one and a half cups of all-purpose flour, one cup of milk, and one beaten egg in a large bowl. Use a whisk to blend the mixture thoroughly. Cover it and allow it to sit at room temperature for no less than one hour. Preheat your oven to 200° about twenty minutes before the batter is ready. Next peel the skins from three large onions and then cut them into quarter-inch-thick slices. Separate the slices into rings and set them aside. Then melt three to four cups of shortening in a skillet and heat it to 375°. Use metal tongs to dip the onion rings into the batter. Then place them in the hot fat. After they turn golden, put them in the preheated oven.

1. This article shows you how to make—
   (A) **French-fried potatoes**　　(B) **onion soup**
   (C) **fried onion rings**　　(D) **pretzels**

2. After blending together the flour, milk, and egg,—
   (A) **let it sit for at least one hour**　　(B) **melt it in a skillet**
   (C) **spread it on the onions**　　(D) **place it in hot fat**

3. Before melting the shortening in the skillet,—
   (A) **put the rings in the oven**　　(B) **preheat the oven to 400°**
   (C) **separate the onion rings**　　(D) **dip the rings in the batter**

4. After dipping the onion rings into the batter,—
   (A) **dip them in flour**　　(B) **put them in the hot fat**
   (C) **mix the flour, milk, and egg**　　(D) **melt the shortening**

DIRECTIONS: First bring home a cardboard carton from your local supermarket. Then cut the four sides of the box down to the height of the tallest rock in your collection. Next take the four strips you just cut from the box and trim them to the same height. Trim a bit more off the ends of the strips so they will fit in the box. Then cut two notches halfway into each strip. Make sure that the notches divide the strips into thirds. Then join the strips crosswise at the notches. Place them in the box. Number the nine compartments in the box and place a rock into each space. Put matching numbers on nine index cards, along with interesting information about each specimen, and file them away.

1. These directions show you how to—
   (A) start a rock collection
   (B) make a display case for rocks
   (C) find interesting rocks
   (D) group your rocks by hardness

2. The sides of the box should be cut down to the height of—
   (A) the smallest of your rocks
   (B) one foot
   (C) the index cards
   (D) the tallest of your rocks

3. The notches you cut in the strips should divide the—
   (A) strips into thirds
   (B) strips in half
   (C) box in half
   (D) box in quarters

4. After putting the rocks into the compartments,—
   (A) trim a bit more off the strips
   (B) divide the strips into thirds
   (C) remove them and file them away
   (D) start a file on your rocks

DIRECTIONS: Approach the bird slowly. Be sure to pick up the bird very carefully. Hold the side that is not injured. The break in the bone is usually under the wing. Disinfect the area with hydrogen peroxide. Be sure to prevent the injured bird from flying. To do this, tie its wing against its body. Use some gauze or a bandage that will be easy to remove later. Make sure that the bandage is not too tight or the bird may have trouble breathing. Then put the bird in a comfortable box. Keep it there for at least ten days. After the wing has healed, remove the bandage. Then allow the bird to fly away.

1. These directions teach you how to—
   (A) catch a bird
   (B) build a bird cage
   (C) heal a bird's broken wing
   (D) feed a bird

2. Look for the broken bone—
   (A) near the head
   (B) on top of the wing
   (C) under the wing
   (D) on the left wing

3. Before putting the bird in a box,—
   (A) let it fly around
   (B) tie its wing to its body
   (C) feed it
   (D) untie the gauze

4. The bird should rest—
   (A) for a day
   (B) for ten days
   (C) without the bandage
   (D) in a tree

DIRECTIONS: First be sure to plan your time carefully from the time you receive the hurricane warning, and avoid any last-second decisions which could leave you marooned. Leave any low-lying areas that may be hit by high tides and strong waves. Don't forget to moor your boat (if you have one) before the storm hits. After securing the boat, do not return to it once the winds pick up. Board up your house windows or protect them with storm shutters and tape. Anchor your outdoor items, such as garbage cans, porch furniture, and heavy garden tools. Store fresh drinking water in clean bathtubs or bottles; your town's water supply may become contaminated. Make sure your battery-operated equipment works. Make sure your car is fueled, but remain indoors during the high winds of the hurricane.

1. These instructions teach you how to—

    (A) survive a storm at sea

    (B) react during a hurricane warning

    (C) live in a storm shelter

    (D) predict hurricanes

2. When you receive the warning, be sure to—

    (A) stay in low areas

    (B) stay in a secured boat

    (C) moor your boat

    (D) remove your storm shutters

3. Before the storm hits, it is important to—

    (A) anchor your garbage cans

    (B) leave your windows open

    (C) drain your car's fuel

    (D) travel to neighbors

4. In addition to storing drinking water, you should also—

    (A) use your batteries

    (B) fuel up your car

    (C) save bottles

    (D) get to low ground

Unit 1 relates a clever experiment for using plants in unusual ways. Here is a simple experiment that focuses on how plants react in certain situations. You can discuss this experiment as you complete Part A.

DIRECTIONS: First, grow a bean plant. After your bean plant has sprouted and is growing nicely, put a carton over it. Then cut a hole in the carton. Wait a couple of weeks. The bean plant will grow up into the carton and out of the hole. This proves that _____ .

A. Exercising Your Skill

Most experiments set out to prove something about the way plants, animals, people, or things behave. And most of the time, the experiments are designed to control certain conditions.

What conditions do you think are being controlled in the bean experiment? Why will the plant grow out of the hole? What does it need that it cannot get inside the carton? Discuss this with your classmates and list the possibilities on the board.

How do you think that the last sentence of the experiment should end? Discuss it with your classmates, listing possible answers on the board. You might want to vote on the best answer.

B. Expanding Your Skill

The bean experiment answers some questions about the action of daylight on bean plants. It also raises some questions. For example, it could be that bean plants always grow upward and always toward the south. If the hole was high up and facing south, you wouldn't have proved anything about the action of daylight on beans. Also, you may have thought the experiment was about all plants. But you have dealt only with beans.

How can the experiment be improved? Suppose you wanted to prove that all plants grow toward the sun.

- How would you change the experiment?
- What conditions or features would you add?

Write down your ideas. Include anything you can think of to improve the experiment. (Don't worry if some of your ideas seem strange, because at this point you're not dealing with a finished product.)

Now share your ideas with your classmates. Treat this sharing as a kind of brainstorming. That means you don't criticize each other's ideas. Even the strangest idea may have something worthwhile in it!

- Which ideas are similar?
- Which things would be hard to do, and which things would be easy?
- Would any of the ideas not work?
- How could they be improved?

C. Exploring Language

Why are experiments written down? For one thing, the experimenter wants to show people what the point of the experiment was and what steps were taken in the experiment. For another thing, the experimenter, or other experimenters, may want to repeat the experiment. The written record becomes a set of instructions. Without that written record, there's nothing to go on.

Think about the bean experiment and the improvements you have discussed. Do you think you're ready to design an experiment? Here is a numbered outline for you to follow. On your paper, write your plans for the experiment using the headings in the outline.

1. Problem or Question
2. What I Want to Prove
3. Materials Needed
4. Procedure
   a. Step 1
   b. Step 2 (and so on)
5. Observations
6. Conclusions

The Problem or Question states in a general way what you want to investigate. For example: How does sunlight affect growing plants?

What I Want to Prove is a narrower statement. For example: Bean plants will grow toward daylight.

After the experiment is done, your Observations tell what you saw or observed as you did the experiment. Your Conclusions tell what you think your Observations mean. Of course, in order to fill in the Observations or Conclusions part, you'll actually have to carry out the experiment.

D. Expressing Yourself

Choose one of these activities.

1. Do the experiment you wrote about in Part C. Complete your write-up with the Observations and Conclusions.

2. Design and write up another experiment using beans or bean plants. Decide on some general question and something you want to prove. For example, you might do an experiment about water (varying amounts) or light (artificial light and/or daylight).

3. Do an experiment on the length of time it takes for certain plants to begin growing or sprouting. Plant the seeds of four or five different vegetables (or flowers) in separate small pots. Put the pots in the same location and give them the same amount of water each day. Keep a record of which one comes up first, second, and so on, and when any obvious changes occur in each one.

DIRECTIONS: The first person in the group starts off by naming anything that is geographical. It could be a city, state, country, river, lake, or any proper geographical term. For example, the person might say, "Boston." The second person has ten seconds to think of how the word ends and come up with another geographical term starting with that letter. The second participant might say, "Norway," since the geographical term has to start with "N." The third person would have to choose a word beginning with "Y." If a player fails to think of a correct answer within the time limit, that player is out of the game. The last person to survive is the champion.

BOSTON
NORWAY
YUGOSLAVIA

---

1. The game may help you with—
   (A) history
   (B) music
   (C) geography
   (D) sports

2. The person trying to answer needs—
   (A) no time limit
   (B) to know geography only
   (C) to ignore the last letters of words
   (D) to know something about spelling and geography

3. Before you choose your own word, think about how—
   (A) the last word starts
   (B) the last word ends
   (C) smart you are
   (D) long the last word is

4. The answers must be—
   (A) in New York
   (B) within the United States
   (C) proper geographical terms
   (D) in the same region

DIRECTIONS: At the call of "Take your mark," get into position. Place the right foot the farthest back with both the knee and toe touching the ground. You will take your first step with your right leg. The toe of your left foot should touch the ground and be even with your right knee. Your hands should be on the ground, behind the starting line. Your fingers should be pointing to the side. Keep your head down, your neck and shoulders relaxed, and arms well spread. As you hear "Get set," raise your right knee and come up on the tips of your fingers. Your hips should be as high as your shoulders. Push off with both feet at the sound of "Go!"

---

1. The directions tell you how to—

   (A) run swiftly   (B) develop footwork
   (C) get a good stride   (D) get a good starting position

2. The toe of your left foot should be—

   (A) outside your arms   (B) even with your right knee
   (C) always up in the air   (D) even with your head

3. Your hands should—

   (A) be on the starting line   (B) face each other
   (C) be on the ground   (D) be kept folded

4. When you hear "Get set,"—

   (A) raise your head   (B) raise your right knee
   (C) lower your right knee   (D) lower your hips

DIRECTIONS: First choose the type of container you like. An attractive disposable flowerpot can be made by cutting off the top of an empty milk carton. Be sure to cover the outside of the container with aluminum foil. An old piano bench can also be converted into a flower container by removing the lid and lining the interior with zinc or copper. Waterproof smaller flowerpots by dipping them in melted paraffin. Allow the paraffin to sink into the pores. Cover the soil in window boxes with brightly colored sand. This keeps loose dirt from flowing over the sides. Paint the inside of flower boxes to discourage insects and preserve the wood. Use clay pots, rather than synthetic containers, for plants that prefer cooler temperatures. Clay keeps the roots about fifteen degrees cooler.

1. These directions will help you—

    (A) **plant seeds** (B) **construct flower containers**
    (C) **paint flower boxes** (D) **make clay pots**

2. After cutting off the top of a milk carton,—

    (A) **line the inside with zinc** (B) **dip it in paraffin**
    (C) **cover the outside with foil** (D) **paint the outside**

3. To waterproof smaller flower pots,—

    (A) **fill them with clay** (B) **dip them in melted paraffin**
    (C) **line them with sand** (D) **use milk cartons**

4. To keep insects away from flower boxes,—

    (A) **line them with foil** (B) **paint the inside**
    (C) **use clay pots** (D) **use brightly colored sand**

DIRECTIONS: Pull some carrots from your garden or buy some at the store. Cut off the green sprouts from one carrot, but leave a little green at the top. Cut the carrot in two pieces, leaving about two inches below the green part. Stick three or four toothpicks into the carrot, the same distance from the green top. Rest the carrot, green part up, in a glass jar. Fill the jar with water to cover about one fourth of the carrot. Place the jar in a lighted place, but not in direct sunlight. Replace the water whenever necessary, and check the carrot after several days. Green sprouts will grow from the top of the carrot.

1. These directions tell you how to—

   (A) use carrots in a salad   (B) get a discount on carrots

   (C) make a salad with carrots   (D) grow new sprouts on a carrot

2. Before cutting the carrot,—

   (A) put toothpicks into it   (B) close the shades

   (C) cut off the sprouts on top   (D) fill the jar with water

3. Cut a piece of carrot about—

   (A) one fourth inch   (B) as long as a toothpick

   (C) two inches long   (D) as long as the sprouts

4. Put four toothpicks into the carrot the same distance from the top—

   (A) so the water will cover them   (B) so the new sprouts will grow

   (C) so the carrot is balanced   (D) so the jar will not tip over

23

DIRECTIONS: First line the bottom of your barbecue grill with heavy aluminum foil to increase the heat and catch the drippings from the meat. Next arrange a base of gravel or a similar material in a level layer about one inch deep. This base should be renewed after every six barbecues. Use charcoal briquets for your fuel. To begin the fire, build a pyramid of briquets and pour a half cup of odorless starting fluid over them. After the fluid has had two minutes to soak, set the briquets alight. Take special care when lighting the briquets. When a gray ash appears on the coals, spread them evenly around the cooking area. Sear your steak quickly on both sides and then cook it more slowly at a distance.

1. This article tells you how to—

    (A) prepare for a picnic
    (B) have an outdoor barbecue
    (C) cook food on a stove
    (D) slice steak

2. Before arranging a gravel base in the grill,—

    (A) put in some briquets
    (B) line the grill with foil
    (C) have your steak ready
    (D) add some gray ash

3. Set the briquets alight—

    (A) right after adding the starter fluid
    (B) two minutes after adding the fluid
    (C) with other hot coals
    (D) after the steak is on the grill

4. Before spreading the coals out,—

    (A) renew the gravel base
    (B) look for a gray ash
    (C) put the steak on the grill
    (D) remove the aluminum foil

DIRECTIONS: Always read the meter dials from the right to the left. This procedure is much easier, especially if any of the dial hands are near the zero mark. If your meter has two dials, and one is smaller than the other, it is not imperative to read the smaller dial since it only registers a small amount. Read the dial at the right first. As the dial turns clockwise, always record the figure the pointer has just passed. Read the next dial to the left and record the figure it has just passed. Continue recording the figures on the dials from right to left. When finished, mark off the number of units recorded. Dials on water and gas meters usually indicate the amount each dial records.

1. These instructions show you how to—

    (A) read a meter
    (B) turn the dials of a meter
    (C) install a gas meter
    (D) repair a water meter

2. Always read the meter dials—

    (A) from top to bottom
    (B) from right to left
    (C) from left to right
    (D) from the small to the large dial

3. As you read the first dial, record the figure—

    (A) on the smaller dial
    (B) the pointer is approaching
    (C) the pointer has just passed
    (D) at the top

4. When you have finished reading the meter, mark off—

    (A) the number of units recorded
    (B) the figures on the small dial
    (C) the total figures
    (D) all the zero marks

DIRECTIONS: After you undress each evening and before you put away your clothes, be sure to air them thoroughly. Always try to hang up your clothes in a cool, dry place. Allow air to circulate in the closet every so often. Use only wooden hangers for heavy items like jackets and coats, to make sure they keep their form. Never hang wet clothes in the closet. Their extra weight may ruin the hanger. After hanging up a garment, always fasten all buttons and secure all zippers. This practice keeps the clothes on the hanger and helps maintain their shape. Use a small whisk broom to occasionally wipe away lint and dirt from your clothes. If brushing doesn't work, press a piece of tape onto the spot and peel off the dirt.

1. These directions teach you how to—

    (A) become a tailor
    (C) keep your closets cool
    (B) keep your clothes fresh
    (D) press your clothes

2. After you undress every night,—

    (A) hang up your wet clothes
    (C) air your garments
    (B) tape your clothes to the hangers
    (D) hang up your clothes in a warm place

3. After you hang up a garment, be sure to—

    (A) unzip the zippers
    (C) fasten the buttons
    (B) dampen it with water
    (D) try to stretch it

4. If brushing doesn't remove dirt from a garment, try—

    (A) a hanger
    (C) circulating air
    (B) a piece of tape
    (D) a vacuum cleaner

UNIT 20

DIRECTIONS: First gather up a small needle, some matching thread, a holder filled with beeswax, the loose button, and the garment. Thread the needle. Be sure to double the thread before knotting. Knot the thread twice to make sure it holds. Then run the thread through the beeswax to strengthen it and prevent tangles. Position the button opposite the buttonhole and in line with the other buttons. Bring the needle up from the underside of the garment and through one hole of the button. Return the needle through the opposite hole in the button and pull firmly. Repeat the process three times for a secure button. Finish the repair by running the needle through the thread on the underside of the fabric and knotting. Reinforce the other buttons while your thread is out.

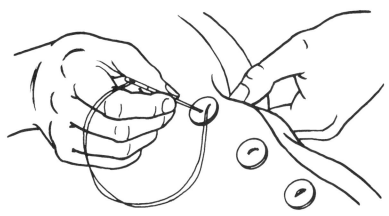

1. This article tells you how to—

   (A) mend a shirt collar
   (C) become a tailor
   (B) repair a ripped dress
   (D) sew on a button

2. Before knotting the thread that has been put through the needle's eye,—

   (A) double the thread
   (C) position the button
   (B) fix the other buttons
   (D) run the thread through the beeswax

3. To prevent the thread from tangling,—

   (A) add a double knot
   (C) run it through beeswax
   (B) double the thread
   (D) start from the underside

4. To finish the repair, run the needle—

   (A) through the opposite hole in the button, and pull
   (C) through the thread on the underside, and knot it
   (B) through the beeswax
   (D) through a flame

27

DIRECTIONS: Always carry a radiotelephone in your boat. If you become stranded, signal the Coast Guard for help. Have a spare engine handy and in good working condition. Be sure to check your spare engine periodically. Your worst danger will come from overexposure to the elements; the sun can cause a rapid loss of body moisture. Should you become stranded, be sure to wear enough clothes to cover your entire body. Wear a hat as well. Make sure that your boat is equipped with quality sunscreening lotions. Never drink any of the salt water, even if you dilute it with fresh water. If your drinking water is in short supply, stay away from foods and soft drinks. Make sure you have a compact mirror (about three inches in diameter) on board for signaling.

1. These instructions tell you how to—
    (A) survive in the desert
    (B) prevent drownings
    (C) make salt water safe to drink
    (D) survive when stranded in a boat

2. The worst danger when stranded is—
    (A) exposure to sun and wind
    (B) lack of water
    (C) attacking fish
    (D) lack of a spare engine

3. If you have little drinking water on board,—
    (A) drink the salt water
    (B) don't eat much food
    (C) eat as much food as possible
    (D) dilute the salt water

4. You can use a mirror to—
    (A) signal other boats
    (B) keep the sun's rays away
    (C) scare the fish away
    (D) work the radio

DIRECTIONS: Be sure to look for simplicity. Remember that good modern furniture should be uncluttered and warm-looking. Be sure that the woods are rich and have interesting grains. Bright upholstery fabrics look well on modern chairs and couches. Don't buy the piece of furniture with the highest price tag; cost is not a good indicator for modern furniture. Make sure that there is an inch-thick dustproofing between the drawers of a chest. Check for mahogany drawer bottoms; this wood is flexible enough to hold most loads. Choose furniture which has matching woodgrains on the drawers or sliding panels of a chest. If you plan to use a modern bookcase for a room divider, be sure to check that both sides are finished.

---

1. These instructions tell you how to—
    (A) **clean your upholstery**
    (B) **build a good bookcase**
    (C) **look for good colonial furniture**
    (D) **look for good modern furniture**

2. Modern chairs look good with—
    (A) **oaken drawer bottoms**
    (B) **bright upholstery**
    (C) **plain-looking fabrics**
    (D) **dark woodgrains only**

3. Between the drawers of a chest, be sure to find—
    (A) **mahogany wood**
    (B) **inch-thick dustproofing**
    (C) **sliding panels**
    (D) **finished wood**

4. Be sure that the drawer bottoms—
    (A) **are made of mahogany**
    (B) **are not flexible**
    (C) **do not have interesting grains**
    (D) **match well with all fabrics**

DIRECTIONS: Wallpaper can be used to make a pleated lampshade. Choose paper with a design you like. Be sure that the paper is six times as wide as the diameter planned for the bottom of the lampshade. After cutting the paper to the proper length and width, use a ruler and pencil to mark off lines. The lines should be a half inch apart. Pleat the paper, using the lines as guides. The pleats will be about a half inch wide. Punch holes through each pleat about two inches from the top of the paper. Next coat both sides of the paper with pure linseed oil. After the paper dries, run a string through the holes and glue the ends together. Fit the shade over your wire frame.

1. These directions tell you how to—
   - (A) clean a dirty lampshade
   - (B) repair a lampshade
   - (C) hang wallpaper
   - (D) make a pleated lampshade

2. The width of the paper must be six times the size of the planned diameter of the—
   - (A) light bulb
   - (B) top of the lampshade
   - (C) bottom of the lampshade
   - (D) wire frame

3. Before you pleat the paper,—
   - (A) punch holes in the paper
   - (B) mark off lines
   - (C) fit it over the frame
   - (D) coat it with linseed oil

4. After running a string through the holes in the shade,—
   - (A) glue the ends together
   - (B) pleat the paper
   - (C) fit it over the frame
   - (D) coat the shade with linseed oil

UNIT 24

DIRECTIONS: In a bowl, blend one egg, one cup buttermilk, and two tablespoons vegetable oil or melted shortening. In another bowl, blend one cup sifted flour with one tablespoon sugar, one teaspoon baking powder, a half teaspoon of baking soda, and a half teaspoon of salt. Add the dry ingredients to the liquids and beat until moistened. Heat a nonstick pan. The pan has reached the correct temperature when water sprinkled on it sizzles. Pour the batter into the pan, forming round cakes. When the pancakes are puffed and full of bubbles, flip them (before the bubbles break) and cook a while longer. Serve. If necessary, keep the pancakes warm in a hot towel in the oven—but be sure the oven is turned off.

1. This article tells you how to—
   - (A) make a pound cake
   - (B) freeze pancakes
   - (C) make an egg batter
   - (D) make pancakes

2. Before measuring out the flour,—
   - (A) blend egg, buttermilk, and oil
   - (B) test the pan to see if it sizzles
   - (C) blend sugar and salt
   - (D) mix the soda and salt

3. After adding the dry ingredients to the liquids,—
   - (A) sift the flour
   - (B) add the sugar
   - (C) strain the batter
   - (D) heat a pan

4. Flip the pancakes—
   - (A) after the bubbles break
   - (B) before the bubbles break
   - (C) before they puff up
   - (D) into a warm towel

31

Have you ever started playing a game before reading all the directions? Confusing, wasn't it? In Unit 13, you read about a word game. Here's another kind of game:

A Trip to Grandma's

The first person says, "I am going on a trip to Grandma's house, and in my suitcase I packed _____ ." Another person says the same thing and adds one more. If someone forgets the list, that player drops out. The winner is the last one left.

If the game is already familiar to you, the directions may seem clear. But if you have never played the game, the directions may be confusing. The directions assume that you already know what is going to happen. They require you to "fill in" too much information that is not given.

A. Exercising Your Skill

How could you improve the directions given above? Discuss improvements with your classmates, or work on your own. If someone already knows the game, list the steps. Don't leave anything out, and don't leave anything to the imagination.

If you are working alone, or if no one in your group knows the game, here are some hints: The object of the game is to remember and repeat a list of items exactly as it was given, and then to add an item of your own. As each player adds an item, the list becomes longer and harder to remember.

Now try rewriting the instructions so they make more sense! Show your version of the game to some friends. See if they can figure out how to play it.

B. Expanding Your Skill

How could you change the game in Part A to make it easier? How could you make it harder?

Hints: You could limit the kinds of things that players can include in the lists. What if each new item had to be in alphabetical order with everything else? Would that make the game easier or harder? What if each new item had to have just one word, or at least two words?

People who invent games for a living are always trying them out on family and friends. Try playing your new version of the game. Do things happen the way you expect them to? Do you need to add any rules or revise the ones you have? Take notes as you play the game. Listen to what your friends say about it. Try out some of the new rules. Make sure you and your friends understand them.

C. Exploring Language

Write a set of instructions for a game that you know how to play. It can be an indoor or an outdoor game, a game for two or more players or a game that has teams. It doesn't have to be complicated; it can be as simple as a Spelling Bee.

What should you include in the game instructions? Here is a list of headings you might include. You probably wouldn't need all of them every time, but you should at least consider them.

Number of players
Object of the game
Materials needed
Setting up
Beginning the game
Order of play
Scoring
Winning the game

You may be able to think of other headings. You might want to use these headings in a different order. That's all right, as long as your directions are clear. Write the directions for your game. Then show your directions to a classmate. See if he or she can figure out how to play it from your directions. If the game is a familiar one, ask your partner to see whether or not the instructions are clear and complete.

D. Expressing Yourself

Choose one of these activities.

1. With a small group of classmates, brainstorm to make up a new game. It could be a word game, a board game, or anything else. You might want to use the headings in Part C as a starting point. Try playing the game in your group, and revise the directions if you need to. Your class may want to put together a booklet of new games that can be played during free time or after school.

2. Choose a familiar game or activity that has no written rules. It might be something as simple as playing catch or touch football, shooting baskets, or having a picnic with friends. Write a set of directions for what you choose. Run through the directions with some classmates who also know the game or activity. If they follow "your" rules, is the game or activity the same as before? Make any necessary changes.

3. Think of a game that you know how to play well, such as a board game or word game. Change the rules. What would happen if you reversed the order of some of the rules? What if the game rewarded cooperation instead of competition? Write the directions for your game, and then try them out on some friends. See if they like the new game better than the old one.

33

DIRECTIONS: First sterilize all utensils and bowls. Heat a gallon of milk in a double boiler to 86°F and stir in four tablespoons of fresh cultured buttermilk. Dissolve some rennet in cool water and stir half the solution in the milk. Let the milk sit and curdle for eighteen hours. Line a colander (a utensil with holes) with muslin and place it over a pot. Drain the curds and whey into the pot. Surround the muslin bag of curd with ice. Put the chilled curd between two boards. Place the whole thing in a cake pan in the refrigerator for eight hours. Put the curd in a bowl and knead a teaspoon of salt into it. Place the salted curd into a cheese press and put the whole arrangement into the refrigerator.

1. These directions will help you to—

    (A) keep milk fresh   **(B) make butter**

    (C) make homemade cheese   **(D) make sour cream**

2. After sterilizing all utensils,—

    (A) heat a gallon of milk   **(B) put some rennet in the curd**

    (C) stir some salt into the milk   **(D) put them into the refrigerator**

3. Before draining the curds and whey,—

    (A) salt the curd   **(B) surround them with ice**

    (C) let the milk curdle   **(D) chill them for eight hours**

4. After adding salt to the curd,—

    (A) chill it with ice   **(B) add some rennet**

    (C) place it in a cheese press   **(D) place it in a muslin bag**

DIRECTIONS: Get a large, clear print. A color print is most effective. You can use a picture of yourself or a picture of the person to whom you intend to send your homemade gift. If you don't have a picture that is large and interesting, you can always use one from a magazine. That is an inexpensive solution. Mount your picture on a thin piece of wood with a high-quality cement. Draw a puzzle pattern with a thin-lined marker. Use a hard coping saw and cut slowly and carefully. You might prefer someone at the local lumberyard to cut your puzzle for you.

1. The article shows you how to—

    (A) **confuse the receiver**   (B) **use a saw**
    (C) **draw**   (D) **make an interesting gift**

2. To solve the problem of obtaining a picture,—

    (A) **draw your own**   (B) **use one from a magazine**
    (C) **hire a photographer**   (D) **use one from a newspaper**

3. When you draw the puzzle pattern, keep—

    (A) **everything the same size**   (B) **everything the same shape**
    (C) **the lines very thin**   (D) **the lines very thick**

4. It is important to—

    (A) **get help if necessary**   (B) **cut one thousand small pieces**
    (C) **use very heavy wood**   (D) **make the pieces circular**

DIRECTIONS: First, collect a few microscope slides and a can of clear lacquer spray. The slides and lacquer must then be stored in the freezer compartment of your refrigerator. During the next snowfall, take the spray and slides from the freezer and place them outside to maintain their cold temperature. Hold the slide on a piece of wood so the heat of your hand doesn't warm it up too much. Spray a thin coat of the lacquer on the slide and hold it outside to accumulate snowflakes. The slide should then be kept outside in the cold and allowed to dry for an hour. You can then bring it in and examine the flakes under a microscope.

1. These directions explain how to—
   - (A) use a microscope to examine slides
   - (B) clean microscope slides
   - (C) preserve snowflakes for examination
   - (D) use a spray can

2. Just before you use the slide and lacquer spray, they must be—
   - (A) stored in the cellar
   - (B) kept warm
   - (C) kept cold in the freezer
   - (D) placed out in the snow

3. The slide should be held on a piece of wood so that—
   - (A) you don't cut yourself
   - (B) the wood becomes cold
   - (C) your hand won't warm the slide
   - (D) your hand stays warm

4. Before you collect the snowflakes,—
   - (A) the slide should warm up
   - (B) it should stop snowing
   - (C) you should examine the lacquer spray
   - (D) you should spray the lacquer on the slide

DIRECTIONS: You can still protect yourself during a storm, even if you are outdoors. First, never take shelter under trees. Lightning generally strikes the highest thing near it, and trees can come down in high winds. Head for a low place—a ditch, a cave, or the bottom of a hill. Lie facedown as flat as you can, with your arms over your head, until the storm passes. If you are in a car during an electrical storm, close the windows and doors and stay there. A car carries lightning into the ground when it is struck.

1. These directions tell how to—

    (A) **figure out directions**   (B) **keep safe outdoors in a storm**

    (C) **find a cave without a map**   (D) **drive safely during a storm**

2. The best place to be in a lightning storm is—

    (A) **playing golf**   (B) **under a tree**

    (C) **as low as possible**   (D) **beneath an underpass**

3. Trees are not safe during an electrical storm because—

    (A) **they can touch wires**   (B) **they can fall in the wind**

    (C) **they attract lightning**   (D) **they can block a car**

4. A car is fairly safe in an electrical storm because—

    (A) **it is warm and dry**   (B) **it grounds electrical charges**

    (C) **it is low**   (D) **it can outrun tornadoes**

DIRECTIONS: As a rule, hang a picture below the eye level of a person standing in the room (but this rule can be bent slightly to suit your tastes). Make sure that a lamp lights the entire picture and that no piece of furniture covers any part of the frame. Try to keep pictures and furniture to scale. When hanging a group of pictures over a couch, be sure to place the bottom of the frame about ten inches above the top of the couch. Place tall pictures on narrow walls and broad pictures on wide walls. Place a group of pictures so that the outside edges of the frames form a square or rectangle. Never allow the picture's hanging device to show.

1. This article teaches you how to—
   - (A) **furnish your living room**
   - (B) **remove a picture from a wall**
   - (C) **hang pictures**
   - (D) **arrange your furniture**

2. Furniture in the room should not—
   - (A) **cover the picture frame**
   - (B) **be under the pictures**
   - (C) **be scaled to the pictures**
   - (D) **be against a narrow wall**

3. Tall pictures should be placed—
   - (A) **on a narrow wall**
   - (B) **above a person's eye level**
   - (C) **two inches above a couch**
   - (D) **on a wide wall**

4. Group pictures so that their outside edges—
   - (A) **are behind a couch**
   - (B) **form a square**
   - (C) **are partially lighted**
   - (D) **are one inch above the couch**

DIRECTIONS: One method (noted as the safest and probably the most popular of all) is to lower your hand net into the water, after you have your fish hooked, and guide the catch into it headfirst. If possible, do not net the fish tailfirst. Never lift the fish from the water and drop it into the net; always keep the net submerged. Land a bass by sticking your thumb into the mouth of the fish and squeezing the lower jaw with the aid of your index finger. The stunned fish can then be lifted into the boat. If you are in a boat with a friend, have your companion land your catch with a gaff hook. Always make sure that the fish is played until tired before landing it.

1. These directions tell you how to—
   (A) use the proper bait
   (C) fish from a dock
   (B) land a fish
   (D) make a fishnet

2. When netting your catch,—
   (A) scoop it up tailfirst
   (C) keep the net underwater
   (B) keep the net above water
   (D) drop the fish into the net

3. Stun a fish by—
   (A) squeezing its tail
   (C) netting it tailfirst
   (B) using a gaff hook
   (D) squeezing its lower jaw

4. A cardinal rule of landing a fish is to—
   (A) keep your net above water
   (C) play it until it is tired
   (B) grab it by the tail
   (D) land it as soon as it is hooked

DIRECTIONS: First be sure to keep the broken ends quiet. Keep the adjacent joints still. Should these joints bend, the muscles will act against the fractured bone and cause motion. Give the victim first aid for shock. Apply a sterile dressing to the fracture if it is compound. Do not try to push back a protruding bone. When you are splinting the fractured area, the end will slip back when the limb is straightened. An ice bag should be used with all fractures, sprains, and dislocations. A simple method of preventing motion of the fragments is to place the limb on pillows. Splints may also be used to keep the limb from moving. Breaks of the ribs or skull bone need no splints as they are held fast by other bones and tissue.

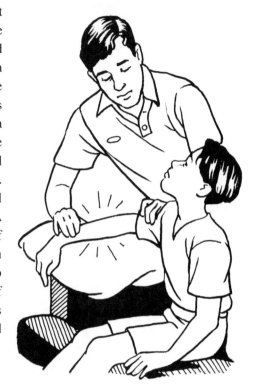

1. This article will help you to—
    (A) **make a splint**
    (B) **care for broken bones**
    (C) **care for bad burns**
    (D) **make a sterile dressing**

2. The first thing to do for a fracture is—
    (A) **keep the broken ends quiet**
    (B) **use an ice bag**
    (C) **push back the protruding bone**
    (D) **make a splint**

3. If the fracture is compound,—
    (A) **move the adjacent joints**
    (B) **don't use an ice bag**
    (C) **push the bone back**
    (D) **apply a sterile dressing**

4. A break which needs no splint is one in the—
    (A) **arm**
    (B) **foot**
    (C) **leg**
    (D) **ribs**

DIRECTIONS: First of all, make a paste of one spoonful of cornstarch (or laundry starch) and a small amount of cold water. Add this solution to a cup of clear water. Put the entire mixture on a burner of the stove for a few minutes. After removing it from the heat, allow it to cool and settle. Next find a clean fountain pen and dip the point in the colorless liquid. Write a message on a piece of paper with your "ink." The words will not appear on the paper. In order to see what you've written, douse the paper with a diluted iodine solution. Make the solution by adding a few drops of tincture of iodine to half a glass of water. The starch in the "ink" and the iodine form a blue compound where they meet.

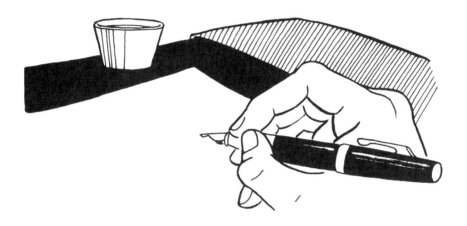

1. These directions show you how to—
   (A) make ordinary ink
   (B) write with "invisible ink"
   (C) make tincture of iodine
   (D) write with iodine ink

2. After adding some cornstarch to cold water, add that solution to—
   (A) tincture of iodine
   (B) your pen
   (C) a cup of clear water
   (D) laundry starch

3. To make your secret writing appear, use—
   (A) pure iodine
   (B) a diluted iodine solution
   (C) a solution of laundry starch
   (D) hot water

4. After using the iodine solution, your writing will appear—
   (A) in an hour
   (B) blue
   (C) green
   (D) red

DIRECTIONS: Start by choosing a light-colored, washable fabric for the background of your design. Any old sheet will do. First wash the material to remove the sizing. Then iron it well so that your spray paint will cover it evenly. Next tape a few old newspapers to the wall and tape your material to the newspapers. Be sure to cover the floor of your spraying area as well. For your stencils, use anything that can be taped or pinned to the fabric. Then arrange your stencils. Spray enamel can be used straight from the spray can, but do not use too much paint; the fabric could become stiff. Make softer colors by using liquid dye; dilute the dye by using four tablespoons of dye to one cup of hot water.

---

1. This article shows you how to—

   (A) **paint newspapers**   (B) **spray designs on fabric**
   (C) **make spray paint**   (D) **make cardboard stencils**

2. Wash your fabric to—

   (A) **flatten it out**   (B) **make it stiff**
   (C) **make sure the paint covers it**   (D) **remove any sizing**

3. When using spray enamel, DO NOT—

   (A) **use it straight from the can**   (B) **wash the fabric first**
   (C) **arrange the stencils**   (D) **use a lot of paint**

4. To dilute dye, mix four tablespoons of dye in—

   (A) **four cups of hot water**   (B) **one cup of spray enamel paint**
   (C) **one cup of hot water**   (D) **one cup of cold water**

DIRECTIONS: First dig a good-sized hole, several feet deep, in a spot not easily seen from the house or garden. The dirt you will be taking from the hole will be left in a pile near the edge to be used as you bury new food garbage. Keep a shovel handy. Throw a can of garbage into the hole and cover it over with a layer of dirt. If necessary, scatter some lime over the dirt to keep bad odors away from the pit. Cover the pit with some sort of screen to keep away stray animals. Leave the refuse in the pit throughout the winter, removing it in time for your summer planting. Throw away any part that has refused to rot. Your fertilizer is now ready.

1. These directions show you how to—

   (A) dig a garden pit   (B) fertilize your garden
   (C) throw out garbage   (D) make fertilizer from garbage

2. To destroy bad odors around the pit,—

   (A) cover the hole with a screen   (B) dig it near the garden
   (C) don't disturb the garbage   (D) scatter some lime in the dirt

3. Before leaving the pit during the winter,—

   (A) cover the pit with a screen   (B) throw away the rotting refuse
   (C) uncover the garbage   (D) sprinkle it with fertilizer

4. When you uncover the pit in the summer,—

   (A) throw away the rotted refuse   (B) throw in some lime
   (C) make a new screen   (D) throw away the unrotted refuse

DIRECTIONS: First you need a bag of marbles. Next draw a circle on the ground. Every player puts one marble in the circle. Now set up to shoot. To shoot your marble, put it on a curved forefinger. Bend your thumb, putting your thumbnail in back of the marble. Shoot the marble by pushing it with your thumb with a snappy motion. The object is to try to shoot one of the marbles out of the ring, using your marble. If you do, you keep that marble. When shooting, you may not raise your hand or move it forward. In an official game, the winner is the player who is the first to win seven marbles. So, "knuckle down" and shoot those "glassies"!

---

1. These directions tell you how to—
   - (A) make a perfect marble
   - (B) collect marbles
   - (C) play with marbles
   - (D) polish marbles

2. The marble to be shot is—
   - (A) placed on your forefinger
   - (B) in back of the thumb
   - (C) put on your thumb
   - (D) the biggest marble

3. When shooting the marble—
   - (A) raise your hand
   - (B) move your hand forward
   - (C) snap it with your thumb
   - (D) push it with your forefinger

4. The object of the game is to—
   - (A) lose seven marbles
   - (B) shoot your marble fast
   - (C) knock the marbles from the circle
   - (D) hold your marble on your thumb

DIRECTIONS: Start on the shady side of the house and work around, avoiding working in the sun. Always wash one side of the house at a time. First, wet down the entire house wall with a hose spray at full intensity. Be sure to work from the bottom up. You will need detergents to loosen soot or oily grime. Squirt a liquid concentrate detergent and water over one section, followed by a strong stream of clean water. Never allow a dirty spot to dry on the surface. Use a hose-brush on stubborn areas. Use a solution of one pound of trisodium phosphate (sold in paint stores) dissolved in a pail of hot water for the most difficult areas. Wear rubber gloves when using this.

1. This article shows you how to—

    (A) paint your house exterior   **(B) shingle your house**

    (C) make a detergent concentrate   **(D) wash your house**

2. Before using detergents,—

    (A) try trisodium phosphate   **(B) begin work at the top of the house**

    (C) allow the water to dry   **(D) wet the entire house wall**

3. An application of liquid detergent and water should—

    (A) be followed by clean water   **(B) replace a hose-brush**

    (C) be allowed to dry   **(D) be done in the sun**

4. Wear rubber gloves when handling—

    (A) detergent concentrate   **(B) the garden hose**

    (C) a hose-brush   **(D) hot water and trisodium phosphate**

DIRECTIONS: First, find out just how tall your friend is. Then have your friend stand beside the tree, the height of which you want to determine. Stand back about forty yards from the tree. Hold a stick upright in your outstretched right hand. Line up the top of the stick with the top of your friend's head. With your thumb, mark the place where you see your friend's feet. Now use the distance between the top of the stick and your thumb as a measuring unit. Line up the top of the stick with the treetop, and see how many times you must move the stick down in order for your thumb to line up with the tree's base. If you multiply your friend's height by the number of times you moved the stick, you will determine the tree's height.

1. The article shows you how to—

    (A) **use a friend**
    (B) **use a stick**
    (C) **measure width**
    (D) **measure height**

2. Your thumb must be lined up with your friend's—

    (A) **thumb**
    (B) **shoulder**
    (C) **feet**
    (D) **head**

3. You really are making a comparison between the height of—

    (A) **your friend and the tree**
    (B) **two friends**
    (C) **your friend and yourself**
    (D) **two trees**

4. In order to calculate the height of the tree, you must—

    (A) **divide**
    (B) **multiply**
    (C) **add and multiply**
    (D) **subtract**

DIRECTIONS: First find a length of loosely woven cloth or wicking. Next locate a box of Epsom salts in your home. (If you have none at home, buy some in a local drug store.) Take the Epsom salts and dissolve as much as possible in a pot of warm water. When the salts are dissolved, pour the water into two drinking glasses. Fill the glasses to the brim. Then place the piece of limp cloth between the glasses, making sure that the ends of the cloth are well immersed. The solution will soak into the cloth and drip from its center. As the Epsom salt solution drips between the glasses, the water will evaporate and the salt will crystallize. Under proper conditions, the crystals will form a real stalactite, such as you find hanging in caves, with a stalagmite forming beneath it.

1. These instructions show you how to—

   (A) make Epsom salts   (B) collect stalactites
   (C) form stalactites   (D) make limp cloth

2. Before putting the salt solution into glasses,—

   (A) hang the cloth between the   (B) soak the cloth in water
       glasses
   (C) dissolve the Epsom salts in   (D) chill the solution
       warm water

3. As the salt solution drips from the cloth,—

   (A) the cloth falls from the glasses   (B) the salt crystallizes
   (C) it forms a wet pool   (D) add more water to the glasses

4. With proper conditions, forming under the stalactite will be—

   (A) a pool of water   (B) a salt cloud
   (C) a stalagmite   (D) nothing

In Unit 25, you read about a way to make homemade cheese. Most people learned how to cook and prepare food by watching their parents or by following recipes in cookbooks. A recipe is a set of directions to follow. It lists the materials (ingredients) and the steps.

A. Exercising Your Skill

By now, most people have tasted yogurt—a form of milk that is something like a custard. Often the yogurt is flavored with fruit. Sometimes it is even frozen and served like ice cream. Basic yogurt is very easy to make. Here's a recipe for it:

Ingredients: One quart of milk and about one tablespoon of plain yogurt. Let stand for one day. Put the milk into a saucepan and heat it to about 100 degrees. When the mixture has set up and become like custard, cover each dish with plastic wrap and refrigerate it. Do not let it boil. Take the saucepan off the heat and stir in the yogurt. Put the dishes in a warm place, covered with a cloth. Pour the mixture into one-cup serving dishes. Yield: 4 servings.

Wait a minute! Something's wrong here! The directions hardly make sense. If you tried to follow them, you would end up either very confused or with a mess on your hands.

You can perhaps see the problem. The steps you are supposed to follow are in the wrong order. Can you use some common sense to put them in the correct order? Rewrite the recipe so that it makes sense. Now compare your rewrite of the yogurt recipe with those of your classmates. Do you all agree? If you can't seem to agree, have someone write each step on a separate line on the board.

B. Expanding Your Skill

Find a simple recipe in a cookbook or use a recipe you know well. Write the steps in a numbered list. Then rewrite the recipe, scrambling the order of the steps. Exchange papers with a classmate and see if you can put each other's recipes in the correct order. The steps in recipes should be easy to figure out because most of them don't work in a reverse order. Here are some things to consider:

- What ingredients do you start with?
- When does food get cut up?
- When does food get heated, or when does it get cooled?
- When does one ingredient get added to another?
- When is food placed into or taken out of bowls or cooking pots?

C. Exploring Language

In the box below are some ingredients and equipment. What egg dish might you make using these things? Decide on a dish and write a recipe. You can write the steps as numbered sentences, or you can write them as a paragraph. Try to imagine that the person you are writing for has very little experience in the kitchen. Give your recipe a title. Then compare your recipe with your classmates' recipes to see if the steps are in the right order.

```
2 to 6 fresh eggs
dash of salt and pepper
1 tablespoon of butter or margarine
2 tablespoons of milk for each egg
a frying pan about 8 to 10 inches in diameter
a wire whisk or egg beater
a large bowl
a spatula
```

D. Expressing Yourself

Choose one of these activities.

1. Think of your favorite cooked food. Do you know how it is prepared? Without looking in a cookbook, try to develop a recipe for the food. List the ingredients, and include amounts to serve four people. List the cooking utensils that are needed. When you have completed your recipe, have a classmate read it over and ask questions about anything that is unclear. Revise your recipe if you need to. If possible, check your recipe against one that is in a cookbook to see how close you've come to the real thing.

2. Have "An Original Recipe" contest with your classmates. First, work together to develop a list of ingredients. The list should be reasonably short and contain ingredients that are fairly easy to obtain. Then work individually to develop your own recipes using as many of the ingredients as possible. You may use any amounts of any of the ingredients. Be creative! When the recipes are completed, pass them around the group. Ask questions, raise objections, and point out problems. Revise your own recipes if you need to. Then take a vote to decide which three recipes are the most "original." If possible, prepare your recipe and bring your "creation" in to class for a tasting party.

3. Write a "recipe" for something other than food. You might have seen similar "recipes" in popular magazines, such as recipes for friendships, recipes for surviving junior high, recipes for improving school spirit, and so on. Your recipe may be serious or humorous. Just be sure to list the "ingredients" and give the steps in the appropriate order.

DIRECTIONS: First find three pipe cleaners. Bend the pipe cleaners into the shape of a head and neck and two arms and two legs. Twist the lower end of the "head and neck" around the middle sections of the "arms and legs" to form the body. Cover the head loop with some cotton and a small piece of white cloth. Sew it in place and paint in a face. To create hair, use yarn or curled strips of paper. Next make a cardboard base about two inches square to support the figure. Cut two slits in the cardboard about one-eighth of an inch apart and slip the feet through these slits. Use cloth or crepe paper to dress the dolls. Simply hold the "clothes" in place with your fingers and tie with thread.

1. These directions teach you how to make—
   (A) **stuffed animals**
   (B) **hand puppets**
   (C) **string puppets**
   (D) **pipe-cleaner dolls**

2. After twisting the pipe cleaners together to form a body,—
   (A) **cover the head with cotton and cloth**
   (B) **make a loop for a head**
   (C) **sew them to cardboard**
   (D) **stand them up**

3. Use yarn to make the—
   (A) **hair**
   (B) **legs**
   (C) **base**
   (D) **clothes**

4. After standing the dolls on a cardboard base,—
   (A) **use cloth to dress them**
   (B) **twist the arms in place**
   (C) **add the hair**
   (D) **cover the head loop with cotton**

DIRECTIONS: First cut off the ends of an empty food can with a rotary can opener. Then carefully cut a strip of metal from the end with an old pair of shears. Stroke the metal strip about twenty times in the same direction. This will magnetize it. Then, using a blunt nail, make a slight dent (not a hole) near the center of the metal strip. Next bend the metal strip at the point of indentation and make two more bends, forcing the dent in the strip to be pointed upward. Cut a slice from a cork and push a pin through the center of the slice. Then place the dent in the strip on the pin. Snip off pieces of the metal strip until it balances on the pin. After testing your creation against another compass, paint the "north" end of the strip.

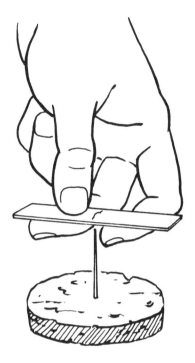

1. This article tells you how to—
   - (A) make a balancing toy
   - (B) balance a pin
   - (C) make a compass
   - (D) make a powerful magnet

2. After cutting out the metal strip,—
   - (A) punch a hole in its center
   - (B) bend it in a circle
   - (C) magnetize it
   - (D) make it into the shape of a pin

3. Before bending the strip,—
   - (A) make a dent in its middle
   - (B) paint its north end
   - (C) balance it on a pin
   - (D) push a pin into a cork

4. After the strip balances on the pin,—
   - (A) test it with another compass
   - (B) paint the whole metal strip
   - (C) magnetize the strip
   - (D) bend the strip

DIRECTIONS: Prepare the soap by scraping some of the soap from one side of the cake. Remove enough to reveal a smooth surface. Let the soap dry for an hour before tracing the pattern. Trace the pattern by placing a blackened piece of paper (penciled side down) on the soap. Place the pattern over this, and trace to obtain an image on the soap. After carving your figure, cut a trench in both base and model and put a toothpick in each. Then heat a piece of soap to jellylike consistency and fill the trenches with it. This will hold the pieces together. After the figure dries for a day or two, polish it with a paper napkin and your fingertips. If you like, color the figure with opaque colors.

1. These instructions show you how to—
  (A) wash your hands with soap
  (B) make soap
  (C) draw with soap
  (D) make a soap sculpture

2. Before tracing a pattern on soap,—
  (A) cut a trench in the base
  (B) heat some soap
  (C) let the soap dry for an hour
  (D) let it dry for a day

3. Cut trenches in base and model—
  (A) after carving the figure
  (B) after polishing the figure
  (C) before carving the figure
  (D) before tracing the pattern

4. After polishing the figure,—
  (A) cut trenches in base and model
  (B) let it dry
  (C) color it
  (D) trace the pattern

DIRECTIONS: First you must find a tile which matches the others on the bathroom wall. Next scrape away the grout (the white substance) from around the tile's edge. Use a screwdriver for this job. When the grout is gone, pry the cracked tile from the wall. Don't pry from the edge, though, or you'll put excess pressure on the surrounding tiles and crack them as well. Chisel a hole in the middle of the cracked tile and pry it off from there. If any cement remains on the wall, scrape it away. Now spread the back of the new tile with mastic, a special adhesive. Center the new tile in its place on the wall and apply some pressure. Finally, fill in the border with new grout. A damp cloth will remove any excess grout.

1. These directions will teach you how to—
   (A) mix grout
   (B) mix a special adhesive
   (C) buy bathroom tiles
   (D) replace a broken tile

2. After finding a matching tile,—
   (A) pry the old tile from the edge
   (B) scrape the grout from the old tile
   (C) mix up some mastic
   (D) put a hole in the old tile

3. Before putting the new tile on the wall,—
   (A) pry off the old tile from the edge
   (B) fill in the border with grout
   (C) don't touch the old cement
   (D) remove any old cement on the wall

4. After the new tile is in place,—
   (A) apply some mastic
   (B) chisel a hole in its middle
   (C) fill in the border with grout
   (D) scrape away the grout

DIRECTIONS: Make sure to chalk an "X" on the wrong side of the fabric when both sides look alike. This assures that you have the right side out as you sew. Use chalk arrows to indicate the direction in which the nap runs on velvet fabrics. Place a piece of white paper under the foot of your sewing machine in order to thread the needle more easily; the eye of the needle will show up more plainly this way. Always thread two bobbins before starting on a large sewing project. Sew buttons in place with elastic thread; it keeps the buttons from ripping out. If your material will show pinholes, use long clips to hold a hem fast. Unstick metal zippers by rubbing them with wax.

1. These directions show you how to—

   (A) **buy a sewing machine**
   (B) **sew up pinholes**
   (C) **become a dress designer**
   (D) **sew more easily**

2. To make sure you have the right side out as you sew,—

   (A) **thread two bobbins**
   (B) **use long pin curl clips**
   (C) **chalk an "X" on the wrong side**
   (D) **rub it with wax**

3. To keep buttons from tearing out,—

   (A) **glue them in place**
   (B) **rub them with wax**
   (C) **sew them on with elastic thread**
   (D) **sew them over pinholes**

4. To hold a hem in place, use—

   (A) **clips**
   (B) **a piece of white paper**
   (C) **elastic thread**
   (D) **a coating of wax**

DIRECTIONS: Is your bicycle in good shape? Are your tires filled with air? Now, before anything else, put on that helmet! Then, get on—just you, no passengers—and ride single file in the same direction as other traffic. Ride only on the right, with the rest of the traffic. Obey all traffic rules. Be ready to brake if you see dangerous things in the road such as boxes, tree limbs, or kids running into traffic after a ball. Signal before you turn, and walk your vehicle across intersections. At night be sure you have reflective clothing or reflective patches on your shoes and helmet.

1. These directions tell you how to—
   (A) fill your tires correctly
   (C) practice bicycle safety
   (B) signal a turn
   (D) find reflective clothing

2. Just before you get on your bicycle,—
   (A) put on your helmet
   (C) check your bike's condition
   (B) watch for children
   (D) walk across the intersection

3. Always ride—
   (A) through the intersection
   (C) going with traffic
   (B) on the sidewalk
   (D) going against traffic

4. Bike riders must take extra caution at night because—
   (A) there is more traffic
   (C) there are fewer police
   (B) drivers cannot see them clearly
   (D) traffic lights stop working

DIRECTIONS: The box should be six to nine inches deep, ten to twelve inches wide, and as long as you care to make it. Use three-quarter-inch white pine, red cedar, or cypress wood. Go to the local lumberyard to have the pieces pre-cut; then assemble them, using screws. Drill half-inch diameter holes in the bottom about eight inches apart to insure proper drainage. If you place the box on a shelf, be sure to put small wedges underneath to allow the water an escape route. When you are finished with the actual construction, paint only the outside. Next fill the window box with a mixture of two parts soil and one part sand and peat moss. Add to this two pints of fertilizer. Then plant your flowers or vegetables.

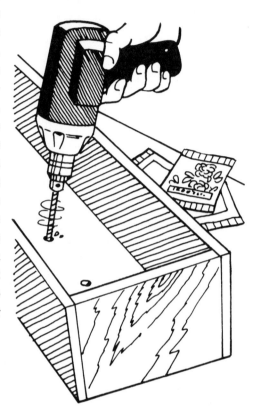

1. This article shows you how to—

   (A) plant vegetables (B) cut lumber
   (C) build a flowerpot (D) build a window box

2. For building the box, you should NOT use—

   (A) white pine (B) plywood
   (C) red cedar (D) cypress

3. Assemble the box with—

   (A) clamps (B) glue
   (C) nails (D) screws

4. Fill the window box with two parts soil and—

   (A) one part sand and peat moss (B) three pints fertilizer
   (C) two parts sand (D) two parts fertilizer

DIRECTIONS: When you want to hang the American flag over the middle of a street, suspend it vertically with the blue field, called the union, to the north on an east-west street. When the flag is displayed with another banner from crossed staffs, the American flag is on the right. Place the staff of the American flag in front of the other staff. Raise the flag quickly and lower it slowly and respectfully. When flying the flag at half-mast, hoist it to the top of the pole for a moment before lowering it to mid-pole. When flying the American flag with banners from states or cities, raise the nation's banner first and lower it last. Never allow the flag to touch the ground.

1. These instructions will teach you how to—
   (A) **make your own flag**   (B) **salute the flag**
   (C) **display the flag**   (D) **fold the flag**

2. On an east-west street, the flag's union should be—
   (A) **pointing down**   (B) **to the south**
   (C) **pointing up**   (D) **to the north**

3. When displayed with another flag, the American flag—
   (A) **must point to the north**   (B) **should be on the right**
   (C) **should be in back**   (D) **must be vertical**

4. Before flying the flag at half-mast,—
   (A) **raise it twice**   (B) **suspend it vertically**
   (C) **hang it upside down**   (D) **raise it to the top**

DIRECTIONS: You will need bricks, three-quarter-inch boards, some varnish, paint, brushes, rags, sandpaper, a tape measure, and a pair of scissors. Be sure to measure carefully the wall space you have available for the bookcase. To begin with, remove all the dust from the bricks and polish them with sandpaper. If you wish, paint the bricks the same color or two shades of one color. Another idea is to cover the bricks with odds and ends of wallpapers or fabrics. Next, sand down the wood shelves and apply two coats of clear varnish or wood stain to them. Separate two shelf areas with four bricks (a good height for hardcover books), and two shelves with three bricks (a good height for paperbacks).

1. This article tells you how to—

   (A) **make a room divider**   (B) **make a simple bookcase**
   (C) **collect bricks**   (D) **care for your books**

2. Before removing the dust from the bricks,—

   (A) **measure your wall space**   (B) **polish them with sandpaper**
   (C) **cover them with wallpaper** (D) **apply varnish**

3. After decorating the bricks,—

   (A) **measure the wall space**   (B) **coat the bricks with stain**
   (C) **sand down the wood shelves** (D) **measure your books**

4. A "three-brick" shelf is good for—

   (A) **hardcover books**   (B) **paperback books**
   (C) **thick books**   (D) **all your books**

DIRECTIONS: Start by collecting as many interesting leaves as you can find. These leaves should be pressed so that you can make a good scrapbook. Put the leaves on several sheets of newspaper on a flat, boardlike surface, and top them with another board. Place heavy objects on the top board to press the leaves and paper together. When the leaves are dry, use tape or glue to secure them to a page of a scrapbook. Place a label beneath each leaf, stating the name of the tree where the leaf was found as well as its uses. To attach the leaves to a slick surface, use a mixture of glue and vinegar in equal parts, pressing until dry.

1. These instructions will help you—
   - (A) buy a scrapbook
   - (B) write a book about leaves
   - (C) start a leaf collection
   - (D) identify leaves

2. Leaves should be pressed—
   - (A) with two boards and heavy weights
   - (B) after they are dry
   - (C) after you write the labels
   - (D) beneath two boards

3. Each leaf's label should note—
   - (A) the color of the leaf
   - (B) the name of the leaf's tree
   - (C) the type of glue used to paste the leaf in
   - (D) how the leaf was found

4. When the scrapbook has slick surfaces, you should mix the glue with—
   - (A) vinegar
   - (B) oil
   - (C) rubber cement
   - (D) water

DIRECTIONS: Keep the left side of your body facing the net. Keep your left foot well out in front of the right one. Your paddle elbow should be slightly bent. Your wrist must be rigid and locked for control. Time your stroke to meet the ball at its highest point. Keep your paddle shoulder high as you start your stroke, and certainly higher than the ball. Swing forward and somewhat downward, so as not to cause a high return. Meet the ball well away from your body. This will prevent a cramped stroke. Make a bold but smooth swing. At the point of contact, the bottom edge of your paddle should be forward at approximately a forty-degree angle from the table. Put some backspin on the ball to keep it low. Follow through straight toward the net.

1. The article teaches you how to—
   (A) **develop table-tennis teamwork**
   (B) **make a table-tennis stroke**
   (C) **block the ball**
   (D) **serve the ball**

2. It is important to—
   (A) **keep the elbow straight**
   (B) **have a loose wrist**
   (C) **have a locked wrist**
   (D) **get the body close to the ball**

3. Upon contact, your paddle should—
   (A) **be perfectly flat**
   (B) **be held loosely**
   (C) **be perpendicular to the table**
   (D) **have a forty-degree tilt**

4. Backspin is necessary—
   (A) **to keep the ball low**
   (B) **to get distance**
   (C) **for power**
   (D) **for a good defense**

UNIT 50

DIRECTIONS: On horseback the thing to remember is the position of your heels, knees, and shoulders. Keep them as low as possible. Point your toes up, and keep your knees well below your hips. Bend your elbows and position them well in front of your hips. Keep your hands about three inches apart. There should be a straight line from the horse's mouth through your hands and forearms to your elbow. Sit as far forward in the saddle as possible. This posture will help you keep your center of gravity in a vertical line with the horse's center of gravity. Your kneecap and the tip of your toe should be in a straight, vertical line. Keep your back straight and your head high.

1. These directions show you the correct way to—

   (A) groom a horse   (B) mount a horse

   (C) dismount a horse   (D) sit on a horse

2. Keep your heels, shoulders, and knees—

   (A) very straight   (B) behind one another

   (C) as loose as possible   (D) as low as possible

3. Your toes should be—

   (A) below the heel   (B) pointed up

   (C) directly below the hips (D) below the knee

4. The horse's mouth and your hands and elbows should be—

   (A) up and down   (B) below one another

   (C) at a right angle   (D) in a continuous line

Units 45 and 47 describe construction projects involving woodworking. Unit 42 tells how to replace a cracked bathroom tile. In your lifetime, you might have to use directions like these—for example: to assemble a child's toy, to hook up a new stereo or computer, to replace a windowpane, or to install a new lock. Directions may be written in list form or in paragraphs. They may include a list of materials, or they may mention the materials as they go along. Usually it is important to follow the steps in a particular order. Read these directions for fixing a dripping faucet.

First, remove the faucet handle. Sometimes this is done by loosening a screw in the middle of the handle. The screw may be hiding under a piece of plastic or chrome trim, which you will have to pry up gently with a screwdriver. Sometimes the faucet handle is a shell that is clipped to the faucet. Look for a little tab peeking through a slot near the bottom of the shell. Press in the tab with the screwdriver and ease the shell off the faucet body. Now you should be able to see the faucet itself. It is usually made of brass. Near the bottom of the faucet, against the sink, the faucet is six-sided like a nut. Put your large wrench around this and unscrew the entire faucet body. Look at the end that was hidden down inside the sink. You should see a brass screw holding in a disc of red or black rubber. That disc is the washer. The washer will probably have a deep groove in it. Unscrew the brass screw and pry out the washer. Put in a new washer and hold it in place with the brass screw. Now screw the faucet body back into the sink and put the handle back on. If you've done everything right, you'll have a dripless sink!

A. Exercising Your Skill

The directions for fixing a faucet are fairly straightforward, but they are perhaps not presented in the best way. Discuss with your classmates how they could be improved or reorganized. Then, on your paper, list the materials and tools that are needed. Next, list the steps to be followed as a series of separate, numbered paragraphs.

Now compare your rewrite with the ones your classmates did. Did you find all the materials and tools? Did you include all the steps? Which form of directions do you think would be more useful to a beginner—the paragraph form or the list you created?

B. Expanding Your Skill

The writer of the directions for fixing a faucet left out two very important steps, one at the beginning and one at the end. Can you figure out what the missing steps are? Write your ideas on a piece of paper. (The answer is somewhere on these two pages, but don't peek! You can find out later if your ideas were right.)

C. Exploring Language

Have you ever built something or done a repair job on a bike or car, or around the house? Did you follow some directions, or were you shown how to do it? Perhaps you had to figure it out for yourself. Choose one of the construction and repair projects below. Try to imagine what tools and materials you would need to complete it. Think of the steps you would take. You can look in repair manuals or instruction books if you like. Then write your own set of directions for completing the project.

> hanging a picture
> painting a wall
> fixing a flat tire
> sewing a torn hem or putting on a patch
>   or replacing a button
> gluing a broken toy
> installing batteries in a toy or camera
> replacing a bulb in a ceiling light
> building a sandbox or birdhouse
> putting up an outdoor swing

D. Expressing Yourself

Choose one of these activities.

1. Pick a construction, craft, or repair project of your own. Write a complete set of instructions telling how to complete it. Be sure to include any essential safety precautions. For example, in the paragraph about repairing the faucet, the first step should have been turning off the water supply to the sink and the last step should have been turning the water supply back on. Did you and your classmates realize that these were the missing steps?

2. Find a project that needs to be done around your home or school. Get permission (and perhaps some help) for the project from an adult. Then read a repair manual or craft book to find out how to build or repair the item. Be prepared to share your experience with your classmates.

3. Many directions come with drawings or photographs or even cartoons showing how something is to be done. One magazine has a "wordless workshop" feature that shows entire projects with only cartoon pictures. Choose a construction, craft, or repair project that interests you. Make a series of drawings or cartoons telling how to complete the project. Try to make them clear enough so that little or no explanation is needed.

Book G

Specific Skill Series

Using the Context

Richard A. Boning

Fifth Edition

SRA/McGraw-Hill
Columbus, Ohio

Cover, Back Cover, Bruce Rowell/Masterfile

SRA/McGraw-Hill

A Division of The McGraw·Hill Companies

Send all inquiries to:
    SRA/McGraw-Hill
    8787 Orion Place
    Columbus, OH 43240-4027

ISBN 0-02-687947-6

    6 IPC 02 01

To the Teacher

PURPOSE:

USING THE CONTEXT has been designed to improve word comprehension and consequently comprehension in general. The reader's attention is directed to language patterns, word form, precise word usage, grammatical correctness, and word recognition. Most important of all, USING THE CONTEXT puts a premium on precise thinking.

FOR WHOM:

The skill of USING THE CONTEXT is developed through a series of books spanning ten levels (Picture, Preparatory, A, B, C, D, E, F, G, H). The Picture Level is for pupils who have not acquired a basic sight vocabulary. The Preparatory Level is for pupils who have a basic sight vocabulary but are not yet ready for the first-grade-level book. Books A through H are appropriate for pupils who can read on levels one through eight, respectively. **The use of the *Specific Skill Series Placement Test* is recommended to determine the appropriate level.**

THE NEW EDITION:

The fifth edition of the *Specific Skill Series* maintains the quality and focus that has distinguished this program for more than 25 years. A key element central to the program's success has been the unique nature of the reading selections. Nonfiction pieces about current topics have been designed to stimulate the interest of students, motivating them to use the comprehension strategies they have learned to further their reading. To keep this important aspect of the program intact, a percentage of the reading selections have been replaced in order to ensure the continued relevance of the subject material.

In addition, a significant percentage of the artwork in the program has been replaced to give the books a contemporary look. The cover photographs are designed to appeal to readers of all ages.

SESSIONS:

Short practice sessions are the most effective. It is desirable to have a practice session every day or every other day, using a few units each session.

SCORING:

Pupils should record their answers on the reproducible worksheets. The worksheets make scoring easier and provide uniform records of the pupils' work. Using worksheets also avoids consuming the exercise books.

To the Teacher

It is important for pupils to know how well they are doing. For this reason, units should be scored as soon as they have been completed. Then a discussion can be held in which pupils justify their choices. (The Integrated Language Activities, many of which are open-ended, do not lend themselves to an objective score; thus there are no answer keys for these pages.)

GENERAL INFORMATION ON *USING THE CONTEXT*:

The meaning of the word *context* should be explained at the outset of instruction. At the earlier reading levels pupils should think of *context* as meaning the *neighborhood* in which a word lives. They should think of it as a clue in identifying new words. This concept can be expanded until the reader conceives of *context* in the fullest sense of the term.

Pupils must understand that it is not desirable to sacrifice accuracy of comprehension for speed. Without rigid time limits, readers can judge each possibility against the total context.

SUGGESTED STEPS:
1. Pupils read the passage. As they come to a missing word, they substitute the word *blank* in its place and proceed until they finish the passage.
2. After pupils read the entire passage, they determine the best choices. If the answers are not immediately obvious, pupils should try each of the choices before making a decision. Common types of incorrect choices include **nonpertinent choice**, **restricted-context choice**, **imprecise choice**, **ungrammatical choice**, and **confused-form choice**.
3. On the Picture Level, pupils read the sentence first. Then they choose the picture that represents the word needed to complete the sentence.

Additional information on using USING THE CONTEXT with pupils will be found in the **Specific Skill Series Teacher's Manual**.

RELATED MATERIALS:

Specific Skill Series Placement Tests, which enable the teacher to place pupils at their appropriate levels in each skill, are available for the Elementary (Pre-1–6) and Midway (4–8) grade levels.

About This Book

Often in your reading you will come across a difficult new word. You may be able to read the word, but you still do not know what it means. One way of finding out a word's meaning is by looking it up in a dictionary. Another way is to use **context**. You can think of context as the "neighborhood" in which a word "lives." A word is never alone. It appears in a sentence with other words, and that sentence has other sentences that come before and after it. These words and sentences are the context of the unknown word.

A word's context often contains clues to its meaning. To find clues, think about the meanings of the other words in the sentence. Look at the sentences that come before and after the sentence that contains the word. Do they give you any clues? Sometimes a writer gives an **example** that can help you figure out the word's meaning. Sometimes you may find a word that has almost the **same** meaning, or a word that means the **opposite**, or even a **definition** of the unfamiliar word, in the same sentence or a nearby one. These are all context clues.

Read the following sentence. Can you guess from the context what word might fit in the blank?

We had our picnic in the shade of an enormous _____ .

Did you guess from the context that the word was probably *tree*? If you did, you were able to tell from the other words in the sentence that the missing word must be a noun. You could also tell that the word names something that can give shade outdoors. It is something that people might have a picnic under. All these context clues helped you know that the word *tree* would make sense.

In this book you will read short paragraphs in which two words have been left out. Choose the correct word for each blank. Context clues in the paragraph will help you decide which words correctly complete the sentences.

A chemical that attacks tooth decay can be squirted onto the decayed area. The liquid softens the decay, allowing it to be scooped out painlessly instead of (1) _____ away. The solution, which works almost immediately, does not (2) _____ the healthy part of the tooth.

1. (A) greased   (B) designed   (C) drilled   (D) mixed
2. (A) foster   (B) affect   (C) fumble   (D) predict

Marching ants cannot swim well. When they come to a stream they do a very strange thing. Some take hold of a root with their strong jaws. Others take hold of fellow ants. Soon there is a "rope" of ants (3) _____ a (4) _____ to the other side. The rest of the ants march across it.

3. (A) holding   (B) swimming   (C) forming   (D) chewing
4. (A) stream   (B) tunnel   (C) subway   (D) bridge

The Smithsonian Institution, a group of museums in Washington, D.C., was (5) _____ with money named in the (6) _____ of James Smithson, an Englishman who had never been to the United States. He wanted the institution established there "for the increase and diffusion of knowledge."

5. (A) destroyed   (B) painted   (C) arranged   (D) established
6. (A) house   (B) will   (C) estimate   (D) friend

The opossum is easily the best actor in the animal world when it "plays possum." So able is the animal to feign death, when frightened or captured, that it is virtually (7) _____ to tell by (8) _____ whether the creature is dead or alive. It remains motionless and limp, with its tongue hanging out of its mouth and eyes open and rolled.

7. (A) easy   (B) impossible   (C) simple   (D) incredible
8. (A) phoning   (B) examine   (C) talking   (D) observation

Louis and Mary Leakey searched for evidence of human origins. In 1931 they found early human bones along with tools in Tanzania, Africa. They named the specimen *homo habilis*, "handy man," or "toolmaker." (9) _____ , in 1978, Mary Leakey discovered footprints of a humanlike species that (10) _____ upright about 3.7 million years ago.

9. (A) Earlier   (B) Soon   (C) Never   (D) Later
10. (A) crawled   (B) sank   (C) slept   (D) walked

American chestnut trees have been destroyed by a deadly bark disease. However, these once noble plants are still struggling to survive. Shoots can be found (11) _____ from old roots, especially in hilly (12) _____ areas of Appalachia. It is possible, therefore, to still see chestnut leaves although the trees are gone.

11. (A) descending	(B) hiding	(C) sprouting	(D) decaying
12. (A) business	(B) wedded	(C) wooded	(D) display

The land which forms at the mouth of a river is called a delta. It is given this name because it resembles the fourth letter of the Greek alphabet, which is shaped somewhat like a small triangle and corresponds to "D." Many of the great (13) _____ of the (14) _____ have deltas.

13. (A) ponds	(B) mountains	(C) rivers	(D) valleys
14. (A) ravine	(B) sea	(C) atmosphere	(D) world

Cows get homesick, too. One named Black Beauty was purchased and transported to a new home a mile away. Some five minutes after reaching her new (15) _____ area, the cow was missing. Nine days later, and one hundred pounds lighter, the homesick cow reappeared at her (16) _____ home.

15. (A) recording	(B) lodging	(C) hangar	(D) mooring
16. (A) mansion	(B) original	(C) colonial	(D) woodland

The English began a tunnel under the English Channel in 1882. They stopped because they feared enemies would use it to (17) _____ England. In 1994, England and France completed a joint project to (18) _____ the two nations with a train tunnel under the Channel.

17. (A) visit	(B) flood	(C) invade	(D) ransom
18. (A) connect	(B) divide	(C) sell	(D) rebuild

If you have baby brothers or sisters, you have (19) _____ seen many weird (20) _____ of creeping. Some babies creep backwards, others sideways. Some do it on hands and toes, others on hands and knees. Babies that never creep at all just sit around until they learn to walk.

19. (A) definitely	(B) probably	(C) never	(D) distinctly
20. (A) models	(B) scenes	(C) styles	(D) shades

UNIT 2

Water pipes in an unheated building will freeze and crack when the outside temperature is freezing. To prevent pipes from breaking, allow water to trickle from each (1) _____ in the building for a day or so. When a building will be (2) _____ for an extended period of time, drain the water system completely.

1. (A) reservoir   (B) axle   (C) faucet   (D) windmill
2. (A) airless   (B) heatless   (C) frozen   (D) motionless

Water in its free state cannot run uphill. If water is transported over an uneven terrain through a pipe, it may (3) _____ to run uphill when traveling from a lower level to a higher level. However, instead of running uphill, it's (4) _____ being pushed by the weight of the water in the pipe behind it.

3. (A) appear   (B) desire   (C) endeavor   (D) start
4. (A) relentlessly   (B) actually   (C) cautiously   (D) usually

---

Is it true that a bullet cannot penetrate the skin of a rhinoceros? From the toughness and the immense thickness of its skin, the hide of the rhinoceros was long believed to be bulletproof. However, it is now known that the skin of the animal is quite soft, except when dried. Then, it becomes exceedingly hard but still (5) _____ by a (6) _____ .

5. (A) edible   (B) manageable   (C) brittle   (D) penetrable
6. (A) bullet   (B) gourmet   (C) chef   (D) tailor

Antarctica is the world's highest, coldest, driest continent. A footprint in Antarctic moss may take ten years to disappear. It has been (7) _____ that it will take a banana peel more than a hundred years to (8) _____ .

7. (A) clutched   (B) estimated   (C) dedicated   (D) expressed
8. (A) produce   (B) migrate   (C) decompose   (D) appear

Insect-eating plants can be found all over the world. These plants devour whatever insects they can trap with their wide and encompassing petals. There are many varieties of insect-eating plants. Some contain water which (9) _____ the insects, others (10) _____ the insects with the aid of acid secretions.

9. (A) deafens   (B) drowned   (C) postpones   (D) dissolves
10. (A) incorporate   (B) digest   (C) welcome   (D) awake

In 1892 Ellis Island, New York, opened as an immigration station for people arriving in America from other countries. Some people had to wait days for permission to enter the United States. Others were refused (11) _____ because of diseases. In 1954 Ellis Island was closed as an immigration center and has since become a tourist (12) _____.

11. (A) criticism   (B) defiance   (C) inheritance   (D) admission
12. (A) carnation   (B) haven   (C) attraction   (D) peninsula

Lobsters, shrimps, crabs, and other crustaceans turn red when they are boiled because heat destroys all but one of the color pigments in their shells—a violet pigment. The (13) _____ water breaks down this violet pigment to form a reddish pigment which gives the cooked lobster its (14) _____.

13. (A) wretching   (B) pouting   (C) boiling   (D) sulking
14. (A) thigh   (B) mirage   (C) symptom   (D) color

A woman boarded a bus in Dallas, Texas, and deposited her $2,000 diamond ring in the fare box. Items such as peach pits, pills, ballpoint pens, bullets, and cigar butts turn up regularly in bus fare boxes. Items not (15) _____ in thirty days are given to the drivers. Fortunately, the woman got her (16) _____ back!

15. (A) discarded   (B) damaged   (C) appraised   (D) claimed
16. (A) memory   (B) ring   (C) bus   (D) bracelet

Robert Bakker's (17) _____ about dinosaurs at first angered other experts. Dinosaurs, he said, were fast moving, not slow. (18) _____ were warmblooded, not coldblooded. And some did not lay eggs, but bore their young alive. Some of Bakker's ideas are accepted today.

17. (A) theories   (B) jokes   (C) stories   (D) bones
18. (A) We   (B) You   (C) It   (D) They

Do you want to confirm a fish story? To prove that the fish you caught is as big as you are claiming it is, make a fish rubbing such as the Japanese made in the 1800s to record the (19) _____ of the fish they caught. They painted or inked the fish, then obtained an (20) _____ by rubbing it on a piece of paper.

19. (A) recipes   (B) sizes   (C) mileage   (D) longitude
20. (A) abbreviation   (B) excursion   (C) impression   (D) apology

9

UNIT 3

Trolley cars are coming back! Before World War I trolleys linked together neighborhoods and cities. With the coming of automobiles and buses, trolleys became almost extinct. Few were left by the 1950s. Now city planners, engineers, and transit operators (1) _____ trolleys can provide the cheap, energy-saving means of (2) _____ needed today.

1. (A) doubt   (B) bellow   (C) believe   (D) imply
2. (A) transportation   (B) excavation   (C) exclamation   (D) communication

---

Karen McNally studies earthquakes. She monitors the shaking earth all over the world. She also teaches geophysics and advises (3) _____ how to make buildings earthquake-safe. McNally hopes scientists will someday be able to (4) _____ major earthquakes accurately.

3. (A) hikers   (B) architects   (C) explorers   (D) painters
4. (A) avoid   (B) outrun   (C) predict   (D) experience

The thief who stole a bicycle in Connecticut was in for a surprise if he opened the carrying bag attached to the bike. It contained a two-foot poisonous copperhead snake. The owner had planned to make it part of a snake collection. Thus far, however, medical authorities have not reported (5) _____ anyone for a copperhead (6) _____ .

5. (A) scolding   (B) visiting   (C) paying   (D) treating
6. (A) penny   (B) collection   (C) snakebite   (D) exhibition

---

Despite your efforts, you'll never find the word "sardine" on a list of fish species, since there is no such fish as a "sardine." A can of sardines can be any (7) _____ , thin-boned fish, from herring to pilchards, as long as it is (8) _____ for packing in oil.

7. (A) armored   (B) tidy   (C) slinky   (D) small
8. (A) inflatable   (B) haulable   (C) suitable   (D) crumbled

---

Some people mistakenly believe onions can prevent disease. An ancient folk custom that has survived to this day is to place onion slices around the house for use in "trapping" (9) _____ that are (10) _____ to humans. The slices are burned each day and replaced with fresh ones.

9. (A) odors   (B) appetites   (C) bacteria   (D) temptations
10. (A) dangerous   (B) novel   (C) offensive   (D) beneficial

UNIT 3

On the first Saturday in October a fiddlers' convention is held on the campus of Athens College in Alabama. Visitors from all over the country are attracted to this mecca of old-time country fiddlin'. Hundreds of (11) _____, not only with fiddles but with banjos and dulcimers, pit their skills against one (12) _____.

11. (A) aviators   (B) scientists   (C) musicians   (D) alligators
12. (A) another   (B) bow   (C) tune   (D) instrument

Most people today would have second thoughts about eating foods that were favorites among some Romans. The brains of peacocks were considered a delicacy. Few could resist mice cooked in honey. Most (13) _____ were (14) _____ when they could serve a food that could not be identified by a guest.

13. (A) mice   (B) hosts   (C) peacocks   (D) guests
14. (A) happiest   (B) delicate   (C) cooked   (D) grave

The pretzel was (15) _____ at one of the monasteries in southern France during the sixth century. Using leftover bread dough, an imaginative monk formed a pretzel to (16) _____ arms folded over in prayer. He called it a pretiola.

15. (A) discounted   (B) burned   (C) invented   (D) reserved
16. (A) reject   (B) represent   (C) assist   (D) disapprove

"The cold shoulder" is an expression which sprang up during the years when knights roamed the land. Wandering knights would usually receive hot meals at any castle, while the (17) _____ peasant would be lucky to be (18) _____ a plate of cold meat. They would likely get a "cold shoulder" of mutton!

17. (A) common   (B) constant   (C) adoring   (D) petite
18. (A) offered   (B) peddled   (C) advanced   (D) reserved

People who spend prolonged periods of time out in the very cold weather are apt to be (19) _____ by frostbite. The most susceptible parts of the body are the fingers, toes, nose, ears, and cheeks. Hard, white areas that tingle or feel numb need to be warmed as quickly as possible, but not with extremely hot (20) _____.

19. (A) informed   (B) criticized   (C) enforced   (D) attacked
20. (A) fees   (B) funds   (C) substances   (D) hiccups

People can actually die of fright or other emotional (1) _____ . Family arguments or breakups, business failures, and even nightmares can set off abnormal heartbeats, called arrhythmias, in people whose hearts appear to be perfectly (2)_____ . Severe abnormalities of the heart can be life-threatening.

1. (A) sentiments   (B) plaques   (C) upsets   (D) harmonies
2. (A) hollow   (B) dishonest   (C) horizontal   (D) normal

Soccer, the fastest-growing team sport, can be played by children regardless of size and ability. Researchers have found that soccer is a comparatively safe activity. In checking 1,292 players, ages seven to eighteen, they (3) _____ a total of thirty-four injuries, or 2.6 per one hundred (4) _____ . Most of the injuries were minor.

3. (A) reported   (B) lipped   (C) kidnapped   (D) immigrated
4. (A) participants   (B) helicopters (C) binoculars   (D) convictions

---

Anyone who has handled a coin has felt its raised edge or border. There are reasons why such a border is there. Not only does this border aid to some extent in handling the coin, but it also serves to protect its (5) _____ from (6) _____ .

5. (A) conversion   (B) absence   (C) face   (D) semicircle
6. (A) tuition   (B) abolition   (C) wear   (D) surgery

In November, around Thanksgiving in the United States, there is a festival in Berne, Switzerland, called Zibelmarit or "onion market." Of all the activities and amusements scheduled, the most unique is a battle of confetti throwing. Children and adults enjoy this (7) _____ playful (8) _____ .

7. (A) weekly   (B) annual   (C) monthly   (D) daily
8. (A) solemnity   (B) ritual   (C) sacrifice   (D) litter

One of the world's strangest birds is the South American hoatzin. This bird's main claim to fame is that its young have claws on their wings as well as their feet! These claws help the leaf-eating hoatzin climb the (9) _____ trees and reach their (10) _____ !

9. (A) barren   (B) contorted   (C) tall   (D) stunted
10. (A) majority   (B) destinies   (C) desserts   (D) meals

It is often supposed that a bullet fired vertically will return to the earth at the same speed with which it left the gun. Such, however, is not accurate since (11) _____ does not pull a bullet through the (12) _____ as fast as a charge of powder drives it.

11.	(A) humidity	(B) gravity	(C) superstition	(D) supposing
12.	(A) water	(B) air	(C) earth	(D) gun

In Grinzing, Austria, drivers of cars have been discouraged in a novel way from speeding. A whole gaggle of geese led by a gooseherd has walked back and forth across the street to slow the traffic. The ambling birds have been more (13) _____ than fines, traffic signs, or radar control in (14) _____ speeding.

13.	(A) scarce	(B) effective	(C) weary	(D) useless
14.	(A) welcoming	(B) admiring	(C) curbing	(D) encouraging

Like animals, the mushroom breathes oxygen and gives off carbon dioxide. Plants do just the opposite. Also like an animal, the mushroom prefers to live in a cave. Some people who have (15) _____ its flesh have a difficult time (16) _____ it from meat.

15.	(A) drunk	(B) sorted	(C) uncovered	(D) eaten
16.	(A) eating	(B) distinguishing	(C) deriving	(D) separate

Survivors of air force disasters prove that (17) _____ will (18) _____ almost anything to keep alive. A meal of one downed flier consisted of monkey meat. Before their rescue, other survivors ate bamboo shoots; still others ate grass, fried bees, snails, snakes, and even butterflies.

17.	(A) airplanes	(B) butterflies	(C) monkeys	(D) people
18.	(A) fight	(B) buy	(C) follow	(D) eat

A most remarkable friendship was that of an adventurous girl and a dolphin on Long Island Sound. The graceful dolphin would tow this girl around the water near Port Jefferson. A school of dolphins would swim about playfully as the girl (19) _____ the fin of her (20) _____ pet and rode happily over the waves.

19.	(A) pinched	(B) clutched	(C) patched	(D) adopted
20.	(A) elaborate	(B) expensive	(C) glamorous	(D) strange

In the last century each town kept its own time, based on the position of the sun. A traveler might have to reset a (1) _____ twenty times in crossing the nation. Finally, after years of confusion, Congress set up the present time (2) _____.

1. (A) trains   (B) watch   (C) direction   (D) destination
2. (A) schedules   (B) days   (C) zones   (D) calendar

What is the most often-played song of all time? It is not by a famous composer. What is probably the most-played song was (3) _____ by two women: Mildred J. Hill and Patty S. Hill of Louisville, Kentucky. These sisters (4) _____ in writing "Happy Birthday to You."

3. (A) opposed   (B) impressed   (C) measured   (D) composed
4. (A) argued   (B) collaborated   (C) applauded   (D) multiplied

---

"Go fly a kite," is exactly what they did. And what a (5) _____ it (6) _____! Villagers in Japan created an aerial monster, circular in shape, weighing half a ton. Hundreds of people and equipment with over 6,000 feet of rope were needed to control the kite in the air.

5. (A) message   (B) bomb   (C) kite   (D) blimp
6. (A) was   (B) dissolved   (C) envisioned   (D) had

In 1935, at sixteen, ballerina Margot Fonteyn danced her first *Swan Lake*. Since then her (7) _____ has been (8) _____. Other outstanding performances include *Sleeping Beauty, Cinderella, Sylvia, Giselle*, and *Firebird*. Her appearances with Rudolf Nureyev, she says, gave her a "second career." In 1956 she was made a Dame of the British Empire.

7. (A) arch   (B) failure   (C) success   (D) rehearsal
8. (A) unbelievable   (B) curtained   (C) minimal   (D) shameful

---

Premature babies sometimes need surgery. One such baby, born two months ahead of schedule, weighed less than three and a half pounds when she required two operations. Five people were needed to take her to the (9) _____ room because of all the (10) _____ and attachments that were keeping her alive.

9. (A) nursery   (B) storeroom   (C) delivery   (D) operating
10. (A) doctors   (B) nurses   (C) machines   (D) interns

UNIT 5

Scientists are developing new "bugs" or microbes that feed on chemicals. One bug will eat its way through crude oil and has the (11) _____ to clean up oil spills. Another bacteria feeds on the chemical known as 2, 4, 5-T as if it were candy. In the future microbes may be used extensively to (12) _____ industrial wastes.

11. (A) illumination (B) potential (C) version (D) criticism
12. (A) combat (B) multiply (C) produce (D) increase

The Sheep-Lending Company, Ltd. of Bonn, West Germany, rents out sheep at ten dollars per sheep per year. Anette von Dorp, a twenty-two-year-old student of agriculture, formed the corporation with her mother and brother. The sheep serve as (13) _____ by keeping areas of (14) _____ short. They also keep lawns well fertilized.

13. (A) models (B) pets (C) lawnmowers (D) animals
14. (A) flowers (B) shrubs (C) bushes (D) grass

Biologists study the tails of humpback whales to learn about the (15) _____ and migrations of these animals. The tail of each whale has its own special notches, scars, and brown algae patches to make it (16) _____. Photographs of over 1,000 humpback whales have been collected and studied at the College of the Atlantic in Maine.

15. (A) habits (B) respiration (C) geography (D) abdomens
16. (A) duplicated (B) imitated (C) repeated (D) unique

The sweetest shop in Paris is "Au Pain de Sucre," located in the middle of the Seine River on St. Louis Island. Customers can buy handmade candy, chocolates, and baskets of sugar. The baskets, which include sugar-loaf cone, different textured sugars, multi-shaped nuggets, and (17) _____ for making taffy, make (18) _____ gifts.

17. (A) muscles (B) paste (C) partners (D) time
18. (A) excellent (B) worthless (C) absurd (D) spicy

Dolphins might well be described as the "hitchhikers of the sea." Clever dolphins allow themselves to be pushed long distances by the bow waves of ships. While they may give the (19) _____ of (20) _____ with ships, they are really moving along at little expense of energy.

19. (A) feeling (B) disguise (C) belief (D) appearance
20. (A) racing (B) dragging (C) propelling (D) driving

A horselaugh is a coarse and loud laugh. The term originated no later than the early eighteenth century, possibly sooner. Some authorities say that "horselaugh" was suggested by the laughlike noise made by horses. It may even be that "horse" in this connection is merely a corruption of "coarse." Certainly, a (1) _____ is (2) _____ .

1. (A) noise   (B) horselaugh   (C) giggle   (D) chortle
2. (A) crude   (B) polite   (C) civilized   (D) gentle

It has been discovered that the water hyacinth just may be the best waste-disposer a water system could have! The pretty flower thrives on garbage! If a water hyacinth is placed in (3) _____ water, the plant drinks in the pollutants and converts them into plant tissue, (4) _____ all the way!

3. (A) sparkling   (B) cleansed   (C) carbonated   (D) polluted
4. (A) wilting   (B) strangling   (C) thriving   (D) starving

---

Women's clothes are buttoned right to left; men's are buttoned left to right. This (5) _____ originated in thirteenth-century France, when men buttoned their own apparel, but women (6) _____ maids to help them dress. Since most people are right-handed, it was handy for the men, and for the maids as they faced the ladies, to button from left to right.

5. (A) proverb   (B) fashion   (C) suspicion   (D) humidity
6. (A) adjourned   (B) dissected   (C) employed   (D) repelled

---

At the age of eighty-eight, Eva Hindler Greene finally received her degree in mining engineering from the Missouri School of Mines and Metallurgy. She had completed the (7) _____ some sixty years (8) _____ , but the school had refused to give a woman that degree. Despite the refusal, she worked as a mining engineer for much of her life.

7. (A) mining   (B) payments   (C) applications   (D) requirements
8. (A) away   (B) before   (C) later   (D) after

It's a strange occupation indeed, and few in the United States are qualified for it. The job is to test the quality of feathers to determine their future use. By squeezing them and tossing them in the air, the feather judge (9) _____ their (10) _____ for use in parkas and other articles of clothing.

9. (A) rejects   (B) determines   (C) doubts   (D) disregards
10. (A) absurdity   (B) cleanliness   (C) priceless   (D) suitability

Skyscrapers were not possible until builders learned to use iron and steel to support many floors. Also, the passenger (11) _____ was invented. The first skyscraper (12) _____ in the United States was the Chicago Home Insurance Building, built in 1883.

11. (A) elevator   (B) fare   (C) train   (D) storage
12. (A) studied   (B) reduced   (C) erected   (D) demolished

Some schools have a "homework hot line." Parents can check on assignments for various classes. Students can no longer claim they don't have any homework or that they forgot the (13) _____. Parents can call the school and get a (14) _____ message about the homework.

13. (A) textbook   (B) teacher   (C) assignment   (D) classmates
14. (A) personal   (B) written   (C) confidential   (D) recorded

Could it happen? It did! The New York City Fire Department usually receives three to eight alarms simultaneously from citizens who think they are the first to see the (15) _____ of a (16) _____. But when a plane once hit the Empire State Building, 150 individuals sent in an alarm, not aware that thousands of others had seen the plane crash into the structure.

15. (A) conclusion   (B) complication   (C) illusion   (D) outbreak
16. (A) storm   (B) crash   (C) fire   (D) distraction

Clams and oysters pump nearly 400 gallons of water through their bodies daily. In this way, they can (17) _____ themselves of bacteria. When shellfish from polluted waters are placed in a clean environment, they soon rid themselves of (18) _____.

17. (A) cleanse   (B) tarnish   (C) refund   (D) bathe
18. (A) pearls   (B) omens   (C) monarchs   (D) pollutants

In the middle ages, glassmakers discovered that if they mixed different chemicals into melted (19) _____, they could create different colors, or stains. Today stained glass (20) _____ let colored sunlight into many churches, government buildings, and private homes.

19. (A) chocolate   (B) ice   (C) glass   (D) wax
20. (A) toys   (B) windows   (C) roofs   (D) porches

In the last century each town kept its own time, based on the position of the sun. A traveler might have to reset a watch twenty times in crossing the nation. Finally, after years of confusion, Congress set up the present time zones.

A. Exercising Your Skill

We plan our lives according to time. Since time is so important, our language is filled with words that are related to it. Some of these words name the ways we measure time. For example, *hour* and *month* are names for units of measure. The thing they measure is time. Other time-related words name objects. They name things we use to keep track of time. The words *calendar* and *clock*, for example, name two of our most familiar timekeepers.

Think about what you know about time. Make two lists of words with the following headings:

Units of Time	Timekeepers
_____	_____
_____	_____
_____	_____
_____	

B. Expanding Your Skill

Compare your lists with those of your classmates. Did you find any new "timely" words to add to yours? Now skim an article about time in the encyclopedia or any other reference book. Can you add more words to your lists? Is there a list of another kind of time words you could make? (Hint: How about adjectives that describe time?)

Now put your time words to work. Write an example of each item on the list, using at least one time word per item. You may use the same time word more than once, but try to use as many different ones as you can. Your examples may be realistic or just plain silly.

A newspaper headline
An advertising slogan
A line from a greeting card
A line from a song
The title of a book
The name of a store
A cheerleader's yell
A recorded greeting on a phone machine
The name of a product
A highway traffic sign
A weather forecast

C. Exploring Language

Think about time as it relates to your life. What do you like and dislike about time? How does time affect your life? What does time mean to you?

Use time words to complete the first paragraph below. Then use your own words to write how you feel about time.

The word _____ comes from the Latin word *kalendae*, which means "calends," the day of the new moon. Its largest unit of time is the _____ , followed (from largest unit to smallest) by _____ , _____ , and _____ .

Of these standard units of time, I think the _____ is the most important. It seems important to me because _____

_____

_____

_____

_____

D. Expressing Yourself

Choose one of these activities.

1. Many people think you can actually "slip" through time—that is, slip between the units of time and enter another system of time or another reality. Some science fiction stories use this idea as a theme. What would happen if you could slip through time? Imagine that you have done just that. Write a description of how you did it and what it's like where you are.

2. Most of the world operates according to the Gregorian calendar. Find out how this system came to be—who, after all, was responsible for our sometimes thirty-day, sometimes thirty-one-day, and sometimes twenty-eight-day (or twenty-nine-day) months. Write a brief explanation.

3. The World Calendar Association wants to change our calendar. Find out how. Then write a paragraph describing the change, and show what the calendar might look like. Or, work with a classmate to create your own calendar. How would you divide up time? What would you call the units of time?

4. In England, an ancient monument known as Stonehenge has been standing for thousands of years. It is made up of huge, roughly cut rocks arranged in a circle. For centuries, people puzzled over Stonehenge. What did it mean to the people who built it? How did they use it? Today scientists believe that Stonehenge served as a kind of calendar. Find out more about this idea. If the scientists' explanation is correct, how did this calendar work? What information did it provide? Write a brief report, and include a diagram of Stonehenge. Use the diagram to help make your report clearer.

Fish in shallow lakes are helped by ice skaters. For people to skate, they must first remove the snow cover. This permits light to filter through the ice. Plants under the ice can continue to give off oxygen, (1) _____ the fish from (2) _____ and increasing their chances for survival.

1. (A) influencing   (B) banning   (C) squeezing   (D) preventing
2. (A) swimming   (B) breathing   (C) suffocating   (D) sunning

Have you tried ultra-pasteurized whipping cream? It has a refrigerator shelf life of sixty to ninety days. Once it's opened, though, you must use it or freeze it. Only when ultra-pasteurized cream is very cold will it whip into (3) _____ peaks. Bowl and beaters can be chilled in the (4) _____ for thirty minutes.

3. (A) volcanic   (B) sunlighted   (C) stiff   (D) mountain
4. (A) avalanche   (B) freezer   (C) cellar   (D) sunshine

Pecans, which were first cultivated by Native Americans, have remained an American specialty. With the (5) _____ of plantings in New South Wales in Australia and Natal in South Africa, these nuts are grown almost nowhere outside America. Nor are they (6) _____ much elsewhere.

5. (A) expression   (B) detail   (C) sincerity   (D) exception
6. (A) breathed   (B) laundered   (C) consumed   (D) confirmed

Scientists now believe that a full moon affects people physically and emotionally. Body enzymes and hormones become more active, while blood pressure, heartbeat, and metabolism increase. Physical problems and diseases become more (7) _____ at this time. Anything can happen to the (8) _____, including an increase in anxiety, aggressiveness, and violent behavior.

7. (A) religious   (B) intelligent   (C) geometric   (D) severe
8. (A) brains   (B) emotions   (C) digestion   (D) respiration

When her father became President in 1963, Luci Johnson was not performing well at school. A Washington, D.C. optometrist discovered that her eyes were at fault. They were unable to function together to discern what her sight revealed. (9) _____ corrected this (10) _____, and Luci went on to make the honor roll in college.

9. (A) Tape   (B) Therapy   (C) Braces   (D) Foresight
10. (A) condition   (B) ability   (C) principle   (D) power

What happens when your leg falls asleep? The nerve impulses and blood (11) _____ to the muscles are temporarily blocked off, but the muscles continue to tense and relax slightly. When you move your leg again, nerve impulses (12) _____ and blood rushes back into the slightly moving muscles. This causes your leg muscles to tingle.

11. (A) venom   (B) type   (C) supply   (D) sugar
12. (A) resume   (B) halt   (C) cease   (D) quit

On February 17, 1864, the first successful submarine attack was made against a surface ship. The Confederate submarine *Hunley* sank the USS *Housatonic*, a thirteen-gun corvette in Charleston harbor. The person (13) _____ for this (14) _____ change in warfare was Captain Hunley, who financed the building of the boat bearing that name.

13. (A) responsible   (B) indicated   (C) suspended   (D) bouyed
14. (A) aquatic   (B) drastic   (C) scenic   (D) admired

The family automobile is the most used vehicle in all history. It hauls the average American over 12,000 miles a year. Seventy-five years ago one traveled approximately 200 miles—by horse, steamboat, or by foot. By the end of the 1960s, Americans were (15) _____ a trillion (16) _____ a year.

15. (A) buying   (B) eating   (C) selling   (D) traveling
16. (A) books   (B) dollars   (C) miles   (D) trees

Waterbeds for babies could prove to be most helpful according to the results of certain new experiments. Doctors at Stanford University and the University of California believe that waterbeds will provide a (17) _____ environment to the one that the premature infants have (18) _____ before birth.

17. (A) different   (B) costlier   (C) noisier   (D) similar
18. (A) tolerated   (B) requested   (C) remembered (D) experienced

---

A woman named Zazel was the first human cannonball. Zazel was fired from a cannon on April 2, 1877, in London, England. The cannon, which was powered by elastic springs, shot her sixty feet into the air. Her act was so (19) _____ that her original engagement was (20) _____ for two years.

19. (A) humdrum   (B) sensational   (C) sensitive   (D) dull
20. (A) prevented (B) extended   (C) restricted   (D) dominated

On October 24, 1901, Anna Edson Taylor was the first person to go over Niagara Falls and (1) _____ . After being released from her barrel, Taylor, a schoolteacher, suggested that others not try "the foolish thing I have done." Ten years later Bobby Leach became the first man to survive the same (2) _____ .

1. (A) die　　　　(B) suggest　　　(C) breathe　　　(D) survive
2. (A) tragedy　　(B) custom　　　(C) aerial　　　　(D) ordeal

Mounds of sandstone from eight feet to twenty-seven feet in diameter can be found in the north-central area of Kansas. The mounds look like bowling balls that were designed for (3) _____ . The sandstone mounds were (4) _____ when erosion disintegrated softer layers of rock that surrounded them.

3. (A) parasites　(B) cattle　　　(C) dwarfs　　　(D) giants
4. (A) decorated　(B) revealed　　(C) infested　　(D) revisited

A geography professor in California once proposed reorganizing the United States so that there would be thirty-eight, not fifty, (5) _____ . He claimed that the new (6) _____ would save the taxpayers money.

5. (A) sizes　　　(B) countries　　(C) cities　　　(D) states
6. (A) collection　(B) preparations　(C) arrangement　(D) institutions

---

If you like to go snowmobiling over ski slopes, chances are you'd enjoy motorcycling on water. You can buy a jet-propelled unsinkable "Wetbike" that rides the waves on skis. Speeds of up to fifty miles per hour are possible. If you should jump or fall off, the (7) _____ motor (8) _____ stops.

7. (A) car　　　　(B) plane　　　(C) boat　　　　(D) bike
8. (A) eventually　(B) ultimately　(C) accidentally　(D) automatically

---

Roller skis are ideal for the summer months when no snow is available. They are made of aluminum and have three wheels, one in the front and two in back. They are fitted with a (9) _____ ratchet so they won't go in reverse. Since roller skis are not equipped with brakes, going downhill can be (10) _____ .

9. (A) rusty　　　(B) primitive　　(C) nonreturn　　(D) noisy
10. (A) dangerous　(B) deliberate　(C) dazzling　　(D) delightful

UNIT 8

The biggest instant camera in the world is (11) _____ at Polaroid headquarters in Cambridge, where it makes extremely accurate copies of famous paintings. The machine measures sixteen by sixteen by sixteen cubic feet. Its interior can (12) _____ twenty people who wear snooperscopes so that they can see in the dark.

11. (A) trudged   (B) housed   (C) resigned   (D) narrated
12. (A) memorize   (B) dissolve   (C) hesitate   (D) hold

Standard light bulbs have an average life of 750 hours. Some bulbs developed for the handicapped give service for 3,500 hours, or up to 5 years. Now a physicist has made a (13) _____ that will last up to 10 years. It combines the (14) _____ of an incandescent lamp with the efficiency of fluorescent lighting.

13. (A) promise   (B) bulb   (C) mistake   (D) gloom
14. (A) convenience   (B) expense   (C) disadvantages   (D) hazards

---

Mexzcapapapetalson has long been a legendary place of wonder and mystery believed to lie deep in the Yucatán jungle. In 1985 archaeologist Brad Savage accidentally discovered that this place had really existed. His team of experts (15) _____ a gigantic "enclosed shopping mall" with ceilings that (16) _____ more than fifty feet over a central waterfall!

15. (A) unearthed   (B) planted   (C) registered   (D) attracted
16. (A) trudged   (B) towered   (C) honored   (D) stunted

Several vegetables, such as cabbage, tomato, broccoli, and sweet potato, are best started in the garden by transplant. This means the seeds are first (17) _____ in small containers (18) _____ . Later, when the plant has a good start, it is ready for transplanting outdoors.

17. (A) planted   (B) found   (C) sealed   (D) concealed
18. (A) secretly   (B) carefully   (C) outdoors   (D) indoors

---

The French princess, Isabella, was only seven when she married King Richard II of England in 1396. The King married her to (19) _____ a long truce with France. Soon afterwards, however, Richard was forced to abdicate and was put in (20) _____ . There he either starved or was murdered, leaving Isabella a widow at eleven.

19. (A) terminate   (B) consider   (C) obtain   (D) discourage
20. (A) debt   (B) prison   (C) charge   (D) action

Designers of movie sets often do intensive research to get authenticity. In the English film *Caesar and Cleopatra*, one set (1) _____ a replica of the night sky as it appeared in 45 B.C. The stars were in the same positions as they were when the (2) _____ meeting of Caesar and Cleopatra took place.

1. (A) rejected   (B) changed   (C) included   (D) burned
2. (A) ludicrous   (B) historic   (C) formal   (D) uneventful

---

Artificial moons and suns are being developed to be turned on or off at will. They would utilize (3) _____ trampoline-shaped reflectors floating in the earth's orbit. The suns, called "solettas," and the moons called "lunettas," would reflect great amounts of heat and (4) _____ which could be put to many uses.

3. (A) enormous   (B) hazardous   (C) miniscule   (D) unknown
4. (A) smog   (B) information   (C) culture   (D) energy

Jacques Cousteau, who is known for his love of the oceans, invented something to help divers spend more time (5) _____ the water's surface. The SCUBA device includes an air tank, so divers need not return to the surface to breathe. SCUBA stands for *self-contained underwater* (6) _____ *apparatus*.

5. (A) beneath   (B) on   (C) above   (D) alongside
6. (A) *breathing*   (B) *bouncing*   (C) *bubbling*   (D) *brave*

Two young people of Storm Lake, Iowa, work as research associates in the study of insect migration. What they do is tag butterflies. Julie Movall and her brother Paul (7) _____ the tag number, place, date, time, whether reared or wild, and sex. They forward the information to a (8) _____ professor in Canada.

7. (A) destroy   (B) record   (C) duplicate   (D) falsify
8. (A) absorbed   (B) acting   (C) university   (D) kindly

Don't be surprised if your toaster, television, or stove becomes talkative. It appears that any CB signal can be picked up by any amplifying gadget if the (9) _____ is close enough. All you need to receive a CB conversation is to have two (10) _____ the proper length in the "talking" object.

9. (A) museum   (B) broadcast   (C) hurricane   (D) waving
10. (A) recorders   (B) wires   (C) projectors   (D) microphones

Most of us get colds, but those who live with people, go to school or work with people, and use public transportation usually get more colds than those who live and work (11) _____ . Why? They're in contact with more infections. People who encounter few others in their daily lives build an immunity, or (12) _____ , to the germs in their environment.

11. (A) together   (B) regularly   (C) alone   (D) allow
12. (A) swelling   (B) hospital   (C) vacuum   (D) resistance

---

Would you like to own a wristwatch with a face smaller than a dime or an aspirin tablet? You can buy a watch of this size! It has a quartz movement so that it doesn't need to be wound. If your eyesight is keen, you might enjoy (13) _____ one of these (14) _____ timepieces.

13. (A) swallowing   (B) postponing   (C) wearing   (D) extinguishing
14. (A) mammoth   (B) miniature   (C) colossal   (D) oversized

---

Despite what you may have heard, the universal distress symbol, S.O.S., does not stand for "Save Our Ship"; in fact, it doesn't stand for anything! It was chosen because it is (15) _____ to transmit and easy to (16) _____ ! It is not an oral signal, either; it's strictly for Morse code!

15. (A) simple   (B) difficult   (C) awful   (D) irresistible
16. (A) except   (B) summarize   (C) describe   (D) remember

A stone forest has been found. The newly found petrified forest is the only one discovered with the trees lying as they fell millions of years ago. Some of the trees are eight and even ten feet in diameter. They all lie in the same direction, (17)_____ that they may have been blown down by a (18) _____ .

17. (A) confirming   (B) proving   (C) indicating   (D) guaranteeing
18. (A) giant   (B) fan   (C) storm   (D) plane

Suppose your uncle asked you for the (19) _____ of the number one followed by one hundred zeros? What would you reply? Nine-year-old Milton Sirotta replied, "A *googol*." And that's just what his uncle, Edward Kasner, a mathematician, decided to call the number. If you don't believe it, look up *googol* in the (20) _____ !

19. (A) sum   (B) answer   (C) name   (D) product
20. (A) atlas   (B) dictionary   (C) cookbook   (D) phone book

"Trolley" systems may one day (1) _____ between Earth and the moon and between Earth and the planets. According to former Apollo astronaut Edwin Aldrin, "They would continue in perpetual cycles among the planets, picking up and dropping off detachable transfer (2) _____ , or taxis, which would carry crew and supplies from the surface of each planet."

1.	(A) shuttle	(B) dangle	(C) collide	(D) dissolve
2.	(A) booklets	(B) vehicles	(C) sounds	(D) conclusions

Ghana, Africa, one of the leading cocoa-producing nations, has developed a new cocoa tree. It starts (3) _____ fruit after two years instead of after five or eight (4) _____ . The new tree will produce 2,000 pounds of dry beans per acre as compared to the 540 pounds per acre produced by older varieties.

3.	(A) bearing	(B) shedding	(C) polishing	(D) consuming
4.	(A) centuries	(B) years	(C) decades	(D) days

Scientists wonder why the people of the Caucasus Mountains area of Russia live so long. Many are well over 100 years old and still active. Is it because of their diet? Their ways of life? Their freedom from worry? The people themselves say that theirs is the land that (5) _____ (6) _____ .

5.	(A) pollution	(B) doctors	(C) death	(D) hospitals
6.	(A) remembered	(B) lost	(C) conquered	(D) forgot

Methane gas in underground coalbeds has caused many mine explosions. The Bureau of Mines has developed a technique for collecting gas. This would prevent explosions and provide fuel. It has been (7) _____ that there is (8) _____ methane gas in mineable coalbeds to take care of the country's natural gas consumption for twelve years.

7.	(A) estimated	(B) guaranteed	(C) approved	(D) insured
8.	(A) inferior	(B) waiting	(C) enough	(D) insufficient

Starboard designates the right side of a ship, but probably very few sailors realize why that term is used. Its origin goes back to the times when vessels were driven by sails and were steered by (9) _____ over the (10) _____ side. This was the "steering paddle," or "steorbord," or "starboard."

9.	(A) farmers	(B) waves	(C) scientists	(D) paddles
10.	(A) seamy	(B) seasoned	(C) right	(D) left

UNIT 10

Underwater hockey, called octopush, is a game that originated in 1954 when divers attempted to add an element of fun to their training programs. A four-pound lead disk, called a "squid," is (11) _____ along the bottom of a pool with a "pusher." The object is to push the "squid" into the other team's (12) _____, or "gully."

| 11. | (A) lumbered | (B) exhaled | (C) propelled | (D) cancelled |
| 12. | (A) caddie | (B) goal | (C) almanac | (D) referee |

Many people know that rats are the enemies of turkeys. They steal their eggs and kill their chicks. Rats can also be (13) _____ of disease germs that (14) _____ the helpless turkey embryos before they have a chance to hatch. Obviously, turkeys are always on the lookout for rats.

| 13. | (A) friends | (B) carriers | (C) preachers | (D) slayers |
| 14. | (A) enrich | (B) retain | (C) kill | (D) nourish |

A pen is a device for writing with a fluid. The first pens were made from reeds; by the seventh century feathers were used. The quills of wing feathers of various birds were cut at an angle, sharpened, and split. (15) _____ pens continued in use until the steel pen was (16) _____ in 1780.

| 15. | (A) Fountain | (B) Quill | (C) Ballpoint | (D) Cartridge |
| 16. | (A) exported | (B) imported | (C) invented | (D) sharpened |

What is the most dangerous occupation? Insurance companies (17) _____ astronauts as their top risks. Other high-risk positions include those of test pilots, bullfighters, performers of stunts, hot-air balloonists, lion tamers, and trapeze artists who carry on their acts without (18) _____.

| 17. | (A) imprison | (B) foil | (C) rate | (D) blindfold |
| 18. | (A) audiences | (B) gallows | (C) canteens | (D) nets |

Even those with the poorest of vision have no problems reading the time from a clock in Milwaukee, Wisconsin. The minute hand is twenty feet long; the hour hand, almost sixteen feet. The (19) _____ of the (20) _____ is more than forty feet high. The illuminated clock can be seen as far away as forty miles.

| 19. | (A) forehead | (B) tick | (C) face | (D) seconds |
| 20. | (A) bomb | (B) feline | (C) clock | (D) tower |

UNIT 11

Can water ever burn? There is a river in Mexico City that has been declared so polluted with waste and chemicals that it is highly flammable. The water is so (1) _____ that inspectors sent to analyze the contents were given injections to (2) _____ disease.

1. **(A)** severe   **(B)** topic   **(C)** sick   **(D)** deadly
2. **(A)** prosper   **(B)** encourage   **(C)** contract   **(D)** prevent

The world's tallest mountain is not Mount Everest near India. The tallest mountain in the world belongs to the United States. It's Mount Kea in Hawaii—some 30,000 feet high. Only the topmost 13,000 feet, however, are above the surface of the sea. The rest (3) _____ below the (4) _____ .

3. **(A)** lies   **(B)** sways   **(C)** entices   **(D)** struggles
4. **(A)** plateau   **(B)** surface   **(C)** trees   **(D)** volcano

A person who is telling a lie produces strange facial expressions. Unusually rapid eye movements, called "micromomentaries," are the most common (5) _____ . These occur at one-sixtieth of a second in someone who is lying, which is much faster than (6) _____ blinks which occur at one-fifth of a second.

5. **(A)** ambition   **(B)** irregularity   **(C)** foliage   **(D)** occupation
6. **(A)** nasal   **(B)** unusual   **(C)** dental   **(D)** normal

On March 26, 1976, a baby boy was born in Norwood Hospital, Massachusetts, at 10:43 P.M. What was so unusual about that? The baby's father, David Hill, had been born on the same day in the same (7) _____ at the same hour—only twenty-seven years (8) _____ !

7. **(A)** hospital   **(B)** town   **(C)** country   **(D)** state
8. **(A)** after   **(B)** following   **(C)** before   **(D)** below

In Sierra Madre, California, a mother hen was killed defending her eggs from a plundering dog. Puff, a cat, decided to help out. The cat patiently sat on the eggs until the chicks hatched. Puff then washed and (9) _____ the motherless (10) _____ as if they were her own kittens.

9. **(A)** ironed   **(B)** folded   **(C)** spanked   **(D)** cuddled
10. **(A)** hens   **(B)** roosters   **(C)** infants   **(D)** chicks

UNIT 11

The windshields of most jet planes are coated with a very fine layer of gold. The layer is so thin that it is (11) _____ . Gold is used as a windshield (12) _____ because it is a good conductor of electricity and makes a fine defroster.

11. (A) transparent   (B) fundamental   (C) antiseptic   (D) monotonous
12. (A) wiper   (B) disinfectant   (C) covering   (D) overlook

---

For centuries most people thought the Earth was flat. Who figured out for sure that the Earth was (13) _____ ? During a lunar eclipse Aristotle noticed that the shadow of the Earth on the moon had a circular shape. He was the first person to back his opinion with a (14) _____ .

13. (A) large   (B) horizontal   (C) round   (D) spinning
14. (A) lie   (B) fact   (C) wish   (D) report

Spanish moss seems to live on nothing. Seen in trees along the Gulf Coast of the United States, the plant is truly a strange one. It is not a parasite, does not harm trees, yet continues to thrive. It catches the dust particles and moisture from the air around it. These give it (15) _____ and (16) _____ .

15. (A) talent   (B) headaches   (C) gloss   (D) food
16. (A) odor   (B) exercise   (C) drink   (D) infection

Would you like to have a watch that chimes the hour, quarter hour, and minutes? Such a pocket watch is now for sale. The 18-karat-gold watch, which took three years of handwork to (17) _____ , also has a perpetual calendar with moon phases. The cost of this (18) _____ pocket watch is $48,000.

17. (A) condemn   (B) complete   (C) approve   (D) correct
18. (A) overloaded   (B) cumbersome   (C) fascinating   (D) unavailable

---

What fruit is (19) _____ like a miniature pair of lungs? It's the fruit of the harpullia, or tulipwood tree. This tree (20) _____ red or orange fruit in a leathery capsule that splits and produces two black, shiny seeds. The fruit is not edible.

19. (A) shaped   (B) skinned   (C) cored   (D) ironed
20. (A) bears   (B) weathers   (C) tempts   (D) reduces

Red tape is the popular name for delay. The term dates back to England during the eighteenth century when it was used to ridicule the delay of government business. People, impatient for action on a particular case, poked fun at the continual (1) _____ and untying of the red tape which bound the legal dispatches and (2) _____ .

1. **(A) tying**   **(B) sewing**   **(C) sorting**   **(D) coloring**
2. **(A) misgivings** **(B) confetti**   **(C) menus**   **(D) documents**

The (3) _____ of throwing something, such as rice or confetti, at the bride after her wedding is not new. The ancient Hebrews (4) _____ cake and nuts; the Britons, biscuits. In Scotland, ancient Rome, Iceland, and other countries, brides have had cakes broken over their heads.

3. **(A) torrent**   **(B) welfare**   **(C) dignity**   **(D) custom**
4. **(A) cracked**   **(B) collapsed**   **(C) narrated**   **(D) hurled**

Without water, a person can live only a week to ten days. What about living without food? Doctors say it depends on circumstances, but with enough water and warm (5) _____ , probable (6) _____ time is two and one-half months. An Irish mayor, for example, went on a hunger strike in prison. He died after seventy-four days of fasting.

5. **(A) wishes**   **(B) surroundings** **(C) inhabitants** **(D) illusions**
6. **(A) arrival**   **(B) construction** **(C) survival**   **(D) destruction**

A commercial art company in Papillion, Nebraska, ran an ad in a newspaper offering "absolutely nothing" for the price of one dollar. Hundreds of calls and letters were received, and some people even sent money. About $230 was (7) _____ to pay for the ad and some bumper (8) _____ which read "Absolutely Nothing."

7. **(A) raised**   **(B) banked**   **(C) printed**   **(D) burned**
8. **(A) fenders**   **(B) lights**   **(C) stickers**   **(D) crops**

How did Ludwig von Beethoven write great symphonies when he was deaf? No one knows for sure. He was twenty-eight when he first began losing his (9) _____ . When he was totally deaf, he must have been able to "hear" the music in his mind, and when he worked at a piano, he may have "heard" by feeling the instrument's (10) _____ .

9. **(A) sight**   **(B) courage**   **(C) taste**   **(D) hearing**
10. **(A) message**   **(B) vibrations**   **(C) notes**   **(D) sonata**

Most people think of dinosaurs as clumsy animals that slowly lumbered around. Why, though, were some anatomical (11) _____ of dinosaurs like those of modern animals that move about quickly and spryly? Some scientists are now (12) _____ that dinosaurs were fast-moving creatures with limb structures like those of fleet-footed ostriches.

11. (A) features   (B) diplomas   (C) splints   (D) acquaintances
12. (A) infected   (B) convinced   (C) fractured   (D) consumed

---

In three hours the sun has been known to bend railroad tracks. This actually happened in Sweden when the sun heated up the icy cold steel rails. Fortunately, a worker (13) _____ the twisted tracks and alerted (14) _____ before a train came through. It took three days to repair the tracks.

13. (A) noticed   (B) disregarded   (C) ignored   (D) forgot
14. (A) authorities   (B) convicts   (C) farmers   (D) nurses

---

Colombian Indians have long used toxins to make lethal blow darts. Similar poisons may soon be used to treat heart and nerve disorders. Eighty chemically related poisons have been extracted from the skins of tropical frogs. These substances are (15) _____ to humans in raw form, but their derivatives can alter the structure of (16) _____ cells.

15. (A) unknown   (B) beneficial   (C) essential   (D) dangerous
16. (A) solitary   (B) dingy   (C) nerve   (D) prison

Rats follow humans almost wherever they go. These crawling, gnawing rodents damage property, spoil food, and carry deadly diseases. Some scientists estimated that rats have caused more human deaths than all of the (17) _____ ever (18) _____. Fortunately, however, they are invaluable laboratory animals used in the study of human diseases.

17. (A) disasters   (B) food   (C) garbage   (D) wars
18. (A) driven   (B) served   (C) gathered   (D) fought

An astonishing fact has been brought out by a research team. According to their study, butterflies taste with their legs! Furthermore, the scientific team claims the butterflies' legs are over 1,500 times as (19) _____ as the human (20) _____ in detecting sweetness of sugar.

19. (A) long   (B) quick   (C) sensitive   (D) impressionable
20. (A) pride   (B) tongue   (C) awareness   (D) emotion

Mexzcapapapetalson has long been a legendary place of wonder and mystery believed to lie deep in the Yucatán jungle. In 1985 archaeologist Brad Savage accidentally discovered that this place had really existed. His team of experts unearthed a gigantic "enclosed shopping mall" with ceilings that towered more than fifty feet over a central waterfall!

A. Exercising Your Skill

A place does not have to be ancient and far away like Mexzcapapapetalson to be mysterious. Places you have visited or even places that you see every day—an abandoned house, a basement or attic, an unexplored street—may have an air of mystery. A natural setting like a beach or meadow may seem filled with mystery at certain times of the day or in certain kinds of weather. Mystery comes not from the place itself but from your own imagination.

Think of a place that seems mysterious to you and make a word chart to describe it. In the center of a sheet of paper, write the name of the place, or make up a name that suits it. Circle the name and draw several lines extending from the circle. On each line, write a word that you could use to convey the mysterious feeling that the place holds for you. Here is an example.

B. Expanding Your Skill

Look over your word chart and share it with your classmates. Can you add any new descriptive words to it?

Look up each of your descriptive words in a dictionary or thesaurus to find synonyms for them. How do the synonyms compare to your original words? Do they give more, or less, of a sense of mystery? Write each of your original descriptive words on a sheet of paper. Beneath each word, write all the synonyms you can find for it. Then think back to your mysterious place. Circle the synonyms that best capture its feeling. Here is an example.

C. Exploring Language

Imagine that you are about to write a mystery or science fiction story or a tale of the supernatural. You want your opening paragraph to catch the reader's attention, arouse curiosity, and set an eerie or mysterious mood. You have decided to begin with a description of a place that will be important to the plot. First, think of a place that would make a good setting for such a story. Picture it in your mind, and jot down some descriptive words, as you did in Part A. Then write the paragraph. Remember—you want your reader to feel a sense of mystery and to wonder, "What strange events are about to happen?"

D. Expressing Yourself

Choose one of these activities.

1. The three places listed in the box are considered legendary, as Mexzcapapapetalson once was. Choose one and do some research on it. Write a report about the place you chose.

Atlantis	Camelot	El Dorado

2. Working alone or with a group of classmates, design a lost city or country. Draw a map and write a brief description of the place. Include some information about the following:

architecture	language
dress	main occupations
education	methods of transportation
geography/landforms	natural resources

3. Find out more information about Mexzcapapapetalson. Then imagine you are a reporter in Brad Savage's archaeological party when the place is discovered. Write a newspaper account of the discovery.

4. Read a science fiction short story about life on another planet. As you read, take notes on the setting. Jot down details that help you picture what this alien environment looks like. Note the landscape, plant and animal life, climate conditions, buildings or other structures—whatever the author includes. Then imagine that you are a filmmaker. You want to turn the story into a movie. In the opening scene, your camera will pan the setting. Using the details from your notes, describe what the camera will see.

An elephant has a very sharp sense of hearing, but is nearsighted and has great difficulty seeing something (1) _____ in front of it. That's why at a zoo or circus you can always see elephants feeling about the floor with their (2) _____ to get at peanuts thrown to them.

1. (A) directly   (B) absolutely   (C) genuinely   (D) positively
2. (A) tusks   (B) ears   (C) trunks   (D) brooms

Some people still practice voodoo. They begin by making a small clay or wax image of an enemy. After sticking pins or thorns into the image, they may burn or bury it. By injuring or destroying the (3) _____, they believe injury or death will come to the (4) _____.

3. (A) enemy   (B) image   (C) voodoo   (D) magician
4. (A) friend   (B) voodoo   (C) enemy   (D) image

Excavations in Paloma, thirty miles from Lima, Peru, may have (5) _____ the oldest American village. Remains and artifacts of a people in the first (6) _____ of a settled existence have been found. Archaeologists believe that six or seven families lived in Paloma 7,700 years ago, and that about twenty families lived there 5,000 years ago.

5. (A) bewildered   (B) unearthed   (C) harpooned   (D) discoverer
6. (A) moments   (B) tubes   (C) vans   (D) stages

The earthworm is built with a (7) _____ device. Its tail is flat. When the worm leaves its (8) _____, it braces its tail in the entrance. If danger threatens, the earthworm uses its tail to snap back in a split second.

7. (A) corkscrew   (B) long   (C) sharp   (D) safety
8. (A) cage   (B) friends   (C) den   (D) hole

Why don't people weigh the same at noon as they do in the morning? Body weight varies throughout the day for different reasons. It can increase after a meal or decrease after exercise and perspiring. The amount of bulk and fiber in the diet (9) _____ body evacuation, which also causes (10) _____ in body weight.

9. (A) refunds   (B) grafts   (C) disables   (D) affects
10. (A) variations   (B) permanence   (C) unwavering   (D) identical

A court case that continued for one hundred years began in Egypt around 1350 B.C. The Neshi family became (11) _____ in a series of court squabbles over about fifty acres of Nile Valley land. In the longest-running case in (12) _____ history, the Neshi family won out.

11. **(A) involved**   **(B) electrocuted**   **(C) abolished**   **(D) televised**
12. **(A) marital**   **(B) medical**   **(C) recorded**   **(D) aviation**

In 1981 rock climbers discovered two birds nesting on a cliff in New Hampshire. The birds turned out to be peregrine falcons, the first (13) _____ in their natural surroundings in the East in almost thirty years. After DDT sprayings in the late 1940s, the falcons had nearly (14) _____, but in 1972 DDT was banned.

13. **(A) engraved**   **(B) mobbed**   **(C) sighted**   **(D) crammed**
14. **(A) mechanized**   **(B) vanished**   **(C) originated**   **(D) tensed**

There is now a restaurant exclusively for canines! Believed to be the first of its kind in the world, the dog restaurant opened in Tokyo amidst a busy shopping center! Dog-sized tables and chairs dot the (15) _____ and the (16) _____ includes raw meat, soup, and fresh milk!

15. **(A) pasture**   **(B) establishment**   **(C) hospital**   **(D) promenade**
16. **(A) buffet**   **(B) fodder**   **(C) breakfast**   **(D) menu**

The three most important horseracing events in the United States are the Kentucky Derby at Churchill Downs, Kentucky; the Preakness at Pimlico Track in Maryland, and the Belmont Stakes at Belmont Park, New York. Only three-year-old horses may (17) _____ these races. When a horse wins all three events, it is called the (18) _____ Crown.

17. **(A) abuse**   **(B) console**   **(C) enter**   **(D) offend**
18. **(A) Duple**   **(B) Hexagonal**   **(C) Triple**   **(D) Septuple**

People who see it can't believe their eyes. Is it a flying mailbox? It's a mailbox, all right, moving on a (19) _____ from its roadside station to the Mullinax patio 100 feet away. Rural Mullinax built it so he and his wife, Alice, don't have to go down the hill to get the (20) _____ .

19. **(A) truck**   **(B) command**   **(C) whim**   **(D) cable**
20. **(A) interest**   **(B) children**   **(C) mail**   **(D) subway**

The dog has been more than a best friend to humans. In cold climates dogs have (1) _____ as bed-warmers. Ladies of fashion once wore live toy poodles or Pekingese dogs as fashion (2) _____ . Until the twentieth century the teeth of dogs were used as money in the Solomon Islands.

1. (A) reduced   (B) served   (C) drilled   (D) transported
2. (A) conferences   (B) editorials   (C) accessories   (D) almanacs

More and more people are painting the flat roofs of their houses with light-colored paint containing aluminum flakes. The lighter roofs (3) _____ heat away during the summer. Conversely, they help reflect house heat back into the house and save a bit on (4) _____ during the winter.

3. (A) unravel   (B) reflect   (C) tarnish   (D) rinse
4. (A) dye   (B) cereal   (C) fuel   (D) ammunition

Who washed her hair on stage during a Broadway musical? If you said Mary Martin you were correct. The show was *South Pacific,* which opened in 1949. The song that prompted the action was "I'm Gonna Wash That Man Right Outta My Hair." Mary Martin (5) _____ the incident in her (6) _____ .

5. (A) accented   (B) pronounced   (C) mentioned   (D) extinguished
6. (A) geography   (B) topography   (C) bibliography   (D) autobiography

"He is quite odd. He eats with a (7) _____ ." This is the way people in Venice described those who used the new eating (8) _____ in the seventeenth century. It was not until the nineteenth century that the fork finally won a place at the dinner table.

7. (A) gulp   (B) straw   (C) song   (D) fork
8. (A) oven   (B) napkin   (C) plate   (D) utensil

Breathing deeply, a nonathletic adult fills his or her (9) _____ with about four liters of air. An athlete can add an extra two liters to that amount. Athletes develop (10) _____ and better working lungs.

9. (A) mouth   (B) stomach   (C) throat   (D) lungs
10. (A) louder   (B) smaller   (C) larger   (D) emptier

It was a very brave or very sick Roman who would visit a doctor. In ancient Rome there were no medical schools. Anyone who wished could practice medicine. Butchers, woodcutters, and stone masons (11) _____ (12) _____ and even performed surgery!

11. (A) prescribed   (B) examined   (C) practiced   (D) referred
12. (A) patients   (B) pulse   (C) hospitals   (D) specialists

---

Sharon, a town in the northwest corner of Connecticut, holds a unique nature festival each summer with special exhibits and trips through woods and fields. (13) _____ to almost everything a (14) _____ lover ever wanted to know concerning snakes and other animals, ferns, wildflowers, and edible wild foods are given at the Sharon Audubon Festival.

13. (A) Lyrics   (B) Answers   (C) Memorials   (D) Furloughs
14. (A) music   (B) wildlife   (C) antique   (D) television

Camels are ill-tempered beasts. They wage dreadful fights, even among themselves. Scraps between them are grim, dangerous affairs. Just let two fight, and other camels (15) _____ the (16) _____ within minutes.

15. (A) call   (B) trample   (C) join   (D) flee
16. (A) police   (B) roars   (C) battle   (D) ground

The training of wild horses is part of a cowhand's job. Known as "breaking a bronco," it is done inside a fenced-off area. Others sit on the fence to enjoy the show. They laugh and poke (17) _____ at the cowhand who is (18) _____ to the turf.

17. (A) guns   (B) rods   (C) fun   (D) horses
18. (A) tossed   (B) hurt   (C) left   (D) helped

Even police officers suffer many embarrassing moments in the line of duty. An annoyed police officer in Atlantic City, New Jersey, rushed to headquarters to find out why he had gotten a ticket for overtime parking. He learned all too quickly that somehow he hadn't recognized his own (19) _____ , a very popular make, and had (20) _____ himself.

19. (A) vehicle   (B) strength   (C) precinct   (D) capacity
20. (A) ticketed   (B) picketed   (C) jailed   (D) arrested

Scientists estimate that a day lasted twenty hours 400 million years ago; but twenty-two hours 4 million years ago due to a decrease in the earth's rotation. Now the (1) _____ rotation has increased slightly. In 1972 the world's timekeepers began adding a "leap second" each year. At present the addition of a "leap second" is (2) _____ only once in every eighteen months.

1. (A) room's   (B) rainfall's   (C) earth's   (D) crop's
2. (A) interesting   (B) destroyed   (C) necessary   (D) pleasing

---

"Button, button, who's got the button?" is an expression that traces far back in history, and one that Mrs. R. Blemster is likely to answer. Her collection consists of more than 10,000 buttons. "Collectors," she says, "are willing to pay large sums of money for buttons." Mrs. Blemster collects buttons, not for (3) _____ but for their (4) _____ .

3. (A) profit   (B) loss   (C) destruction   (D) waste
4. (A) bulk   (B) nourishment   (C) awkwardness   (D) beauty

A five-centimeter (two-inch) rose tree called Innovation was presented at an (5) _____ in Paris in 1986. The roses on the tree measured two centimeters (.8 inch) in diameter. It took French (6) _____ ten years to develop this dwarf rose.

5. (A) atlas   (B) execution   (C) accident   (D) exhibit
6. (A) horticulturists   (B) divers   (C) hairdressers   (D) chefs

---

Would you believe that there once existed a Society for the Prevention of People Being Buried Alive? Patents were even secured to help the members in their task! Someone invented an (7) _____ bell to be placed in the coffin; this would be rung should the "corpse" wake up (8) _____!

7. (A) enchanted   (B) electric   (C) antique   (D) insistent
8. (A) prematurely   (B) alone   (C) neighbors   (D) underground

---

In 1945 a Persian cat named Baby became a seeing-eye cat. The cat's mistress, Carolyn Swanson, lost her eyesight in that year. Swanson grew to trust Baby as her guide on daily walks. Baby would swish her tail against Swanson's legs whenever it was (9) _____ to cross a (10) _____ intersection.

9. (A) cautious   (B) healthy   (C) security   (D) unsafe
10. (A) school   (B) street   (C) shopping   (D) rural

UNIT 15

The world's first nuclear-powered ship, the *Savannah*, is a museum that can be visited at Patriot's Point, South Carolina, across the river from Charleston. The (11) _____ passenger-and-cargo vessel first sailed in 1962 to (12) _____ peaceful uses of atomic energy. It visited thirty-seven foreign ports before being taken out of service in 1970.

11. **(A) contagious**   **(B) transparent**   **(C) combination**   **(D) medical**
12. **(A) pollute**   **(B) demonstrate**   **(C) disobey**   **(D) obstruct**

A redwood tree of the United States' northwest coast stands between 200 and 275 feet tall. Its (13) _____ does not rot easily. It also resists disease and insect attack. The redwood's main enemies are people, (14) _____ use its beautiful wood for buildings and furniture.

13. **(A) wood**   **(B) width**   **(C) structure**   **(D) height**
14. **(A) where**   **(B) which**   **(C) who**   **(D) why**

In eighteenth century England some unusually (15) _____ punishments were often meted out for minor crimes. Over 200 types of crimes were (16) _____ by death. A person could be executed for stealing rabbits, associating with gypsies, or cutting a tree on public land. Today such crimes would be misdemeanors or felonies at most.

15. **(A) pleasing**   **(B) eternal**   **(C) severe**   **(D) simple**
16. **(A) addressed**   **(B) punishable**   **(C) negated**   **(D) admirable**

Have you ever poured coffee grounds down the sink? Did someone tell you they would scour the grease from your drains? It's not true, according to an (17) _____ from the plumbing industry. Just like sand, coffee grounds will stay in the pipes and cause (18) _____ problems.

17. **(A) organist**   **(B) administration**   **(C) authority**   **(D) exile**
18. **(A) diplomatic**   **(B) plumbing**   **(C) academic**   **(D) discipline**

In Japan people traditionally give gifts to relatives and business associates at year-end, in December, and at midyear, in July. They express their gratitude and wishes for continued good relations. If relations aren't satisfactory, presents help (19) _____ them. Over ten percent of the yearly total of department store sales (20) _____ in July, with over sixteen percent in December.

19. **(A) improve**   **(B) perturb**   **(C) destroy**   **(D) waste**
20. **(A) accuse**   **(B) entitle**   **(C) labor**   **(D) occur**

UNIT 16

Madagascar is a large island two hundred fifty miles off the coast of southern Africa. It is the fourth largest in the world, only (1) _____ in (2) _____ by Greenland, New Guinea, and Borneo. The majority of people in Madagascar live off the land and are either cattle-raisers or rice farmers.

1. (A) sculptured   (B) punctuated   (C) leased   (D) exceeded
2. (A) mirth   (B) camouflage   (C) brawn   (D) area

If you find a shoebox-sized radiosonde made of cardboard and plastic, return it to the National Weather Service. A prepaid mailbag is included inside it. Important (3) _____ needed for weather forecasting comes from radiosondes. These instruments rise into the atmosphere (4) _____ to balloons and then parachute to earth.

3. (A) punctuation   (B) decoration   (C) voting   (D) information
4. (A) summoned   (B) transcribed   (C) attached   (D) mailed

---

A chain letter is the term applied to a good luck message or a threat of bad luck if the recipient does not send copies to others. Since such messages contain threats, they are not mailable on postal cards or on the outside of mail. They are only (5) _____ when sent in (6) _____ with the postage prepaid.

5. (A) secretive   (B) mailable   (C) concealed   (D) esteemed
6. (A) trucks   (B) molecules   (C) submarines   (D) envelopes

---

"How old are you?" is not the most tactful of questions. The answer could well be, "It's none of your business!" A fan asked movie star Gloria Swanson how (7) _____ she was. Miss Swanson insisted on (8) _____ the fan's age. When the fan replied that she was seventy-seven, Miss Swanson said, "That makes us the same age."

7. (A) heavy   (B) intelligent   (C) wealthy   (D) old
8. (A) ignoring   (B) knowing   (C) doubling   (D) calculating

---

Would you believe that the legendary bare-fisted champion, John L. Sullivan, was once knocked out by an elderly woman named Hessie Donahue? On an (9) _____ tour John and Hessie would (10) _____ the crowds by "boxing," but one day, the 145-pound Hessie hit Sullivan with a right hook and knocked him out!

9. (A) exhibition   (B) exasperating   (C) achievement   (D) urgent
10. (A) irritate   (B) delight   (C) manipulate   (D) bore

The most expensive set of false teeth ever fitted for an other-than-human mouth went to a donkey! A very popular (11) _____ at the Tokyo Zoo, a donkey known as Ichimonji lost all of its teeth by the time it was twenty-nine. The Tokyo (12) _____ School came through, though, with $2,000 worth of new teeth.

11. (A) collection   (B) display   (C) performance   (D) attraction
12. (A) Elementary   (B) Secondary   (C) Medical   (D) Engineering

---

Noted visitors are frequently presented with the keys to a city. The ceremony traces back to ancient times when towns in Europe were fortified and visitors could only enter or leave through doors that were locked. The keys today are presented to distinguished visitors of a city simply as a (13) _____ of (14) _____.

13. (A) symptom   (B) guarantee   (C) forerunner   (D) token
14. (A) disgrace   (B) honor   (C) freedom   (D) evil

The Opera House in Sydney, Australia, is an architectural spectacle. It was (15) _____ over a period of fourteen years at a cost of 100 million dollars. There are four main (16) _____ halls: the Opera Theatre, the Concert Hall, the Drama Theatre, and the Film Theatre.

15. (A) obstructed   (B) transmitted   (C) constructed   (D) decoded
16. (A) performing   (B) political   (C) meditating   (D) balloting

---

Radar traps catch more than speeding motorists. One in New Jersey nabbed a speeding and riderless horse! A police car gave chase; four others were to follow. The five cars cornered the horse, but it escaped. Finally, it was again cornered and police lassoed the runaway. It was taken to police headquarters to (17) _____ its (18) _____.

17. (A) write   (B) await   (C) log   (D) escape
18. (A) bail   (B) journey   (C) owner   (D) trader

The Chesapeake Bay Bridge Tunnel is considered one of the seven engineering wonders of today's world. It spans the mouth of the Chesapeake Bay between Cape Charles and Virginia Beach, Virginia. The (19) _____, 17.6 miles long, is a (20) _____ of trestled highway above the water, two tunnels under the water, and four artificial islands.

19. (A) establishment   (B) structure   (C) building   (D) organization
20. (A) spectrum   (B) program   (C) nest   (D) combination

When Elizabeth Blackwell graduated from medical school in Geneva, New York, in 1849, she became the first woman doctor of modern times. After further studies in France and England, Elizabeth (1) _____ to the United States where she started a free clinic and later (2) _____ the New York Infirmary and Training School.

1. (A) certified   (B) financed   (C) previewed   (D) returned
2. (A) pasteurized   (B) discovered   (C) founded   (D) violated

---

The weight of a person depends more on his or her genes than on eating habits learned as a child. Studies not only have (3) _____ the importance of genetic influences, but have determined that a mother's weight is more closely (4) _____ to her children's future weights than the father's is.

3. (A) adjusted   (B) refunded   (C) proved   (D) ignored
4. (A) subscribed   (B) sustained   (C) donated   (D) related

---

Pemmican, a Native American food, has become popular with campers and hunters of today. A lightweight, high-energy food, it doesn't take up much room in a backpack. Bars can be purchased in camper-supply stores or by mail order. To (5) _____ your own pemmican, you'll (6) _____ dried chipped beef, peanuts, raisins, and beef suet.

5. (A) invent   (B) make   (C) hire   (D) purchase
6. (A) consume   (B) waste   (C) swallow   (D) need

Our senses yield false impressions under certain circumstances. A room, for example, might appear warm to a person coming in from outside where it is cold. Yet the same room may feel cold to someone who enters from a still warmer room. Humans can distinguish between (7) _____ and (8) _____ only relatively.

7. (A) impressions   (B) feelings   (C) rooms   (D) hot
8. (A) outside   (B) impression   (C) cold   (D) temperature

It is popularly believed that some of the houses in Virginia were built of bricks brought over from England. Historians, however, are agreed that very few, if any, bricks used in the colonies were (9) _____ from (10) _____. All the bricks used in making houses in Virginia during the seventeenth and eighteenth centuries seem to have been made here.

9. (A) manufactured   (B) departed   (C) imported   (D) assigned
10. (A) Mars   (B) England   (C) America   (D) Virginia

Few skeletal remains of elephants have been found in Africa. Scientists say the flesh is quickly stripped from the skeletons by other animals and the bones widely scattered. Local people believe the elephants go to a certain (11) _____ spot to (12) _____—the Valley of Ivory. Many dream of finding this place with its wealth of tusks.

11. (A) populated   (B) busy   (C) obvious   (D) isolated
12. (A) rejoice   (B) die   (C) relax   (D) drink

The world's largest known accumulation of gold is housed under the Federal Reserve Bank Building in New York City. Stacks of gold bars weighing twenty-seven pounds apiece are piled high in this underground (13) _____ which is divided into individual (14) _____ for foreign countries, central banks, and international monetary organizations.

13. (A) igloo   (B) generator   (C) coffin   (D) vault
14. (A) hemispheres   (B) compartments   (C) narratives   (D) coffins

After surgery, doctors may prescribe various drugs to relieve pain. Some doctors prescribe electrical stimulation, whereby tiny currents of electricity are applied to the skin several times a day. This electrical technique not only (15) _____ pain but keeps the patient (16) _____ rather than doped up from drugs.

15. (A) measures   (B) induces   (C) relieves   (D) intensifies
16. (A) comfortable   (B) sleepy   (C) serene   (D) alert

The Mount Rushmore monument in South Dakota turned out quite differently than anyone had at first expected. It was originally intended to show the faces of Kit Carson, Jim Bridger, and John Colter—all western legends. But the sculptor (17) _____ and (18) _____ four Presidents instead.

17. (A) objected   (B) cheered   (C) agreed   (D) worked
18. (A) asked   (B) suggested   (C) named   (D) mistook

One cactus plant grows as tall as a four-story building. With its thick stem and fingerlike arm, it can weigh ten tons. The saguaro plant can endure for long periods—as much as two years—without a drop of water. Of course, it shrinks. When (19) _____ does (20) _____ , it swells up like an accordion.

19. (A) autumn   (B) rainfall   (C) research   (D) linoleum
20. (A) depart   (B) play   (C) beware   (D) come

More and more bank tellers are being protected from the gunfire of robbers. Bullet-resistant plastic or glass barriers are erected above the tellers' counters. These transparent (1) _____ have not only succeeded in (2) _____ harm to the tellers but have helped reduce the number of bank holdups.

1. (A) shields   (B) recorders   (C) microphones   (D) gangplanks
2. (A) fostering   (B) encouraging   (C) ministering   (D) preventing

---

Many young birds are afraid to test their wings. They must sometimes be pushed off a limb or a cliff by their mothers before they learn to fly. This is not so with the megapode. These birds are hatched fully feathered and are able to fly from the (3) _____ as soon as they (4) _____ from the shell.

3. (A) nest   (B) moment   (C) residence   (D) flutter
4. (A) evolve   (B) emerge   (C) develop   (D) impact

A San Mateo, California, dentist, Dr. Ursula Dietrich, sells her own special brand of toothpaste for animals. She believes the brushing of the teeth to be an (5) _____ part of a pet's (6) _____. The lips of the animal are gently raised while the brushing is done. Pets reportedly enjoy the procedure.

5. (A) innocent   (B) adaptable   (C) obscure   (D) essential
6. (A) grooming   (B) heredity   (C) tradition   (D) property

---

The Oklahoma Territory was officially opened on April 22, 1889, with the report of a pistol shot. Within twenty-four hours about 50,000 settlers had staked their claims, but some had jumped the gun and entered prematurely. Thus, Oklahoma's (7) _____—the Sooner State—was born! Some (8) _____ too soon!

7. (A) reputation   (B) quest   (C) nickname   (D) alias
8. (A) derived   (B) lingered   (C) achieved   (D) arrived

The pupils of anyone's eyes will change in size during a period of mental (9) _____. Give someone material to memorize, then ask the person to repeat the material. The pupils will expand as the person is given the memory work, contract during the actual memorization, and expand again as the person (10) _____ the material memorized.

9. (A) concentration   (B) abbreviation   (C) measurement   (D) specification
10. (A) receives   (B) persuades   (C) cooperates   (D) recites

The Appalachian Trail, which stretches from Springer Mountain in Georgia to Mount Katahdin in Maine, attracts many hikers, some of whom travel its entire (11) _____ . The trail extends 2,050 miles through fourteen states. Although it sometimes takes hikers over paved roads, the (12) _____ quality of the trail is most appealing.

11. (A) conference   (B) distance   (C) semester   (D) revolution
12. (A) wilderness   (B) metropolitan   (C) aquatic   (D) dormitory

---

People often ask, "Why are there holes in Swiss cheese?" These holes are produced by the liberation of gases caused by bacterial action during the process of fermentation. The holes are half an inch in diameter. This type of cheese (13) _____ in the mountains of Switzerland, but can also be (14) _____ in other parts of the world.

13. (A) dissolved   (B) terminated   (C) originated   (D) sputtered
14. (A) expanded   (B) treacherous   (C) startled   (D) produced

---

A rickshaw is a two-wheeled carriage pulled by a person. Usually found in the Orient, the rickshaw was (15) _____ by Jonathan Scobie, an American minister living in Japan. He designed it in the 1860s as a means of transportation for his wife, who was (16) _____ disabled.

15. (A) propelled   (B) invented   (C) discovered   (D) replaced
16. (A) since   (B) athletically   (C) physically   (D) visibly

---

Scientists wondered how trout made their way to the high mountain lakes of Colorado. Ute Indian history gives us the answer. In the summer deer fled high into the mountains. The Ute people (17) _____ trout to these lakes in deerskin (18) _____ so they would have fish to eat while hunting.

17. (A) flew   (B) guided   (C) carried   (D) swam
18. (A) canoes   (B) bags   (C) streams   (D) bottles

Millville, New Jersey, could be called the Holly City of America. In 1926 the owner of a local company sent fresh holly cuttings to forty-six customers as a holiday greeting. People receiving the holly were so appreciative that sending holly became an annual (19) _____ . Nearly three thousand boxes were being mailed out by 1953, when Millville's nickname became (20) _____ .

19. (A) conference   (B) tradition   (C) problem   (D) spotlight
20. (A) quarterly   (B) futile   (C) uniform   (D) official

Zoologists in England have developed fiberglass electronic eggs to study the habits of breeding birds. The fake eggs, suitably colored and sized, are used to replace normal eggs in birds' nests. Inside the (1) _____ eggs are high-frequency radios which (2) _____ information about temperature, light, and humidity.

1. (A) genuine   (B) abstract   (C) false   (D) edible
2. (A) extinguish   (B) transmit   (C) eliminate   (D) defrost

---

The driver of a soft-drink truck came to the rescue of a woman whose car was on fire. He grabbed a 64-ounce bottle from his truck, shook it (3) _____ , then (4) _____ the soft drink over the engine. Almost immediately the flames were extinguished.

3. (A) ominously   (B) sluggishly   (C) vigorously   (D) slightly
4. (A) advertised   (B) smeared   (C) sprayed   (D) drank

Groundhog Day, February 2: The groundhog emerges from its burrow but does not see its shadow. According to an old tradition, this means six more weeks of cold weather. Why does the groundhog interrupt its (5) _____ at this time of year? It is awakened by (6) _____ and ventures out to find food.

5. (A) independence   (B) activity   (C) hibernation   (D) progress
6. (A) impatience   (B) curiosity   (C) danger   (D) hunger

The duckweed is the tiniest of all flowers. It is a floating or (7) _____ freshwater plant, so named because ducks like to eat it. The duckweed is only about 1/50th of an inch long and 1/63rd of an inch wide. Very small roots or no roots at all are a (8) _____ of this plant.

7. (A) waterproofed   (B) rooting   (C) submerged   (D) flying
8. (A) misgiving   (B) deterrent   (C) characteristic (D) fascination

---

Have you ever wondered how many oranges an orange tree could yield in one harvest? A spokesperson for the Florida Citrus Mutual announced that one tree will produce from 1,000 to 1,200 oranges. This amount depends on the size of the oranges, not the (9) _____ of the (10) _____ .

9. (A) kind   (B) name   (C) size   (D) color
10. (A) baskets   (B) tree   (C) harvest   (D) farm

The Trojans and Greeks had fought ten years without a decisive victory. Then, according to legend, the Greeks offered the gift of a huge, wooden horse to their enemy as a (11) _____ gesture. Greek soldiers, (12) _____ inside the horse, came out at night and opened the gates of Troy to their army. The Trojan defeat followed.

11. **(A)** peace   **(B)** superstitious   **(C)** negative   **(D)** threatening
12. **(A)** confused   **(B)** contented   **(C)** concealed   **(D)** condemned

---

Why stay in a confined position on an airline flight when you can exercise and improve your (13) _____ well-being? At least one airline has installed a forty-five minute (14) _____ program on flights. Soft music can be tuned in on one of the headset channels to accompany the program, which shows simple exercises to do in or near your chair.

13. **(A)** spiritual   **(B)** financial   **(C)** physical   **(D)** intellectual
14. **(A)** alphabetical   **(B)** reading   **(C)** survival   **(D)** exercise

---

Animals are sometimes classified as either carnivorous or herbivorous. A carnivorous animal eats meat and a herbivorous animal eats plants. You are correct in (15) _____ that "carn" must (16) _____ to meat and "herb" must have something to do with plants.

15. **(A)** ascending   **(B)** prescribing   **(C)** assuming   **(D)** consenting
16. **(A)** indicate   **(B)** relate   **(C)** revolve   **(D)** mean

---

Goalball is played blindfolded. The game was developed in Germany after World War II to provide blind veterans with (17) _____ and exercise. It is played on an indoor court with a ball shaped like, but heavier than, a basketball. The ball has bells inside to help players keep (18) _____ of it during a game.

17. **(A)** merchandise   **(B)** recreation   **(C)** weapons   **(D)** commission
18. **(A)** straight   **(B)** smug   **(C)** track   **(D)** hold

---

The moon follows a cycle, which lasts a month. For half the month, the moon wanes, or appears to grow smaller. For the other half of the month, the moon waxes, or appears to (19) _____ in size. The moon continues to wax until it is (20) _____ .

19. **(A)** add   **(B)** diminish   **(C)** contract   **(D)** increase
20. **(A)** around   **(B)** completely   **(C)** full   **(D)** luminous

More and more people are painting the roofs of their houses with light-colored paint containing aluminum flakes. The lighter roofs reflect heat away during the summer. Conversely, they help reflect house heat back into the house and save a bit on fuel during the winter.

A. Exercising Your Skill

Color is an important part of our lives. It keeps us warmer or cooler. It attracts our attention. It soothes us and excites us. Look around you. How many different colors do you see? Count them. You don't have to be exact; make an estimate. Chances are there are several times more colors than you count. Think about the colors and the words used to name colors. Make a list of as many colors as you can think of. Try to list at least twenty.

Now make a color wheel like the one to the right. Divide it into six sections labeled *red*, *orange*, *yellow*, *green*, *blue*, and *purple*. Fill each section with the names of the appropriate colors from your list. Some of the colors may seem appropriate for two sections. For example, suppose you have listed the color aqua. Does aqua belong in the blue section or in the green section? Check the dictionary. If your dictionary defines aqua as "greenish-blue," put it in the blue section. If the definition is "bluish-green," put it in the green section. If both definitions are given, the choice is up to you.

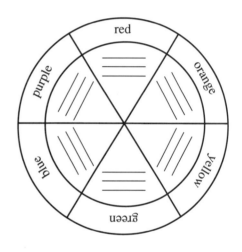

B. Expanding Your Skill

Read over your color wheel. Put a check next to those words that have other meanings, such as *orange* and *peach*. (They name fruits as well as colors.) Then compare your wheel with those of your classmates. Can you add new color words to yours?

Discuss how we describe color. What words do we use? What do the following words mean when used to describe color?

> brilliant   dark   deep   light   pale   strong

Find out the meanings of these color words:

> primary   secondary   hue   shade   value

C. Exploring Language

Look around you. Let your eyes wander. Are there some things in the room that "catch" your eye more than others? Are they colorful? For most people, colors have the power to draw attention. They also have the power to stir certain feelings. For instance, blue is a restful color. Red is an exciting color.

Choose one of the colors that caught your eye as you looked around the room. Write a paragraph describing it. The object isn't important, just focus on the color. Describe it by making comparisons. You can make three different kinds of comparisons: (1) You can compare it to feelings and emotions; for example, "It is a peaceful shade of blue." (2) You can compare it to things that have the same color—"It is the color of asparagus and of my cat's eyes." (3) You can compare it to things that you experience through your other senses—hearing, smell, taste, and touch. For example, "It is like the sound of a trumpet," or "It is like the feel of stepping into a warm bath." Use all three kinds of comparisons in your paragraph.

D. Expressing Yourself

Choose one of these activities.

1. The state of Vermont is named for a color. Find out what language the name comes from and what it means. How did the state get that name?

2. Pigment (paint) colors are different from light colors. Find out how they are different and what makes them so. Start by finding out what the primary colors are for each.

3. A rainbow arcing across the sky is always a breathtaking sight. At one time, people attached magical meanings to this spectacle, but today most people accept the scientific explanation. Find out how scientists explain rainbows. See if you can answer these questions: When do rainbows appear? Why do they form an arc? Why do they have separate bands of color?

4. Did you know that the first film for taking color photographs was invented by two musicians? Their names were Leopold Godowsky and Leopold Mannes. People called them "crackpots," but we have them to thank for the color pictures we take and for the color movies we watch. Read about these fascinating men, and write a brief report about the double life they led.

5. Gemstones are the most richly colored of all natural objects. They have long been treasured as a feast for the eyes. Make a chart that lists the names of several kinds of gems, their color (or colors—some have more than one), and where they are found. You might want to include an extra column for interesting facts about the gems. If you list more than one gem of a particular color, group them by color.

Have you ever tasted "perry," a cider that is pressed from fresh pears rather than apples? This (1) _____, which is widely known in England, can also be purchased during the fall in upstate New York. Perry is only (2) _____ for two or three months, though, since pears have a much shorter storage life than apples.

1. (A) ammonia   (B) sausage   (C) beverage   (D) lichen
2. (A) consuming   (B) quotable   (C) apparent   (D) available

Some women from India have red marks, called tikas, painted on their foreheads. They were once symbols of (3) _____ and worn by all married (4) _____ . Today they are worn only for decorative purposes. They may be in the shape of a circle, a diamond, or a teardrop.

3. (A) wedding   (B) chemistry   (C) misconduct   (D) marriage
4. (A) relatives   (B) technicians   (C) women   (D) musicians

The first woman mayor in America, twenty-seven-year-old Susanna Medora Salter, was elected by a two-thirds majority in April of 1887. The (5) _____ part of the (6) _____ was that Salter was not aware she was one of the candidates until she arrived at the polling station that day!

5. (A) gloomiest   (B) quickest   (C) wisest   (D) strangest
6. (A) situations   (B) frustration   (C) election   (D) votes

Inspired by the life-saving exploits of St. Bernards in snowy regions, owners of some French beaches are employing huge Newfoundland dogs as lifeguards! The dogs are fitted with rubber handles attached to their backs as they swim out to swimmers in (7) _____. They keep people (8) _____ until help arrives!

7. (A) discomfort   (B) remorse   (C) distracting   (D) distress
8. (A) amused   (B) afloat   (C) distracted   (D) endangered

Two sociologists have (9) _____ that many people are unaware of much of the lawbreaking going on around them. A crime—the breaking into a locked car—was staged. The "thief," who pretended to have lost the car keys, was even able to (10) _____ the services of a passerby who helped unlock the car with a coat hanger!

9. (A) imagined   (B) gestured   (C) determined   (D) discredited
10. (A) advertise   (B) secure   (C) disdain   (D) witness

Eula McClaney, born in Alabama in 1913, worked as a sharecropper until she was twenty-six. Then she began to make money in real estate. She later operated a (11) _____ for people who are emotionally disturbed. Her memorabilia is (12) _____ in the Schomburg Collection for Research in Black Culture in the New York Library.

11. (A) plow   (B) residence   (C) mortgage   (D) printer
12. (A) patented   (B) refused   (C) housed   (D) shattered

When it is time for soldiers to be in their quarters and for all lights to be put out, taps are sounded. This is a military signal most often sounded by a bugle or trumpet in the evening. Its origin is uncertain. Taps are also sounded over the (13) _____ of a (14) _____ soldier.

13. (A) table   (B) door   (C) birthplace   (D) grave
14. (A) happy   (B) lazy   (C) dining   (D) departed

Are you angry? It often shows on your face by creases between the eyebrows just above the bridge of your nose. A Native American who wanted to express the word "anger" through (15) _____ language would raise a closed (16) _____ to the same point between the eyebrows, and with the pad of the thumb encircle the area.

15. (A) musical   (B) sign   (C) foreign   (D) silently
16. (A) window   (B) issue   (C) fist   (D) coffin

The coconut is a mainstay of life in the Pacific. It (17) _____ both food and drink. The meat is also fed to livestock. The coconut even provides threads for (18) _____ and soap for washing.

17. (A) encourages   (B) neglects   (C) provides   (D) discourages
18. (A) fuel   (B) cloth   (C) oil   (D) food

The electronics industry has made radios, TVs, computers, cameras, and stereo (19) _____ smaller and smarter. Watches, besides telling time, can store data that can be (20) _____ by pressing a button.

19. (A) machinery   (B) musicians   (C) equipment   (D) strategy
20. (A) speculated   (B) oppressed   (C) humiliated   (D) retrieved

United States pennies minted after 1981 weigh nineteen percent less than the "copper pennies" (1) _____ before that time. The older pennies contain mostly copper with a five percent mixture of zinc, while the new, lighter-weight pennies contain mostly zinc with just a (2) _____ of copper.

1. **(A) quizzed**   **(B) bloated**   **(C) produced**   **(D) injected**
2. **(A) episode**   **(B) coating**   **(C) definition**   **(D) twitch**

Mikey is a six-foot-four, two-hundred-pound robot who sings, dances, and tells jokes. He can be hired to host or emcee a party or any (3) _____ that requires an attention-getter. Mikey's other (4) _____ include blinking eyes and a right arm that can hand out food or leaflets.

3. **(A) resort**   **(B) partly**   **(C) partition**   **(D) event**
4. **(A) heralds**   **(B) successors**   **(C) features**   **(D) spirits**

Need a pair of shoes? It's best to buy them in the late afternoon or evening when your feet have expanded. Be sure the shoes are (5) _____ enough for bone (6) _____ . When unlaced, you should be able to insert a finger behind your heel. The most comfortable walking shoes have low heels.

5. **(A) rigid**   **(B) roomy**   **(C) tidy**   **(D) noisy**
6. **(A) therapy**   **(B) movement**   **(C) decay**   **(D) mutiny**

Many plant names arise from similarities in shape, size, or color to more familiar plants. Squirrel corn is not corn. It is, instead, a small white flower. Blue-eyed grass is really an iris. Dogtooth violets are not violets, but lilies. It is rather odd how we (7) _____ many (8) _____ plants.

7. **(A) water**   **(B) ruin**   **(C) misname**   **(D) mislead**
8. **(A) familiar**   **(B) model**   **(C) bloom**   **(D) harsh**

The captain of a nine-ton boat (9) _____ it through a Florida inlet. Suddenly, the vessel stopped dead in forty feet of water as if it had struck a sandbar. What the boat had (10) _____ was a humpback whale coming up for air. It lifted all but the rear of the vessel from the water!

9. **(A) navigated**   **(B) excavated**   **(C) negotiated**   **(D) revised**
10. **(A) theorized**   **(B) encountered**   **(C) irrigated**   **(D) allied**

In 1873 Ellen Swallow Richards was (11) _____ a chemistry degree from the Massachusetts Institute of Technology, making her America's first professional woman (12) _____. During twenty-seven years as a professor at M.I.T., she wrote many books on chemistry and nutrition. It was Richards who started the first public-school lunch program.

11. (A) averted   (B) inflated   (C) forgiven   (D) granted
12. (A) engineer   (B) chemist   (C) economist   (D) archaeologist

---

Doctors have a simple test for diagnosing the disease diabetes in children. By having a child press one hand against the other, they can determine whether or not a child has joint stiffness, which is a(n) (13) _____ warning of diabetes. Of 169 young patients with diabetes for more than four and a half years, eighty-two (14) _____ joint stiffness.

13. (A) irregular   (B) reminder   (C) reliable   (D) elaborate
14. (A) invaded   (B) organized   (C) dissolved   (D) demonstrated

---

Cars painted in dull colors are hard to see from a distance and are more often (15) _____ in accidents than red or yellow cars. Bright orange is the most noticeable color from afar. Cars best-observed in traffic and from a distance are multicolored, the best (16) _____ being white and black, yellow and blue, or green and red.

15. (A) involved   (B) avoided   (C) refreshed   (D) prohibited
16. (A) appliances   (B) combinations   (C) machines   (D) contractions

---

It is a common misbelief that horsehairs will turn into snakes if placed in water. Those with a minimum knowledge of natural history know that a hair never turns into a snake. The belief probably arises from the fact that some worms (17) _____ the (18) _____ in the horse's tail.

17. (A) confuse   (B) resemble   (C) separate   (D) distinguish
18. (A) bridle   (B) hairs   (C) braid   (D) swish

Root beer, ginger ale, or any other soda will bubble after a container of it is opened. This is because it contains carbon dioxide, a colorless gas, that has dissolved under pressure. When the container is opened, the pressure is (19) _____. The liquid cannot hold as much carbon dioxide, so the (20) _____ bubbles out of the beverage.

19. (A) interpreted   (B) enclosed   (C) curled   (D) released
20. (A) aircraft   (B) detergent   (C) excess   (D) anger

Coyotes are nocturnal—they are out and about mostly at night. These doglike animals can (1) _____ to many (2) _____ . Their nightly howls are heard in the mountains of Maine, on the deserts of the Southwest, and even in the suburbs of Los Angeles.

1. (A) grow   (B) adapt   (C) respond   (D) alternate
2. (A) environments (B) qualities   (C) differences   (D) seasons

---

Bats are a nuisance if they get under the shingles of a house. Small enough to crawl through cracks, they often roost in places you can't get at. Bats will bite just like rats and other (3) _____, so be (4) _____ . If you are bitten, go at once for treatment for tetanus and rat bite fever.

3. (A) reptiles   (B) rodents   (C) birds   (D) fowl
4. (A) spiteful   (B) careful   (C) joyful   (D) bashful

Glass coins stamped with hieroglyphical symbols were discovered some years ago at the Tomb of Thebes. This glass could have been molded only in hot metal molds. Until this discovery it was, and still is, commonly (5) _____ that this (6) _____ of blowing glass was invented at the Boston and Sandwich Glass Company, Sandwich, Cape Cod.

5. (A) doubted   (B) questioned   (C) believed   (D) suspected
6. (A) method   (B) ritual   (C) custom   (D) sheen

The spitting snake is well named. It received its name from the fact that it ejects a poisonous spray from its mouth, often for a distance of ten to fifteen feet. The venom is apparently (7) _____ for the (8) _____ of its victim. Sharp pain and temporary blindness result as the snake prepares for its meal.

7. (A) better   (B) aimed   (C) worse   (D) good
8. (A) eyes   (B) teeth   (C) tongue   (D) ears

Warts can be an embarassing problem. Nerves and emotional stress have a great deal to do with them. Some specialists use hypnosis as a cure. Other (9) _____ include (10) _____ by freezing or by electrolysis. Whatever you do, don't pick warts, as this can spread them. Most disappear by themselves.

9. (A) problems   (B) treatments   (C) falsehoods   (D) causes
10. (A) removal   (B) devouring   (C) controlled   (D) neglect

Is it possible that a coin thrown into the air could land heads-up fifty times in (11) _____ ? Only if a million people each tossed a coin ten times every minute for forty hours a week is there a (12) _____ that there could be fifty straight heads once in nine centuries!

11. (A) condition   (B) impression   (C) succession   (D) oppression
12. (A) slogan   (B) remembrance   (C) resolution   (D) probability

---

A battle that lasted thirty-six days, in which 6,821 Americans were killed, and 19,217 wounded, has been immortalized in bronze. In Arlington National Cemetery tourists can see the (13) _____ , bronze sculpture of four Marines putting the American (14) _____ atop Mt. Suribachi on the island of Iwo Jima. The battle of Iwo Jima took place in 1945.

13. (A) minuscule   (B) warily   (C) large   (D) defenseless
14. (A) ancestry   (B) flag   (C) cuisine   (D) politics

Did you know that your feet contain one-fourth of the 206 bones in your body? Each foot contains twenty-six bones that are connected by thirty-three joints and tied together with 200 (15) _____ . When you consider all the pressure your feet get from your body weight, you can understand why they are so (16) _____ constructed.

15. (A) strings   (B) arteries   (C) ligaments   (D) chains
16. (A) crudely   (B) weakly   (C) flimsily   (D) marvelously

---

The first sports event in America was a horse race in 1665. It was held at the Newmarket Course in Nassau County, New York, less than fifteen miles from the present-day Belmont Race Track. (17) _____ in the colonies, horse races were (18) _____ by George Washington and Thomas Jefferson.

17. (A) Exploited   (B) Unrestricted   (C) Unfavorable   (D) Popular
18. (A) conducted   (B) galloped   (C) enjoyed   (D) measured

---

Carmen Miranda was the queen of samba (a Latin American dance) during the 1930s and 1940s. Her dancing and singing, featured in Broadway shows and Hollywood movies, brought her worldwide fame. Her outlandish (19) _____ included turbans overflowing with fruit. These were (20) _____ from the turbans of native women of Brazil.

19. (A) speeches   (B) costumes   (C) manners   (D) paintings
20. (A) copied   (B) kidnapped   (C) nestled   (D) concluded

A meteorite obtained from the Antarctic ice cap was being sliced for study at the Smithsonian Institution in Washington, D.C. Suddenly, researchers couldn't cut any further! X-rays (1) _____ that they had hit the first bits of diamond ever (2) _____ from outer space, probably formed by a collision that crushed carbon.

1. (A) provoked	(B) revealed	(C) receded	(D) dispelled
2. (A) stampeded	(B) postponed	(C) recovered	(D) purchased

If you have, or plan to start, a strawberry patch, you might want to save your old sheets and bedspreads as Margaret Szabo does. She then uses them to keep her (3) _____ warm. When frost threatens, Szabo makes sure the strawberries in her (4) _____ are snugly wrapped up in the soft materials.

3. (A) family	(B) strawberries	(C) attitude	(D) artifacts
4. (A) cakes	(B) market	(C) patch	(D) refrigerator

"Who's going to throw out the garbage today?" How often has that been said in your home? Be careful, however, before you do toss it out. A torn painting was recovered by one garbage collector and is now valued at $8,000. Before you throw out the trash, remember, (5) _____ isn't always (6) _____ .

5. (A) garbage	(B) money	(C) mink	(D) collection
6. (A) pure	(B) art	(C) valuable	(D) garbage

Some people boast that they can identify a friend's handwriting. This may be so. Tests show, however, that more than half of the people cannot identify their own handwriting. A study presented to a group of New York psychologists concluded that identification of handwriting should not be reliable (7) _____ for use in (8) _____ .

7. (A) connections	(B) theory	(C) evidence	(D) guess
8. (A) colleges	(B) hospitals	(C) jails	(D) courts

Japanese scientists have found a cure for paroxysmal dysacusis, a disease of the blood vessels in the inner ear which causes deafness. Thirty-two of thirty-nine patients who (9) _____ treatment had their hearing ability restored. (10) _____ masks, the patients inhaled pressurized oxygen for one hour. This increased blood circulation in their ears.

9. (A) rejected	(B) relished	(C) resented	(D) received
10. (A) Wearing	(B) Fashioning	(C) Adjusting	(D) Refusing

The oldest living thing ever discovered on earth is not certain. But a claim can be put in for a pine tree found in Nevada. Its rings indicate that it is almost 5,000 years old. That would make the tree (11) _____ than the (12) _____ of ancient Egypt.

11. (A) younger   (B) taller   (C) heavier   (D) older
12. (A) rings   (B) chowders   (C) aisles   (D) pyramids

It has been proven that our modern letter "O" began as a sketch meant to represent the human eyeball in its socket! As time went on, the drawing was made more simple by eliminating the outline of the socket. The letter "O" is (13) _____ in that it alone has not been (14) _____ for the past 2,700 years!

13. (A) unique   (B) absurd   (C) explosive   (D) authentic
14. (A) aboard   (B) restored   (C) changed   (D) revoked

Does traveling at 1,800 miles per hour on a supersonic airliner seem fast to you? By the early twenty-first (15) _____ it may seem slow. A rocket-liner could be in use then which would (16) _____ passengers from one side of earth to the other in just forty-five minutes.

15. (A) century   (B) decade   (C) generation   (D) era
16. (A) adapt   (B) transport   (C) calculate   (D) dissemble

When Alfred Ely Beach proposed that a subway be built beneath New York City, people laughed at him. So, using his own money and telling no one, he built part of his proposed system. The project took twenty-six months and, until its (17) _____ in 1870, was a (18) _____ to all but the workers.

17. (A) comment   (B) completion   (C) climax   (D) appointment
18. (A) secret   (B) joy   (C) shock   (D) success

Starving people have been known to boil shoes to make leather soup. The soup sustained them but was far from (19) _____ . Shoes that are made in India from the (20) _____ of water buffalos might prove more appetizing. The hide is said to be delicious when boiled for hours, sun-dried, and cooked in deep fat.

19. (A) filled   (B) irregular   (C) admirable   (D) tasty
20. (A) hides   (B) sniffs   (C) shudders   (D) hiccups

In 1981, at ninety-two years of age, Cathleen Nesbitt played the part of Rex Harrison's mother in a revival of the (1) _____, *My Fair Lady*. In trying to (2) _____ some of her old friends who had since passed away she said, "It's extraordinary how many people seem to die young—in their early 80s."

1. (A) hurricane (B) minstrel (C) musical (D) funeral
2. (A) locate (B) hoist (C) avoid (D) misplace

Residents of Aberdeen, Washington, enjoy its reputation as the wettest town in the United States, averaging 80 to 112 inches of rain a year. Of course, almost every (3) _____ in the town sells (4) _____. To prove they enjoy the rain, the almost 20,000 residents hold an annual Rain Fair.

3. (A) house (B) store (C) school (D) church
4. (A) rainwear (B) books (C) glasses (D) fairs

A memento of a tornado that hit Omaha, Nebraska, in 1975 is on display in one of the city's parks. It is a twenty-two-foot-high piece of art fashioned by a sculptor from eleven thousand pounds of twisted (5) _____. The steel came from a warehouse which stood directly in the path of the (6) _____.

5. (A) minds (B) viewpoints (C) steel (D) flesh
6. (A) tornado (B) promotion (C) train (D) cloudburst

Some wrasse and parrotfish go to sleep in homemade sleeping bags which are really mucous cocoons, open at both ends so that water can pass through. The transparent bags, (7) _____ by glands under the fishes' gill covers, may contain a deadly substance that (8) _____ hungry moray eels.

7. (A) misjudged (B) produced (C) revised (D) wrinkled
8. (A) repels (B) organizes (C) notifies (D) moderates

Why not plant a flower clock? The (9) _____ of many flowering plants open or close at specific (10) _____. African marigolds, for instance, open at seven in the morning. Evening primroses open at six in the evening, and white waterlilies close an hour later.

9. (A) stems (B) roots (C) blisters (D) blossoms
10. (A) days (B) times (C) colors (D) chimes

Moving walkways, escalators, and elevators move more people throughout the world than any other form of mass (11) _____, such as planes, trains, buses, or ships. An (12) _____ 70 billion passengers travel up, down, and across areas on moving stairs, platforms, and ramps each year.

11. (A) advertisement (B) correspondence (C) transportation (D) registration
12. (A) honorary   (B) estimated   (C) imaginary   (D) abbreviated

Did you ever hear a mouse sing? Some can do exactly that. There are numerous cases of mice creating musical sounds like the chirping, twittering, or warbling of birds. Some of the more common species of (13) _____ seem to (14) _____ the best. The singing mouse is not a myth.

13. (A) dogs   (B) mice   (C) spiders   (D) cats
14. (A) sing   (B) play   (C) dance   (D) hum

The province of British Columbia, Canada, has great natural power sources. Its rivers hold the (15) _____ of producing a hydro-electric capacity of more than forty thousand megawatts—sufficient to turn on every light bulb in California! A dam on the Peach River, five hundred miles northeast of Vancouver, will (16) _____ some of this power.

15. (A) survival (B) equation (C) moderation (D) potential
16. (A) reject   (B) forfeit   (C) harness   (D) transcribe

The height of a mountain peak sometimes will change following a disaster. Once Mt. Everest in Asia, highest of all peaks in the world, gained 198 feet almost instantly. It happened during a severe earthquake in Assam. After the (17) _____, Mt. Everest was 29,200 feet above sea (18) _____.

17. (A) flood   (B) construction (C) quake (D) demolition
18. (A) breeze (B) voyages   (C) front (D) level

Have you heard of an air ambulance? It is really a flying hospital equipped with medical equipment. A flying hospital includes a special (19) _____ bed, cardiac monitors, oxygen, respirator, drugs, and an air-ground telephone. Each flight carries a medical (20) _____. So far there are only four of these medical transporters in the United States.

19. (A) stretcher (B) musty   (C) carved   (D) flower
20. (A) guarantee (B) narrative (C) attendant (D) disaster

An ortolan is a small bird that is esteemed as a table delicacy in Europe. It is usually stuffed, roasted, flamed with liquor, and served under a napkin. The diner lifts the napkin, (1) _____ under it to sample the aroma of the roasted bird which is then (2) _____ — bones, beak, and all.

1. (A) complaining   (B) humming   (C) peeking   (D) dismissing
2. (A) electrocuted   (B) pasteurized   (C) devoured   (D) deposited

---

Those who accidentally swallow metal objects need not worry. An electromagnet at the end of the cord can be swallowed to tug the object from the stomach. For example, when the magnet reaches the round end of an open safety pin, the power is switched on to pull out the (3) _____ with is point (4) _____ .

3. (A) pin   (B) tenant   (C) vial   (D) stomach
4. (A) sharpened   (B) upward   (C) protruding   (D) downward

---

Frogs breathe in a peculiar way. Since a frog has no ribs, its breathing is not accompanied by the expansion and contraction of its chest. The air must be swallowed in order to reach the lungs. A frog can go for a considerable period of time without breathing because it gets (5) _____ of its (6) _____ supply through its skin.

5. (A) ounces   (B) tons   (C) part   (D) none
6. (A) muscular   (B) talent   (C) lotion   (D) oxygen

Jumping rope is the latest alternative to jogging. Advantages are that it doesn't require as much space, it can be done in private, and it doesn't depend on good weather. Physical fitness experts agree that (7) _____ rope helps build up endurance, raises the pulse rate, stretches muscles, loosen up joints, and (8) _____ agility and coordination.

7. (A) pulling   (B) snagging   (C) braiding   (D) skipping
8. (A) destroys   (B) hinders   (C) improves   (D) prohibits

When journalists visit Beijing, China, they are amazed by the secretaries who work there! Being a (9) _____ in China must be one of the most (10) _____ jobs in the country! They must master the art of using the Chinese typewriter, which has up to 7,100 characters!

9. (A) recorder   (B) dignitary   (C) physician   (D) secretary
10. (A) difficult   (B) figurative   (C) generous   (D) playful

Have you ever eaten with a spork? This (11) _____ of a spoon and a fork is an ingenious device that can save you time and energy while you go about your daily living. With a single utensil, you get the (12) _____ of two.

11. **(A) interruption**   **(B) quantity**   **(C) transparency**   **(D) combination**
12. **(A) shuffles**   **(B) nutrients**   **(C) least**   **(D) function**

You can find out the age of an elephant seal by studying a cross section of one of its permanent canine teeth. By counting the number of concentric rings, you can (13) _____ the animal's (14) _____ to within a month, up to age twenty in the male and to age thirteen in the female.

13. **(A) experience**   **(B) develop**   **(C) choose**   **(D) learn**
14. **(A) age**   **(B) disease**   **(C) handicap**   **(D) ailment**

What do your fingernails and a beaver's teeth have in common? Not much, except the ability to grow continually. A beaver's teeth never need trimming, though, because beavers (15) _____ wood all day long. They feed on bark and small twigs, and they use their (16) _____ to build dams from logs and branches.

15. **(A) gather**   **(B) polish**   **(C) grind**   **(D) drill**
16. **(A) teeth**   **(B) leaves**   **(C) bones**   **(D) fur**

There is only one spot in the United States where a house could be built with each corner in a different state. That spot is at the meeting point of Colorado, Utah, New Mexico, and Arizona. Since the (17) _____ is on a (18) _____ and since little vegetation grows there, no house has ever been built on that spot.

17. **(A) site**   **(B) sketch**   **(C) camp**   **(D) architect**
18. **(A) paper**   **(B) plateau**   **(C) trip**   **(D) loan**

Do you think that plants can live in the Dead Sea? The usual answer is that no living thing can live in its waters. Yet Dr. B. Elazari-Volcani has found seventeen species of the one-celled lower plants known as algae. The Dead Sea is not as (19) _____ as it is commonly (20) _____ to be.

19. **(A) colorful**   **(B) dangerous**   **(C) lively**   **(D) dead**
20. **(A) proved**   **(B) dreamed**   **(C) believed**   **(D) confirmed**

Moving walkways, escalators, and elevators move more people throughout the world than any other form of mass transportation, such as planes, trains, buses, or ships. An estimated 70 billion passengers travel up, down, and across areas on moving stairs, platforms, and ramps each year.

A. Exercising Your Skill

Transportation moves us and our possessions from one place to another. We move, they move. We move them, and in some cases, they move us. Think about different forms of transportation. How many different kinds do you ride in or on during a week? How many in a day? How many do you see but don't use? How many do you know about but have never even seen? Now think about how things move. Think of the words we use to describe movement. Make two lists, one of words that name forms of transportation (like *plane* and *boat* and *rocket* and *rickshaw* and . . .), the other of words that describe **how** things move (like *slowly* and *quickly* and *bumpily* and . . .). Write your words under the following headings:

Forms of Transportation	How Things Move
_____	_____
_____	_____
_____	_____
_____	_____

B. Expanding Your Skill

Compare your list with your classmates' lists. Can you add any means of transport to your list? Were you surprised at a vehicle that you forgot?

On a sheet of paper, copy each sentence below. Try to fill in the blanks with words from your lists that make sense. If you find that you must think of a new word to complete a sentence, add that word to the appropriate list.

Example: The ___rocket___ lifted _forcefully_ into the air.

1. The _____ plodded _____ across the desert sands.
2. The _____ floated _____ down the stream.
3. The _____ plowed _____ through the snow.
4. The girl on a _____ zigzagged _____ along the sidewalk.
5. The _____ carried us _____ to the next floor.
6. The _____ sped _____ across the lake.
7. The _____ carried its load _____ up the mountain.
8. The _____ sailed _____ over the treetops.
9. The _____ rolled _____ down the country road.
10. The _____ and rider galloped _____ through the canyon.

C. Exploring Language

Do you want to go for a ride? Right now? What would you like to try today? A kayak? A cable railroad? A hot-air balloon? How about a ride around town in a stagecoach? If you could take any form of transportation—one you had never taken—what would you choose? Picture yourself in or on it. Write a paragraph telling about the ride. What is it like? What sounds do you hear? How fast are you going? What does the movement feel like? How do *you* feel—are you excited, more scared than you thought, bored?

D. Expressing Yourself

Choose one of these activities.

1. Liftaway, boneshaker, and horseless carriage were early names for three commonly used modern means of transportation. Can you figure out what they are?

    (Have you given up? A liftaway is an elevator; it lifts you away. A boneshaker is a bicycle. Early bicycles had metal-rimmed wheels; roads were a lot rougher than they are now. When you rode a bicycle, your bones got a good shaking. A horseless carriage is, of course, a car. Early cars looked like carriages without horses.) Think up similar descriptive names for four other modes of transportation.

2. Imagine life without the automobile—or bus or truck. How would we get to school and to work? How would we visit our relatives a hundred miles away? What do you think would happen? Write a paragraph about how our lives would change.

3. What is the history of the elevator? Who invented it? When? How was the first elevator powered? How have elevators changed? Write a brief report.

4. Choose a place that is across the continent from where you live. If you wanted to visit that place, how could you get there? By bus? Train? Plane? Find out which forms of transportation are available. Would you need more than one kind? How much would each cost, and how long would each take? Call airlines, bus companies, and train stations. Organize the information on a chart, so that you can compare cost versus time.

5. Invent your own fantasy form of transportation. Write a lively magazine article telling what it looks like, how it works, and what it does. Explain what its special advantages are. Also mention its drawbacks. (Every vehicle has some!) Include an illustration with the article.

Book **G**

Specific Skill Series

Locating the Answer

Richard A. Boning

Fifth Edition

SRA/McGraw-Hill
Columbus, Ohio

Cover, Back Cover, ZEFA/Germany/The Stock Market

SRA/McGraw-Hill   &

A Division of The **McGraw·Hill** *Companies*

Printed in the United States of America.

Send all inquiries to:
   SRA/McGraw-Hill
   8787 Orion Place
   Columbus, OH 43240-4027

ISBN 0-02-687957-3

 5 6 IPC 02 01

To the Teacher

PURPOSE:
As its title indicates, LOCATING THE ANSWER develops pupils' skill in finding *where* sought-for information can be found within a passage. Pupils must carefully read and understand each question, grasp phrase and sentence units, and discriminate between pertinent and irrelevant ideas.

FOR WHOM:
The skill of LOCATING THE ANSWER is developed through a series of books spanning ten levels (Picture, Preparatory, A, B, C, D, E, F, G, H). The Picture Level is for pupils who have not acquired a basic sight vocabulary. The Preparatory Level is for pupils who have a basic sight vocabulary but are not yet ready for the first-grade-level book. Books A through H are appropriate for pupils who can read on levels one through eight, respectively. **The use of the *Specific Skill Series Placement Test* is recommended to determine the appropriate level.**

THE NEW EDITION:
The fifth edition of the *Specific Skill Series* maintains the quality and focus that has distinguished this program for more than 25 years. A key element central to the program's success has been the unique nature of the reading selections. Nonfiction pieces about current topics have been designed to stimulate the interest of students, motivating them to use the comprehension strategies they have learned to further their reading. To keep this important aspect of the program intact, a percentage of the reading selections have been replaced in order to ensure the continued relevance of the subject material.

In addition, a significant percentage of the artwork in the program has been replaced to give the books a contemporary look. The cover photographs are designed to appeal to readers of all ages.

SESSIONS:
Short practice sessions are the most effective. It is desirable to have a practice session every day or every other day, using a few units each session.

To the Teacher

SCORING:

Pupils should record their answers on the reproducible worksheets. The worksheets make scoring easier and provide uniform records of the pupils' work. Using worksheets also avoids consuming the exercise books.

It is important for pupils to know how well they are doing. For this reason, units should be scored as soon as they have been completed. Then a discussion can be held in which pupils justify their choices. (The Integrated Language Activities, many of which are open-ended, do not lend themselves to an objective score; thus there are no answer keys for these pages.)

GENERAL INFORMATION ON *LOCATING THE ANSWER*:

At the earlier levels the answer to the question is worded much the same as the question itself. As the books increase in difficulty, there is less correspondence between the phrasing of the question and the phrasing of the answer.

SUGGESTED STEPS:

1. Pupils read the question *first* and then look for the answer.

2. Pupils use the range finder (sentence choices) in Books B–H. The letters or numbers in the range finder (below the question) indicate which sentences must be read to locate the answer to the question. In the Picture Level, the pupils decide which picture answers the question. For Preparatory and A levels, the number before the question tells the paragraph to read.

3. Pupils read the sentences with the question in mind. (On the Picture Level, pupils look at the pictures. On the Preparatory and A levels, pupils read the paragraph.)

4. When using Books B–H, pupils write (in the space on the worksheet) the letter or number of the sentence that answers the question. On the Picture Level, pupils write the letter of the correct picture choice. On the Preparatory and A levels, pupils write the letter of the correct word choice.

Additional information on using LOCATING THE ANSWER with pupils will be found in the **Specific Skill Series Teacher's Manual**.

RELATED MATERIALS:

Specific Skill Series Placement Tests, which enable the teacher to place pupils at their appropriate levels in each skill, are available for the Elementary (Pre-1–6) and Midway (4–8) grade levels.

About This Book

People read for different reasons. You may read a story just for fun. You may read a letter from a friend to find out what your friend has been doing. You may read a book or an article to find the answer to a question.

Reading to find information is different from other reading. You are reading with a particular purpose. This means that you have to know what you are looking for. You need to read with your questions in mind. You can think of this as searching for something you have lost. You don't know where the lost object is, but you know what you are looking for.

Knowing what you are looking for can help you decide where to look. You wouldn't look for a missing shoe in the refrigerator. You might look for it under your bed or in the closet. You wouldn't look for the answer to a question about whales in a paragraph about dolphins. You would try to find the answer in a paragraph about whales.

Knowing how to locate information is an important reading skill. For each unit in this book, you will find ten questions about a piece of writing. The answers to the questions appear in that piece of writing. Your job is to locate the answers. You do not actually answer the questions. Instead, you tell **where** to find the answers.

Read this paragraph. Which sentence answers the question "Under which President did Frances Perkins serve as secretary of labor?"

(1) Frances Perkins was active in government for much of her life. (2) She became the first woman Cabinet member in the United States in 1933. (3) Perkins served as secretary of labor under President Franklin D. Roosevelt from 1933 until 1945. (4) In 1946, President Truman appointed her to the United States Civil Service Commission.

The answer is in sentence (3).

As you work on each unit in this book, read the questions first. Look at the five numbers below each question. Then look for the answer in the sentences with those five numbers in the piece of writing. Read the sentences with the question in mind. Tell which sentence gives the answer.

UNIT 1
Main Street, U.S.A.

(1) Indianapolis, capital of Indiana, is one of the few large cities in the world that is not located on a navigable body of water. (2) Yet the city is now the largest state capital in the United States. (3) Because Indianapolis lay in the path of westward expansion, overland transportation found its way here. (4) The city became a leading railway center. (5) More interstate highways go through Indianapolis than through any other major city in America.

(6) As Indianapolis grew, it became a leader in manufacturing. (7) It was an early leader in the automotive industry. (8) At one time eighteen car manufacturers had their headquarters here. (9) Improvements in automotive construction and design were tested at a bicycle track called the Bicycle Oval. (10) Eventually, these early car makers were absorbed by larger manufacturers, but today the city remains a leader in the production of automobile parts.

(11) The Bicycle Oval is now called the Motor Speedway. (12) It is still used by car manufacturers to test new equipment. (13) Now testing is done at a classic American sporting event, the Indianapolis 500. (14) It is said that all major developments in automobiles first proved themselves in this grueling race. (15) Among the many improvements that emerged were high-compression engines, four-wheel brakes, and hydraulic shock absorbers.

(16) In other industries too Indianapolis is a leader. (17) The city ranks high in the production of airplane and truck engines. (18) More telephones are produced in Indianapolis than in any other city in the world. (19) Flourishing industries like these have attracted labor from other states. (20) For this reason, Indianapolis grew phenomenally in population in the decades after World War II, zooming from twenty-sixth to eleventh among American cities. (21) The Indianapolis area, including suburbs, is now home to over 1,160,000 people.

(22) Indianapolis is proud of the part the city and state have played in wars fought by America. (23) In the center of the city is the Soldiers and Sailors Monument, 284 feet tall, the third tallest shaft in the United States. (24) Directly to the north is the five-block-long Memorial Plaza. (25) Here are found the World War Memorial and the national headquarters of the American Legion.

(26) Indianapolis is also a center for government and culture. (27) The state capitol building, with its magnificent copper dome, stands in the heart of the city, surrounded by other government offices. (28) Indiana and Purdue Universities have campuses in the city. (29) Indianapolis is home to the Indianapolis Colts professional football team and the Indiana Pacers of the National Basketball Association. (30) Indianapolis has its own symphony orchestra. (31) It also has a Museum of Indian Heritage. (32) Over seventy-five successful writers have come from the city.

(33) Many visitors note that the spacious streets of the city look familiar. (34) There is a reason. (35) The heart of Indianapolis, called the Mile Square, was laid out by one of the planners of Washington, D.C.

(36) Few visitors fail to be impressed by the personality of this city. (37) There is a combination of northern activity, southern charm, and heartland practicality. (38) For this reason, it has often been called "Main Street, U.S.A."

UNIT 1
Main Street, U.S.A.

1. What is the largest state capital in the United States?
   Sentence   (1)   (2)   (3)   (4)   (5)

2. How many car manufacturers had their headquarters there?
   Sentence   (6)   (7)   (8)   (9)   (10)

3. What were three improvements in automobiles?
   Sentence   (11)   (12)   (13)   (14)   (15)

4. Where are the most telephones produced?
   Sentence   (15)   (16)   (17)   (18)   (19)

5. Is the population of Indianapolis greater than one million?
   Sentence   (19)   (20)   (21)   (22)   (23)

6. Did Indianapolis play a role in America's wars?
   Sentence   (22)   (23)   (24)   (25)   (26)

7. Of what metal is the state capitol dome made?
   Sentence   (25)   (26)   (27)   (28)   (29)

8. Does Indianapolis have an orchestra?
   Sentence   (28)   (29)   (30)   (31)   (32)

9. Do visitors find the city looks familiar?
   Sentence   (31)   (32)   (33)   (34)   (35)

10. What is the heart of Indianapolis called?
    Sentence   (34)   (35)   (36)   (37)   (38)

UNIT 2
Cinderella City

(**1**) Few people had heard of Fort Dallas in 1894. (**2**) It was just a dusty little village on Biscayne Bay in south Florida. (**3**) Out in the bay was an island containing a mangrove swamp. (**4**) Today the village is known as Miami, a modern city with a glittering skyline, and counting suburbs, over $1\frac{1}{2}$ million people. (**5**) The swamp has been replaced with one of the most glamorous resorts in the world—Miami Beach.

(**6**) What caused this swift and remarkable change? (**7**) After a killing frost hit upper Florida in 1894, a woman from Fort Dallas mailed flowers to a railroad builder. (**8**) She wanted to show that frost rarely strikes Miami. (**9**) Impressed, the railroad builder extended the line's tracks to include what is now called Miami. (**10**) Since then, Miami has become a "Cinderella City."

(**11**) With more than three hundred days of sunshine a year, this resort is one of the leading tourist cities in the nation. (**12**) Each year millions of visitors arrive in this sunshine capital, many of them during the winter months. (**13**) To provide accommodations for this army of tourists, the Miami area has the greatest concentration of hotels in the United States. (**14**) Natives call people who own homes in the North and spend winters in Florida "snowbirds."

(**15**) Many northerners, mindful of the chilly weather back home, stay to build businesses. (**16**) The city now has over two thousand manufacturing plants. (**17**) Miami is now a leader in the garment industry, second only to New York City. (**18**) It is also prominent in the making of furniture, metal products, and transportation equipment.

(**19**) In natural resources, Miami is wealthy. (**20**) Among fishing ports it ranks as a leader. (**21**) Fish are so plentiful that tourists fish from bridges in the city. (**22**) No so well known is the fact that the Miami area is a national leader in freshwater fishing. (**23**) There are over thirty thousand lakes in Florida—more than in any other state. (**24**) Freshwater bass are caught for commercial sale as well as for sport. (**25**) Out of every hundred residents in the city, forty-two engage in fishing.

(**26**) Miami is also a leading processor of food. (**27**) Two of every three oranges and nine of ten grapefruit grown in the country come from Florida. (**28**) Most are shipped north through Miami. (**29**) Because of the soil and the sun, the city also ships winter-grown vegetables and fruits to northern cities. (**30**) South of the Miami area is where most of the southern Florida crop of winter vegetables and fruits is grown. (**31**) So valuable is the land that an acre commands four times the value of similar land in the North.

(**32**) Because about two-fifths of Miami's population is of Cuban origin, it is a resort city with a Spanish accent. (**33**) Approximately 650,000 Miami-area residents have Cuban roots. (**34**) Many large corporations with South American offices have set up branches in Miami. (**35**) Here Hispanic professional and business people employ their bilingual skills.

(**36**) Many visitors pour into the city around the winter holidays for the King Orange Jamboree. (**37**) This begins in mid-December, and the highlight is reached on New Year's night with the Orange Bowl football game between two outstanding college teams.

1. Did Miami Beach begin life as a mangrove swamp?

   Sentence   (1)   (2)   (3)   (4)   (5)

2. Do frosts rarely strike Miami?

   Sentence   (5)   (6)   (7)   (8)   (9)

3. How many days of sunshine does Miami get each year?

   Sentence   (9)   (10)   (11)   (12)   (13)

4. During what season do many tourists visit Miami?

   Sentence   (12)   (13)   (14)   (15)   (16)

5. Why do many people from the North establish businesses in Miami?

   Sentence   (15)   (16)   (17)   (18)   (19)

6. Is commercial fishing restricted to the ocean?

   Sentence   (20)   (21)   (22)   (23)   (24)

7. Is the percentage of oranges grown in the Miami area higher than the percentage of grapefruit?

   Sentence   (25)   (26)   (27)   (28)   (29)

8. Are all winter fruits and vegetables in southern Florida grown south of Miami?

   Sentence   (29)   (30)   (31)   (32)   (33)

9. How much does an acre of land cost south of Miami?

   Sentence   (30)   (31)   (32)   (33)   (34)

10. How many people with Cuban roots live in the Miami area?

    Sentence   (33)   (34)   (35)   (36)   (37)

UNIT 3
Eden of the West

(1) In a recent poll experts were asked to name the best American cities in which to live. (2) The one that surpassed all others, in the experts' judgment, was San Diego, California. (3) One expert even described it as being close to an urban Garden of Eden.

(4) What does San Diego have that merits such praise? (5) One asset is physical—location and climate. (6) The city is situated surrounding a magnificent harbor on the coast of southern California, close to the Mexican border. (7) Much of it is on high or hilly land that catches the balmy Pacific breezes. (8) Palm-lined bays and ocean beaches make it a paradise for enthusiasts of swimming, surfing, boating, fishing—or just sunning. (9) Landlubbers enjoy the abundant golf courses and tennis courts. (10) Rain rarely interrupts the sunshine. (11) The yearly rainfall is only about ten inches, and the annual temperature averages a pleasing sixty-three degrees Fahrenheit.

(12) Another asset of San Diego is its economy. (13) Residents find employment in manufacturing, scientific research, marketing, shipping, fishing, agriculture, and tourism. (14) Among the goods manufactured in and around the city are electronic and aerospace equipment, marine products, and clothing. (15) Laboratories conduct nuclear and oceanographic research. (16) Many Portuguese-American families earn their living at tuna fishing. (17) The city is home also to thousands of Mexican-Americans and Philippine-Americans.

(18) The cry of "Anchors aweigh!" is a familiar one in sparkling San Diego Bay, one of the world's best natural harbors. (19) Not only do merchant ships dock there, but the U.S. Navy maintains one of its larger bases there as well. (20) Many a sailor, enchanted by the city during a tour of duty, has returned to settle in the area after retirement.

(21) Despite its clean, modern look, San Diego has a history dating back far beyond that of many older eastern cities. (22) The bay was discovered by Spanish ships in 1542—over three quarters of a century before the Pilgrims landed in Massachusetts. (23) Franciscan missionaries settled the area in 1769. (24) In the early 1800s, under Mexican rule, it became a thriving port for shipping cattle hides. (25) After California became an American state, the completion of the Santa Fe railroad and the discovery of gold in the hills spurred the city's growth. (26) Buildups of defense-related facilities and industries helped cause the city to spurt from forty-third in population in 1940 to eighth in 1980—with a phenomenal growth rate of twenty-five percent between 1970 and 1980 alone. (27) Between 1980 and 1988 the population jumped another twenty percent, to over one million.

(28) San Diego's millions of yearly visitors come not just for a swim or a sail. (29) High on the city's list of attractions is its world-famous zoo, one of the largest anywhere. (30) The zoo also operates a wild-animal park where endangered species are preserved. (31) Tourists also flock to Sea World, the world's largest aquarium, and to the Fleet Space Theater, the nation's largest planetarium. (32) Theaters, concert halls, colleges, and museums (including the Aerospace Museum) round out the attractions of one of America's most attractive cities, San Diego.

UNIT 3
Eden of the West

1. Is San Diego located near the Mexican border?

   Sentence   (**2**)   (**3**)   (**4**)   (**5**)   (**6**)

2. Is it more often rainy or sunny in San Diego?

   Sentence   (**6**)   (**7**)   (**8**)   (**9**)   (**10**)

3. What is the average annual temperature?

   Sentence   (**8**)   (**9**)   (**10**)   (**11**)   (**12**)

4. Does San Diego manufacture any aerospace equipment?

   Sentence   (**11**)   (**12**)   (**13**)   (**14**)   (**15**)

5. Where does the U.S. Navy maintain one of its largest bases?

   Sentence   (**15**)   (**16**)   (**17**)   (**18**)   (**19**)

6. Have many sailors settled in San Diego after retirement?

   Sentence   (**19**)   (**20**)   (**21**)   (**22**)   (**23**)

7. In what year did missionaries settle the area?

   Sentence   (**23**)   (**24**)   (**25**)   (**26**)   (**27**)

8. What caused the rapid growth in population after 1940?

   Sentence   (**25**)   (**26**)   (**27**)   (**28**)   (**29**)

9. What is the population of San Diego?

   Sentence   (**27**)   (**28**)   (**29**)   (**30**)   (**31**)

10. What is the name of the nation's largest planetarium?

    Sentence   (**28**)   (**29**)   (**30**)   (**31**)   (**32**)

UNIT 4
Canada's Meeting Place

(1) On the Canadian side of Lake Ontario, across that huge lake from Niagara Falls, lies the bustling city of Toronto. (2) Home to over 600,000 people, it is the capital of the province of Ontario. (3) Among Canadian cities, Toronto is second in size only to Montreal. (4) Toronto and its suburbs contain over $2\frac{1}{2}$ million people, giving it Canada's largest metropolitan-area population.

(5) Toronto may not be Canada's largest city, but it is number one in many respects. (6) It is the country's chief center of finance, communications, and industry. (7) The daily volume handled by the Toronto Stock Exchange is the greatest in Canada and third greatest in North America. (8) The city ranks first in Canada in printing, publishing, moviemaking, and television production. (9) The following are other leading industries: slaughtering; meat packing; and the manufacture of clothing, machinery, electrical goods, and furniture. (10) In all, almost six thousand industrial companies produce over $7 billion worth of goods a year.

(11) The first inhabitants of the site of Toronto were Iroquois Indians. (12) *Toronto*, in fact, is an Indian word meaning "meeting place." (13) In the early 1700s the French built a fur-trading post, a mission, and a fort in the vicinity. (14) It was not until 1793, long after the French had been driven out by the British, that the area saw a permanent settlement. (15) At first the town was named York. (16) It did not adopt its present name until 1834.

(17) World Wars I and II brought rapid industrial expansion to the Toronto area, as well as sizable growth in population. (18) Today this clean, beautiful city has become a center not only of commerce but also of culture and recreation. (19) Toronto has its own symphony orchestra, opera company, and ballet company, as well as the nation's second largest collection of Canadian art. (20) The Royal Ontario Museum in the city is Canada's largest museum. (21) Residents and visitors alike enjoy the city's six thousand acres of parks. (22) They can gape and gawk at exhibits at the world's largest annual fair, the Canadian National Exhibition. (23) Sports fans can cheer major league hockey, football, and baseball. (24) The Hockey Hall of Fame is located in one of Toronto's parks.

(25) True to its Indian designation as a meeting place, Toronto has long been a center of transportation. (26) Located on the St. Lawrence Seaway, it can ship its manufactured goods around the world by sea. (27) Toronto International Airport is the busiest in the nation.

(28) Toronto is quite a contemporary city. (29) It was the world's first city to have a computer-controlled traffic signal system. (30) Beneath its downtown streets runs Canada's first subway. (31) Toronto's modernistic City Hall—two gracefully curved office towers sheltering a low, clamshell-shaped council building—is an architectural gem.

(32) Dominating the city's skyline is the tallest freestanding structure in the world, the Canadian National Tower. (33) This soaring shaft is not a building but a TV transmitting mast. (34) It exceeds the height of the world's tallest building, Chicago's Sears Tower, by 368 feet. (35) At 1,140 feet there is a revolving restaurant. (36) In clear weather diners can see seventy-five miles. (37) In stormy weather their digestion may be upset by some of the two hundred lightning bolts that strike the tower each year.

1. Does Toronto rank first in any way?

   Sentence   (1)   (2)   (3)   (4)   (5)

2. Who were the first inhabitants of Toronto?

   Sentence   (7)   (8)   (9)   (10)   (11)

3. Was a mission built there in the early 1700s by the French?

   Sentence   (11)   (12)   (13)   (14)   (15)

4. What is the name of Canada's largest museum?

   Sentence   (16)   (17)   (18)   (19)   (20)

5. Where is the Hockey Hall of Fame located?

   Sentence   (21)   (22)   (23)   (24)   (25)

6. How does its location on the St. Lawrence Seaway benefit Toronto?

   Sentence   (23)   (24)   (25)   (26)   (27)

7. Is Toronto a contemporary city?

   Sentence   (24)   (25)   (26)   (27)   (28)

8. Was Canada's first subway built in Toronto?

   Sentence   (29)   (30)   (31)   (32)   (33)

9. What is the tallest freestanding structure in the world?

   Sentence   (31)   (32)   (33)   (34)   (35)

10. Is it possible to see a great distance from the tower's restaurant on clear days?

    Sentence   (33)   (34)   (35)   (36)   (37)

UNIT 5
Center of the Crescent

(**1**) This southern city declared its own independence from England a year before the rest of the nation. (**2**) Until the California gold rush of 1849, this city and its surrounding area topped the nation in gold production. (**3**) Today the city is the heart of the nation's foremost textile-producing region. (**4**) The city is Charlotte, North Carolina.

(**5**) With a population of 373,000, Charlotte is the largest city in the Carolinas. (**6**) Moreover, it is the center of a metropolitan area whose population exceeds 1,300,000. (**7**) Charlotte lies in the south central part of the state. (**8**) It is close to the South Carolina border. (**9**) This region is part of a broad, fertile plateau. (**10**) Called the Piedmont, the plateau extends across the center of North Carolina. (**11**) To the east lies the Atlantic coastal plain, and to the west lie the beautiful Blue Ridge Mountains.

(**12**) It was in 1750 or so that the first European settlers first set foot on the site of Charlotte. (**13**) They were mostly Scotch-Irish and Germans who had migrated from colonies further north. (**14**) As a name for their village, they chose that of the queen of England at the time. (**15**) She was Charlotte of Mecklenburg, actually a German. (**16**) Despite this homage to the queen, the town soon became one of the colonies' hottest centers of revolution. (**17**) In May 1775, over a year before the national Declaration of Independence was drafted in Philadelphia, citizens of the Charlotte area reportedly signed their own Mecklenburg (County) Declaration of Independence. (**18**) Charlotte's spirit was showing the colonies the way.

(**19**) Charlotte has continued to play a role in America's development. (**20**) Two distinguished Presidents, Andrew Jackson and James Polk, were born in the area. (**21**) In the first half of the nineteenth century, gold from mines around Charlotte contributed to America's wealth. (**22**) During this era Charlotte was the gold capital of the country, and a U.S. mint was established there.

(**23**) Today the gold is gone. (**24**) The mint has been rebuilt as an art museum. (**25**) But the Charlotte region prospers from a new kind of wealth—manufacturing. (**26**) The city is the heart of a large industrial area known as the Carolinas Crescent. (**27**) It extends more than two hundred miles, from Raleigh, N.C., to Greenville, S.C. (**28**) With over twelve hundred wholesale businesses and a hundred trucking terminals, Charlotte is the region's hub of manufacturing, distribution, and selling. (**29**) It is one of America's chief trucking centers.

(**30**) Abundant labor and proximity to cotton-growing areas have helped make the Piedmont region around Charlotte the nation's leading producer of textiles. (**31**) In the city itself, in addition to clothing and other textiles, factories produce processed foods and meat as well as bakery and dairy products. (**32**) Machinery, metals, chemicals, computers, and paper are also prominent products.

(**33**) Residents of Charlotte enjoy their city's mild climate. (**34**) Its elevation keeps it cooler in summer than the hot, humid coastal areas. (**35**) For culture, the city has museums, a symphony orchestra, and a campus of the University of North Carolina. (**36**) Sports fans cheer basketball and hockey at the new thirteen-thousand-seat coliseum. (**37**) Car enthusiasts come from all over the Crescent, and beyond, to watch world and national auto races at the Charlotte Motor Speedway.

UNIT 5
Center of the Crescent

1. What happened in 1849 to cause the city of Charlotte to lose its standing as the nation's top gold producer?

   Sentence   **(1)**   **(2)**   **(3)**   **(4)**   **(5)**

2. Which is the largest city in the Carolinas?

   Sentence   **(5)**   **(6)**   **(7)**   **(8)**   **(9)**

3. What is the name of the plateau extending across the center of North Carolina?

   Sentence   **(8)**   **(9)**   **(10)**   **(11)**   **(12)**

4. Who were the first non-Native American settlers to migrate to Charlotte?

   Sentence   **(13)**   **(14)**   **(15)**   **(16)**   **(17)**

5. In what year was the Mecklenburg Declaration of Independence signed?

   Sentence   **(17)**   **(18)**   **(19)**   **(20)**   **(21)**

6. Does Charlotte still play a role in America's development?

   Sentence   **(18)**   **(19)**   **(20)**   **(21)**   **(22)**

7. What took the place of gold to prosper Charlotte's economy?

   Sentence   **(23)**   **(24)**   **(25)**   **(26)**   **(27)**

8. How far does the Carolinas Crescent extend?

   Sentence   **(27)**   **(28)**   **(29)**   **(30)**   **(31)**

9. What helps to keep Charlotte cooler in summer than the coastal areas?

   Sentence   **(31)**   **(32)**   **(33)**   **(34)**   **(35)**

10. Is there a famous auto speedway located in Charlotte?

    Sentence   **(33)**   **(34)**   **(35)**   **(36)**   **(37)**

UNIT 6
The City That Care Forgot

(1) New Orleans is often called "America's Most Interesting City." (2) The ground level of the city is actually *lower* than that of the Mississippi River, and its waters must be held back by levees, or banks of earth. (3) Visitors are sometimes startled to look up and see large ocean-going vessels steaming by above the level of their heads!

(4) Because of its European flavor and gaiety, the city is also known as "The Paris of America." (5) "Crescent City" is still another name for New Orleans, because the city lies in a bend, or crescent, of the Mississippi.

(6) Only New York City is a larger American port. (7) In trade with Latin America, New Orleans outstrips every other port in the United States. (8) The city is also a ship-building center. (9) It specializes in the manufacture of aluminum and chemicals. (10) A new space-age industry is the production of rocket boosters.

(11) Because of the warm, moist climate, almost any crop can be grown here, including rice, cotton, and sugar cane. (12) Tobacco and even bamboo grow well. (13) The city contains one of the largest sugar-refining plants in the world.

(14) Above all, New Orleans is known for its unique atmosphere. (15) Lacy iron grillwork decorates many of the homes in the Vieux Carré, or the French Quarter, the oldest part of the city. (16) The houses themselves are of Spanish design. (17) Both French and Spanish blood flow in the veins of members of the oldest families. (18) These people, known as Creoles, may speak French as well as English.

(19) In the days following the Louisiana Purchase, the intruding Americans and aristocratic Creoles became rivals in the sugar trade. (20) Duels flared up. (21) The slightest insult could result in a challenge. (22) "Pistols for two; breakfast for one" became a common expression.

(23) In time the easygoing charm of the Creoles cast its curious spell on newcomers. (24) Now the entire city is influenced by the Creole culture. (25) People of all national backgrounds eat Creole dishes of rice, seafood, and sauces. (26) Restaurants in New Orleans that feature these foods are considered among the finest in the world. (27) Even more than for its food, New Orleans is known as the home of America's unique contribution to music—jazz. (28) Basically Afro-American with Creole influences, jazz was made famous in New Orleans by such legendary musicians as Louis Armstrong.

(29) This basic love of food, music, and enjoyment finds an outlet in many celebrations. (30) A Mid-winter Sports Carnival is held during the Christmas holidays, ending with the Sugar Bowl college football game on New Year's Eve. (31) Other sporting events are held in the huge Superdome, the world's largest indoor stadium. (32) Starting on January 6, the city gets ready for Mardi Gras—or "Fat Tuesday." (33) This is the last day before Lent. (34) Parades are held and prizes awarded for costumes. (35) Visitors who arrive for the festivities claim that the city works its magic on all newcomers.

(36) It is easy to see why New Orleans is also known as "The City That Care Forgot."

UNIT 6
The City That Care Forgot

1. Was it necessary for New Orleans to erect any structures because of the location of the city?

    Sentence   (**1**)   (**2**)   (**3**)   (**4**)   (**5**)

2. Why is New Orleans called "Crescent City"?

    Sentence   (**3**)   (**4**)   (**5**)   (**6**)   (**7**)

3. What port is larger than New Orleans?

    Sentence   (**6**)   (**7**)   (**8**)   (**9**)   (**10**)

4. In addition to shipping, does New Orleans engage in any other activity related to the sea?

    Sentence   (**8**)   (**9**)   (**10**)   (**11**)   (**12**)

5. What kind of refining plants does the city contain?

    Sentence   (**10**)   (**11**)   (**12**)   (**13**)   (**14**)

6. Is New Orleans known for its atmosphere?

    Sentence   (**13**)   (**14**)   (**15**)   (**16**)   (**17**)

7. What is another name for the French Quarter?

    Sentence   (**15**)   (**16**)   (**17**)   (**18**)   (**19**)

8. What event was followed by conflict between Creoles and outsiders?

    Sentence   (**17**)   (**18**)   (**19**)   (**20**)   (**21**)

9. Is there any indication that, in the duels, one of the two participants did not survive?

    Sentence   (**20**)   (**21**)   (**22**)   (**23**)   (**24**)

10. Is there a basic love of food and music in New Orleans?

    Sentence   (**25**)   (**26**)   (**27**)   (**28**)   (**29**)

In Units 1 through 6, you read passages about several cities in the United States and Canada. You can find additional information about these places, and other places in the world, in an atlas or an almanac.

An **atlas** is a reference book of maps. The maps may be of cities, states, countries, regions, or the entire world. The locations shown on the maps in an atlas are listed alphabetically in an index at the back of the book.

An **almanac** is a reference book that is published each year. It gives information about people, places, events, awards, and records. The facts listed often cover many years.

A. Exercising Your Skill

From the definitions above, and from what you already know, decide where you would look *first* for the answers to each of the questions below. Write the number of each question under one of these headings on your paper: *Atlas, Almanac*.

1. Who was awarded the Nobel Prize for Peace in 1987?
2. What major mountain range lies on the east coast of Chile?
3. How many people lived in Charlotte, North Carolina, in 1980?
4. What is the zip code of San Clemente, California?
5. Is Iowa located north or west of Kansas?
6. What is the capital city of Guatemala?
7. Where were the 1984 winter Olympics held?
8. Which motion picture won the Academy Award for "best picture" in 1975?
9. How many Canadian provinces share a border with Montana?
10. Where is the Bay of Fundy located?

B. Expanding Your Skill

Look at the parts of indexes below. The first is from an atlas; the second is from an almanac. Number your paper, and tell on which page you would look for information about each phrase.

Atlas

Map Area	Page
Jackson, the capital of Mississippi	22
James River, South Dakota	23
Japan, a country in Asia	51

Almanac

Subject	Page
Structures	
bridges	488
dams	489
skyscrapers	485
tunnels	487

1. the Sea of Japan
2. the location of Jackson
3. the mouth of the James River
4. major cities in Japan

5. the World Trade Center
6. the Golden Gate Bridge
7. the Holland Tunnel
8. the Hoover Dam

C. Exploring Language

Look at the section of a town street map below. Locations can be found within one or more squares on the map. Each square is lettered and numbered. On your paper, write six questions that can be answered from the information labeled on the map. The answers should be in the form of lettered and numbered squares on the map. Example: *In which map square can you find Markham Road?* (Answer: square C-2)

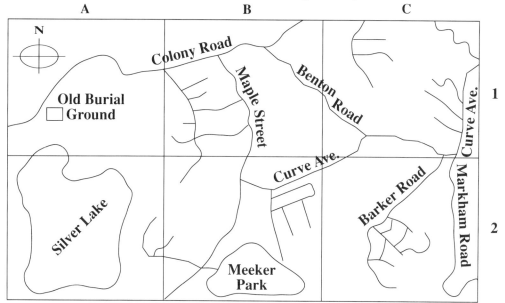

D. Expressing Yourself

Choose one of these activities.

1. With a group of classmates, make up a Class Almanac. Give facts about the size of your class and list notable events of the year. Give awards to real or imaginary people for categories such as the following:

   Person Who Laughed the Most in *(year)*
   Person Who Studied the Hardest in *(year)*
   Most Artistic Person
   Most Athletic Person

   Use your imagination and sense of humor.

2. Work with a partner. Make a map of the area where your school is located. Identify such things as major roads, parks, bodies of water, land forms, or important landmarks. Compare your map with your classmates' maps.

UNIT 7
Room to Grow

(1) Everyone has heard of a town springing up almost overnight. (2) But Oklahoma City was born in a matter of hours. (3) On April 22, 1889, the government offered tracts of land to homesteaders near a tiny railroad station on the Canadian River in central Oklahoma. (4) At noon that day a bugle rang out, and the rush was on to stake out claims. (5) By nightfall the tiny hamlet had become a tent city of ten thousand people.

(6) Today Oklahoma City continues to boom in ways undreamed of when it was a tent town. (7) Besides being the state capital, it is a leading aviation center, where important divisions of the Federal Aviation Administration are located. (8) Here research is done on aeromedicine. (9) New methods to improve the safety records of airlines are developed. (10) Oklahoma City is also the headquarters of Tinker Air Force Base, an important supply and repair station, and the city's largest single employer, with over 25,000 workers.

(11) The city has used its space-age skills to help create a new industry. (12) Because of its vast computer facilities, Oklahoma City is a leader in providing computer information on credit card owners.

(13) Oklahoma City has found wealth below ground as well as above it. (14) The city lies in the heart of a rich oil field. (15) There are dozens of multimillion-dollar oil-related industries in the city. (16) The Oklahoma City area has about 980 oil wells. (17) The city is one of the leading refiners of oil in the nation.

(18) The oil business received a boost in 1928 when oil was discovered under the city itself. (19) In 1936 oil was discovered on the grounds of the state capitol building. (20) Today there are eighteen oil derricks on the capitol grounds. (21) They have produced millions in revenue for the state treasury.

(22) Livestock is a major industry. (23) Here can be found the nation's fourth largest cattle market. (24) The city is headquarters for one of the largest meat-packing firms in the world. (25) In the surrounding area ranchers raise hundreds of thousands of beef cattle. (26) Oklahoma is the nation's fourth largest cattle-growing state. (27) In honor of this western heritage, Oklahoma City maintains the Cowboy Hall of Fame. (28) Here there are authentic western paintings and equipment used by cowhands. (29) Each year the city plays host to the National Rodeo Finals.

(30) Oklahoma City has a large Native American Indian population. (31) It has more Native Americans than any other state. (32) The word *Oklahoma* comes from the Choctaw language—*okla* means "people," and *homma* means "red." (33) In the State Historical Society Museum in Oklahoma City is the largest collection of Indian relics in the world. (34) These include famous war bonnets and peace pipes.

(35) Oklahomans look with confidence to the future. (36) Although their city ranks thirty-third in population, it is one of the largest in area. (37) "That's to give us plenty of room to grow," they explain.

1. What did the government offer homesteaders in 1889?

   Sentence   **(1)**   **(2)**   **(3)**   **(4)**   **(5)**

2. What happened at noon on April 22, 1889?

   Sentence   **(2)**   **(3)**   **(4)**   **(5)**   **(6)**

3. Does Tinker Air Force Base employ many city residents?

   Sentence   **(6)**   **(7)**   **(8)**   **(9)**   **(10)**

4. Does Oklahoma City provide computer information?

   Sentence   **(9)**   **(10)**   **(11)**   **(12)**   **(13)**

5. Are there many wealthy oil-related industries in the city?

   Sentence   **(11)**   **(12)**   **(13)**   **(14)**   **(15)**

6. Do the capitol grounds have any unusual features?

   Sentence   **(16)**   **(17)**   **(18)**   **(19)**   **(20)**

7. Does Oklahoma City pack any of its own products?

   Sentence   **(20)**   **(21)**   **(22)**   **(23)**   **(24)**

8. What is raised on ranches in surrounding areas?

   Sentence   **(24)**   **(25)**   **(26)**   **(27)**   **(28)**

9. Does Oklahoma have more Native Americans than any other state?

   Sentence   **(29)**   **(30)**   **(31)**   **(32)**   **(33)**

10. How does Oklahoma City rank in population?

    Sentence   **(33)**   **(34)**   **(35)**   **(36)**   **(37)**

UNIT 8
Big D

(**1**) As only a stagecoach stop, Dallas felt it was doomed unless it could persuade the railroad to come to town. (**2**) Finally in 1872, after twenty-five years of pleading, the Houston and Texas Central brought the first train to Dallas. (**3**) Neither the town nor the railroad knew it, but at that moment a mighty city was born.

(**4**) Today the stagecoach stop is a modern city of gleaming towers that rise above the prairie by the Trinity River in central Texas. (**5**) It is now known affectionately to its over 900,000 citizens as "Big D." (**6**) Dallas is the eighth largest city in the nation today and the leading transportation center in the Southwest. (**7**) It services a marketing area that occupies one-fifth of the entire nation. (**8**) Early terminal merchants gave the city its start. (**9**) These merchants set up stores at the end point of the railroad. (**10**) At first they sold to townspeople and farmers. (**11**) Later they sent out salespeople to other towns, and a trading area was launched. (**12**) In wholesale trade Dallas leads America in the sale of giftwares. (**13**) It is also a leader in the sale of apparel and home furnishings.

(**14**) Retail stores in Dallas have many customers throughout the state and the Southwest. (**15**) One department store, Neiman-Marcus, has customers around the world. (**16**) This large and successful store caters to the city's desire for the unusual. (**17**) "His and hers" airplanes have been offered for hundreds of thousands of dollars. (**18**) Ermine bathrobes are sold for thousands.

(**19**) World War II brought many defense-related industries to Dallas. (**20**) The manufacture of aircraft and missile parts and electronic equipment has declined but continues to be a major industry. (**21**) Because of its location, a number of companies have moved their home offices to Dallas. (**22**) More oil firms have headquarters in Dallas than in any other city in the United States. (**23**) Dallas houses more insurance companies than any other city in the Southwest.

(**24**) As an exhibition center, Dallas ranks among the leaders. (**25**) More than five hundred fairs, exhibits, and festivals are held here each year. (**26**) Nearly three million people visit the State Fair of Texas in Dallas, making it the largest annual fair in the United States.

(**27**) Dallas is the oil center of the nation. (**28**) More than three-fourths of the United States' known oil reserves lie within five hundred miles of the city. (**29**) Dallas is the headquarters of more oil firms than any other city.

(**30**) More cotton is grown in Texas than in any other state. (**31**) Dallas is a leading cotton center and a leading manufacturer of cotton gins. (**32**) It is also a leading apparel center. (**33**) It is one of the three principal fashion centers in the United States.

(**34**) The Dallas-Fort Worth Airport is one of the busiest in the world. (**35**) It covers seventeen thousand acres, more than the island of Manhattan. (**36**) This giant airport serves over forty million passengers a year. (**37**) It is designed to handle more freight than any seaport in the world and more aircraft than the New York area's LaGuardia, Kennedy, and Newark airports combined.

(**38**) The tiny railroad center has come a long way indeed!

UNIT 8
Big D

1. Was Dallas a stagecoach stop?

   Sentence   (1)   (2)   (3)   (4)   (5)

2. What is Dallas called by its citizens?

   Sentence   (4)   (5)   (6)   (7)   (8)

3. Where did early merchants set up stores?

   Sentence   (9)   (10)   (11)   (12)   (13)

4. What special distinction does Dallas have as a wholesale center?

   Sentence   (11)   (12)   (13)   (14)   (15)

5. Is Dallas a leader in the sale of home furnishings?

   Sentence   (12)   (13)   (14)   (15)   (16)

6. When did many defense-related industries start in Dallas?

   Sentence   (16)   (17)   (18)   (19)   (20)

7. Why have many companies moved their home offices to Dallas?

   Sentence   (21)   (22)   (23)   (24)   (25)

8. Which state grows the most cotton?

   Sentence   (26)   (27)   (28)   (29)   (30)

9. Does Dallas produce any cotton gins?

   Sentence   (29)   (30)   (31)   (32)   (33)

10. How many acres does the airport cover?

    Sentence   (34)   (35)   (36)   (37)   (38)

UNIT 9
Gateway to the West

(**1**) To early French settlers, life in the small fur-trading post was often hard. (**2**) At times they called their settlement *Pain Court*, which means "short of bread." (**3**) Now, two hundred years later, the trading post is the populous city of St. Louis. (**4**) It is the busiest port on the inland Mississippi River. (**5**) It has a wide variety of industries that employ one-third of its workers.

(**6**) St. Louis is a major manufacturing city. (**7**) Transportation equipment is its leading product. (**8**) Only Detroit and Flint, Michigan, produce more automobiles. (**9**) Railroad cars and barges come from its factories. (**10**) In aviation and the aerospace industry, St. Louis is also a leader. (**11**) The city is the home of the largest aerospace manufacturer in the world. (**12**) It was this company that produced the space capsule that carried America's first astronaut beyond the earth. (**13**) St. Louis got an early start in the aerospace field. (**14**) In 1927, a group of St. Louis investors put up the money for a young aviator to attempt a solo transatlantic flight. (**15**) His name was Charles A. Lindbergh, and he named his plane the *Spirit of St. Louis*.

(**16**) What caused the growth in manufacturing? (**17**) One reason is that St. Louis is the heart of the only industrial area which produces all six basic metals—iron, lead, zinc, copper, aluminum, and magnesium. (**18**) Another reason is the favorable location of the city. (**19**) It is situated at the center of the Mississippi River, just below the point where it merges with the Missouri. (**20**) Because of this location, St. Louis has long been a transportation hub. (**21**) It is second only to Chicago as a rail and trucking center.

(**22**) Prosperity first began for St. Louis because it lay in the path of the westward expansion. (**23**) It became a jumping-off place for wagon trains heading west. (**24**) The city learned to trade with wagon trains. (**25**) It began manufacturing items to sell. (**26**) It even got an early start in the paint business by providing paint to traders for Native American Indians, who daubed it on their faces.

(**27**) A German settler who became highly impressed with St. Louis wrote a number of enthusiastic letters about it to friends at home. (**28**) Before long, waves of German immigrants poured into the city, giving it a Germanic flavor, which it has to this day.

(**29**) Successful German brewers brought their skills with them and gave St. Louis a new industry. (**30**) Today the city is a brewing center. (**31**) The world's largest brewing company is headquartered here. (**32**) The product of the brewers is so popular that waiters serve it to audiences at concerts of the world-famous St. Louis Symphony.

(**33**) The city is also famous for its widely respected newspaper, the *Post Dispatch*. (**34**) One of the founders of the newspaper was Joseph Pulitzer, who established the coveted Pulitzer Prizes. (**35**) These are awarded annually for excellence in journalism, letters, and music.

(**36**) Despite its achievements, St. Louis has never forgotten its early days as a wagon station, when it became known as the "Gateway to the West." (**37**) In tribute to those times, a huge steel arch has been erected. (**38**) It is 630 feet high, the tallest monument in the world. (**39**) Appropriately, it is known as the Gateway Arch.

UNIT 9
Gateway to the West

1. What does *Pain Court* mean?

   Sentence (**1**) (**2**) (**3**) (**4**) (**5**)

2. Besides barges, what other large equipment is manufactured in St. Louis?

   Sentence (**6**) (**7**) (**8**) (**9**) (**10**)

3. Who put up money for a transatlantic flight?

   Sentence (**11**) (**12**) (**13**) (**14**) (**15**)

4. Does St. Louis enjoy any unique advantage in the field of resources?

   Sentence (**16**) (**17**) (**18**) (**19**) (**20**)

5. Who wrote enthusiastic letters about St. Louis?

   Sentence (**23**) (**24**) (**25**) (**26**) (**27**)

6. What gave St. Louis a Germanic flavor?

   Sentence (**24**) (**25**) (**26**) (**27**) (**28**)

7. For what publication is the city famous?

   Sentence (**29**) (**30**) (**31**) (**32**) (**33**)

8. How often are Pulitzer Prizes awarded?

   Sentence (**32**) (**33**) (**34**) (**35**) (**36**)

9. How did St. Louis pay tribute to its early days?

   Sentence (**33**) (**34**) (**35**) (**36**) (**37**)

10. Does the Gateway Arch stand higher above ground than the Washington Monument?

    Sentence (**35**) (**36**) (**37**) (**38**) (**39**)

UNIT 10
Where History Is Made

(1) This large city does almost no manufacturing and very little wholesale trade. (2) Yet without the important service it provides, businesses everywhere would quickly grind to a halt. (3) Chaos would reign in all other leading cities. (4) As you may have guessed, the "product" we are talking about is government, and the city is the capital of the United States, Washington, D.C.

(5) In a single year Congress must deal with as many as ten thousand separate bills and resolutions. (6) Few reach the floor, but all are handled in committees. (7) To keep the wheels of government turning, more than 370,000 people work for the federal government. (8) The government employs more people than does any kind of private business in the city.

(9) Washington has many distinctions. (10) It leads the nation in education. (11) More than fifteen percent of its adults have had four years or more of college. (12) More scientists can be found here than in any other city. (13) Since larger incomes are earned by trained people, Washington has the highest median income of any city. (14) Of all American cities, Washington has the highest portion of black citizens—seventy per-cent—most of whom are employed in keeping our government operating.

(15) Information is the lifeblood of the city. (16) The Library of Congress houses the largest and most comprehensive warehouse of information in the world. (17) It contains 84 million items on hundreds of miles of shelves! (18) In addition to books, these items include manuscripts, maps, photographs, and documents. (19) Papers of the Presidents all the way back to Washington are found here. (20) The library is open to the public. (21) It is considered by writers and scholars to be one of the finest in the world.

(22) Washington has many important government buildings and historic shrines. (23) These include the Capitol itself, the White House, the Supreme Court, the Lincoln Memorial, the Washington Monument, the Pentagon, Arlington Cemetery, the Smithsonian Institution, the headquarters of the Federal Bureau of Investigation and of many other gov-ernment agencies, and the Bureau of Engraving and Printing. (24) Tens of millions of dol-lars in paper money is printed here every day.

(25) It was only after long debate that Washington became the location for the capital of the United States. (26) Prior to this, the capital had been located at various times in seven other cities—Philadelphia, Baltimore, Lancaster (Pa.), Princeton, Annapolis, Trenton, and New York. (27) In 1791 Congress approved a site on the Potomac River between Maryland and Virginia and designated it the District of Columbia.

(28) Fittingly, the city that grew on the site was named in honor of our first President, who had picked the location on which to build the Capitol. (29) Unlike most cities, Washington was planned on paper before any of its buildings were erected. (30) As a result, the city is spacious rather than crowded. (31) The central part of the city resembles a huge green park with broad, tree-lined boulevards and splendid views of its great struc-tures.

(32) Every spring tourists flock to Washington. (33) They watch in fascination as the city goes about the business of making history.

UNIT 10
Where History Is Made

1. How many people in Washington work for the federal government?

   Sentence   (**3**)   (**4**)   (**5**)   (**6**)   (**7**)

2. Does the government or private business employ more people?

   Sentence   (**5**)   (**6**)   (**7**)   (**8**)   (**9**)

3. Does Washington rank first among cities in scientists?

   Sentence   (**10**)   (**11**)   (**12**)   (**13**)   (**14**)

4. What city has the highest median income?

   Sentence   (**12**)   (**13**)   (**14**)   (**15**)   (**16**)

5. How are most of seventy percent of Washington's population employed?

   Sentence   (**14**)   (**15**)   (**16**)   (**17**)   (**18**)

6. Do writers esteem the Library of Congress?

   Sentence   (**19**)   (**20**)   (**21**)   (**22**)   (**23**)

7. How much paper money is printed in Washington each day?

   Sentence   (**23**)   (**24**)   (**25**)   (**26**)   (**27**)

8. Prior to Washington, was the capital of the United States established in seven cities?

   Sentence   (**26**)   (**27**)   (**28**)   (**29**)   (**30**)

9. Is the heart of Washington a business district?

   Sentence   (**28**)   (**29**)   (**30**)   (**31**)   (**32**)

10. Are tourists attracted by anything other than landmarks, historic shrines, and the beauty of the city itself?

    Sentence   (**29**)   (**30**)   (**31**)   (**32**)   (**33**)

UNIT 11
Land of Magic

(1) Far to the west, said the legend, was a magic land of sunshine, where fruit grew in all seasons. (2) Curious mountain dwellers who journeyed to the small Spanish village found the legend true. (3) But they reported that the settlement did not look as if it ever would grow as large as its name—*El Pueblo de Nuestra Señora la Reina de Los Angeles de Porciuncula*.

(4) Today those mountaineers would not recognize the once sleepy Spanish settlement. (5) The name has been shortened to Los Angeles, but the town itself has grown to enormous size. (6) More than seven million people live in and around the city, drawn by the climate that beckoned those first visitors. (7) Los Angeles is now the second largest metropolitan area in the United States.

(8) It ranks even higher in industry than it does in population. (9) Among industrial cities, it is first in the nation. (10) Los Angeles is the aerospace production capital of the world. (11) Of course, no other city produces as many motion pictures and television films. (12) Los Angeles is also a major music-recording center. (13) In garment manufacturing it is also a leader. (14) It is a top producer of sports clothing. (15) Los Angeles is a leading producer of automobiles. (16) As a center of fish canning, it is likewise in the forefront. (17) It rivals Akron, Ohio, as a producer of tires. (18) Construction and publishing are also important industries.

(19) From the beginning this seemed to be a land where anything was possible. (20) In the 1890s oil was discovered in the magic city. (21) People drilled wells in their basements and on their front lawns. (22) Many became millionaires. (23) Some of these wells are still producing. (24) When Los Angeles needed a harbor, it built one. (25) It is the largest constructed harbor in the world. (26) When Los Angeles needed water, it built the longest aqueduct known—235 miles.

(27) In 1886, the railroads offered passage from Kansas City to Los Angeles for only $1. (28) Newcomers poured into the city, drawn by the warm climate. (29) Later came tourists, curious to see real motion pictures and television shows being filmed. (30) They visited Disneyland and the stretch of shops on Wilshire Boulevard known as the Miracle Mile. (31) Today, visitors are amazed at the variety of activities available. (32) Skiing in the mountains and surfing at the seashore are both within an hour's drive. (33) For those who enjoy spectator sports, Los Angeles has much to offer. (34) There are professional football, baseball, basketball, and hockey, and there are outstanding college teams such as those of the University of Southern California and the University of California at Los Angeles. (35) For those who want to relax or observe nature, the city has over three hundred parks. (36) Griffith Park is one of the world's largest city parks. (37) Lovers of culture can enjoy the Los Angeles Philharmonic Orchestra.

(38) For those visitors who wish a rare glimpse into the past, there are the La Brea tar pits. (39) In these pits are the bones of unwary animals trapped in the tar as long as a million years ago. (40) On view are the remains of such long-extinct animals as the saber-toothed tiger and the mastodon.

(41) The people of Los Angeles come from a wide variety of ethnic backgrounds. (42) People from Latin America make up about 28 percent of the city's population. (43) There are more Mexican-Americans than in any other city—more than half a million. (44) Half a million black Americans constitute the city's second largest ethnic group. (45) Other ethnic groups include Americans of Japanese, Chinese, and Filipino origins. (46) All Los Angeles' citizens work hard to keep the city one of America's top centers of industry, education, and recreation.

UNIT 11
Land of Magic

1. What has happened to the name of the town itself?

   Sentence   (**1**)   (**2**)   (**3**)   (**4**)   (**5**)

2. Have industry and population generally kept pace with each other?

   Sentence   (**6**)   (**7**)   (**8**)   (**9**)   (**10**)

3. Is Los Angeles the aerospace production capital of the world?

   Sentence   (**9**)   (**10**)   (**11**)   (**12**)   (**13**)

4. Is Los Angeles a center of fish canning?

   Sentence   (**14**)   (**15**)   (**16**)   (**17**)   (**18**)

5. Is Los Angeles the home of any publishers?

   Sentence   (**18**)   (**19**)   (**20**)   (**21**)   (**22**)

6. When was oil discovered in Los Angeles?

   Sentence   (**20**)   (**21**)   (**22**)   (**23**)   (**24**)

7. Does Los Angeles have a constructed harbor?

   Sentence   (**25**)   (**26**)   (**27**)   (**28**)   (**29**)

8. Does Los Angeles have a professional football team?

   Sentence   (**31**)   (**32**)   (**33**)   (**34**)   (**35**)

9. Where were the bones of long-dead animals found?

   Sentence   (**36**)   (**37**)   (**38**)   (**39**)   (**40**)

10. Are there various ethnic groups in Los Angeles?

    Sentence   (**40**)   (**41**)   (**42**)   (**43**)   (**44**)

UNIT 12
Crossroads of the Nation

(1) In the heart of America, just about midway between the East and West Coasts, lies Omaha, Nebraska. (2) It is situated amid feed-grain farmland just east of the vast range where millions of head of cattle graze. (3) As a result, Omaha has become one of the world's leading cattle markets and meat-packing centers. (4) Located on the west bank of the busy Missouri River, Omaha also became a major transportation center early in its history. (5) The development company that founded the town in 1854 chose the site because of all these natural advantages. (6) Omaha's progress since then indicates that it chose well.

(7) This city of over 300,000 took its name from the Omaha Indians, one of several Native American tribes who inhabited the area. (8) They hunted the millions of buffalo that roamed the plains. (9) The city's future as a transportation junction was foreshadowed when the famous Lewis and Clark expedition, exploring the Louisiana Purchase territory in 1804, found the site on their route. (10) The land was not heavily settled until the 1850s, after the U.S. government obtained the Nebraska Territory from the Native Americans by treaty. (11) The new town soon prospered as a point of departure for wagon trains heading for western gold.

(12) It was the coming of the transcontinental railroad, however, that really put Omaha "on the map" in the 1860s and 1870s. (13) The Union Pacific and other railroads laid their routes through it. (14) One of the first railroad bridges across the Missouri River, in 1873, accelerated the city's development. (15) Its proximity to cattle lands led it to mushroom as a hub of commerce connected with shipping, feeding, and slaughtering cattle. (16) Today Omaha is still one of the nation's leaders in these activities. (17) Millions of cattle are slaughtered here annually. (18) They await their fate in the Union Stockyards, one of the world's largest.

(19) Modern Omaha, however, is not a one-industry town. (20) Since World War II manufacturing has flourished. (21) Principal products include electrical and telephone equipment, farm equipment, metalwork, and published materials. (22) Only three U.S. cities surpass Omaha as a rail center. (23) Its railroad terminal is one of the nation's busiest. (24) The rail and highway networks that converge on the city have given it the nickname "Crossroads of the Nation."

(25) One non-farm business in which Omaha has become a leader is insurance. (26) Statistics show that Omaha is now the country's fourth greatest center for the insurance business. (27) The world's largest private health insurance company has its headquarters here. (28) So do about thirty-five other insurance firms.

(29) There is more going on in the Omaha area than business. (30) Near the city is Offutt Air Force Base. (31) Offutt is no ordinary air base. (32) It is the global headquarters of the U.S. Air Force's Strategic Air Command. (33) From sophisticated, computerized control panels here, America's long-range bombers throughout the world are monitored, directed, and kept on the alert.

(34) Among the Omaha area's noted institutions is Boys Town, a community that takes in homeless and needy boys. (35) It was once the subject of a well-known movie.

(36) To college baseball players and fans, the name Omaha means glory. (37) It is here that the annual College World Series is played every June. (38) The winner is the undisputed champion of the college baseball world—until next year.

1. What river runs east of Omaha?

    Sentence   (1)   (2)   (3)   (4)   (5)

2. Does Omaha have any natural advantages?

    Sentence   (3)   (4)   (5)   (6)   (7)

3. What signaled the city's future as a transportation junction?

    Sentence   (8)   (9)   (10)   (11)   (12)

4. Did the transcontinental railroad have any influence on Omaha's growth?

    Sentence   (12)   (13)   (14)   (15)   (16)

5. What accelerated the city's development in 1873?

    Sentence   (14)   (15)   (16)   (17)   (18)

6. Is Omaha a one-industry town?

    Sentence   (18)   (19)   (20)   (21)   (22)

7. What are three principal products manufactured in Omaha?

    Sentence   (21)   (22)   (23)   (24)   (25)

8. Has Omaha become a leader in the insurance business?

    Sentence   (25)   (26)   (27)   (28)   (29)

9. Is Offutt an ordinary air base?

    Sentence   (29)   (30)   (31)   (32)   (33)

10. How long does the champion of the college baseball world reign?

    Sentence   (34)   (35)   (36)   (37)   (38)

In Units 7 through 12, you read about these cities in the United States: Oklahoma City, Oklahoma; Dallas, Texas; St. Louis, Missouri; Washington, D.C.; Los Angeles, California; and Omaha, Nebraska. You could skim or scan material to find more information about these cities.

To scan: move your eyes quickly over the written material until you find the fact or facts you are looking for

To skim: read a passage quickly to get the main idea(s)

A. Exercising Your Skill

Use the definitions above to decide whether you would skim or scan material in a newspaper to get each of the following types of information. Number your paper from 1 to 8; then write *skim* or *scan* next to each number.

1. the prices of two sale items in an advertisement
2. the general idea of a speech given by the governor
3. the telephone number of a person selling a bicycle
4. the time and location of a movie you want to see
5. what led up to a petition being signed by voters
6. the names of the state senators on a certain committee
7. the effects of a hurricane on several communities
8. the arguments for and against supporting a certain regulation

B. Expanding Your Skill

Play this game with a classmate. The first underlined word in each line of words is repeated exactly *at least* once more in the line. Scan the line until you find it and point to the word *each time it appears*. Do this for each underlined word in each line. See who can finish scanning all the lines for the underlined words first.

• incline	income	inclined	invite	incline	include
• cycle	cycles	cycled	cycling	cycle	cyclone
• through	through	thorough	thought	threw	through
• brow	brew	brow	borrow	brow	brawl
• receive	receipt	received	receive	recall	recipe
• prepare	prepare	pretend	prepared	protect	prepare
• write	written	white	writer	write	wrote
• suspect	suspect	suspense	suppose	suspend	suspect
• lunch	launch	lurch	laundry	lunch	lawn
• arrive	arose	arrival	arrive	arisen	arrived
• robot	robotics	robot	rotate	robber	robot
• visible	visible	vision	visible	valuable	visit
• remain	remember	remainder	remain	retain	remained
• trial	trail	trial	triangle	tried	trial
• spend	spent	spend	spin	spend	spanned

C. Exploring Language

Read each paragraph below. On your paper, write at least two detail questions for each paragraph that can be answered by scanning the paragraph.

1.   Above all, New Orleans is known for its unique atmosphere. Lacy iron grillwork decorates many of the homes in the Vieux Carré, or the French Quarter, the oldest part of the city. The houses themselves are of Spanish design. Both French and Spanish blood flows in the veins of members of the oldest families. These people, known as Creoles, may speak French as well as English.

Questions: _____
        _____

2.   In the days following the Louisiana Purchase, the intruding Americans and aristocratic Creoles became rivals in the sugar trade. Duels flared up. The slightest insult could result in a challenge. "Pistols for two; breakfast for one" became a common expression.

Questions: _____
        _____

3.   In time the easygoing charm of the Creoles cast its curious spell on newcomers. Now the entire city is influenced by the Creole culture. People of all national backgrounds eat Creole dishes of rice, seafood, and sauces. Restaurants in New Orleans that feature these foods are considered among the finest in the world. Even more than for its food, New Orleans is known as the home of America's unique contribution to music—jazz. Basically Afro-American with Creole influences, jazz was made famous in New Orleans by such legendary musicians as Louis Armstrong.

Questions: _____
        _____

D. Expressing Yourself

Choose one of these activities.

1. Cut a news article out of a newspaper. Paste it on a sheet of paper. Then make up four or five questions about details that can be found by scanning the article. Exchange articles and written questions with a classmate. See who can find the answers to the other's questions first.

2. Look in a book of short stories, such as *Aesop's Fables*. Choose a story to act out as a skit with three or four classmates. Tell the story through dialogue, voice tones, facial expressions, and body movements. After the skit, ask students in the audience to summarize the main idea of the story, and then to point out one or two traits about each character in the story.

(**1**) Few cities in history have shown a growth rate like that of Chicago. (**2**) In 1820 the city consisted of ten or twelve houses and a store or two. (**3**) Now it is the third largest city in the nation, and still it continues to grow before our eyes. (**4**) Thousands of new buildings are constructed every year. (**5**) More than seven million people now live in and around the city. (**6**) Every month new skyscrapers reach into the air. (**7**) To paraphrase poet Carl Sandburg, Chicago is a brawny young giant with big shoulders, a colossus of the prairies.

(**8**) Youngest of all major cities in the world, Chicago is in an ideal location to keep growing. (**9**) Astride the crossroads of the nation, it is the largest railroad center in the world. (**10**) No other city in the land is a larger trucking center. (**11**) Even though the city, located on Lake Michigan, is more than seven hundred miles from the ocean, it is the largest inland port in the world. (**12**) Ships from far-off Europe find their way here through the St. Lawrence Seaway and the Great Lakes. (**13**) O'Hare Airport is the world's busiest commercial airport. (**14**) Overall, Chicago is the leading transportation center in the United States.

(**15**) Chicago began life in 1779 as a small trading post on the Chicago River. (**16**) A farsighted black freedman named Jean du Sable did a flourishing fur business with Native American Indians. (**17**) When his trading post became a fort and then a city, it was named Chicago. (**18**) This is the Native American word for the wild onions found in the area.

(**19**) Today Chicago still continues to set astonishing records. (**20**) The greater Chicago area is a leading maker of steel in the country. (**21**) It produces more steel than Great Britain, France, West Germany, Italy, or Belgium. (**22**) Chicago leads the nation in the mail-order business and in wholesale distribution. (**23**) Its location in the heart of North America's farmland makes it the world's largest grain market.

(**24**) Chicago is the convention hub of America. (**25**) Each year the city plays host to more than a thousand conventions. (**26**) In 1860 Abraham Lincoln was nominated for President at the Republican convention held here. (**27**) Since then over a third of all major political conventions have taken place in Chicago.

(**28**) But Chicago did not achieve success without problems. (**29**) At one time pollution from the Chicago River threatened the city. (**30**) Undaunted, engineers reversed the course of the river so that clean Lake Michigan waters would flow into it! (**31**) Today it is one of the few rivers that runs backwards. (**32**) On another occasion the city seemed to be sinking. (**33**) A positive-minded person named Cheseborough jacked up buildings and covered the area with twelve feet of earth. (**34**) The extra height gave the city a new lease on life. (**35**) Even the famous fire of 1871 could not snuff out the spirits of the lusty young giant. (**36**) The entire central city was destroyed. (**37**) But citizens built anew—this time with steel and concrete. (**38**) For good measure they invented the skyscraper. (**39**) Today Chicago's impressive skyline includes the world's tallest building, the 1,454-foot Sears Tower.

(**40**) Among those who have contributed to Chicago's progress is the noted social reformer Jane Addams, who established housing for poor immigrants in 1899. (**41**) Chicago is the largest American city ever to have a woman mayor—Jane Byrne. (**42**) Elected in 1979 by a record eighty percent landslide vote, she worked vigorously to keep Chicago one of America's most vital cities.

(**43**) The small trading post of Jean du Sable has come a long way.

UNIT 13
City of the Big Shoulders

1. What specific statistic illustrates the continued annual growth of Chicago?

    Sentence   (1)   (2)   (3)   (4)   (5)

2. What is the world's busiest commercial airport?

    Sentence   (9)   (10)   (11)   (12)   (13)

3. What did the trading post become before it became a city?

    Sentence   (14)   (15)   (16)   (17)   (18)

4. What does the Native American word *chicago* mean?

    Sentence   (18)   (19)   (20)   (21)   (22)

5. How does Chicago rank in the mail-order business?

    Sentence   (21)   (22)   (23)   (24)   (25)

6. Who was nominated for President in Chicago in 1860?

    Sentence   (24)   (25)   (26)   (27)   (28)

7. What was a threat to the city at one time?

    Sentence   (27)   (28)   (29)   (30)   (31)

8. What was the Chicago fire not able to do?

    Sentence   (34)   (35)   (36)   (37)   (38)

9. Is the world's tallest building part of Chicago's skyline?

    Sentence   (36)   (37)   (38)   (39)   (40)

10. Who established housing for poor immigrants in 1899?

    Sentence   (39)   (40)   (41)   (42)   (43)

UNIT 14
Motor City

(1) Would this be a good place to build a trading post? (2) Antoine de la Mothe Cadillac looked with approval at the high bluffs overhead. (3) Then, with a signal he stopped his flotilla of canoes. (4) From this position the river could be guarded from all directions. (5) He and his crew put ashore to build their fort on the Detroit River. (6) It was 1701.

(7) That tiny settlement has grown into the nation's sixth largest city—Detroit. (8) The city has won fame in an area Cadillac could not foresee. (9) It is now known as the "Motor City," home of the nation's automobile industry. (10) Although less than one percent of the United States' population lives in Detroit, about twenty-five percent of the nation's automobiles are built here. (11) More cars and trucks are made here than in any other city in the United States.

(12) Why is Detroit the place where the automotive industry has flourished? (13) Long before the car was invented, a carriage and bicycle business thrived here. (14) The city was filled with mechanics who understood vehicles and wheels. (15) The invention of the combustion engine brought about the birth of the automobile.

(16) The Detroit River itself played a major role. (17) Joining Lake Erie and Lake St. Clair, it is a strait: a narrow body of water connecting two larger bodies of water. (18) *Ville d'etroit* (city of the strait) was the name given to Cadillac's original settlement. (19) The river today is one of the world's busiest inland waterways. (20) Thus there has been no shortage of easily available raw materials for the auto-making plants of the area.

(21) Not surprisingly, the roads around Detroit grew with the automotive industry. (22) The first mile of concrete highway in the nation was built in the city.

(23) Detroit leads in other industries too. (24) It is a leader in the production of chemicals. (25) The industry received a boost when it was learned that Detroit was sitting on top of a salt mine a thousand feet beneath the earth. (26) A layer of salt thirty-five feet thick is mined through the use of a tunnel system almost sixty-nine miles long.

(27) Detroit is also a recording center. (28) Black musicians and business people have built this business into a multimillion-dollar industry, with a galaxy of associated companies. (29) The type of music they developed is known as "Motown" or the "Detroit Sound," and was made famous by such singing stars as Diana Ross. (30) Recordings are made in ten different languages, including German, Japanese, Spanish, Portuguese, and Italian.

(31) Its nearness to large lakes makes Detroit a leading city for pleasure-boating. (32) This and other water sports attract thousands to Metropolitan Beach, the largest freshwater beach in the world.

(33) Detroit has done much rebuilding. (34) Cobo Hall, a prime example of this, is one of the largest convention facilities in the world.

(35) In downtown Detroit you will find the Veterans Memorial Building. (36) It was on this spot, almost three hundred years ago, that Cadillac decided to come ashore and build his fort. (37) In doing so, he unknowingly laid the foundation for an industrial empire.

UNIT 14
Motor City

1. Did the possibility of attack influence Cadillac in selecting the location for his trading post?

   Sentence   (1)   (2)   (3)   (4)   (5)

2. What city leads in the manufacture of cars and trucks?

   Sentence   (7)   (8)   (9)   (10)   (11)

3. Was the automotive industry the first business that flourished in Detroit?

   Sentence   (10)   (11)   (12)   (13)   (14)

4. What made the invention of the modern automobile possible?

   Sentence   (13)   (14)   (15)   (16)   (17)

5. What is a strait?

   Sentence   (16)   (17)   (18)   (19)   (20)

6. What grew along with the automotive industry?

   Sentence   (18)   (19)   (20)   (21)   (22)

7. Where was the first concrete highway in the nation built?

   Sentence   (22)   (23)   (24)   (25)   (26)

8. By what other name is "Motown" known?

   Sentence   (25)   (26)   (27)   (28)   (29)

9. What is an excellent example of Detroit's rebuilding?

   Sentence   (30)   (31)   (32)   (33)   (34)

10. How long ago did Cadillac build his fort?

    Sentence   (33)   (34)   (35)   (36)   (37)

UNIT 15
Nickname City

(**1**) Why has Nashville, Tennessee, been given so many nicknames? (**2**) It is called the "Wall Street of the South," "Music City, U.S.A.," and the "Athens of the South." (**3**) This wide range of nicknames reflects this city's characteristics and modern-day development.

(**4**) Until European settlers arrived in the 1700s, this region was populated mainly by Native Americans of the Shawnee tribe. (**5**) In 1806 Nashville became a city. (**6**) During the 1800s it grew as a port for steamboats traveling up and down the Ohio and Mississippi Rivers. (**7**) As the river trade grew, farm income increased. (**8**) Later the creation of the Tennessee Valley Authority in 1933 boosted Nashville's growth. (**9**) This federal project was created to develop the area's natural resources and to help the economy of the region.

(**10**) Located in the fertile, bowl-shaped Nashville Basin, the city has always relied on farming for much of its income. (**11**) The climate here is generally mild. (**12**) The temperature usually goes no higher than 80 degrees Fahrenheit in the summer and no lower than 40 in the winter. (**13**) Corn and other vegetables are important regional farm products, but livestock is the major agricultural money-maker in the Nashville area. (**14**) Meat-packing plants thrive in the basin region, and dairy farms are numerous. (**15**) What this farming area is probably most famous for are its Tennessee Walking Horses.

(**16**) Industry is also important in modern Nashville. (**17**) The city houses over 650 industrial plants. (**18**) Nashville is a national leader in producing printed materials. (**19**) Other major products are aircraft parts, food products, glass heating and cooking equipment, phonograph records, tires, and trucks. (**20**) As the major investment banking center of the South, Nashville won its nickname "Wall Street of the South." (**21**) The city is the home of one of the largest life insurance companies in the nation. (**22**) In addition, the headquarters of one of the country's largest hospital management companies is located here. (**23**) The world's largest automobile glass plant can be found here also.

(**24**) It was during the 1950s that Nashville gained its reputation as "Music City, U.S.A." (**25**) Today the city ranks second in the nation in music recording; in country-music recording, it is the leader. (**26**) Nashville boasts more than 180 recording companies, 23 recording studios, and about 450 song-publishing firms. (**27**) Opryland, a large outdoor theme park, proudly houses The Grand Ole Opry House. (**28**) The radio program "Grand Ole Opry" is broadcast here. (**29**) This program is the longest running radio show in the United States. (**30**) It is hardly surprising that the "home of country music" attracts visitors from all over the world!

(**31**) Nashville has many other popular tourist spots. (**32**) President Andrew Jackson's stately mansion, the Hermitage, is now a public museum. (**33**) Jackson and his wife, Rachel, are buried on the grounds. (**34**) The city's fine examples of historic architecture lure students as well as visitors. (**35**) Nashville became known as the "Athens of the South" because of its many buildings in the Greek classical style. (**36**) The campuses of Nashville's fifteen colleges and universities are where the majority of these buildings are located. (**37**) The world's only full-size replica of the Parthenon, an ancient Greek building, is probably the most notable.

(**38**) The rich combination of tradition and progress makes Nashville a popular city to live in and to visit. (**39**) Whether its appeal is as the "Wall Street of the South," "Music City, U.S.A.," or the "Athens of the South," Nashville has enough southern hospitality and modern conveniences to please just about everyone.

UNIT 15
Nickname City

1. What do Nashville's nicknames reflect about the city?

    Sentence **(1)**   **(2)**   **(3)**   **(4)**   **(5)**

2. Was Nashville ever a port?

    Sentence **(2)**   **(3)**   **(4)**   **(5)**   **(6)**

3. Why was the Tennessee Valley Authority created?

    Sentence **(7)**   **(8)**   **(9)**   **(10)**   **(11)**

4. Is livestock important to Nashville's economy?

    Sentence **(11)**   **(12)**   **(13)**   **(14)**   **(15)**

5. Can dairy farms be found around Nashville?

    Sentence **(13)**   **(14)**   **(15)**   **(16)**   **(17)**

6. Is Nashville a thriving publishing center?

    Sentence **(17)**   **(18)**   **(19)**   **(20)**   **(21)**

7. Does Nashville have any ties to the automobile industry?

    Sentence **(22)**   **(23)**   **(24)**   **(25)**   **(26)**

8. Does Nashville have much for tourists to see?

    Sentence **(27)**   **(28)**   **(29)**   **(30)**   **(31)**

9. Who is interested in Nashville's historic architecture?

    Sentence **(32)**   **(33)**   **(34)**   **(35)**   **(36)**

10. Does Nashville offer southern hospitality?

    Sentence **(35)**   **(36)**   **(37)**   **(38)**   **(39)**

UNIT 16
Haven of Freedom

(1) Philadelphia owes its appearance and design in part to the London fire of 1666. (2) William Penn, Philadelphia's founder, instructed that the new city be made of brick and that buildings be placed apart in rectangular blocks, to reduce the likelihood of fire spreading. (3) His plan proved successful; Philadelphia is one of the few large American cities that has never had a major fire.

(4) Today the city is the fifth largest in the nation. (5) It still retains much of the past. (6) Located in the southeastern tip of Pennsylvania, Philadelphia is the largest freshwater port in the world. (7) Its docks line the Delaware River for a hundred miles, from the city to the Atlantic Ocean, making it the nation's twelfth largest port. (8) It is one of the nation's leaders in foreign trade. (9) Regular departures are scheduled to two hundred ports in a hundred foreign nations.

(10) Manufacturing is Philadelphia's leading source of income. (11) The city is a national leader in the fabrication of metals, the processing of food, the manufacturing of textiles, and printing and publishing. (12) The Philadelphia area is also the leading center of oil refining on the East Coast. (13) The publishing industry got its start when Benjamin Franklin founded the *Pennsylvania Gazette* and *Poor Richard's Almanac*. (14) Today the city is the home of many textbook publishers.

(15) In attracting citizens, Penn also showed his foresight. (16) Because he wanted Philadelphia to be a haven of freedom, he encouraged those of all beliefs to locate here. (17) People of every creed and color responded. (18) So many Germans migrated to Philadelphia that the section where they lived is known to this day as Germantown.

(19) Philadelphia has always been famed as a center of education. (20) In the 1800s the nation's first art school and first medical school were established here. (21) Women's education was advanced by the founding of one of the first colleges for women, as well as the first medical school and first art school for women. (22) Today the city boasts five of the country's leading medical schools.

(23) The city has many historic shrines. (24) These include Independence Hall, where the Declaration of Independence was signed and the Constitution was written. (25) The Liberty Bell is on display here. (26) Nearby is the house where Betsy Ross is said to have made the first American flag. (27) Not far outside the city lies Valley Forge, where the Continental Army camped during the bitter winter of 1777-1778.

(28) Philadelphia is a leading banking center. (29) The first bank in the United States was organized here in 1780, and its founders helped finance the Revolution.

(30) Much of old Philadelphia lives on in its streets and red brick houses. (31) One of these streets, Elfreth's Alley, is said to be the oldest residential street in continuous use in the United States.

UNIT 16
Haven of Freedom

1. How did William Penn reduce the likelihood of fire spreading?

    Sentence   (1)   (2)   (3)   (4)   (5)

2. Is Philadelphia the world's largest freshwater port?

    Sentence   (5)   (6)   (7)   (8)   (9)

3. Is Philadelphia located on the Atlantic Ocean?

    Sentence   (7)   (8)   (9)   (10)   (11)

4. Why did William Penn want people of all beliefs to locate in Pennsylvania?

    Sentence   (12)   (13)   (14)   (15)   (16)

5. What reminder exists in Philadelphia today of the immigration of earlier times?

    Sentence   (16)   (17)   (18)   (19)   (20)

6. Where were the nation's first art and medical schools established?

    Sentence   (17)   (18)   (19)   (20)   (21)

7. Does Philadelphia have any leading medical schools today?

    Sentence   (22)   (23)   (24)   (25)   (26)

8. How does Philadelphia rank as a banking center?

    Sentence   (24)   (25)   (26)   (27)   (28)

9. Who helped finance the Revolution?

    Sentence   (26)   (27)   (28)   (29)   (30)

10. What is special about Elfreth's Alley?

    Sentence   (27)   (28)   (29)   (30)   (31)

UNIT 17
Mile High City

(**1**) Denver is known as the "Mile High City," because the State Capitol Building of Colorado stands on land exactly a mile above sea level. (**2**) The city is also known as the "Nation's Second Capital," because only Washington, D.C. contains more U.S. government facilities. (**3**) Thirty-eight thousand people work for the federal government, as well as thousands more for the state. (**4**) Denver is called the "Queen City of the Plains," because it is the largest city in the region and stands at the edge of the prairie that lies at the foothills of the Rockies.

(**5**) Next to the government, the chief employer is industry. (**6**) Denver is home to the world's largest makers of luggage and of hoses. (**7**) Processed food, sporting goods, tires, toys, and defense and space equipment are other major products.

(**8**) Despite modern industry and a modern skyline, Denver retains much of its past. (**9**) On Capitol Hill are the Victorian mansions of the silver and cattle barons. (**10**) Department stores carry cowboy boots and Stetsons along with the latest styles from Los Angeles and New York. (**11**) Visitors find they can pan gold and, if they work hard enough, can make $50 per day. (**12**) The big annual event in the region is the National Stock Show and Rodeo held in January.

(**13**) Originally the city was a mining camp, founded by prospectors who discovered gold near a Native American Indian village on the Platte River. (**14**) Although Denver no longer has its gold and silver booms, mining is still an important industry. (**15**) Now the metals all have a space-age sound—vanadium, cadmium, and uranium. (**16**) The nearby Climax Molybdenum Mine is one of the largest underground mines in the world.

(**17**) Long a leading occupation, the cattle business continues to boom. (**18**) Denver is the home of one of the largest cattle-feeding lots in the world. (**19**) So many cattle are fed here that computers must be used to analyze the feeding mixtures in different lots.

(**20**) Denver also serves as a distribution center for a vast area. (**21**) This is the largest trading area in the nation, extending from Canada to Mexico and covering one-third of the United States.

(**22**) Tourism is another important source of income. (**23**) Drawn by cool mountain air and more than three hundred days of sunshine each year, over seven million tourists visit the city annually. (**24**) The humidity is low, and the annual rainfall totals only fourteen inches. (**25**) Visitors are impressed with the backdrop of mountains just to the west.

(**26**) Denver is also the gateway to the Rocky Mountain ski areas. (**27**) Skiers from all over the nation come here to test their skill at Vail, Aspen, and other ski resorts.

(**28**) The Denver Mint is second only to Fort Knox in its supply of gold. (**29**) All American coins minted today are made in Denver or Philadelphia. (**30**) The Denver Mint produces over forty million pennies each day.

(**31**) Visitors are also attracted by the nearby Air Force Academy. (**32**) Close at hand is NORAD. (**33**) This is the home of the North American Air Defense Command. (**34**) It is buried beneath Cheyenne Mountain under a quarter mile of granite. (**35**) Military teams scan the radar screen twenty-four hours a day to keep America safe from surprise air attacks.

(**36**) The attractive Denver area has been growing rapidly in population. (**37**) In eight years it has climbed from twenty-seventh to twenty-first among the nation's metropolitan areas, exceeding Seattle, Washington; Miami, Florida; Milwaukee, Wisconsin; and Cincinnati, Ohio. (**38**) The "Mile High City" is riding high.

1. What city contains more U.S. government buildings than Denver?

    Sentence **(1)**   **(2)**   **(3)**   **(4)**   **(5)**

2. Where are the world's largest makers of luggage located?

    Sentence **(4)**   **(5)**   **(6)**   **(7)**   **(8)**

3. Is Denver a leader in the production of defense and space equipment?

    Sentence **(6)**   **(7)**   **(8)**   **(9)**   **(10)**

4. Do Denver's industry and skyline reflect its past?

    Sentence **(8)**   **(9)**   **(10)**   **(11)**   **(12)**

5. What is the name of one of the largest underground mines?

    Sentence **(12)**   **(13)**   **(14)**   **(15)**   **(16)**

6. How are computers used in the cattle business?

    Sentence **(16)**   **(17)**   **(18)**   **(19)**   **(20)**

7. How far does the Denver trading area extend?

    Sentence **(20)**   **(21)**   **(22)**   **(23)**   **(24)**

8. Why do many people go to Vail and Aspen?

    Sentence **(25)**   **(26)**   **(27)**   **(28)**   **(29)**

9. How many pennies are produced daily at the Denver Mint?

    Sentence **(29)**   **(30)**   **(31)**   **(32)**   **(33)**

10. How many cities has Denver exceeded in population in the past several years?

    Sentence **(34)**   **(35)**   **(36)**   **(37)**   **(38)**

(**1**) Pittsburgh has proven itself to be a strong, vital city. (**2**) As the steel center of America, Pittsburgh's economy suffered when the steel industry began to decline in the late 1940s. (**3**) Thousands of workers needed to find new jobs to support their families. (**4**) Fortunately, a modern service industry had been quietly growing and offering workers training and employment. (**5**) Pittsburgh is now an important center for two thriving industries—computer services and health care.

(**6**) Pittsburgh is located in southwestern Pennsylvania, where the Allegheny and Monongahela rivers meet and form the Ohio River. (**7**) The area where the three rivers converge is called the "Golden Triangle," Pittsburgh's downtown area. (**8**) The park at the tip of the "Golden Triangle" houses the British Fort Pitt. (**9**) The city has over 720 bridges—more than any other city in the nation. (**10**) Most of the population lives in suburbs in the rolling hills across the bridges. (**11**) Cable cars take commuters and tourists up and down the steep hills along the river.

(**12**) The Iroquois were the earliest residents of the Pittsburgh area. (**13**) Then, at various times, the French and British occupied the area, but in 1758, Britain won control. (**14**) After the Revolutionary War Pittsburgh was nicknamed "Gateway to the West." (**15**) At that time the city served as a popular starting point for pioneers traveling west. (**16**) As pioneer settlers in the west needed goods from the east, the trade business grew. (**17**) Before long Pittsburgh became a manufacturing center. (**18**) In the mid-1800s the Civil War boosted Pittsburgh's growing steel industry because the Union Army needed arms. (**19**) Railroads were also being built across the country. (**20**) As the nation's transportation industry grew, the steel and aluminum industries boomed. (**21**) As a result, between 1870 and 1900 Pittsburgh's population climbed from 86,076 to 321,616. (**22**) Later, during World War II, Pittsburgh produced more steel than Germany and Japan together!

(**23**) The economic benefits of the steel industry were great, but Pittsburgh suffered negative effects, too. (**24**) The smoke from the factories caused so much pollution that, by the 1940s, streetlights were needed during the middle of the day. (**25**) In 1946 the city began a massive program to clean buildings and to clear the air. (**26**) During the 1950s and 1960s many other kinds of companies moved their headquarters to Pittsburgh.

(**27**) Today, although the steel industry is still important to Pittsburgh's economy, other industries have taken root. (**28**) Hospitals in Pittsburgh are among the best in the world. (**29**) Pittsburgh has become an important technological research and development center. (**30**) Warehouses are being replaced by skyscrapers. (**31**) There is a strong push to turn factories along the river into ultra-modern research and manufacturing centers.

(**32**) Pittsburgh also has a thriving cultural scene. (**33**) The Pittsburgh Symphony is world-famous. (**34**) The Pittsburgh Ballet Theater, Opera Company, Public Theater, and Civic Light Opera are all highly respected. (**35**) The Carnegie Institute, founded by steel manufacturer Andrew Carnegie, includes both the Museum of Natural History and the Museum of Art. (**36**) Other attractions include The Aviary, with its exotic tropical birds, and the Phipps Conservatory, which displays flowers from all over the world. (**37**) The city also boasts more than 2,500 acres of parks. (**38**) In addition, sports fans here cheer on their champion professional and collegiate baseball, football, and hockey teams.

(**39**) The city's business and cultural activities have helped attract many residents to Pittsburgh. (**40**) Whether people come for business opportunities, for cultural events, or for a place to live, they usually find more reasons to stay than they had expected!

UNIT 18
City of Champions

1. Does Pittsburgh have any modern industries?

   Sentence   (1)   (2)   (3)   (4)   (5)

2. Where do most of the people of Pittsburgh live?

   Sentence   (6)   (7)   (8)   (9)   (10)

3. How are cable cars used in the city?

   Sentence   (8)   (9)   (10)   (11)   (12)

4. Did the French ever occupy the Pittsburgh area?

   Sentence   (11)   (12)   (13)   (14)   (15)

5. Why was Pittsburgh called the "Gateway to the West"?

   Sentence   (15)   (16)   (17)   (18)   (19)

6. How did the transportation industry's growth affect the steel industry?

   Sentence   (20)   (21)   (22)   (23)   (24)

7. Is the city turning old factories into new research centers?

   Sentence   (27)   (28)   (29)   (30)   (31)

8. Are there many cultural activities in Pittsburgh?

   Sentence   (28)   (29)   (30)   (31)   (32)

9. Does Pittsburgh have a symphony?

   Sentence   (31)   (32)   (33)   (34)   (35)

10. Do people come to Pittsburgh for reasons other than business?

    Sentence   (36)   (37)   (38)   (39)   (40)

UNIT 19
Where It All Began

(1) Boston is a city that faces the future while it looks back upon its past. (2) Situated at the head of Massachusetts Bay, it presents a study in contrasts. (3) Soaring glass and steel skyscrapers tower over colonial church steeples. (4) Early mills stand near modern electronics plants.

(5) Boston is one of the world's leading leather dealers. (6) It surpasses all others in the production of shoes. (7) No other American city has as large a wool market. (8) But Bostonians point out that the success of today owes much to the past. (9) Early Boston skippers were so successful that they created new industries. (10) As their coffers over-flowed from trade, they built an entire manufacturing town, the present city of Lawrence, Massachusetts. (11) They also insured their own ships, creating the insurance industry in America. (12) They lent their money to others, who built manufacturing industries and started the banking industry. (13) Today Boston is one of the leading financial centers in America. (14) Although it ranks eighteenth in population, only two other cities do more financial business.

(15) Family fortunes, earned ten generations ago, still survive under shrewd Yankee management. (16) Instead of supplying capital for cod fishing, they now support space-age industries such as electronics—another area in which Boston is a leader.

(17) Boston is an important educational center. (18) Approximately 150,000 students attend forty-seven colleges and universities in the area. (19) Early colonists sent their children to school as young as three years of age. (20) In 1635 Boston became the home of the first high school in the English-speaking American colonies, Boston Latin School. (21) The school is still in operation. (22) Boston is also the home of the colonies' first kindergarten and the first university, Harvard. (23) Many industries throughout the nation send executives to the Harvard School of Business for special courses.

(24) In medicine Boston is also a leader. (25) Hospitals here are world-famous for the specialists on their staffs. (26) Medical students arrive from all over the world for advanced work. (27) Patients who wish special care stream in from all points, including distant countries. (28) The first public health department was founded here two centuries ago by a silversmith named Paul Revere.

(29) The city is also famous for outstanding citizens and families. (30) In colonial times the Adams family produced two Presidents. (31) In recent times the Kennedy family, descended from Irish immigrants, has presented the nation with two senators and a President.

(32) Many historic shrines are found in the city, including Faneuil Hall, "The Cradle of Liberty." (33) There is also the home of Paul Revere, one of the oldest houses in America. (34) Some of the early cobblestone streets can be found in Boston much as they were two hundred years ago. (35) Each year thousands of tourists come to visit Boston, "the city where it all began."

UNIT 19
Where It All Began

1. Where is Boston located?

   Sentence (**1**)   (**2**)   (**3**)   (**4**)   (**5**)

2. Does any other American city have as large a wool market?

   Sentence (**6**)   (**7**)   (**8**)   (**9**)   (**10**)

3. Does Boston's past contribute to its success today?

   Sentence (**8**)   (**9**)   (**10**)   (**11**)   (**12**)

4. What manufacturing city grew from the overflow of trade riches?

   Sentence (**9**)   (**10**)   (**11**)   (**12**)   (**13**)

5. What American industry did the Boston skippers create?

   Sentence (**11**)   (**12**)   (**13**)   (**14**)   (**15**)

6. In what new industry has Boston become a leader?

   Sentence (**14**)   (**15**)   (**16**)   (**17**)   (**18**)

7. Were there any high schools in the 1600s?

   Sentence (**17**)   (**18**)   (**19**)   (**20**)   (**21**)

8. Where do many industries send executives for special courses?

   Sentence (**21**)   (**22**)   (**23**)   (**24**)   (**25**)

9. Who founded the first public health department?

   Sentence (**24**)   (**25**)   (**26**)   (**27**)   (**28**)

10. What house, one of the oldest in America, is located in Boston?

    Sentence (**29**)   (**30**)   (**31**)   (**32**)   (**33**)

In Units 13 through 19, you read about some goods and services in the cities of Chicago, Detroit, Nashville, Philadelphia, Denver, Pittsburgh, and Boston.

A. Exercising Your Skill

When you buy food or other goods or services, you receive a bill or a receipt that tells you how much something costs or how much money you owe and for what. On your paper, draw a word map like the one below. From what you know about bills, choose the words or phrases from the box that tell about goods or services for which you might receive a bill. Write the goods and services at the end of the lines.

car repair	pizza	playground	library
friendship	elevator ride	doctor's visit	new sneakers
plane ticket	ocean view	movie rental	magazine
birthday party	eye exam	TV program	sunshine

B. Expanding Your Skill

Look at the menu below. Decide which lettered part or parts of the menu answer each question. Number your paper 1 through 6. Next to the number, write the letter or letters that show the answer. If you can't find the answer to a question on the menu, write "no answer."

Boston Lunch Room
M E N U

A
- #1 Special—An Old-time Favorite!
  Boston Baked Beans in Pot
  apple, celery, and walnut salad
  roll & butter $5.75

B
- #2 Special—Catch of the Day!
  Baked Boston Scrod
  green beans, mashed potato
  roll & butter $7.85

C
Both specials include a beverage.
Add 5% state sales tax.

1. What is included in the #2 special?
2. How much does the #1 special cost, not including tax?
3. Can you get just a glass of milk at this restaurant?
4. What percentage is the tax you have to add?
5. What do both specials include?
6. Are hamburgers served at this restaurant?

C. Exploring Language

Look at this advertisement for a back-to-school sale. On your paper, write five questions that can be answered with information in the advertisement.

Back-to-School Sale

Sale Week: 8/31-9/6   Sale Hours: 9 AM - 9 PM Mon-Sat
                                              9 AM - 5 PM Sun

30% off ticket price on these items:
- five-pocket jeans   - three-ring binders
- windbreaker jackets   - three-hole punched paper
- heavy-duty bookbags   - pens and pencils

Reduced prices on these items: sweaters, shirts, slacks, raincoats

---

Look at this copy of a cash register slip for items purchased at a paper-goods store. Notice that TX means sales tax. On your paper, write five questions that can be answered with information on the slip.

Thank You for Shopping
at Supplies-Galore
3/06/91

Quantity	Item	Price
1	tote	3.25
1	pkg. legal pads	10.75
1	pkg. AA batteries	2.98
1	box fine-line pens	8.50
		$25.48 Sub
		1.21 TX
		$26.69 Tot

D. Expressing Yourself

Choose one of these activities.

1. Make up an advertisement for a service that you would like to take advantage of. Give information about the service, its cost, and how to arrange for the service. Use your imagination when making up the service. You might think about this advertising lead as a starter: We Clean Your Room for You!

2. Look at several advertisements in a newspaper or magazine. Choose one that catches your interest. List the information that makes the product or service impressive, special, or worth exploring.

UNIT 20
City of Skyscrapers

(1) In sheer size alone this city staggers the mind. (2) More than seven million citizens can be found here. (3) Only nine states each have more people. (4) No other city in the world has so many tall buildings. (5) The highest soar 110 stories into the air. (6) On overcast days you cannot even see the tops. (7) Of course, we are talking about the largest city in the nation—New York, the "City of Skyscrapers."

(8) Servicing New York's residents—plus hundreds of thousands of suburbanites who commute here daily—is a monumental task. (9) To maintain law and order there is a police force larger than an army division. (10) It takes forty thousand farms to supply New Yorkers with milk, and four million cattle a year to satisfy their appetite for beef. (11) There are enough telephone wires in the city to stretch around the earth five hundred times. (12) The longest tunnel in the world—105 miles—is only one of two tunnels needed to convey from upstate the billions of gallons of water New Yorkers use daily. (13) The world's busiest subway system carries a billion passengers a year on 230 miles of track under and over the city's streets to over 450 stations. (14) Among them is Grand Central, the world's largest railroad station. (15) The port of New York is the largest and richest in the world, and the busiest in America, handling over 150 billion pounds of cargo a year. (16) It has a navigable waterfront of 755 miles and can berth 391 ships at a time.

(17) New York is located in the southeastern corner of New York State, at the mouth of the Hudson River. (18) The city is made up of five boroughs—Manhattan, Queens, the Bronx, Brooklyn, and Staten Island. (19) If Brooklyn were a separate city, it would be the fourth largest in the United States!

(20) From the beginning, New York has been a melting pot. (21) In 1650 in the Dutch village of New Amsterdam, there were only fifteen hundred inhabitants, but they spoke eighteen different languages. (22) Today the city is made up of ethnic neighborhoods of people from dozens of different lands. (23) You can find any kind of restaurant you wish, from Armenian to Yugoslavian. (24) Newspapers are printed here in dozens of different languages.

(25) New York leads all American cities in manufacturing and service industries. (26) The city has nearly twenty thousand manufacturing establishments. (27) In New York, especially in the famous garment district of Manhattan, more than one-fourth of all America's clothing is produced. (28) New York is the nation's publishing and printing center. (29) More American publishers and other communication media have headquarters here than anywhere else. (30) New York is also the financial and banking capital of the world. (31) The Wall Street area is the home of the New York and the American stock exchanges, where thousands of fortunes have been made—and lost. (32) One New York bank boasts the world's largest vault—350 by 100 feet, with forty-four-ton doors. (33) Besides Wall Street, other famous New York streets are Fifth Avenue, Park Avenue, and Broadway. (34) Broadway is the theater capital of America.

(35) The sights and sounds of Manhattan attract sixteen million tourists and convention delegates each year. (36) In a sense they are returning home. (37) New York is the place where the ancestors of many of them first stepped ashore in their new country. (38) Most visitors agree that the view of New York's soaring towers, sweeping bridges, sparkling harbor, and majestic Statue of Liberty is unequaled anywhere on earth. (39) The splendor and excitement of the "City of Skyscrapers"—or the "Big Apple" as it has come to be called—will always be a magnet for visitors and residents.

UNIT 20
City of Skyscrapers

1. Do more than nine states each have a population of at least seven million people?

    Sentence   (1)   (2)   (3)   (4)   (5)

2. How many times would all the telephone wires in the city encircle the earth?

    Sentence   (7)   (8)   (9)   (10)   (11)

3. Does New York have the busiest port in the United States?

    Sentence   (12)   (13)   (14)   (15)   (16)

4. What is the phrase that has described New York from the beginning?

    Sentence   (17)   (18)   (19)   (20)   (21)

5. Is there any indication that the inhabitants of early New Amsterdam came from many different countries?

    Sentence   (18)   (19)   (20)   (21)   (22)

6. Does New York have ethnic neighborhoods?

    Sentence   (22)   (23)   (24)   (25)   (26)

7. Is New York a publishing center?

    Sentence   (26)   (27)   (28)   (29)   (30)

8. Where is the theater capital of America?

    Sentence   (32)   (33)   (34)   (35)   (36)

9. Why do many tourists who visit New York feel they are returning home?

    Sentence   (33)   (34)   (35)   (36)   (37)

10. Does New York have more than one nickname?

    Sentence   (35)   (36)   (37)   (38)   (39)

(**1**) Minneapolis was well named. (**2**) *Minne* is a Sioux word meaning "water," and *polis* is a Greek word for "city." (**3**) Twenty-two lakes are found inside the city limits. (**4**) Minneapolis straddles the mighty Mississippi River and is located in southeastern Minnesota, about 350 miles northwest of Chicago.

(**5**) This northern city is a leading flour center. (**6**) Farmers in the surrounding area have always produced an abundance of wheat. (**7**) In 1885 a new process was developed here for milling flour. (**8**) Ample local water power quickly made Minneapolis the "flour city of the United States." (**9**) Although milling has since spread elsewhere, four of the nation's leading millers still have headquarters here. (**10**) Minneapolis is also a leader in the processing of cake and biscuit mixes as well as breakfast cereals.

(**11**) Because it is situated in the center of rich farmland, Minneapolis has become both a manufacturing and a distributing center for farm implements. (**12**) It is also a leader in the manufacture of electrical equipment for industry.

(**13**) In distributing its own products throughout the region and the nation, Minneapolis has become a busy transportation center. (**14**) It ranks third nationally in truck and rail traffic. (**15**) Much shipping is done on the Mississippi. (**16**) Minneapolis is the northernmost major port on the river.

(**17**) This attractive city is considered one of the most beautiful in the upper Midwest. (**18**) In addition to the lakes already mentioned, the city is the home of Minnehaha Falls, immortalized by Longfellow in the poem "The Song of Hiawatha." (**19**) There are 153 parks here. (**20**) Maple trees line pleasant streets. (**21**) In spring and summer the entire city itself resembles a huge park.

(**22**) Because Minneapolis is the gateway to the lake country of northern Minnesota, it is often called "Vacation Capital." (**23**) The state has more than twenty thousand lakes. (**24**) Most famous, perhaps, is Lake Itasca. (**25**) Out of this lake flows the mighty Mississippi. (**26**) At this point it is just a stream ten feet wide and less than two feet deep.

(**27**) Thousands of people from Minneapolis and all over the nation own cottages in the lake country. (**28**) Few states have more summer cottages per capita than Minnesota.

(**29**) In addition to boating and swimming, many other sports are enjoyed. (**30**) Nearly one person in every five goes hunting each year. (**31**) It is claimed that no other city sells such a large number of fishing licenses. (**32**) Even in the winter, people fish through the ice. (**33**) Huts are dragged out onto frozen lakes. (**34**) Many of them are furnished with carpets and easy chairs to make fishing more comfortable.

(**35**) In spectator sports, citizens of Minneapolis are a hardy lot. (**36**) At National Football League games, when the Minnesota Vikings play, parties are held in the parking lot. (**37**) Even in the snow, fans gather to share refreshments and chat.

(**38**) Every season is good for outdoor sports in the Midwest's "Vacation Capital."

1. Does Minneapolis straddle the Mississippi River?

   Sentence   **(1)**   **(2)**   **(3)**   **(4)**   **(5)**

2. What natural resource played an important role in the quick development of Minneapolis?

   Sentence   **(4)**   **(5)**   **(6)**   **(7)**   **(8)**

3. How many leading millers have headquarters in Minneapolis?

   Sentence   **(8)**   **(9)**   **(10)**   **(11)**   **(12)**

4. Does the location influence any specific industries?

   Sentence   **(10)**   **(11)**   **(12)**   **(13)**   **(14)**

5. Does Minneapolis distribute its products throughout the nation?

   Sentence   **(13)**   **(14)**   **(15)**   **(16)**   **(17)**

6. Is Minneapolis a port?

   Sentence   **(15)**   **(16)**   **(17)**   **(18)**   **(19)**

7. How would one describe Minneapolis during the spring and summer?

   Sentence   **(18)**   **(19)**   **(20)**   **(21)**   **(22)**

8. What is perhaps Minnesota's most famous lake?

   Sentence   **(22)**   **(23)**   **(24)**   **(25)**   **(26)**

9. Does Minnesota exceed any other states in the number of summer cottages per capita?

   Sentence   **(24)**   **(25)**   **(26)**   **(27)**   **(28)**

10. Are boating and swimming popular sports?

    Sentence   **(29)**   **(30)**   **(31)**   **(32)**   **(33)**

UNIT 22
Capital of the Northwest

(1) Seattle is located on the eastern edge of Puget Sound in the state of Washington. (2) It is known as the "Capital of the Northwest," because it is the largest city in the region, as well as the leading industrial, financial, and supply center. (3) Seattle is also known as the "Gateway to the Orient and Alaska," because of the shipping business it conducts with those areas.

(4) The city is blessed with beauty and natural resources. (5) Ocean liners can be glimpsed in Elliot Harbor. (6) All around are tree-covered mountains that remain snow-capped most of the year. (7) Towering above the surrounding peaks, and visible from the city, is 14,410-foot Mount Ranier. (8) The stand of timber in these mountains is one of the richest in the country. (9) As a result, lumbering has become a highly diversified industry in and around Seattle. (10) Much of this lumber is used for structural purposes. (11) The city produces plywood, furniture, office and school supplies, pulp, and paper. (12) Even bark is processed into insulating board. (13) Sawdust becomes fuel briquettes or is fed to cattle.

(14) The Seattle area has cool summers and abundant moisture. (15) During the summer cool air moves in from the Gulf of Alaska. (16) During the winter prevailing winds blow in from warmer latitudes. (17) Only twice has the temperature passed one hundred degrees Fahrenheit, and it has never sunk to zero. (18) Seattle is as far north as St. John's, Newfoundland, yet its temperature permits flowers such as camellias and azaleas to grow.

(19) Power is supplied by hydroelectric plants in the area. (20) The Columbia River, which flows through the state, has a potential of providing one-third of the power for the entire United States. (21) Aluminum, which requires a great deal of power to process, is one of the chief products in the area. (22) Because of the large supply of this metal, Seattle is one of the leading aircraft-building centers in the United States. (23) Thanks to the abundance of power, electric rates are low in Seattle. (24) This has resulted in attracting new industry.

(25) Seattle is one of the leading ports in the nation. (26) It is one day's shipping time closer to Japan than any other American port and is a leader in trade with the Orient. (27) It is also a leader in trade with the Canadian province of British Columbia and with Alaska. (28) The largest fishing fleet on the West Coast can be found in Seattle. (29) In volume of Alaskan king crab, salmon, and halibut brought in, Seattle is a world leader.

(30) Few areas have as many facilities for outdoor recreation. (31) Hunting and both fresh- and saltwater fishing are excellent. (32) In no other place in the world is there as heavy a concentration of pleasure boats. (33) One out of every four adult residents owns a boat. (34) A number of people live on houseboats, many of them quite lavish. (35) During the first two weeks of August, the annual Seafair is held on nearby Lake Washington. (36) This show features water carnivals, boat races, and even hydroplane races.

(37) Downtown Seattle offers many diversions also. (38) A trip on the monorail can whisk you to the Civic Center and the futuristic 607-foot Space Needle observation tower in ninety seconds. (39) The city is ranked among the ten leading cities in the nation by those who rate restaurants. (40) In many ways, life is good in the "Capital of the Northwest."

1. Is Seattle called the "Capital of the Northwest" for more than one reason?

   Sentence   (1)   (2)   (3)   (4)   (5)

2. How does the stand of timber compare with others in the country?

   Sentence   (5)   (6)   (7)   (8)   (9)

3. Is any product of the lumber industry used to feed cattle?

   Sentence   (9)   (10)   (11)   (12)   (13)

4. Where do the prevailing winds come from in the winter?

   Sentence   (14)   (15)   (16)   (17)   (18)

5. What river flows through Washington?

   Sentence   (19)   (20)   (21)   (22)   (23)

6. How does aluminum help Seattle make a significant contribution to modern transportation?

   Sentence   (21)   (22)   (23)   (24)   (25)

7. Is electricity expensive in Seattle?

   Sentence   (23)   (24)   (25)   (26)   (27)

8. Does Seattle have a fishing fleet?

   Sentence   (26)   (27)   (28)   (29)   (30)

9. When is the annual Seafair held?

   Sentence   (31)   (32)   (33)   (34)   (35)

10. Does the Seafair feature any unusual form of transportation?

    Sentence   (36)   (37)   (38)   (39)   (40)

UNIT 23
City on the Move

(1) Atlanta, the capital of Georgia, has been called the "Pacesetter of the South," because it leads that area in industry and transportation. (2) At times Atlanta is known as the "Gate City of the South," because it lies at the extreme end of the Alleghenies. (3) Much east-west traffic passes through the city. (4) Atlanta is also known as the "Phoenix of the South." (5) Even though it was burned to the ground twice, each time it sprang forth anew from the ashes, like the bird of mythology.

(6) Now, because of its growth, Atlanta is known as the "City on the Move." (7) Population in the city and surrounding area is nearing the two million mark—one-third of all Georgia's people. (8) The city is the financial and merchandising center of the Southeast. (9) The Merchandise Mart is America's second largest wholesale showroom under one roof. (10) In the 1960s more new jobs were created here than anywhere else in the nation, and retail sales doubled. (11) Today most of the country's top five hundred corporations have offices in Atlanta. (12) Many black Atlantans have risen to prominent positions in the city's government and corporations, including Maynard Jackson, who was the first black to become mayor of a large southern city.

(13) Why this growth? (14) Following World War II, industry began to move into the Southeast. (15) Northern manufacturers were attracted by climate, lack of congestion, and plentiful available labor. (16) Atlanta, largest city in the largest southeastern state, led in this growth.

(17) Atlanta is a large transportation center. (18) The newly expanded Hartsfield International Airport is the world's largest in floor space and number of gates, and one of the nation's busiest. (19) Only twelve cities have more registered trucks. (20) Atlanta is the southeastern hub of the Interstate Highway System and is the focal point for three major interstate arteries. (21) For over a century it has been the railroad center of the South. (22) It is served by thirteen different railway systems.

(23) Recently Atlanta decided to rebuild its downtown area. (24) The result is one of the most attractive downtown sections in the United States. (25) Skyscrapers soar skyward, including the world's tallest hotel, the seventy-story Peachtree Center Plaza. (26) More than thirty major new buildings have been erected in recent years.

(27) Below the downtown streets lies Underground Atlanta, a restored business district of the city, just as it was before the turn of the century. (28) The streets are lighted by gas. (29) Many charming shops and more than thirty restaurants attract a constant stream of visitors.

(30) Located 1,050 feet above sea level, Atlanta has a climate that encourages year-round sports, including boating and auto racing. (31) The new municipal stadium is home for the Atlanta Braves baseball team and the Atlanta Falcons football team. (32) Atlanta has a sports history that goes back to the city's beginnings. (33) The area, in fact, was won as a trophy by the Creek Indians as a result of a ball game with the Cherokees. (34) Later the land was ceded to the United States government.

(35) Another tourist attraction is Stone Mountain, located fifteen miles east of the city. (36) This is the largest exposed mound of granite in the world. (37) It is five miles in circumference and soars 850 feet above the plains.

(38) Many permanent residents have been attracted from the North. (39) They too want to be part of the "City on the Move."

1. How many times was Atlanta burned to the ground?

   Sentence   **(1)**   **(2)**   **(3)**   **(4)**   **(5)**

2. What is one of America's largest wholesale showrooms under one roof?

   Sentence   **(6)**   **(7)**   **(8)**   **(9)**   **(10)**

3. Who was the first black person to become mayor of Atlanta?

   Sentence   **(10)**   **(11)**   **(12)**   **(13)**   **(14)**

4. What advantages attracted northern manufacturers?

   Sentence   **(13)**   **(14)**   **(15)**   **(16)**   **(17)**

5. What place has Atlanta had in the growth experienced by the Southeast?

   Sentence   **(15)**   **(16)**   **(17)**   **(18)**   **(19)**

6. Is Atlanta a focal point for major interstate arteries?

   Sentence   **(17)**   **(18)**   **(19)**   **(20)**   **(21)**

7. What word best describes Atlanta's downtown section?

   Sentence   **(21)**   **(22)**   **(23)**   **(24)**   **(25)**

8. What is found beneath the downtown streets?

   Sentence   **(26)**   **(27)**   **(28)**   **(29)**   **(30)**

9. Is Atlanta above sea level?

   Sentence   **(29)**   **(30)**   **(31)**   **(32)**   **(33)**

10. Who later got the land won by the Creeks?

    Sentence   **(34)**   **(35)**   **(36)**   **(37)**   **(38)**

UNIT 24
Enchanting City

(1) Santa Fe has been called the most unique city in America. (2) This colorful, enchanting city is located in the heart of New Mexico, "Land of Enchantment." (3) Santa Fe enjoys a special distinction: it is the oldest state capital still in existence.

(4) This city's history is as rich and colorful as its appearance. (5) Before Spanish colonists arrived in the early 1600s, Pueblo Indians (Native Americans) lived in the area. (6) Several Pueblo communities still exist. (7) After Mexico won its independence from Spain in 1821, Santa Fe became the capital of a Mexican province. (8) In 1830 New Mexico became a United States territory, and in 1912 it was officially granted statehood. (9) Santa Fe's Spanish and Mexican roots are still very evident and continually attract new residents as well as visitors.

(10) Trade was a key factor in Santa Fe's early development. (11) During the 1800s Santa Fe was at the western end of the Santa Fe Trail. (12) First used only by pack horses, this trail later became the route taken by wagons for travel and trade between Santa Fe and Independence, Missouri. (13) Other important trading centers were located along the trail in Colorado, Kansas, and Arkansas. (14) In the 1860s and 1870s railroads gave Santa Fe's economy a huge boost. (15) When railroad trade developed between the eastern United States and Mexico, Santa Fe became a natural stopping and trading point.

(16) Today government jobs employ most of Santa Fe's approximately fifty thousand residents. (17) Many people also work in the tourist trade. (18) Unlike some modern cities, Santa Fe has deliberately kept its historic appearance and charm intact. (19) The narrow, winding streets are still dotted with adobe dwellings. (20) *Adobe* is the Spanish name for sun-dried bricks or houses built with these bricks.

(21) Visitors come for the beauty of the town as well as for the natural beauty of the land around it. (22) Santa Fe is at the edge of the Rio Grande River basin and at the foothills of the Southern Rocky Mountains. (23) At over 6,950 feet above sea level, it is one of the highest cities in America. (24) Spectacular sunsets and richly colored mountains thrill visitors and residents alike.

(25) The nearby pueblos, where the Pueblo people live, also attract many visitors. (26) *Pueblo* means "community" or "village" in Spanish. (27) There are nineteen of these pueblos in New Mexico and over half of them are near Santa Fe. (28) The authentic Native American dancing and craftmaking fascinate the visitors who flock to these villages.

(29) Because Santa Fe has been and still is home to many artists, people often come here just to see the art. (30) It is not surprising, then, that Santa Fe is also home to many museums and over a hundred art galleries. (31) And, as a special form of Native American art, pottery has long flourished here. (32) In addition, the city's outdoor opera is a popular warm-weather event, and in the nearby mountains skiing can be enjoyed almost all year round.

(33) The charms of Santa Fe are varied and numerous. (34) Visitors come to see Native American pueblos. (35) Others are lured by the unique artwork. (36) Nature lovers come for the color and splendor of the scenery. (37) Whatever their interests, most people find even more than what they were looking for in Santa Fe!

UNIT 24
Enchanting City

1. Has Santa Fe been described as unique?

   Sentence   (**1**)   (**2**)   (**3**)   (**4**)   (**5**)

2. Who lived in the area before the early 1600s?

   Sentence   (**4**)   (**5**)   (**6**)   (**7**)   (**8**)

3. What factor was a key to Santa Fe's early development?

   Sentence   (**10**)   (**11**)   (**12**)   (**13**)   (**14**)

4. Where was Santa Fe on the Santa Fe Trail?

   Sentence   (**11**)   (**12**)   (**13**)   (**14**)   (**15**)

5. Who employs most of Santa Fe's citizens?

   Sentence   (**16**)   (**17**)   (**18**)   (**19**)   (**20**)

6. What river is Santa Fe near?

   Sentence   (**18**)   (**19**)   (**20**)   (**21**)   (**22**)

7. How high above sea level is Santa Fe?

   Sentence   (**23**)   (**24**)   (**25**)   (**26**)   (**27**)

8. What fascinates visitors to the pueblos?

   Sentence   (**25**)   (**26**)   (**27**)   (**28**)   (**29**)

9. Are there many art galleries in Santa Fe?

   Sentence   (**29**)   (**30**)   (**31**)   (**32**)   (**33**)

10. What is a popular outdoor musical event?

    Sentence   (**32**)   (**33**)   (**34**)   (**35**)   (**36**)

(**1**) Baltimore was named after Lord Baltimore, founder of the colony of Maryland. (**2**) The city began as a small port on Chesapeake Bay, established to help local tobacco growers get their product to European markets. (**3**) But shippers quickly noted that the port was sheltered on the tidewater and was free from ice and storms. (**4**) In time these factors made the port more important than the tobacco crop itself.

(**5**) Today more than 51 million tons of cargo move through the thriving port of Baltimore each year. (**6**) The city is the fourth largest port on the East Coast and is sixth largest in the nation.

(**7**) Because it lies closer to the Midwest than any other eastern seaport does, Baltimore is a transportation center. (**8**) Cargoes are sped to and from the Midwest and other points by a network of railways. (**9**) Baltimore is an important railroad center. (**10**) It had forged to the front in this area by the 1850s. (**11**) Fifty trucklines help to move the mountains of cargo that pass through here yearly.

(**12**) Baltimore is the eleventh largest city in the nation. (**13**) Over half of its workers are engaged in manufacturing. (**14**) The area's leading industry is steel. (**15**) In colonial times iron was discovered in the area. (**16**) The fashioning of muskets and cannonballs for the Revolutionary War led to Baltimore becoming an important steel center. (**17**) The city is the home of one of the largest steel mills in the world.

(**18**) Grateful merchants of the past century made important contributions to their city. (**19**) Johns Hopkins left $7 million for a new university and hospital. (**20**) Today the school of medicine and the hospital make up one of the world's leading medical centers. (**21**) The center specializes in cancer research.

(**22**) Until a great fire in 1904, the appearance of Baltimore had changed little over the decades. (**23**) Vast areas consisted of rows of Georgian brick homes with white marble steps. (**24**) The ritual was born for Baltimore citizens to scrub their steps regularly. (**25**) Some of these homes still exist and give parts of the city the appearance of London.

(**26**) Baltimore is a famous seafood port. (**27**) Oysters from Chesapeake Bay are highly prized. (**28**) Other favorite delicacies are Maryland soft-shell crab and diamondback terrapin. (**29**) An especially popular place to enjoy these and other seafoods is the city's newly revitalized waterfront, with its promenade and pavilions.

(**30**) Baltimore is rich in history. (**31**) In the War of 1812, American privateers from the city harassed the British. (**32**) In retaliation, the British attempted to burn the city. (**33**) After a spirited battle at Fort McHenry, the British were repulsed. (**34**) During the battle the American flag at the fort survived a twenty-five-hour bombardment. (**35**) The sight of this flag still waving inspired an onlooker named Francis Scott Key to write "The Star-Spangled Banner."

(**36**) Defenders in the battle were honored with the construction of the Battle Monument two years after the war. (**37**) This is America's first major war memorial. (**38**) Baltimore is also the home of the first Washington Monument, erected in 1815. (**39**) Fittingly, Baltimore is known as the "Monumental City."

UNIT 25
Monumental City

1. How did Baltimore help local tobacco farmers?

   Sentence   **(1)**   **(2)**   **(3)**   **(4)**   **(5)**

2. Was Baltimore a sheltered port?

   Sentence   **(3)**   **(4)**   **(5)**   **(6)**   **(7)**

3. How does the location of Baltimore make it a transportation center?

   Sentence   **(5)**   **(6)**   **(7)**   **(8)**   **(9)**

4. When did Baltimore become an important railroad center?

   Sentence   **(7)**   **(8)**   **(9)**   **(10)**   **(11)**

5. How many of Baltimore's people work in manufacturing?

   Sentence   **(12)**   **(13)**   **(14)**   **(15)**   **(16)**

6. What action aided medical science?

   Sentence   **(16)**   **(17)**   **(18)**   **(19)**   **(20)**

7. Does Baltimore resemble London in any way?

   Sentence   **(21)**   **(22)**   **(23)**   **(24)**   **(25)**

8. Has the port of Baltimore become well known for anything other than steel?

   Sentence   **(26)**   **(27)**   **(28)**   **(29)**   **(30)**

9. Was Francis Scott Key a participant in the battle of Fort McHenry?

   Sentence   **(31)**   **(32)**   **(33)**   **(34)**   **(35)**

10. Where is the first Washington Monument located?

    Sentence   **(35)**   **(36)**   **(37)**   **(38)**   **(39)**

In Units 20 through 25, you read passages that gave a lot of information about the cities of New York, Minneapolis, Seattle, Atlanta, Sante Fe, and Baltimore. Information is sometimes visually summarized on graphs. Two types of graphs are line graphs and circle graphs.

A **line graph** shows how information changes over a period of time or from situation to situation.

Example: Rainfall in Midtown

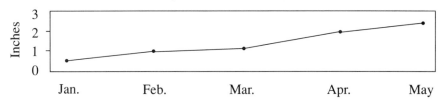

A **circle graph** shows the percentage that each part takes up in a whole.

Example: Colors in Midtown Flag

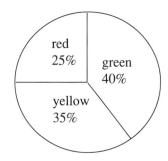

A. Exercising Your Skill

You could organize this type of daily information on a graph: the average amount of time spent doing homework over a five-day period. What other types of day-to-day information could you organize on graphs? Would a line or a circle graph be best for each example? List a few examples on your paper. Compare your list with your classmates' lists. See if they thought of any examples that you did not think of.

B. Expanding Your Skill

Decide which type of graph should be used to organize the following items of information. List the number of each item under the heading *Line* or *Circle* on your paper. Then compare your lists with your classmates' lists.

1. number of students playing after-school sports over a four-month period
2. percentage of students in a class reading each of five possible books for a book report
3. amount of space taken up by each of ten types of vegetables in a garden
4. number of pottery pieces found in each of four sites
5. amount of a budget given over to each of five areas of spending

C. Exploring Language

Look at the line graph below. On your paper, write three or four sentences that say in words what the graph shows.

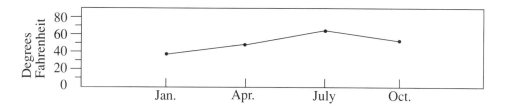

Average Temperature in Seattle

Study the circle graph below. On your paper, write three or four sentences describing what the graph shows.

Types of Pets Owned by Students

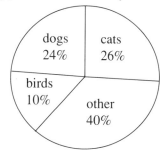

D. Expressing Yourself

Choose one of these activities.

1. Make up a circle graph showing the following types of information about yourself: in a twenty-four hour period, the percentage of time spent sleeping, eating, in school, with family, playing, reading, watching TV. Use real percentages, or make them up.

2. With a partner, use a social studies or geography book that you both have. Find a passage with some facts that can be organized on a line or a circle graph. Prepare the graph together.

Book D

Specific Skill Series

Getting the Facts

Richard A. Boning

Fifth Edition

SRA/McGraw-Hill
Columbus, Ohio

Cover, Back Cover, Kennan Ward/The Stock Market

SRA/McGraw-Hill

A Division of The **McGraw·Hill** *Companies*

Send all inquiries to:
    SRA/McGraw-Hill
    8787 Orion Place
    Columbus, OH 43240-4027

ISBN 0-02-687964-6

10 11 12 IPC 03 02 01

To the Teacher

PURPOSE:
GETTING THE FACTS is designed to develop skill in recalling factual information from a single reading. The material is structured so that there is no "turning back" for the answer. The story is on one side; the questions are on the reverse. Readers must take as much as they can from one reading. The knowledge that they cannot turn back to the story helps them gain skill in GETTING THE FACTS.

FOR WHOM:
The skill of GETTING THE FACTS is developed through a series of books spanning ten levels (Picture, Preparatory, A, B, C, D, E, F, G, H). The Picture Level is for pupils who have not acquired a basic sight vocabulary. The Preparatory Level is for pupils who have a basic sight vocabulary but are not quite ready for the first-grade-level book. Books A through H are appropriate for pupils who can read on levels one through eight, respectively. **The use of the *Specific Skill Series Placement Test* is recommended to determine the appropriate level.**

THE NEW EDITION:
The fifth edition of the *Specific Skill Series* maintains the quality and focus that has distinguished this program for more than 25 years. A key element central to the program's success has been the unique nature of the reading selections. Nonfiction pieces about current topics have been designed to stimulate the interest of students, motivating them to use the comprehension strategies they have learned to further their reading. To keep this important aspect of the program intact, a percentage of the reading selections have been replaced in order to ensure the continued relevance of the subject material.

In addition, a significant percentage of the artwork in the program has been replaced to give the books a contemporary look. The cover photographs are designed to appeal to readers of all ages.

SESSIONS:
Short practice sessions are the most effective. It is desirable to have a practice session every day or every other day, using a few units each session.

To the Teacher

SCORING:

Pupils should record their answers on the reproducible worksheets. The worksheets make scoring easier and provide uniform records of the pupils' work. Using worksheets also avoids consuming the exercise books.

It is important for pupils to know how well they are doing. For this reason, units should be scored as soon as they have been completed. Then a discussion can be held in which pupils justify their choices. (The Integrated Language Activities, many of which are open-ended, do not lend themselves to an objective score; thus there are no answer keys for these pages.)

GENERAL INFORMATION ON *GETTING THE FACTS*:

GETTING THE FACTS varies in content. It contains stories about mysteries and unexplained happenings, remarkable people, and odd customs. It was the author's intention to include stories that would help stretch the imagination, spark new hobbies, promote admiration for outstanding achievements, and develop a sense of wonder about our world. Interest ratings were obtained from junior and senior high students as well as elementary school pupils. The stories included in GETTING THE FACTS are those to which the readers reacted most strongly.

There is only one correct answer for each question. The incorrect answers may very well be true and make sense. The readers may know that they are true from their own experiences. The only correct answer choice, however, is the one that is stated in the story. GETTING THE FACTS means getting the facts from a particular story. It really means knowing whether or not something was stated. This must be made clear to pupils.

SUGGESTED STEPS:

1. Pupils read the story. (In the Picture Level books, the pupils look at the pictures.)
2. After completing the story, pupils turn to the questions on the reverse side and choose the letters of the correct answers.
3. Pupils write the letters of the correct answers on the worksheets.
4. Pupils may return to the story only after their answers have been recorded and scored.

RELATED MATERIALS:

Specific Skill Series Placement Tests, which enable the teacher to place pupils at their appropriate levels in each skill, are available for the Elementary (Pre-1–6) and Midway (4–8) grade levels.

About This Book

A **fact** is something that can be proved true. It is something that can be checked. These statements are facts.

- The earth is 92.9 million miles from the sun.
- George Washington was born on February 22, 1732.

There are facts in everything you read. Read this paragraph:

There are trees that really walk. They grow in Florida. These trees have long roots that reach out like legs. As the roots grow out, they pull the tree along.

These are facts from the paragraph:

- There are trees that walk.
- They grow in Florida.
- They have long roots that reach out like legs.
- The roots pull the tree along.

A short piece of writing that presents facts on one subject is called an *article*. Reading an article for facts is not the same as reading a story just for fun. You should read more slowly when you are reading to find out new information. To understand the information, you may need to figure out the meanings of new words. To remember the facts, you may need to read part of the article again.

In this book, you will read articles on many different subjects. After you have read an article, turn the page to find ten questions about it. The correct answers to the questions are facts from the article. The incorrect answers may be true and make sense, but the only correct answer choice is the one that is stated in the article. "Getting the Facts" means getting the facts from a particular article. Only by reading the article carefully can you answer the questions correctly.

CONTENTS

UNIT 1
Salty Waters

Can you imagine tying rocks to your feet so you won't drown? Imagine water so "thick" that a swimmer would float like a cork. Then why the rocks? You'd need the rocks to keep from tipping over and floating head down. Does this sound like a tall tale, a legend from the distant past? It isn't! The "thick" water is in the Dead Sea, a salt lake that lies on the border between Israel and Jordan. It is set in a deep valley, with golden-brown walls rising 4,000 feet above it.

From the air, the Dead Sea looks like a sparkling blue lake about fifty miles long and ten miles wide. It contains the saltiest water on earth. It is so salty that few people would care to swim in it.

The Dead Sea is so salty that no fish or plants can live in it. One legend says that the air above the Dead Sea will kill birds that fly overhead. That's not true. The air above the Dead Sea is perfectly safe. However, few birds would bother to fly over it—after all, it contains nothing for them to eat!

How did the Dead Sea get to be so salty? Imagine fresh water flowing into a lake. Once the water is in the lake, it has nowhere to go because the lake is at the lowest point on earth. Then imagine the sun beating down. Some of the water evaporates, changes from a liquid into a gas. The water started out with tiny amounts of salt in it. Almost all water has some salt, which it picks up from the ground. Now imagine this process happening for thousands of years. The water keeps coming in and then evaporating. The salt stays behind. The water that stays behind grows more and more salty.

What good is the Dead Sea if nothing grows in it and nobody goes there for vacation? The edges of the sea contain some valuable minerals. These are dug up and sold.

1. The water in the Dead Sea is very—

   (A) thin   (B) thick   (C) cold

2. Swimmers in the Dead Sea would—

   (A) float   (B) sink   (C) sing

3. This is because the Dead Sea contains a lot of—

   (A) ice   (B) dirt   (C) salt

4. From the air, the Dead Sea looks like a—

   (A) pile of salt   (B) blue lake   (C) huge ocean

5. The Dead Sea is about—

   (A) 10 miles long   (B) 4,000 feet deep   (C) 50 miles long

6. The Dead Sea contains no—

   (A) water or rocks   (B) salt   (C) fish or plants

7. A bird flying over the Dead Sea would—

   (A) be killed   (B) find no food   (C) see no water

8. Fresh water contains tiny amounts of—

   (A) iron   (B) animals   (C) salt

9. When water evaporates, salt—

   (A) stays behind   (B) also evaporates   (C) turns to stone

10. The edges of the Dead Sea contain—

    (A) gold   (B) minerals   (C) trees

UNIT 2
The Beautiful Road

Today we repair or replace roads every few years. The Inca civilization built their road system to last. And they built it over five hundred years ago.

The Inca civilization was in the Andes Mountains in South America. They lived in what is now Peru. Their empire stretched for thousands of miles. They went everywhere on foot, so they built five thousand miles of roadway.

The main Inca road was called Capac Nan. This means "Beautiful Road." It was paved and had gutters and curbs. It was lined with trees to provide shade for travelers. The road went along high mountain ridges, through deep valleys, and across bridges over rivers.

The main branch of Capac Nan covered the same distance as that from London to New York. Much of the system is crumbling today. But some parts of it can still be traveled in comfort.

The Incas used their road to get important news to all parts of their empire. The news was delivered by runners. The runners were trained from the time they were children. They had to learn to run fast at high altitudes with little oxygen.

The runners were set up in relay systems. Each one would run about two miles and then give his news to the next runner. The runners could cover about 250 miles each day. This is about the same rate as the Pony Express traveled in the United States. But the Pony Express used—you guessed it—horses!

UNIT 2
The Beautiful Road

1. The Inca people lived in the—

   (A) Andes   (B) Rockies   (C) Alps

2. The country of Peru is in—

   (A) Europe   (B) South America   (C) England

3. The Incas traveled on—

   (A) carts   (B) foot   (C) boats

4. Trees were planted along the road to provide—

   (A) fruit   (B) firewood   (C) shade

5. The Inca road covered thousands of—

   (A) miles   (B) valleys   (C) gutters

6. The Incas delivered news by—

   (A) runners   (B) horse   (C) radio

7. The runners started their training as—

   (A) teenagers   (B) children   (C) adults

8. At high altitudes, there was little—

   (A) oxygen   (B) shelter   (C) food

9. Each runner would pass his news to the next runner after two—

   (A) miles   (B) days   (C) naps

10. The Inca runner system could cover 250 miles each—

    (A) week   (B) day   (C) hour

UNIT 3
The Biggest Creature of All

Can you name the largest animal that has ever lived? Is it the elephant? Or is it the extinct animal of long ago, the dinosaur? If you chose either one, you're wrong. The largest animal that has ever lived on Earth is alive today. It is the great blue whale.

An adult blue whale is longer than two city buses. Its heart is the size of a taxicab. It can weigh as much as 170,000 tons. To feed its enormous body, the blue whale takes in forty-five tons of water at a gulp. It then strains the water through hundreds of bony plates to take out three to four tons of krill, its food, each day.

Blubber is a whale's fat. In the blue whale, the blubber may equal one third of the animal's total weight. The blubber is rich in oil, which is why people have hunted the blue whale for so long.

Surprisingly, though the blue whale is huge, it is not slow. It was able to outrun sailing ships for 300 years. Then steamships allowed whale hunters to catch up to the giant. So many blue whales were killed that the species almost became extinct. Now blue whales are protected and biologists believe they are making a comeback.

Scientists have reported seeing blue whales off the California coast. These whales are not as easy to find as those that sing, jump, or travel in large packs. Still, anyone who does spot a blue whale thinks the day has been a success!

UNIT 3
The Biggest Creature of All

1. The largest animal that has ever lived is the—

   (A) dinosaur   (B) elephant   (C) blue whale

2. The largest animal that has ever lived is—

   (A) on land   (B) alive today   (C) not living today

3. The blue whale is longer than—

   (A) two city buses   (B) ten trains   (C) a mile

4. The blue whale takes in water at the rate of—

   (A) 170 tons   (B) 45 tons   (C) 4 tons

5. The blue whale eats—

   (A) blubber   (B) oil   (C) krill

6. Blubber is a whale's—

   (A) fat   (B) skin   (C) fins

7. People have hunted the blue whale for its—

   (A) oil   (B) krill   (C) song

8. It surprises people to learn that the huge blue whale is—

   (A) fast   (B) fat   (C) sleepy

9. Whalers started catching blue whales when they had—

   (A) submarines   (B) steamships   (C) canoes

10. Blue whale numbers are increasing because they are—

    (A) having twins   (B) hunted   (C) protected

UNIT 4
Floating Giants

Icebergs are "born" in the coldest parts of the world. There the land is covered with ice. The ice moves slowly over the land to the sea. The waves of the sea break off huge pieces of ice. These pieces are new icebergs. They are ready to start lives of their own. This is how icebergs are "born."

Not all icebergs are the same size. Some are only twenty or thirty feet long. Others are as large as mountains. The largest icebergs are seventy or even eighty miles long. These icy giants may reach five hundred feet into the sky. This is as high as a fifty-story building. No wonder icebergs are often called "floating giants."

We can see only a small part of an iceberg. Most of it is hidden under the water. The part under the water is nine times as large as the part above the water. That is why a ship can never sail too close to an iceberg. The part of the iceberg hidden under the water could rip open the bottom of the ship and make it sink. Icebergs have also been known to roll over. Who would want to be caught underneath? An iceberg may weigh as much as ten thousand elephants!

Icebergs may live for many years. Those that float around in the coldest water often live for fifty or even a hundred years. Those icebergs that drift into warmer water have shorter lives. They melt after only a few years.

The great white mountains of ice split in two when they melt. Cracking icebergs sound like thunder. The sound can be heard many miles away. Perhaps it is the floating giant's way of saying, "Get one last look, everybody. I'm starting to melt!"

UNIT 4
Floating Giants

1. Icebergs are "born" where the land is covered with—

    (A) ice   (B) water   (C) boats

2. Ice moves over the land—

    (A) quickly   (B) slowly   (C) sadly

3. Large pieces of ice are broken off by—

    (A) waves   (B) wind   (C) whales

4. Icebergs are—

    (A) small   (B) not all the same   (C) mountains
    size

5. The longest icebergs are—

    (A) eight feet   (B) eight miles   (C) eighty miles

6. Most of an iceberg is—

    (A) growing   (B) hidden   (C) above the water

7. In very cold water, icebergs may live—

    (A) one year   (B) 100 years   (C) 500 years

8. Icebergs that drift into warm water may live—

    (A) a few years   (B) 100 years   (C) forever

9. When icebergs melt, they often split—

    (A) forward   (B) in front   (C) in two

10. When icebergs split, they sound like—

    (A) waves   (B) thunder   (C) babies

UNIT 5
Funny Money

Money! What do you "see" when you hear this word? Do you picture a round metal coin? Do you think of paper money? Most likely you think of one or the other. The money we see and use is made of paper or metal. But the money of long ago was not at all like the money we use today.

Coins were not always made of metal. Soap was once money to the people of Mexico. Lumps of coal were used as coins by the people of England. Stone money was used on the Pacific Ocean island of Yap.

Even food was used as money. In Russia, "coins" of cheese could be used to buy things. Bricks of tea leaves were used as money in Tibet. The tea leaves were first boiled in water. They were then pressed into hard brick shapes.

Coins were not always round. The coins of old China were once in the shape of a knife. In another land coins were made in the shape of a fish. Square money is still used by the people of India. Money in the shapes of rings and bracelets is also still seen in some parts of the world. Ring money is easy to carry.

Did you ever hear anyone say, "Money doesn't grow on trees"? Is it true? Did money ever grow on trees? In far-off Malaysia, people once made their own small trees out of tin. Small, round tin coins were joined to the trunk of the tin-money trees. People just broke off the money they needed! Wouldn't it be nice if all people had money trees of their own?

1. The money we see and use today is made of—

    (A) wood   **(B) gold**   **(C) paper or metal**

2. Soap was once used as money by the people of—

    (A) Mexico   **(B) Canada**   **(C) Ireland**

3. People in England once used money made of—

    (A) coffee   **(B) sugar**   **(C) coal**

4. Stone money was used by the people of—

    (A) India   **(B) England**   **(C) Yap**

5. In Russia, coins were once made of—

    (A) monkeys   **(B) cheese**   **(C) bread**

6. Before tea leaves were made into money, they were—

    (A) eaten   **(B) baked**   **(C) boiled**

7. Coins of old China were once made in the shape of—

    (A) knives   **(B) sheep**   **(C) cars**

8. In India we can still find—

    (A) wet money   **(B) fat coins**   **(C) square coins**

9. Ring money is easy to—

    (A) make   **(B) carry**   **(C) eat**

10. The people of one country once made—

    (A) money trees   **(B) money games**   **(C) stones**

UNIT 6
How to Get There from Here

You know how important a map is to show you where things are. Early civilizations thought maps were important, too. The oldest map on record gives the outlines of a person's estate. Perhaps he wanted everyone to know which land was his.

Mapmaking became more important when people started exploring. If travelers kept maps of where they had been, the trip would be easier for the next person. Unfortunately, early maps were not very scientific. People did not know what lay across the seas or over the next mountain. They imagined the seas to be full of monsters that would sink ships. Often a mapmaker would draw these so-called monsters right on a map.

Early maps were made from available materials. The Arctic people used both dark and light colored animal skins. They cut the shapes of their islands from the dark skins. Then they sewed the shapes to the large, light skin, representing the ocean. South Pacific islanders used shells and bits of coral to represent their islands on maps.

Early mapmakers disagreed about which directions were important. Some put east at the top of their maps, because the sun rises from that direction. Others put the direction of the prevailing winds at the top. Winds were very important to sailors.

In the second century A.D. an Egyptian named Ptolemy began to improve mapmaking. He moved it from art into science. First, he put north at the top of his maps. And, as an astronomer, he based his maps on a round Earth. He tried to make the distances between lands on a map more accurate. Ptolemy's maps were so good that they were still used hundreds of years after his death.

1. The earliest recorded map shows a person's—

   (A) ship   (B) island   (C) estate

2. Mapmaking became more important because of—

   (A) drawing   (B) exploring   (C) astronomy

3. Early maps were not very—

   (A) artistic   (B) interesting   (C) scientific

4. Some people imagined that ships were sunk by—

   (A) monsters   (B) storms   (C) rocks

5. The Arctic people used dark animal skins to represent—

   (A) the ocean   (B) islands   (C) monsters

6. Early mapmakers had different ideas about—

   (A) direction   (B) winds   (C) sailing

7. Some thought east was the most important because of—

   (A) sunset   (B) sunrise   (C) eclipses

8. The direction of the prevailing winds was important to—

   (A) sailors   (B) islanders   (C) artists

9. Ptolemy's map skills grew from his work as an—

   (A) Egyptian   (B) astronomer   (C) Inuit

10. Ptolemy determined that the direction at the top of a map should be—

    (A) north   (B) east   (C) winds

In Unit 5 you read about different kinds of money. Some money is made of metal, but other money has been made from stone, coal, tea, and even cheese. Think about the money you use. What is it made of? What colors and shapes does it have? Then read the following paragraph about money.

Money is a useful tool for buying things. Without money, we would have to use other things—work, products we had made, or foods we had grown—to trade for things we wanted. What makes money work? Money must have a value of its own. Some of the first coins were made of very rare and expensive metals, like gold and silver. It was easy to carry a few coins that might be worth a whole cow or a day's work. These days, few coins are actually made of rare and expensive metals. In fact, much of our money is made of paper.

A. Exercising Your Skill

Answer these questions about the paragraph you just read.

1. What is most money made out of today?
2. What must money have in order to make it work?
3. What could we use for trading if we didn't have money?
4. What were some of the first coins made out of?
5. What is one reason why money is useful for spending rather than for trading?

B. Expanding Your Skill

United States Presidents from the past are pictured on some coins and on paper money. Find out who some of these Presidents are and which kinds of money their faces appear on. On your paper, make a list of the names you find out about. Beside each name, write the name of the coin or bill that carries that President's picture.

C. Exploring Language

Look at the fronts and backs of three different coins. What words are printed on the front of every coin? Write the words on your paper. What words are printed on the back of every coin? Write these words. See if you can find out what the non-English words (a national **motto**) mean. Look up the entry for this motto in a big dictionary. Write what the motto means and what language it is printed in.

Now choose one coin and write a description of it. Include details about its color, shape, and size, and about the pictures and words printed on it.

D. Expressing Yourself

Choose one of these things.

1. Choose one of the kinds of "funny money" you learned about in Unit 5. It could be the cheese money of Russia, Malayan coins from the trunk of a tin-money tree, or some other kind of money. Write three or four sentences describing this money—what it is made of, what it looks like, and what you imagine it might have been worth in terms of what a person might have been able to get in exchange for it.

2. Role-play a "trade" with a partner. You have a certain kind of money (one of the kinds you read about or a kind you invent for the skit). Your partner has a product or service you want to buy. Act out how you would bargain with each other during this "trading" situation.

3. Design your own money system. What would the money be made of? What would it look like? Would your money system include something called "coins," or would you call these things something else? What name would you give each "coin"? Draw pictures of the different kinds of money in your money system. Write a sentence or two about each picture, explaining what the money is and what its value is.

UNIT 7
The Elephant Bird

The first people who visited Africa came back with strange stories. Their stories were about a giant bird. The name of the bird was the elephant bird.

The elephant bird was very large. One story told how it could eat baby elephants. Another story told how the bird would drop rocks on ships that passed by. Still another story told of how the bird carried a person away in its claws! People liked to hear such stories, but not all of them were true. People began to wonder. Was the elephant bird real? "No bird could grow that large," people said.

Today we know for a fact that the elephant bird really did live. How do we know? Bones of the bird have been found. The bones were dug out of the ground on the island of Madagascar, off the east coast of Africa. Eggshells of the elephant bird have also been found.

The bones show that the elephant bird was a giant, taller than the tallest human being. It was ten feet high. It was also very heavy. An elephant bird often weighed a thousand pounds. The eggs of the elephant bird were the largest eggs ever laid—the size of basketballs. People who find the eggshells today make them into water jugs. The jugs can hold over eight quarts of water.

No one knows how the elephant bird got its name. We do know that it was too heavy to fly, so not all the stories about it are true. Did it really eat baby elephants? We do not know, but why do you think it was called the elephant bird?

UNIT 7
The Elephant Bird

1. The elephant bird was said to feed on—

    (A) grass   (B) baby elephants   (C) horses

2. The elephant bird was said to drop rocks on—

    (A) homes   (B) people   (C) ships

3. The stories about the bird were—

    (A) disliked   (B) all true   (C) not all true

4. Bones of the elephant bird have been—

    (A) found   (B) made   (C) painted

5. The elephant bird lived near—

    (A) China   (B) New York   (C) Africa

6. The elephant bird was taller than the tallest—

    (A) human   (B) tree   (C) building

7. The elephant bird weighed—

    (A) 1,000 pounds   (B) 100 pounds   (C) 2,000 pounds

8. The egg of the elephant bird was as large as a—

    (A) mountain   (B) river   (C) basketball

9. Eggshells of the elephant bird are used for—

    (A) holding food   (B) washing babies   (C) water jugs

10. No one knows how the elephant bird got its—

    (A) nest   (B) name   (C) food

UNIT 8
Is Anything Down There?

What is it that swims in Loch Ness? No one knows. Those who have seen it, or say they have seen it, call it "the monster." They have named it the Loch Ness Monster.

Loch Ness is a long and very deep lake in Scotland. Since the year 565, many people there have told of seeing a strange animal with a long, snakelike neck and a small head. Most of those who have seen it say the Loch Ness Monster is dark, has a hump like a camel, and is about fifty feet long.

Some people have taken pictures of the beast. However, none of the pictures came out clearly, and one film that was said to be of the monster turned out to be a fake. But the pictures do seem to show a dark animal with a long neck, a small head, and a long body.

Some people think that the "thing" in Loch Ness is a rock or a log floating in the lake. "But how can a rock swim?" ask those who believe in the monster. "Besides, do rocks or logs have necks and heads?" Some say it is not a rock or log, but only a seal. Those who have seen the creature say that no seal ever grew that big. Scientists have taken pictures underwater but have found nothing.

Perhaps we will never know what it is that lives in the waters of Loch Ness. Maybe it is a monster. Maybe it is not. Someday you might be lucky enough to get a close look at the thing in the lake. Perhaps you will be sitting in a boat just a few feet from the monster as it rises out of the water!

1. People have seen the monster since the year—
   (A) 1622   (B) 1799   (C) 565

2. The monster has been seen by over—
   (A) 1,000 people   (B) 10 monsters   (C) 1,000 children

3. The neck of the monster is said to be—
   (A) green   (B) long   (C) short

4. People who see the monster say it has—
   (A) a fat head   (B) a small head   (C) no head

5. The monster is said to be about—
   (A) twenty-five feet   (B) fifteen feet   (C) fifty feet

6. The pictures taken of the monster—
   (A) are clear   (B) were never taken   (C) are not clear

7. Some people think that the monster is a—
   (A) rock   (B) boat   (C) person

8. Other people say the monster is a—
   (A) giant bird   (B) seal   (C) snake

9. Some people say it could not be a seal because a seal is—
   (A) dark   (B) too big   (C) much smaller

10. Perhaps someday you will see the monster—
    (A) up close   (B) far away   (C) eat its meal

UNIT 9
Little Rocket of the Airways

Everything about the hummingbird is small. The egg from which it is hatched is about the size of a jellybean. The nest in which it is born is the size of a walnut. A baby hummingbird is only the size of a bee. When fully grown, it is all of two inches long and weighs less than a penny. It weighs so little that it can stand on a blade of grass and the grass hardly bends!

No bird can match the hummingbird in flight. It can hang in midair without moving up or down, backward or forward. The long, strong wings move so quickly that they can hardly be seen. By studying them in slow motion, scientists know their wings beat more than sixty times each second. You can hear them. They make a humming sound. That is how the hummingbird got its name.

The hummingbird is as fast as it is small. It zips, dips, and darts at speeds greater than fifty miles an hour. It can fly backward or sideways and can rise straight into the air like a little rocket. The bird has been known to fly five hundred miles without stopping for rest.

The hummingbird is a fearless fighter. It will pick fights with birds of all sizes. It is as likely to go after a crow or a hawk as a moth or a bee. It will fly at its enemies like a bullet, using its sharp bill as a weapon.

Hummingbirds spend most of their time in the air. Their feet are weak and not meant for walking. But then, a bird is born to fly—and no bird can fly like the little rocket of the airways, the hummingbird.

UNIT 9
Little Rocket of the Airways

1. The hummingbird's egg is the size of a—

   (A) **jellybean**   (B) **pea**   (C) **watermelon**

2. A hummingbird's nest is the size of—

   (A) **an ant**   (B) **a bird**   (C) **a walnut**

3. The hummingbird weighs less than—

   (A) **nothing**   (B) **a penny**   (C) **a drop**

4. The hummingbird's wings beat sixty times each—

   (A) **minute**   (B) **hour**   (C) **second**

5. The wings of the hummingbird make a—

   (A) **burning sound**   (B) **humming sound**   (C) **crying sound**

6. Hummingbirds can fly faster than—

   (A) **50 miles an hour**   (B) **lightning**   (C) **airplanes**

7. Hummingbirds take nonstop flights of—

   (A) **fancy**   (B) **500 miles**   (C) **1,000 miles**

8. The hummingbird likes to—

   (A) **sing**   (B) **walk**   (C) **fight**

9. The hummingbird uses its pointed bill as a—

   (A) **spoon**   (B) **bullet**   (C) **weapon**

10. Of all the birds, the hummingbird is the best—

    (A) **worker**   (B) **flyer**   (C) **eater**

UNIT 10
Island of the Past

Did you ever wonder what it was like to live in the old days? There is a place where you can find out. It is called Mackinac Island.

On this island, instead of "Beep, beep!" you hear "Clippety clop," "Giddyap!" and "Whoa!" on the streets. No automobiles are allowed. Many people ride in horse-drawn carriages. The people like it this way—just as it was in the old days.

Mackinac Island is in the American Great Lakes. Many people spend summer vacations there because of the island's beautiful trees and sandy beaches. But they go there also to enjoy the old-fashioned life. They ride around in shiny black carriages pulled by pairs of handsome horses. These carriages look like the stagecoaches in Western movies—only smaller. They have big wooden wheels, and the driver sits on top up front, holding the horses' reins. The driver wears a bright red coat and a black high hat.

Not everybody rides in carriages. Some people saddle up and ride horseback. Others pedal along on bicycles or just walk. Nobody seems to miss the cars.

Long ago only Native Americans lived on Mackinac. They believed it was the oldest island in the world. They said the island was created by piling earth on the back of a giant turtle. In the frontier days, hunters, trappers, and soldiers used Mackinac as an important base.

Today the people of Mackinac like to remember their past. They have repaired an old fort and many old houses and stores. One house is even older than the United States! The people show visitors through these old buildings and tell them about the old days. If you ever want to return to the past, just take a trip to Mackinac.

1. You could find out what life in the old days was like at—
   (A) **Rhode Island**   (B) **Coney Island**   (C) **Mackinac Island**

2. People ride in carriages pulled by—
   (A) **horses**   (B) **tractors**   (C) **goats**

3. Mackinac Island is in the—
   (A) **Great South Bay**   (B) **Great Salt Lake**   (C) **Great Lakes**

4. The driver of the carriage holds the—
   (A) **wheels**   (B) **horses' reins**   (C) **saddle**

5. The driver wears a—
   (A) **red hat**   (B) **red coat**   (C) **black coat**

6. Nobody seems to miss—
   (A) **trains**   (B) **cars**   (C) **trucks**

7. Native American legends say the island is the world's—
   (A) **oldest**   (B) **smallest**   (C) **noisiest**

8. People on the island repaired—
   (A) **an old bus**   (B) **an old fort**   (C) **an old rug**

9. One house is older than—
   (A) **Canada**   (B) **Russia**   (C) **the United States**

10. The people show visitors—
    (A) **movies**   (B) **old buildings**   (C) **shells**

UNIT 11
Unusual Suppers and Snacks

Why don't you surprise your family? Just wait until the next time they ask what you want for supper. Just say, "How about kangaroo-tail soup?" See what they say. They may be surprised to learn that this soup is sold in some stores.

Maybe members of your family are tired of always having the same kinds of meats. Tell them about buffalo meat. Quite a few people like the taste. There is baby octopus, too. You can find fresh baby octopus in some fish stores.

Most people like to eat a little snack between meals. Perhaps you can get your family to buy snails, which come from France. You might want your snails as a bedtime snack. Frogs' legs, roasted grasshoppers, and ants are also eaten as snacks. If your family members agree to buy the ants, ask them to get the chocolate-covered kind. They are crunchy.

Will your family think that your taste is a little strange? If so, tell them of the food eaten by people of long ago. In past times people ate fern plants, spiders, worms, and crunchy dandelions. Mouse pie was a favorite, too. A bear's paw was a treat, though it had to be cooked a long time before it was tender enough to eat. People said it had a sharp taste!

Ask your friends in for dinner. Give them something new to eat—something they have never tasted before. Don't say a word. Wait until they have finished. Then you can tell them what they have been eating. Won't they be in for a surprise!

UNIT 11
Unusual Suppers and Snacks

1. When your family asks what you want to eat—

   (A) say nothing   (B) surprise them   (C) laugh

2. Fresh baby octopus can be found in—

   (A) a zoo   (B) some fish stores   (C) America

3. Snails that we buy for food come from—

   (A) France   (B) Italy   (C) Japan

4. A food people like for snacks is—

   (A) bear's ears   (B) camel's hump   (C) frogs' legs

5. Chocolate-covered ants are—

   (A) large   (B) crunchy   (C) dirty

6. People of long ago ate—

   (A) tigers   (B) butterflies   (C) spiders

7. Dandelions are said to be—

   (A) crunchy   (B) sour   (C) bitter

8. A bear's paw is said to have a—

   (A) sharp taste   (B) sweet taste   (C) flat taste

9. The story says to ask your friends in for—

   (A) breakfast   (B) lunch   (C) dinner

10. Don't tell your friends what they have eaten until they—

   (A) ask you   (B) have finished   (C) are seated

UNIT 12
Rights for Lefties!

Did anyone ever pay you a left-handed compliment? That means that someone said something about you that sounded nice but really wasn't. Have you ever read about a sinister character in a ghost story? *Sinister* means "evil," but the word comes from a Latin word that means "on the left hand"!

Where did such awful ideas about lefties get started? For one thing, there are very few left-handed people—no more than one in eight or one in ten people. That makes lefties very easy to notice. Among some ancient peoples, like the Incas of South America, being left-handed was lucky. Among other peoples, being different in any way was considered unlucky.

Whether you are left-handed or right-handed depends on your parents. If both parents are lefties, half their children will be lefties. If both parents are righties, chances are only about one in fifty that any of their children will be a lefty. You can see that there will be far more righties than lefties!

This is a right-handed world. Imagine writing with your left hand. As soon as you write a word, your hand covers it up. If you rest your writing hand on the paper, you will immediately smudge what you wrote. Think about turning pencil sharpeners, doorknobs, or any clock or toy that is wound up. Even scissors and rulers are right-handed. Most musical instruments are right-handed. A lot of companies are now making special scissors, rulers, musical instruments, and so on for the lefties of the world.

Some people think lefties are smarter than righties. That may or may not be true, but there are certainly some famous lefties: singer Judy Garland; rock star Paul McCartney; tennis stars John McEnroe and Jimmy Connors; movie stars Julia Roberts and Robert Redford; skating star Dorothy Hamill; and baseball great Babe Ruth.

UNIT 12
Rights for Lefties!

1. A left-handed compliment—

   (A) is really good   (B) is silly   (C) only sounds good

2. *Sinister* means "on the left hand" and also—

   (A) "evil"   (B) "wonderful"   (C) "brotherly"

3. The number of lefties is about—

   (A) two in fifty   (B) one in a hundred   (C) one in ten

4. The ancient Incas of South America thought being left-handed was—

   (A) silly   (B) evil   (C) lucky

5. If both of your parents are lefties, you—

   (A) will be a lefty   (B) will be a righty   (C) might be a lefty

6. If both of your parents are righties, chances are that you are—

   (A) right-handed   (B) left-handed   (C) lucky

7. Left-handed writing is easy to—

   (A) read   (B) do   (C) smudge

8. Most wind-up objects or things with cranks are—

   (A) left-handed   (B) right-handed   (C) easy to handle

9. John McEnroe and Jimmy Connors are—

   (A) a rock group   (B) inventors   (C) tennis stars

10. Famous lefty Babe Ruth played—

    (A) tennis   (B) baseball   (C) rock music

The Second L A P
Language Activity Pages

In Unit 11 you read about many strange foods. Maybe you would prefer a sandwich. You can still find some really different foods in the everyday sandwich. Read about them in the paragraph that follows.

In almost every country, people serve food inside some kind of bread or pastry. Our typical sandwich—a piece of meat between two slices of bread—was invented in England. Peanut butter and bananas as a filling came much later! You may have had tacos—thin corn pancakes that have been fried and then wrapped around shredded meat. The people of Wales have given us meat pasties—a triangle of pastry with meat and vegetables baked inside. The Italians have provided calzones—bread baked around cold cuts and cheese. The Chinese or Vietnamese egg roll is a rice pancake wrapped around shreds of meat and vegetables and then fried.

A. Exercising Your Skill

Think of the foods you have read about. Which ones would you be willing to try? Which ones would you avoid? Read "Strange Suppers and Snacks" in Unit 11 again, and then reread the paragraph above. Copy the following headings on your paper. List as many foods as you can think of under each heading.

Foods I Would Try	Foods I Would Avoid

B. Expanding Your Skill

What other foods can you think of? Which are your favorites? Choose one food that you haven't read about yet. On your own paper, write a few sentences describing this food and why you like it. Also include a sentence that explains why you think other people should try this food.

33

C. Exploring Language

You know a lot about food. You know what people usually eat for breakfast, lunch, dinner, and snacks. Think about what you know from your own experience and from what you have read and seen on television. Imagine that you own your own restaurant. What would be on the menu, or list of foods, in your restaurant? Divide your menu into five sections. Then write the following headings on your paper. For each heading, list the names of four or five different foods.

Soups	Salads	Main Dishes	Vegetables	Desserts
_____	_____	_____	_____	_____
_____	_____	_____	_____	_____

D. Expressing Yourself

Choose one of these things.

1. Imagine that you are going to interview a person who is known for being a good cook. This person might be someone in your family, a friend, a neighbor, or a cook in a local restaurant. Write a list of questions that you could ask this person. If possible, set up an actual interview with the person and report to your class what you find out.

2. Role-play an interview with a partner who is pretending to be a famous cook. Make up a list of questions to ask of "the famous cook." Your partner (the "famous cook") can make up likely answers as you ask your questions.

3. Write a short story that tells about some experience you have had in which food played an important part. Did you have to go without food for a long time? Did you try some new food? Did you spill tomato sauce on your aunt's new tablecloth? Your story can be about a time that was odd, exciting, or funny.

UNIT 13
Deer on the Doorstep

Would you be surprised to open your front door and find a four-hundred-pound deer standing there? Would you think it odd to see two deer strolling down the middle of your town's busiest street? In most towns, such sights would certainly be strange. In Waterton, Canada, they are common.

Every winter dozens of mule deer come into Waterton from the nearby hills and woods. They are called mule deer because they have long ears, like mules. The deer roam through the town. They cross lawns and gardens and climb onto porches. They walk down the middle of streets and even along sidewalks. At busy corners cars screech to a stop as the deer cross, paying no attention to traffic lights.

The people of Waterton are so used to the deer that they hardly notice them—until the animals start eating their trees and bushes. Unlike most deer, these mule deer are not at all afraid of people. They do not dash off when someone tries to shoo them away from eating a tree on a front lawn. This is the only thing the people of Waterton do not like about the deer. The deer eat off so much bark and so many leaves that many lovely bushes and trees die. No garden in Waterton is safe.

Have you already figured out why the deer like to spend their winter "vacations" in Waterton? Of course—there is plenty of food there. In the mountains and forests, many deer die each winter because deep snow covers the grass and bushes they feed on. The deer come to town for other reasons too. There they are safe from their natural enemies, mountain lions and coyotes. Also, they find warmer shelter behind houses.

The people of Waterton have learned to get along with the deer, even though the animals get in the way. The deer too have had to learn to put up with people who get in their way—all the visitors who come to Waterton to take their pictures!

UNIT 13
Deer on the Doorstep

1. It might be strange to see two deer walking on—
   (A) a kitchen floor (B) the busiest street (C) a rooftop

2. These sights are common in—
   (A) Waterton (B) Jollytown (C) New York City

3. The deer come from nearby—
   (A) zoos (B) kingdoms (C) woods

4. The deer do not watch—
   (A) street signs (B) crossing guards (C) traffic lights

5. The deer are not afraid of—
   (A) mice (B) fireworks (C) people

6. In Waterton the deer find plenty of—
   (A) money (B) soda (C) food

7. Besides mountain lions, enemies of the deer are—
   (A) rabbits (B) coyotes (C) cats

8. The deer find shelter behind—
   (A) houses (B) flowers (C) buses

9. People in Waterton have learned to get along with the—
   (A) visitors (B) children (C) deer

10. Visitors take the deer's—
    (A) pictures (B) toys (C) mail

UNIT 14
Names, Names, Names

People like to give names to everything they see. They give names to towns, cities, streets, lakes, rivers, parks, and mountains. Some of the names are funny. Some are sad. Other names are just downright silly. We do not always know how names came to be chosen, but names dot our maps.

Sometimes the names of people are used to name places. There are places called David, Ruth, Nick, and Charles. Even the last names of people are used. Our country's capital is Washington, the name of our first President. There is a city called Lincoln. Other places have names as common as Smith and Jones.

Almost every animal has a place named after it. How would you like to live in a place called Buzzard's Bay? Or would Spider, Beaver, Black Snake, or Buffalo be more to your liking? Animals are favorites when it comes to naming places.

Would you like to live in a town with a happy name? New Hope, Sunrise, Beauty, Smile, and Goody are pleasant names. Would you like to live in Lovely, Blessing, or Jollytown? What about living in Christmas or Santa Claus? All of these are names of places in our country. There are places with names that are not so happy. They are Worry, Strain, Broken Arrow, and Devil's Tower. Such names could hardly make us smile. There are also many silly names. Stone, Busy, Hi Hat, Sparks, and Dime Box are but a few.

The longest place name in our country is that of a lake. It reads Chargoggagoggmanchaugagoggchaubunagungamaugg. It is an American Indian word and means "You fish on your side of the lake, and I'll fish on mine."

1. When people see things, they like to—

    (A) **draw them**   (B) **name them**   (C) **eat them**

2. One first name that was used to name a place is—

    (A) **Tom**   (B) **Bill**   (C) **Nick**

3. Our capital is named for—

    (A) **an animal**   (B) **a person**   (C) **Lincoln**

4. Places named after animals are—

    (A) **small**   (B) **few**   (C) **many**

5. When most people hear the name "Goody," they—

    (A) **shudder**   (B) **leave**   (C) **smile**

6. A happy name found in the story is—

    (A) **Black Snake**   (B) **Worry**   (C) **Jollytown**

7. A sad name found in the story is—

    (A) **Smile**   (B) **Broken Arrow**   (C) **Tears**

8. A silly name found in the story is—

    (A) **No Money**   (B) **Dancing Bear**   (C) **Dime Box**

9. The longest place name in our country was given to—

    (A) **a fish**   (B) **a lake**   (C) **an island**

10. The longest place name in our country was thought of by—

    (A) **teachers**   (B) **American Indians** (C) **swimmers**

UNIT 15
American Indian Feathers

Have you ever seen the feathers on a real American Indian arrow? Have you ever taken a good look at them? If you have, you know that some of the feathers are marked. They may also be cut, split, or colored. In days of long ago, the Plains Indians wore these in different ways. Some wore their feathers straight up. Others wore them sideways or hanging down.

The markings and the ways the feathers were worn tell us a lot about the Plains Indians. Not many people of today know what the markings mean. The feathers tell a story of what a warrior did in battle. They tell why the warrior had the right to wear them. Feathers were somewhat like medals.

Plains Indian warriors who were very brave in battle could wear a feather straight up. They had to kill an enemy or touch a live enemy in battle and escape. If anyone touched an enemy who was hurt and got away, they could wear a feather sideways. The first warrior to touch a dead enemy could wear a feather hanging down.

The colors and markings of each feather meant something, too. For some groups, the white feather showed that a warrior had killed an enemy. A red spot on a feather meant the same thing. Sometimes a little piece was taken out of the side of the feather. This showed that the warrior had taken the scalp of an enemy. A red feather showed that the warrior had been hurt in battle. A split feather showed that the owner had been hurt many times.

The next time you see a picture showing Plains Indians of long ago, look at the feathers they are wearing. What can you tell about them from their feathers?

UNIT 15
American Indian Feathers

1. You must look carefully at feathers to see how they are—

   (A) **marked**   (B) **gathered**   (C) **pinned**

2. Today, few people know the meaning of—

   (A) **bird feathers**   (B) **feather beds**   (C) **American Indian feathers**

3. Feathers tell what the Plains Indians did in—

   (A) **camp**   (B) **battle**   (C) **school**

4. A warrior who touched an enemy who was hurt could wear a feather—

   (A) **sideways**   (B) **backward**   (C) **forward**

5. A feather hanging down meant that the wearer was the first to touch—

   (A) **a dead enemy**   (B) **a friendly enemy** (C) **an arrow**

6. To show that he had killed an enemy, the warrior wore a—

   (A) **white feather**   (B) **purple feather**   (C) **blue feather**

7. A warrior who had taken the scalp of an enemy wore a—

   (A) **cut feather**   (B) **whole feather**   (C) **blue feather**

8. If a warrior had been hurt in battle, he wore a—

   (A) **bandage**   (B) **red feather**   (C) **green feather**

9. A warrior who had been wounded many times wore a—

   (A) **split feather**   (B) **necktie**   (C) **big feather**

10. American Indian arrow feathers can tell—

   (A) **birds**   (B) **stories**   (C) **pens**

UNIT 16
The Woman Who Wouldn't Give Up

It would not be long now. The ship offshore must soon be torn apart by the storm. It was 1838, and one of the worst storms in history was roaring along the coast of England. The lighthouse keeper looked out at the ship. "It will be gone in a few more minutes," he said sadly.

His daughter, Grace Darling, could see the people on the ship. Some knelt in prayer. "Can't we save them?" she asked. "Isn't there any way to help them?"

"No one can take a lifeboat out in that water," he answered. "The waves are too large."

Grace had great courage. She simply did not know how to give up. Filled with pity, she raced to the lifeboat. Her father followed. He pleaded with her not to get into the boat, but she would not listen. Her father could not let her go alone. He too climbed in. The two of them rowed frantically. Each wave seemed ready to hurl them into the sea.

Suddenly there was a terrible roar. The storm had split the ship in two. People were clinging to each half. Their deaths could not be far off.

Grace and her father rowed faster. Soon they reached the ship and began filling the lifeboat with survivors. Then father and daughter brought their lifeboat safely to shore.

To this day, a small statue stands above the grave of Grace Darling. Sailors from all over England visit it. People still honor the young woman who did not know how to give up.

UNIT 16
The Woman Who Wouldn't Give Up

1. The storm took place in—
   (A) 1900   (B) 1800   (C) 1838

2. The storm roared along the coast of—
   (A) France   (B) Ireland   (C) England

3. The lighthouse keeper's daughter was named—
   (A) Grace   (B) Mary   (C) Frances

4. His daughter wanted to—
   (A) help   (B) run   (C) swim

5. Her father said the waves were too—
   (A) fast   (B) large   (C) strong

6. She was filled with—
   (A) pity   (B) fear   (C) doubt

7. She and her father—
   (A) rowed   (B) called for help   (C) swam

8. The ship—
   (A) overturned   (B) sank   (C) split in two

9. Father and daughter filled the lifeboat with—
   (A) life jackets   (B) survivors   (C) oars

10. Above the grave of the young woman lifesaver is a—
    (A) lifeboat   (B) statue   (C) tree

UNIT 17
Lights in the Night Sky

Is there life on other planets? Do visitors from outer space fly over our cities and towns? Some people think so. But, of course, no one knows for sure.

People sometimes report seeing strange-looking lights in the night sky. Some believe the lights are spaceships. They say these spaceships give off light as they zoom through the sky. Some pilots have reported seeing small flying objects flash past their planes. They have said these objects look like dishes or saucers. That is where the term "flying saucers" came from.

In the last fifty years, thousands of people have seen these lights from the ground and from the air. Some have taken pictures of these "flying saucers." They are said to fly much faster than airplanes and dart out of sight very quickly.

Many of these lights in the sky have been explained. Sometimes they are meteors, or satellites, or weather balloons. Sometimes airplanes are even mistaken for flying saucers.

However, scientists say there could be life on some faraway planets. They say that whoever lives there could know more than we do on Earth. These life forms could be ahead of us in technology. They could be curious about our world, just as we would be curious about them. Who knows? Maybe someday we will have a chance to answer these questions.

1. Some people say that the strange lights could be—

   (A) pretty   (B) spaceships   (C) green

2. The spaceships are said to look like—

   (A) airplanes   (B) people   (C) saucers

3. The lights have been seen by—

   (A) few people   (B) thousands   (C) nobody

4. The flying objects are said to fly faster than—

   (A) airplanes   (B) light   (C) kites

5. The flying objects are said to be rather—

   (A) small   (B) large   (C) ugly

6. When some people hear about flying saucers, they are—

   (A) doubtful   (B) funny   (C) bored

7. Some of these lights in the sky are really—

   (A) costly   (B) slow   (C) meteors

8. Sometimes the flying saucers are really—

   (A) dishes   (B) birds   (C) airplanes

9. Scientists think there could be life on—

   (A) some planets   (B) the sun   (C) the rainbow

10. Whoever might live on other planets could be—

    (A) tired   (B) boring   (C) curious about Earth

UNIT 18
Up, Up, and Away

How would you like to fly to school? Would you like to zip through the air like a bird? Someday you may be able to do just that. All you would need is your flying belt. You would be able to fly anywhere with just the push of a button!

You can't get a flying belt yet. But the belts have been tested by the U.S. Army. The army thinks that soldiers with flying belts could jump over fences and fly across rivers.

The flying belt would have a small jet engine strapped on a person's back. A small tank holds jet fuel. When you press a button, the engine sends out a strong blast of air that pushes against the ground. That push sends you up into the air. The flying belt can take you as high as you want to go. You can even change your speed and direction. To land safely, you slowly cut down the force of the blast.

The flying belt could be used not only by the army. Lifeguards could zoom over the water and save people in no time at all. Firefighters could fly to a fire. The flying belt might even help people get to work more quickly.

The flying belt could be used for fun, too. It would be light, small, and easy enough for anyone to use. If you would like to "blast off" into the future, save your money. You could be first in your neighborhood to have a flying belt.

1. Someday you may be able to fly like a bird with—

   (A) a flying fish   (B) a flying belt   (C) fly paper

2. Flying belts are still not ready to be—

   (A) sold   (B) steamed   (C) frozen

3. Flying belts would help the army—

   (A) eat   (B) sleep   (C) cross rivers

4. A flying belt is strapped on a person's—

   (A) back   (B) bicycle   (C) car

5. You will go up when a strong blast of air pushes against the—

   (A) wings   (B) nose   (C) ground

6. To come down, you just cut the force of the—

   (A) words   (B) wings   (C) blast

7. The flying belt could be used by—

   (A) birds   (B) doctors   (C) lifeguards

8. The flying belt would help people get to—

   (A) work   (B) the attic   (C) the basement

9. The flying belt could be used for—

   (A) fun   (B) work only   (C) police work only

10. If you would like a flying belt, save your—

    (A) steam   (B) money   (C) friends

UNIT 19
Girl Without Fear

Eight-year-old Mabel Stark had no fear of tigers. Someday she hoped to train wild animals and make them obey her. After watching her first circus, Mabel knew that nothing else would make her happy.

Mabel never changed her mind. Years passed before she got her chance. One day she asked the owner of a circus if she could get into the cage with the wild tigers. At first the circus owner only laughed, but at last he agreed. Into the cage stepped Mabel, alone with three tigers. She spoke to them in a firm voice. The tigers roared but did just what Mabel told them to do. She walked out unhurt. The circus owner asked her to join the circus.

People came from miles around to see the "Girl Without Fear." They cheered as she put the animals through their tricks. In a cage filled with sixteen wild tigers, Mabel had complete control over the beasts. She made them walk over wires and turn over on their backs. She even made one tiger ride on the back of a horse.

In one of her acts, Mabel liked to wrestle with a tiger. The sight of the girl in the claws of a tiger made people shudder with fear. For this act Mabel wore a white leather suit. This suit kept the sharp claws of the tiger from hurting her.

When asked what it takes to become a wild-animal trainer, animal trainers always answer, "You must believe in yourself. You must know you can control wild animals. Never be mean to them. Even wild animals know if you don't like them. Above all, you must never show any fear." Mabel Stark truly deserved to be called the "Girl Without Fear."

1. When Mabel was eight years old, she said she was not afraid of—

    (A) big people   **(B) tigers**   **(C) circuses**

2. Mabel wanted to train wild animals after she saw her first—

    (A) circus   **(B) zoo parade**   **(C) movie**

3. When Mabel first asked to get into the cage, the owner—

    (A) said she could   **(B) fainted**   **(C) laughed**

4. Mabel spoke to the tigers in a voice that was—

    (A) soft   **(B) firm**   **(C) loud**

5. When Mabel got into the cage, the tigers—

    (A) ate her   **(B) smiled**   **(C) roared**

6. In the cage, Mabel worked with—

    (A) music   **(B) sixteen tigers**   **(C) five lions**

7. Mabel made one tiger ride on the back of a—

    (A) truck   **(B) lion**   **(C) horse**

8. When Mabel would wrestle with a tiger, people would—

    (A) shudder   **(B) hide**   **(C) run away**

9. Mabel wore a leather suit in order to—

    (A) look pretty   **(B) keep warm**   **(C) protect herself**

10. In order to train wild animals, one must—

    (A) feed them   **(B) always be happy**   **(C) never show fear**

In Unit 17, you read a story about flying saucers. Read these two paragraphs from the story:

> In the last thirty years, thousands of people have seen these lights from the ground and from the air. They have taken pictures of these "flying saucers." The saucers are said to fly much faster than airplanes. They can dart out of sight very quickly and are often said to be rather small. Any creatures in them would have to be small, too—perhaps only three or four feet tall.
>
> Many people laugh when they hear of flying saucers. They say there are no such things. They say that flying saucers are just rays of light that have bounced from the ground up into the air. Some people think they are light rays from the sun. Others believe they are rainbows, clouds, or maybe nothing at all.

A. Exercising Your Skill

What have people observed about flying saucers? Make up a "fact list" about flying saucers based on what you have just read. Divide your list into these two sections:

1. **In Favor of Flying Saucers**
2. **Against Flying Saucers**

Write the section headings on your paper. List at least three supporting facts—or facts that tell about the main idea or heading—under each heading.

B. Expanding Your Skill

Write a report that has two paragraphs. Use the headings and lists of facts you wrote for Part A. Turn each of the headings into a main idea sentence. Use the facts in supporting sentences. Then give your report a title. Compare your report with your classmates' reports. See how close their main idea sentences and facts are to yours.

C. Exploring Language

Imagine that you have seen something not easily believed—a flying saucer, a flying elephant, an alligator in the subway, a dragon, or anything else. First, draw a picture of what you "saw." Then write a paragraph describing the thing you saw. Include at least five facts in your description. Try to make the facts as believable as possible.

D. Expressing Yourself

Think about flying saucers and other hard-to-believe things. Then choose one of these things.

1. Write a newspaper story about what you imagined in Part C. Use the facts you wrote and the picture you drew. Add any other information, such as the date and location, to make your event seem real.

2. Using the hard-to-believe thing you thought of, or some other hard-to-believe thing or event, write a newspaper story explaining why it was not real. (The flying elephant, for instance, may actually have been a huge balloon in a parade!)

3. As you know, some people believe they have seen flying saucers, while other people think such things are ridiculous. When can you believe what you see? Magicians can make us "see" things that aren't there. Or they can make disappear things that we thought we could surely see. What would convince you that something existed? Discuss this with a small group of your classmates. Work with them to make a list of the facts or ideas that would convince you and those in your group that something hard to believe really "is."

UNIT 20
The Yeti

The people of Tibet call it a Yeti. *Yeti* means "Wild Person of the Mountains." A Yeti is a creature that is part human and part beast. People who live in Tibet believe in the Yeti. They tell strange stories about it.

There are even those who say they have seen a Yeti. They say it is about the size of a tall person. It is covered with reddish-brown hair. The face is flat like a monkey's. The head comes to a point. Most often the Yeti walks on two legs. When it is frightened, it runs on all fours. Its voice is loud and is often heard in the evening.

"How strange a Yeti must look!" visitors to Tibet say. "Is there really such a thing?" they ask. A few have gone to the high mountains of Tibet to find out. They want to get a look at the Wild Person of the Mountains. Some people even hope to bring back a Yeti.

So far, no one has been lucky enough to capture a Yeti. But large footprints have been found. Pictures of the tracks have been taken. They show that the Yeti has four toes and walks with bare feet in the mountain snow. Some people say these footprints are the tracks of a bear. Others say they are the tracks of a monkey. The people of Tibet say the tracks are made by the Yeti.

No one really knows who or what has made these tracks. No one even knows what a Yeti really is. Those who come from far away still look for the Yeti. The people of Tibet do not. "After all," they say, "who in their right mind would want to get close to the Wild Person of the Mountains?"

UNIT 20
The Yeti

1. *Yeti* means a wild person of the—

   (A) snow   (B) caves   (C) mountains

2. A Yeti is said to be the size of a—

   (A) dog   (B) tall person   (C) small person

3. The hair of a Yeti is said to be—

   (A) reddish brown (B) black   (C) gray

4. The face of a Yeti is supposed to be flat like that of a—

   (A) horse   (B) monkey   (C) dog

5. When a Yeti runs on all fours, it is said to be—

   (A) frightened   (B) happy   (C) sad

6. People say that a Yeti is most often heard in the—

   (A) morning   (B) afternoon   (C) evening

7. Those who wish to find the Yeti go to—

   (A) the zoo   (B) Tibet   (C) Spain

8. So far, a Yeti has not been—

   (A) caught   (B) searched for   (C) talked about

9. The pictures of the footprints show that the Yeti has—

   (A) dirty feet   (B) four toes   (C) six toes

10. Some people say that the tracks are those of—

    (A) a bear   (B) an elephant   (C) a goat

No one would hire little Lillian. She seemed too small to be an acrobat. At last she got a job in a small theater, but disaster soon struck. A ring snapped, and she fell thirty feet to the stage. Lillian hurt her ankles and was on crutches. "You're lucky you weren't killed," the manager said. "Give up this crazy idea while you are still alive."

But Lillian knew that the slip had been the fault of the ring. "I'm going on again tonight," she told the manager. He stared in disbelief. Then he changed his mind.

"If you wish," he said. In his greedy mind, he knew that the brave girl would attract a large crowd. It would be good for business.

That night Lillian climbed up on the stage on crutches. Then she handed them to her helper. A huge crowd waited in silence. News of the tiny girl and her accident had spread throughout New York. Lillian announced that she would do a stunt called "the plange." In this stunt she would hold on to just one ring with one hand and whirl her entire body over her wrist. This was the most difficult stunt in the circus. Only the strongest people could do it. Few would even attempt it.

People watched tensely. The manager rubbed his hands together briskly. The house was packed. Lights dimmed. Drums rolled. Then Lillian began to hurl her body up into the air. It went right over her wrist. As she did, the audience began to pick up the count. They chanted in amazement, "One, two, three—." Still Lillian continued to whirl. At the count of sixty she stopped. The crowd rose to its feet. For fifteen minutes they applauded wildly. In all of circus history, she was the first to do this dangerous stunt so many times.

The manager rushed to her side. He promised to give her a small raise if she would appear every night. But an agent from Barnum and Bailey was present and signed her to a large contract. Little Lillian had become the biggest star in the world of the circus!

1. It seemed that Lillian was too—

   (A) young   (B) small   (C) timid

2. She was given a job by the owner of a—

   (A) movie studio   (B) carnival   (C) small theater

3. Lillian fell when a ring—

   (A) slipped   (B) snapped   (C) spun

4. She fell to the—

   (A) stage   (B) ground   (C) roof

5. Lillian hurt her—

   (A) knees   (B) feet   (C) ankles

6. Lillian gave her crutches to—

   (A) the manager   (B) her helper   (C) the audience

7. Lillian swung up over her—

   (A) wrist   (B) knees   (C) crutches

8. The audience began to—

   (A) boo   (B) sing   (C) count

9. The stunt was performed—

   (A) fifteen times   (B) sixty times   (C) three times

10. The audience applauded for—

    (A) fifteen minutes   (B) ten minutes   (C) five minutes

A shiny black creature sees a fish twelve feet below the surface of the water. The creature dives, catches the fish in its teeth, and brings it to the surface. Is this creature a seal? No, it is a dog—the world's best swimming dog. Such dogs have been called "the dogs that think they are seals."

It's easy to guess the name of this kind of dog. It's called the water dog. It comes from a country called Portugal (say "PORT you gull"), across the ocean. For years and years the fishers of Portugal took water dogs along in their boats. These dogs helped the fishers in wonderful ways. They would jump into the water and herd the fish into the fishers' nets. If a fish escaped, a water dog would swim after it, catch it in its mouth, and bring it back to the net—without harming the fish.

The water dog can do even more amazing things. Its hind legs are so strong that it can leap right out of the water into a boat. It can swim from one fishing boat to another, carrying a message. In a war long ago, the Spanish navy used water dogs to swim from ship to ship with messages. An old, old story tells of a drowning sailor who was pulled from the sea and saved by a water dog.

Today, however, very few people know about the water dogs of Portugal. When the fishers got motorboats with radios, they didn't need their dogs as much. Nearly all the water dogs were forgotten and died. By 1960 there were only fifty water dogs left in the whole world.

Then an American named Mrs. Miller heard about the water dogs. She brought two of them to America. She took care of them and the puppies they soon had. Today there are many children and grandchildren of those two water dogs. They are gentle and make wonderful pets. You can buy one, but because they are rare, they are expensive. You'd better have $500!

1. The shiny black creature is a—

   (A) horse　　　　**(B) dog**　　　　(C) fish

2. These animals think they are—

   (A) farmers　　　**(B) monkeys**　　　(C) seals

3. The fishers took their dogs in their—

   (A) boats　　　　**(B) trucks**　　　(C) stores

4. The dogs would not harm the escaped—

   (A) fisher　　　　**(B) boat**　　　(C) fish

5. A dog can swim between boats, carrying a—

   (A) bottle　　　　**(B) message**　　　(C) tale

6. The sailor in the story was—

   (A) singing　　　**(B) drowning**　　　(C) eating

7. Instead of dogs, fishers used—

   (A) radios　　　**(B) nets**　　　(C) telephones

8. The number of water dogs in 1960 was—

   (A) fifty　　　**(B) eighteen**　　　(C) two

9. The American woman's name is—

   (A) Mrs. Farmer　　**(B) Mrs. Fisher**　　(C) Mrs. Miller

10. The price of a water dog today is about—

    (A) $100　　　**(B) $250**　　　(C) $500

UNIT 23
The Magic Man

Harry Houdini could do almost anything. He could walk through a brick wall. He could escape from a trunk with a rope around it. He could even make an elephant disappear! Harry Houdini, you see, was a magician. He was not just a good magician. There has never been a magician like him.

Nearly any magician can make a rabbit disappear. Such an act was too easy for Harry Houdini. He used the biggest animal he could find, an elephant. Harry put the animal into a big box on the stage. A second later he opened the box and the elephant was gone! How did he do such a trick? Most people have no idea.

Maybe the Great Trunk Trick was his best. First, Harry's hands were tied behind his back and he was put into a sack. The sack was tied and placed inside the trunk. The trunk was locked. Then ropes were put around it. Within a second Harry would pop out and take a bow. How the people clapped!

How could a person walk through a brick wall? The Great Houdini did it almost every day. He had the brick wall made right on the stage. People saw it being made. Small screens were then put on both sides of the wall. People stood on both sides of the brick wall to see that Harry did not go around it. Harry would stand on one side of the wall. In a second he would be on the other side. People could hardly believe their eyes.

Even today no one knows how Harry did all these tricks. They were only tricks. He said so himself. However, magicians never give away their secrets. Harry Houdini, the Magic Man, never did.

UNIT 23
The Magic Man

1. Harry Houdini could walk through a—
   (A) needle   (B) mountain   (C) brick wall

2. Harry Houdini made an elephant—
   (A) cry   (B) dance   (C) disappear

3. Houdini was a—
   (A) movie star   (B) magician   (C) writer

4. In the Great Trunk Trick, Harry's hands were—
   (A) empty   (B) tied   (C) warm

5. A rope was placed around—
   (A) the trunk   (B) Harry   (C) the wall

6. Houdini walked through a wall almost every—
   (A) hour   (B) day   (C) year

7. The brick wall was made on the—
   (A) porch   (B) ground   (C) stage

8. On both sides of the brick wall there were—
   (A) people   (B) bricks   (C) rabbits

9. Even today no one knows how Harry—
   (A) did his tricks   (B) liked people   (C) made the wall

10. Magicians never give away their—
    (A) money   (B) secrets   (C) rabbits

UNIT 24
Seagoing Bottles

Can you imagine finding a bottle with a message inside—or perhaps one containing money? Not long ago a child in New York found a bottle that had been washed up on the beach. Inside was $1,700! After waiting a year, the youngster was allowed to keep the money.

Bottles sometimes contain notes from a person who is shipwrecked. A bottle was once found on a beach in Japan. Inside was a message. It read, "Thirty people and forty ponies are starving." It had been sent two hundred years before. It had come to shore on a beach near the hometown of the person who had written the message!

Bottles may travel thousands of miles over the oceans. They may drift as far as a hundred miles in a day. Over fifty years ago a fisher placed a bottle into the North Sea just to see how far it would go. This bottle has been picked up many times. Each time it has been placed back into the water. It has circled the world five times!

Somewhere on the high seas may be the most valuable bottle of all. It contains a message written by a ship's captain. A storm was raging, and the captain feared the ship might go down. The captain placed a message into a bottle so that the world would know of the ship's difficulties. The message was addressed to the King and Queen of Spain. If you are the finder, this message will be worth a fortune to you. It is signed "Christopher Columbus."

The next time you visit the beach, keep a close watch. You may find a bottle cast up on the sand. A seagoing treasure may have come home to rest.

1. Bottles sometimes contain—

    (A) food   (B) messages   (C) maps

2. The bottle found by the youngster in New York contained—

    (A) $100   (B) $1,700   (C) $1,000

3. The Japanese bottle arrived late by—

    (A) 200 years   (B) 100 years   (C) 75 years

4. In a single day a bottle may travel—

    (A) 2 miles   (B) 100 miles   (C) 50 miles

5. The fisher put the bottle into the North Sea—

    (A) over 50 years ago   (B) 20 years ago   (C) 5 years ago

6. This bottle has circled the globe—

    (A) two times   (B) three times   (C) five times

7. The captain feared the ship might—

    (A) be late   (B) be captured   (C) sink

8. The ship's captain wrote a message to the King and Queen of—

    (A) England   (B) Portugal   (C) Spain

9. The message was signed by—

    (A) Hernando Cortez   (B) Christopher Columbus   (C) Myles Standish

10. You may find a bottle washed up on the—

    (A) sand   (B) grass   (C) street

UNIT 25
The Special Olympics

The Olympics are some of the most exciting sports events in the world. But there is another Olympics about which you may not have heard. This is the Special Olympics, for people with mental disabilities.

People with mental disabilities learn more slowly than other people. Sometimes they have trouble controlling the actions of their arms and legs. Sometimes they also have physical disabilities. For many years, everyone thought that mentally disabled people could not take part in sports. They were wrong.

The first Special Olympic Games were held in Chicago in 1968. One thousand people competed in many events. Since then Special Olympics programs have been organized in all fifty states. Canada takes part, too. Today over a million people participate in the Special Olympics.

Mentally disabled persons over the age of eight may take part in the Special Olympics. These people may also have physical disabilities. People have run in races using crutches or walkers. A young girl entered the long jump event with an artificial leg. A blind runner raced around the track with the help of his coach's voice. A deaf basketball team planned their plays using sign language.

Winning is wonderful for people who may never have had much success. But training for and entering the Special Olympics is also important. The participants become more confident. They learn how to concentrate in order to play well. Then they use that concentration in school to improve their schoolwork. Like anyone else, they feel great when they prove they can do something well.

1. People with mental disabilities often learn—
   (A) slowly   (B) quickly   (C) walking

2. No one thought people with mental disabilities could play—
   (A) fair   (B) sports   (C) music

3. The first Special Olympics Games were held—
   (A) in 1968   (B) last year   (C) last century

4. They were held in—
   (A) Canada   (B) all the states   (C) Chicago

5. Today the number of people taking part is more than—
   (A) one million   (B) one thousand   (C) ten thousand

6. In order to take part, a person must be at least—
   (A) twenty-one   (B) a teenager   (C) eight

7. People have entered races using—
   (A) cars   (B) crutches   (C) skates

8. A girl with an artificial leg entered the event called—
   (A) swimming   (B) long jump   (C) basketball

9. A deaf basketball team planned its plays using—
   (A) sign language   (B) lip reading   (C) hearing aids

10. The Special Olympics helps mentally disabled people become—
    (A) isolated   (B) arrogant   (C) confident

Unit 20 told about the Yeti, the wild person of the mountains of Tibet. Read this story about a wild person—or thing—that's a bit closer to home.

For almost 200 years, the story has gone around concerning a giant human—or ape—or bear—that lives in the northwestern part of our continent, near the coast. The local word for the creature is Sasquatch, which means "wild person of the woods." Another name is Bigfoot.

One man, Albert Ostman, claims he was carried away by a Sasquatch in 1924. He was camping out when a huge creature grabbed him, sleeping bag and all, and carried him for thirty miles to a clearing in the woods. There, Ostman was astonished to see a whole family of Sasquatch. After a week, Ostman escaped. He didn't tell anyone right away because he knew no one would believe him. When he did finally talk, Ostman said that the Sasquatch was between seven and eight feet tall. It had a square head and very long arms and was covered with hair. The members of the Sasquatch family could talk with each other, but Ostman did not know the language.

No one agrees about what the Sasquatch is, or even if it exists, but at least a hundred people claim to have seen the creature since 1920.

A. Exercising Your Skill

Imagine that you have come face-to-face with a Sasquatch. Draw a picture of what you might have seen. Use the facts in the story above to help you.

B. Expanding Your Skill

Read again about the Yeti in Unit 20. Make a list of the ways in which the Yeti and the Sasquatch are similar. Then make a list of the ways in which they are different. Compare your two lists with your classmates' lists.

C. Exploring Language

Imagine that you are a Sasquatch. You have been captured by some campers in the Rocky Mountains. What do you see? What do the campers look like? What are your feelings? Write a report that your other Sasquatch friends would believe.

D. Expressing Yourself

Choose one of these activities.

1. Put on a skit with a classmate. One of you takes the part of a Yeti. The other takes the part of a Sasquatch. You have both seen, in the distance, a small figure. The figure walks upright. It has very thick feet and wrinkled skin. When it gets warm, it takes some of the skin off! Its footprint shows no toes at all, but it leaves a funny pattern in the mud. What is the creature? Is it a small Yeti ancestor? Is it a young Sasquatch playing tricks? Could it be a new kind of bear? Or is it one of those creatures from the legend of the humans? Have a friendly argument about what you have seen. Make up your own explanations for the strange feet, skin, and so on.

2. Imagine that no one has ever seen an elephant. A friend comes back from a trip to the zoo—or to Africa. He or she claims to have seen a huge gray animal. It has a long nose that reaches the ground. It has legs like tree trunks. Two of its "teeth" grow out of the side of its mouth and are each three feet long! How would you respond? How would you "explain" each of the things your friend has seen? Write what you would say to your friend. You may want to present the friend's description and your response, or explanation, as a skit.

Book G

Specific Skill Series

Getting the Main Idea

Richard A. Boning

Fifth Edition

SRA/McGraw-Hill
Columbus, Ohio

Cover, Back Cover, Jonathan Scott/Masterfile

SRA/McGraw-Hill
A Division of The **McGraw·Hill** Companies

Send all inquiries to:
    SRA/McGraw-Hill
    8787 Orion Place
    Columbus, OH 43240-4027

ISBN 0-02-687977-8

        6 IPC 02 01

To the Teacher

PURPOSE:
GETTING THE MAIN IDEA is designed to assist pupils in grasping the central thought of a short passage. This skill is not only one of the most important of all major skills, but one which must be developed from the earliest stages.

FOR WHOM:
The skill of GETTING THE MAIN IDEA is developed through a series of books spanning ten levels (Picture, Preparatory, A, B, C, D, E, F, G, H). The Picture Level is for pupils who have not acquired a basic sight vocabulary. The Preparatory Level is for pupils who have a basic sight vocabulary but are not yet ready for the first-grade-level book. Books A through H are appropriate for pupils who can read on levels one through eight, respectively. **The use of the *Specific Skill Series Placement Test* is recommended to determine the appropriate level.**

THE NEW EDITION:
The fifth edition of the *Specific Skill Series* maintains the quality and focus that has distinguished this program for more than 25 years. A key element central to the program's success has been the unique nature of the reading selections. Nonfiction pieces about current topics have been designed to stimulate the interest of students, motivating them to use the comprehension strategies they have learned to further their reading. To keep this important aspect of the program intact, a percentage of the reading selections have been replaced in order to ensure the continued relevance of the subject material.

In addition, a significant percentage of the artwork in the program has been replaced to give the books a contemporary look. The cover photographs are designed to appeal to readers of all ages.

SESSIONS:
Short practice sessions are the most effective. It is desirable to have a practice session every day or every other day, using a few units each session.

SCORING:
Pupils should record their answers on the reproducible worksheets. The worksheets make scoring easier and provide uniform records of the pupils' work. Using worksheets also avoids consuming exercise books.

It is important for pupils to know how well they are doing. For this reason, units should be scored as soon as they have been completed. Then a discussion can be held in which pupils justify their choices. (The Integrated Language Activities, many of which are open-ended, do not lend themselves to an objective score; thus there are no answer keys for these pages.)

GENERAL INFORMATION ON *GETTING THE MAIN IDEA:*

There are several ways by which teachers can help pupils identify main ideas.
A. **Topic Words:** Pupils tell in a word or two the topic of the paragraph.
B. **Key Question Words:** Pupils learn that questions can begin with special words: *Why, Where, When, How,* and *What.*
C. **Place Clues:** Pupils become aware of paragraph structure. They learn that the main idea is often stated in the first or last sentence.
D. **Space Clues:** Pupils learn that the central thought of a paragraph is not limited to a single sentence, even though it may be stated in one sentence.
E. **Turnabout Clues:** If the main idea is stated in one sentence, pupils learn to change that sentence into a question and see if the whole paragraph answers it.
F. **General and Specific Ideas:** Pupils understand that some words are more general or inclusive than others. Pupils compare sentences to determine which are more inclusive and which are supporting sentences.

SUGGESTED STEPS:

1. Pupils read the passage. (On the Picture Level, they look at the picture.)
2. After reading each passage (or looking at the picture), the readers select its main idea. The choices are on the opposite page (or below the picture/passage, at the Picture, Preparatory, and A levels).

Additional information on using GETTING THE MAIN IDEA with pupils will be found in the **Specific Skill Series Teacher's Manual**.

RELATED MATERIALS:

Specific Skill Series Placement Tests, which enable the teacher to place pupils at their appropriate levels in each skill, are available for the Elementary (Pre-1–6) and Midway (4–8) grade levels.

About This Book

A picture, a paragraph, or a story is about something. It has a topic, or subject. The **main idea** tells about the subject. The main idea of a paragraph is the most important idea the writer is trying to state. You can think of a main idea as being like a tree. The tree has many parts—a trunk, roots, leaves, branches. All these parts together add up to make the whole tree. In the same way, the **details** in a paragraph add up to tell about the main idea.

Sometimes, the main idea is stated in a sentence. This is often the first or last sentence in a paragraph. In the following paragraph, the main idea is stated in the first sentence. The other sentences in the paragraph are details. They tell more about the main idea.

Metric units increase or decrease by tens. For example, the basic unit, the *meter*, has ten parts called *decimeters*. A decimeter has ten parts called *centimeters*, which are made up of ten *millimeters* each. Long distances are measured in *kilometers*, units of one thousand meters each.

Sometimes, there is no main idea sentence. Then you need to think about the information in all of the sentences and figure out what the main idea is. Read this paragraph. Ask yourself, "What is the paragraph mainly about?"

The smallest monkey is the pygmy marmoset, which measures only about six inches long, not including the tail. Woolly monkeys have a body length of fifteen to twenty-three inches. The mandrill's body length may be as long as thirty-two inches.

This sentence tells the main idea:
Monkeys vary greatly in size.

In this book, you will read paragraphs. Then you will decide what each paragraph is mainly about. You will use the information in the paragraph to figure out the main idea.

UNIT 1

1.   Someday scientists may actually perfect a machine that can translate one language into another. Translation machines have been invented, and some are even used for certain tasks, but improvements are needed. As an example of the problems of machine translation, consider the word *like*. In one sentence, it may mean "similar to," as in "He is like his father." In another sentence, it may mean "enjoy eating," as in "They like ice cream." The translating machine once digested the sentence "Time flies like an arrow." Out came the translation: a Russian sentence that meant "Time flies like to eat arrows."

2.   The first woman employee of the U.S. Forest Service began as a clerk in New Mexico. Anita Kellogg wished to be a forest ranger. In 1920, she took a civil service examination for a ranger job—a lonely and hard post in the rugged Southwest—and passed it. She wasn't made a ranger, however, because she was a woman. She was made a fiscal agent to pay firefighters. Somehow, she got into the thick of a big forest fire in the Gila National Forest and performed so ably that she was given a commendation and an increase in pay. However, discrimination caused Anita Kellogg to fall short of her great ambition— to become the first female forest ranger.

3.   A vast cedar forest once covered the now barren slopes of the Lebanese mountains. Early civilizations used the trees to build their houses and ships. The interior of King Solomon's temple was made entirely of cedar from Lebanon. The first recorded forestry law—to preserve these cedars—was enacted by the Roman Emperor Hadrian. Unfortunately, rulers who followed Hadrian lacked his foresight, and for centuries the area was stripped. Four hundred trees near Basharri in northern Lebanon are all that remain of the once-vast forest. However, if nitrogen-fixing shrubs are planted to restore and enrich the soil, the area could once again become productive forest land.

4.   The high-spirited, playful porpoise is usually considered to be a friendly, lovable sea creature, while the shark is held to be dangerous and hostile. How can the peaceful porpoise swim around in the same ocean as the aggressive shark? There's no need to worry about the porpoise, for it can take very good care of itself. When provoked, it will attack a shark, hitting it at top speed in the tender portion of the abdomen, ripping it open. The porpoise is also capable of damaging the shark's gills by vigorous, top-speed bumping, thus destroying the shark's breathing apparatus.

5.   The notion that a horseshoe is lucky dates from ancient times. The grounds for the belief vary widely. In ancient times, iron was considered a sacred metal. Another theory is that the horseshoe acquired its magical reputation because it is similar in shape to the crescent moon, once considered a symbol of good luck. Still another theory is that the superstition is somehow related to the mystic number seven, the number of nails in a horseshoe. At any rate, the belief goes back to the time of the Romans. In modern times, President Truman hung a horseshoe above the door of his office in the White House.

1. The paragraph tells mainly—

    (A) how translation machines work
    (B) how translation machines are used for certain tasks
    (C) why the word *like* needs careful translation
    (D) why improvements are needed in translation machines

2. The paragraph tells mainly—

    (A) how Anita Kellogg tried to become a forest ranger
    (B) what forest rangers do
    (C) where Anita Kellogg took a civil service examination
    (D) how many female forest rangers there are today

3. The paragraph tells mainly—

    (A) who tried to preserve the Lebanese forests
    (B) what the interior of King Solomon's temple was like
    (C) how early civilizations used cedar trees
    (D) what has happened to the cedar forests of Lebanon

4. The paragraph tells mainly—

    (A) why a shark is considered dangerous and hostile
    (B) how fast a porpoise can swim
    (C) how a porpoise protects itself against a shark
    (D) how a shark breathes with its gills

5. The paragraph tells mainly—

    (A) why the horseshoe is considered a lucky symbol
    (B) why the number seven is lucky
    (C) what President hung a horseshoe outside his office
    (D) how the horseshoe resembles the moon

UNIT 2

1.   That furry Australian marsupial known as the koala bear is not much like true bears. Most bears will eat small animals, such as mice and rats. They also like grass, eggs, garbage, and snakes. Some bears even enjoy ice cream, soda, hot dogs, and hamburgers. But the koala has different eating habits. It will eat only the leaves of one type of tree—the eucalyptus. The koala will starve to death rather than eat anything else.

---

2.   The Japanese are famous for their genius in producing small things. They have produced small cars, radios, and trees. Japan now has a farmer who has worked for a decade to produce tiny pigs called minipigs. This farmer's desire to go from "maxi" to "mini" was stimulated by the wide use of pigs in space control and medical research. The average adult hog weighs four hundred pounds. The minipig does not exceed sixty pounds. Each minipig costs one hundred dollars. American researchers are very interested in using minipigs.

---

3.   How would you relish a bird on your dinner table with its feathers intact? In fashionable homes of long ago this was the custom. Ducks, swans, and even peacocks were actually served this way. The bird was first skinned, stuffed, and roasted. Then, after it was allowed to cool, the skin was carefully sewed on again. Placed on a large platter, the bird was brought to the dining hall, much to the delight of the guests. Once the bird was sufficiently admired, its covering was pulled away, and the guests would begin to eat.

---

4.   Astrid Lindgren of Sweden started writing stories for children when she slipped on an icy sidewalk and sprained her ankle. Pippi Longstocking, the name she invented for the girl with red hair and freckles, became famous in books translated around the world. Ms. Lindgren lets Pippi do anything she wants—go to bed as late as she likes, buy lots of candy, and have magical powers. Pippi has become one of the most popular characters in children's books.

---

5.   You may think that certain modern shoe styles are ridiculous, but you should have seen fourteenth-century shoes! The "rage" in shoe fashion back then was long, upturned toes, often decorated with bells. The toes, stuffed with hay, curled upwards and then sometimes even curved back down again. This odd style was worn throughout Europe by nobles and commoners alike. The toes of some shoes were so long that little chains attached to the knees held them up and prevented the wearer from tripping. Many rulers forbade the silly style. Even so, people persisted in wearing such outlandish footwear until the fashion finally died out of its own accord.

1. The paragraph tells mainly—

    (A) why the koala likes eucalyptus leaves
    (B) what most bears in the wild prefer to eat
    (C) where the native habitat of koalas is located
    (D) what koalas and true bears like to eat

---

2. The paragraph tells mainly—

    (A) how to train minipigs
    (B) where minipigs are produced
    (C) what American researchers think about minipigs
    (D) why the Japanese have produced minicars

---

3. The paragraph tells mainly—

    (A) which kinds of birds have been used for food
    (B) what people ate long ago
    (C) how birds were prepared for eating long ago
    (D) why people have enjoyed looking at birds

---

4. The paragraph tells mainly—

    (A) why Pippi Longstocking became so popular
    (B) how the character Pippi Longstocking was invented and developed
    (C) why Astrid Lindgren named her character Pippi Longstocking
    (D) how Astrid Lindgren began telling stories to her children

---

5. The paragraph tells mainly—

    (A) who wore unusual shoes in the fourteenth century
    (B) how a fashion died out of its own accord
    (C) why silly shoe styles change
    (D) what kinds of shoes were worn in the fourteenth century

UNIT 3

1.   The Great Depression that struck America in the 1930s was in every respect a catastrophe. Yet ecologists realize now that it did have one beneficial effect. Before the Depression, in the 1920s, raccoon-fur coats were a popular fad. So many raccoons were slaughtered for their fur that some scientists feared the animal would become extinct. But with the Depression came poverty. Few could afford such coats. As a symbol of times that were gone, they went out of fashion. The raccoon gained a new lease on life.

2.   What a remarkable creature is the electric eel! This snakelike fish can produce an electrical charge that lasts only two thousandths of a second, but it can send out more than four hundred of these per second, totaling six hundred volts. A car battery gives only twelve volts! Even if the electric eel produced this amount of electricity for twenty minutes continuously, all it would need would be a rest of five minutes to "recharge its batteries." It's a shame that someone can't harness its power. Can't you just hear the service station attendant say, "Want your oil and eel checked?"

3.   In southwestern Ohio lies the largest and best-known of the Native American earthworks, or mounds. It is Great Serpent Mound and is believed to have been built by the Adena culture. In the form of a coiled snake, the mound is twenty feet wide and five feet high. If it were "uncoiled" it would stretch for a quarter mile. The site is protected today, and thousands of visitors come each year to admire it and think about the culture that built it.

4.   In Congress, when one legislator agrees to vote for a bill that another legislator wants and then expects a similar favor in return, it is called "logrolling." The term goes back to frontier times in America. When a pioneer planned to build a log cabin, the neighbors would gather and cut trees, roll the logs to the site of the building, and help to construct the house. In return, the new home owner was expected to give the neighbors similar help. This practice, called logrolling, eventually also became part of the political vocabulary of America.

5.   Triton is the name of Neptune's large moon. Part ice and part rock, it is slightly smaller than Earth's moon. Though it is the coldest object in the solar system, Triton amazed scientists when they saw evidence in *Voyager* photographs that the planet has active volcanoes. It joins Earth and Io, Jupiter's small moon, as the only three volcanically active bodies in the solar system. Triton also has a variety of surface patterns. Because of one bumpy area of its terrain, scientists have nicknamed Triton "the cantaloupe moon."

1. The paragraph tells mainly—

   (A) why raccoons are slaughtered today
   (B) why people in the 1920s liked raccoon coats
   (C) how a bad event can cause something good
   (D) how bad effects of an event can spread

2. The paragraph tells mainly—

   (A) why the eel's power has never been harnessed
   (B) what the voltage of a car battery is
   (C) how long the electric eel's charge lasts
   (D) why the electric eel is a remarkable creature

3. The paragraph tells mainly—

   (A) about the Adena people
   (B) how long Great Serpent Mount is
   (C) the description of Great Serpent Mound
   (D) about the fight to protect Great Serpent Mound

4. The paragraph tells mainly—

   (A) why legislators do favors for each other
   (B) how "logrolling" entered the political vocabulary
   (C) how frontier people helped each other build log cabins
   (D) what pioneers did with logs

5. The paragraph tells mainly—

   (A) about how cold Triton is
   (B) how much like Earth's moon Triton is
   (C) how Triton got its nickname
   (D) about the characteristics of Triton

1.   The manatees of the Caribbean and dugongs of the Indian Ocean are curiosities among fish. They are the only remaining species of Serenia, or "moon creatures." They have a human facial appearance and feed standing upright in the water. They hold their flippers out like arms. Their secretive habits and their peculiarity of coming out mostly at night in the moonlight, combined with their human appearance, cause fear and superstition among fishers of the region. Manatees are probably how the legend of mermaids got started. They might also have been a prototype for the many fictional creatures of the deep.

2.   Queen Nefertiti was one of the greatest women of ancient Egypt. Her name means "Behold, the beautiful woman comes!" Although she was beautiful and rich, she was unspoiled, kind, and gentle. As a girl, Nefertiti played with Akhenaton, the future king of Egypt. In 1369 B.C., the sixteen-year-old Akhenaton became king. Soon after, he married Nefertiti, who became queen of Egypt at fifteen. Akhenaton and Nefertiti had six children, all girls. One of their daughters married King Tutankhamen and became queen of Egypt like her mother.

3.   The library in Blue River, Oregon, is one of the most unusual libraries in the world. If you want to borrow a book from this little one-room library, you don't need a card. There's no time limit on borrowing, and everything is free. The 7,500-book library is on the "honor system." It was begun several years ago by Mrs. Frances O'Brien, who decided that the four little communities around Blue River needed a place to borrow books.

4.   Dr. Peter Mark Roget was an English doctor of the early 1800s whose name is remembered for an accomplishment that had no relation to the practice of medicine. Roget decided that it would be useful to group words according to ideas they expressed instead of the usual alphabetical dictionary listing. The first edition of his list was published in 1852. Many editions followed, and Dr. Roget never stopped adding to his list. To this day, *Roget's Thesaurus* of synonyms and antonyms is used by almost everyone interested in words in the English language. New editions of this handy reference book appear constantly.

5.   Because of the threat of German submarines attacking Allied ships without warning in World War I, a device was needed to detect the submarine before they struck. A French scientist named Longevin developed a system known as sonar, which could locate objects submerged in water. Sound beams were sent through the water. If such a sound beam struck no obstacle, it would eventually fade out. If the sound beam hit a submarine or other object, it would bounce back as an echo. The direction of the echo and the time it took to return would enable the sonar operator to determine exactly where the submarine or other obstacle was.

1. The paragraph tells mainly—

   (A) where Serenia fish live
   (B) when Serenia fish are visible
   (C) what Serenia fish are like
   (D) why Serenia fish act like people

2. The paragraph tells mainly—

   (A) whom Queen Nefertiti married
   (B) when Nefertiti became queen
   (C) who Queen Nefertiti was
   (D) what the name *Nefertiti* means

3. The paragraph tells mainly—

   (A) how Blue River supports its library
   (B) who Mrs. Frances O'Brien is
   (C) why the Blue River Public Library is unusual
   (D) where the Blue River Public Library is

4. The paragraph tells mainly—

   (A) where Dr. Roget practiced medicine
   (B) when Dr. Peter Mark Roget lived
   (C) how *Roget's Thesaurus* came into being
   (D) what words are contained in Roget's book

5. The paragraph tells mainly—

   (A) how sonar was used to detect submarines in World War I
   (B) how sound beams travel through the water
   (C) how Allied ships were attacked in World War I
   (D) what underwater echoes tell people

1.   There are many hardy people who enjoy riding surfboards in the winter as well as in the summer. Winter surfers wear special wet suits, which eliminate most of the cold. They wear gloves and special boots, which keep them fairly warm. Their heads get coldest of all. "In February, your hair freezes," said one surfer. Still, whenever the waves are rolling as they like them, even if the temperature drops below the freezing mark, a few dedicated people always manage to find the courage to brave the cold and go surfing.

2.   Zimbabwe is the name of a stone ruin that stands in the country of Zimbabwe, Africa. This ruin was first viewed by a European in the sixteenth century. The name *Zimbabwe* comes from the Shona-speaking Karanga tribe. It is a contraction of either *dzimba woye* ("venerated houses") or *zdimba dza mabwe* ("stone house"). A thirty-foot-high wall, tapering from a thickness of seventeen feet at the base to three feet at the top, encloses an imposing windowless tower as well as remnants of other structures. Carbon-14 dating tests reveal that the site was continuously occupied by humans from the Stone Age until the eighteenth century. The reason the hilltop complex was abandoned may be shrouded in mystery forever.

3.   Only one of the Japanese women reached the pinnacle. Tiny Junko Tabei succeeded where so many men and women had failed. Standing 4'9" and weighing ninety-four pounds, she was the first woman to reach the top of treacherous Mt. Everest. She had been climbing for fifteen years and had scaled every Japanese mountain. What was left, then, but to try the tallest peak in the world? In 1992, she became the first woman to climb the highest mountains on Earth's seven major regions.

4.   Beauty practices, such as manicuring and coloring the nails, were known to ancient peoples. An excavation at the royal tombs at Ur of the Chaldees in Babylonia revealed a gold manicure set used by someone in the year 3200 B.C., making it over five thousand years old. Famous queens, namely Nefertiti and Cleopatra of Egypt, painted their fingernails and toenails different shades of red to enhance their physical attractiveness. For hundreds of years, women of the aristocracy in Spain also used color on their nails. It seems that throughout history, people have recognized nail care as being an important part of good grooming.

5.   Which weather events do you think are the most dangerous? People who keep track of such statistics say flooding kills more Americans each year than any other weather factor. About 140 people die in floods each year. Another 100 are killed by lightning strikes, 80 people are killed by tornadoes, and an equal number by hurricanes. You don't often hear of people dying in hailstorms, but it does happen. In 1888, a hailstorm in India killed 246 people.

1. The paragraph tells mainly—

    (A) when many people go surfing
    (B) what surfing in the winter is like
    (C) why February is a good month for surfing
    (D) where winter surfing takes place

2. The paragraph tells mainly—

    (A) how the name *Zimbabwe* originated
    (B) what is known about the stone ruin called Zimbabwe
    (C) where Zimbabwe is located
    (D) why Zimbabwe was abandoned in the 1700s

3. The paragraph tells mainly—

    (A) what it is like to climb Mr. Everest
    (B) how many mountains Junko Tabei climbed
    (C) about Junko Tabei's climbing accomplishments
    (D) why the other women failed to reach the pinnacle

4. The paragraph tells mainly—

    (A) how old the practice of manicuring and coloring the nails is
    (B) why Cleopatra manicured and colored her nails shades of red
    (C) how color enhances the appearance of nails
    (D) why a manicure set was placed in a tomb

5. The paragraph tells mainly—

    (A) how many Americans die each year due to severe weather
    (B) how to protect oneself from severe weather
    (C) why people in India are uncomfortable with hailstorms
    (D) why it is important to stay away from lightning

UNIT 6

1.   The loveliness of carnations has helped to make them very popular flowers in today's world. Carnations were just as well known in the sixteenth century—not to look at but to eat! Candied carnation was a dessert fit for royalty. It was made by dipping fresh carnations into egg white and powdered sugar. Carnation jam and carnation relish were also treats, although the recipes haven't been handed down. During the reign of Queen Elizabeth I, carnations were added to wines and other beverages to flavor the drinks. Flowers on the dinner table were as common as they are today, only then they were part of the meal!

2.   Unusual place names seem to be characteristic of Newfoundland, Canada. Many of these names indicate difficult times, love and romance, or creatures of the sea, land, or sky. For example, Bareneed, Famish, Gut, Empty Basket, Gripe Point, and Misery Point certainly suggest hard times. Things apparently improved, however, when romance took over, for one also discovers Sweet Bay, Heart's Desire, Heart's Delight, Cupids, Parsons Pond, and Paradise—plus Tickle Cove, and Ha Ha Bay. Animals are also well represented with Lion's Den, Hare's Ears Point, Bear's Cove, Penguin Island, Pigeon Island—and, with a noble display of fairness, Goose Bay and Gander Bay.

3.   Dorothea Dix was one of the most vigorous and distinguished women who ever lived. In an age when women were supposed to be quiet housewives, she spent a long life fighting bravely for "lost causes," though she was semi-invalid. Dorothea was born in Maine in 1802, where she lived a life of grinding poverty. She moved to Boston to live with relatives and began to teach school. Later, she got a job teaching Sunday School in jails, which opened her eyes to the terrible conditions there and in other institutions. She traveled all over the world to document the horrors of insane asylums, poorhouses, and jails—and to bring these evils to public attention.

4.   You probably eat a lot more Chinese food than you think you do. Italians may not be happy, but here is the truth about spaghetti. Originally, it was an Oriental dish. Marco Polo, the famous Italian trader and explorer, brought spaghetti back from his trips to China and introduced it to Europe. Sauerkraut may sound German, but the Chinese were eating it in 200 B.C. Because of its vitamins, sauerkraut was fed to the laborers working on that large-scale public works project, the Great Wall of China.

5.   How cold does it get in the Arctic and Antarctic regions? If someone tells us eighty below zero Fahrenheit, that really doesn't mean much. It helps our understanding, though, if we consider that at such a temperature frost forms inside a lit kerosene lamp! A running reindeer gives off so much body heat that a fog is formed so dense we can't see the animal. Dropped mercury becomes flat and solid instead of spattering into little balls. Perhaps most instructive of all, one's breath instantly forms into ice crystals that clash together and can actually be heard!

1. The paragraph tells mainly—

    (A) what a carnation dessert is

    (B) how carnations were once used for foods

    (C) how carnations have been popular throughout history

    (D) why carnations were added to wines and other beverages

2. The paragraph tells mainly—

    (A) why most names in Newfoundland suggest romance

    (B) what unusual names are found in Newfoundland

    (C) what animals are represented in Newfoundland names

    (D) how many Newfoundland names suggest hard times

3. The paragraph tells mainly—

    (A) where and when Dorothea Dix was born

    (B) who brought the evils of prisons to America's attention

    (C) how Dorothea Dix overcame poverty

    (D) where Dorothea Dix worked as a teacher

4. The paragraph tells mainly—

    (A) why the Italians may not be happy about spaghetti's origin

    (B) why the Chinese ate sauerkraut

    (C) that spaghetti and sauerkraut are actually Chinese foods

    (D) why Marco Polo ate spaghetti

5. The paragraph tells mainly—

    (A) why the Arctic and Antarctic regions are so cold

    (B) what happens to dropped mercury in very cold temperatures

    (C) what coldness really means in the Arctic and Antarctic regions

    (D) how cold affects a kerosene lamp

A. Exercising Your Skill

Part of Unit 1 talks about something that affects many people at one time or another—superstitions. Read the following paragraphs about superstitions. Then, on your paper, write a sentence that sums up the main idea of each paragraph.

1.   How most superstitions came into being is not known, but they have been passed along from old to young year after year. Why is this? Some people claim the reason is really a force of habit, while others say it is the result of our interest in magic. Whatever the reasons, many people seem to like relying on some good-luck piece, or on making a wish to protect them from bad luck. That is why many of us are likely to make a wish when we see a shooting star or go out of our way to avoid having a black cat cross our path.

Main idea of the paragraph: _____

2.   The wishbone from a chicken can be a kind of superstition. Grasp one end of the bone with your little finger, while a friend grasps the other end. Close your eyes and make a wish, then pull. If you get the larger part of the wishbone, it is said that your wish will come true, but only if you don't tell anyone. People in Sweden make wishes on ginger snaps. Holding the cookie in one hand, they hit it with the other. If the cookie breaks into three pieces, they can make a wish. If it breaks into more than three, well, they can eat the cookie anyway. The French people wish on wine, the English when stirring a Christmas pudding, and the Russians on finding two filbert nuts in one shell. Of course, nearly everyone wishes when blowing out the candles on a birthday cake!

Main idea of the paragraph: _____

B. Expanding Your Skill

Write a title for each paragraph in Part A. Remember that a good title sums up the main idea in a very few words.

Paragraph One: _____   Paragraph Two: _____

Now compare your titles with your classmates' titles. How many had the same or similar titles?

On your paper, write two supporting ideas from each paragraph that helped you choose the title you wrote.

	Paragraph One		Paragraph Two
1.	_____	1.	_____
2.	_____	2.	_____

C. Exploring Language

Choose one of your own superstitions, if you have any, or choose a commonly held superstition. If you need help thinking of a superstition, use the sayings listed below that are or may be based on superstitions. Write a paragraph explaining why you or other people have that particular superstition. Explain what you think the superstition means. Be sure to include a main idea sentence in your paragraph.

- Eat an apple before going to bed
  And you'll make the doctor beg his bread.
  (Or: An apple a day keeps the doctor away.)

- Onion's skin, very thin
  Mild winter coming in.
  Onion's skin, very tough
  Coming winter, cold and rough.

- Give a sick person a plant rather than a bouquet of flowers.

- Put money into a purse or wallet before giving it as a gift.

- Find a penny and pick it up
  And all day long you'll have good luck.

- If you spill salt, throw a pinch of it over your shoulder.

D. Expressing Yourself

Choose one of these activities.

1. Working with three of your classmates, make up a new superstition. Write down some ideas about why you decided on the superstition. Then explain it to the class in an oral presentation.

2. Draw a picture illustrating the effects of a superstition on someone. Show your drawing to the class to see if they can guess what superstition the picture illustrates.

3. Play a game of charades. You and your classmates take turns acting out and trying to guess a particular superstition.

4. Most libraries have books on the subject of superstitions and old sayings that may be based on superstitions. Choose a superstition or saying and find out about its origin. Report your findings in class.

1. In 1940, an exhibit of rural-life paintings in a New York City gallery caused quite a stir. The artist's name was Anna Mary Moses, but everyone called her Grandma! Grandma Moses was eighty years old, an unusual age for an artist's first exhibit. Her simple country scenes attracted much attention. Grandma Moses had spent most of her life farming and homemaking. After her husband died, she spent more and more time painting. Until she died at 101, Grandma Moses created the primitive rural pictures for which she gained her fame. She truly became the "grand old lady of American art."

2. The War of 1812 was, in many ways, the strangest war in the history of the United States. Two days before it began, England stated that it would repeal those laws that were the chief cause of all the trouble. News of England's action didn't reach the United States until the war was in full swing. Also, the Battle of New Orleans, perhaps the fiercest battle of the war, took place fifteen days after the peace treaty was signed. To top this series of oddities, both England and the United States claimed to have won the war.

3. Most people who lived in fifteenth-century England actually believed that geese grew on trees. The geese trees were thought to be found on islands somewhere near Scotland. The trees supposedly bore barnacles as fruit. Ripened barnacles then fell into the sea and developed into geese, or so reported the leading botanists and zoologists of the time. The existence of the trees was just taken for granted. Although the belief in tree-grown geese has long since disappeared, the official scientific term—*barnacle goose*—is still used today in the classification of geese.

4. William Kelly, an ironworker in Kentucky, made big pots out of iron. He was always hoping that he could find a way to make stronger pots. One day, Kelly was heating the iron to make his pots. As he melted the iron over a charcoal fire, a cold breeze came through his shop and hit the melted metal. The iron turned white-hot. When it cooled, Kelly found the oxygen in the air had turned his iron into something stronger—steel. In England, a man named Henry Bessemer (1813–1898) found the same thing. The two eventually got together and formed a steelworks.

5. Comic strips reach a larger audience than do stories by the most famous writers. The funny papers have a great impact on the millions of their fans, children and adults alike. People can't seem to read the funny papers and forget them. In the Blondie comic strip, when Blondie didn't know what to name her baby, thousands of readers sent her possible names. Cartoon characters like Snoopy sell hundreds of products a year. Readers often complain if the characters die or do something they don't like. In a way, comics are nothing to laugh at!

UNIT 7

1.   The paragraph tells mainly—

   (A) who Grandma Moses was and how she won fame
   (B) where Grandma Moses' paintings were exhibited
   (C) when Grandma Moses began painting
   (D) why Grandma Moses chose to paint

2.   The paragraph tells mainly—

   (A) why the War of 1812 was strange
   (B) when the Battle of New Orleans occurred
   (C) who won the War of 1812
   (D) when England repealed the troublesome laws

3.   The paragraph tells mainly—

   (A) why geese grew on trees
   (B) what strange ideas people have had throughout history
   (C) what is inside barnacles
   (D) where geese were once believed to have come from

4.   The paragraph tells mainly—

   (A) how the process of making iron was invented
   (B) who William Kelly was
   (C) how the process of making steel was discovered
   (D) who Henry Bessemer was

5.   The paragraph tells mainly—

   (A) why Blondie is a popular comic strip
   (B) why comics are funny
   (C) how many famous writers are comic strip fans
   (D) how great an effect comic strips have on their fans

UNIT 8

1.   More stories have been told and written about the mystery of the *Mary Celeste* than about any other ship in the annals of the sea. In 1872 the *Mary Celeste* was found sailing off the Azores. Nobody was aboard! Maybe there had been a mutiny. Perhaps the crew had escaped after ridding the ship of its officers and then perished at sea. Maybe everyone deserted the ship for some unknown reason with the intention of returning. Possibly an unfavorable wind came up, taking the ship forever out of reach. The mystery remains.

2.   You have probably heard that the parts of a split worm will go on living. The front end of an angleworm that is sliced in two near the center will grow another tail. The hind half, however, will produce a second tail at the cut end. This "new" worm will have two tails and no head! Eventually it will die from hunger. If only a few front segments are cut off a whole worm, new segments grow back. When more than five or six segments are removed, the total number are rarely regenerated.

3.   The largest and heaviest horses in the world are the great shires weighing over two thousand pounds and standing as high as eighteen hands (six feet) at the shoulder. The shires are draft horses—used for pulling heavy loads. In 1924 two shires in England pulled a world-record load for horses: fifty-six tons. Back in the Middle Ages, when English knights were seeking a breed of horse that could carry a warrior in full armor into battle, they chose the shire. In fact, the horses themselves wore armor from head to hoof.

4.   When or where the game of chess originated has never been authenticated, but it is believed to be the oldest game in the world. The name *chess* comes from the Persian *shah mat*, which means "the king is dead." Such a meaning could indicate that the Persians started chess, although the origin of the game has been attributed to almost every early civilization. One of the most popular theories is that the Hindus of India began to play chess as a substitute for war because it was against their religion to kill people. If this theory is correct, chess began about five thousand years ago.

5.   It was only in the 1960s that a major surgical discovery made life more bearable for hundreds who suffer from arthritis. Until then, most sufferers from this disease were relieved only by hot soaks and aspirin, the latter not well tolerated by many. Then came a breakthrough. Doctors found materials that could bear weight and were self-lubricating and slip-proof. With these, they began replacing diseased hip joints. Unsure of lasting results, they cautiously used the method only on older people. The operation proved such a success that today surgeons use the principle to replace various joints such as shoulders, elbows, knees, and ankles. The method is used only on joints that are nonfunctioning or extremely painful.

1. The paragraph tells mainly—

    (A) what happened in 1872
    (B) what the mystery of the *Mary Celeste* is about
    (C) why there are mysteries of the sea
    (D) how the crew escaped

---

2. The paragraph tells mainly—

    (A) how an angleworm can grow new parts
    (B) why an angleworm grows new parts
    (C) what happens when an angleworm is cut in two
    (D) how angleworms reproduce themselves

---

3. The paragraph tells mainly—

    (A) how the shire horses acquired their name
    (B) what makes the shire horses special
    (C) what the world's strongest horses pulled
    (D) how the English knights went into battle

---

4. The paragraph tells mainly—

    (A) where and when the game of chess may have begun
    (B) why the Hindus played chess as a substitute for war
    (C) where the name *chess* comes from
    (D) when chess first became a popular game

---

5. The paragraph tells mainly—

    (A) how aspirin helps arthritis sufferers
    (B) what discovery helps arthritis sufferers
    (C) when a major surgical discovery was made
    (D) how arthritis causes diseased joints

1.   Everyone knows that pigs have short curly tails. Have you ever wondered which way their tails curl? Most people haven't. However, a farm and livestock study group in the state of Michigan wanted to find out the answer to that question. Their investigation showed that 50 percent of pigs' tails curl clockwise, $18\frac{2}{3}$ percent curl counterclockwise, and $31\frac{1}{3}$ percent curl both ways. Now you know. Very clever are those Michigan agricultural researchers!

2.   Deborah Sampson, born on December 17, 1760, in Plymouth, Massachusetts, lived an incredible life. She taught herself to read and write and earned enough money for her own schooling for a short time. Before she was twenty, she taught school, a brave task since she had had very little formal education herself. When the Revolutionary War broke out, Deborah's extraordinary life really began. She disguised herself in a man's suit, enlisted in the American army in 1778, and served for the entire term of the war under the name of Robert Shirtliffe!

3.   One of the bleakest places in the world is the island of Ascension, in the middle of the South Atlantic. It is inhabited by about two hundred people who take care of a cable station. Ascension is volcanic, covered for the most part with barren lava and other volcanic material. Swimming in the sea is impossible because of sharks and undertow. Ships must anchor a half mile off shore. Yet the residents seem to like the place. Maybe it's because of the weather. It seldom rains, and a sea breeze always keeps it pleasantly cool.

4.   The moon isn't made of green cheese, but it does have the hiccups. At least that's what a group of M.I.T. scientists discovered. Automatic seismic stations left on the moon by the astronauts indicate that once a month the gravitational pull of the earth gives the moon's deep, rocky interior a case of creaking, popping seismological hiccups! These little moonquakes, which are very weak by earth standards, take place regularly and always at the same locations, some four hundred to six hundred miles deep. How can the moon be cured of its hiccups? It can't hold its breath or breathe into a paper bag. It might as well continue to hic along.

5.   One of the most powerful telescopes in the world is in Russia. It uses a mirror nearly twenty feet in diameter. So great is this telescope's range that it could see a candle's light fifteen thousand miles away! Yet this giant scope may be dwarfed in the near future. American astronomers are contemplating an incredibly huge telescope with a set of mirrors thirty yards across. That is nearly one-third the length of a football field! Even this is tiny compared with a radiotelescope being built in New Mexico. Shaped like a Y, it has arms each thirteen miles long!

1. The paragraph tells mainly—

    (A) why pigs have short curly tails
    (B) what ways pigs' tails curl
    (C) when pigs' tails curl
    (D) what causes pigs' tails to curl

2. The paragraph tells mainly—

    (A) why Deborah taught herself to read and write
    (B) why Deborah pretended to be a man
    (C) how Deborah enlisted in the American army
    (D) what Deborah did

3. The paragraph tells mainly—

    (A) why swimming is impossible in Ascension
    (B) how many people live in Ascension
    (C) what one of the world's bleakest places is like
    (D) why residents like Ascension

4. The paragraph tells mainly—

    (A) what scientists know about the moon
    (B) what hiccuplike moonquakes are
    (C) where the quakes in the moon occur
    (D) how moonquakes and earthquakes differ

5. The paragraph tells mainly—

    (A) how big the largest telescopes are getting
    (B) how a radiotelescope works
    (C) what can be seen through a radiotelescope
    (D) why scientists want bigger telescopes

1.   Miners needed to get rid of their gold as quickly as they got it out of the ground. During the California gold rush days, miners were being murdered at a rate of more than one a day. Any miner with gold was in danger of death and would have been happy to have the gold safeguarded and delivered to San Francisco or back home. Out of this need was born the Wells Fargo Company. Wells Fargo stagecoaches carried the miners' gold through bandit-filled mountains to the safety of a city bank. Wells Fargo became the name of a firm that miners could trust.

2.   When did weatherproof overshoes, or galoshes, originate? More than two thousand years ago, Roman armies invaded a land called Gaul. The Roman soldiers noticed that the Gauls wore a strange type of shoe. Soon Roman shoemakers began to copy it. They called it a *gallicia*, meaning "a Gaulish shoe." It was especially serviceable in bad weather. Today the sole of such a shoe is usually made of rubber or synthetic material rather than wood, but the shoe is very similar in style to the kind worn by the Gauls. Doesn't the word *galosh*, meaning "a high overshoe," sound like the word *gallicia*—a Gaulish shoe?

3.   Patience Wright, who became known as the "Promethean Modeler," was the first European settler born in America who pursued the art of sculpture. The famous artist later changed her medium to colored wax and used it throughout her career to make likenesses in low relief and in the round. She took her craft to England in 1772, and her genius, personality, and keen initiative soon won her critical acclaim. Ms. Wright then traveled to France, where she modeled busts of Benjamin Franklin and many members of royalty. In addition, Patience Wright also was appointed draughtsperson of the Philadelphia Mint and created the designs on the first United States coins.

4.   Vaqueros from Mexico were among the first cowhands in North America. The English-speaking people who became involved in the American cattle industry in the 1800s learned a great deal from these vaqueros. Early ranchers in the Southwest learned to ride mustangs and drive long-horned cattle in ways that were traditionally Mexican. The cowhand's saddle and dress, the art of roping, the roundup, and the branding of stock were all borrowed directly from Mexican-Americans. No other industry or occupation in the United States shows such a direct Mexican influence.

5.   Jazz is the only form of music native to the United States. It grew from a number of African-American musical forms, including gospel songs, spirituals, slave songs, and minstrel show music. Eventually it combined with elements of European music. The first organized form of jazz was ragtime, which was made up of musical compositions played on the piano. Scott Joplin was a famous ragtime composer in the early 1900s. Today, jazz practitioners are some of the most well-known international composers and musicians.

1. The paragraph tells mainly—

    (A) how many miners were murdered

    (B) where Wells Fargo carried the gold

    (C) why city banks were safe

    (D) how the Wells Fargo Company came into being

2. The paragraph tells mainly—

    (A) when and where galoshes originated

    (B) why people wear galoshes

    (C) who the Gauls were

    (D) where the land of Gaul was located

3. The paragraph tells mainly—

    (A) why Patience Wright went to France

    (B) why Patience Wright went to England

    (C) what Patience Wright's accomplishments were

    (D) why Patience Wright changed her medium

4. The paragraph tells mainly—

    (A) where vaqueros came from

    (B) how Mexican ways influenced America's first cowhands

    (C) when Americans first became cowhands

    (D) how the cowhands in the Southwest dressed in the 1800s

5. The paragraph tells mainly—

    (A) about the life of Scott Joplin

    (B) where gospel music came from

    (C) about the origins of jazz

    (D) how jazz musicians became famous

1.   Can you imagine a birthday cake weighing $17\frac{1}{2}$ tons? This gigantic confection, made in honor of our country's Bicentennial, stood in the center of a San Francisco department store and dazzled everyone with its splendor. This cake, the world's largest, was decorated with a ton of colorful historical paintings made out of icing. It stood thirty feet high and took over 11,500 pounds of flour to make. Other ingredients were 20,500 eggs, 5,100 pounds of sugar, and a 200-pound "pinch" of salt. The birthday cake cost $100,000 to make, but the "bakers" hoped to earn back their expenses by selling two-pound pieces at about six dollars each.

2.   A supervisor at the famous St. Louis Zoo in Missouri once checked on a disturbance occurring among the chimpanzees. It seemed that a young chimp was bothered by a loose baby tooth. Its comrades were trying to help by extracting the tooth. Not one of the chimpanzees, including the victim itself, could pull the tooth. The zookeeper, amazed at the chimps' understanding of the problem at hand, gave the suffering chimp a pair of pliers. The animal soon got the idea and pulled out its own loose tooth. Afterward, the whole group looked angrily at the tooth, bit it, and even jumped on it. The zookeeper had a hard time getting that tooth away from them!

3.   The first famous American newspaperwoman was Nellie Bly, who, in 1889 at the age of twenty-two, captured the attention of the world when she went around the earth on a stunt mission for the *New York World*. Nellie, whose real name was Elizabeth Cochrane, was trying to beat the time of fictional Phileas Fogg, hero of Jules Verne's novel, *Around the World in Eighty Days*. She rode on ships and trains, sampans and horses—and she made it in seventy-two days, easily beating Fogg's time. Her career made her name a synonym for the female star reporter for many decades after her outstanding reportorial feats.

4.   One of the most colorful sights in historic San Francisco is the cable car. Only two other cities in the world—Wellington, New Zealand, and Hong Kong—have anything remotely resembling it. The cable cars, first installed on the steep hills of San Francisco in 1873, were so well built that some of the original ones are still running. They are powered by a cable that runs underneath the streets. San Franciscans love their cable cars; they have parties, weddings, and political rallies on them. In 1947, the mayor, after urging that the cable cars be scrapped and replaced with buses, was resoundingly defeated in the next election!

5.   If a giant anteater's parents told it "Hold your tongue!" that would be quite an order. The anteater's tongue is up to three feet long! This strange creature, as you might imagine, needs quite a long head to house that tongue. The animal's name signals what its sticky tongue is used for. When the anteater spies an anthill or termite colony, it first rips the place open with its six-inch claws. Then out flashes the tongue and zap! Hundreds of the tiny insects get an unexpected tour of the anteater's stomach. These insects are the anteater's only food.

1.   The paragraph tells mainly—

   (A)   what the Bicentennial cake was like
   (B)   how the Bicentennial cake was decorated
   (C)   where the Bicentennial cake was located
   (D)   what the Bicentennial cake cost

2.   The paragraph tells mainly—

   (A)   why all the chimpanzees were angry
   (B)   what bothered a young chimpanzee
   (C)   how a chimp's loose tooth caused a disturbance
   (D)   why the young chimpanzee's tooth was loose

3.   The paragraph tells mainly—

   (A)   how Nellie Bly became world famous
   (B)   how Phileas Fogg became world famous
   (C)   what newspaper Nellie Bly worked for
   (D)   when Nellie Bly became world famous

4.   The paragraph tells mainly—

   (A)   what Hong Kong cable cars are alike
   (B)   how cable cars operate
   (C)   how important San Francisco's cable cars are to its citizens
   (D)   why San Francisco's mayor wanted to scrap the cable cars

5.   The paragraph tells mainly—

   (A)   how the anteater's parents speak to it
   (B)   how long the anteater's claws are
   (C)   why the anteater needs a long tongue
   (D)   why the anteater likes ants and termites

UNIT 12

1.   Mary Edwards Walker, who was born in Oswego, New York, in 1832, was a woman ahead of her time. She first became a teacher, then earned a medical degree. At the marriage ceremony to her doctor husband, Mary wore trousers and had the word *obey* taken out of the customary wedding vows. She then continued to practice medicine under her maiden name. During the Civil War, she volunteered as an army physician and became the first woman to receive a commission as an assistant surgeon. Taken prisoner, she spent four months as a Confederate prisoner of war. Mary Walker is the first woman to have received the nation's highest decoration for valor, the Congressional Medal of Honor.

2.   Some dairy experts know how to make cows give more milk. If they are kept cool, cows will yield more milk. Since it is too expensive to air-condition a barn, the cows' heads and necks can be kept comfortable by having special cooling devices put around them. Cows whose heads were kept cool gave twenty percent more milk than cows that were allowed to suffer from the summer heat. Elsewhere, a farmer-musician discovered that cows gave more milk if music was played for them. The farmer said that the better the music was, the better the milk. The cows gave most while listening to Mozart.

3.   It is a fact that animals can warn people of natural disasters. Some animals tried to do so at Skoplje, Yugoslavia, on the day of one of the world's worst recorded earthquakes. Zookeepers ran to investigate when lions and tigers paced their steel cages restlessly. Police were puzzled when tame pigeons took flight out of town. One family was awakened when a pet canary, trying to fly away, beat its wings against the cage. That morning the earth beneath Skoplje moved and thundered. Seconds later, the city lay in ruins. During the recovery period, people recalled the odd behavior of those animals. The townspeople realized too late that the animals' warnings could have saved many lives.

4.   Bees make a humming noise that baffled science for many years. How is this sound produced? It was learned that bees make the sound by moving their wings rapidly. A bee may flap its wings at the rate of 440 times per second. In a hive there are certain bees known as "fanners." These bees have but one function. By rapidly beating their wings, they keep the air moving through the hive. Long before humans thought of air conditioning, bees were using it.

5.   According to superstition, the number of happy months you will have during the year depends on the number of falling autumn leaves you catch in your hand. Even if you catch only one leaf before it reaches the ground, you will be spared colds during the coming winter. The behavior of growing leaves is said to indicate weather conditions also. You can forecast rain if the leaves turn their undersides up or if they suddenly make a rustling noise. In the spring, if the oak tree sprouts leaves first the summer will be dry, but if the ash sprouts first the summer will be wet.

1. The paragraph tells mainly—

    (A) why Mary Edwards Walker earned a medical degree
    (B) how Mary Edwards Walker became an army surgeon
    (C) what military decoration Mary Edwards Walker received
    (D) what Mary Edwards Walker did in her lifetime

2. The paragraph tells mainly—

    (A) why barns can be air-conditioned
    (B) how cows can be made to produce more milk
    (C) what cooling devices can be used on cows
    (D) how cows are affected by music

3. The paragraph tells mainly—

    (A) where a severe earthquake occurred in Yugoslavia
    (B) why Skoplje had a severe earthquake
    (C) how Skoplje's animals tried to warn the townspeople
    (D) how the animals' warnings saved many lives

4. The paragraph tells mainly—

    (A) what air conditioning is
    (B) how many times per second a bee flaps its wings
    (C) what bees do with their wings
    (D) how many tasks the "fanner" has

5. The paragraph tells mainly—

    (A) how you can have happy months
    (B) how leaves are involved in superstition
    (C) how leaves indicate weather conditions
    (D) how oak and ash trees sprout

A. Exercising Your Skill

Inventions come from many places. In the following paragraph, you will read about some of them.

> Teri Pall invented the cordless telephone. Stephanie Kwolek invented Kevlar®, which is used in bulletproof vests. Mary Kies came up with a method of weaving bonnets. In 1809 Kies was the first woman to obtain a U.S. patent for her invention. Women have invented many of the items we take for granted in our modern world. They had to overcome many barriers to be accepted as inventors. Often they stayed in the background, making suggestions to husbands, brothers, or sons, who would then take out a patent for an invention in their own name. Would it surprise you to know that there is evidence that Cyrus McCormick's reaper and Eli Whitney's cotton gin were based on women's ideas?

Write the main idea sentence. _____

B. Expanding Your Skill

Every paragraph has a main idea, but sometimes that idea is unstated. Every paragraph also has supporting sentences. They tell more about the main idea, even when it is not directly stated. Read the paragraph below.

> In the early days of flying, barnstorming was a popular form of entertainment for people. Fliers would travel around the country, often landing in fields and sleeping in farmers' barns. They would perform in air shows at fairs and carnivals to earn money. Their shows consisted of stunt flying, jumping with parachutes, and wing walking. People loved to watch the shows, but sometimes they made the exhibitions even more dangerous. Spectators would run into the fields in front of oncoming planes, and the planes would often crash. Bessie Coleman, Harriet Quimby, and hundreds of other early pilots were killed while performing adventurous flying stunts.

Write the main idea, and tell if it is stated or unstated.

_____

Write two details that support the main idea.

_____

_____

C. Exploring Language

Choose one of these main idea sentences (completing it, if necessary) and expand it into a paragraph of five or six sentences. Be sure that each of the sentences that you write supports the main idea. Finally, write a title for your paragraph.

1. My favorite invention is _____ .
2. The idea that women cannot do the same tasks as men is nothing more than prejudice.
3. The skies are so vast and dangerous that it is surprising how few accidents there are today.
4. I first spotted the UFO on _____ at _____ .

D. Expressing Yourself

Choose one of these activities

1. Imagine you were asked to be a pilot in the days of barnstorming. Write a paragraph or two explaining why you would or would not accept the challenge. Be sure to back up your main argument with supporting ideas.

2. Think of an invention that would make your life easier. What might it be? What would it look like? Draw a picture illustrating how your invention works.

3. Set up an informal debate in which four students argue for, and four others argue against, having women as fighter pilots in the military. Let each speaker have one minute to present an argument. The rest of the class can vote for the side with which they agree.

4. Look up the story of another famous woman, such as Barbara Jordan. Present your findings in an oral report to the class.

UNIT 13

1.   Over two thousand years before Columbus, dwellers of Mexico began building one of the world's most incredible cities. A people called the Zapotecs leveled a mountain summit on which they erected stone temples and tombs. They accomplished this without beasts of burden or even knowledge of the wheel. Stones weighing up to four tons were dragged up a trail that circled the mountain. At its zenith, the Zapotecs' city covered fifteen square miles! About A.D. 1000 the Zapotec civilization declined. Not until 1932 did an archaeologist discover the mountain's full splendor.

2.   From 1716 to 1718, Edward Teach plundered cargo vessels and American coastal cities. With his long black beard tied in braids with ribbons, Blackbeard (as he was called) presented a terrifying picture. In the thick of battle the British pirate stuck long lighted matches into his hat, framing his fierce face in fire and smoke. Blackbeard and his bloodthirsty band of buccaneers created so much terror along the coast that a ship was sent to take him dead or alive. Caught off the North Carolina coast on November 21, 1718, and badly wounded, Blackbeard was captured and beheaded.

3.   Can you imagine a diamond that weighs eight hundred carats? That was the original size of the Kohinoor diamond, a name that means "mountain of light." Successively owned by several East Indian monarchs, it was first heard of in the West in 1663. In 1739 a Persian king conquered Delhi and got the diamond. Murdered on his way home, the king, as he was dying, passed the diamond to his Afghan bodyguard. Years later, the disowned grandson of the bodyguard secretly departed to India with the stone. When the British conquered India in 1849, the Kohinoor, by then weighing "only" 106 carats, was presented to Queen Victoria. Later it became part of Queen Mary's crown.

4.   Once an ant closes its jaws on an object, it holds on no matter what the consequences are. Even if its head is cut off, it will often maintain its grip. In South America and other parts of the world, some people use this characteristic to heal wounds. When a person receives a cut, the edges of the wound are held together. The open jaws of a large ant are placed against the cut. The infuriated ant clamps its jaws together, one on each side of the cut. The people then cut off the body of the ant, leaving just the jaws to keep the wound effectively stitched.

5.   Successful advertisers have used scented ads in newspapers and magazines to promote such wares as soaps, cosmetics, flowers, and fruits. A meat packer in California decided to get into the act and use this technique, but it backfired! The company ran a scented ad that smelled like bacon, the product it wished to promote. Dogs all over the area got a whiff of it and ran for what they thought was a tasty meal. There was hardly a newspaper on a porch anywhere that some keen-nosed dog hadn't grabbed, run away with, and torn to pieces to find the "bacon."

1. The paragraph tells mainly—

    (A) how Columbus found the Zapotecs
    (B) how large the Zapotecs' city was
    (C) when the Zapotecs lived
    (D) what the Zapotecs achieved

2. The paragraph tells mainly—

    (A) how Edward Teach tied his beard
    (B) how Blackbeard terrified people
    (C) when Blackbeard lived
    (D) why Blackbeard stuck matches under his hat

3. The paragraph tells mainly—

    (A) who first owned the Kohinoor diamond
    (B) what the history of the Kohinoor diamond is
    (C) why the Kohinoor diamond lost weight
    (D) how the Kohinoor diamond became part of Queen Mary's crown

4. The paragraph tells mainly—

    (A) how helpful ants are
    (B) how clever the people of South America are
    (C) how wounds are effectively treated
    (D) how ants are used to bind wounds

5. The paragraph tells mainly—

    (A) how one scented ad backfired
    (B) why some advertisers have used scented ads
    (C) where the meat-packing company was located
    (D) how soaps are promoted

1.   Have you seen a U.S. two-dollar bill? Many of your grandparents and great-grandparents were no doubt quite familiar with this denomination of U.S. money. The first two-dollar bill was printed in 1862, the year that paper money was first issued. This so-called "deuce" continued in circulation until the 1960s, when the government decided to stop printing these bills because they were not used much and were often confused with other bills. Collectors hoarded the last of these discontinued deuces. The two-dollar bill was reintroduced in 1976 as a U.S. Bicentennial gesture, but public response was negative. The deuce was doomed once more.

2.   Grace O'Malley was a pirate, although she swore the English queen drove her to it. In the sixteenth century, Grace and her family ruled several Irish islands. The British raided her islands and killed one of her sons. On that day, Grace became a pirate. She attacked British ships and kept their treasures. Having grown up sailing around her islands, she was an excellent sailor. Grace could make surprise attacks from nowhere and hide in hidden channels only a native would know. Grace O'Malley became known as Queen of the Pirates.

3.   The firefly fish, which lives in the Banda Sea in the East Indies, is named for the sort of searchlight it carries below each eye. The searchlight is a semicircular spot somewhat larger than the eye and located just below it. A colony of bacteria nourished by secretions from the fish provides the light. The firefly fish has a unique way of flashing the light on and off. It just covers or uncovers the area by means of a black fold of tissue, which has a function similar to an eyelid's.

4.   What is the oldest object in the city of London, England? If someone asked you, you might offer the name of a castle or abbey. In each case you would be wrong, for the oldest object in London is the London Stone. Originally a tall, upright stone on Cannon Street, it is today a mere fragment embedded in the wall of Saint Swithin's Church. Its history goes back to the New Stone Age and carries with it sacred associations. The London Stone is mentioned in an early Saxon document. Medieval kings used it after their coronations. The kings struck it with their swords as a token of the city's submission to them.

5.   Martha Berry was one of those people who inspire others. Born into a well-to-do Georgia family in 1867, she decided early in life to dedicate herself to helping the less fortunate folk in the sparsely-settled mountain regions of her state. Her first school was started in 1902 in a log cabin on her farm—with only five boys. From that humble beginning, the Berry Schools grew. Students worked for the school in return for tuition. Berry College, just one of the Berry Schools, is today a vibrant tribute to the unceasing efforts of Martha Berry.

1.   The paragraph tells mainly—

   (A) when the first two-dollar bill was introduced
   (B) why people hoarded two-dollar bills in the 1960s
   (C) what collectors do with two-dollar bills
   (D) what the history of the two-dollar bill has been

2.   The paragraph tells mainly—

   (A) why the British killed Grace O'Malley's son
   (B) how Grace O'Malley became the Queen of the Pirates
   (C) what Irish islands Grace O'Malley ruled
   (D) why the English queen's ships raided the Irish islands

3.   The paragraph tells mainly—

   (A) how the firefly fish turns its light off
   (B) where the firefly fish lives
   (C) how the searchlight of the firefly fish works
   (D) why some fish need bacteria

4.   The paragraph tells mainly—

   (A) who used the London Stone after coronations
   (B) what the oldest object in London is
   (C) how old the London Stone is
   (D) where the London Stone is mentioned

5.   The paragraph tells mainly—

   (A) how Martha Berry helped the less fortunate
   (B) what college today is named after Martha Berry
   (C) how many boys attended Martha Berry's first school
   (D) when Martha Berry started her first school

1.   You've surely caught a cold from a relative, classmate, or friend—no matter how hard you tried to avoid it. In fact, it's not as easy to catch a cold as you might think. Medical researchers at the University of Wisconsin tried an experiment. Twenty-four married couples, mostly students, volunteered to risk a cold for science. One person in every couple was intentionally given nose drops containing a known cold virus. Each couple spent a lot of time in close contact. Yet in only thirty-eight percent of the cases was a wife able to "give" her cold to her husband or a husband "give" his cold to his wife. This study suggests that the idea of the common cold spreading like wildfire from person to person may be just a myth.

2.   Many reptiles look fearsome, which is an important part of their defense system. Since many reptiles are small and harmless, their strange appearances can help frighten away predators. Some reptiles also hiss loudly or swell up their bodies to appear dangerous. The Australian frilled lizard puffs up a folded "collar" around its neck so that it suddenly looks many times larger. And a North American turtle called the stinkpot releases a terrible smell that would give a skunk pause.

3.   There were few jobs in Ireland during the 1820s, so many Irish people came to America to work, digging the Erie Canal for eight cents a day. There were a few Yankee farmers and other immigrants digging "Clinton's ditch," but is was mostly the Irish who cleared the trees from Albany to Buffalo. Half the time they waded deep in chilly muck, kept warm by a flannel shirt and a slouch cap. Swamp fever killed many good workers, but there were always more to take their place and work from sunrise to sunset six days a week until 1825, when the Erie Canal was finished.

4.   The flightless penguins are certainly not visually oriented birds. They can't tell their mates from other penguins by sight. Instead, they identify their partners by the sounds of their voices. Penguins searching for their mates go from nest to nest sounding their calls. When they pick the wrong nests, they are pecked and driven off to other ones. When the right mate is discovered, there follows a period of excited bowing and crooning. Even though this seems like very strange behavior to most of us, it's the customary conduct of our webfooted friends, the penguins.

5.   The tallest monument in the United States is the Gateway Arch in St. Louis, Missouri. This graceful arch symbolizes the city's role as the gateway to the West. Higher than the Washington Monument and twice the height of the Statue of Liberty, the Gateway Arch is said to be strong enough to withstand a wind of 150 miles per hour or more. Between the legs of the sixteen-ton steel arch are underground exhibits that tell of America's westward expansion. Trains whisk visitors up through the legs to the top of this curved steel structure, where sightseers can enjoy one of the finest views of America's heartland.

1. The paragraph tells mainly—

    (A) how to catch cold
    (B) what research has discovered about catching colds
    (C) why people catch colds
    (D) why married people catch more colds than unmarried people

2. The paragraph tells mainly—

    (A) how bad the stinkpot smells
    (B) how reptiles defend themselves
    (C) how some reptiles make themselves bigger
    (D) how reptiles catch their prey

3. The paragraph tells mainly—

    (A) why the Erie Canal was built
    (B) who the builders of the Erie Canal were
    (C) what "Clinton's ditch" was
    (D) where the Erie Canal was built

4. The paragraph tells mainly—

    (A) how penguins identify their mates
    (B) why penguins can't fly
    (C) what happens when penguins pick the wrong nests
    (D) why penguins sometimes bow and croon

5. The paragraph tells mainly—

    (A) what the Gateway Arch in St. Louis is like
    (B) how the Gateway Arch compares with the Washington Monument
    (C) what can be seen from the top of the Gateway Arch
    (D) what the Gateway Arch symbolizes

1.   All his life Ulysses Smith had one terrible thought—what if he were accidentally buried alive? He made an unusual request in his will. He asked that, when he was buried, there be a shaft over his head up to the surface of the ground, with a glass placed on top of the shaft. He also asked that a stick be placed in his coffin so that if he woke up, he could break the glass. He also wanted a bell so he could ring for help. Ulysses Smith was buried, as he requested, in Middlebury, Vermont. The glass was never broken and the bell was never rung.

2.   During her fabulous career in opera, American singer Risë Stevens sang more than forty roles during thirty-five years. She appeared in the world's great opera houses and became especially famous for her record album, *Carmen*. At her peak, she was considered the world's greatest mezzo-soprano. When she left the stage, Risë Stevens became a voice coach, then lived in the Virgin Islands for three years. Back in New York, she again coached music and singing. Later she became president of the Mannes College of Music.

3.   Have you ever heard of a "voiceprint"? It is a weapon for criminologists. Like a fingerprint, it is extremely valuable to the police in identifying criminals. Its developer, Dr. Kersta, says that it is as accurate as a fingerprint and has great value in kidnapping cases. When a kidnapper uses the telephone to demand ransom or to give instructions, tapes are made of the speaker's voice. The tapes are then compared with voices on file or with the actual voices of the suspects. According to Dr. Kersta, no two voices are identical.

4.   Seagulls and other large birds snatch fish from water for their meals. Nature, however, has a way of evening things out. Birds swimming on the water's surface may be caught and eaten by a certain large European catfish. Another fish, the common angler, is known as the goosefish because geese, ducks, gulls, and other aquatic birds have been found in its stomach. Often attaining a length of four or five feet, the ugly, voracious angler is evidently not particular about what it eats with its enormous mouth, which is so big that in some places the fish is called the "mouth fish" or "allmouth."

5.   During World War I, one of the acts committed by the Germans that turned world opinion against them was the execution of a British nurse, Edith Cavell. Fifty-year-old Cavell had come to Belgium some years before 1915 to start a nurses' training school. When the war broke out, the Germans advanced across Belgium, and many retreating English soldiers donned civilian clothes to evade them. Edith Cavell hid many of these soldiers in her hospital. She was caught, tried, and sentenced to death. Despite a world outcry, the Germans carried out the sentence. Edith Cavell, shot by a firing squad, became a famous martyr.

1. The paragraph tells mainly—

   (A) how Ulysses Smith finally died
   (B) why Ulysses feared being buried alive
   (C) where Ulysses Smith was buried
   (D) what precautions Ulysses Smith took against being buried alive

2. The paragraph tells mainly—

   (A) what Risë Stevens did after leaving opera
   (B) how long Risë Stevens was an opera singer
   (C) what Risë Stevens' career has been like
   (D) how many opera roles Risë Stevens learned

3. The paragraph tells mainly—

   (A) why kidnappers use the telephone
   (B) how voiceprints differ from fingerprints
   (C) how voiceprints help the police
   (D) why two voices are never identical

4. The paragraph tells mainly—

   (A) how some birds eat fish
   (B) how some fish eat birds
   (C) how long the angler fish is
   (D) how goosefish swallow whole birds

5. The paragraph tells mainly—

   (A) why Edith Cavell went to Belgium
   (B) why Edith Cavell hid English soldiers in her hospital
   (C) why English soldiers donned civilian clothes
   (D) how the execution of Edith Cavell turned world opinion against Germany

1.   Are you aware that Americans are the only Western people who use a fork in the left hand to cut food but then shift the fork to the right hand to eat it? Since the fork was not used in England until the late 1700s, it was rare or unavailable to pioneer American colonists. Not until the 1870s were forks universally accepted in the United States. The early American custom was to eat with the knife in the right hand and to spear food on its point—aided by a spoon and the fingers. When the fork was introduced, the custom of eating right-handed had become too much of a habit to be changed.

---

2.   The Chinese invented paper almost a thousand years before Europeans did. In A.D. 105 Tsai Lun found that plant fiber ground up and soaked in water would dry into a usable item on which to write. A Chinese chemist, Pi Cheng, invented movable type in 1040, about 400 years before Johannes Gutenberg developed it in Germany. In 1090 the Chinese invented the magnetic compass. This led to long-distance ocean travel and worldwide exploration and trade.

---

3.   Deserts are fascinating ecosystems. Because they have so little water, any animal or plant that lives in a desert must adapt in some way. The kangaroo rat literally does not drink any water. It gets moisture from seeds. Cacti and other desert plants have root systems that spread out over a large area just below the ground's surface. These roots quickly collect any rain that falls then store it in stems that can expand to hold lots of moisture. The spines on the cacti's outsides keep desert animals from taking the water for themselves.

---

4.   Many cities eager to be rid of pigeons have tried repellents, electric shock, poisons, and open hunting seasons, but the perennial guests still seem to increase in numbers. However, in Grigny, France, the problem was solved almost before it began. The architect of the newly opened town square thought it looked unfinished and believed gigantic statues twenty feet high would make the square strikingly beautiful. They did. However, the local pigeons were horrified. One look at the monstrous statues and the pigeons took off like arrows sprung from bows!

---

5.   Born in New York City in 1850, Charlotte Ray was not only the first African American woman to become a lawyer in the United States, but also the first woman allowed to practice law in a court in the District of Columbia. She had attended a school in Washington, D.C., and then taught at Howard University. Charlotte Ray was graduated from the law department of Howard in 1872 and the following month was accepted by the District of Columbia bar. In addition to her brilliant legal work, she was known to have great interest in the women's suffrage movement.

1. The paragraph tells mainly—

   (A) when the fork was first used in England
   (B) when forks became popular
   (C) how an American eating custom originated
   (D) how the colonists ate their food

2. The paragraph tells mainly—

   (A) how to make paper and movable type
   (B) how Gutenberg learned from Tsai Lun
   (C) about Chinese inventions
   (D) about how the magnetic compass works

3. The paragraph tells mainly—

   (A) how the kangaroo rat gets moisture
   (B) how animals and plants survive in the desert
   (C) about the widespread root system of desert plants
   (D) about why the desert has so little water

4. The paragraph tells mainly—

   (A) what methods have been used to repel pigeons
   (B) why many cities are eager to get rid of pigeons
   (C) how pigeons keep increasing
   (D) when pigeons should be frightened away

5. The paragraph tells mainly—

   (A) where Charlotte Ray received a legal education
   (B) where Charlotte Ray was born
   (C) why Charlotte Ray taught at Howard University
   (D) what Charlotte Ray's career was like

UNIT 18

1.   Alaska's national parks are comprised of over 41 million acres of wilderness land, more than the total of the rest of the U.S. national parks. One of Alaska's parks features the highest mountain in North America, Mount McKinley in Denali National Park. The Athapaskan people call the peak *Denali,* or "the high one." Another park, Katmai, is the site of Mount Novarupta, a volcano that erupted in 1912 in the worst blast of this century. Glacier Bay, as you might guess, contains many glaciers—more than 20. And Wrangell-St. Elias Park contains nine of the tallest peaks in the United States.

2.   Knowledgeable and experienced scuba divers looking for a good place to locate sunken ships would do well to head for the tiny Atlantic islands of Bermuda, 50 miles off Cape Hatteras, North Carolina. This island group sits in the middle of an estimated five hundred wrecked ships, most of them in shallow waters. These wrecks span over 450 years of history. The ships include treasure galleons, sailing ships, and even steel-hulled freighters. Many seafarers, coming unexpectedly upon these islands, have lost their lives or have seen their ships ruined there. In fact, Bermuda's first settlers were shipwrecked sailors.

3.   A terrible explosion occurred in Russia on June 30, 1908. Trees were blasted apart thirty miles from the explosion's center, an earthquake wave passed twice around the world, and the nights for two months afterward were startlingly bright over two continents! Today, scientists call it recorded history's most awesome explosion. How fortunate that it happened in barren central Siberia and not in a heavily populated area of the world! Most authorities who have checked the site suspect that a meteor struck the earth. It is believed that a strike of this size occurs about once in every two thousand years!

4.   When a skunk is approached by an enemy, it stamps its feet and waits for a response. If it still feels frightened or threatened, it turns its back on its attacker and squirts an amber-colored liquid from the glands beneath its tail. This foul-smelling spray, released four or five times in rapid succession, can project as far as twelve feet, burn the enemy's eyes and skin, and cause temporary blindness, yet it never gets on the fur of the skunk itself, nor is it ever used against other skunks.

5.   The steamer *Eastland*, out of Chicago, had been considered rather unstable for some time. When overcrowded, it had been known to tilt while cruising. Nevertheless, in 1915 more than two thousand passengers, many of them toddlers and children, crowded on board for a picnic cruise. Before the *Eastland* even left its dock, it suddenly keeled over. More than eight hundred people were drowned. After the ship was raised and all the dead removed, many people thought the vessel would be scrapped. Instead, it was renovated successfully. It became the U.S.S. *Wilmette* and served as a training ship for naval recruits.

1. The paragraph tells mainly—

    (A) the characteristics of Alaska's national parks
    (B) why the Athapaskan people call one peak *Denali*
    (C) why there are so many glaciers in Alaska
    (D) the number of acres that make up Alaska's park system

2. The paragraph tells mainly—

    (A) how scuba drivers search for sunken ships
    (B) who Bermuda's settlers were
    (C) why Bermuda is a good place to search for sunken ships
    (D) how many treasure ships have been wrecked around Bermuda

3. The paragraph tells mainly—

    (A) how powerful the 1908 explosion in Siberia was
    (B) how scientists checked the explosion in Siberia
    (C) why the meteor dropped into a barren, unpopulated region
    (D) who witnessed the meteor's fall

4. The paragraph tells mainly—

    (A) why a skunk stamps its feet and waits
    (B) how far a skunk can spray
    (C) how a skunk wards off an enemy
    (D) why a skunk never uses its spray against other skunks

5. The paragraph tells mainly—

    (A) why the steamer *Eastland* was not stable
    (B) when the *Eastland* tragedy occurred
    (C) what happened to the steamer *Eastland*
    (D) where the *Eastland* tragedy happened

UNIT 19

1. One of the most memorable snowstorms in the eastern part of the United States was the blizzard of 1888. Conditions were particularly bad in New York City during this storm. Twenty-one inches of snow fell, but it piled up in drifts that observers said reached second-story windows. At one point, the wind blew at eighty-four miles per hour, and the thermometer dipped to four below zero Fahrenheit. All transportation came to a halt. Four hundred people lost their lives. One of the few persons to profit from the snow was a store owner who sold twelve hundred pairs of rubber boots.

2. Imagine your mother being arrested for voting in a Presidential election! In 1872 police arrested Susan B. Anthony for this crime. At her trial the judge asked, "You voted as a woman, did you not?" She answered that she had not voted as a woman but as a citizen of the United States. Refusing to pay a $100 fine, Ms. Anthony became a leader in the cause of equal rights and opportunities for women. In 1920 Congress passed the nineteenth amendment, giving women the right to vote. Ms. Anthony, who had died fourteen years earlier, deserves much of the credit for its passage as one of the first women's rights leaders—the suffragists.

3. In old Europe elaborate fountains often graced the centers of cities. In modern American cities, fountains are making a dramatic comeback. Planners of many skyscrapers and urban centers are including exciting fountains in their designs. These fountains usually stand in plazas or parks where passersby can enjoy their beauty. Some fountains spout many-colored jets of water into the air. In others, water rushes or gurgles over concrete blocks of varying shapes and sizes. Architects feel that fountains offset the plainness of tall buildings. City dwellers find them oases of beauty.

4. When ships were driven ashore in storms, they often lost their cargoes to plunderers, who would come upon the shipwrecks and make off with the goods. Some of these pirates even lured ships ashore by running up and down the dunes with lanterns. Others tied a lantern to a horse's neck and rode up and down the dunes. To the approaching ships, the moving lights appeared to be other vessels moving along the coast. When the ships attempted to follow the same course, they became stranded on the shoals. The crafty pirates then seized the cargoes and often killed the crews as well.

5. Cynthia Westover Alden, born in Iowa in 1858, did not let the sex discrimination of the times stand in her way. She became an expert shot and skilled rider of horses, and she acquired an intimate knowledge of wild animals and nature. After graduating from the State University of Colorado, she took a four-year course in a commercial college and became a skilled mathematician. In New York she was appointed a custom-house inspector, learning many different languages to help her communicate with the immigrants with whom she worked. She became the only woman to hold a position by appointment in any New York City department when she was named private secretary to a commissioner.

1. The paragraph tells mainly—

    (A) how 400 people lost their lives in the blizzard of 1888
    (B) what the blizzard did to transportation in New York City
    (C) how a store owner made large profits
    (D) how severe the blizzard of 1888 was

2. The paragraph tells mainly—

    (A) why Susan B. Anthony was put in jail
    (B) what a judge said to Susan B. Anthony
    (C) why Congress passed the nineteenth amendment
    (D) how Susan B. Anthony helped the cause of women

3. The paragraph tells mainly—

    (A) who builds city fountains
    (B) how fountains in cities are built
    (C) what city fountains do
    (D) why fountains are appearing in cities

4. The paragraph tells mainly—

    (A) why sailors fear shoals
    (B) why ships' cargoes were valuable
    (C) how plunderers caused shipwrecks
    (D) how storms caused shipwrecks

5. The paragraph tells mainly—

    (A) what Cynthia Alden accomplished
    (B) when Cynthia Alden was born
    (C) where Cynthia Alden became a private secretary
    (D) how languages helped Cynthia Alden in her job

A. Exercising Your Skill

Cynthia Westover Alden, whom you read about in Unit 19, was not the only woman to challenge her times. Read these paragraphs about another truly liberated nineteenth-century woman.

1.   Have you ever heard of Annie Oakley? She became a famous "show off"! Annie Oakley learned to shoot when she was just seven years old on her parents' farm in Ohio. But it was Thanksgiving Day in 1876 when Oakley won her first important shooting match. On that day fifteen-year-old Oakley beat Frank Butler, a world-famous trick shooter. Not only did Oakley win the fifty-dollar prize, she also won the heart of her opponent. Within two years Oakley and Butler were married. Soon after, Annie Oakley was the star of her own trick-shooting act. Oakley joined Buffalo Bill Cody's Wild West Show and traveled all over the world. Everywhere she performed, she won over audiences with her remarkable trick shooting. Kings and queens, presidents, and ordinary people cheered wildly every time Annie Oakley appeared.

2.   Annie Oakley's real name was Phoebe Ann Moses. Early on, well before she decided to make a career of trick shooting, Phoebe Ann Moses decided that she did not like her name. In fact, she so hated the name Phoebe that she refused to answer to it. "Call me Annie," she insisted, and the name stuck. Then, when she turned fifteen, Annie left the family farm to live in Cincinnati with her sister Lyda and Lyda's husband, Joe Stein. One day Joe and Lyda mentioned that they were thinking of moving out of the city into one of the small towns nearby—Hyde Park, or Oakley. Annie liked the sound of "Oakley" and decided on the spot to adopt that as her last name.

On your paper, write a main idea sentence for each paragraph.

- Main idea for Paragraph One: _____
- Main idea for Paragraph Two: _____

Now think of a good title for the whole passage. The title should, of course, relate to the topic. It should also be worded in such a way that it will create interest and curiosity. Write a title on your paper. Then compare your title with your classmates' titles.

B. Expanding Your Skill

Work with a small group of classmates to make a chart comparing Annie Oakley with another famous woman. List similarities and differences based on personal traits, goals, and achievements. Compare your group's chart with your classmates' charts.

C. Exploring Language

Read the paragraphs below. Then write a title on your paper for each paragraph.

(Title)
_____

One of the most famous people in America in the nineteenth century was William S. Cody. Pony Express rider, buffalo hunter, Indian scout, adventurer, Cody was known as "Buffalo Bill." In 1883 he organized a Wild West show because he wanted people in the East to know what the West was really like. Although critics panned the show as one of the worst ever produced, the public loved it. As one observer noted later, the show "captured the imagination of a public that was still fascinated by the romance of the West."

(Title)
_____

Annie Oakley would ride into the arena on a snow-white horse. She wore a buckskin blouse and skirt and carried her rifle. First her husband Frank Butler would toss some glass balls into the air. Oakley would shoot and break them, all the while riding at a full gallop. Then Butler would hold a coin between his fingers and Annie would shoot this away. Next, it was a playing card whose spots she shot out. Finally, still galloping wildly around the arena, she snuffed out the flames on several lighted candles.

D. Expressing Yourself

Choose one of these activities.

1. With another classmate, act out the shooting match between Annie Oakley and Frank Butler on Thanksgiving Day in 1876. (Use no props, not even toy guns.)

2. Put yourself in Annie Oakley's or Frank Butler's place just after the shooting match between the two. Remember that Oakley has defeated Butler, a world-famous trick-shot artist. Imagine what each might have said to the other. Write a dialogue showing their conversation. If possible, act it out with a classmate.

3. *Annie Get Your Gun* is a musical play about Annie Oakley. See if you can find a copy of this play in your school library or local public library. Write a short paragraph telling who wrote the play, when it was published, who the characters are, and other details that interest you.

1.   Can you picture the masked raccoon of our woodlands entering a department store during the night? When this actually happened in Montgomery County, Pennsylvania, it stirred up some mystery and excitement. The raccoon is a creature with great curiosity—and a sweet tooth. This particular raccoon shopped about until it stumbled onto a display of chocolate candy. What a feast the animal had in that lonely store! But by mistake, the raccoon also knocked a telephone off its cradle. An operator, hearing heavy breathing over the phone, summoned the police. The masked burglar was soon carried away—in a box trap!

2.   Knott's Berry Farm in Buena Park, California, is one of the most popular amusement parks in the United States. It used to have a Corkscrew ride, which carried its passengers up a seventy-foot incline, dropped them into the rush of gravity, and whipped them around two complete barrel rolls, while spinning them upside down twice at speeds up to forty-five miles per hour. Passengers were riveted to cockpit-like seats by centrifugal force, with the added safety of a foam rubber and iron shoulder harness. It sounds hair-raising, but the ride was surprisingly smooth, according to those who braved the challenge. The centrifugal force was so powerful that a dime held in an outstretched palm during the ride did not budge.

3.   The porcupine's diet is unbelievable. The "quill-pig" of our north woods will eat axe handles, canoe paddles, and shovel handles. It even has been known to eat half the floor out of a small cabin and the bottom out of a heavy aluminum kettle. The animal is constantly in search of salt. In the Pennsylvania mountains, a spreader being used to put cinders and salt on highways was parked for several days behind a remote shed. When the operator returned, it was discovered that a hungry porcupine had visited and eaten the rubber tires off the wheels!

4.   Sound cannot travel in a vacuum. It must have some medium through which it can pass, such as liquid, solid, or gas. Sound travels through dry air at about seven hundred miles per hour. This is about the speed of a bullet fired from a rifle. Sound travels about four times this speed through water. Sound can travel even faster through the ground than through the air. This explains why Native Americans of old would put their ears to the ground in order to hear approaching buffalo or horses. In general, most liquids and solids transmit sound at a faster rate than air does.

5.   Coco Chanel, born in the Auvergne area of France, was one of the world's greatest fashion designers. She introduced many fashion "firsts" and started many fashion trends, including the famous Chanel suit. Her famous perfume, Chanel No. 5, first appeared in 1922. She chose that number because she believed it was lucky. In her own woolen factory she created exclusive fabric designs in soft colors. Chanel loved to be copied. Whatever style she wore, other women rushed to buy. She died in 1971, but her fashion business continues.

UNIT 20

1. The paragraph tells mainly—

    (A) why a raccoon has great curiosity

    (B) how one raccoon stirred up excitement

    (C) why raccoons like shopping centers

    (D) why the telephone operator called the police

---

2. The paragraph tells mainly—

    (A) how amusement parks in the United States rank in attendance

    (B) what the Corkscrew ride at Knotts Berry Farm was like

    (C) why centrifugal force is powerful

    (D) where Knott's Berry Farm is located

---

3. The paragraph tells mainly—

    (A) how porcupines eat rubber tires

    (B) why the diet of a porcupine is unbelievable

    (C) where porcupines live

    (D) what a "quill-pig" is

---

4. The paragraph tells mainly—

    (A) how fast sound travels through the water

    (B) why Native Americans put their ears to the ground

    (C) how quickly solids transmit sounds

    (D) how quickly sound travels in different mediums

---

5. The paragraph tells mainly—

    (A) what Coco Chanel's career was like

    (B) what Chanel's fashions were like

    (C) why Chanel liked the number five

    (D) how Chanel discovered her perfume

UNIT 21

1.   Satellites that resemble flying pencil sharpeners, floating windmills, and swooping beetles are launched by the United States Orbital Geophysical Observatory. Each satellite is designed to carry special kinds of instruments and to travel in a specific path or orbit, televising images that describe electromagnetic radiation in unexplored regions in space. One satellite with the letters "EGO" circles around the earth gathering information about interplanetary dust and energy particles. These bits of data, when classified and interpreted, help astronomers to gain a clearer understanding about the earth's position in the solar system and to isolate forces that cause changes in the Earth's physical environment.

---

2.   Lena Horne is one of this country's most popular singers. Her success took a long time and a lot of hard work. She was born in Brooklyn in 1917. Her parents were separated. Her mother was a traveling actress, so Lena lived with her grandmother when she was very young. She was placed in many foster homes as she grew up until, at age sixteen, she became a dancer in a New York nightclub. That was the beginning of her very successful career as an entertainer. In the early 1940s she went to Hollywood, where she became the first African-American woman in the history of films to sign a long-term contract. In 1995 she was still playing to sellout audiences.

---

3.   For most Americans today, doing the wash means pressing a button on a machine. How launderers of old would have loved such a luxury! Homer's *Odyssey* describes how clothes were washed about 1000 B.C. They were placed in shallow water, pounded clean by feet, then left to dry in the sun. Soap that could easily be made from common materials was not invented until almost 2,000 years later, in Arabia. The first crude, hand-operated "washing machines" appeared only about two hundred years ago. Not until 1922 was the agitator—the basis of modern automatic washers—invented.

---

4.   Of all animals, perhaps the horse can be the warmest friend or meanest enemy! Many curious tales are told about the likes and dislikes of racehorses, for example. One famous horse couldn't win a race when it lost the company of its pal, a pony. Another enjoyed the company of a goat! Many famous horses were warmly attached to grooms. One horse wouldn't permit anyone in the stall while its groom was sleeping there. It didn't want the groom disturbed. Sometimes, though, a horse will dislike the groom. Many stable hands have quit because a horse bit or kicked them at every opportunity.

---

5.   No one remembers in what year the automobile heater was invented, but it is known that Augusta M. Rogers, a woman from Brooklyn, New York, received a patent for an automobile heating system that was not dependent on fire. Ms. Rogers also obtained patents for an improved folding chair and a special canopy meant to protect people against such annoying insects as mosquitoes. She invented all these things in a period of just four years. The car heater was the invention of which she probably was most proud.

1.   The paragraph tells mainly—

   (A) why the satellites have different shapes
   (B) how satellites aid our understanding of the Earth and space
   (C) what instruments detect electromagnetic radiation in space
   (D) where the satellites travel

2.   The paragraph tells mainly—

   (A) how Lena Horne climbed to success
   (B) why people like Lena Horne's voice
   (C) who Lena Horne's mother was
   (D) why Lena Horne became an actress

3.   The paragraph tells mainly—

   (A) how most Americans do their wash today
   (B) how common soap was invented
   (C) how clothes were washed through the ages
   (D) how ancient people used solar energy in washing

4.   The paragraph tells mainly—

   (A) why a horse enjoyed the company of a goat
   (B) why horses dislike grooms
   (C) what some horses' likes and dislikes have been
   (D) what happened to a horse when it lost its friend

5.   The paragraph tells mainly—

   (A) why Augusta M. Rogers invented a car heater
   (B) how Augusta M. Rogers invented a car heater
   (C) what Augusta M. Rogers invented
   (D) where Augusta M. Rogers lived

1.   Some plants and animals are called "living fossils" because they have continued to live on Earth long beyond the extinction of other species related to them. One living fossil is the tuatara, a small New Zealand animal somewhat like a lizard. The tuatara is related to a group of reptiles that became extinct millions of years ago. *Tuatara* is a Maori word meaning "peaks on the back." The animal has a crest of scales running down its back and tail. Tuataras mature very slowly. They are still growing at age sixty and may live to be 120.

2.   Robins, those cheerful, red-breasted birds long associated with the return of spring, have always fascinated bird watchers. The birds are often seen staring raptly at the ground before them, heads cocked attentively to one side as if straining to hear welcome sounds. This has caused widespread speculation that the birds may be listening for earthworms and waiting for the worms to appear, providing a succulent meal for the robins. In fact, the robins are not listening; they are trying to see clearly. Their problem is that they do not have bifocal vision, and so their concentration (plus vision) is better with only one eye in use. Hence, their heads are cocked expectantly to the ground.

3.   When Grace Darling was seventeen, her father relented and let the girl, who loved the ocean so much, help him in the Longstone Lighthouse. On the Northumbrian coast, storms were fierce, currents dangerous, and rocks tricky. One morning in 1838, during a raging storm, Grace was sure she heard faint cries in the wind. When dawn broke, she and her father saw survivors clinging to part of a wrecked ship. Though the waves and the winds were treacherous, Grace insisted that they attempt a rescue. Under the conditions it was a miracle, but Grace and her father saved ten lives. News of her heroism spread till Grace Darling herself became somewhat of a tourist attraction in Great Britain.

4.   A person choking to death is powerless. The victim cannot speak or breathe, turns blue, collapses, and dies in four minutes. Never beat the victim's back, lift the arms, or force water down the throat. The victim's survival depends on someone administering the "Heimlich Maneuver," which has been described in articles and demonstrated on television. The food choking the victim must be dislodged immediately. To accomplish this, the rescuer gets behind the victim, whether sitting or standing, then makes a fist of one hand, grabs it with the other hand, and presses sharply into the choker's abdomen with a quick upward thrust. This dislodges the food, and the victim breathes again.

5.   Millions of European immigrants came to America, lived in ghettos, and struggled all their lives for survival. Perhaps forty years passed before immigrants could save enough money to retire and make the journey "home" to the old country. When they got there, they discovered that they were "foreigners" in their birthplace and that they were regarded as "American." Often they came back to live their retirement in America, for they knew now that America had become their real "home."

1. The paragraph tells mainly—

    (A) the characteristics of the reptile family

    (B) what the Maori word *tuatara* means

    (C) the characteristics of the tuatara

    (D) the reason there are living fossils

2. The paragraph tells mainly—

    (A) what the robin looks like

    (B) why robins cock their heads attentively

    (C) what robins have to do with spring's return

    (D) why robins listen for earthworms

3. The paragraph tells mainly—

    (A) how Grace Darling became famous because of a sea rescue

    (B) what happened one morning in 1838

    (C) what the coasts of Northumbria were like

    (D) who helped Grace save the survivors

4. The paragraph tells mainly—

    (A) what choking is

    (B) why food causes choking

    (C) how to save a person from choking to death

    (D) how long it takes a person to choke to death

5. The paragraph tells mainly—

    (A) how long it took immigrants to retire

    (B) where European immigrants were forced to live

    (C) why the immigrants recognized America as their real home

    (D) what Europeans thought of Americans

1.   The paper checks people write have become more personalized than ever before. Included along with the names, addresses, and telephone numbers of the checking account owners are individualized designs and special colors. But one of the most personalized checks ever issued was made of steel, not paper. The $1,500 check, which weighed over twelve pounds and was a foot high and two feet long, was issued in 1932 by an electrical company in Cleveland, Ohio, to the winner of an arc-welding contest. The endorsement was welded on the back, and marked "paid" by the bank with a rifle, the word *PAID* being spelled out with bullet marks.

2.   In recent times we have witnessed tremendously high money judgments awarded by courts to various people. Nevertheless, perhaps none can match the amount awarded by a court on March 6, 1922, of more than 300 trillion dollars. The judgment was won by Henry B. Stuart of San Jose, California. He was owed it under a note for $100 with interest at ten percent compounded monthly. The debtor, a Mr. George Jones, paid nothing on the note from 1897 to 1922, so the interest just kept accumulating. The final amount owed was exactly $304,840,332,912,685.16. Not surprisingly, George Jones declared bankruptcy.

3.   If you were looking down at tide pools or coral reefs, you might say, "Oh, what pretty flowers!" Many plants grow there. But the "flowers" you see might not be flowers at all. They might be animals. Many "plants" of the seashore are really animals instead of plants. Some of the animals even have plant names. These animals hold tightly to the rocks or shells on the floor of the sea. These "flowers," known as sea anemones, are but a part of the strange life that shares the planet that we call home.

4.   Scientists in Stockholm, Sweden, have developed equipment that applies "artificial respiration" to polluted lakes. The device pumps compressed air and a chemical mixture into the water to reduce the number of nutrients. It was tested on a small dying lake in Sweden. As a result of pollution, oxygen in the hundred-foot-deep lake had been exhausted to within sixteen feet of the surface. Several months after the device was lowered into the lake, the water cleared, the oxygen content returned to normal, and new plant growth was cut in half. While these results have not occurred in other experiments, scientists hope to perfect the device for use in the future.

5.   Belle Boyd, born in 1843, was a Confederate spy whose daring efforts helped the success of several military actions in the Civil War. On one occasion at Front Royal, Virginia, she overheard Union plans at General Shield's staff meeting. She rode quickly to the nearest Confederate camp and revealed the secrets. She also helped Stonewall Jackson save several bridges. Belle was arrested twice for spying. The second time, in 1863, she was exchanged for an important Union prisoner. She then left for England with letters from President Jefferson Davis and became a successful actress. She returned after the war, continued her stage career, and married the officer who had captured her.

1. The paragraph tells mainly—

    (A) how paper checks have become personalized

    (B) how an unusual check was marked "paid"

    (C) who issued a check to the winner of an arc-welding contest

    (D) what one of the most unusual checks ever issued was

2. The paragraph tells mainly—

    (A) who Henry B. Stuart is

    (B) why George Jones lost a court judgment

    (C) how interest on a note is calculated

    (D) what the most money awarded by a court was

3. The paragraph tells mainly—

    (A) how animals cling to rocks and shells

    (B) how sea animals might be mistaken for plants

    (C) how plants manage to survive in the sea

    (D) where plants live

4. The paragraph tells mainly—

    (A) how long it takes to clear polluted water

    (B) why oxygen is important

    (C) what pollution is

    (D) how a new device combats lake pollution

5. The paragraph tells mainly—

    (A) how Belle Boyd helped Stonewall Jackson

    (B) why Belle Boyd was a Confederate spy

    (C) why Jefferson Davis sent Belle Boyd to England

    (D) how daring and successful Belle Boyd was

1.   Sausages were probably first made around 1500 B.C. by the Babylonians. At the time of Caesar, the sausage gained a sinful reputation because it was so popular and closely identified with wild, extravagant festivals. When the Christian era began, the festivals and the sausages were banned. However, people still demanded them, so the sausages were secretly sold until the ban was finally lifted. By the Middle Ages, sausages were so widespread that they were named for the towns in which they originated: Genoa, Vienna, Bologna, and Frankfurt. In America the first sausage, pemmican, came from the Indians, who combined chopped dried beef and dried berries. Today, America has over two hundred types of sausages.

2.   Dorothy Harrison Eustis taught the first Seeing Eye dogs used in the United States. She had seen German shepherd dogs being trained to guide war-blinded soldiers in Switzerland. Her unusual school started there in 1923. Like the Europeans, she trained German shepherds. Bred to herd sheep, these dogs also were protective and big enough to pull back in a harness to relay signals to masters. They were taught to guide a blind person on steps and through heavy traffic. Later, Seeing Eye dogs were trained at kennels in Morristown, New. Jersey. It was perhaps the most outstanding service to the blind since the invention of the Braille system of letters.

3.   In Santa Fe, New Mexico, Michael Naranjo has an art studio. This young sculptor was blinded by a hand grenade in Vietnam, and his eyes are artificial. His sculptures are not. During his hospital stay, Naranjo, who had been an artist, made hundreds of clay models of animals and people, expressing his visionary recollections through his hands. He is now a famous sculptor and has won many awards. His most recent victory over his blindness is a monumental twelve-foot bronze called "Taos War Dancer."

4.   The Japanese are noted for their kite flying. Engaging in kite battles is one of their favorite sports. At the Cherry Blossom Festival, kite "wars" provide the principal excitement of the day. Kite flyers by the thousands gather in fields for the battles. Kite strings are covered with glue and powdered glass. Once the sky is filled, the flyers cross kite strings. Each pulls a line back and forth against the kite string of an opponent. Soon one string cuts through the other. For the loser, the battle is over. For the winner, other battles lie ahead.

5.   Why are many children's banks shaped in the form of a pig? During the Middle Ages, metal was scarce and expensive. Household utensils were made of a clay known as pygg. In time all dishes were known as pygg. In those days people did not save their money in a bank. They placed it in a jug or jar. The container was known as a "pyggy bank," Centuries later a manufacturer was asked to produce a pyggy bank. Not knowing the origin of the term, the manufacturer mistakenly produced a bank in the form of a pig, and the idea became popular!

1. The paragraph tells mainly—

    (A) when the Babylonians invented sausages
    (B) where sausages were first eaten
    (C) why the Christians banned sausages
    (D) what the history of sausages is

2. The paragraph tells mainly—

    (A) who taught the first Seeing Eye dogs used in America
    (B) what kind of dogs were first used as Seeing Eye dogs
    (C) where Seeing Eye dogs were later trained in America
    (D) where Dorothy Eustis established her first school

3. The paragraph tells mainly—

    (A) where Michael Naranjo's studio is located
    (B) how a young sculptor overcame his blindness
    (C) how a young sculptor was blinded
    (D) why Michael Naranjo became a sculptor

4. The paragraph tells mainly—

    (A) how popular kites are
    (B) why the Japanese enjoy kite flying
    (C) how Japanese kite strings get broken
    (D) what Japanese kite battles are like

5. The paragraph tells mainly—

    (A) what dishes were once made of
    (B) what dishes were once called
    (C) how a misunderstanding resulted in the piggy bank
    (D) why household utensils were not made of metal

1.   Would you like to live about two hundred miles from both Paris and London? Then move to the Channel Islands, which lie in the English Channel between southern England and northern France. However, these islands are such sunny havens of peaceful agricultural beauty (famed for low-price markets, surfing, sailing, golf, castles, walks, and bike paths) that they've been forced to make it very difficult for aliens to obtain citizenship. There are two main islands, Guernsey and Jersey, and several smaller ones. The mini-islands of Sark and Herm allow no automobiles. On Herm, there are no roads—only hills, beaches, and woods. All the islanders enjoy the pleasant climate, with year-round average temperatures of 58–60 degrees.

2.   Though most of today's household "sponges" are artificial, the natural sponges used by previous generations were the actual skeletons of a unique animal species. For centuries most people thought that sponges were plants, because they seem just pulpy masses with no organs, growing out of rocks. Yet the sponge contracts when touched, and it "eats" tiny plants and animals from water flowing through its cells. Though it lacks a brain, a stomach, a heart, lungs, blood, or muscles, it does have a mouthlike "osculum." It has a skeleton but no bones; in fact, the red, orange, yellow, green, brown, or black mass once used by humans was the creature's skeleton.

3.   At twenty, Mary Patten learned about navigation while circling the world in her husband's clipper ship, *Neptune's Car*. In July 1856, she was again aboard the *Car* when it left New York Harbor, bound for San Francisco. As the ship rounded Cape Horn, Captain Patten was stricken with brain fever. His wife was suddenly the only person who could navigate and command the ship. During the next fifty-six days, she nursed her husband and guided the huge ship through pounding storms off Cape Horn. She averted a mutiny led by the first mate and finally brought the *Car* safely to San Francisco after 134 days at sea.

4.   You may never have heard of a waltzing mouse, but there is such a breed. This kind of mouse is produced by selective breeding. It is believed to be of Japanese origin. The waltzing mouse has the habit of suddenly interrupting whatever it is doing and spinning around rapidly like a top. One mouse may spin around in circles, and another may move in a straight line. It is believed that this waltzing is caused by an inherited defect in the inside of the ears. This defect interferes with the mouse's balance.

5.   When the publisher suggested that she write a book about girls, the author panicked. She insisted that she couldn't. However, she and her family needed money, so she agreed to try. Called a "tomboy," she thought she knew nothing about girls. Finally, she decided the story would be about the troubles and pleasures experienced by her and her sisters. Her publisher read the story but didn't find it exciting. Maybe he didn't know enough about girls. He gave the story to many girls to read, and each loved it more than the one before. Louisa May Alcott's *Little Women* became an instant success. Today it is a classic.

UNIT 25

1. The paragraph tells mainly—

    (A) why it is difficult to become a citizen of the Channel Islands
    (B) why the Channel Islands are a good place to live
    (C) why automobiles are not allowed on certain islands
    (D) where low-price markets are located

2. The paragraph tells mainly—

    (A) why sponges come in different colors
    (B) why people use artificial sponges today
    (C) what sponges are used for
    (D) what a natural sponge really is

3. The paragraph tells mainly—

    (A) how Mary Patten nursed her husband back to health
    (B) why Mary Patten sailed the ship around Cape Horn
    (C) how Mary Patten saved her husband's ship and its crew
    (D) why the first mate led a mutiny

4. The paragraph tells mainly—

    (A) what the origin of the waltzing mouse is
    (B) how the waltzing mouse got its name
    (C) what the effects of heredity are
    (D) how a waltzing mouse is tamed

5. The paragraph tells mainly—

    (A) how famous Louisa May Alcott became
    (B) how girls enjoyed reading *Little Women*
    (C) how Louisa May Alcott came to write *Little Women*
    (D) why Louisa May Alcott wanted to be a writer

A. Exercising Your Skill

Unit 23 describes the daring work of Belle Boyd during the Civil War. American women have always been ready to help in the defense of their country. Read the following paragraph about two such women.

> On June 11, 1814, a British warship sailed into the harbor of Scituate, Massachusetts. The Redcoats meant to capture the town, for the two countries were at war. Soldiers boarded small boats and prepared to row ashore. Two young sisters, Abigail and Becky Bates, watched the preparations from a lighthouse on a point of land at the entrance to the harbor. They knew there were no Minutemen in Scituate to defend the town. Somehow they would have to stop the British themselves. Abigail got the idea first. She took her father's fife and drum from his room in the lighthouse. Then quickly the two girls ran to a spot behind the dunes, where the British could not see them. Becky carried the drum, Abigail the fife. As the British force rowed closer and closer, they began to hear the notes of the hated Colonial marching tune, "Yankee Doodle." Thinking a force of Minutemen was waiting to fight them, the British returned to their ship. Within an hour they sailed away, never to return. Scituate had been saved.

On your paper, write a sentence that sums up the main idea of the paragraph. Then write a "catchy" title. Compare your sentence and title with those of your classmates.

B. Expanding Your Skill

Sentences in a passage generally should support the main idea. Read the paragraph to decide what the main idea is. Find the two sentences that do *not* support the main idea.

> Before the American Civil War began in 1861, many slaves fled their owners in the South in an attempt to reach Canada and freedom. Canada is the largest country in North America. Few runaways were successful. Hunger claimed many, who reluctantly returned to their owners. Bounty hunters tracked down many others. Then, just before the Civil War began, the number of successful escapes increased dramatically. The reason was the "Underground Railroad." Women especially helped form this noted escape route. One of the leaders was Laura Haviland, a Quaker widow, who operated a rest stop in Ohio. The Civil War lasted until 1865.

On your paper, write the two sentences that do not support the main idea.

1. _____
2. _____

C. Exploring Language

Write four or five sentences to complete each of these paragraphs. Give each paragraph a title.

(Title)
_____

1. People should help their country in time of need. _____
    _____
    _____
    _____
    _____

(Title)
_____

2. If I had been with Abigail and Becky Bates, I would have _____
    _____
    _____
    _____
    _____

D. Expressing Yourself

Choose one of these activities.

1. Prepare a two- or three-minute talk about some person whom you admire. The person should be living. Be sure to include strong supporting ideas for your opinions. Present the talk before your classmates.

2. Form a panel with several of your classmates. Choose a discussion leader, or moderator. Think about what you already know about heroes, living or dead, real-life or fictional. What traits do they have that you admire? What, in your own opinion, makes a hero? Who are some of your heroes? If you could become best friends with just one hero, who would that be? Discuss the subject of heroes.

3. Find out how Dolley Madison, wife of James Madison, the fourth President of the United States, showed bravery during the War of 1812. Write a report or give a talk explaining her bravery.

4. Write a newspaper story telling how a police officer or firefighter showed bravery in a dangerous situation. Be sure to include the five **W**s: *Who, What, When, Where,* and *Why (or How)*. Add a headline for your story. Then draw a "photo" type of illustration such as might be printed with the story in the newspaper.

Book **G**

Specific Skill Series

Drawing Conclusions

Richard A. Boning

Fifth Edition

SRA/McGraw-Hill
Columbus, Ohio

Cover, Back Cover, James D. Watt/Masterfile

SRA/McGraw-Hill

A Division of The McGraw·Hill Companies

Send all inquiries to:
  SRA/McGraw-Hill
  8787 Orion Place
  Columbus, OH 43240-4027

ISBN 0-02-687987-5

  6 7 IPC 02 01

To the Teacher

PURPOSE:
DRAWING CONCLUSIONS helps develop one of the most important interpretive skills. Pupils learn to look beyond the writer's literal statements to reach an unstated but logical conclusion based on those statements and sometimes their phrasing. In DRAWING CONCLUSIONS the correct conclusion is the most logical one for pupils to reach from only the information presented.

FOR WHOM:
The skill of DRAWING CONCLUSIONS is developed through a series of books spanning ten levels (Picture, Preparatory, A, B, C, D, E, F, G, H). The Picture Level is for pupils who have not acquired a basic sight vocabulary. The Preparatory Level is for pupils who have a basic sight vocabulary but are not yet ready for the first-grade-level book. Books A through H are appropriate for pupils who can read on levels one through eight, respectively. **The use of the *Specific Skill Series Placement Test* is recommended to determine the appropriate level.**

THE NEW EDITION:
The fifth edition of the ***Specific Skill Series*** maintains the quality and focus that has distinguished this program for more than 25 years. A key element central to the program's success has been the unique nature of the reading selections. Nonfiction pieces about current topics have been designed to stimulate the interest of students, motivating them to use the comprehension strategies they have learned to further their reading. To keep this important aspect of the program intact, a percentage of the reading selections have been replaced in order to ensure the continued relevance of the subject material.

In addition, a significant percentage of the artwork in the program has been replaced to give the books a contemporary look. The cover photographs are designed to appeal to readers of all ages.

SESSIONS:
Short practice sessions are the most effective. It is desirable to have a practice session every day or every other day, using a few units each session.

SCORING:
Pupils should record their answers on the reproducible worksheets. The worksheets make scoring easier and provide uniform records of the pupils' work. Using worksheets also avoids consuming the exercise books.

To the Teacher

It is important for pupils to know how well they are doing. For this reason, units should be scored as soon as they have been completed. Then a discussion can be held in which pupils justify their choices. (The Integrated Language Activities, many of which are open-ended, do not lend themselves to an objective score; thus there are no answer keys for these pages.)

GENERAL INFORMATION ON *DRAWING CONCLUSIONS*:

The questions in DRAWING CONCLUSIONS do not deal with direct references; thus the answers do not use the same words as the paragraphs. On the Picture Level, the readers examine the picture for the correct answer. The Preparatory, A, and B levels contain primarily indirect references; that is, the answers are found in the paragraphs but with slightly different wording. Some easy conclusions are also included. As the books advance in challenge, there are more difficult conclusions, involving less obvious relationships. The conclusions also become more dependent on qualifying words such as "mostly," "all," "some," or "only."

In DRAWING CONCLUSIONS the readers are asked to find an example, note a contrast, generalize, see cause and effect relationships, detect a mood, see an analogy, identify a time or place relationship, make a comparison, or anticipate an outcome.

It is important that the teacher ask pupils to find in the paragraph the specific information relevant to the tentative conclusion. Then pupils must test the conclusion against the information provided. When the emphasis is placed on finding evidence to prove answers and when the pupils put themselves in roles of detectives, not only does their ability to draw conclusions rapidly improve, but they also have fun.

Pupils must know that a conclusion is a judgment made. It must be supported by strong evidence. In DRAWING CONCLUSIONS the correct answer is one that is either highly likely or certain.

Some alternate answer choices may be true. The answer that is accepted as correct, however, must not only be true but must have supportive evidence in the paragraph. The clue may hinge on a single word, involve a phrase or a sentence, or encompass the paragraph as a whole.

RELATED MATERIALS:

Specific Skill Series Placement Tests, which enable the teacher to place pupils at their appropriate levels in each skill, are available for the Elementary (Pre-1–6) and Midway (4–8) grade levels.

About This Book

When you read, you can often figure out things that the writer doesn't tell you directly. You do this by thinking about the information the author does tell you. When you figure out something the author does not state directly, you are **drawing conclusions**.

Good readers draw conclusions as they read. They use the information the writer gives them to figure out things that the writer does not say. Read this paragraph. What conclusion can you draw about the information in the following paragraph?

> You might be surprised to know that the type of engine used in modern cars is similar to one installed on a bulky, three-wheeled carriage in 1885. Since 1885, almost all cars have been powered by gasoline engines. Today's compact, speedy cars are highly developed versions of those early cars.

Did you figure out that the engines in the three-wheeled carriage and in modern cars are both gasoline-powered? Did you also figure out that today's cars are faster than the earlier ones? You can draw these conclusions from the information the writer gives.

In this book, you will read paragraphs. After you read each paragraph, choose the best conclusion from three possible choices. Use the information in the paragraph to figure out the correct answer.

1.   Tarantula! The name strikes terror into most who encounter the spider. Little wonder. Covered with hair and having a leg spread of up to ten inches, the giant arachnid is not exactly what you would like to find on your pillow. Yet, though its bite can be painful, the tarantula is generally harmless to humans. Generations of people nevertheless believed that a tarantula's bite caused the "dancing sickness," which made victims leap into the air and run about hysterically, making strange noises—a condition called tarantism. In Italy it was once believed that the exhaustive dancing of the vigorous tarantella would cure this condition. In fact, the name of the spider is supposed to come from the town of Taranto, Italy, where tarantula-like wolf spiders abound.

2.   Natural materials such as stones, leaves, and clay have been used by both humans and animals to make things. A wasp called the potter wasp builds its nest from clay. After the clay dries in the sun, the nest will last for a long time and will not rot. Human potters also make containers from clay. The particles in soil are easily formed into shapes such as bowls, vases, or pots. Human potters probably dried their creations in the sun before they learned how to create high heat in a kiln. Both wasps and humans end up with very strong, long-lasting containers.

3.   Oceanography as a field of study had its beginnings in the 1870s with the voyage of the *Challenger*. This was the first deep-sea expedition organized on a large scale for the sole purpose of conducting a scientific study of the oceans. On its three-and-a-half year journey the *Challenger* obtained more detailed information than had been collected since people first ventured upon the ocean. Among the discoveries were the presence of sea life at astonishing depths and the fact that all oceans have the same chemical makeup. The historic British-sponsored voyage laid the foundation for one of the most exciting fields of science.

4.   In the Himalayan Valley north of India the expression "Every dog has its day" is true, because one day a year is set aside as "Dogs' Day." On that day humans revere dogs as fellow creatures in the brotherhood of all living things. Every dog, down to the filthiest cur, receives choice foods, a garland of flowers hung around its neck, and the red spot of Hindu holiness imprinted on its forehead. The following morning the dogs return to their life of receiving kicks, curses, and thrown stones for next 364 days.

5.   George Eliot was the pen name for Mary Ann Evans, a famous novelist. Ms. Evans was born in England in 1819. Her childhood and youth were spent in the peaceful countryside. Her home life was strict and religious. She later wrote about members of her family. When she began to write books, Ms. Evans took the pen name of George Eliot to avoid the prejudice against women writers. Her stories portrayed women characters so realistically, however, that other writers began to suspect the truth—that "George Eliot" was a woman.

1. You can conclude that—

   (A) wolf spiders are excited by the tarantella
   (B) the tarantula's reputation is undeserved
   (C) superstition can be very close to fact
   (D) tarantulas seek out people's pillows

2. You can conclude from this paragraph that—

   (A) potter wasps use containers made by humans
   (B) human potters copied potter wasps' behavior
   (C) clay pottery is easily shattered
   (D) clay must be shaped while it is wet

3. The paragraph leads to the conclusion that—

   (A) the discoveries were of no consequence
   (B) previous deep-sea expeditions had other purposes
   (C) the *Challenger* was probably an American ship
   (D) the trip was extremely short

4. The paragraph suggests that the dogs in the Himalayan Valley—

   (A) have a wonderful life
   (B) usually have a hard life
   (C) are well fed and happy
   (D) are loyal to their masters

5. The paragraph suggests that—

   (A) no one is certain that George Eliot was a woman
   (B) Ms. Evans only imagined there was prejudice against women writers
   (C) many people would not accept women writers
   (D) because of prejudice, Ms. Evans died in poverty

UNIT 2

1. Gazing across the arid, rocky Moroccan plain, one can hardly realize that 1,800 years ago the thriving Roman city of Volubilis stood there, amid an area rich in vegetation, yielding abundant harvests of grain. With a population estimated at fifty thousand, Volubilis was the capital of the Romans' North African province of Mauretania. The remains of its well-laid-out streets and triumphal arch give hint to the grandeur that was Rome. Visitors can see the ruins of a Roman bakery, oil mills, the market place, and the main shopping street, lined by a row of tall posts.

2. The buffalo was not only meat for the American Indians of the plains; it was just about everything. Hides were fashioned into tepees, boats, clothing, rugs, bedding, and shields. Buffalo bones were made into clubs, tools, and sled runners. Sinews provided sewing materials, bindings, and bowstrings. All edible parts provided food. From the buffalo horns Indians made cups and ladles. Even the eye sockets in the buffalo skulls were used. Hair was drawn through the two openings to make it into rope. The tail? It was made into a fly swatter!

3. Spelunkers, those people who explore the mysterious corridors far beneath the earth's surface, have made significant contributions to humanity. By their discovery of the tools, weapons, and paintings of the Stone Age, spelunkers have helped unravel the mystery of our past. Their descent into eerie caverns has brought numerous wonders to light: underground rivers, ice caves, bones of strange and extinct animals, and blind fish that have dwelt in darkness for untold centuries. Spelunkers have also measured and mapped the world's caves. Their efforts have opened the marvels and delights of the underground world to the millions who visit caves annually.

4. In Mexico and most other Latin American countries, December 28, *Dia de los Inocentes* (Day of the Innocents), is the day when practical jokers are in their glory. How much pleasure the Mexicans get out of this special day is revealed by an incident which occurred several years ago. It was reported in the Mexican newspapers that a new volcano was erupting near Nuevo Laredo. Readers were shocked, since the area had never experienced volcanic eruptions before; in fact, it was quite level. The story closed with a reminder that the date was December 28!

5. Humans can speed across the earth's surface faster than any other mammal, but not on their own two legs. The fastest human has run at only twenty-two miles per hour. Some elephants can do twenty-five m.p.h. in short dashes. A race horse has been clocked at forty to fifty m.p.h. To measure the real speed of mammals, one has to consider the antelope and the gazelle. Some of them have attained speeds of sixty to sixty-five m.p.h. But the fastest of all land animals is the cheetah. It has been timed at seventy m.p.h.—though it can maintain this speed for only a mile.

1. You can conclude that—

   (A) the Romans were conquered by the Moroccans
   (B) climate can change greatly over centuries
   (C) the Romans were more primitive than we had thought
   (D) human cleverness can tame the desert

2. From the paragraph you can tell that American—

   (A) Indians killed no other animals but buffalo
   (B) Indian warriors did not use the buffalo
   (C) Indians used the buffalo all year
   (D) Indian women used the buffalo more than the men

3. It is clear that—

   (A) all caves are tourist attractions
   (B) all the world's caves have been mapped
   (C) the underground world is more exciting than outer space
   (D) Stone Age people once occupied caves

4. The paragraph suggests that the *Dia de los Inocentes* is most like our—

   (A) April Fools' Day
   (B) Halloween
   (C) Fourth of July
   (D) Christmas

5. You can conclude from the paragraph that—

   (A) some horses can run faster than any cheetah
   (B) an antelope can catch a cheetah within a mile
   (C) some gazelles can run faster than any horse
   (D) some humans can run faster than any elephant

1.　More than fifteen million dollars waits in a Swiss bank for a missing woman known only as Bracha. The money was left to her in 1965 by Samuel Weingarten, who had survived the German concentration camps to become a wealthy businessman in Switzerland. Bracha had nursed Weingarten back to health, and they fell in love. Weingarten went to Switzerland, and they planned to meet. However, something went awry, and they never did. Weingarten never forgot the nurse, Bracha, and she will be a rich woman if she is ever found.

2.　Fishing can be frustrating unless the angler realizes that fishing is really hunting, and that the fish is a clever animal with good vision, a keen sense of smell, excellent hearing, and an instinct to survive. Fish see colors, so people wearing clothing that doesn't blend with the surroundings had better bring along their own food. Chances are they won't be eating fish. Shadows on the water, noisy oars, heavy steps on the shoreline, and conversation are all warnings to fish that an enemy is after them. As in hunting, the key to successful fishing is respect for the quarry.

3.　In the past, humans have been slow to act against the threatened extinction of wild animals. Thus they have lost forever many of those animals not able to adapt to changes in their environment. With the loss, however, people have acquired appreciation for their natural heritage and increased their knowledge of what they must do to protect it. They have resolved to try to preserve from extinction creatures that are few in numbers, such as the California condor and the whooping crane. Concerned people hope that these creatures will not suffer the same fate as the great auk, the passenger pigeon, and the heath hen.

4.　In Canada, a reference to London could be to the city of London, England, or the city of London, Ontario. It becomes more confusing if one starts talking about streets with such names as Oxford, Waterloo, or York, since there are streets in both Londons bearing these names. The Canadian London also has such world-famous names as Hyde Park, Covent Garden, Pall Mall, Piccadilly, and Trafalgar. The North American London even has a St. Paul's Cathedral and a Blackfriars Bridge, and, just as in London, England, it crosses a river by the name of Thames!

5.　House-sitters care for other people's homes or apartments while they are away. If you are a house-sitter and live in a big city or a college town where there are always people coming and going, you can usually manage year-round, rent-free living. The best idea is to find a wealthy family who owns two or more seasonal homes and who will pay the house-sitter's travel expenses to go from one house to another. If you don't mind living in the North during the winter and in the South during the summer, it can be a very nice, very inexpensive life.

1. The paragraph suggests that—

   (A) Bracha was killed by the Germans
   (B) Bracha never loved Weingarten
   (C) the money may never be given to Bracha
   (D) the bank would never let Bracha have the money

2. The paragraph suggests that when fishing, you should—

   (A) use a motorboat
   (B) stand close to the water
   (C) not wear a red jacket
   (D) tell jokes to keep from becoming bored

3. You can tell that—

   (A) there are no more passenger pigeons in the world
   (B) there is almost no chance of saving the California condor
   (C) humans caused the extinction of the whooping crane
   (D) today humans do not care about their heritage

4. The paragraph suggests that the two Londons—

   (A) have much in common
   (B) were founded in the same year
   (C) have the same number of people
   (D) are rivals

5. House-sitters must be people who enjoy—

   (A) having their own homes
   (B) living in the South
   (C) moving from place to place
   (D) living in a big city

1.   It is believed by many that a bull will attack anything colored red. It isn't true because bulls are colorblind. They will react the same way regardless of the color that is used to tease them. It is the movement of the bullfighter's cape, not the color, that causes the bull to react. Actually, anything waved in front of a bull will excite the animal and make it charge. In fact, since the bull is colorblind, waving a white cape or white cloth would probably get a quicker response, since the bull can see it better.

2.   *Raisin sec* is a French phrase meaning dried grape. Raisins evolved in the warm lands along the Mediterranean Sea, where grapes that dried on the vine were found to have a wonderful sweet flavor. The drying process was begun on a larger scale, and the raisins became important in Mediterranean trade. Raisins are still produced in France and Spain, where dried grapes are dipped in boiling water to give them a glossy sheen and to soften the skin. Australia has also become an important producer. The world's leading producer of raisins today is the United States, where over one-third of California's annual grape crop is used to make raisins.

3.   In battles of ancient times, elephants were feared in war almost as much as missiles are today. Heavy metal plates covered the sides and heads of the enormous animals. Swords were strapped to their trunks. Poisoned daggers were fastened to their tusks. Elephants carried soldiers armored with chain metal and carrying swords or javelins. Opposing armies had specially trained troops whose job it was to deal with these huge four-legged weapons. Catapults were used to hurl objects with flaming tar or sulphur at the elephants, sometimes causing the elephants to stampede through their own troops, destroying everything in their path. The ancient general Hannibal used elephants with his army in his famous crossing of the Alps.

4.   Animal Gourmet in New York City is a store that sells the fanciest of foods for dogs. For instance, you can buy special dog appetizers of liver paté and shrimp served on rye bread. For main courses, your dog can sample steak *tartare*, Swedish meatballs, and fancy French *boeuf bourguignon*. For desserts, there are "pupcakes" and special doggy ice cream. Dogs who are celebrating their birthdays can even have a piece of doggy birthday cake made of liver and dog meal, complete with frosting. The Animal Gourmet provides even the most demanding canine with its palate's delight.

5.   Six-pack rings are everywhere. They end up on beaches after picnics or are blown into rivers when people discard them. Diving birds can get one ring caught around their neck and hook another ring to a pillar. They can drown or strangle. Pelicans can get rings stuck around their bills. To protect wildlife, simply cut through each plastic circle before you discard your own six-pack rings. And pick up and snip any others that you see.

1. You can conclude that if a bull were in a field near you, you should—

    (A) quickly remove your red coat

    (B) run for the fence

    (C) quickly put on a white coat

    (D) stand still

2. You can conclude from the paragraph that—

    (A) over two-thirds of California's grapes are used for jam

    (B) French and Spanish raisins are better than U.S. raisins

    (C) raisins are produced in sunny climates

    (D) American raisins are better than French or Spanish raisins

3. You can tell that—

    (A) Hannibal rode atop an elephant in battle

    (B) all ancient armies used elephants

    (C) elephants were not always successful in attacks

    (D) the elephants remained calm even when attacked

4. The paragraph does *not* tell—

    (A) whether the Animal Gourmet caters to cats

    (B) where the Animal Gourmet is

    (C) what kinds of food the Animal Gourmet provides

    (D) whether the Animal Gourmet provides foreign foods

5. You could conclude from this paragraph that—

    (A) people are very careful about discarding six-pack rings

    (B) six-pack rings are useful items

    (C) a pelican with a ring around its beak could starve

    (D) diving birds try to dive through the rings

1.   Apple cider was the most popular drink in America in the eighteenth century—by far. Though tea, coffee, hot chocolate, and other beverages were easily available to the early settlers, they simply preferred cider—and it was cheaper than most drinks. John Adams, our second President, drank a large cup of cider each morning before breakfast and lived to the age of ninety-one. It has been estimated that in the year 1767, more than one barrel of cider per capita was drunk in Massachusetts. In the nineteenth century, the amount of cider used was even greater.

2.   Crime in the streets was a terrible problem for the Romans. Those famous Roman roads that crisscrossed the Empire weren't safe for anyone. Organized highway robbers made traveling the Empire's roads extremely dangerous. The Appian Way in the third century was at the mercy of a band of six hundred robbers for two years. The leader was kept informed about each traveler who was approaching and exactly what was being transported. Each time the Roman government broke up one crime ring of robbers, another immediately took its place. Crime plagued Rome even after the Empire fell!

3.   Because of its ferocious face, huge chest, enormous muscles, and massive jaw, the gorilla has become a symbol of terror to humans. Truthfully, of all the anthropoid apes it is probably the least offensive. When a gorilla believes it is in danger, it puts on a blood-curdling and terrifying act to frighten away an intruder. When it is finished acting it sits down and, using the palms of its hands, thumps the ground. If this doesn't frighten the trespasser, the gorilla turns and moves away. Rarely does it attack, even if advanced upon, nor does it ever make an unprovoked attack.

4.   How did desert communities grow corn, squash, cotton, and beans? The Hohokam people lived along the Gila River in Arizona until about 1450. They built a fine irrigation system to take advantage of all moisture. They built canals to follow the land's natural slope and the river's curve. To prevent canal water leaking into the desert, they lined their canals with clay, which made them waterproof. When Europeans settled there in 1868, long after the Hohokam left, they found the old canals still usable.

5.   Driving northwest of Portland, Oregon, Gail Beveridge noticed that the car she was passing had its brake lights blinking. She slowed down, followed the car, and recognized the light pattern as Morse code for S O S. Ms. Beveridge called the police, who stopped the car on the pretext of a speeding violation. The driver got out of the car, whispered, "Help, shotgun!" and fled to the patrol car. The hitchhiker riding in the car was taken into custody. Police found a sawed-off shotgun on the passenger side of the car.

UNIT 5

1. The paragraph suggests that—

   (A) there was no shortage of cider in 1767
   (B) early Americans had only cider to drink
   (C) drinking cider killed President Adams
   (D) after 1767, cider became less popular

---

2. The paragraph suggests that the highway robbers were—

   (A) constantly in danger
   (B) all captured
   (C) well organized
   (D) really honest citizens

---

3. The paragraph implies that gorillas—

   (A) do not have many battles
   (B) live only in Africa
   (C) are really fierce animals
   (D) have a gentle appearance

---

4. You can figure out that—

   (A) the Hohokam built their irrigation system to last
   (B) crops such as corn, cotton, and beans need little water
   (C) the Hohokam did not want to live with Europeans
   (D) water passes easily through clay

---

5. You can tell that—

   (A) the hitchhiker was just about to murder the driver
   (B) Ms. Beveridge had learned Morse code in the army
   (C) the hitchhiker did not realize the driver was signaling
   (D) the signaling car was speeding

UNIT 6

1.   That small, still voice that tells us something is morally wrong is known as our conscience. Sometimes it takes a long time till the voice of conscience is heard. Officials of a city in Utah received two dollars from a woman who wrote that two years earlier she had used a picnic area without paying the required dollar fee. It wasn't that she'd meant not to pay; she had just forgotten. "I apologize for my dishonesty," she wrote, and added another dollar "to cover inflation and interest." Another case was that of a Californian who finally paid a parking ticket he had owed to the city of Dallas, Texas, for thirty-two years.

2.   Although it's totally inside Swiss borders, Campione is actually part of Italy. People there use Swiss money, and the Swiss postal system delivers their mail. Their police force, however, is made up of ten Italians. According to Swiss law, the police can't carry their guns on Swiss soil to reach Campione. When they are coming from Italy, they take a boat across Lake Lugano to the Swiss border. There they surrender their guns to the Swiss border patrol, which accompanies them to Campione and returns the guns. It seems like a game, but it's done to show that each nation respects the laws of the other.

3.   Misers are a peculiar breed. One penny pincher named Ida Wood was so money mad that she declared herself, secretly of course, a human bank. Trusting neither banks nor the stock market, she carried her entire savings around on her person. A money belt around her waist hid $750,000 until she was ninety-three. Ida lived in a shabby apartment, refused visitors, ate raw fish, and smoked cigars. Nothing, however, shocked people more than her hospital stay. The nurse who dressed her in a hospital gown found the money belt—containing nearly a million dollars!

4.   Many of us have looked at paintings and wondered which way they should be hung. With modern works of art especially, it is sometimes a problem to know which is the top or bottom. Don't worry if you are confused. Even the experts make mistakes. *Le Bateau*, a painting by the famous artist Henri Matisse, was hung upside down at an exhibit in the Museum of Modern Art in New York City. An estimated 116,000 people viewed *Le Bateau* for two months before the error was discovered!

5.   Persistent collectors of rare plant specimens have endangered more than three thousand American plant species. The giant fawn lily and the Nevada primrose are now listed as "commercially exploited." One commercial collector dug up 700,000 rattlesnake orchids and acres of cacti. Private collectors have randomly picked such rare plants as the ram's head, lady's slipper, or leathery grape fern. Picnickers plunder public parks. Once plant predators decide they want a rare specimen, almost nothing can stop them. The destruction of habitats to create farms, strip mines, houses, highways, and other developments has also killed many of the scarce plants.

1. You can conclude that the people paid because they—

    (A) were afraid of being caught
    (B) wanted to get something off their minds
    (C) hadn't known previously that the money had to be paid
    (D) were too poor to pay earlier

2. The paragraph suggests that—

    (A) both nations are satisfied with this arrangement
    (B) the Swiss mistrust the Italians
    (C) the people of Campione would rather be Swiss
    (D) Campione's location has caused a touchy international situation

3. The paragraph suggests that Ida Wood—

    (A) was frequently ill
    (B) didn't believe in luxuries
    (C) carried mostly coins in her money belt
    (D) had a large family

4. From the paragraph, you can conclude that—

    (A) modern art is not very popular
    (B) Matisse's painting looked good either way
    (C) people who visited the museum knew nothing about modern art
    (D) Matisse painted *Le Bateau* upside down

5. The paragraph suggests that—

    (A) there are no more rattlesnake orchids
    (B) people should not picnic in parks
    (C) flowers are really not important
    (D) some plant species may soon be extinct

The First L A P
Language Activity Pages

A. Exercising Your Skill

Do you enjoy riddles? Did you ever stop to think that when you solve a riddle, you are really **drawing a conclusion**? A conclusion is a decision or judgment you make based on facts and information. Read the following riddles, and think about the information each one contains. Write the answers on your paper.

1. Two boys were born in the same hospital on the same day. They have the same father and mother, but they are not twins. How can you explain this?
2. A woman drove all the way from Boston to Los Angeles without knowing she had a flat tire. How is that possible?
3. What five-letter word has six left when you take two letters away?
4. If the blue house is on the left side of the road and the brown house is on the right side of the road, where is the White House?
5. If a father bull eats three bales of hay and a baby bull eats one bale, how much hay will a mother bull eat?
6. A dog was tied to a fifteen-foot rope, but it walked thirty feet. How was it able to do this?
7. Two softball teams played a game. One team won, but no man touched base. How was that possible?
8. How can you jump off a fifty-foot ladder without getting hurt?
9. A police officer saw a truck driver going the wrong way down a one-way street but didn't give the truck driver a ticket. Why not?
10. What is pronounced like one letter, is spelled with three letters, and is a part of every person and animal?

B. Expanding Your Skill

Take turns asking and answering the riddles. Did everyone come up with the same answers? Why or why not? Discuss the information given in each riddle that led to your answers. In some cases, the humor of the answer depended on information that was *not* given. Discuss the important facts that were left out of riddles 2, 6, and 9, for example. Then turn this page upside down to check the answers to the riddles.

Answers: 1. they are two of a set of triplets; 2. the flat tire was her spare tire; 3. sixty; 4. Washington, D.C.; 5. there's no such thing as a mother bull; 6. the rope wasn't tied to anything; 7. the teams were all-women teams; 8. jump off the first rung; 9. the truck driver was walking; 10. eye

18

C. Exploring Language

What makes a joke funny? In order to understand the humor of a joke, you need to draw conclusions about it. Read each of the following jokes. On your paper, answer the questions about the jokes.

1. A woman went into a clothing store and asked the clerk, "May I try on that dress in the window, please?" "No, madam," the clerk answered. "You'll have to use the fitting room like everyone else."

   What had the woman really meant?

2. One day Larry's grandmother said to him, "There are two words I want you to promise me you'll never use. One word is swell and the other is rotten." "Sure, Grandma," said Larry. "What are the two words?"

   What was Larry's misunderstanding?

3. On seeing that his friend Mike looked sad, Leo asked him, "Is anything the matter?" "My doctor told me I can't play golf," replied Mike. "Oh, has he played golf with you too?" asked Leo.

   What is the difference between what the doctor meant and what Leo thinks the doctor meant?

D. Expressing Yourself

Choose one of these activities.

1. Create riddles of your own to ask your classmates. See whether they can guess the answers to your riddles by using the information you provide. Have them explain how they arrived at the answers.

2. Play "Twenty Questions" with your classmates. The leader thinks of an item. The others ask questions that can be answered only by *yes* or *no*. Then they put the clues together to draw a conclusion about the item.

3. Put on a comedy show for your class. Work with one or two of your classmates. Tell jokes to the class. If you don't know any jokes, get a book of jokes from the library. Try to memorize the jokes rather than read them.

1.   Beneath that sweet white mound of whipped cream, pouring its fragrant juices into the shortbread, is that favorite of American berries—the strawberry. Appropriately, the strawberry, a plant of the rose family, is a member of the group *Fragaria*, meaning "fragrance." But whence the name *strawberry*? Perhaps you've picked strawberries. Noting that the plump red berries seemed scattered or strewn randomly among the plant's leaves, Anglo-Saxons of ancient England called it *streoberie*, meaning "strewn berry." The strawberry plant does not reproduce by seeding but sends out runners that grow along the ground and root in the soil, producing new plants. Since strawberries grow in every state in the Union, there should be no shortage of strawberry festivals to delight us wherever we roam.

2.   Sailors of the waters off Africa tell about a strange island of dogs. On charts of the Indian Ocean, it is listed as Juan de Nova. Centuries ago the mariners of many lands, including pirates, landed on this island west of Madagascar to take aboard fresh water and coconuts. Sometimes, ships' dogs were left behind. There were no people, but the dogs managed to survive on sea gulls and turtle eggs. In time, the dogs began hunting in packs. Sailors who went ashore on Juan de Nova told frightening stories about savage dogs that howled like wolves. It was, they said, an island ruled by dogs!

3.   When a cat's tail begins flipping from side to side, it is a signal that the animal is excited or annoyed and is ready to scratch or pounce. If a barking dog appears, automatically the cat's tail stiffens and straightens, its back rises into a hump, and every body hair fluffs out from the sudden tightening of muscles. Shorter spinal muscles draw the backbone into an arch and hold the tail rigid. Tightening muscles beneath the skin pull the hairs straight up. All this is performed unconsciously by that special area of the cat's brain that flashes emergency messages to the proper muscles.

4.   Most historians omit the fact that Union and Confederate soldiers sometimes acted like good friends during some battles of the Civil War. Once, troops ran out of trenches and shook hands like old pals! In one period, the soldiers of both sides bathed together in the Rapidan and Rappahannock rivers between the firing lines. Later, during the siege of Vicksburg, there were truces during which they picked blackberries side by side. As Confederate troops marched toward Gettysburg, a little girl dashed out and waved a Union flag at them. The Confederate general politely tipped his hat in salute, and the troops, following behind, all did the same!

5.   There are certain animals which can be called "assistants." On more than one occasion people have reported seeing birds feeding a crippled bird or one not otherwise able to feed itself. Hunters report cases of elephants helping a wounded companion, pushing and guiding the animal until it is out of danger. Even more remarkable are instances of mutual help between animals belonging to different species. Photographs are available of a bird feeding a goldfish. The bird held pieces of food in its beak and transferred them to the mouth of the hungry goldfish.

1. You can tell that—

   (A) strawberries have been known for centuries

   (B) strawberries do not grow in California

   (C) strawberries grow only in America

   (D) *streo* means "straw" in Anglo-Saxon

2. The paragraph does *not* tell—

   (A) why ships' dogs were left behind

   (B) why pirates landed on Juan de Nova

   (C) what the dogs ate

   (D) where Juan de Nova is located

3. In danger or emergency, a cat—

   (A) stiffens and fluffs only if it chooses to

   (B) tries to imitate a dog

   (C) lengthens its spinal muscles

   (D) cannot stop its body from stiffening and fluffing

4. The paragraph suggests that during the Civil War—

   (A) the Confederate general was actually a Union spy

   (B) there were very few bloody battles

   (C) many soldiers had no natural hatred for the enemy

   (D) most soldiers refused to fight against their friends

5. The "assistant animals" can best be compared to—

   (A) domestic animals

   (B) farmers

   (C) nurses

   (D) generals

1.   Scientists have fossil evidence of life going back billions of years. But most fossil studies concentrate on only the last 600 million years. Why? Organisms with skeletons or other hard parts did not appear on Earth until about 600 years ago. Most life before that was made of soft material. Would you rather search for fossils of jellyfish or those of shelled organisms?

2.   During colonial days, as increasing numbers of people came from Europe to New England, the area began to get crowded. Farmers would find animals straying onto their property from a nearby farm, and sometimes a cow or a pig would destroy part of a garden. So the people got together and built town pounds—big stone corrals with walls high enough to hold any farm animal. One person in each area was named poundkeeper, whose job was to round up any animal that got away from the farm where it belonged. The poundkeeper would put the animal in the pound until its owner paid a fine to get it back.

3.   Pablita Velarde, a Pueblo Indian girl, made many paintings of Indian women at their daily chores such as molding clay into large jars and caring for their families. She also painted the ceremonial dances of the Pueblos. The vivid portraits attracted attention outside the reservation, and she was asked to do murals for many buildings. She perfected a form of earth painting, grinding clays into painting colors on an Indian grinding stone. Velarde's work has won many prizes. One of her paintings was presented by the President of the United States to the Prime Minister of Denmark.

4.   A woman who had the courage to believe in her goals when things went against her was Lucy Beeman Hobbs. Through hard work and determination, she became America's first woman dentist. During the 1850s, while working as a teacher, she decided to study dentistry. Schools refused to admit her. After working for a dentist, she began her own practice. Lucy Hobbs still wanted to go to dental school. In 1865 she finally was admitted as the first and only woman student at the Ohio College of Dental Surgery. Her persistence had won.

5.   Are you a "workaholic"? It's not a disgrace if you are, but it might be good for you to vary your lifestyle with some recreation. Typical workaholics are perfectionists who demand never-ending work of themselves and often of others as well. They get up early and go to bed late, frequently existing on three or four hours of sleep a night and taking catnaps at any time or place. The opposite of workaholics are "playaholics," who sleep late, and when they do finally arise, are looking forward to play instead of work.

1. You can conclude from the paragraph that—

    (A) organisms without skeletons do not leave good fossils
    (B) fossils formed earlier than 600 million years ago are buried too deep
    (C) life has only been on Earth for 600 million years
    (D) jellyfish fossils are very easy to find

2. From the paragraph you can understand that—

    (A) the more animals there were, the less the poundkeeper had to do
    (B) the owners usually got their animals back
    (C) it would have been easier to build fences around all the farms
    (D) in Europe there had been animal pounds

3. From the paragraph you can conclude that Pablita Velarde—

    (A) painted mostly buildings
    (B) has never been recognized as an artist
    (C) painted mostly Indians and Indian life
    (D) used only bright colors in her paintings

4. From the paragraph you can see that—

    (A) Lucy Hobbs became the most famous American dentist of the 1800s
    (B) discrimination against women was unusual in the mid-1800s
    (C) there were no dental colleges in this country until after 1865
    (D) people could practice dentistry in the 1850s without completing dental school

5. The paragraph suggests that—

    (A) a life style balanced between work and recreation is best
    (B) being a "workaholic" is the best way for a person to live
    (C) "workaholics" are in better health than "playaholics"
    (D) most people would like to work for a "workaholic"

UNIT 9

1.   Have you ever climbed above the timberline of a high mountain? Trees stop growing at that altitude because they cannot survive the freezing temperatures and the battering winds. Because the water in the ground above the timberline stays frozen much of the year, large plants cannot obtain sufficient water. Only lichens, mosses, and stunted vegetation can endure there. Just below the timberline are evergreen trees, whose tough, pointed needles can withstand the harsh climate more easily than can the broad leaves of other trees. Since the timberline is dependent on climate and latitude, it is much higher on some mountains than on others.

2.   The Irish, or white, potato was first grown in South America and brought to Europe by Spanish explorers. In some nations it became a major part of the diet. The typical Russian at one time ate more than a pound of potatoes a day. Potatoes kept the Germans alive during two world wars. Perhaps the champion potato eaters of all were the Irish of previous centuries. The Irish, lacking meat, ate potato bread, potato soup, and potato cakes—as well as boiled, baked, and fried potatoes. The average citizen ate as much as eight pounds of potatoes in a single day. Small wonder that white potatoes became known as Irish potatoes!

3.   From the top of Buffalo Bill Dam, Wyoming, one is introduced to a series of fantastic but often dramatically lifelike formations sculptured by wind and rain. The Holy City is a fantastic collection of spires resembling churches. The outline of the Laughing Pig is directly over the highway. There are also rocks resembling an elephant's head, a bear, a camel, and a boy and his dog. A tower-like structure is appropriately called Chimney Rock. Even with no snow, there are four old people on a toboggan! Most would agree that Chimney Rock is one of the most spectacular rock formations in existence!

4.   It's all aboard for Silverton, Colorado! People who board this train at Durango, Colorado, actually relive an 1882 adventure. Not far out of the station an abundance of wildlife, including deer, elk, bear, and a mountain lion, comes into view. As the train winds through San Juan National Forest, passengers can see over 140 species of wild grass and three hundred different flowering plants such as Colorado's state flower, the blue columbine. When the train arrives in Silverton, passengers leave to stroll around town, shop, and have dinner before the trip back to Durango. The tracks of this narrow-gauge railroad were laid in 1882.

5.   Io, Jupiter's closest satellite, has more volcanic activity than any other body in the solar system, including Earth. Io's volcanoes erupt with sulfur, which colors the moon's surface with shades of red and yellow. Astronomers have fun calling Io "the pizza moon." But Io's volcanoes are not caused by the moon's interior heat, as on Earth. Io is caught in an orbit between Jupiter and another moon, Europa. The gravitational pull from these two larger bodies keeps Io constantly bulging and stirred up. This keeps the moon constantly erupting.

1. On a high mountain, a broad-leafed oak or maple tree would be found—

    (A) just above the timberline
    (B) just below the timberline
    (C) well below the timberline
    (D) anywhere above the timberline

2. You can tell that the Irish potato was—

    (A) the main part of the Irish diet
    (B) a delicacy
    (C) eaten in only one form
    (D) introduced by the Russians

3. The rock formations were produced by—

    (A) modern humans
    (B) cave people
    (C) nature
    (D) Buffalo Bill

4. You can conclude that people who take the train to Silverton are nearly all—

    (A) business persons
    (B) hunters
    (C) prospectors
    (D) tourists

5. You can conclude that—

    (A) people will be able to travel to Io someday
    (B) the gravitational pull from Earth's moon does not affect our planet the same way that Jupiter and Europa affect Io
    (C) only moons and planets with sulfur have volcanoes
    (D) Io's volcanoes can be controlled by scientists on Earth

1.   The Yellow River in northern China annually left enormous deposits of silt along its course, which in turn raised the level of its bed and forced the waters to spill across its banks on an average of once every two years. In time, the people learned to build dikes and dams and to harness the unpredictable river with canals and irrigation systems. Still, during the last three thousand years of recorded history, the Yellow River has changed its course nine times. Each time it moves, the river causes untold damage and takes the lives of thousands of people. No wonder it is referred to as "China's Sorrow"!

2.   The reason your feet, unlike those of birds, might get frostbitten if you were to go barefoot outdoors in freezing weather, is that your body's heating system is different from a bird's. When you go out in the cold, a special temperature regulator in you brain sends out signals that tighten muscles and reduce the flow of blood in the tiny blood vessels under your skin. Since birds do not have such a heat regulator, the blood vessels do not tighten and the blood flow is not reduced. Moreover, a bird's body temperature is higher than a human's. These two factors prevent a bird's feet from freezing.

3.   The orange and black monarch butterfly of North America is famous for its seasonal migration. At summer's end, the monarchs gather in huge flocks and begin to wing their way south. Led by their marvelous instincts, giant swarms of migrating monarchs, each group numbering in the thousands, make their way along the same routes their ancestors took. Flying by day and resting at night, the monarchs finally arrive at winter quarters hundreds of miles away. There they gather in the identical trees that their ancestors chose as resting places in generations past. Birds will not bother the brightly colored monarch butterfly, because it smells and tastes bad to them.

4.   Was it the tax on tea or the mark of the broad arrow that angered the American colonists more? It's hard to say. By carving the sign of the broad arrow, the English reserved trees of the New World for the Crown's use. Great white pines, for example, were so marked to become masts for the king's ships. The angry colonists needed these pines for American wagons, barrels, fuel, and other uses. The pioneer people prized the white pines so highly that they used them as symbols of their new country on the early flags. One of the colonial flags at the battle of Bunker Hill had a green pine tree on a white background.

5.   Maine has cold and snowy winters, so it's not surprising that this is where the heated snow shovel has been invented—by a plumber. The heated shovel looks like an ordinary shovel, but the blade part is hollow. It contains a coil which conducts heat throughout the shovel. The coil is fed from a battery carried in the shovel shaft. That battery can be repowered by attaching a power cord on the shovel to a line going to house current. The shovel keeps the user's hands warm and sends snow sliding easily off the blade.

1. The paragraph suggests that the Chinese—

   (A) now have complete control of the Yellow River
   (B) worship the Yellow River
   (C) still can't completely control the Yellow River
   (D) transport goods on the Yellow River

2. You can conclude that if birds had a temperature regulator they would—

   (A) feel the cold less
   (B) want to fly farther north in winter
   (C) all die in summer
   (D) feel the cold more

3. From the paragraph you can tell that—

   (A) the monarch butterfly is enormous
   (B) the monarch butterfly has amazing migrating instincts
   (C) the monarchs fly at night
   (D) changes in migrating patterns occur in each new generation

4. You can conclude from the paragraph that—

   (A) England paid the colonies for the trees they used
   (B) some of the trees eventually were used for weapons
   (C) England placed a tax on trees in the colonies
   (D) white pines were excellent wood

5. The paragraph suggests that ordinary snow shovels—

   (A) have blades that snow sticks to
   (B) are too small for efficient use
   (C) are too heavy
   (D) have short handles

1.   The elephant's trunk is a muscular extension of a nose and upper lip grown together. As it is closely allied with the motor and sensory areas of the brain, the trunk is under delicate voluntary control, giving it great skill of movement. It can pick up a pin from the ground, uncork a wine bottle, open a slipknot, toss up and catch a baseball, trigger a gun, open a gate, and ring a bell. Some elephants have been trained to use their trunks to sweep paths and walkways with brooms and to carry garden watering pots.

2.   You've probably noticed that pennies and nickels have smooth edges, but silver or mostly silver coins—dimes, quarters, and half dollars—have milled, or grooved, edges. Gold coins also have milled edges. Coins were milled to stop people from stealing money. People used to pare, or shave, the edges of valuable coins, particularly gold coins. Over time the gold and silver shavings they gathered could add up to quite a bit of money. With the edges of coins milled, the paring became visible. Since copper and nickel coins were not valuable enough to be pared, their edges were not milled.

3.   Spring fever has often been thought of as a feeling of renewed enthusiasm for life. However, in some modern studies about spring's effect on humans, researchers say it brings feelings of hopelessness. When chronobiologists—scientists who study the body's natural rhythms—put the data of many medical records into a computer, the computer showed that depression and ulcers appear most often in the springtime. The study of body rhythms is a new field of science—one that will continue to prove useful in the understanding of human behavior, and especially in our ideas about spring fever.

4.   In the middle 1800s, a young black man, Elijah McCoy, was very interested in mechanical engineering. After many frustrating months of job hunting and encountering prejudice, McCoy had to accept a position as a railroad coal shoveler. He soon saw how inefficient locomotives were. At that time, trains frequently had to stop in order to be lubricated. Working on the problem for months, McCoy devised a way to accomplish the lubrication while the machines were moving. He also invented other devices. It was because of his talents that a popular phrase was created. Whenever railroad people wanted to buy equipment, they would make sure they got "the real McCoy."

5.   The Colorado Railroad Museum is keeping alive an important part of the state's colorful history which might otherwise be forever lost. The railroads of a century ago made it possible for Colorado to take advantage of its natural resources. To break the isolation of remote areas, the rails climbed over the treacherous passes, bored under walls of granite, clung to cliff ledges, and fought with violent rivers for room on narrow canyon floors. The museum dramatically tells the story—with the help of a replica of an 1880 depot, fifty-three locomotives, freight cars, cabooses, and wooden coaches.

1. An elephant's trunk serves as—

    (A) its eyes and ears
    (B) an arm and a hand
    (C) a leg and a foot
    (D) another head

2. You can tell that—

    (A) if gold coins were issued today, they would not have milled edges
    (B) the U.S. is the only country that mills edges of coins
    (C) quarters will continue to have milled edges
    (D) copper is rarer than silver

3. You can conclude that the new scientific evidence about spring fever—

    (A) does not agree with the chronobiologists' findings
    (B) does not reach accurate conclusions
    (C) will not prove very useful to the average person
    (D) does not agree with what most people believe

4. You can tell that—

    (A) no one knew what McCoy had invented
    (B) McCoy never received a penny for his inventions
    (C) McCoy coined the phrase "the real McCoy" himself
    (D) McCoy's inventions were highly successful

5. The paragraph suggests that building railroads in Colorado must have—

    (A) required an enormous effort
    (B) taken very little time
    (C) cost little money
    (D) been without any purpose

1.   The unusual thresher shark is able to attack fish better than any other shark. *Alopias* has a tail, or at least the upper half of a tail, as long as its body, fifteen feet or more. Other deep-feeding sharks drive schools of fish upward. The thresher, feeding near the surface, "surrounds" the smaller fish by circling them, moving its incredible tail, and herding them inward. They feel the tail before they see the shark. Suddenly, from somewhere on the outside of the circle, the blunt-headed *Alopias* is having dinner.

2.   A recent study of telephone use reinforces popular beliefs about the speech habits of Americans in different regions. New Englanders, for example, have long been noted for not wasting words in conversation. They carry this trait to the telephone, too. A recent survey of forty-four states disclosed that Rhode Island and Vermont residents made the shortest phone calls, with residents of Maine, Massachusetts, New Hampshire, and Connecticut close behind. In contrast to the tight-lipped New Englanders, garrulous Texans made the longest calls of all.

3.   Shivering in the cold will warm you up. Your muscles have to exercise in order for you to shiver. The work done by your muscles makes you warmer even though you don't consciously make them work. A sudden shutdown occurs in the little tubes that carry warm blood just underneath your skin. This causes the blood to remain deeper down in your body where it helps to warm your heart, liver, and other important organs. Your skin may feel chilly when you shiver, but your insides are actually warming up.

4.   There are some people who will tell you to remove food from cans immediately after opening them or else the reaction among the food, can, and air will make the food poisonous. The premise is false. Food in an opened can will not become poisonous any faster than it would if removed, because it is the airborne bacteria that cause food to spoil, not the metal of the container. To prevent food left in a can from spoiling, cover the can. Acid foods left in metal containers may develop an undesirable taste, but it is not the taste of poison.

5.   Colonial settlers valued the wood of the white cedar for its remarkable ability to resist water and rot. During the 1700s, most of the shingles used for houses were made from trees growing in New Jersey cedar swamps. By the 1800s, the trees had been used up. However, one day some sunken logs floated to the swamp's surface. Although they had been under water for centuries, the logs still contained excellent timber. When lumberjacks discovered that the bottom of the swamp was lined with fallen white cedar trees, "cedar mining" began in the New Jersey swamps and continued until the Civil War!

1. You can tell that the thresher uses its tail like a—

   (A) gun
   (B) lasso
   (C) whip
   (D) boat

2. You can conclude that Texans—

   (A) like New Englanders
   (B) dislike New Englanders
   (C) like to talk
   (D) talk only to other Texans

3. You can conclude from the paragraph that—

   (A) in hot weather your insides are cold
   (B) the colder it gets, the warmer you will be
   (C) when you shiver, your skin freezes
   (D) shivering is a way nature protects you

4. You can conclude from the paragraph that—

   (A) some foods will taste bad if left in open cans
   (B) bacteria are attracted more to metal than to other substances
   (C) cans are safer than any other place for storing food
   (D) some foods will become poisonous if left in open cans

5. You can tell that cedar mining in Jersey swamps—

   (A) has ended
   (B) will continue
   (C) was a total failure
   (D) was important during the 1700s

A. Exercising Your Skill

A **conclusion** is a decision or judgment you make that is based on facts and information. A **syllogism** is a method of reasoning in which two statements are made. From the two statements, a conclusion is drawn in a third statement. Think about the example below:

Statement A: All birds lay eggs.
Statement B: Robins are birds.
Conclusion: Robins lay eggs.

Read each of the following pairs of statements. Think about the information given in Statement A and Statement B of each pair. Use that information to draw a conclusion. Write the conclusion on your paper.

1. Statement A: All living things need oxygen to grow.
   Statement B: Plants are living things.
   Conclusion: _____

2. Statement A: All islands are surrounded by water.
   Statement B: Nantucket is an island.
   Conclusion: _____

3. Statement A: All planets in our solar system revolve around the sun.
   Statement B: Mars is a planet.
   Conclusion: _____

4. Statement A: All citrus fruits are good sources of vitamin C.
   Statement B: Oranges and grapefruits are citrus fruits.
   Conclusion: _____

B. Expanding Your Skill

Discuss the conclusions you wrote in Part A. Explain how each pair of statements led to your conclusion. Then write your own syllogism. Include two statements of fact followed by a third statement in which you draw a conclusion based on those facts.

C. Exploring Language

Read the following paragraphs. Study the conclusions that follow each. Write the one conclusion that can be correctly drawn from each paragraph. Tell what information in the paragraph supports that conclusion.

1. An island is a body of land surrounded by water. Hawaii is made up of eight major islands and 124 smaller islands. The largest of the islands is called Hawaii.

   A. Hawaii is a state.
   B. No map is large enough to show all 132 of Hawaii's islands.
   C. Each of the Hawaiian Islands is surrounded by water.

2. The farther a planet is from the sun, the colder it is. Pluto is the ninth planet from the sun. Neptune is the eighth planet from the sun.

   A. Pluto is colder than Neptune.
   B. Neptune is colder than Pluto.
   C. Neptune and Pluto are the same temperature.

3. Phoenician sailors in the year 2000 B.C. used a block of soda to hold their cooking pot over the fire. The soda and sand turned into a bubbly liquid which, when cooled, turned into glass.

   A. The sailors paid no attention to safety.
   B. Heated soda and sand cool very rapidly.
   C. Glass can be made by heating soda and sand.

D. Expressing Yourself

Choose one of these activities.

1. Work in two teams to create syllogisms; omit the conclusion that can be drawn. Teams take turns reading their pairs of statements to the other team. A correct conclusion scores one point for the guessing team. An incorrect conclusion scores a point for the other team.

2. On an index card, write a conclusion about something your class has read or knows about. Exchange conclusions with a classmate, and write two statements that would lead to that conclusion.

3. Think of a syllogism. Then get three index cards. Write the first statement on one card, the second statement on a second card, and the conclusion on the third card. Shuffle the cards. Ask your classmates to put the syllogism in the right order.

1.   The frigate bird, because of its impressive size and wing span of seven and a half feet, has been called a "feathered airplane." It can float high in the air for hours without moving its wings—rising in spirals or soaring slowly along, piloting its flight by effortlessly changing the angle of its "planes." At the close of the day, it settles in the bushes or mangrove trees along the shore. However, it must take off from high places because its feet are weak and clumsy. The frigate bird dwells in the tropics, seldom being seen farther north than the coasts of Florida or southern California.

2.   Would you believe that the most common substance on earth other than air—sea water—is now being made artificially and sold to aquariums, laboratories, and hatcheries, some of which are situated on the seacoast itself? Even aquariums like Mystic, Connecticut's, on saltwater Long Island Sound, employ artificial sea water for convenience and content control. Creating artificial sea water is far more complicated than merely dumping a few pounds of salt into a tank of water. Levels of nitrogen, phosphorus, oxygen, bacteria, and salt must be maintained in delicate balance over extended periods.

3.   A neutron star is very dense and massive. That is, it is relatively small, but very tightly packed and very heavy. A rotating neutron star gives off radio waves. These waves travel through space and can be measured on Earth as pulses. The pulses are so regular that they were originally mistaken for signals from intelligent civilizations. In fact, astronomers called the first pulsars LGMs, which stands for "little green men."

4.   The world's greatest camouflage experts are not in any army but in the world of nature. The larva of the moth *Amphidasis cognataria*, for example, survives by imitating its environment. It is more difficult for birds such as warblers and finches to find *Amphidasis* larva than any other insect, for the moth is spruced up like a rose twig and transfixes itself at the same angle as the twig it imitates. Its skin is green, spotted, and colored like leaf scars. To fool its enemies totally, the moth arranges its tiny pink forefeet to resemble the bud of the twig it is imitating. Even the keen eyesight of birds fails to see through its disguise.

5.   Most people know that *two bits* refers to a quarter, but few people know how the term originated. In the colonial days in America, when coins of all nations circulated freely, the most popular coin was the Spanish dollar, also called a *piece of eight*. To make change for small purchases, it became customary to cut the coin into pie-shaped pieces. One-eighth was worth twelve and one-half cents and was called a *bit*. Two bits became twenty-five cents; four bits, fifty cents; and six bits, seventy-five cents. Imagine what those sharp-pointed little *bits* did to colonists' pockets!

1. The frigate bird can *not*—

   (A) control the angle at which it flies
   (B) glide easily through the air
   (C) do a running takeoff from the ground
   (D) ever be seen on the northern California coast

2. The paragraph implies that—

   (A) the earth has more sea water than air
   (B) Mystic's aquarium contains only freshwater fish
   (C) some natural sea water is not chemically balanced
   (D) it is not profitable to make artificial sea water

3. It is likely that pulsars are named for—

   (A) intelligent civilizations in space
   (B) a neutron star's size and mass
   (C) a neutron star's regular waves
   (D) astronomers on Earth having fun

4. You can conclude that—

   (A) *Amphidasis* larva is the favorite food of birds
   (B) the larger a creature is, the poorer its eyesight
   (C) the rosebush itself can sense that the larva is there
   (D) blending with the surroundings is good protection

5. You can conclude that—

   (A) the colonies coined their own money
   (B) paper money was common in the colonies
   (C) colonists' pockets often developed holes
   (D) Spanish dollars were made of solid gold

UNIT 14

1.   A single oak tree may produce 50,000 acorns in a good year. But very few of these will take root as oak seedlings. Many of the acorns will be eaten by animals. Others will end up in places that do not support tree growth—in water or on rocky surfaces. Many seedlings that do take root may still be eaten by animals before they can mature, or be crushed into the ground by moving animals or people. If you ever see a huge oak, you'll know that it was one of the lucky ones.

2.   In some regions spiders exist in enormous numbers. In certain areas the estimated number of spiders ranges from eleven thousand per acre in a woodland to over two million in grassy areas. Being insect-eaters, they do a great amount of good under the right circumstances. Spiders in Athens, Greece, have eliminated infestations of bedbugs, since a single spider is capable of eating thirty to forty bedbugs in one day. Even the ill-reputed black widow spider is beneficial. One black widow devoured 250 houseflies as well as a variety of other insects. However, it is true that spiders do not discriminate between the harmful and beneficial insects, killing both.

3.   During the Victorian era, the English believed in "a sound mind in a healthy body." The country overflowed with health devices that were either useful or useless, harmful or harmless. While they slept, girls with large ears wore Claxton's Ear-Cups. People with muscle and joint problems used Zander's Mechanical Exercisers and underwent agonizing pain. The most unusual invention was the battery-operated Electrophatic Belt. When strapped around the waist, the gadget delivered a series of mild electric shocks. Advertisements announced the belt's ability to act upon all organs of the body, thereby reducing general weakness. The one thing the belt could not do was to survive advancing medical knowledge.

4.   The poet Katherine Lee Bates, who was born in Falmouth, Massachusetts, in 1859, had very strong ties to her native state. Bates was educated at Wellesley College and later taught there for forty years. Although Massachusetts has first claim to her fame, she actually belongs to the entire nation. Her words to the patriotic hymn "America the Beautiful" have made her immortal. Katherine Bates is said to have been inspired to write the lyrics when standing atop Colorado's 14,100-foot Pikes Peak. From this rooftop of America, the beautiful spacious skies seem endless, and the purple Rocky Mountains do tower majestically above the fruited plain that unfolds eastward toward amber waves of grain.

5.   On the north bank of the Thames River, just east of the city of London, is found the Tower of London. It has been used as an ancient fortress, a prison, and a royal residence. Primarily a museum today, it houses the glittering royal treasures of the English rulers—armor, ancient weapons, and a collection of torture instruments. Many famous people, including Queen Elizabeth I (while still a princess) and Sir Walter Raleigh, were held prisoner in the Tower; some were beheaded there. As recently as World War II, spies were executed within the Tower's forbidding walls.

1. You can conclude from the paragraph that—

    (A) acorns take root in water
    (B) animals do not like oak trees
    (C) many more acorns are produced than become new trees
    (D) huge oak trees grow only where there are no animals

2. The paragraph suggests that spiders—

    (A) do more harm than good
    (B) do more good than harm
    (C) are more numerous than bedbugs
    (D) are taking over the world

3. You can conclude from the paragraph that the—

    (A) Electrophatic Belt was effective
    (B) Victorians valued the mind more than the body
    (C) Victorians placed little value on the mind or the body
    (D) Electrophatic Belt was not effective

4. You can conclude from the paragraph that—

    (A) Katherine Bates died at age forty
    (B) Wellesley College is in Massachusetts
    (C) Pikes Peak is in Massachusetts
    (D) Katherine Bates was poorly educated

5. The story mentions—

    (A) the names of spies executed during World War II
    (B) four uses to which the Tower of London has been put
    (C) precisely how old the Tower of London is
    (D) exactly how many prisoners were held at the Tower of London

UNIT 15

1.   We tend to think of canals as modern engineering feats. Yet one of the world's great canals dates from the sixth century B.C. Nature had given the Chinese no easy way to transport goods from the fertile lands of the south to the arid regions of the north. They, therefore, dug a canal ninety miles from Lake Tai Hu to the Yangtze River and called it *Yon Ho*, or Grand Canal. Seven centuries later, the Sui Dynasty commanded five and a half million peasants to widen and deepen the canal and line it with rocks so it would no longer be choked by silt. Eventually extended to 1,200 miles, the Grand Canal is still in use today.

2.   Since 1750, bands of roving British gypsies have held a reunion each June near Appleby, a little town in the north of England. At Crowning Fair Hill just outside of town, eight hundred or so colorful wagons, campers, trailers, and motor homes gather on a thirty-two-acre campsite. At the fair, gypsies show and sell horses. The gypsies are superb horse breeders and traders. A good horse can bring in as much as $1,000. The gypsies also sell donkeys, sheep, and cattle. Many of the fifteen thousand gypsies in Britain attend the annual reunion.

3.   Different birds eat different foods. Worms are not the choice of all birds. Hawks and owls prefer to dine on mice and rabbits. Vultures eat dead animals, and flycatchers gulp down unlucky flies and mosquitoes. Woodpeckers eat carpenter ants and bark beetles. The clue to what a bird eats is in the shape of its beak. Wide-billed ducks scoop up plants and animals from the mud. Finches are seed eaters because their short, fat beaks can break open hard shells. The hook-beaked birds—owls, hawks, and eagles—tear flesh, and the nuthatches' thin beaks act as tweezers to select tiny insects among leaves.

4.   Ocean water gets colder and saltier at greater depths. The sun's light can only penetrate a few hundred meters into the water. In the upper layers of the ocean, the sun's light heats the water and powers photosynthesis in ocean plants. This explains why shallow bays, such as Chesapeake Bay, and coastal areas of the ocean are full of both plant and animal marine life.

5.   To users of snowmobiles in North America, who number more than ten million, the machine is a source of fun and recreation, but it didn't start out that way. It was invented as a practical means of transportation in the snow country of northern Canada. The first one was called the "Ski-Dog." The inventor gave this original snowmobile to a friend, to use on missionary journeys among the Ojibway Indians around St. James Bay. The primitive machine was loud, heavy, hard to use, and got stuck in snowdrifts, but it was a vast improvement over dogsleds.

1. The paragraph suggests that the original Grand Canal—

    (A) was one hundred miles long
    (B) was used for swimming
    (C) wasn't completely satisfactory
    (D) didn't require much work

2. You can tell from the paragraph that gypsies—

    (A) love to sing
    (B) buy many horses
    (C) move a great deal
    (D) hate to camp

3. You can tell that hook-beaked birds eat—

    (A) seeds
    (B) insects
    (C) meat
    (D) plants

4. From this paragraph you can conclude that—

    (A) deep-sea divers must wear goggles
    (B) deeper waters have less life than shallow waters
    (C) ocean plants prefer deeper water
    (D) coastal areas have particularly cold water

5. You can tell from the paragraph that the snowmobile—

    (A) wasn't any better than the dogsled
    (B) hasn't changed its name
    (C) has changed in its purpose
    (D) was invented by a missionary

UNIT 16

1.   Malaria has killed more people than all of history's wars and plagues, including the Black Death. Victims it doesn't kill suffer nearly unbearable fevers, chills, and weaknesses. Once it was believed that the cause of malaria was air coming from swamps or marshes, hence the term *malaria* from *mal aire* (bad air). Prior to 1740, it was called "chills" or "fever," or even "the shakes." There were terrible outbreaks of malaria in the fourth and fifth centuries B.C. and in the sixth through nineteenth centuries A.D. Malaria still kills about two million people annually!

2.   In 1883, British troops were stationed in India, a part of the British Empire. Every morning as part of their routine, the soldiers used to roll around in the mud in full uniform. The mud was for protection to camouflage the sparkling white British uniforms. Without mud, the soldiers were sitting ducks for the enemy, targets easy to hit. One day their colonel explained the mud bath to a visiting British clothes manufacturer, who returned to England to make new uniforms for the soldiers, copying that mud color. The outfits that the manufacturer made were called *khaki*, the Indian word for mud!

3.   Commercial egg distributors take advantage of the popular belief that brown eggs are more nutritious and richer than white ones. The truth is that the color of an eggshell is unrelated to its richness. Analysis of the chemical composition of both eggs confirms that fact. All eggs, regardless of color, are designed by nature for the maturation of chicks, so they all contain more than enough nourishment in a limited space. Strange as it may seem, light-colored eggs are generally selected by New Yorkers, whereas dark-colored eggs are preferred by Bostonians.

4.   The first woman to swim the English Channel four times was San Diego-born Florence Chadwick. In her first attempt in 1950, she beat the speed record set by her idol, Gertrude Ederle. During a span of nineteen years Chadwick won the San Diego Bay race a total of eight times, and in 1950 she conquered the Channel in thirteen hours and twenty minutes, a new world's record for women. During the next five years, Chadwick swam the Channel three more times, becoming the first woman to swim it both ways. She made the most of her fame, advising a swimwear company and opening Florence Chadwick Swimming Schools in New York City.

5.   The last of the great five-masted, square-rigged ships vanished without leaving a trace. The *Kobenhavn*, sailing from Buenos Aires to Australia, radioed in December 1928, that all was well aboard—and was not heard from again! Though sturdily built and equipped with adequate boats and lifesaving gear, the vessel simply disappeared from sight. Had the *Kobenhavn* been caught in a swift and violent storm? Had an iceberg sent the iron-hulled ship to its doom? Its fate and that of the sixty people aboard remain one of the unsolved mysteries of the sea.

40

1. You can tell from the paragraph that—

    (A) deaths from malaria are increasing
    (B) malaria is always fatal
    (C) a cure for malaria has not been found
    (D) malaria did not exist before 1740

2. You can tell that—

    (A) rolling in the mud served no purpose
    (B) the new uniforms were white
    (C) the soldiers' khaki outfits were properly named
    (D) the color of uniforms is unimportant

3. You can conclude that—

    (A) Bostonians prefer dark eggs because Boston gets less sunlight than New York
    (B) distributors know that brown eggs are better
    (C) white eggshells turn brown when cracked
    (D) it is not known why Bostonians and New Yorkers differ in egg preference

4. The paragraph suggests that—

    (A) it is not difficult to swim the English Channel
    (B) Florence Chadwick was handicapped
    (C) Gertrude Ederle was a famous swimmer
    (D) Florence Chadwick never won a trophy

5. As possible causes of the disappearance, the writer suggests—

    (A) forces of nature
    (B) a defective ship
    (C) a mutinous crew
    (D) poor leadership

1.   In ancient and medieval days, pepper was considered so valuable it was used as money. People would weigh out little bits of it, as if it were gold, to purchase articles or pay their rent. When the Gothic armies stormed ancient Rome and took over the city, they demanded a ransom that included three thousand pounds of pepper. Often, when a medieval father made up his daughter's dowry—the possessions she brought to her husband when she married—pepper was one of the most valuable items. In those times, pepper was nothing to sneeze at.

---

2.   A biologist in New Zealand says that a species of crow can make and use tools. Gavin R. Hunt observed crows pulling twigs from a branch. He watched as they used their beaks to shape a hook at the end of a twig. They also removed leaves from the twig and trimmed off the bark to make the tool smooth. Finally, they used the hooked tool to remove worms and other tasty insects from holes in trees and logs.

---

3.   It has been said that the history of North America has been written on a beaver skin. This is just another way of saying that the beaver, perhaps more than any other animal in history, is responsible for the exploration and colonization of the continent. The relentless search for more and more beaver pelts to supply the world with hats and coats went on for three centuries. The commercial value of the furs spurred the creation of trading posts, which later expanded into cities. It also caused the colonists from various nations to engage in long and bloody conflicts.

---

4.   The zipper is a relatively new invention. In 1893 a Chicago engineer filed the first patent for a crude "slide fastener." It didn't work very well, but even when the design was dramatically improved in 1913, the public still wasn't ready. The problem was not mechanical, but moral. Many people of that day did not believe that the zipper was proper for clothes. It offered speed and convenience, but somehow it seemed indecent to get in and out of clothes that quickly. Today, zippers are everywhere and are accepted by just about everyone.

---

5.   Waves that move over shallow water have enormous strength. Even four-foot-high waves have been known to drag a four-thousand-pound block of concrete twelve feet and turn it on its side. Waves have taken stones weighing about seven thousand pounds from a twenty-foot seawall and tossed them over the wall. One block of cement weighing over five million pounds was carried away by violent waves during a storm. What incredible power waves possess!

1. You can conclude that in ancient times—

   (A) a husband paid his bride's father for her

   (B) pepper was common at meals

   (C) gold was unknown

   (D) pepper was not sprinkled freely on food

2. From this paragraph, you can conclude that—

   (A) crows are intelligent animals

   (B) crows and chimpanzees live together

   (C) crows have few ways to gather food

   (D) crows share their tools with one another

3. You can tell that the search for beaver—

   (A) wasn't really important

   (B) resulted in good and bad

   (C) took place only in Europe

   (D) didn't last very long

4. The zipper—

   (A) came before buttons

   (B) achieved popularity in the 1890s

   (C) was never designed for women

   (D) became most popular within the last 70 years

5. You can tell that—

   (A) only the size of a wave determines the wave's strength

   (B) the deeper the water, the more destruction is caused

   (C) there is almost no limit to the force of waves

   (D) it is only during storms that the power of waves is recognized

1.   Years ago there was a mystery about blood transfusions. They saved some lives, but in many other cases the patients died, apparently from the transfusions themselves! Then in 1900 a Viennese scientist, using a microscope and blood from two associates, proved that there are different blood types and, more important, that mixing types when transfusing blood can cause the patient's death. Today there is no reason to fear death from a blood transfusion, for all blood is classified before transfusions are given. Blood banks and hospitals keep their supplies of blood according to type, and each donor's blood is analyzed before being used.

2.   Hawaii's famous Mauna Loa is the largest volcano in the world. It looms 13,680 feet above the ocean and extends 18,000 feet below the sea, giving a total height of over 31,000 feet—the world's largest mountain mass. Half the island of Hawaii is covered with old lava flows from this volcano. When Mauna Loa starts shaking and rumbling, residents of Hilo, the nearest city, do not panic. They know from past eruptions that the lava flows slowly enough for them to evacuate in time.

3.   Covington, the seat of Kenton County, Kentucky, is known not only as a breeding center of thoroughbred horses, but also as the town that has the smallest church in the world, the church of Monte Cassino. With walls only eight feet high and a belfry so small that it cannot hold a bell, the church resembles a mausoleum from the outside. The inside of the church can accommodate only three people at a time, sitting on rough wooden benches facing a tiny altar. Built in 1850 by Benedictine monks, it was named after the first Benedictine monastery in Italy.

4.   Practically any state road map will disclose a score of unusual town names. Some communities seem to sound as if they were named for birds or animals. For example, Ohio has many "bird towns": *Martin, Robins, Parrot,* and *Cygnet*. Virginia has a *Cuckoo* and a *Horsey*. There's an *Elephant* in Montana and a *Shy Beaver* in Pennsylvania. Kentucky comes up with *Hippo* and *Mousie*. New Jersey, on the other hand, seems to prefer parts of animals such as *Hensfoot, Crow's Foot,* and *Colt's Neck*. Reading a road map these days can seem very much like paging through a zoology text!

5.   The strongest earthquake to hit the United States occurred not on the west coast, but in the middle of the country. On February 7, 1812, a "super quake" struck New Madrid, Missouri, on the Mississippi River. The shock rang church bells in Boston and changed the course of the Mississippi River. It formed two large lakes. Aftershocks shook the area for two years. The death toll was low only because few people lived in that area at the time.

1.   If the patient had type A blood and the donor had type B, the—

   (A) donor could die
   (B) patient would get well
   (C) patient could die
   (D) donor would get healthier

2.   You can conclude that—

   (A) Hawaii is mostly a flat island
   (B) no people live anywhere near Mauna Loa
   (C) Mauna Loa's eruptions have killed no one recently
   (D) it is possible to climb all 31,680 feet of Mauna Loa

3.   From the paragraph you can *not* tell—

   (A) what Covington is known for
   (B) why the church was built so small
   (C) where the first Benedictine monastery was
   (D) what the church looks like from outside

4.   The paragraph suggests that zoology deals with—

   (A) geography
   (B) animals
   (C) towns
   (D) maps

5.   The paragraph suggests that—

   (A) aftershocks are worse than the original quake
   (B) the effects of earthquakes can be felt at a distance
   (C) only the west coast has "super" earthquakes
   (D) few people died in the quake because they were not home

1.   Humans have measured time almost since they first became aware of its passage. For centuries sundials and hourglasses were the world's only time-telling devices. A variation of the hourglass was the water clock, which measured time by the amount of water dropping through an opening in a jar. It was first used in 2000 B.C. in Egypt. The mechanical clock, developed during the Middle Ages, is powered by a weight dropping or a spring uncoiling at a regulated interval. Yet such clocks were notoriously inaccurate until the 1600s, when a Dutch scientist installed pendulums into clocks. Since the time of a pendulum's swing never changes, a pendulum can control a clock's rate precisely.

2.   New roses don't evolve quickly. To develop a new strain, the rose fanciers may spend half their lifetimes carefully grafting one variety of the flower to the bush of another, thus crossing two strains. Years after their first attempts, they may still be crossing hybrids from the first union in order to develop a new blossom with all the qualities the modern flower must have. When that happy goal is reached, rose enthusiasts then go right out and apply for a patent on their "invention." From then on, the new rose is exclusively theirs to sell.

3.   Every year during the festival of Setsubun, held the first few days of February in Japan, the head of the household casts out demons by using beans! Dressed in ancient costume—black kimono, ceremonial coat, and divided skirt—he or she tours the house, carrying a box of roasted beans. In each room, the beans are thrown out the window with the shout, "Out with the devil!" Then more beans are scattered around the room to the chant, "In with the good luck!" This ritual supposedly assures the family good fortune and health for the coming year.

4.   "Excuse me, ma'am, have you got the time?" You may be surprised that the lady you asked does not respond, blink, or make any gesture whatsoever. Laughing, you finally realize you've been hoodwinked! At Madame Tussaud's Waxworks Museum in London, some wax likenesses are so convincing and so casually placed among the crowds of some two million visitors a year that it's very possible to make this error. All this genius stems back to Madame Marie Tussaud herself. She learned the strange art of duplicating people's forms from her doctor uncle—who sought only to improve his knowledge of anatomy by modeling human parts in wax.

5.   If you have ever been in a building that was more than two hundred years old, you may have noticed how small the doorways and windows seemed. It's no mystery. People were shorter two hundred years ago. The average height of soldiers in America's War of Independence was 5 feet 4 inches. Even in the last fifty years Americans have grown taller. In 1920 the average height for men was 5 feet $7\frac{1}{4}$ inches. Today it is nearly 5 feet 9 inches. The most amazing increase in height in the world has occurred in Japan. Recently the height of the average Japanese jumped $2\frac{1}{4}$ inches in ten years.

1. In the year 1500 people probably—

   (A) wore pendulum wrist watches
   (B) were often not on time
   (C) counted the swings of pendulums
   (D) carried large water jars everywhere

2. The paragraph suggests that rose breeders—

   (A) are foolish
   (B) must have patience
   (C) can't protect their new strains
   (D) are always successful

3. The paragraph does *not* tell—

   (A) when the festival occurs
   (B) how the ceremony originated
   (C) what is thrown out the window
   (D) what the ritual is supposed to accomplish

4. The paragraph suggests that—

   (A) Madame Tussaud's Waxworks cheats its visitors
   (B) Madame Tussaud's wax figures are all kept in glass cases
   (C) people don't mind being deceived at the Waxworks
   (D) Madame Tussaud's first wax figure was of her uncle

5. The paragraph suggests that—

   (A) only Americans and Japanese are getting taller
   (B) many people in the world are getting taller
   (C) average heights of people will probably increase no further
   (D) only men, not women, are getting taller

A. Exercising Your Skill

A good detective uses clues to draw a **conclusion** about a crime. A good reader uses clues provided by the writer to draw a conclusion about a piece of writing. How good a detective are you? Read each of the sets of clues below. On your paper, write what you think is happening in each case.

EVENT 1

astronauts waving	shuttle on launch pad	TV cameras
"Ignition!"	Kennedy Space Center	pillar of flame
deafening roar	"Liftoff!"	crowded beaches

What is happening? _____

EVENT 2

interstate highway	suitcases on car roof	road maps
"Are we there yet?"	family in car	motels
fast food places	license plates	gas stops

What is happening? _____

EVENT 3

ticket line	popcorn and candy	dark theater
huge green monster	screams	"I can't look!"
whirring projector	cold air conditioning	soft seats

What is happening? _____

EVENT 4

crowds of people	tokens	city
tracks	"Hold that door!"	underground

What is happening? _____

EVENT 5

earth	lots of water	"Plant six inches apart"
seeds	sunshine	"Oh, my aching back!"

What is happening? _____

B. Expanding Your Skill

Compare the conclusions you drew about each event with your classmates' conclusions. Did everyone arrive at the same conclusions? Why or why not? Discuss the clues that led to each conclusion. What other clues might have helped you draw that conclusion? On your paper, write additions to the list of clues for each event.

C. Exploring Language

On page 48, you drew conclusions about events that were each based on several facts. See how good you are at drawing conclusions based on just three facts! Read each of the following items. Draw a conclusion about what is happening.

1. "Quiet on the set!" "Places, everyone." "Lights, camera, action!"
2. "Thirty seconds!" "Contact light!" "Houston, Tranquility Base here. The *Eagle* has landed."
3. "My assistant will enter the cabinet." "Watch closely as I pass the hoop over and around all sides." "Abracadabra!"
4. "Keep your eyes on ring three." "It's the greatest show on Earth!" "Bring in the clowns!"
5. "Open wide." "Do you brush after every meal?" "I'm afraid you have a cavity."
6. "This is your captain speaking." "Fasten your seat belts." "We are presently climbing to 30,000 feet."
7. "May I see your license, please?" "I clocked you at 75 miles an hour." "I couldn't have been, Officer!"
8. "Quiet, please." "You'll find *Newsweek* in the periodicals room." "Look it up in the card catalog."
9. "My name is Tad, and I'll be your waiter tonight." "There are several specials." "I'll have the chicken in orange sauce."
10. "It makes a grinding noise." "Let's get it up on the lift." "You may need an engine overhaul."

D. Expressing Yourself

Choose one of these activities.

1. Work together with a group of classmates to plan and act out a scene. You may want to use the items in Part C for ideas. Have your other classmates draw a conclusion about what is happening. Ask them to explain their reasoning.

2. Make up a list of clues about an event. Then trade lists with a classmate. Write a few sentences that draw a conclusion about the clues on your classmate's list.

3. Write a paragraph describing an event. Then exchange papers with a classmate. Circle the important clues in your classmate's sentences.

1.   The Ford Trimotor, affectionately nicknamed the *Tin Goose*, contributed more than any other airplane to the development of American civil aviation into a giant industry. The *Tin Goose* brought our country's first transcontinental air service. In fact, as a direct result of the use of this mechanical pioneer, America witnessed its first complete airfreight operations, its first modern commercial airport, and the first meals aboard planes for passengers. Despite all this, the reign of the *Tin Goose* as the leading airplane of the United States was very brief—only from the late 1920s to the early 1930s.

---

2.   There have been many unusual wills, but none was stranger than that of Daisy Alexander. She wrote her will and sealed it in a bottle, which she threw into the Thames River in England. Twelve years later, Jack Wurm, an unemployed American, found the bottle on a beach in San Francisco. He opened it and read, "To avoid confusion, I leave my entire estate to the lucky person who finds this bottle, and to my attorney, Barry Cohen, share and share alike. Daisy Alexander, June 20, 1937." Daisy, a descendant of Isaac Singer, inventor of the sewing machine, was a wealthy woman. Jack Wurm inherited more than six million dollars.

---

3.   A fifteen-foot-tall olive tree was recently uprooted by a bus in a traffic accident in Greece. Parts of the split tree were immediately replanted in the same spot, then surrounded by a protective steel fence. The Greek government took these steps to save the tree because it is believed to be the tree under which Plato taught. Estimated to be 3,000 years old, the gnarled tree grew along the "Sacred Way" highway between Athens and the nearby port of Piraeus—until it was hit by the bus. According to legend, Plato taught philosophy in the shade of this historic tree over 2,300 years ago.

---

4.   A person gets a "second wind," or the return to normal breathing, after an interim loss of breath during a period of prolonged physical exertion. The heart adjusts to the rate of breathing. Running uses an above-normal amount of energy, resulting in rapid breathing and loss of breath. However, by continuous running a person adjusts to the gait and regains normal respiration. The sudden action of starting to run creates large amounts of lactic acid in the muscles, and a rapid heart caused by automatic impulses of the nervous system. The second wind is attained when the runner's heart action is fast enough to take care of the extra energy.

---

5.   Fire was one of the worst enemies of the early American and Canadian colonists. The danger of fire was always with them. The popular belief that all settlers built log cabins is wrong. Log cabins came much later. The early settlers lived in simple grass-thatched houses with a large stone fireplace in the middle. Chimneys were wooden and lined with clay. Often the clay grew hot and dry and chipped off. Then the fireplace's flames would reach the wood, and before long the house was ablaze. To protect the settlers from Indians, the houses were built very close together. Thus, when one house burned, the whole town usually caught fire.

1. You can conclude from the paragraph that—

   (A) another name for the Ford Trimotor was the *Spruce Goose*
   (B) the Ford Trimotor crashed many times
   (C) meals were not served aboard planes before 1920
   (D) the Ford Trimotor was a small plane

2. Daisy Alexander probably—

   (A) knew that Wurm would find the bottle
   (B) was in love with Barry Cohen
   (C) had no relatives that she cared deeply for
   (D) knew that the will would not be legal in England

3. You can tell that—

   (A) the Greeks love philosophy
   (B) there are many buses in Greece
   (C) Athens is a port
   (D) Plato is a very famous Greek

4. You can conclude that—

   (A) only athletes in top condition get a second wind
   (B) there is also a third wind
   (C) getting a second wind is normal
   (D) a second wind is harmful to health

5. The paragraph suggests that the early colonists had—

   (A) no way to keep warm
   (B) one enemy
   (C) two enemies
   (D) very sturdy homes

1.   Humans' fascination with emeralds has existed since ancient times. Orientals decorated statues of love gods and goddesses with the green gems. Romans believed that wearing an emerald made a person lucky in love. Cleopatra captivated Mark Antony by wearing emeralds from her own mines to set off her beautiful reddish hair. The emperor Nero, on the other hand, believing that emeralds relieved eyestrain, had an emerald lens ground for himself. Other powers attributed to emeralds include curing indigestion, protecting sailors from drowning, foretelling the future, and improving intelligence, speech, or memory.

2.   When the Spanish invaded Mexico in the 1500s, they were busy looking for gold, so they overlooked the beautiful gardens of the Aztec Indians. Among the American Indian peoples, the Aztecs were outstanding creators of gardens. Flowers and plants, avocado trees, and pineapples flourished. Before the Spanish left, they took samples of the food plants. However, many varieties of unusual flowers were left behind unnoticed and unappreciated. Three hundred years later, visiting botanists rediscovered the Aztec gardens. The Aztecs were finally recognized as the excellent gardeners they were.

3.   Who is "the most calculating woman in the world"? It's Shakuntala Devi from Calcutta, India. She has a command of numbers that enables her to out-calculate a computer and to solve complex arithmetic problems almost instantaneously. To the question, "What is the cube root of 274,077,577,255,219,853,331,128,661?" Ms. Devi, in less than twenty seconds, answered, "649,567,821." Her gift for numbers is a mystery. She has not had the aid of any formal education. Many believe her power borders on ESP (extrasensory perception). Ms. Devi hopes to show people that they should depend less on computers and more on themselves.

4.   When John Davis' wife, Sarah, died in 1930, he decided to build a memorial to her that would be different. The Davis Memorial in Mt. Hope Cemetery in Hiawatha, Kansas cost about $50,000 and consists of a set of life-sized figures. The unusual feature of the memorial is that the figures depict John and Sarah at various times since their marriage. They appear first as newlyweds, then as a middle-aged couple, and finally in old age. The last statue shows John sitting alone after Sarah's death—her vacant chair beside him.

5.   Did you know that an "alarm system" used by an English king some three hundred years ago is still maintained today? The "system" is a flock of ravens kept in the Tower of London. The birds are fed by public funding. When the tower was built centuries ago, ravens congregated there in their constant search for garbage to eat. Those same birds cried out a warning to King Charles II one night when his enemies tried to attack. The ruler afterwards ordered that the birds, whose frightened croaks saved his life, be protected and given a food allowance.

1.   The author implies that—

(A) Cleopatra dyed her hair
(B) Cleopatra loved Nero
(C) emeralds have great powers
(D) emeralds are still popular

2.   You can tell from the paragraph that the Spanish invaded Mexico—

(A) to acquire wealth
(B) many years before Columbus' voyage to America
(C) to civilize the Aztecs
(D) to study the many beautiful flowers

3.   The paragraph suggests that—

(A) Ms. Devi uses computers
(B) Ms. Devi cheats
(C) formal education is a waste of time
(D) Ms. Devi is unusual

4.   You can tell that—

(A) John Davis hoped for another wife
(B) Sarah Davis wanted a great memorial
(C) John Davis was wealthy
(D) John Davis killed his wife

5.   You can conclude from the paragraph that King Charles II—

(A) was grateful to the ravens
(B) died at a young age
(C) had very few enemies
(D) lived far from the Tower of London

1.   Thirteen is considered an unlucky number all over the world. This superstition goes back over two thousand years. France forbids persons from living in a house with that number. The number that follows 12 is $12\frac{1}{2}$, and then 14. In Italy, games based on numbers never use the unlucky thirteen. Some sailors refuse to leave port on the thirteenth day of the month. Even in practical, businesslike America, many tall buildings skip the thirteenth floor, and many airliners omit the number thirteen on the seats of their planes.

2.   The signal light that guards the shore of Scituate, Massachusetts, about midway between Boston and Plymouth, is truly unique. The beacon that flashes from Minots Light spells out "I love you" in nautical code for all sailors to see. The signal light has resisted change for over a hundred years. At one time, when the Coast Guard tried to improve the aging equipment, this original coded message was altered. Because of public protests, the Coast Guard agreed to back down on any plans to change the message itself. The loving signal was restored, much to the satisfaction of the local citizens and sailors worldwide who continue to rely on its guiding rays of light.

3.   Gold is considered precious because it is probably the first metal known to humans, it can be found in a free state, and it is one of the softest of all metals. Early civilizations took advantage of its flexibility to fashion it into any shape desired. Since gold is not perishable, it became a means of storing value for the future. Later, it was made into coins and became a medium of exchange. Today brokers store gold in vaults and give a written guarantee to deliver the gold when due.

4.   What one person says and how another interprets it are often two different things. A few years ago a TWA jet received word from the controller at Dulles Airport that the plane was "cleared for approach." The pilot immediately took the plane down to "approach altitude" but crashed into a mountain, killing ninety-two passengers. Later, in the investigation, the controller said that "cleared for approach" means that the plane could descend to approach altitude if there were no obstacles in the way. The pilot understood the expression to mean that there were, in fact, no obstacles in the way.

5.   Picture symbols help travelers from foreign countries find their way around. The U.S. Department of Transportation has thirty-four symbol signs that make life easier for visitors to our country. It's easy to figure out what these symbol signs mean. For example, a letter P crossed by a red bar inside a red circle means no parking. An umbrella and glove under a question mark indicates Lost and Found. A burning cigarette crossed by a red bar inside a red circle means no smoking. A red cross stands for first aid. Any questions? Look for a big question mark inside a circle.

1. You can conclude that—

    (A) the French are not very superstitious
    (B) many Italians are sailors
    (C) most blocks in France have fewer than thirteen houses
    (D) in some hotels, the floor after the 12th is the 14th

2. The paragraph suggests that—

    (A) citizens of Scituate were not respected by the Coast Guard
    (B) most people are reluctant to give up traditions
    (C) a pair of young lovers once drowned off Scituate
    (D) "I love you" can be seen farther than any other signal

3. You can tell from the paragraph that—

    (A) gold will decay with age
    (B) gold has remained highly valued throughout history
    (C) gold coins are less valuable than silver ones
    (D) people today like to carry large amounts of gold with them

4. This paragraph suggests that—

    (A) Dulles is the nation's most dangerous airport
    (B) flying is the most dangerous form of travel
    (C) communicating clearly is important
    (D) the pilot was guilty in the crash

5. The paragraph suggests that—

    (A) the U.S. Department of Transportation is in Washington
    (B) not many umbrellas are lost
    (C) the signs are designed for people who don't speak English
    (D) a red bar indicates danger

UNIT 23

1.   We usually admire rich people. Yet among Pacific Northwest Indian tribes, chiefs would achieve worthy reputations by giving away most of their possessions at feasts called *potlatches*. This Nootka Indian word means "giving." The most common possession disposed of was blankets, though sometimes canoes, animal hides, and even houses were given away. Chiefs who desired enduring fame among their people might give away everything they owned—even the clothes on their backs. One extremely generous Kwakiutl chief was named "Chief Throw Away." Of course, when another chief potlatched, the first chief was expected to receive a good share of the second chief's possessions. Thus no chief stayed poor for long.

2.   Elizabeth Blackwell was the first woman to receive a medical degree in the United States. At first, schools of medicine rejected her because she was a woman. Then, almost as a joke, the Geneva Medical College in upstate New York accepted her application. In 1849, she was the top student in her graduating class. She soon discovered that hospitals didn't want her either, so she started her own—the New York Infirmary for Women and Children. Later, she expanded the infirmary to include a Women's College. Finally in England, she became a full professor at the London School of Medicine for Women.

3.   Fortunately, teeth stop growing in humans and in several other animals when the roots of the teeth close after the teeth have reached a certain size. However, the teeth of rodents, elephants, and wild boars remain open at the roots; new material is added, and their teeth continue to grow. This peculiarity is beneficial to gnawing rodents, as the continual growth of their teeth prevents them from being worn away. Yet it can also be hazardous. Some teeth may grow crooked, or the lower jaw may be displaced. The continued growth of these nonfunctional teeth may close the animal's mouth or force the teeth through the upper jaw, penetrating the brain and causing death.

4.   An old circus tradition forbids two clowns from having the same funny face. This tradition is very carefully observed. When young men or women decide to become professional clowns, they must send a drawing of their chosen face to the secretary of the International Circus Clown Club. The secretary then paints each new face on an eggshell and compares it with others in the vast collection of faces in the club's office in Croydon, England. Should the new face look too much like an existing clown face, the secretary tells the new clown to design a different one. Without doubt, it is the face that gives each clown an individual trademark.

5.   Early colonists in America made their own cosmetics—rather strange ones by today's standards. A woman might wrap her face in bacon to soften her skin. Or she might grind eggshells and scent the dust with perfume to make face powder. Sucking on a lemon was supposed to make lips redder. Hair was powdered with sifted flour mixed with plaster of Paris and perfume. Men stuck small pieces of silk on their faces as decorations, and they had special little rooms called "powder closets" in which they would whiten their wigs!

1. The writer seems to feel that—

    (A) most chiefs were greedy
    (B) some chiefs were cheated in potlatches
    (C) potlatches didn't hurt the chiefs
    (D) Indians who were not chiefs disliked potlatches

---

2. The paragraph suggests that Elizabeth Blackwell succeeded in spite of—

    (A) a lack of funds
    (B) a prejudice toward women
    (C) her young age
    (D) her moving to London, England

---

3. From the paragraph you can tell that—

    (A) it is not good for rodents to grow
    (B) it would be better for human teeth to keep growing
    (C) everything in nature works perfectly
    (D) what is good for an animal may also cause problems

---

4. You can conclude that—

    (A) most professional clowns have sent a drawing to England
    (B) there are very few professional clowns in the world
    (C) clown faces are all very similar
    (D) the Circus Clown Club is just a joke

---

5. You can tell that the early colonists—

    (A) believed a "natural look" was best
    (B) paid a great deal for their cosmetics
    (C) were concerned about their appearance
    (D) spent a great deal of time working

UNIT 24

1.   How far can the unaided eye see? From the top of a skyscraper or a mountain, you may enjoy a fifty- to seventy-five-mile view. Yet on a clear night, away from city lights, if you turn your eyes to the heavens you will see an object so far away that even if you could travel at the speed of light—186,000 miles a second—you would need thousands of lifetimes to reach it. This most remote object visible to the naked eye is the galaxy of Andromeda, a vast group of countless stars 12 quintillion miles distant. Its light takes two million years to reach Earth! To the eye it appears as a beautiful hazy spiral cloud about the size of the moon.

2.   The well-known phrase "to let the cat out of the bag" does not refer to the rescuing of a cat. Its beginning traces back to the methods of marketing at the county fairs of old England, where suckling pigs were often sold wrapped in a sack. Dishonest merchants would take advantage of an unsuspecting customer and hand over a sack containing a cat instead of a piglet. Usually the switch would not be discovered until the buyer returned home. A suspicious buyer, however, would insist on opening the sack at the fair to examine the content and thus "let the cat out of the bag"—expose the fraud.

3.   Over hundreds of centuries Egypt has created mummies, pyramids, picture writing, and beautiful objects of art. In addition, this civilization built the first lighthouse, more than a thousand years ago. At a time when sea travel was almost unknown and the world was still believed by most people to be flat, the Egyptians invented the lighthouse to warn sailors that they were approaching dangerous waters. On a small island called Pharos, just outside the harbor of Alexandria, they built a great tower. In the tower a fire of coal or wood cast a light that could be seen for miles in the worst storms.

4.   What if you could buy your own island? What would you look for? Be sure that the island is accessible to guests and to delivery of food and fuel, and that it has fresh water, adequate soil to keep vegetation, good drainage, and safe swimming conditions. Consider the Sea Islands off the Georgia coast, as well as islands in Long Island Sound, along the coast of Maine, and in Puget Sound. Other areas to consider are the South Pacific, the Mediterranean, and the Caribbean. In most of the world, foreigners are prohibited from legally owning property, so purchasing an island in a foreign country can be very complicated.

5.   Volcanoes are generally considered to be destructive, but they do produce some good effects. Farmers who live near a volcano often have excellent crops because volcanic ash provides minerals that make the crops thrive hardily. Farmers in the vicinity of a volcano wait for an eruption to subside. Then they haul back the ashes in order to sprinkle them on the land. People in Iceland find volcanoes useful in another way. They employ the steam from volcanoes to heat their homes and greenhouses. In Italy the steam from volcanoes is also used to advantage—to run generators that provide electricity.

1. The paragraph suggests that—

    (A) the moon is 12 quintillion miles distant
    (B) no one from Earth will ever reach Andromeda
    (C) light travels more slowly than spaceships
    (D) city lights aid us in viewing the heavens

2. You can conclude that—

    (A) all merchants were dishonest in old England
    (B) cats were outlawed in England
    (C) English buyers had reason to be suspicious
    (D) English cats were worth more than pigs

3. You can conclude that Alexandria was—

    (A) an Egyptian queen
    (B) a small island
    (C) an Egyptian port
    (D) the name of a lighthouse

4. You can conclude that—

    (A) people are rushing to buy the available islands
    (B) owning an island may be the answer to all a person's problems
    (C) South Pacific islands are more in demand than North American islands
    (D) owning an island may present more problems than the buyer realizes

5. You can tell from the paragraph that—

    (A) volcanoes cause only destruction
    (B) farmers dread the side effects of volcanic ash
    (C) volcanoes can produce power
    (D) people in Iceland have steam-engine railroads

1.   For people living in the jungles of Central and South America and in the Caribbean Islands, a poisonous plant provides the bread of life. This plant is the cassava. It has other names—manioc, rumu, casabi, and, appropriately, bitter cassava. It is surely one of the world's strangest food plants, for in its natural state it is poisonous. Its bitter root contains prussic, or hydrocyanic acid—a colorless, highly poisonous, often deadly, liquid. Some of this poison is removed by washing the roots; the rest disappears by cooking. Cassava starch is the source of tapioca and is used for laundry starch. Cassava flour or meal is made into bread.

2.   Light produced without heat or electricity is no longer a dream, thanks to the scientific creation of chemical light. This kind of light can even be poured from a can! Motorists stranded on dark highways can merely spray the chemical on the highway as a warning to approaching drivers. A highway coated with chemical light is many thousands of times as bright as one bathed in moonlight. Manufacturers of the product see many uses for it, particularly in emergency lighting systems. There is only one major drawback—chemical light begins to dim within a few hours after being used.

3.   "Dear, please go out to the garden and change the water on the tomatoes." Someday this odd request may not seem strange at all. With the world running short of fertile land, biologists are turning with increasing interest to hydroponics—the raising of plants in water. A seedling is simply removed from the earth, its roots are cleansed of dirt, and it is "planted" in a tray of water. Sand or water-absorbent minerals help hold the plant upright. To the water are added chemical nutrients. Costs of hydroponics equipment and nutrients are high, however, and few trained personnel exist. The most practical application of hydroponics may become the growing of food on long space voyages.

4.   The smallest antelope in the world is the royal antelope, one of Africa's tiny-hoofed mammals. It stands only eight inches high at the shoulders. This antelope's small horns are less than an inch long, scarcely sticking out above the hair. Its legs are as thin as a person's little finger, and its hoofmarks are the size of a fingernail. Little wonder that the shy animal of the tropical forest is easily frightened! Despite its small size, it races away in bounds nine feet long at the first sign of danger.

5.   Dolphins navigate in clear or murky water by means of an echo-chamber system similar to that employed by bats. The dolphin emits a series of clicking sounds, sometimes at ranges which humans cannot hear. By bouncing these clicks off objects in the neighborhood, this intelligent animal is able to navigate in complete darkness. Experimenters, working with dolphins wearing blindfolds, report that the dolphins were able to find their way through mazes using their natural "radar." The way in which these clicks are produced has not yet been determined by scientists.

1. You can tell that the poison must be removed before the cassava—

   (A) is used for starching clothes
   (B) can be made into rumu
   (C) will lose its bitterness
   (D) can be used as food

2. From the paragraph you can *not* tell—

   (A) how chemical light helps stranded drivers
   (B) what some uses of chemical light are
   (C) if chemical light completely disappears within 24 hours
   (D) how chemical light compares with moonlight

3. In the near future we are *not* likely to see—

   (A) any practical application of hydroponics
   (B) a shortage of trained personnel
   (C) a shortage of fertile land
   (D) huge hydroponic farms worldwide

4. You can tell from the paragraph that the royal antelope—

   (A) is so helpless it is nearly extinct
   (B) is bold despite its small size
   (C) has powerful legs for its size
   (D) lives in all parts of the world

5. The paragraph suggests that dolphins rely greatly on—

   (A) other friendly fish
   (B) their sense of hearing
   (C) blindfolds when swimming
   (D) their sense of sight

A. Exercising Your Skill

Good readers use the information a writer provides to draw **conclusions**. Incorrect conclusions are those that are not supported by the evidence. Read the following story. On your paper, write what you think happened to the people in the adventure.

> Cora and Jed liked farming. They liked caring for the animals and helping in the fields. They particularly liked eating the fresh vegetables, fruit, and eggs produced on their family farm. Out in the fields one day, Cora looked to the west and saw clouds piling up. She said to Jed, "We better get the animals in, it's going to storm soon." The two urged the slow-moving cows and sheep into the barn and then secured the shutters on their home. As the wind increased the power went off. Jed turned on a battery-powered radio and heard a weather prediction of severe weather. The children were used to these warnings and entered the storm shelter to wait out the wind. They knew their parents would take shelter in town, where they had gone shopping.
>
> The wind howled fiercely and the rain poured down for more than half an hour. When the storm subsided, they emerged into the backyard, which was washed clean by the rain and sparkling with sunlight. It was also littered with debris. Suddenly Jed laughed and pointed to the upright water trough where the animals drank. "Look, it's totally empty," he said. "It should be filled after all that rain."

B. Expanding Your Skill

Following are the solutions that have been offered regarding the mystery of the empty water trough. Read each conclusion below, and discuss it with your classmates. Share you own conclusion with your classmates, and discuss the evidence that led you to draw that conclusion.

1. The cows and sheep had gotten out of the barn and drunk all the water.
2. The storm had included a tornado cloud that littered the yard with debris and also sucked up the water from the trough.
3. The storm had forced something sharp through the side of the trough, which the children could not see but which had caused the water to leak out.

C. Exploring Language

Read the following passage, and think about the information the writer provides. Then choose one of the possible conclusions about the event. (If you prefer, write your own conclusion.) On your paper, list the evidence that led you to choose that conclusion.

Bruce Gernon's flight from Andros Island in the Bahamas to Palm Beach, Florida, on December 4, 1970, began in an ordinary way. The first hint of something unusual was a "strange, cigar-shaped cloud." Gernon tried to avoid the cloud, but it seemed to come right at him. Suddenly, he was in a tunnel surrounded by white clouds swirling around the plane. The plane seemed to go faster, and for a few moments, Gernon and his father—who was serving as copilot—experienced weightlessness. Gernon's navigational equipment would not work, and he could not make radar contact.

Then the plane left the tunnel. Ahead, Gernon saw an island. He thought it must be another island in the Bahamas, but he soon recognized it as Miami Beach. He was stunned—this was impossible! After landing, he checked his clock and fuel gauge. A trip that normally took about 75 minutes had taken only 45 minutes! In addition, the plane had burned twelve fewer gallons of fuel than usual.

1. Gernon had flown through a time warp that shortened the distance between the Bahamas and Florida.
2. Gernon's plane had been caught in a rapid air current that pushed it toward Florida at a high rate of speed. Because of the air pushing it, the plane used less fuel than usual.
3. Gernon was mistaken about the time the trip had taken and the amount of fuel the plane had used.

D. Expressing Yourself

Choose one of these activities.

1. Form two teams to create paragraphs from which a conclusion can be drawn. The members of a team take turns reading their paragraphs to the other team. A correct conclusion scores one point for the answering team. An incorrect conclusion scores one point for the asking team.

2. Work with two other classmates. Each of you chooses one of the possible conclusions listed in Part C. Have a debate where each of you defends your conclusion. Let the rest of the class decide who gave the most convincing argument.

Book **G**

Specific Skill Series

Detecting the Sequence

Richard A. Boning

Fifth Edition

SRA/McGraw-Hill
Columbus, Ohio

Cover, Back Cover, Wayne Lynch/Masterfile

SRA/McGraw-Hill

A Division of The McGraw-Hill Companies

Send all inquiries to:
    SRA/McGraw-Hill
    8787 Orion Place
    Columbus, OH 43240-4027

ISBN 0-02-687997-2

    6 IPC 02 01

To the Teacher

PURPOSE:

DETECTING THE SEQUENCE helps develop the important ability to determine time relationships—the order in which things happen. Proficiency in this often taken-for-granted skill is necessary in all kinds of academic and nonacademic reading, from narration to process explanation.

FOR WHOM:

The skill of DETECTING THE SEQUENCE is developed through a series of books spanning ten levels (Picture, Preparatory, A, B, C, D, E, F, G, H). The Picture Level is for pupils who have not acquired a basic sight vocabulary. The Preparatory Level is for pupils who have a basic sight vocabulary but are not yet ready for the first-grade-level book. Books A through H are appropriate for pupils who can read on levels one through eight, respectively. **The use of the *Specific Skill Series Placement Test* is recommended to determine the appropriate level.**

THE NEW EDITION:

DETECTING THE SEQUENCE has been designed to help improve students' skills in identifying the sequence of events within a reading selection. In this series, the variety of questions helps develop students' understanding of multiple ways of expressing time relationships. Questions are text-dependent rather than picture-dependent.

SESSIONS:

Short practice sessions are the most effective. It is desirable to have a practice session every day or every other day, using a few units each session.

To the Teacher

SCORING:

Pupils should record their answers on the reproducible worksheets. The worksheets make scoring easier and provide uniform records of the pupils' work. Using worksheets also avoids consuming the exercise books.

It is important for pupils to know how well they are doing. For this reason, units should be scored as soon as they have been completed. Then a discussion can be held in which pupils justify their choices. (The Integrated Language Activities, many of which are open-ended, do not lend themselves to an objective score; thus there are no answer keys for these pages.)

GENERAL INFORMATION ON *DETECTING THE SEQUENCE*:

DETECTING THE SEQUENCE helps develop sequence skills through three general types of questions: (1) those that focus directly on when an event happened; (2) those that focus on which of several events happened first (or last) among the events mentioned; and (3) those that focus on whether a particular event happened before, at the same time as, or after another. The teacher should make clear to students that a question reading "Which happened first (last)?" means "Which happened before (after) any of the *other answer choices*?" (not "Which happened first [last] in the entire reading selection?").

Answering questions in DETECTING THE SEQUENCE involves more than just reading for facts. Most questions require pupils to establish the time relationships between two separately stated ideas by utilizing time clues in the text. (On the Picture Level, pupils examine two pictures illustrating a sequence of events, and determine which event happened first.)

SUGGESTED STEPS:

On all levels above Picture, pupils should read each story carefully. At the end of each statement they should try to form a picture in their minds so that they will clearly understand what happened first, second, and so forth. As they read, pupils should look for key words that serve as sequence clues, such as *then, before, soon, finally, later, while, when,* and *now.* After finishing the story, pupils should review it mentally. Without looking at the story, they should be able to recall the sequence in which events occurred. If they cannot do this, they should reread the story. Pupils should then answer the questions on their worksheets. In answering, pupils may look at the story as often as necessary.

RELATED MATERIALS:

Specific Skill Series Placement Tests, which enable the teacher to place pupils at their appropriate levels in each skill, are available for the Elementary (Pre-1–6) and Midway (4–8) grade levels.

About This Book

In real life, things happen in a certain order. You do one thing. Then you do another thing. This is called *sequence*. Sequence is the order in which things happen. Another name for *sequence* is *time order*.

Story events happen in a certain order, too. In a story, something happens. Then something else happens. Often one event causes the events that follow.

The events in a story are usually told in the order in which things happened. The paragraph below uses this order.

> Mr. Chung yawned. He folded the newspaper neatly and placed it on the table. He put the cat out, locked the doors, and trudged slowly up the long flight of stairs.

Sometimes, events may be told out of order. Read the sentence below. Use clues to figure out the correct order of events.

> Before he got on his bike, Sam checked the tires.

Did Sam get on his bike first or check the tires first? The word *before* tells you that he checked the tires first.

Now read these sentences.

> While Dad fixed the pancakes, the rest of us started packing. Unfortunately, as a result of yesterday's rain, some of the clothes were still damp.

Which of these events happened first: the packing, the rain, or fixing the pancakes? Which two things happened at the same time? How can you tell?

Words like *after*, *before*, *while*, *then*, *next*, *first*, and *last* are clues to the sequence of events. Phrases such as *having done this* or *as a result* also give clues. Another clue to the sequence is the natural order of events. Could you ride your bike before you got on it? Could you pour a glass of juice before you opened the container?

In this book, you will read many different kinds of stories and articles. As you read, look for clues that let you know the order in which things happened. Then answer questions about the sequence of events.

UNIT 1
Honeybee Society

Did you know that some ancient cultures used to honor honeybees? They did so because they believed that the social organization of a honeybee colony provided a model for living and working together in harmony. The organization of a colony is based on the three different types of bee—queen, worker, and drone—each having its own tasks to perform at different times in its life. When all bees perform their tasks properly, the colony is in harmony.

The queen is the one bee in the entire colony that produces eggs. To do so, she mates with six or more drones over a period of a few days. When eggs are passing through a queen's body, she decides whether they will become female or male bees, depending upon whether she fertilizes them or not. Fertilized eggs become female queens or workers; unfertilized eggs become male drones. The queen then deposits her fifteen hundred or more eggs in cells in the hive. After the eggs hatch into bees, the care, feeding, and defense of these young bees is taken over by female workers.

The female worker bees spend the first weeks of their lives cleaning and polishing the cells, or compartments, in the hive. When they are a little older, they begin repairing the hive and building cells, feeding and caring for the queen and the developing bees, controlling the temperature in the hive, and working to convert nectar into honey.

The oldest workers function as field bees. In the field, a worker locates and collects nectar from flowers. It stores the nectar in a honey sac in its throat, then flies back to the hive with its cargo. Once at the hive, the worker deposits the nectar in the mouth of a younger worker, who then deposits it in a cell and next begins converting it to honey.

After depositing its nectar, the field bee proceeds to tell the other field workers where the nectar flowers are located. She does this by performing what looks like a circular dance. The other workers follow her, imitating her movements. The type and number of movements in a dance seem to tell the other bees the approximate location of the flowers. At this time, they also pick up the scent of the flowers from which the nectar has come. With this information, the other workers take off to gather nectar themselves. Once enough nectar has been gathered and converted into honey, young and old workers work together to store the honey in airtight cells with wax caps.

Male bees are drones, and their one function is to mate with the queen and provide her with the fertilizing material with which she can determine the sex of future bees. After a drone has mated with a queen, the drone dies. Drones still in the hive when autumn comes are driven out by worker bees.

Following this organizational pattern, a typical honeybee colony can support over sixty thousand bees at its peak each year.

UNIT 1
Honeybee Society

1. **Which of these happens first?**

    (A) The queen mates with drones.

    (B) The queen determines the sex of developing bees.

    (C) The worker bees begin caring for the developing bees.

    (D) The queen deposits eggs in cells in the hive.

2. **Which of these do the female workers do first?**

    (A) repair the hive

    (B) clean and polish the cells

    (C) feed and care for the queen

    (D) control the temperature in the hive

3. **What does a worker bee do after depositing nectar in a cell?**

    (A) cleans and polishes hive cells

    (B) looks for flowers in the fields

    (C) feeds and cares for the queen

    (D) converts the nectar into honey

4. **Which of these happens last?**

    (A) An older worker tells other workers where the flowers are.

    (B) An older worker gathers nectar in the field.

    (C) An older worker deposits nectar in the mouth of a younger worker.

    (D) Many older workers fly off to gather nectar in the field.

5. **What happens to the drone after it mates with a queen?**

    (A) It dies.

    (B) It is driven out of the nest.

    (C) It collects nectar from flowers.

    (D) It cares for developing bees.

The painter looked at the blank piece of canvas for about a second. Then he started to paint. He put one color after another onto the canvas. Shapes began to form. A tree could be seen. Then a river appeared. Other trees showed up in the back of the picture. Sunlight could be seen through the clouds. Then, just seconds later, the painter stepped back. He was finished. Right there, in front of everyone, he had made a wonderful painting. It had taken less than sixty seconds.

Who is this painter who can finish a picture in a minute or less? His name is Morris Katz, and he is listed as the world's fastest painter in the *Guinness Book of World Records*. Some of his paintings, in fact, have been placed in the Guinness Book of Records Museum located in the Empire State Building in New York City.

Morris Katz has set all kinds of records with his paintings. He finished a complete painting in less than forty-three seconds. Once, he painted for twelve straight hours and completed 103 paintings. That is one painting every seven minutes!

Morris Katz got started in all of this in an unusual way. He first took up "speed painting," as he calls it, when he was twenty-four years old. Why? Because, he says, he wanted to make paintings that were not expensive. "I wanted to paint a good painting and be able to sell it to all the nice people who can't afford $2 million for a painting." Most of Katz's paintings sell for around $30. For that price, you get to watch him paint and to hear him talk to you about the painting he is making.

How does it work? Well, Katz often paints at street fairs and carnivals. Once he is there, he sets up his equipment. People start coming to him almost at once. He puts all of his paints on a large block. The paint is several inches deep because he uses so much of it in a short amount of time. Then Katz gets out bathroom tissue, which he uses as his "brush." The soft paper, he says, helps him make paintings "without effort and without complications." Katz uses so much when he paints that he buys about ten thousand rolls of bathroom tissue each year. He also uses a palette knife, which has a short, thick blade that can spread paint quickly. Katz thinks it works faster and better than any brush, and it is much easier to clean.

When his paints and paper are ready, Katz begins. Using the palette knife, he paints the background. Then, with knife and tissue paper, he puts the shapes on the canvas. It is all so fast that you can hardly see what he is doing. All the while, he chats with the people around him. "Here's a mule," he giggles, "and here's de-tail." (Katz's jokes are one reason people come back to him again and again.) Then, just seconds later, he is finished. Swiftly, he puts the picture in a frame. Then, in less than eight seconds, he staples the painting to the frame. It is all over. Now the painting just has to dry.

Morris Katz finished over 180,000 paintings by the age of fifty-six. Imagine how many more paintings he will finish in his lifetime!

UNIT 2
The Fastest Painter in the World

1. **What happened after the sunlight could be seen through the clouds in one picture?**
   (A) Katz stepped back.
   (B) Katz set up his paints.
   (C) Shapes began to form.
   (D) Katz thought about what he might paint.

2. **When did Katz take up "speed painting"?**
   (A) before he was twelve
   (B) after he was fifty-six
   (C) when he was twenty-four
   (D) when he was eighteen

3. **What happens first when Morris Katz prepares to paint?**
   (A) He takes out bathroom tissue.
   (B) He puts all of his paints on a large block.
   (C) He applies color with a palette knife.
   (D) He puts the canvas into a frame.

4. **When does Katz paint the background of a painting?**
   (A) at the same time he adds the shapes
   (B) just after his paints and paper are ready
   (C) after he paints in the people
   (D) just before he puts the picture in a frame

5. **What happens last?**
   (A) Katz's hands move quickly over the canvas.
   (B) Katz puts the picture in the frame.
   (C) Katz staples the picture into the frame.
   (D) Katz uses the knife and paper.

UNIT 3
John Muir

In 1892 the Sierra Club was formed. In 1908 an area of coastal redwood trees north of San Francisco was established as Muir Woods National Monument. In the Sierra Nevada mountains, a walking trail from Yosemite Valley to Mount Whitney was dedicated in 1938. It is called John Muir Trail.

John Muir was born in 1838 in Scotland. His family name means "moor," which is a meadow full of flowers and animals. John Muir loved nature from the time he was small. He also loved to climb rocky cliffs and walls.

When John was eleven, his family moved to the United States and settled in Wisconsin. John was good with tools and soon became an inventor. He first invented a model of a sawmill. Later he invented an alarm clock that would cause the sleeping person to be tipped out of bed when the timer sounded.

Muir left home at a young age. He took a thousand-mile walk south to the Gulf of Mexico in 1867 and 1868. Then he sailed for San Francisco. The city was too noisy and crowded for Muir, so he headed inland for the Sierra Nevadas.

When Muir discovered the Yosemite Valley in the Sierra Nevadas, it was as if he had come home. He loved the mountains, the wildlife, and the trees. He climbed the mountains and even climbed trees during thunderstorms in order to get closer to the wind. He put forth the theory in the late 1860s that the Yosemite Valley had been formed through the action of glaciers. People ridiculed him. Not until 1930 was Muir's theory proven correct.

Muir began to write articles about the Yosemite Valley to tell readers about its beauty. His writing also warned people that Yosemite was in danger from timber mining and sheep ranching interests. In 1901 Theodore Roosevelt became president of the United States. He was interested in conservation. Muir took the president through Yosemite, and Roosevelt helped get legislation passed to create Yosemite National Park in 1906.

Although Muir won many conservation battles, he lost a major one. He fought to save the Hetch Hetchy Valley, which people wanted to dam in order to provide water for San Francisco. In late 1913 a bill was signed to dam the valley. Muir died in 1914. Some people say losing the fight to protect the valley killed Muir.

1. **What happened first?**
    (A) The Muir family moved to the United States.
    (B) Muir Woods was created.
    (C) John Muir learned to climb rocky cliffs.
    (D) John Muir walked to the Gulf of Mexico.

2. **When did John Muir invent a unique form of alarm clock?**
    (A) while the family still lived in Scotland
    (B) after he sailed to San Francisco
    (C) after he traveled in Yosemite
    (D) while the Muir family lived in Wisconsin

3. **What did John Muir do soon after he arrived in San Francisco?**
    (A) He ran outside during an earthquake.
    (B) He put forth a theory about how Yosemite was formed.
    (C) He headed inland for the Sierra Nevadas.
    (D) He began to write articles about Yosemite.

4. **When did John Muir meet Theodore Roosevelt?**
    (A) between 1901 and 1906
    (B) between 1838 and 1868
    (C) between 1906 and 1914
    (D) between 1868 and 1901

5. **What happened last?**
    (A) John Muir died.
    (B) John Muir Trail was dedicated.
    (C) Muir's glacial theory was proven.
    (D) The Sierra Club was formed.

How would it be possible to recreate an ancient style of pottery that had died out as long ago as the 1300s? One pottery maker, Maria Martinez, was determined to try.

Born in 1887 on the San Ildefonso Pueblo in New Mexico, Maria had her early education at St. Catherine's Indian School in Santa Fe, New Mexico. From the time she was a young girl, however, Maria's passion was pottery making, and she spent most of her free time crafting traditional coiled pots for her pueblo. These were used in Pueblo ceremonies or sold to tourists. What Maria really wanted to do, however, was find out how the ancient Anasazi Indians had crafted their pots and achieved the highly polished black finish that characterized them. She spent many years trying to learn this ancient method.

In 1913, Maria married Julian Martinez, an archeological worker and painter. The Martinezes began to work together on pottery making, with Maria shaping the pots and Julian painting them with simple but fascinating ancient designs. The Martinezes still hadn't discovered the old Anasazi method for producing the pots, however.

Then their luck changed. The director of the archeological program that Julian worked for gave the Martinezes some fragments of Anasazi pots that had been found during a dig. By studying the fragments and by experimenting, the couple found out how the old potters had probably produced their pots. They found that they had to use local clay and polish the damp pots carefully. The pots then had to be buried in sheep or horse manure in carefully regulated fires. From this, a process called carbonization took place, and the pots came out with the highly polished black surfaces that had distinguished the old Anasazi pieces.

After this method was rediscovered and put into practice, Maria Martinez's pots started to come into demand. One of her first pots was purchased by John D. Rockefeller. After that, her pottery became internationally known, and pots signed by Maria Martinez were greatly sought after. Even with fame, Maria and Julian continued to work quietly together until his death in 1943. She then continued her craft with the help of other Pueblo workers and family members. She never sought personal wealth or fame, but she encouraged and promoted other local craftspeople to learn her methods and to produce pots of their own.

Although she didn't seek personal recognition, Maria Martinez did receive many awards. She was named Outstanding Indian Woman by the Indian Fire Council of 1934; she was given the Craftsmanship Award by the American Institute of Architects in 1954; and she received the American Ceramic Society Award in 1968. Her pots were also exhibited at many world fairs, at the Smithsonian Institution, at the American Museum of Natural History, and at many other museums.

Maria Martinez dedicated the rest of her life to her craft, even teaching her method in the University of California's summer program—where she instructed pupils by having them observe directly and participate. She died in 1980, having realized her personal dream and having given new life to Pueblo Indian art.

1. **When did Maria Martinez first show an interest in pottery?**

   (A) after meeting the archeological program director

   (B) after marrying Julian

   (C) after making pots for Pueblo ceremonies

   (D) as a young girl

2. **What happened after the Martinezes received the Anasazi pot fragments to study?**

   (A) Maria and Julian were married.

   (B) Julian painted the pots that Maria shaped.

   (C) The couple found out how to achieve carbonization of the pots.

   (D) The couple sold the pot fragments to tourists and collectors.

3. **In the old Anasazi method, what step came after polishing the damp pots?**

   (A) burying them in manure

   (B) signing them

   (C) painting figures on them

   (D) taking them out of the fire

4. **Which of these happened last?**

   (A) Maria crafted pots for Pueblo ceremonies.

   (B) John D. Rockefeller bought one of Martinez's pots.

   (C) The Martinezes decoded the ancient Anasazi method.

   (D) Maria and Julian Martinez married.

5. **Which of these happened last?**

   (A) Maria Martinez was named Outstanding Indian Woman by the Indian Fire Council.

   (B) Maria Martinez received the American Ceramic Society Award.

   (C) Maria and Julian Martinez taught the method to other Pueblo potters.

   (D) Maria Martinez made a pot that John D. Rockefeller bought.

What do most people think about when they think of dogs? Do they think of friendly pets or of fierce animals that can capture galloping deer, zebras, and other game?

On Africa's Serengeti Plain, there are only a few pet dogs but many wild ones. These dogs are small, with spotted coats and long, pointed faces. They are speedy and strong, and packs of these dogs can capture and kill animals the size of antelopes.

When these dogs hunt, it is exciting. They begin by roaming an area until they see a likely target, usually an animal that is smaller, younger, or perhaps weaker than the other ones in its herd. Then the pack of dogs begin the chase, which can last for hours. Usually, they catch up with the escaping animal. Then, working together as a pack, they quickly kill and eat their prey.

Usually, wild dogs are born in January and February. One mother dog may have eight to ten pups, which she hides in a hole underground. Then, after two weeks, they begin to come out once in a while to run a bit, follow their mother around, and sometimes even play with the older dogs. Then they go back into the safety of their underground den. As the days go by, the pups spend more and more time outside. They also switch from a diet of their mother's milk to one of meat brought to them by dogs returning from the hunt. Play is the main part of their lives. Their play, however, is really training for their lives as hunters because they learn to follow and pick up the scent of other animals. Wrestling with each other, they learn how to pull animals to the ground.

By the time the pups are ten weeks old, they begin to look more like the other dogs in the pack. Though small, they are already learning the ways of the older animals. Soon they are ready to follow the pack wherever it goes. During the first three months of the pups' life, the pack usually remains as much in one place as it can. Once the pups are ready, though, the pack moves on. Moving, of course, allows the dogs more chances for hunting prey and for finding water during the long dry season that comes to the Serengeti Plain each year.

The young dogs have a hard life because game is not easy to find. Also, disease and lack of water can claim many of them. However, the pups are not really ready to become hunters until they are about a year old, when they have become both fast enough and strong enough to help bring down large animals.

For many years, professional hunters used to kill the dogs. Then people became concerned about animal protection and campaigned for laws to protect the dogs. Soon such laws were passed, and now the dogs are protected. As a result, life may become a bit easier for these unusual members of the dog family.

1. **What happens first?**

    (A) The dog pack works together to bring down the prey.

    (B) The dog pack begins the chase.

    (C) The dog pack attacks its prey.

    (D) The dog pack roams an area to find an animal.

2. **When are pups first hidden underground?**

    (A) when they switch to a diet of meat

    (B) two weeks after birth

    (C) at birth

    (D) after they are fully grown

3. **When do the pups start playing with older dogs?**

    (A) after they are six months old

    (B) after they are about two weeks old

    (C) when they are less than a week old

    (D) not until they are over a year old

4. **What happens first?**

    (A) The pups begin to look more like the other dogs.

    (B) The pups are ready to follow the pack.

    (C) The pups are ready to become hunters.

    (D) The pack moves on.

5. **What happened last?**

    (A) Professional hunters killed the dogs.

    (B) Dogs became protected by laws.

    (C) People became concerned about protecting the dogs.

    (D) The dogs became tame.

UNIT 6
Time for Magic

To do some magic tricks, you must prevent your "audience" from seeing what you do with your hands. For others, you have to buy special equipment to perform the trick. Here is a trick, however, that only requires a clock, a pencil, and some paper. The only "trick" is being able to count!

Start by getting an old clock with a large round face. The large face will allow everyone to see the numbers, even from far away.

Then ask for someone from your audience to help you. Point to the clock and say that you are going to do a trick that uses the numbers on the clock. Then ask your assistant to think of any hour between one and twelve and to let you know when he or she has done that. Remind your assistant, however, that he or she is not to tell you what the number is. Then give him or her a pencil and paper on which to write the number. He or she should then hold the paper in one hand or put it in a pocket.

Now take back the pencil and wave it around for effect. Use the pencil to tap numbers on the face of the clock. Tell your helper to start silently counting the taps with the number that comes *after* the number he or she has written down on the paper. (If your helper doesn't understand, explain it this way: "For example, if you picked the number four, you should count the first tap as five, then six, and so on. If you picked twelve, you should count the first tap as one, two, and so on.") Tell the person to call out, "Stop!" when he or she reaches the number twenty. To everyone's surprise, at that moment you will be pointing at the hour your assistant wrote on the piece of paper.

Here's how the trick works. Begin tapping any numbers at all. Do this for the first seven taps. Keep track of how many numbers you are tapping—this is important! Then, when it is time for your eighth tap, tap your pencil against the twelve on the clock. For the ninth tap, hit your pencil against the number eleven. For the tenth tap, hit the ten. Continue around the clock backward until your assistant calls, "Stop!" Ask the person what number you are pointing to. Then have the person take out the piece of paper and read the number that was written down. The numbers will be the same. When the person acts surprised, just take your bows.

UNIT 6
Time for Magic

1. **What does the magician do before the trick begins?**
   (A) gets a clock, pencil, and paper
   (B) makes marks on a clock
   (C) chooses a number between one and twelve
   (D) taps on a clock

2. **What happens first?**
   (A) The magician taps on the face of the clock.
   (B) The person from the audience writes down a number.
   (C) The magician bows to the audience.
   (D) The person from the audience starts to count.

3. **When should the person from the audience call, "Stop"?**
   (A) when he or she reaches the number twelve
   (B) after he or she counts backward from ten
   (C) when he or she counts to twenty
   (D) after fifteen seconds

4. **When does the magician tap backward around the clock?**
   (A) before the person from the audience thinks of a number
   (B) while the person from the audience is still counting
   (C) after the person from the audience finishes counting
   (D) while the person from the audience is thinking of a number

5. **What happens last?**
   (A) The magician points to the number chosen by the person from the audience.
   (B) The person from the audience reads the number on the paper.
   (C) The magician takes a bow.
   (D) The person from the audience looks surprised.

17

In Unit 6, you learned about a simple magic trick that can make your friends stand up and take notice. What is it that makes people enjoy magic so much? For a magic trick to work—to appear "magic"—it's important to do things in the right order.

Now read about another trick that you can learn to do with just a little practice.

For this trick, you will need an assistant who knows exactly how the trick is done.

Ask two volunteers to join you on stage. Hold up a long piece of rope, about four or five feet in length, and ask them to make sure it is really one piece and not two taped together. Next, have your assistant stand between the two volunteers and face the audience. Your assistant should hold his or her arms close to the body, keeping both hands behind the back in fists and with both thumbs held straight out.

Then, stand right behind your assistant, facing his or her back. Put the center of the rope over your assistant's head and in front of his or her chest. After this, pretend to "wrap" the rope around your assistant's body. What actually happens is this: When you bring each end of the rope behind your assistant, loop the ends around his or her thumbs. To the audience, it will appear that you're crossing the ends over each other and around your assistant's body; actually, however, each end will go back to the side where it came from!

Now hand the volunteers the ends of the rope and ask them to pull. When the rope begins to move, your assistant should lower his or her thumbs. Suddenly, the rope snaps around—just as if it came right through the assistant's body!

A. Exercising Your Skill

Think about the order in which things are done—or need to be done beforehand—for the rope trick. What happens first? What happens next? What time-order words help you know the sequence in which events happen? Read the list of steps below. (Some have not yet been included in the story.) On your paper, write the events in their correct order.

Show the rope to the volunteers from the audience. Talk about wrapping the rope around your assistant.

Stretch out the rope behind your assistant's back.

Ask for two volunteers from the audience.

Show the audience each end of the rope as you hand it to a volunteer.

B. Expanding Your Skill

Imagine that you are getting the instructions for the rope trick ready to publish in a "how-to" book about magic tricks. What other steps will you add? Think about what steps have to be done before the performance and what the magician should do or say at the close of the performance. Write an introduction and a conclusion to the instructions, adding these steps. Then compare what you wrote with what your classmates wrote. Discuss with them the reasons for adding each of the steps.

C. Exploring Language

Imagine that you are explaining a magic trick to someone. Every step must be described in just the right order so that the trick will work perfectly.

Now read the list of steps below. Decide what order they should be in. On your paper, write directions for the trick. Make sure you put the steps in the right order. Also make sure you add time-order clue words that will help someone do the trick correctly.

The Dime That Disappears

Make your hand with the dime in it into a fist.

Ask a volunteer from the audience to come up and help you.

Just before you do the trick, place a blob of sticky, wet soap on the fingernail of your middle finger.

The dime is now hidden from view on the back of your hand, stuck to the soapy fingernail.

Make sure the dime is flat in the center of your palm.

With your fist closed, press the dime into the soap.

Show your audience that your palm is now empty.

Open up your hand again.

Ask the volunteer from the audience to place the dime in the palm of your hand.

Take out a dime and tell your audience that you can make it disappear—but you'll need a helper to do it.

D. Expressing Yourself

Choose one of these activities.

1. Imagine that you are a magician doing tricks in front of an audience. A big part of your act will be what you say—how you get people interested in watching your magic tricks and how you make them respond to those tricks. Choose one of the tricks described on these two pages. Write down what you would say or do to make those tricks "come alive" and be exciting or "magical" for your audience.

2. Write a newspaper review about a magician's performance. Describe what happened, how the audience reacted, and what you thought of the magic act. Write a headline for your article.

3. Make a poster advertisement for your own magic act. In the center, draw a picture of yourself dressed as a magician. Then, using words and pictures, let people know what wonderful magic tricks they will see if they come to your show. Give your ad a title.

UNIT 7
The Greatest Prank of All Time

People love practical jokes—as long as the jokes aren't on them. For many years, America's college students have loved pranks and stunts more than anyone else has. One college—the California Institute of Technology—has been the most successful of all in creating unusual stunts.

Cal Tech, as it is called, has been the leader of the world of college stunts for many years. Back in 1972, students pulled off a prank in which they made an entire room "disappear." This is how they did it. A student lived in a large building, called a dormitory, with many other students. At one time, he was away from his dormitory room for an entire week, and that is when the other students in the dormitory set to work. First, they put plaster over the student's door. Next, they repainted the whole wall and even put new baseboards along the wall. Then, to top it off, they moved a light to a spot right in the middle of where the door of the room should have been. When the student returned to the dormitory late on a Sunday night, he was amazed to find that he had no room to go to. To make matters worse, everyone in the dorm pretended not to know him at all. Soon he was banging on the walls looking for his room. The student's "friends" finally confessed.

Cal Tech's biggest prank, however, took place way back in 1960. Called the Great Rose Bowl Prank, it was seen by almost thirty million people on national television. Each New Year's Day, a famous football bowl game is held in Pasadena, California. For the 1960 game, students at Cal Tech decided to make a few unannounced changes. One of the teams, the University of Washington, had a famous cheering display. Thousands of students would sit in the stands holding different cards. On the cards were colors, letters, and even parts of drawings. At various times, cheerleaders would call out the name of a card ("blue 3," "red 6," and so on). When all the cards were up, a word or picture would be formed.

The day before the big football game, however, a Cal Tech student pretended to be a reporter for an area newspaper. In an "interview" with the Washington cheerleaders, the student learned how the card system worked. Later that night, Cal Tech students sneaked into the rooms of the Washington cheerleaders. Working quickly, they replaced the carefully ordered Washington cards with special cards they had made. The job wasn't easy. In fact, over two thousand cards had to be marked and set up in perfect order for the stunt to work.

On New Year's Day, everyone waited for the Washington halftime show. The first eleven Washington card shows went off perfectly. Number twelve, though, was supposed to show the Washington mascot, a dog called a husky. Instead, a beaver appeared on the cards in the grandstands. Then number thirteen was supposed to spell out the word *Washington*. It did—but backward. At that point, cheerleaders began to think something was up—but no one seemed to know exactly what. No one else, including the TV announcers, had caught on. However, moments later, everything was clear. Number fourteen showed the words *Cal Tech* in giant letters across the stands. People at home fell silent, and TV announcers stopped talking. The Washington marching band stopped in its tracks, and soon they just wandered off the field, completely confused. Finally, the cheerleaders simply gave up trying to go on with their show.

For years, people talked about that day. Cal Tech had pulled off "the greatest college prank of all time."

1. **What happened first?**

   (A) A Cal Tech student returned to his dormitory.

   (B) Other students pretended not to know the student.

   (C) Cal Tech students plastered over the door to the young man's room.

   (D) Students put new baseboards in the hall.

2. **When did students confess what they had done to their fellow student?**

   (A) before he went away for a week

   (B) after he banged on the walls

   (C) before they repainted the hall

   (D) as he came into the dorm

3. **What happened before a Cal Tech student pretended to be a reporter?**

   (A) Over 2,000 cards were marked and set in order by Cal Tech.

   (B) Cal Tech students decided to make some changes in the cheering display.

   (C) Cal Tech students replaced the Washington cards.

   (D) The football game took place.

4. **When did everyone finally realize what had happened at the Rose Bowl?**

   (A) before display number thirteen

   (B) during display number fourteen

   (C) after display number fifteen

   (D) before the game began

5. **What happened last?**

   (A) The Washington cheerleaders stopped their show.

   (B) The Washington band walked off the field.

   (C) TV announcers became confused.

   (D) The words *Cal Tech* appeared in the Washington grandstands.

UNIT 8
Giant Tortoises of the Galapagos

The Galapagos (say "guh LAH puh gohs") Islands are in the Pacific Ocean, off the western coast of South America. They are a rocky, lonely spot, but they are also one of the most unusual places in the world. One reason is that they are the home of some of the last giant tortoises left on earth.

Weighing hundreds of pounds, these tortoises, or land turtles, wander slowly around the rocks and sand of the islands. Strangely, each of these islands has its own particular kinds of tortoises. There are seven different kinds of tortoises on the eight islands, each kind being slightly different from the other.

Hundreds of years ago, thousands of tortoises wandered around these islands. However, all that changed when people started landing there. When people first arrived in 1535, their ships had no refrigerators. This meant that fresh food was always a problem for the sailors on board. The giant tortoises provided a solution to this problem.

Ships would anchor off the islands, and crews would row ashore and seize as many tortoises as they could. Once the animals were aboard the ship, the sailors would roll the tortoises onto their backs. The tortoises were completely helpless once on their backs, so they could only lie there until used for soups and stews. Almost 100,000 tortoises were carried off in this way.

The tortoises faced other problems, too. Soon after the first ships, settlers arrived bringing pigs, goats, donkeys, dogs, and cats. All of these animals ruined life for the tortoises. Donkeys and goats ate all the plants that the tortoises usually fed on, while the pigs, dogs, and cats consumed thousands of baby tortoises each year. Within a few years, it was hard to find any tortoise eggs—or even any baby tortoises.

By the early 1900s, people began to worry that the last of the tortoises would soon die out. No one, however, seemed to care enough to do anything about the problem. More and more tortoises disappeared, even though sailors no longer needed them for food. For another fifty years, this situation continued. Finally, in the 1950s, scientists decided that something must be done.

The first part of their plan was to get rid of as many cats, dogs, and other animals as they could. Next, they tried to make sure that more baby tortoises would be born. To do this, they started looking for wild tortoise eggs. They gathered the eggs and put them in safe containers. When the eggs hatched, the scientists raised the tortoises in special pens. Both the eggs and tortoises were numbered so that the scientists knew exactly which kinds of tortoises they had—and which island they came from. Once the tortoises were old enough and big enough to take care of themselves, the scientists took them back to their islands and set them loose. This slow, hard work continues today, and, thanks to it, the number of tortoises is now increasing every year. Perhaps these wonderful animals will not disappear after all.

UNIT 8
Giant Tortoises of the Galapagos

1. **What happened first?**

   (A) Sailors took tortoises aboard ships.

   (B) The tortoise meat was used for soups and stews.

   (C) Tortoises were put onto their backs.

   (D) Settlers brought other animals to the islands.

2. **What happened soon after people brought animals to the islands?**

   (A) Tortoise eggs were kept in safe containers.

   (B) Scientists took away as many animals as they could.

   (C) The animals ate the tortoises' food and eggs.

   (D) The tortoises fought with the other animals.

3. **When did people start to do something to save the tortoises?**

   (A) in the 1500s

   (B) in the 1950s

   (C) in the early 1900s

   (D) in the 1960s

4. **What happens right after the tortoise eggs hatch?**

   (A) The scientists take the tortoises back to their islands.

   (B) The scientists get rid of cats, dogs, and other animals.

   (C) The sailors use the tortoises for food.

   (D) The scientists raise the tortoises in special pens.

5. **What happened last?**

   (A) The tortoises began to disappear.

   (B) The number of tortoises began to grow.

   (C) Scientists took away other animals.

   (D) Tortoises were taken back to their home islands.

People love races of all kinds. Cars, people, horses, even dogs race to the cheers of millions of people each year. One special race is called the triathlon. In a triathlon, a person may race on a bike, then swim, and finally run. A triathlon is a unique event, but even more interesting is a special quadrathlon that was held in Montpelier, Vermont, every year. (A quadrathlon has four parts instead of three.) This contest tested more than just people's athletic strength and endurance. It also tested their skills as cooks!

This odd contest was held at the New England Culinary Institute, where people learn cooking and other related trades. Most of the students went on to careers in restaurants and hotels. Kitchen work is hard, as the students knew. That is why, as student Tom Hassenauer said, "The fitter you are, the less stress there is in the kitchen." With that in mind, Hassenauer dreamed up a special quadrathlon for the students at this cooking school. The first one was held in 1983.

Each team was made up of five people—a runner, a bike rider, a food server, and two cooks. At the start, the bike rider raced up and down hills for six to eight miles. All the while, he or she carried a heavy bag of groceries. Once the rider arrived at the school, he or she handed the groceries to the team's "first cook," who chopped vegetables, peeled potatoes, and generally prepared the food for cooking. Then he or she placed everything on plates and set them on trays. The team runner then raced with the trays two and one half miles to the second kitchen.

Next, working as fast as he or she could, the main cook, at the second kitchen, finished preparing the meal. The biggest problem, of course, was that many things were often missing. Food may have fallen from the rider's grocery bags or from the runner's trays. The cook had to make do with whatever was left. Then, when the meal was finally ready, the cook put the food on plates and handed it to the server. In this final part of the event, the server brought the meal to the judges.

How was the quadrathlon scored? Teams were given points for speed. They also got points for how good the food actually tasted. Finally, points were given for how well the server presented the meal to the judges and how well he or she cleaned up.

The judges tried to keep the race as difficult as possible. To achieve this, they often put strange things into the grocery bags in order to make it harder for cooks to think of dishes to make. One year, for instance, a cook was given one chicken, a beet, three eggs, a stick of butter, a carrot, some rice, some noodles, and an orange. Finding something to cook from all that must have been some challenge!

Does the cooking quadrathlon interest you? Well, if you want to try something even more difficult, you might enter Montpelier's special winter quadrathlon. The contest, developed after the regular quadrathlon, requires the team members to cross-country ski instead of run or bike. In this contest, at least, there is no problem keeping things cold!

1. **What happened first?**

    (A) The meals were cooked.

    (B) Riders carried bags of food.

    (C) Meals were served to the judges.

    (D) Runners raced to the first kitchen.

2. **What happened right after the first cook prepared the food?**

    (A) The cook placed the food on trays.

    (B) Food fell from the bags.

    (C) Judges received the food.

    (D) A bike rider brought food to the kitchen.

3. **What happened just before the main cook finally cooked the meal?**

    (A) The cook gave the food to the server.

    (B) The runner raced with the food.

    (C) The food was put on trays.

    (D) The rider delivered the food.

4. **What happened first to the food after it was cooked?**

    (A) A server took it to the judges.

    (B) It was packed in grocery bags.

    (C) A bike rider carried it to the next stop.

    (D) It was placed on trays.

5. **What happened last?**

    (A) The special winter quadrathlon was developed.

    (B) Tom Hassenauer came to the New England Culinary Institute.

    (C) Montpelier hosted the first quadrathlon.

    (D) Tom Hassenauer thought up the quadrathlon.

UNIT 10
Charles Lindbergh

Charles A. Lindbergh is remembered as the first person to make a nonstop solo flight across the Atlantic, in 1927. This feat, when Lindbergh was only twenty-five years old, assured him a lifetime of fame and public attention.

Charles Augustus Lindbergh was more interested in flying airplanes than he was in studying. He dropped out of the University of Wisconsin after two years to earn a living performing daredevil airplane stunts at country fairs. Two years later, he joined the United States Army so that he could go to the Army Air Service flight-training school. After completing his training, he was hired to fly mail between St. Louis and Chicago.

Then came the historic flight across the Atlantic. In 1919, a New York City hotel owner offered a prize of $25,000 to the first pilot to fly nonstop from New York to Paris. Nine St. Louis business leaders helped pay for the plane Lindbergh designed especially for the flight. Lindbergh tested the plane by flying it from San Diego to New York, with an overnight stop in St. Louis. The flight took only 20 hours and 21 minutes, a transcontinental record. Nine days later, on May 20, 1927, Lindbergh took off from Long Island, New York, at 7:52 A.M. He landed at Paris on May 21 at 10:21 P.M. He had flown more than 3,600 miles in $33\frac{1}{2}$ hours. His flight made news around the world. He was given awards and parades everywhere he went. He was presented with the U.S. Congressional Medal of Honor and the first Distinguished Flying Cross. For a time, Lindbergh toured the world as a U.S. goodwill ambassador. He met his future wife, Anne Morrow, in Mexico, where her father was the United States ambassador.

During the 1930s, Charles and Anne Lindbergh worked for various airline companies, charting new commercial air routes. In 1931, for a major airline, they charted a new route from the east coast of the United States to the Orient. The shortest, most efficient route was a great curve across Canada, over Alaska, and down to China and Japan. Most pilots familiar with the Arctic did not believe that such a route was possible. The Lindberghs took on the task of proving that it was. They arranged for fuel and supplies to be set out along the route. On July 29, they took off from Long Island in a specially equipped small seaplane. They flew by day and each night landed on a lake or a river and camped. Near Nome, Alaska, they had their first serious emergency. Out of daylight and nearly out of fuel, they were forced down in a small ocean inlet. In the next morning's light, they discovered they had landed on barely three feet of water. On September 19, after two more emergency landings and numerous close calls, they landed in China with the maps for a safe airline passenger route.

Even while actively engaged as a pioneering flier, Lindbergh was also working as an engineer. In 1935, he and Dr. Alexis Carrel were given a patent for an artificial heart. During World War II in the 1940s, Lindbergh served as a civilian technical advisor in aviation. Although he was a civilian, he flew over fifty combat missions in the Pacific. In the 1950s, Lindbergh helped design the famous 747 jet airliner. In the late 1960s, he spoke widely on conservation issues. He died August 1974, having lived through aviation history from the time of the first powered flight to the first steps on the moon and having influenced a big part of that history himself.

UNIT 10
Charles Lindbergh

1. **What did Lindbergh do before he crossed the Atlantic?**

   (A) He charted a route to China.

   (B) He graduated from flight-training school.

   (C) He married Anne Morrow.

   (D) He acted as a technical advisor during World War II.

2. **What happened after Lindbergh crossed the Atlantic?**

   (A) He flew the mail between St. Louis and Chicago.

   (B) He left college.

   (C) He attended the Army flight-training school.

   (D) He was given the Congressional Medal of Honor.

3. **When did Lindbergh meet Anne Morrow?**

   (A) before he took off from Long Island

   (B) after he worked for an airline

   (C) before he was forced down in an ocean inlet

   (D) after he received the first Distinguished Flying Cross

4. **When did the Lindberghs map an air route to China?**

   (A) before they worked for an airline

   (B) before Charles worked with Dr. Carrel

   (C) after World War II

   (D) while designing the 747 airliner

5. **What event happened last?**

   (A) Lindbergh patented an artificial heart.

   (B) The Lindberghs mapped a route to the Orient.

   (C) Lindbergh helped design the 747 airliner.

   (D) Lindbergh flew fifty combat missions.

UNIT 11
Frederick Douglass

In 1841 a young man addressed an antislavery meeting in Massachusetts. He talked about what it was like to be separated from one's family as a child. He talked about being beaten and overworked. He talked about learning how to read and write in secret. He talked about what it was like to be a slave. Perhaps one of the reasons the listeners were so impressed with the speaker was because he had been a slave himself.

Frederick Douglass was born into slavery in 1818 in Maryland. His last name was Bailey, the name of his mother. First he was separated from his mother, then his grandmother. He eventually was sent to work for a family named Auld. Sophia Auld did not know that slaves were not to be taught to read or write, so she taught Frederick how to do both. By the time her husband stopped her, Frederick had learned enough to progress on his own.

Later Frederick worked for a man named Covey, who often beat him. One night Frederick resisted the beating and the two men fought for two hours. This was a dangerous thing for a slave to do, but Covey finally gave up. Frederick was never beaten again.

In 1836 Frederick and other slaves tried to escape. Someone betrayed them and the attempt failed. Shortly after that, Frederick met Anna Murray, a free black woman, and the two fell in love. In 1838 Frederick planned another escape, and this time he successfully reached New York City. He and Anna were married shortly thereafter. Frederick decided to change his last name to symbolize his new freedom. He took the name Douglass from a character in a book a friend of his was reading at the time.

Frederick Douglass's presence was a tremendous boost to the antislavery movement. Anyone who had doubts about the morality or violence of slavery had only to listen to the articulate ex-slave describe his former life. After President Lincoln issued the Emancipation Proclamation in 1863, Douglass helped recruit black soldiers to fight for the Union in the Civil War. He died in 1895 after a long, full life.

1. **When did Frederick Douglass learn to read?**

   (A) after he escaped from slavery

   (B) while he lived with the Aulds

   (C) while he lived with his grandmother

   (D) after he married Anna Murray

2. **What happened after Sophia Auld stopped teaching Frederick?**

   (A) He forgot everything he had learned.

   (B) He asked other slaves to teach him.

   (C) He continued to learn on his own.

   (D) He decided reading was not important.

3. **What happened first?**

   (A) Douglass addressed an antislavery meeting.

   (B) Douglass resisted the beating of a man named Covey.

   (C) Douglass took a new name.

   (D) Douglass escaped from slavery.

4. **When did Frederick Douglass meet Anna Murray?**

   (A) after he escaped from slavery

   (B) after he reached New York

   (C) in between his escape attempts

   (D) at an antislavery meeting

5. **What happened last?**

   (A) Douglass recruited black soldiers to fight for the Union.

   (B) President Lincoln issued the Emancipation Proclamation.

   (C) Frederick Douglass married Anna Murray.

   (D) Frederick Douglass spoke at an antislavery meeting.

UNIT 12
White-Water Rafting

When Dana Hammond and her family went rafting on the Colorado River, they really didn't know what to expect. They had seen some pictures in which light rubber rafts bounced along the rapidly flowing water, sometimes going completely under the water. None of these pictures, however, was as exciting as the real thing.

The family's voyage began calmly enough. Their four guides had two large rafts, loaded with all the necessary supplies for a two-day journey. Also aboard was a life jacket for each person to wear at all times. They set out early in the morning, and for the first few minutes, the trip seemed to be progressing easily. The wide, calm river and peaceful sandy beaches along the water's edge made Dana wonder why rafting was considered such an exciting sport.

Within an hour, though, Dana wished she had never had that thought. Suddenly, the river became narrow, and the water rushed over large rocks. It was the roughest stretch of water Dana had ever seen. The rafts had to fight their way through the rapids. At times, the fronts of the rubber rafts were completely under the water. Everyone held on tightly, though, and at last, the water grew quieter. Ben, the head guide, led the rafts to a calm spot on the riverbank. Everyone stretched out on the ground and rested. All too soon, however, Ben had everyone back in the boats. "All right," he said loudly. "You've seen what it's like. Now let's get going."

For the rest of the day, the group pushed down the river. They rushed through rapids. They stopped for lunch on a sandbar in the middle of the river. They even spent an hour exploring a fifty-foot waterfall that stood right on the bank of the river. By four o'clock, the passengers were so tired they could hardly move. As head guide, Ben did not seem tired at all, but he looked for a good camping spot and brought the boats in for the night. That night, Dana would sleep better than she had ever slept before. Before turning in, she and the other passengers ate a wonderful dinner, which Ben and the guides had prepared. Then, sitting around the campfire, the family listened to the guides' stories of their adventures on the river. By nine o'clock, Dana's eyes started to close—all by themselves. "Turn in, everybody," Ben said firmly. "You'll all be up by first light."

True to his word, Ben had everyone up and moving by dawn. After a quick breakfast, they were out on the river again. This time, the water was even rougher than before. Dana got a seat in the "horn"—the front part of the boat—and got a close-up view of the action. She held onto the safety ropes as the boat plunged in and out of the water. It was the roughest ride so far.

Around noon, Ben had the boats pulled ashore. After lunch, everyone hiked through the canyon, and Dana managed to take some pictures of two wild burros roaming the area. A few hours later, the group was back on the water. That evening, they pulled into shore for the last time. The family was almost sad to leave the boats, but the trucks and vans were already there to pick them up and bring them back to the "real" world. Dana, though, can hardly wait to go back again. Next year, she says, she'll ride the "horn" for the whole trip.

UNIT 12
White-Water Rafting

1. **Which of these happened first?**

   (A) The raft went through the rapids.

   (B) Dana saw some pictures of rafts on the Colorado River.

   (C) People boarded the two rafts.

   (D) The group ate on a sandbar.

2. **What did the family do just before turning in for the night?**

   (A) They listened to stories about adventures on the river.

   (B) They hiked around the canyon.

   (C) They explored a fifty-foot waterfall.

   (D) They met the trucks and vans.

3. **When did Dana ride in the horn?**

   (A) on the morning of the first day

   (B) on the afternoon of the first day

   (C) on the morning of the second day

   (D) on the afternoon of the second day

4. **When did Dana take pictures of wild burros?**

   (A) before the family rode the roughest rapids of all

   (B) when the family pulled into shore for the last time

   (C) before Dana rode the "horn"

   (D) while the family hiked through the canyon

5. **Which of these happened last?**

   (A) The group left at dawn.

   (B) The guides told stories of their adventures on the river.

   (C) Dana said she'll ride in the horn all the time.

   (D) The trucks and vans arrived.

In Unit 12, you read about a girl who went white-water rafting on the Colorado River with her family. Think about other outdoor adventures people can have. Then read the following story.

Megan crawled forward a few more inches. "It's okay," she called back to her teacher and friends. "There's plenty of room ahead."

Soon, Megan and the others were standing in a small "room" deep under the ground. The walls were a shiny dark green. "It looks like a whole wall of jewels," gasped Manuel, who was standing right next to Megan.

It had taken the group almost three hours of climbing and crawling to get to this small room. All five of these people were experienced cavers (or *spelunkers*, as they are sometimes called). They had been planning this trip for several weeks. Now, far inside the cave, they knew that all the preparation and effort had been worthwhile.

Megan and her friends had never even heard of caving before their science teacher, Ms. Rodriguez, came to Lane Junior High School. But Ms. Rodriguez had been exploring caves since she was a teenager. Her excitement over her hobby spread to some of her students. Soon, a Caving Club was formed. Now, eighteen months later, the members were on their third trip underground.

A. Exercising Your Skill

Think about the order in which things happen in this part of the story. What happened first? What happened next? What words help you know the order in which the events happened? Are there any words that tell you how long some of the events took?

Now read the list of events below. On your paper, write the events in the order in which they happened in the story.

The Caving Club went on its third trip.
Ms. Rodriguez came to teach at Lane Junior High School.
The group climbed and crawled for three hours.
The Caving Club was formed.
The cavers decided that all of their work had been worthwhile.
Megan led the group into the underground "room."
The club took its first trip.
The club began planning its third trip.
The cavers saw the jewellike walls of the underground "room."

B. Expanding Your Skill

What do you think might happen next in this story? On your paper, write five events that you think might happen. Number them to show the order in which they would take place. With a group of classmates, share and discuss the events each of you wrote. Ask your classmates if they agree or disagree with the order in which you listed the five events. Have them give reasons for their answers.

C. Exploring Language

Imagine that you are describing the Caving Club members' experiences on this day. What might the young cavers find? What problems might arise? What adventures might they have?

On your paper, complete this part of the story in your own words (one or more for each blank). Be on the lookout for places where you can use time-order clue words.

For a few moments, the group explored _____ . Suddenly, Ms. Rodriguez noticed _____ . _____ everyone gathered around her, Ms. Rodriguez said, "This is a *most* unusual find! These are _____ ."

Holding the _____ in his hands, Todd whispered, "Let's see what else we can find in here." _____ the group spread out. For almost _____ they quietly examined every inch of the room.

_____ a cry from Wilma broke the silence. " _____ !" she cried as everyone rushed to her side.

"What is it?" asked _____ .

"I'm not _____ ," said Ms. Rodriguez. "But it certainly isn't like anything we've ever seen in a cave before." _____ she suggested, "Let's see what other treasures this little room has to offer."

With that, they went back to their _____ . They worked until everyone grew hungry. _____ after a brief break for lunch, they _____ . It was _____ when Megan suddenly came upon another room. Hurriedly, they worked together to _____ . _____ , however, it was time to head back.

_____ they came out of the cave entrance and climbed into the van, they all agreed that this had been _____ .

D. Expressing Yourself

Choose one of these activities.

1. Think about what the cavers might have discovered. Could it be a treasure of some kind? Could it be something left by someone a long time ago? Could it be a unique-looking cave formation or perhaps an unusual creature rarely seen anywhere else? On your paper, write another paragraph to add to the story telling what the cavers discovered. Make sure the sequence of events in your discovery paragraph is clear.

2. Turn the entire story of the Caving Club into a play. Include directions that tell the actors what to do and when—crawl, wave, stand up, and so on. Also include directions that tell the actors how long each action is supposed to take. After you finish writing the story in play form, assign parts and produce the play. Put on the play for the class or other classes in your school.

3. Use encyclopedias or other reference books to learn about caving. How do people learn about this sport? What equipment do they need? Where and when do they go caving? What kinds of things do they do? Why does caving excite people? Write a short report about caving and read it aloud in class. Plan the order of your facts carefully.

UNIT 13
A Whale of a Tale

Have you ever been stuck somewhere? Perhaps you were walking in the woods and became caught in a sticky swamp, or perhaps you were stuck in the middle of a busy street for a few moments while cars raced by you. Experiences like these can be quite disturbing. However, can you imagine what it must be like to be trapped suddenly by giant sheets of ice—so that you have almost no room to move and no way out? That is exactly the situation that faced three gray whales in 1988. Their story is an exciting "escape" story.

In early autumn, three young gray whales were traveling along the north coast of Alaska, headed west on a path whales had used for ages. Suddenly, however, huge packs of ice closed together, forming a solid wall for the whales to break through. They couldn't swim under the ice either because they would have to surface to breathe, and the ice pack was too long. The whales, therefore, were cut off from the open water of the Beaufort Sea, and they were trapped in two small pools of water. They faced almost certain death in this foodless prison.

The whales were soon discovered by Alaskan Inuit hunters, who reported what they had found. It was then that government officials in Alaska and in Washington, D.C., heard and took action. They sent experts of all kinds to help. Then people interested in the environment also took action. Just a few days after the hunters' discovery, people all over the world had learned of the whales' problem from newspaper and television stories and had begun to offer their help. The nearby community of Barrow, Alaska, became flooded with people who had come to save the whales. More reporters began to arrive as well, and soon, news broadcasts and newspapers were filled with daily reports on the condition of the whales. Even politicians began to comment on the whales. However, despite all the attention from television and politicians, it was the cooperation of thousands of people that finally freed the whales from their trap.

The people of Barrow, for example, worked around the clock to help the whales escape from their icy trap. Ice was cut and moved away as fast as possible. Oil companies lent equipment. Their chain saws helped cut breathing holes for the whales so that they could stay alive under the thick ice. The oil companies also lent a giant ice smasher that helped break up the ice surrounding the whales. They donated a piece of equipment that moved over the ice and opened up the first part of a channel through which the whales could swim to the open sea.

Help came from as far away as Minnesota. There, two people heard about the trapped whales and decided to do what they could. They sped to Alaska, bringing with them de-icing machines to cut a path through the ice for the whales.

Finally, other nations offered their help, too. The Soviet Union sent navy icebreakers. These giant ships helped cut through the thick ice that was the whale's last obstacle to freedom. After that, there was a channel for the whales to swim through. One of the whales had already died, but the two survivors slowly made their way to freedom. When they did, people over much of the world gave a sigh of relief.

UNIT 13
A Whale of a Tale

1. **What happened first?**
    (A) Three young gray whales became trapped by ice.
    (B) Alaskan Inuit hunters discovered three young whales.
    (C) A Soviet icebreaker created a channel through the ice off Alaska.
    (D) Three young gray whales traveled west along the north coast of Alaska.

2. **What happened just before the whales were cut off from the open water of the Beaufort Sea?**
    (A) They were discovered by Inuit hunters.
    (B) Huge packs of ice closed together.
    (C) Government officials took action.
    (D) Barrow became flooded with people.

3. **When did people beyond Alaska learn of the whales?**
    (A) after newspapers reported the trapped whales
    (B) after Inuit people reported the trapped whales
    (C) before Inuit people reported the trapped whales
    (D) the same day the whales were first trapped

4. **When did icebreakers from the Soviet Union clear part of the channel?**
    (A) near the end of the rescue
    (B) at the beginning of the rescue
    (C) before the rescue began
    (D) after the first whale got stuck

5. **What happened last?**
    (A) Icebreakers arrived from the Soviet Union.
    (B) People cut breathing holes for the whales.
    (C) The whales reached the open sea.
    (D) Politicians talked about the whales.

UNIT 14
A Long Time to Wait for a Letter

What do you do after you send someone a letter? If you are like most people, you probably start checking the mailbox the day after you send your own letter. If that is the way you are, you might feel sorry for a group of sailors who served on the U.S.S. *Caleb Strong* during World War II. In 1944, the *Caleb Strong* went from Newport News, Virginia, to Oran, Algeria. During that time, ninety-three of the sailors on board wrote letters to people back home. Over 250 letters were written during the trip, but none of them reached the people they were sent to—until 1987!

What happened? Well, when the *Caleb Strong* arrived in Algeria, the sailors gave the letters to one of their shipmates who would soon be returning to the United States. He promised to mail the letters as soon as he returned home, but, unfortunately, he failed to keep his promise.

According to Meg Harris, a spokesperson for the postal service, the sailor simply forgot. After the war, he stored the letters in his aunt's attic in Raleigh, North Carolina. At last, in June 1987, someone noticed the letters and took them to the local post office. The postal workers, however, did not know what to do about the forty-three-year-old letters.

Finally, the postal service decided to deliver the mail. Unfortunately, this proved to be more difficult than it might have appeared. One set of letters, for example, was addressed to a sailor's girlfriend. This woman, however, had married someone else long ago. She did not even want to see four letters from a boyfriend she had not seen in forty years.

The Veterans Administration in Washington, D.C., went to work and helped find many of the people. Radio and television stations also helped, but luck helped most of all. For instance, the postmaster in Raleigh, North Carolina, recognized one of the names on the letters. Someone he knew also looked over the envelopes. That person recognized two names and helped forward the letters to the right people. In Washington, D.C., one postal service manager noticed a name on one envelope that looked like the name of a baseball player for the Boston Red Sox and the Baltimore Orioles. With the help of the Major League Baseball Players' Alumni Association, this man finally received his letter.

Meg Harris says that not all the letters have been so easy to deliver either to the senders or to receivers. One of the sailors, for example, was named Smith. "He won't be easy to find," she explained. She also expected to have trouble finding Raoul Alvarez because Alvarez is also a common name. Surprisingly, though, Raoul Alvarez turned out to work in a post office in California. His letter, which was addressed to Terry Espinosa, was quickly delivered to his wife, whose name in 1944 had been Terry Espinosa. She was thrilled to see the old letter that her husband had sent her.

UNIT 14
A Long Time to Wait for a Letter

1. **What happened first?**

   (A) A sailor said he would mail all the letters.

   (B) The post office received the letters.

   (C) The U.S.S. *Caleb Strong* sailed from Virginia to Algeria.

   (D) A sailor forgot to mail the letters.

2. **When were the letters written?**

   (A) before World War II

   (B) after World War II

   (C) while the ship was sailing to Algeria

   (D) after the shipmate returned home

3. **When did the sailor store the letters in his aunt's attic?**

   (A) before World War II

   (B) during World War II

   (C) after World War II

   (D) in June 1987

4. **What happened last?**

   (A) The Veterans Administration helped find many of the people.

   (B) Someone noticed the letters.

   (C) Someone took the letters to the local post office.

   (D) The postal service decided to deliver the mail.

5. **When did Raoul Alvarez and his wife get their mail?**

   (A) just before he took a job with the postal service in California

   (B) while he was working for the postal service in California

   (C) before the *Caleb Strong* returned to the United States

   (D) while he was in Algeria

UNIT 15
Dr. David Livingstone, African Explorer

You may be familiar with the quote "Dr. Livingstone, I presume?" That is the famous greeting that Sir Henry Morton Stanley is said to have spoken when he found the previously missing Dr. David Livingstone in the heart of Africa. Do you know, however, how Dr. Livingstone came to be there in the first place?

Born in Scotland in 1813, David Livingstone worked in a cotton mill as a young boy to finance his own education. Later, Livingstone studied medicine at a university in Glasgow. In 1840, the young man went to Africa as a medical missionary. His first stop was at Kuruman, a settlement near the Kalahari Desert in present-day Botswana. While at Kuruman, Livingstone met and married Mary Moffat. In 1849, the two crossed the Kalahari Desert together and were the first Europeans to see Lake Ngami.

From 1852 to 1856, Livingstone went alone on an expedition to try to find a route to the African interior from one of the coasts. On this trip, he traveled all the way to Luanda on the west coast. From Luanda, Livingstone journeyed back to the Zambezi and followed that river north to its mouth in the Indian Ocean. It was on that leg of the trip that he discovered Victoria Falls of the Zambezi River in 1855.

Livingstone returned to Great Britain in 1856 and published his book *Missionary Travels and Researches in South Africa*, which made him famous. During this time, he was also received at the English court by Queen Victoria and was made a Fellow of the Royal Geographical Society.

Returning to Africa in 1858, Livingstone led an expedition to explore the Shire River and regions around Lake Nyasa. At that time, he became increasingly concerned about the inhumanity of slave traders in Africa. In 1865, Livingstone returned again to England and published *Narrative of an Expedition to the Zambezi and Its Tributaries*. In this second book, he told the European people about the horrors of the slave trade.

In 1866, an expedition was financed for Dr. Livingstone to search for the source of the Nile River. He reached Lake Tanganyika in 1869, but then communications from him ceased, and people became concerned about his safety. Livingstone was resting at Ujiji in 1871 when a rescue party led by Sir Henry Morton Stanley came upon him, and Stanley uttered the now-famous greeting. After that, Stanley and Livingstone explored more of the Lake Tanganyika area together. Then Livingstone continued alone in search of the source of the Nile River. It was on this expedition, around May 1, 1873, that Livingstone died in what is now Zambia.

Dr. David Livingstone is regarded as one of the foremost European explorers of Africa, providing some of the first accurate information for the formulation of modern maps. He is also recognized as being a pioneer in the movement to end the African slave trade.

UNIT 15
Dr. David Livingstone, African Explorer

1. **Which of these did David Livingstone do first?**
   (A) became a missionary
   (B) studied medicine
   (C) married Mary Moffat
   (D) worked in a cotton mill

2. **Which of these areas did Dr. Livingstone visit last?**
   (A) Kuruman
   (B) Lake Nyaša
   (C) Luanda
   (D) Victoria Falls

3. **When did Dr. Livingstone publish a book telling about the slave trade?**
   (A) after Stanley found him
   (B) during his first visit to England
   (C) during his second visit to England
   (D) while resting at Ujiji

4. **What happened first?**
   (A) Livingstone discovered Victoria Falls.
   (B) Livingstone was met by Stanley at Ujiji.
   (C) Livingstone began searching for the source of the Nile River.
   (D) Livingstone and his wife discovered Lake Ngami.

5. **What happened last?**
   (A) Stanley and Livingstone explored more of the Lake Tanganyika area.
   (B) An expedition was financed for Livingstone to search for the source of the Nile River.
   (C) Stanley uttered his now-famous greeting.
   (D) Livingstone reached Lake Tanganyika.

UNIT 16
Pocahontas, the Peacemaker

The story of how the girl Pocahontas saved John Smith's life is well known to most grade-school children. Pocahontas did even more to establish peaceful relations between New World and Old World people, however.

Pocahontas was the daughter of Powhatan, chief of a powerful league of over thirty tribes of Algonquian-speaking Indians (Native Americans) in the area around Jamestown, Virginia, in the early 1600s. The young girl's given name was Matoaka, but she was called Pocahontas, meaning "the playful one." In 1607, Pocahontas' life became even more interesting. At that time, a group of English colonists arrived on her people's land and settled very close to her village. Her father, Powhatan, made no aggressive moves against the settlers at first, but he did feel that they represented a threat to the Indian nation.

By 1608, it began to appear that the English settlers were not going to leave on their own as others before them had. It was at that time that one settler was captured while hunting. The prisoner, John Smith, was brought to Powhatan. According to one source, Smith's future was about to be decided when Pocahontas cried out for him to be saved. In the Algonquian culture, that kind of request could save a prisoner's life, so Smith was spared. Smith stayed in the village for several weeks after that and became good friends with many of the Algonquians.

Several braves then returned John Smith to Jamestown and on their return to Powhatan told the chief that the settlers were very ill and starving. Pocahontas overheard this. She did not want these people to die, so she brought food to the settlement on a regular basis during that time. Many said that it was Pocahontas who kept the colony going.

Over time, however, tension mounted between the Jamestown settlers and the Algonquians, and eventually Pocahontas was forbidden by Powhatan to visit the English settlement. Around that time, the new governor of Jamestown, Samuel Argall, had Chief Powhatan's daughter taken as a hostage to be traded for English prisoners and some rifles that the Algonquians had taken. Powhatan's reply to the capture was that he would return the prisoners but not the guns. In fact, Powhatan was quite certain that the settlers would never harm Pocahontas.

Meanwhile, in the Jamestown settlement, Pocahontas was being treated very well. She had many friends there already and was allowed to visit from house to house. During her long stay, she took on the religion of the settlers, and she also took the English name Rebecca. It was during this time that she met John Rolfe, a settler who had introduced tobacco growing to the Virginia colony. Rolfe asked permission to marry Rebecca. Permission was granted by the governor of the colony and, ten days later, by Powhatan. Every Jamestown settler, two of Rebecca's uncles, and two of her brothers attended the wedding. This union was followed by eight years of peace between the Indians and the English and was often referred to as the "Peace of Pocahontas."

The Rolfes had one son, Thomas. After Rebecca Rolfe's untimely death in her early twenties, John and Thomas Rolfe continued to live and work in Jamestown.

1. **Which of these happened first?**

   (A) John Smith was taken captive.

   (B) Pocahontas met John Rolfe.

   (C) Pocahontas saved John Smith's life.

   (D) Jamestown was settled by the English.

2. **When was Pocahontas taken hostage?**

   (A) before she brought food to the settlement

   (B) after she met John Rolfe

   (C) after Powhatan told her she could no longer visit the English settlement

   (D) before she saved John Smith

3. **When did Pocahontas take the name Rebecca?**

   (A) when she was a child

   (B) after the birth of her son, whom she named Thomas

   (C) after she married John Rolfe

   (D) while she was a captive at Jamestown

4. **What happened after Pocahontas married John Rolfe?**

   (A) Powhatan would not return the rifles to the English.

   (B) There were eight years of peace between the Algonquian Indians and the English.

   (C) Pocahontas took on the religion of the settlers.

   (D) Pocahontas met a settler who had introduced tobacco growing to the Virginia colony.

5. **Which of these happened last?**

   (A) Algonquians came to a wedding at Jamestown.

   (B) John Rolfe introduced tobacco as a crop.

   (C) Rebecca Rolfe died.

   (D) The Algonquian Indians and the English enjoyed eight years of peace.

UNIT 17
Maple Syrup the Old-fashioned Way

Maple syrup can be one of the most delicious treats imaginable. It can be poured over pancakes or waffles, and it can be made into wonderful desserts. Years ago, it was used in place of sugar by American colonists. In fact, three hundred years ago, people in New England even delayed celebrating Thanksgiving for several days because they did not have enough maple syrup to make their pies and desserts!

How is this wonderful syrup made? First, people wait for the very first signs of spring, usually in February or early March. Even though snow is usually still on the ground, the days are just beginning to get warm enough for sap to start flowing inside the sugar maple trees from which the syrup will come.

When the perfect weather arrives, people gather up their "tapping tools" and head off to the sugar maple trees, which they begin to "tap." First, they drill a hole into the tree. Next, they hammer a spout into the hole. A small tree gets one spout, but a large tree can get two or even three spouts at a time. As soon as the spout is in, sap starts dripping out of the tree. Everyone then rushes to hook a piece of plastic tube to the spout. The end of the tube is put into a large bucket, where the sap begins to collect.

Everyone then waits for the buckets to fill. This might take several days or even weeks. Then the buckets are collected and taken to a barn or other large area where the next step, "boiling down," takes place. The sap that comes from the trees contains a lot of water that can be removed by this process.

Boiling down is a fairly simple process. First, a large barrel is filled with sap. The sap slowly drips from this barrel down into a pan that sits over a fire. The sap boils inside the pan, then flows down into another pan that is set slightly lower. The sap is boiled again in this second pan, where it gets hotter and hotter. The syrup is almost ready when most of the water has been boiled away. This can take an entire day. During this time, people check the temperature of the sap.

Once the temperature is just right, the sap—now syrup—is taken away from the fire and strained by pouring it through layers of cotton or other cloth. This gets rid of the minerals still left in the syrup. Although these minerals are not harmful to people, they do make the syrup look cloudy.

Once the syrup is put into jars, the process has almost been completed. All that remains to be done is to seal the jars and put labels on them so people know what is inside. Then all anyone has to do is to dig into a stack of pancakes dripping with fresh, homemade maple syrup.

1. **What happens first?**

   (A) Spouts are put into trees.

   (B) Plastic tubes are put into large buckets.

   (C) Holes are drilled in the trees.

   (D) Sap collects in buckets.

2. **What happens right before everyone rushes to hook a piece of plastic tube to the spout?**

   (A) A spout is hammered into the hole in the tree.

   (B) Sap starts dripping out of the tree.

   (C) The sap collects in a bucket.

   (D) Everyone waits for the buckets to fill with sap.

3. **What happens soon after a barrel is filled with sap in the boiling-down process?**

   (A) Buckets begin to fill.

   (B) Labels are put on syrup jars.

   (C) Plastic tubes are used.

   (D) The sap boils in a pan over a fire.

4. **When does syrup get strained?**

   (A) while it is coming from the trees

   (B) before it drips out of the second pan

   (C) before it is heated a second time

   (D) after it has reached just the right temperature

5. **What happens last?**

   (A) The syrup is put into jars.

   (B) Water is removed.

   (C) The syrup is boiled once more.

   (D) The syrup is put into a large barrel.

UNIT 18
A Leader of His People

Cesar Chávez was born in 1927 in Arizona. His parents had immigrated to the United States from Mexico. During Chávez's earliest years, the family lived on a small farm, raising vegetables and chickens. Then, when Chávez was seven, the family lost the farm. They became migrant workers, traveling up and down California, following the fruit and vegetable harvests, finding work when and where they could. It was a difficult life. The work was extremely hard and the pay very low. In 1939, there were more than 300,000 migrant workers in California. Workers who complained about poor pay or the terrible working conditions quickly found themselves out of work. There were always other out-of-work migrants waiting to take over their jobs.

Chávez often picked peas from dawn until dusk for less than a penny a pound. He worked in the damp soil until the skin on his fingers cracked and bled. At night, the family stayed in the miserable labor camps provided by the growers. The tiny shacks were usually unheated and without running water. Often as many as fifty families shared a single bathroom. Once, when they had no work and no money, the Chávez family lived for an entire winter in a cold, wet tent. Through all of this, young Cesar tried to get an education. It wasn't easy. Because his family moved so often, Cesar attended thirty different schools during one six-year period.

Cesar Chávez found his first steady job in 1952, when he was twenty-five years old. He married and settled down to raise a family. By the early 1960s, however, conditions for migrant workers were no better than they had been when Chávez was young. Chávez decided that he must help the farm workers form a union to protect themselves and demand fair treatment from the growers. Even though he had a family and little money, Chávez quit his job and began traveling around the state, talking to workers.

In September 1962, the union was officially formed. In 1965, Chávez and the United Farm Workers Association began what was to become a five-year battle with the California grape growers. Union members carried on a strike against the growers. Because the strikers refused to give up and the growers refused to give in, the strike dragged on.

In 1967, Chávez made a bold move. He sent fifty workers to New York City to picket stores where California grapes were sold. He urged stores and the public to stop buying California grapes. Slowly the grape boycott spread across the country. Despite all this, the growers stood fast. By this time, most union members had sold everything they owned. Chávez announced that he would go on a fast (hunger strike) to draw attention to the pickers' cause and to rally his workers around the union's nonviolent principles. After twenty-five days without food, Chávez felt that the danger of violence was past and he ended his fast. His union was more determined and united than ever.

Finally, in 1970, the grape growers gave in and signed the first union contracts with farm workers. It had been a long and bitter battle, and it was only the first of many for Cesar Chávez. He had established the success of his methods, and he had demonstrated the importance of unity and nonviolence in the struggle for a better living for migrant workers and their families.

UNIT 18
A Leader of His People

1. **Which of these events happened first?**

   (A) The Chávez family was out of work and lived in a tent.

   (B) The Chávez family became migrant workers.

   (C) The Chávez family lost the farm.

   (D) The Chávez family raised chickens and vegetables.

2. **When did Chávez get his first steady job?**

   (A) after he married

   (B) before he got an education

   (C) before he decided to help form a union

   (D) after he began traveling around the state to talk to workers

3. **Which of these events took place before Cesar Chávez founded the farm workers' union?**

   (A) the grape boycott

   (B) the United Farm Workers' strike

   (C) Chávez's quitting his job

   (D) Chávez's hunger strike

4. **When did Chávez begin a five-year battle with California grape growers?**

   (A) before the union was formed

   (B) after the workers went on strike

   (C) after 1967

   (D) before fifty workers went to New York City to picket

5. **Which of these events happened last?**

   (A) Chávez went on a hunger strike.

   (B) The grape growers signed the first union contracts with farm workers.

   (C) Workers went to New York City to picket.

   (D) The grape boycott spread across the country.

UNIT 19
Rachel Carson

Rachel Carson was born in 1907 in Pennsylvania. She always wanted to be a writer, even as a child. Her story "A Battle in the Clouds" was printed in *St. Nicholas* magazine in 1918. She was paid $10.00 for her story!

Rachel studied literature in college but also had to take some science courses in order to graduate. Her biology teacher, Mary Scott Skinker, taught her subject with so much passion that Rachel decided to change her major to biology. But she loved writing, too. Would she have to choose between the two?

Carson earned a master's degree in marine biology from Johns Hopkins University in 1932. But there were few jobs for women scientists in those days. She began writing radio scripts for the Bureau of Fisheries. This work paid about $20.00 per week. Carson was thrilled to find a job in which she could combine science with writing. Later a full-time job paying $2,000 per year opened up at the Bureau.

Soon Carson's writing was in great demand. *Under the Sea Wind,* a book about the creatures of the sea, was published in 1941. It combined fictional stories about sea animals and plants with factual science in an interesting way. Not many writers could do that. *The Sea Around Us* followed ten years later.

Carson began to learn about the environmental threats to life both in the oceans and on land. She studied the effects of pesticides used to control mosquitoes and other insect pests. DDT had indeed reduced diseases carried by mosquitoes. But it was also killing bees, grasshoppers, birds, and other animals.

In 1962, Carson published *Silent Spring*. The title was inspired by the fact that pesticides were reducing bird and wildlife populations, making each spring more silent than the last. The book caused a tremendous controversy. Chemical manufacturers called Carson a hysterical woman and worse. Others were supportive. Scientists praised the accuracy of her research. The *New York Times* said she should win the Nobel Prize. President John F. Kennedy read the book and set up an advisory committee to investigate the dangers of pesticide misuse. Carson herself testified before a Senate committee in 1963.

The use of DDT was severely restricted in 1972 by the Environmental Protection Agency, which was formed in 1970. Many people feel that Carson's work led to the formation of the EPA. Unfortunately Carson did not live to see the results of her efforts. She died of cancer in 1964.

UNIT 19
Rachel Carson

1. **What happened first?**

   (A) *Under the Sea Wind* was published.

   (B) *Silent Spring* was published.

   (C) *The Sea Around Us* was published.

   (D) "A Battle in the Clouds" was published.

2. **When did Rachel Carson decide she wanted to be a writer?**

   (A) after she graduated from Johns Hopkins

   (B) after she decided to study biology

   (C) when she was a child

   (D) after the success of *The Sea Around Us*

3. **When did Rachel fall in love with science?**

   (A) when she had Mary Scott Skinker as a teacher

   (B) when she began to research DDT

   (C) when she decided to combine writing and science

   (D) when she was taking literature courses

4. **What happened last?**

   (A) DDT was restricted.

   (B) The EPA was formed.

   (C) Rachel Carson died.

   (D) Rachel Carson testified before Congress.

5. **When did Carson make about $20.00 per week?**

   (A) when she was writing for *St. Nicholas* magazine

   (B) when she published *Silent Spring*

   (C) when she worked full-time with the Bureau of Fisheries

   (D) when she wrote radio scripts for the Bureau of Fisheries

The Third L A P
Language Activity Pages

In Unit 14, you read about how the postal service has tried to deliver letters that are over forty years old. Now read about how the postal service goes about delivering your letters every day.

Mail is gathered from all the many drop boxes in your community. These drop boxes may be on a street corner, in a building, or even in front of the post office. Next, the mail is taken to the post office. There the letters are put into large bags. The bags are then rushed to sorting centers.

The mail is sorted so that it can be sent to the right places as quickly as possible. The first step is to send the letters through a machine called an *edger-feeder*. This machine sorts out the envelopes according to size. The envelopes then go to another machine, a *facer-canceler*. This second machine arranges the envelopes so that they face the same way. It places a cancellation mark on the envelope over the stamp. This mark shows where the letter is being sorted, what time it was sorted, and other information.

Then the letters go to a very special third machine, an *optical character reader*. This machine "reads" the numbers of the zip code on the envelopes. As it reads those numbers, the machine sends the letters to different areas, depending on where they are addressed to. That way, all the letters going to California can be placed together, all those going to Alaska together, and so on.

A. Exercising Your Skill

Think about the order in which things happen in the passage above. What happens first? What happens next? Read the list of events below. On your paper, write the events in the order in which they happened. Add time-order clue words to some of the sentences to help make the order clear.

The optical character reader reads the zip codes.
People place mail in the postal service drop boxes.
Bags of mail are rushed to sorting centers.
An edger-feeder machine sorts out the envelopes by size.
Letters are put into large bags.
The optical character reader sorts the letters, by zip codes, according to destination.
The facer-canceler arranges the envelopes and applies the cancellation mark.
Mail is taken to a post office.
Mail is picked up from the drop boxes.

B. Expanding Your Skill

What might happen next as the mail is being sent to your home? On your paper, write three events that you think might happen. Put them in the appropriate order. Compare your sentences with your classmates' sentences. Are they similar or different?

48

C. Exploring Language

The mail was not always moved and delivered so easily. One of the most famous chapters in the history of mail delivery is the story of the Pony Express, which sent horses and riders across two thousand miles of America, from St. Joseph, Missouri, to Sacramento, California. On your paper, complete the story of the Pony Express in your own words (one or more for each blank).

The Pony Express began in 1860, when the mail took up to three weeks to get from the East Coast to the West Coast. The mail traveled by train only as far as Missouri, where the railroad lines ended. Two members of Congress set up a special _____ to solve the problem of getting mail _____ . Horses were bought, riders were _____ , and stations were _____ . _____ , on April 3, 1860, the Pony Express _____ .

Here is how the system worked. A rider started out on a fresh horse from the first station. _____ he rode ten to fifteen miles. When he arrived at the next station, he _____ and galloped off. _____ , on the fresh horse, he went on for the next ten or fifteen miles _____ . The rider repeated this four or five times until he had covered about sixty to _____ miles. _____ , at what was called a home station, riders were changed. The new horse and rider _____ . In this way, the mail was kept moving _____ , night and day.

The Pony Express worked so fast and efficiently that mail could cross the country in only ten days. _____ , however, _____ the beginning of the telegraph made the Pony Express _____ . _____ , in 1861, after the telegraph lines reached all the way to the West Coast, the Pony Express _____ .

D. Expressing Yourself

Choose one of these activities.

1. Think about what it must have been like to have ridden for the Pony Express. What dangers would you have faced? What would it feel like to ride a galloping horse for about seventy-five miles each day? On your paper, write what a day in the life of a Pony Express rider might have been like. If you wish, underline the time-order words that give clues to when things happen in your story.

2. Using encyclopedias or other reference books, research another "chapter" in American history that relates to communication. Your topic might be the invention of the telegraph, telephone, or television; the expansion of the railroad in the West; the recent development of overnight express-mail delivery; or any other topic that you prefer. When you take notes, include words that signal the order of the events. Use your notes for a brief report. Give your report a title, and then present the report orally in class.

UNIT 20
A Long, Hard Journey

In 1976, Sichan Siv was crawling through the jungle, trying to escape from Cambodia. By 1989, however, Sichan Siv was working in the White House, in Washington, D.C., as an advisor to the President of the United States. How had this strange journey come about?

Like millions of Cambodians, Siv was a victim of a bloody civil war. One of the sides in this war was the Cambodian government. The other was a group called the Khmer Rouge. When the Khmer Rouge won the war, the situation in Cambodia got worse. Many people were killed, while others were forced into hard labor. Sometimes entire families were wiped out.

Siv came from a large family that lived in the capital of Cambodia. After finishing high school, Siv worked for a while with a Cambodian airline company. Later, he taught English. After that, he took a job with CARE, an American group that was helping victims of the war.

Siv had hoped to leave Cambodia before the Khmer Rouge took over the country. Unfortunately, however, he was delayed. As a result, he and his family were taken from their homes and forced to labor in rice fields. After a while, Siv managed to escape. He rode an old bicycle for miles, trying to reach Thailand where he would be free and safe. For three weeks, he slept on the ground and tried to hide from the soldiers who were looking for him. Caught at last, he was afraid he would be killed. Instead, he was put into a labor camp, where he worked eighteen hours each day without rest. After several months, he escaped again; this time he made it. The journey, however, was a terrifying one. After three days of staggering on foot through mile after mile of thick bamboo, Siv finally made his way to Thailand.

Because he had worked for an American charity group, Siv quickly found work in a refugee camp—a place where others who had also fled from their homes could stay. Soon, however, he was on his way to the United States. He arrived in June of 1976 and got a job—first picking apples and then cooking in a fast-food restaurant. Siv, however, wanted more than this; he wanted to work with people who, like himself, had suffered the hardship of leaving their own countries behind. Siv decided that the best way to prepare for this kind of work was to go to college. He wrote letters to many colleges and universities. They were impressed with his school records from Cambodia, and they were impressed with his bravery. Finally, in 1980, he was able to study at Columbia University in New York City. After finishing his studies at Columbia, Siv took a job with the United Nations. He married an American woman and became a citizen. After several more years, he felt that he was very much a part of his new country.

In 1988, Siv was offered a job in the White House working for President Reagan's closest advisors. It was a difficult job, and he often had to work long hours. However, the hard work was worth it, because Siv got the opportunity to help some refugees in his work.

UNIT 20
A Long, Hard Journey

1. **What happened first?**

   (A) Siv worked for CARE.

   (B) Siv got a job with a Cambodian airline.

   (C) Siv went to Columbia University.

   (D) Siv worked in a refugee camp in Thailand.

2. **What happened after Siv escaped the first time?**

   (A) He and his family had to work in rice fields.

   (B) He was sent to Thailand.

   (C) He was forced to teach English.

   (D) He was sent to a labor camp.

3. **What happened after Siv spent several months in a labor camp?**

   (A) He escaped again.

   (B) He was afraid he would be killed.

   (C) He worked in a rice field.

   (D) The Khmer Rouge took over the country.

4. **When did Siv go to the United States?**

   (A) before he worked in the rice fields

   (B) after he had escaped to Thailand

   (C) after he worked picking apples

   (D) before he took a job with CARE

5. **What happened last?**

   (A) Siv became a United States citizen.

   (B) Siv went to work at the United Nations.

   (C) Siv went to work at the White House.

   (D) Siv finished his studies at Columbia University.

UNIT 21
Dogsled Racer

Young Jennie Hutchins is a "musher." No, that's not someone who likes a strange kind of breakfast cereal. It is someone who races sleds in the snow. It is one of the most unusual and exciting sports in North America. All of Jennie's family enjoys dogs and sledding. Her parents make the slim, beautiful sleds and also help train the dogs. Jennie and her brother Nathan were getting ready for a race. And when someone from the Hutchins family races, everyone goes.

On the day of the race, the Hutchinses get up early. By the time the sun comes up, the dogs are barking and yelping, and Jennie and Nathan give them special hugs. The two children are junior sled racers. Because the rules for these young racers say they must train the dogs that they race, both Jennie and Nathan are especially close to their dogs. Someday, those dogs will be the lead dogs in a team.

Right after breakfast, Jennie's father and older brother, Willie, put the sleds into a trailer hooked to their car. Next, they put the dogs' harnesses in as well. While all this is going on, Jennie loads the Siberian Huskies into the trailer, where each dog has its own special spot.

When everything is aboard the trailer, the family sets out. They drive carefully, since they do not want to upset the dogs or let the sleds spill out. Finally, they arrive in Stowe, Vermont, where the junior race is to be held.

Everything is quickly unloaded. Jennie and her mother put Jennie's dog, Frosty, into the harness. Jennie is entering a one-dog race. Other races have more dogs pulling the sleds, but, for this race, Frosty will be the only dog pulling Jennie's light sled.

When everything is set, Jennie moves to the starting line. The racers do not leave all at once, but one at a time. The judges use stopwatches to time each racer from the starting line to the finish line. The race covers about a mile and a half.

When the starter waves his arm, Jennie cries out, "Hike! Hike!" Then Frosty jumps forward, pulling Jennie and the sled along. Soon the strong dog is speeding over the snow. Frosty's big, broad paws, like snowshoes, keep the dog from sinking into the snow.

As Frosty and Jennie charge over the snow, Jennie can tell that she is making good time. Zooming around corners, she digs a heel into the snow to slow the sled. Once the sled has rounded the corner, Jennie lifts her heel and the sled jumps forward again. There is no need to tell Frosty to go faster. The dog just loves to run, even pulling the sled and rider.

At last, the finish line is in sight. As they cross, Jennie wonders whether she and Frosty have won. An hour later, she hears the news—she has finished second, and Nathan has finished third. It has been a good day for the Hutchins family. Now that Jennie and Nathan's race is over, everyone goes to work to make sure that Willie is ready for his upcoming race.

1.   **What happens first?**

(A) Mr. Hutchins and Willie put the sleds into the trailer.

(B) Jennie loads the dogs into the trailer.

(C) The family eats breakfast.

(D) The dogs' harnesses are put into the trailer.

2.   **What happens after Frosty is put into the harness?**

(A) The family eats breakfast.

(B) Willie helps load the sleds.

(C) Jennie moves to the starting line.

(D) The dogs go to their special spots in the trailer.

3.   **What does Jennie do after the sled rounds corners?**

(A) She yells, "Hike! Hike!"

(B) She tells Frosty to go faster.

(C) She lifts her heel from the snow.

(D) She digs her heel into the snow.

4.   **When does Jennie learn who has won the race?**

(A) as soon as she crosses the finish line

(B) when she yells, "Hike! Hike!"

(C) as soon as Nathan comes in

(D) an hour after she crosses the finish line

5.   **What happens last?**

(A) Jennie finishes the race.

(B) Nathan finishes the race.

(C) Everyone helps Willie get ready for his race.

(D) Jennie knows she has made good time.

UNIT 22
Race in the Desert

Every year since 1986, some of the world's most daring runners have gathered in the desert of Morocco. They are there to take part in one of the most difficult races in the world. The Marathon of the Sands, as it is called, covers over 125 miles of desert and mountain wilderness. The runners complete the course in fewer than seven days, and they run with their food, clothing, and sleeping bags on their backs.

The Marathon of the Sands was founded in 1986 by Patrick Bauer. His idea was to give the runners, who come from all over the world, a special kind of adventure. Most of the runners in this race have found that they form deep friendships with the other runners during their days and nights in the desert. Facing terrible heat and complete exhaustion, they learn much about themselves and each other.

For most of the runners, though, the challenge of the race is the main reason for coming. On the first day, for example, they run fifteen miles across a desert of sand, rocks, and thorny bushes. Few runners finish the day without blistered and raw feet. They also suffer from a lack of water. (They are allowed less than nine quarts of water during each day of the race.) Most of all, they are exhausted when they arrive at their campsite for the night.

The second day, the runners are up at 6:00 A.M. Within a few hours, it is 100°F, but the runners do not hesitate. They must cover eighteen miles that day. That night, they rest. They must be ready for the next day's run.

On the third day, the runners must climb giant sand dunes—the first they have faced. Dust and sand mix with the runners' sweat. Soon their faces are caked with mud. After fifteen miles of these conditions, the runners finally reach their next camp.

The race continues like this for four more days. The fourth and fifth days are the worst. On the fourth day, the runners pass through a level stretch and a beautiful, tree-filled oasis, but then, on this and on the next day, they cross more than twenty-one miles of rocks and sand dunes. The temperature soars to 125°F, and many runners cannot make it. Helicopters rush fallen runners to medical help. Runners who make it to the end of the fifth day know that the worst is over, however.

On the sixth day, heat and rocks punish the racers terribly. In the Valley of Dra, the wind picks up and, as the desert heat is thrust against them with great force, they grow more and more exhausted.

The seventh day is the last, with only twelve miles to be covered. The dusty, tired, blistered runners set out at daybreak. Near the finish line, children race along with the runners, for everybody has caught the excitement. The ones who have run the whole marathon know they have accomplished what most people could not even dream of. "During the hard moments," says one contestant who has raced here twice, "I'd think, 'Why am I here?' Then I'd realize I was there to find my limits."

UNIT 22
Race in the Desert

1. **What happens first?**

   (A) The runners face their first sand dunes.

   (B) The runners cross through the Valley of Dra.

   (C) The runners set out across fifteen miles of desert.

   (D) The runners ask themselves, "Why am I here?"

2. **When do the runners climb the first giant sand dunes?**

   (A) on the first day

   (B) after the second day

   (C) after the fourth day

   (D) before they must cover 18 miles in one day

3. **When do the runners cross 21 miles of rocks?**

   (A) before they meet throny bushes

   (B) when they reach the Valley of Dra

   (C) after they pass through an oasis

   (D) after the wind picks up

4. **When do the racers reach the Valley of Dra?**

   (A) before the seventh day

   (B) on the fourth day

   (C) after the sixth day

   (D) before they reach the oasis

5. **What happens last?**

   (A) The runners' faces become caked with mud.

   (B) Children race along with the runners.

   (C) Temperatures reach 125°F.

   (D) The fifth day ends.

UNIT 23
King of the Fads

Have you ever tried using a Hula Hoop? Have you ever played with a Slinky or a Rubik's Cube? If not, maybe you've tried on a pair of Mickey Mouse Club ears at one time or another. All of these objects are "fads"—things that are hugely popular before they suddenly disappear.

Most people forget about fads after a while, but Ken Hakuta is not like most people. In fact, he is "King of the Fads." In his office, he has thousands of examples of fads. His files and bookcases are filled with everything from Mickey Mouse telephones to pet rocks. However, the most interesting objects in Hakuta's office are not the fads from the past, even though he has thousands of them around for people to look at. No, the really fascinating aspect of Hakuta's work is the plans and models for fads of the future.

Hakuta became interested in fads in a strange way. Until a few years ago, he was in the import-export business near his home in Washington, D.C. Most of the goods he brought into the United States were "normal" items such as radios and fabrics. In 1983, though, a strange package arrived for him from his parents in Tokyo, Japan. The package contained six "Wacky Wallwalkers" for Hakuta's children. A Wacky Wallwalker looks like a small octopus. To play with one, you simply throw it against a wall. Once the Wacky Wallwalker is attached to the wall, it begins to crawl downward—all by itself.

Hakuta took them everywhere he went. He took them to offices and restaurants, where people stopped and took notice. They loved these strange objects. Realizing that the toys would be a hit, Hakuta soon found himself in the Wacky Wallwalker business.

Hakuta must have known what he was doing because Wacky Wallwalkers became one of the great fads of 1983 and 1984. In fact, over 150 million of them were sold. They were even supposed to be part of the advertising campaign used to make people see a 1980s James Bond movie. After that, Hakuta's fad business expanded rapidly. People all over the world wrote to tell him about their ideas for new toys and fads, and they even sent him working models of their inventions. They continue to do so.

Right now, Hakuta has some "great" new inventions ready to start selling. There is the "tornado in a bottle," for example. This is a bottle filled with dark liquid. When you shake it, a tiny tornado swirls around and sweeps over a small town inside the bottle. One of Hakuta's favorite inventions is a battery-run cat's paw. You are supposed to use it whenever you discover mice in your home.

One of the strangest items of all, however, is "dried water." Hakuta discovered the product at one of the Fad Fairs that he runs each year. What is dried water? Well, explains Hakuta, it is made up of small tablets that can be carried around more easily than containers of water. Whenever you need or want water, just add some water to the tablets. Believe it or not, Hakuta says with a smile, they have already sold quite a few of these tablets. It shows, says Hakuta, just how wild fads can really be.

1. **What happened first?**

   (A) Hakuta discovered dried water tablets.

   (B) Hakuta invented the "tornado in a bottle."

   (C) Hakuta was in the import-export business.

   (D) Hakuta got six Wacky Wallwalkers in the mail.

2. **When does a Wacky Wallwalker start crawling by itself?**

   (A) before it is taken from its package

   (B) after it hits the wall

   (C) before it is thrown

   (D) after it reaches the floor

3. **When did Hakuta decide Wacky Wallwalkers would be a hit?**

   (A) before he took them to offices and restaurants

   (B) after he took them to offices and restaurants

   (C) when his parents sent them to him from Tokyo

   (D) before he worked in the import-export business

4. **Which invention did Hakuta sell first?**

   (A) tornado in a bottle

   (B) dried water

   (C) Wacky Wallwalkers

   (D) battery-run cats' paws

5. **What happened last?**

   (A) Wacky Wallwalkers were a success.

   (B) Wacky Wallwalkers were used to help sell a movie.

   (C) Hakuta moved to Washington, D.C.

   (D) People sent Hakuta ideas for new toys.

UNIT 24
"One Small Favor"

On August 26, 1920, the nineteenth amendment to the Constitution of the United States—which gave women the right to vote—became law. In the words of that amendment, "The right of citizens of the United States to vote shall not be denied or abridged by the United States or by any state on account of sex." Incredibly, the nation was then 125 years old.

The fight for the right of women to vote was a long and difficult battle. It actually began in 1648 in the colony of Maryland, long before there was a United States of America. The first person to speak out in the defense of a woman's right to vote was Margaret Brent.

Margaret Brent had come to America with her brother and sister years before 1648. Like many others who came before and after her, she was excited by the stories she heard about opportunities in the colonies. The Brents worked hard and prospered in the Maryland colony, acquiring several large parcels of land, which they operated as farms. Margaret Brent especially attracted the attention of Governor Leonard Calvert, who was quite impressed with her business abilities. A wealthy man himself, Calvert sought out her advice in matters of money. What is more, the governor saw to it that Margaret Brent sat in the Maryland assembly. There she learned firsthand about bills the members of the assembly were debating—bills that might well affect the fortunes of Governor Calvert himself. She served the governor well on that account, but one can be sure he was not so pleased with her fiery sense of justice.

Margaret Brent, you see, was allowed to *sit* in the assembly. She was even allowed to speak on occasion, but she was not allowed to vote. This latter restriction irritated her. She was so disturbed by the notion that a woman was not considered equal to a man that she determined to speak out against it. Her opportunity came during a meeting of the assembly. There was a pause during one of the many debates that mark any session of a legislature. Taking advantage of the lull, Brent rose to her feet and fixed her eyes upon the members of the assembly. Without waiting to be recognized, she began to speak.

She wished to ask, Brent said, "one small favor" of the assembled body. Since she had been permitted to act like a member of the assembly for several weeks, she argued, there was no reason she could see to be denied any rights accorded to members. She was asked what she meant. Her reply was that she should be permitted to vote in the assembly. The men were outraged, but Brent stood her ground firmly. The debate ran on for hours, with Brent slowly winning the members to her side. Sensing what was happening, the speaker of the assembly abruptly ended the session in spite of the howls of many who were present.

Margaret Brent never did win the right to vote. Nevertheless, her strong efforts in that behalf mark the first public voice in the struggle for women's rights.

UNIT 24
"One Small Favor"

1. **Which of these events happened last?**
   - (A) Brent asked for "one small favor."
   - (B) Women won the right to vote.
   - (C) The Brents acquired land.
   - (D) Governor Calvert appointed Margaret to the assembly.

2. **What was the first thing Brent did when she reached the colonies?**
   - (A) She went to work for the governor.
   - (B) She took her seat in the assembly.
   - (C) She ran farms with her family.
   - (D) She spoke out for women's rights.

3. **Which of these events happened first?**
   - (A) Margaret Brent sat in the Maryland assembly.
   - (B) The United States became a nation.
   - (C) Margaret Brent met Governor Calvert.
   - (D) Maryland's first public speech for women's rights was made.

4. **What happened after Brent had sat in the assembly for several weeks?**
   - (A) She met the governor.
   - (B) She decided to speak for women's rights.
   - (C) She advised the governor.
   - (D) She acquired several parcels of land.

5. **Which of these events happened last?**
   - (A) Brent asked that she be permitted to vote in the assembly.
   - (B) The speaker of the assembly ended the session.
   - (C) Brent began to speak without waiting to be recognized.
   - (D) Brent rose to her feet and fixed her eyes upon the members of the assembly.

UNIT 25
A Powerhouse of a Drummer

When young Terri Carrington plays the drums, people listen. There aren't many female drummers in either jazz or rock and roll. However, people have been listening to Carrington since she was ten years old. Now that she's in her twenties, they listen even more. That's because she plays better than ever.

Carrington comes by her talent naturally. Her grandfather was Matt Carrington, who played drums with some of the greatest names in jazz as well as with one of the very first rock stars of all time, Chuck Berry. Terri Carrington's father also performed with big-name musical groups—playing the saxophone, though, not the drums. While Terri was growing up, music was always a part of the Carrington house. Young Terri's mother played the piano almost every day, and her father would sit with Terri on his knee, listening to the best recordings of classic jazz.

Terri Carrington started with music at the age of five, when she found her father's old saxophone in their house in Medford, Massachusetts. The young girl showed instant talent. At the age of seven, however, she faced a problem—her baby teeth were coming out, so she could no longer hold the mouthpiece of the saxophone in her mouth.

Terri Carrington could not bear to be without music. So, exploring the basement of the family home, she came across her grandfather's old set of drums. In no time at all, the young girl was playing them.

By the age of ten, Terri was ready to perform, and the young drummer appeared in Kansas with the band of jazz trumpeter Clark Terry at the Wichita Jazz Festival. The next year she performed with such famous jazz musicians as Dizzy Gillespie, Oscar Peterson, and Elvin Jones.

Terri Carrington graduated from Medford High School at the age of sixteen. Then she headed off for the Berklee College of Music in Boston. She had won a scholarship to go to the college when she had been only eleven! While at Berklee, she played the drums with everyone from singer Harry Belafonte to Stan Getz and "Cannonball" Adderly. The teen-ager had become a sensation in the jazz world.

In 1986, she tried out for a band being formed by saxophone player Wayne Shorter and won the job over thirteen other drummers. From then on, big things began to happen. Her first record, *Real Life Story*, broke out in the top twenty jazz albums of 1989. She switched to television, taking a job on a popular late-night show. She also began to play other kinds of music as well. Soon her rhythm and blues drumming was earning her as much attention as her work in jazz. In fact, she says, she'll play any kind of music at all, but she prefers beating the drums.

1. **What happened first?**

   (A) Terri Carrington started playing the saxophone.

   (B) Terri Carrington started playing the drums.

   (C) Terri Carrington performed with Clark Terry.

   (D) Terri Carrington won a scholarship to the Berklee College of Music.

2. **When did Terri Carrington switch to drums?**

   (A) just before her baby teeth began to come out

   (B) while her baby teeth were coming out

   (C) when she turned six

   (D) after she won a scholarship to college

3. **When did Terri Carrington appear at the Wichita Jazz Festival?**

   (A) before she was seven

   (B) when she was eight

   (C) when she was ten

   (D) after she turned eleven

4. **When did Carrington win a job with Wayne Shorter over thirteen other drummers?**

   (A) in 1986

   (B) in 1989

   (C) at age ten

   (D) at age sixteen

5. **What happened last?**

   (A) Carrington played with Harry Belafonte.

   (B) Carrington graduated from Medford High School.

   (C) Carrington played with Dizzy Gillespie.

   (D) Carrington's record broke into the top twenty.

The Last L A P
Language Activity Pages

In Unit 25, you read about a young woman who is becoming known as one of the best drummers in the world. Now read about a group of young people who want to have their own band.

All four members of the Jetts were nervous. Al, the lead guitar player, paced up and down. Over in the corner, Luisa tapped her fingers in rhythmic beats. She always seemed to be practicing her drumming, even while everyone was waiting to go out on stage.

It had taken the Jetts two years of hard work and long practice sessions, and they finally were about to go out on stage for their first big performance. They had played for parties and school dances, but they had never before played at a real rock concert. Even though they were only the warm-up band, it was still a thrill!

During the past two years, they had practiced night after night. They had worked to convince people that a live band, rather than records or tapes, would make a wonderful attraction at a party. At first, they had played without being paid—just to get experience and to get their name known. Finally, people had begun to notice them, and they were on their way to becoming something more than an amateur rock-'n'-roll band.

Suddenly, they heard their name being announced over the public-address system. The crowd gave a loud cheer. "All right," whispered Luisa, "now let's show them what a *real* band can do!"

A. Exercising Your Skill

Think about the order in which things happen in the story. What happened first? What happened next? What words help you know the order in which the events happened? Are there any events that you think may have happened before the actual beginning of the story?

Read the list of events below. On your paper, write the events in the order in which they happened or probably happened.

The Jetts got jobs playing at parties.
The Jetts heard their name over the public-address system.
The Jetts first got together and formed their band.
People began to notice the Jetts.
The Jetts practiced night after night.
The group waited backstage nervously.
The group headed out onto the stage as the crowd cheered.

B. Expanding Your Skill

What do you think might happen next in the story? List five events that you think might happen. Number them to show the order in which they would take place. Then compare your list of events with your classmates' lists. Are they similar or different? Discuss the order and give your reasons for putting the events in the order you chose.

C. Exploring Language

Think about what it must feel like to be giving your first real concert as a member of a band. How would you feel about the performance or the audience? How would you act backstage? What kinds of music do you think you would want to play?

On your paper, complete the story in your own words (one or more for each blank). Be sure to use words that will help your readers know the order in which things happen.

Quickly, the Jetts got themselves arranged behind the curtain. They smiled _____ . Still, they were _____ . _____ , even before the curtain opened, Luisa began _____ . By the time the curtain was fully open, the Jetts _____ . The crowd _____ . Al and Dina started singing, and the whole hall seemed to _____ . _____ the place _____ .

The group kept it up for _____ . Within minutes, people were in the aisles _____ . Every player was playing _____ . They had played in front of audiences before. _____ , however, they felt that _____ .

_____ the Jetts rushed from the stage, the audience _____ . They didn't want them _____ . _____ , in a flash, the group was _____ . _____ Al's voice sang to the music of his guitar, the band knew they could _____ .

D. Expressing Yourself

Choose one of these activities.

1. Think about what might happen to the Jetts after this concert. Do you think they will be a success? What do you think the next step in their career might be? Put your thoughts down on paper. Add time-order clue words to show the sequence in which events might happen. Then write an ending for the story in Part C.

2. Imagine that you work for a rock magazine. You have just heard the Jetts' concert. Now you are going to write a review of the Jetts and their music. Think about what you saw and heard. Then write your review. Be sure to tell what happened in the correct order. Tell your readers what you thought of the Jetts' performance, and give reasons for your opinions.

3. Write an advertisement for the Jetts' next concert. Imagine that your ad will be broadcast over the radio. To appeal to listeners, your words should be fresh, lively, and vivid and should make people think that the Jetts are the greatest new group in the world! Then present your ad orally to your class as a radio commercial.

Book D

Specific Skill Series

Identifying Inferences

William H. Wittenberg

Fifth Edition

SRA/McGraw-Hill
Columbus, Ohio

Cover, Back Cover, John Downer/Masterfile

SRA/McGraw-Hill
A Division of The **McGraw·Hill** *Companies*

Send all inquiries to:
 SRA/McGraw-Hill
 8787 Orion Place
 Columbus, OH 43240-4027

ISBN 0-02-688004-0

 9 10 11 IPC 03 02 01

To the Teacher

PURPOSE:

IDENTIFYING INFERENCES is designed to develop one of the most difficult interpretive skills—arriving at a *probable* conclusion from a limited amount of information. IDENTIFYING INFERENCES requires the readers to *read between the lines*. They must utilize previously acquired knowledge and past experiences in order to fully comprehend the message of the text.

FOR WHOM:

The skill of IDENTIFYING INFERENCES is developed through a series of books spanning ten levels (Picture, Preparatory, A, B, C, D, E, F, G, H). The Picture Level is for pupils who have not acquired a basic sight vocabulary. The Preparatory Level is for pupils who have a basic sight vocabulary but are not yet ready for the first-grade-level book. Books A through H are appropriate for pupils who can read on levels one through eight, respectively. **The use of the *Specific Skill Series Placement Test* is recommended to determine the appropriate level.**

THE NEW EDITION:

The fifth edition of the *Specific Skill Series* maintains the quality and focus that has distinguished this program for more than 25 years. A key element central to the program's success has been the unique nature of the reading selections. Nonfiction pieces about current topics have been designed to stimulate the interest of students, motivating them to use the comprehension strategies they have learned to further their reading. To keep this important aspect of the program intact, a percentage of the reading selections have been replaced in order to ensure the continued relevance of the subject material.

In addition, a significant percentage of the artwork in the program has been replaced to give the books a contemporary look. The cover photographs are designed to appeal to readers of all ages.

SESSIONS:

Short practice sessions are the most effective. It is desirable to have a practice session every day or every other day, using a few units each session.

SCORING:

Pupils should record their answers on the reproducible worksheets. The worksheets make scoring easier and provide uniform records of the pupils' work. Using worksheets also avoids consuming the exercise books.

It is important for pupils to know how well they are doing. For this reason, units should be scored as soon as they have been completed. Then a discussion can be held in which pupils justify their choices. (The Integrated Language Activities, many of which are open-ended, do not lend themselves to an objective score; thus there are no answer keys for these pages.)

GENERAL INFORMATION ON *IDENTIFYING INFERENCES:*

The difference between a *conclusion* and an *inference*, as presented in this series, is that a conclusion is a logical deduction based upon conclusive evidence, while an inference is an "educated guess" based upon evidence that is less than conclusive. Read this sample:

> Captain Fujihara quickly parked the fire truck, grabbed his helmet, and rushed into the house at 615 Oak Street.

You can *conclude* that Captain Fujihara knows how to drive because that ability was required to park the fire truck. You can *infer* that there is a fire at 615 Oak Street because Captain Fujihara took his helmet and rushed into that house. This is an inference because firefighters do rush to put out fires. It is an inference because there may be another reason for the firefighter's rushing to the house. Captain Fujihara may live there and be late for supper. Thus an inference is supported by evidence, but the evidence is not necessarily conclusive.

SUGGESTED STEPS:

1. Pupils read the text. On levels C-H, after reading, pupils examine the statements that follow the text to determine whether each is a factually true statement (T), a false statement (F), or a valid inference (I). ("True" statements are those about which the reader can be *certain* from the text.) On lower levels, pupils determine which statement about the text or picture is probably true.
2. Then pupils reexamine the text or picture for evidence to support their decisions.
3. Pupils record their answers on the worksheets.

RELATED MATERIALS:

Specific Skill Series Placement Tests, which enable the teacher to place pupils at their appropriate levels in each skill, are available for the Elementary (Pre-1–6) and Midway (4–8) grade levels.

About This Book

In a story, a writer does not tell the reader everything. A careful reader is able to make educated guesses about things the author does not tell. An educated guess is a guess that is based on facts the author provides plus the reader's own knowledge and experience. For example, an author may write the following in a story:

Janet clutched a handkerchief tightly in her fingers. Sobbing, she raised her hand to wipe away the tears that trickled down her cheeks.

You can make an educated guess that Janet is sad, based on the fact that she is crying and on your own knowledge that people sometimes cry when they are sad.

This kind of educated guess is called an **inference**. You cannot be certain that your inference is correct. In the example above, Janet may be crying because she has hurt herself. Or she may be crying because she is very happy. Other details in the story will help you make the best possible guess.

In this book, you will read short stories. Then you will read four sentences about each story. You will have to decide whether each sentence is true (T), false (F), or an inference (I). A true statement tells a fact from the story. A false statement is one that is not true. An inference says something that is *probably* true based on facts in the story and your own knowledge and experience. More than one sentence about one story may be true, false, or an inference. You must read each sentence carefully to decide which it is.

1.   "Be sure to wear your warmest coat," advised Mother. "It can get very cold in the mountains."

"Don't worry about me," said Judy. "No one knows better than I do how cold it can get in the mountains. I'm taking my heaviest coat, two sweaters, and a blanket."

---

2.   "It was so cold last night that the water on the streets froze," said Barbara. "People who are driving should drive very carefully."

"The roads are slippery," agreed Marion. "I hope my brother gets home safely. Whenever he drives, I worry about him. My parents worry about him, too."

---

3.   Bill opened the newspaper. He turned the pages rapidly until he found the comics. Then he sat on his bed and began to read. It wasn't long before Bill's mother could hear him laughing. Bill's mother said to herself, "I'll bet Bill is reading the comics again."

---

4.   "Wow! How tall is that building, Aunt Amy?" asked Juan.

"That's the World Trade Center, Juan," Aunt Amy replied. "It's 110 stories tall."

"I saw some tall skyscrapers in San Francisco," Juan went on, "but New York City takes first place!"

---

5.   "Would you like to play checkers?" asked Bonnie. "I got a new checker set for my birthday. I must warn you, though, I'm a pretty good player."

"Don't worry about me," said Mark. "I'm a good checker player too. As a matter of fact, I can beat everyone else in my class at school."

UNIT 1

		T	F	I
1.	(A) Mother told Judy to wear warm clothes.	☐	☐	☐
	(B) Mother told Judy to have fun swimming on her trip.	☐	☐	☐
	(C) Judy had been to the mountains before.	☐	☐	☐
	(D) Judy was taking two sweaters to the mountains.	☐	☐	☐

		T	F	I
2.	(A) Marion's parents never worry about her brother.	☐	☐	☐
	(B) Marion's brother is not an excellent driver.	☐	☐	☐
	(C) Marion has at least one brother.	☐	☐	☐
	(D) Marion worries about her brother when he drives.	☐	☐	☐

		T	F	I
3.	(A) Bill often reads the comics.	☐	☐	☐
	(B) Bill sat on a chair to read the comics.	☐	☐	☐
	(C) Bill and his mother weren't in the same room.	☐	☐	☐
	(D) Bill's mother could hear Bill laughing.	☐	☐	☐

		T	F	I
4.	(A) Juan has been to San Francisco.	☐	☐	☐
	(B) Juan and Aunt Amy are in New York City.	☐	☐	☐
	(C) The World Trade Center is 110 stories tall.	☐	☐	☐
	(D) Aunt Amy doesn't know anything about the World Trade Center.	☐	☐	☐

		T	F	I
5.	(A) Bonnie was just learning how to play checkers.	☐	☐	☐
	(B) Mark was afraid to play checkers with Bonnie.	☐	☐	☐
	(C) Bonnie and Mark are not in the same class.	☐	☐	☐
	(D) Bonnie received a checker set for her birthday.	☐	☐	☐

1. "Ouch! I've got a splinter in my finger," cried Rosa. "I knew I shouldn't have climbed over the wooden fence." Rosa ran into the house to find her mother. She knew that it would be bad to leave the splinter in her finger for a long time.

---

2. "I call my dog Jumbo because it's so big," said Ralph. "My friend calls her pet cat Fluffy because it's so soft."

    "Those are good names," said Tom. "Last week I got a pet dog. I think a good name for my new dog would be Lightning."

---

3. Cathy heard someone yelling for help. She ran to the backyard to see who was in trouble. What she saw made her laugh. A cat was in a tree, and Cathy's little sister wanted someone to help it. "Don't worry," said Cathy to her sister. "Cats can get out of trees whenever they want to."

---

4. Bobby saw Father lying on the sofa. He looked peaceful with his eyes closed and his hands resting on his stomach. Bobby took his roller skates and quietly left the room. A few minutes later, Bobby's mother asked where Bobby was. Father said that Bobby had gone roller-skating.

---

5. "What did you eat for breakfast?" asked Juan. "I had my favorite—eggs, toast, juice, and a large glass of milk."

    "You were lucky," said Luis. "My alarm clock didn't go off this morning, and I got up late. But I'm going to eat a really big lunch."

UNIT 2

			T	F	I
1.	(A)	Rosa got a splinter in her toe.	☐	☐	☐
	(B)	Rosa wanted her mother to take out the splinter.	☐	☐	☐
	(C)	Rosa climbed over a fence.	☐	☐	☐
	(D)	Rosa ran to find her father.	☐	☐	☐

			T	F	I
2.	(A)	Tom's dog is a fast runner.	☐	☐	☐
	(B)	Ralph has a pet cat.	☐	☐	☐
	(C)	Tom likes the names Jumbo and Fluffy.	☐	☐	☐
	(D)	Ralph's pet is named Fluffy.	☐	☐	☐

			T	F	I
3.	(A)	Cathy hurried to see who was in trouble.	☐	☐	☐
	(B)	Cathy told her sister not to worry.	☐	☐	☐
	(C)	Cathy doesn't have any brothers or sisters.	☐	☐	☐
	(D)	The person that Cathy heard yelling was her sister.	☐	☐	☐

			T	F	I
4.	(A)	Father was resting in an easy chair.	☐	☐	☐
	(B)	Father wasn't sleeping when Bobby went skating.	☐	☐	☐
	(C)	Bobby doesn't have a pair of roller skates.	☐	☐	☐
	(D)	Bobby's mother wondered where Bobby was.	☐	☐	☐

			T	F	I
5.	(A)	Luis didn't eat breakfast.	☐	☐	☐
	(B)	Juan ate eggs and bacon for breakfast.	☐	☐	☐
	(C)	Juan liked the breakfast he ate.	☐	☐	☐
	(D)	Luis will be very hungry by noon.	☐	☐	☐

1. "I must get into the habit of remembering my lunch," said Gina. "I left it on the school bus twice last week. And one day I even forgot to take it out of the house." Gina was glad when it was suppertime. She was extremely hungry.

2. "Don't step on the new sidewalk," warned Mr. Jefferson. "The cement is still soft. I'm guarding the sidewalk so people will not write their names in it."

    "That's a good idea," said Tony, "but it looks as if Billy was here before you started guarding the sidewalk."

3. Mrs. Rojas is going to retire next month. She has been working in the same department store for almost twenty-five years. On her last day of work, her friends at the store are going to have a party to honor Mrs. Rojas. Her friends are also going to give her a gold watch.

4. "Can you identify this old coin?" asked James. "I found it when I was digging in the garden."

    Father looked at the coin. "It's certainly an old coin, but I can't tell what country it's from. Let's take the coin and show it to Mrs. Barry."

5. Jean saw an envelope in the street. She picked it up and looked inside. It was filled with money! Jean counted it and found that there was $2,000 in the envelope. Jean took the money to the police station. A few days later, a woman named Rita came to Jean's house. She gave Jean a reward.

UNIT 3

		T	F	I
1.	(A) Gina rides to school on a bus.	☐	☐	☐
	(B) Gina always buys her lunch at school.	☐	☐	☐
	(C) Today Gina had forgotten her lunch again.	☐	☐	☐
	(D) Gina sometimes forgets to do things.	☐	☐	☐

		T	F	I
2.	(A) Mr. Jefferson warned Tony about the soft cement.	☐	☐	☐
	(B) "Billy" was written in the sidewalk.	☐	☐	☐
	(C) Mr. Jefferson didn't want the sidewalk damaged.	☐	☐	☐
	(D) The cement in the sidewalk was fairly hard.	☐	☐	☐

		T	F	I
3.	(A) Mrs. Rojas has worked in the same store for many years.	☐	☐	☐
	(B) Mrs. Rojas is almost twenty-five years old.	☐	☐	☐
	(C) Mrs. Rojas retired last month.	☐	☐	☐
	(D) Mrs. Rojas' friends are going to give her a present.	☐	☐	☐

		T	F	I
4.	(A) James used the coin to buy seeds.	☐	☐	☐
	(B) Mrs. Barry knows a great deal about coins.	☐	☐	☐
	(C) Father could tell that the coin was old.	☐	☐	☐
	(D) James found the coin at the beach.	☐	☐	☐

		T	F	I
5.	(A) Jean found the money in a pocketbook.	☐	☐	☐
	(B) Jean took the money to the police station.	☐	☐	☐
	(C) The lost money belonged to Rita.	☐	☐	☐
	(D) Jean found the money in a street.	☐	☐	☐

1. "What hours is the library open?" asked Carla. "I have a report to do for school, and I need to get a book."

"The library opens at 9 A.M. on Saturdays, and it doesn't close until 9 P.M.," said Julia. "You have a lot of time to get there."

---

2. "Can you get my ball?" asked Robert. "I threw it too high, and it landed on the roof."

"I can't get the ball without a ladder," said Robert's older brother. "We'll have to wait until our neighbor, Mr. Green, comes home from work. Then I'll be able to get your ball."

---

3. Sachi yawned, stretched, and smiled as thoughts of an enchanted forest crossed her memory. She jumped out of bed and shivered from the cold. She threw on her warmest robe and headed downstairs toward the welcome smells of fresh juice and warm oatmeal.

---

4. "I'm so hungry that I could eat everything in the refrigerator!" exclaimed Joe. "What time is supper?"

Joe's mother smiled. It seemed as if Joe was always hungry. "We'll be eating in about an hour," she said. "Eat a carrot or two until supper is ready."

---

5. "Did you see the fish I caught yesterday?" asked Cathy. "It nearly pulled me out of the boat!"

"Yes," said Judy. "I did see the fish you caught, and today we're supposed to go fishing again. I surely hope I catch a fish this time. Even if I don't, camping is really fun."

		T	F	I
1.	(A) Carla had to do a report for school.	☐	☐	☐
	(B) Julia knew when the library was open.	☐	☐	☐
	(C) Carla went to the library on Saturday.	☐	☐	☐
	(D) Carla didn't have time to get to the library.	☐	☐	☐

		T	F	I
2.	(A) Robert hit the ball over the roof.	☐	☐	☐
	(B) Mr. Green has a ladder.	☐	☐	☐
	(C) Robert's brother hid his ball.	☐	☐	☐
	(D) Mr. Green has a job.	☐	☐	☐

		T	F	I
3.	(A) Sachi had been dreaming.	☐	☐	☐
	(B) Sachi's bedroom was on the first floor.	☐	☐	☐
	(C) Sachi felt cold.	☐	☐	☐
	(D) Sachi was going to eat breakfast.	☐	☐	☐

		T	F	I
4.	(A) Joe had to wait about an hour for supper.	☐	☐	☐
	(B) Mother was angry because Joe wanted to eat.	☐	☐	☐
	(C) Joe said that he was hungry.	☐	☐	☐
	(D) Mother told Joe not to eat anything until suppertime.	☐	☐	☐

		T	F	I
5.	(A) Judy didn't see Cathy's fish.	☐	☐	☐
	(B) Cathy was in a boat when she caught her fish.	☐	☐	☐
	(C) The fish that Cathy caught was very big.	☐	☐	☐
	(D) Judy likes to go camping.	☐	☐	☐

1.   Birds had been eating the strawberries in Mrs. Garcia's window box. After all the work she had done, the birds were eating the berries that she had grown for her family. Suddenly, Mrs. Garcia had an idea! "I will put a pinwheel in my window box," she thought. "That will keep the birds away."

---

2.   The boys were walking across a field when they heard a strange sound. They looked and then began yelling and running. A huge bull was rushing toward them! Juan was the first to leap over the fence to safety. It was a minute or two later before Bobby and Carl jumped the fence.

---

3.   "You don't deserve to go to the movies," said Father. "Your brother worked hard cleaning the closet, but you didn't help at all."

"I know I should have helped," said Linda, "but I became so interested in my book that I forgot. I promise to help next time."

---

4.   "Whose car is that in the driveway?" asked Bonnie. "It's the kind of car I'd like to own someday."

"That car belongs to a friend of your sister," said Mother. "She came to pick up your sister. They're going to the museum to see a new exhibit of French paintings."

---

5.   "Do you intend to go to Jim's party or not?" asked Barbara. "You keep changing your mind."

"It depends," said Mark. "If I can shoot baskets with Uncle Bill, I'll shoot baskets. If I can't shoot baskets with Uncle Bill, then I'll go to Jim's party."

UNIT 5

			T	F	I
1.	(A)	Berries were growing in Mrs. Garcia's window box.	☐	☐	☐
	(B)	Mrs. Garcia liked the birds in her window box.	☐	☐	☐
	(C)	The birds made Mrs. Garcia unhappy.	☐	☐	☐
	(D)	Mrs. Garcia thought the birds would like the pinwheel.	☐	☐	☐

			T	F	I
2.	(A)	Juan can run faster than the other boys.	☐	☐	☐
	(B)	The boys were not frightened by the bull.	☐	☐	☐
	(C)	The boys heard the bull before they saw it.	☐	☐	☐
	(D)	The bull couldn't jump the fence.	☐	☐	☐

			T	F	I
3.	(A)	Linda liked the book she was reading.	☐	☐	☐
	(B)	Linda wanted to go to the movies.	☐	☐	☐
	(C)	Linda's father cleaned the closet.	☐	☐	☐
	(D)	Linda said she would help next time.	☐	☐	☐

			T	F	I
4.	(A)	Bonnie's sister owns the car in the driveway.	☐	☐	☐
	(B)	Mother didn't know whose car was in the driveway.	☐	☐	☐
	(C)	Bonnie likes the style of the car in the driveway.	☐	☐	☐
	(D)	Bonnie's sister is going to a museum.	☐	☐	☐

			T	F	I
5.	(A)	Barbara asked Mark a question.	☐	☐	☐
	(B)	Mark didn't want to shoot baskets.	☐	☐	☐
	(C)	Mark said he'd never go to one of Jim's parties.	☐	☐	☐
	(D)	Mark enjoys shooting baskets very much.	☐	☐	☐

1. Everyone in the neighborhood was happy. A carnival was coming to town. There would be many rides, shows, and plenty of delicious food. Rosa was especially happy. Her cousin, Cindy, was coming to visit for a few days. Now they would have things to do that were fun.

---

2. "Look at the way your dog is scratching," said Louis. "It must have fleas."

"My pet does have fleas," said Rita. "I've washed the dog with special soap and used cans of flea powder. Nothing seems to work. The fleas will be gone soon, though. Tomorrow my dog is going to a dog doctor."

---

3. Marion loved a certain necklace, but she didn't have enough money to buy it. Marion thought, "I can do one of two things. I can save my money for weeks to buy the expensive necklace, or I can buy a cheaper necklace." The next day, Marion got a job working in a store after school.

---

4. Corey and Jo slid further down in their seats. They hid their heads behind Corey's jacket.

"I guess *Animals on Parade* would have been a better choice," said Corey. "This is too scary."

"I agree," said Jo as she spotted the nearest exit.

---

5. Tom woke up. He heard a strange noise. Tom listened carefully, but he couldn't tell what it was. He got out of bed and looked in the living room, but the noise wasn't coming from there. Then Tom went into the bathroom. He turned a faucet handle and went back to bed.

UNIT 6

		T	F	I
1.	(A) People would be able to eat at the carnival.	☐	☐	☐
	(B) Rosa was afraid that Cindy wouldn't like the carnival.	☐	☐	☐
	(C) Rosa traveled a long way to visit Cindy.	☐	☐	☐
	(D) Many people were happy that a carnival was coming to town.	☐	☐	☐

		T	F	I
2.	(A) Rita had forgotten to use flea powder on her dog.	☐	☐	☐
	(B) Rita believed the doctor would get rid of the fleas.	☐	☐	☐
	(C) Rita has a dog for a pet.	☐	☐	☐
	(D) Rita had tried to get rid of her dog's fleas.	☐	☐	☐

		T	F	I
3.	(A) Marion waited to buy the expensive necklace.	☐	☐	☐
	(B) Marion doesn't like to wear jewelry.	☐	☐	☐
	(C) Marion got a job cutting lawns.	☐	☐	☐
	(D) Marion needed more money to buy the expensive necklace.	☐	☐	☐

		T	F	I
4.	(A) Corey and Jo were watching a movie.	☐	☐	☐
	(B) They used Corey's jacket to keep warm.	☐	☐	☐
	(C) Corey and Jo agreed they had made a poor choice.	☐	☐	☐
	(D) Jo was planning to leave.	☐	☐	☐

		T	F	I
5.	(A) Tom called for his parents.	☐	☐	☐
	(B) Tom was in bed when he first heard the noise.	☐	☐	☐
	(C) Tom heard water dripping.	☐	☐	☐
	(D) Tom looked first in the bathroom for the noise.	☐	☐	☐

"Be sure to wear your warmest coat," advised Mother. "It can get very cold in the mountains."

"Don't worry about me," said Judy. "No one knows better than I do how cold it can get in the mountains. I'm taking my heaviest coat, two sweaters, and a blanket."

A. Exercising Your Skill

In the passage above, Judy is preparing for some cold weather in the mountains. Sometimes a story will tell you directly that the weather or the season is causing a character to feel hot or cold. In other stories, you can tell whether a character is feeling hot or cold from clues in their actions. Practice recognizing these types of clues. Choose a partner and take turns completing the following sentences.

1. My _____ get cold first.
   Sometimes my _____ turns red in the cold.

2. It is hot where I live in the month of _____ .
   I wear _____ and _____ in hot weather.

Now with your partner, take turns making up other sentences like the ones above and completing them. The sentences should tell about what people do when they are hot, and what they do when they are cold. You can say the sentences out loud or write them on your paper.

B. Expanding Your Skill

Share your sentences with other groups. Did some others think of different sentences from yours? Continue to think about feeling hot or cold. On your paper, draw idea wheels like the ones below. Add as many words or phrases as you can think of to each wheel.

C. Exploring Language

Read the sentences below. Imagine that they are written under the pictures in a family photograph book. On your paper, write what you think is happening in each picture. Then write what you think the weather is like.

1. Tess steps to the edge of the board, holds her nose, and jumps in!
   Tess is _____ .
   The weather is _____ .

2. Sean and Luz toss one heavy shovelful after another to clear a path.
   Sean and Luz are _____ .
   The weather is _____ .

3. Mom and Dad take turns pushing the noisy machine back and forth across the lawn.
   Mom and Dad are _____ .
   The weather is _____ .

Now draw a "family album" picture of you and a friend or member of your family having fun on a vacation. Then, under the picture, write a title or sentence to go with it.

D. Expressing Yourself

Choose one of these activities.

1. With three or four other students, make up a story and take turns telling parts of the story to the rest of the class. The story should tell about something that usually happens in either the spring or the fall. Don't name the season in the story. After the story is finished, see if your classmates can guess what the season is.

2. Draw pictures for a travel advertisement. The scenes might be anything from a warm, tropical climate for swimming, to a brisk, snowy climate for skiing. Write sentences under each picture to make people want to visit the area you have drawn. Ask classmates whether your advertisement is convincing or not.

1.   "How long will it take for my broken leg to heal?" asked Tony. "I'm supposed to run in an important race in three weeks."

"Don't plan to run in that race," said the doctor. "Your leg will be in a cast for six weeks. After that, your leg will be as good as new."

---

2.   "Please go to the store for me," said Mother. "I need a gallon of milk. Your Aunt Jane is coming for supper, and I want to be sure to have enough of everything." Billy grabbed his umbrella and hurried to the store. He was glad to help because his Aunt Jane was coming.

---

3.   "The weather forecast on TV said it would rain today," said Carla, "but the sun is shining. I would have gone on a picnic if I'd known it was going to be a nice day."

"The weather cannot always be forecast correctly," said Mrs. Foster, "but you still have time to go on a picnic."

---

4.   "Sit! Roll over! Come! See how my dog obeys," said Jean. "I taught my dog many commands by rewarding it when it did something correctly."

"I should have used your system of giving a reward," said Gina. "I worked with my dog for three weeks, and it didn't learn to obey one command."

---

5.   "What I love most about a sailboat," said Robert, "is that it's so quiet. The boat sails across the water so silently that it's almost like floating through the air."

"I agree," said Mr. Green. "I also like sailboats because they don't need gasoline to operate, only the wind."

UNIT 7

		T	F	I
1.	(A) Tony won't be able to run in an important race.	☐	☐	☐
	(B) It will take eight weeks for Tony's leg to get better.	☐	☐	☐
	(C) Tony will be able to run in races after six weeks.	☐	☐	☐
	(D) Tony had his broken arm in a cast.	☐	☐	☐

		T	F	I
2.	(A) Mother needed a gallon of milk.	☐	☐	☐
	(B) There were dark clouds in the sky.	☐	☐	☐
	(C) Billy helped by going to the store.	☐	☐	☐
	(D) Mother wanted Billy to go to the drugstore.	☐	☐	☐

		T	F	I
3.	(A) The weather forecast on TV was correct.	☐	☐	☐
	(B) Mrs. Foster wanted to go on a picnic.	☐	☐	☐
	(C) Carla likes to go on picnics.	☐	☐	☐
	(D) The weather forecast said it was going to rain.	☐	☐	☐

		T	F	I
4.	(A) Jean didn't punish her dog.	☐	☐	☐
	(B) Jean and Gina both have pets.	☐	☐	☐
	(C) Jean's dog will roll over when it's told to.	☐	☐	☐
	(D) Gina's dog will sit when it's told to.	☐	☐	☐

		T	F	I
5.	(A) Robert likes sailboats because they aren't noisy.	☐	☐	☐
	(B) Sailboats need gasoline for fuel.	☐	☐	☐
	(C) Mr. Green doesn't like sailboats because they're so quiet.	☐	☐	☐
	(D) Mr. Green and Robert both like sailboats.	☐	☐	☐

1.   "Let me take your picture," said Rick. "I just got a new camera for my birthday, and I'm anxious to use it."

"Okay," said Joe. "Take a picture of me sitting in my brother's new car. I'd love to have a copy of the picture to show to my friends."

---

2.   "Will you run an errand for me?" asked Mr. French. "I need some milk and bread, but I can't go to the store. My foot is still too sore to walk on."

"Sure," said Emily. "I'll walk to the store. It will take me only a few minutes."

---

3.   The sign on the building read "All-Cities Young Folks Talent Show—Practice Today at 2:00 P.M." A bus pulled up with Ms. Velez and several laughing, chattering youngsters. Each carried a musical instrument, dancing clothes, or sheets of music. The youngsters cheered when Ms. Velez said, "Practice begins in fifteen minutes!"

---

4.   Almost every book that Ralph reads is about airplanes. When he isn't reading about airplanes, Ralph enjoys building model planes. He even built one that has wings eight feet across. Ralph says, "I can't wait until I'm old enough to learn how to fly a real airplane."

---

5.   Julia cried with pleasure as her sled sped swiftly downhill. Suddenly, a squirrel ran directly in front of the sled. Julia screamed! Then, just at the last second, the squirrel jumped out of the way. Julia breathed a sigh of relief as her sled finally stopped at the bottom of the hill.

UNIT 8

		T	F	I
1.	(A) Joe got a camera for his birthday.	☐	☐	☐
	(B) Rick wanted to take Joe's picture.	☐	☐	☐
	(C) Rick knows how to use a camera.	☐	☐	☐
	(D) Joe has a brother.	☐	☐	☐

		T	F	I
2.	(A) Emily said she would get milk for Mr. French.	☐	☐	☐
	(B) Emily drove her car to the grocery store.	☐	☐	☐
	(C) Mr. French said he had a sore toe.	☐	☐	☐
	(D) Mr. French doesn't live far from the store.	☐	☐	☐

		T	F	I
3.	(A) There were dancers in the group.	☐	☐	☐
	(B) It was about 1:45 P.M.	☐	☐	☐
	(C) The show would include young people from one city only.	☐	☐	☐
	(D) The youngsters were in the show.	☐	☐	☐

		T	F	I
4.	(A) Ralph knows how to build large model airplanes.	☐	☐	☐
	(B) Ralph spends a lot of time reading.	☐	☐	☐
	(C) Ralph is afraid to fly in an airplane.	☐	☐	☐
	(D) Ralph is not old enough to be a pilot.	☐	☐	☐

		T	F	I
5.	(A) Julia arrived safely at the bottom of the hill.	☐	☐	☐
	(B) The squirrel wasn't hit because Julia stopped the sled.	☐	☐	☐
	(C) The squirrel wasn't hit because Julia was traveling slowly.	☐	☐	☐
	(D) Julia thought surely the sled would hit the squirrel.	☐	☐	☐

1. "I want to be a doctor when I grow up," said Rosa. "I think it would be wonderful to help people who are sick."

"That would be wonderful," agreed Judy, "but I'd rather be a teacher. Teachers help people, too, and it would be fun to work with young children."

2. James was excited about going horseback riding at the farm. He had never been horseback riding before, but he was anxious to try. However, when James saw the size of the horses at the farm, he said, "I'm not going to ride on those horses. I'd be afraid to fall off!"

3. Linda had never been prouder. She had just won a trophy for bowling the highest game in the school bowling tournament. Dozens of boys and girls had bowled, but Linda had beaten them all. Now she was glad that she had spent all those hours practicing.

4. "I think I'll have pancakes for breakfast," said Bill. "I never eat pancakes at home, but when I'm on vacation I often order them." A few minutes later, a waiter brought Bill his pancakes. Bill poured molasses on the pancakes and said, "Now that's what I call a delicious-looking breakfast."

5. "Mrs. Rojas is a wonderful gardener. Everything she plants grows beautifully. Look at her flowers," said Marion, "and look at her vegetable garden. Every plant is healthy."

"She's a great gardener; she reads a lot," said Carla. "Before she plants something new, Mrs. Rojas reads everything she can about it."

UNIT 9

		T	F	I
1.	(A) Rosa would like to help people who are sick.	☐	☐	☐
	(B) Rosa and Judy both want to help people.	☐	☐	☐
	(C) Rosa is still going to school.	☐	☐	☐
	(D) Judy wants to become a nurse.	☐	☐	☐

		T	F	I
2.	(A) The horses at the farm are very large.	☐	☐	☐
	(B) James is an experienced horseback rider.	☐	☐	☐
	(C) At first, James wanted to go horseback riding.	☐	☐	☐
	(D) James went horseback riding in a park.	☐	☐	☐

		T	F	I
3.	(A) Linda wasn't very happy about winning.	☐	☐	☐
	(B) Linda's score was higher than anyone else's who bowled.	☐	☐	☐
	(C) Only girls were allowed to bowl in the tournament.	☐	☐	☐
	(D) Linda had prepared for the bowling tournament.	☐	☐	☐

		T	F	I
4.	(A) Bill frequently eats pancakes at home.	☐	☐	☐
	(B) Bill is on vacation.	☐	☐	☐
	(C) Bill is sorry he ordered pancakes.	☐	☐	☐
	(D) Bill put something on his pancakes.	☐	☐	☐

		T	F	I
5.	(A) Mrs. Rojas wouldn't be a great gardener if she didn't read so much.	☐	☐	☐
	(B) Mrs. Rojas often reads about growing plants.	☐	☐	☐
	(C) Mrs. Rojas doesn't like to grow flowers.	☐	☐	☐
	(D) Mrs. Rojas has a vegetable garden.	☐	☐	☐

1.　"Look at all the dark clouds," said Father. "Hurry! We have to close the windows." Father and the children quickly closed the windows. Just as the last one was closed, it started to pour.

"That was close," said Cathy. "When Mother gets home, she'll be happy to find that nothing got wet."

2.　"A messenger just brought a package for you," said Barbara. "It's a big package, but it's not very heavy."

"Oh, I know what it is," said Mother. "I had a new frame put on your father's picture. I'm going to give it to him for his birthday. I asked the store to deliver it."

3.　Tracy's younger cousin, Meg, looked up, up, up! The man with the large sign seemed to be about eight feet tall. He walked with long, stiff-looking steps.

"Don't you think he looks funny?" asked Tracy.

"No!" answered Meg, as she ducked behind her cousin to get out of the huge person's way.

4.　Dozens of people clapped as the woman got out of a taxi. "I loved your last movie," shouted one fan. "May I have your autograph?" pleaded another. The woman smiled and signed several autographs.

"I'm glad that you like my acting," said the woman as she entered a hotel with her suitcases.

5.　"My aunt likes the mountains," said Juan. "Next year she's going to rent a cabin there. Then I'll be able to spend my vacation in the mountains."

"That sounds nice," said Marion, "but what do kids do to have fun in the mountains?"

		T	F	I

1.
(A) Mother helped to close the windows.
(B) Only a few things in the house got wet.
(C) Father knew it would rain because of the clouds.
(D) The windows were closed just in time.

2.
(A) The messenger had given the package to Barbara.
(B) The package was too heavy for Barbara to carry.
(C) Father will soon have a birthday.
(D) Mother had asked to have the package delivered.

3.
(A) Tracy is older than Meg.
(B) The man was carrying a sign.
(C) Meg thought the man was funny.
(D) The man scared Meg.

4.
(A) The woman didn't have time to sign autographs.
(B) The woman in the taxi was an actress.
(C) The woman was going to stay at the hotel.
(D) Many people saw the woman get out of the taxi.

5.
(A) Marion has never spent time in the mountains.
(B) Juan's aunt owns a house in the mountains.
(C) Juan intends to go to the mountains next year.
(D) Juan had been to his aunt's cabin in the mountains.

1.   A fortune in gold is in a ship in the ocean. The ship sank over one hundred years ago. Numerous attempts have been made to recover the treasure, but they all have failed. Now, new diving equipment allows divers to go deeper than ever before. Maybe the treasure will finally be recovered.

---

2.   "Oh! Oh! I can feel rain on my face. Where did you get this tent?" asked Jessica. "If it keeps raining, we're going to get soaked."

"The tent belonged to my aunt," said Amber. "I guess I should have waterproofed it."

---

3.   "Didn't it hurt when the doctor took the piece of glass out of your hand?" asked Bobby.

"No," replied Louis. "The doctor made my hand numb before he took out the glass. He said I was lucky. I could have been more seriously hurt when I fell and put my hand through the window."

---

4.   "My older sister will graduate from high school this year," said Robert. "She doesn't know what she'll do then. Maybe she'll get a job, or maybe she'll go to college."

"My brother graduated last year," said Linda. "Then he joined the navy. He likes to sail on the ocean."

---

5.   Bonnie didn't see the slow leak in the rowboat she rented. She put her fishing equipment into the boat and rowed to the middle of the lake. After a while, however, Bonnie's feet were getting wet. Bonnie saw the leak and rowed quickly toward shore. Luckily, she reached shore before the boat could sink.

UNIT 11

		T	F	I
1.	(A) The ship contains a very valuable cargo.	☐	☐	☐
	(B) The ship lies in very deep water.	☐	☐	☐
	(C) No one has tried to get the gold.	☐	☐	☐
	(D) The ship sank many years ago.	☐	☐	☐

		T	F	I
2.	(A) Jessica was afraid they'd get very wet.	☐	☐	☐
	(B) Amber had bought the tent a short time ago.	☐	☐	☐
	(C) The tent leaked.	☐	☐	☐
	(D) Jessica was glad the sun was shining.	☐	☐	☐

		T	F	I
3.	(A) Louis had gotten hurt when he had an accident.	☐	☐	☐
	(B) The doctor had taken glass out of Louis' arm.	☐	☐	☐
	(C) It had hurt when the glass was removed.	☐	☐	☐
	(D) The doctor had said that Louis was lucky.	☐	☐	☐

		T	F	I
4.	(A) Linda's brother is still in the navy.	☐	☐	☐
	(B) Robert's sister knows what college she'll attend.	☐	☐	☐
	(C) Robert is younger than his sister who will be graduating.	☐	☐	☐
	(D) Robert is Linda's brother.	☐	☐	☐

		T	F	I
5.	(A) The boat sank, but Bonnie was safe.	☐	☐	☐
	(B) Bonnie knows how to row a boat.	☐	☐	☐
	(C) Bonnie rented the boat to go fishing.	☐	☐	☐
	(D) Bonnie's feet got wet.	☐	☐	☐

UNIT 12

1.   As Ms. Cohen passed out the test papers, the students waited to begin writing the answers.

Dianne put several newly sharpened pencils in her tray, then whispered "Good luck!" to her friend Zack.

Zack only half-smiled back. He looked uncomfortable—as if he'd rather be anyplace else.

---

2.   "Look at this advertisement," said Jane. "It says that you can buy a camera for only twelve dollars. That's quite a bargain!"

"Not really," said Jim. "That same camera usually costs ten dollars at the department store. My aunt says it's cheap because it's not a very good camera."

---

3.   "I had an interesting conversation with Julia," said Rick. "She was telling me all about her trip last summer. Did you know that she rode in a helicopter?"

"No, I didn't," answered Rosa. "I wonder if she liked riding in the helicopter. It must have been exciting."

---

4.   The fire engine raced down the street with its siren blaring. Cars and trucks pulled to the side of the road to let it pass. Firefighters clung to the fire engine as it turned a sharp corner. Then it roared down the next street at high speed.

---

5.   The tigers paced back and forth in their cages. The monkeys swung from limb to limb. Even the elephants walked nervously about. "There's going to be a big storm," said Mr. Jefferson, the zookeeper. "I can feel it in my bones. And just look at those dark clouds drifting toward us."

UNIT 12

		T	F	I
1.	(A) Zack was comfortably waiting for the test.	☐	☐	☐
	(B) Dianne had several pencils ready for writing.	☐	☐	☐
	(C) Zack hadn't prepared well for the test.	☐	☐	☐
	(D) Dianne and Zack didn't know each other.	☐	☐	☐

		T	F	I
2.	(A) Cameras usually cost more than twelve dollars.	☐	☐	☐
	(B) The camera in the advertisement was really a bargain.	☐	☐	☐
	(C) Jim's aunt wouldn't buy the camera.	☐	☐	☐
	(D) You can buy a camera at the department store.	☐	☐	☐

		T	F	I
3.	(A) Julia had taken a trip last summer.	☐	☐	☐
	(B) Julia had told Rosa all about her trip.	☐	☐	☐
	(C) Rick and Julia had ridden in the helicopter together.	☐	☐	☐
	(D) Rosa has never been in a helicopter.	☐	☐	☐

		T	F	I
4.	(A) Cars and trucks got out of the fire engine's way.	☐	☐	☐
	(B) The fire engine wasn't going very fast.	☐	☐	☐
	(C) The fire engine was on its way to a fire.	☐	☐	☐
	(D) Firefighters were riding on the fire engine.	☐	☐	☐

		T	F	I
5.	(A) Mr. Jefferson works in a zoo.	☐	☐	☐
	(B) Mr. Jefferson was expecting a mild rainfall.	☐	☐	☐
	(C) There were dark clouds in the sky.	☐	☐	☐
	(D) The coming storm bothered the animals.	☐	☐	☐

Almost every book that Ralph reads is about airplanes. When he isn't reading about airplanes, Ralph enjoys building model planes. He even built one that has wings eight feet across. Ralph says, "I can't wait until I'm old enough to learn how to fly a real airplane."

A. Exercising Your Skill

The story tells that Ralph is interested not only in real airplanes but also in model airplanes. Airplanes are one of the things that move through the air. What other types of living and non-living things can you think of that move through the air? On your paper, write the headings below. For each, write as many words as you can think of that name things that move through the air. The first items are given as examples.

Things That Move Through the Air

Living Things	With Motors	Toys or Sport Things
bat	airplane	kite

B. Expanding Your Skill

Choose one of the things you wrote under the headings for Part A. Write three or four sentences that describe the thing, but don't name it. That way, your sentences can serve as a kind of riddle. Then read your sentences to a classmate and see if he or she can guess what you are describing.

C. Exploring Language

Read the following paragraphs about imaginary creatures that move through the air or in the sea. On your paper, write the last sentence of each paragraph, telling what you think the creature is and where it usually travels—in the air, on the land, in the sea, or any combination of these places.

1.   Some people think I am ugly because my skin has big green scales, my wings are spiky-looking like a bat's, and I breathe smoke and fire. Many people are afraid of me. But actually I can be very kind. I am a _____ , and I travel _____ .

2.   Some say I make a big splash. I am half human, half creature. My shiny, silver-green fin is strong and quite lovely, as is my long, flowing hair. Sometimes on my hair I wear a wreath of tiny shells and flowers. I am a _____ , and I travel _____ .

D. Expressing Yourself

Choose one of these activities.

1. Play a word-association game with a partner. One player writes the name of something that flies, such as a bee. The other player says the first words that come to mind—or words that tell about it—such as *buzz*, *honey*, *queen*, and *sting*. Each word is worth one point. Take turns writing and saying words for ten minutes. The player with the most points wins.

2. In many mystery stories, clues are given so that the detective can figure out "who dunnit." With a partner, make up a mystery story about something that flies. Give your story a catchy title. For example, some titles might be "The Confusing Kite," "The Baffling Balloon Mystery," or "The Case of the Haunted Helicopter." Tell the mystery to your classmates, but don't give away the ending. Ask *them* to solve it.

1. "My favorite dessert is ice cream," said Tony, "and my favorite flavors are vanilla and chocolate. I could eat ice cream every day and never get tired of it."

"I like ice cream, too," said Jean, "but it's not my favorite dessert. My favorite dessert is strawberry shortcake."

---

2. The bus departed at exactly six o'clock. Lois was glad that she was on the bus. She was going to visit a friend. Lois had brought two magazines and a newspaper for the trip. She knew the trip would seem shorter if she kept busy. She had also taken along an apple and two sandwiches.

---

3. "I don't believe it, but I read that an explorer found dinosaurs living in Africa," said Judy. "The explorer said she recorded the roar of the dinosaurs."

"I read that, too," said Marsha. "I also read that she'll soon be returning to take their pictures. Wouldn't it be wonderful if there really were living dinosaurs?"

---

4. "Did you see the mystery on television last night?" asked Billy. "I couldn't figure out who stole the money until the last minute of the program. It was a great mystery."

"No, I didn't see it," said Gina. "I was listening to a concert on the radio."

---

5. "You can't go into that store," said James. "The owner told you never to go back after you broke the window."

"Don't worry," said Bob. "I'll wear a disguise. I'll wear a hat and dark glasses." Bob went into the store, but in a few minutes the owner told him to leave.

UNIT 13

		T	F	I
1.	(A) Jean doesn't like the taste of ice cream.	☐	☐	☐
	(B) Tony and Jean both like desserts.	☐	☐	☐
	(C) Tony's favorite flavor is strawberry.	☐	☐	☐
	(D) Jean likes the flavor of strawberries.	☐	☐	☐

		T	F	I
2.	(A) Lois took something to read on the trip.	☐	☐	☐
	(B) The bus left at noon.	☐	☐	☐
	(C) Lois was going on a long trip.	☐	☐	☐
	(D) Lois was happy to take the bus trip.	☐	☐	☐

		T	F	I
3.	(A) Judy and Marsha had both read about the explorer.	☐	☐	☐
	(B) The explorer said that dinosaurs are always quiet.	☐	☐	☐
	(C) Marsha hopes that there aren't real dinosaurs.	☐	☐	☐
	(D) The explorer hadn't taken pictures on her first trip.	☐	☐	☐

		T	F	I
4.	(A) Gina likes music more than mystery shows.	☐	☐	☐
	(B) Billy enjoyed the mystery on television.	☐	☐	☐
	(C) The mystery Billy saw was about a kidnapping.	☐	☐	☐
	(D) Billy watched television last night.	☐	☐	☐

		T	F	I
5.	(A) Bob had broken a window in the store.	☐	☐	☐
	(B) The owner wanted Bob to work in the store.	☐	☐	☐
	(C) Bob's disguise didn't fool the owner.	☐	☐	☐
	(D) Bob was afraid to go into the store.	☐	☐	☐

1.   "Be careful walking across the floor," warned Juan. "This is an extremely old house, and the floors aren't too sturdy."

"We shouldn't be in here anyway," said Louis. "The sign on the house says to enter at your own risk. I don't want to take any risks."

---

2.   Whizzing smoothly along to the steady *clack-clack* of wheels on rails, Cara and Hector noticed that Cara's father had dozed off.

"I guess I'll have to point out the sights, Hector," said Cara. "One of my favorites is just ahead."

"Great!" said Hector. "I'll write about it in my diary."

---

3.   A medal was given to Mrs. Garcia for bravery. While going shopping, Mrs. Garcia had seen a house on fire. She could hear someone screaming. Mrs. Garcia had rushed into the house even though it was on fire and full of smoke. A few minutes later, she had come out carrying a young boy.

---

4.   "Did you see the enormous catfish Maria caught in the river?" asked Joe. "It was the largest fish I've ever seen!"

"The fish Maria caught wasn't that large," remarked Helen. "As a matter of fact, it was a small catfish. Most catfish are much larger."

---

5.   The diamond from Father's ring was missing. His whole family began looking for the stone. Father had been washing dishes, so they looked in the sink. He had been watching TV, so they looked in the den. Suddenly Judy exclaimed, "Here it is! I found the diamond in the cookie jar."

UNIT 14

			T	F	I
1.	(A)	The house had been built many years ago.	☐	☐	☐
	(B)	The sign said it was safe to enter.	☐	☐	☐
	(C)	It was Juan's idea to go into the house.	☐	☐	☐
	(D)	It might be dangerous to walk in the house.	☐	☐	☐

			T	F	I
2.	(A)	Cara's father was staring out the window.	☐	☐	☐
	(B)	Cara, Hector, and Cara's father were on a plane.	☐	☐	☐
	(C)	Cara had been on that trip before.	☐	☐	☐
	(D)	Hector planned to write about the things he saw.	☐	☐	☐

			T	F	I
3.	(A)	It was the boy that Mrs. Garcia had heard screaming.	☐	☐	☐
	(B)	It was a brave act to enter the burning house.	☐	☐	☐
	(C)	Mrs. Garcia had accidentally set the house on fire.	☐	☐	☐
	(D)	Mrs. Garcia had not been badly burned.	☐	☐	☐

			T	F	I
4.	(A)	Joe doesn't know much about fishing.	☐	☐	☐
	(B)	Helen said Maria had caught a small fish.	☐	☐	☐
	(C)	Maria had caught a large fish in the lake.	☐	☐	☐
	(D)	Joe thought Maria had caught a huge fish.	☐	☐	☐

			T	F	I
5.	(A)	Judy found Father's ring in the sink.	☐	☐	☐
	(B)	Father had been eating cookies.	☐	☐	☐
	(C)	Father sometimes watches television.	☐	☐	☐
	(D)	Father owns a diamond ring.	☐	☐	☐

1. A swarm of bees flew into the classroom. The teacher was astonished because it had never happened before. Many pupils screamed as they rushed out of the room. Luckily, only two pupils were stung. It seems that a truck carrying the bees had just tipped over. The bees had flown out of the truck and into the school.

---

2. "If that dog is lying on the couch again, I'm going to teach it a lesson," said Father. Father hurried into the living room. The dog was lying on the rug. "I'm glad the dog's not on the couch," said Father. "Maybe it's finally learning not to lie on the furniture."

---

3. Something woke up Mrs. Kern. She listened and heard a sharp noise repeated over and over. "What could be making that noise so early in the morning?" she wondered. Mrs. Kern looked out the window. There was a woodpecker pecking at a tree. "I guess the woodpecker is hungry," said Mrs. Kern.

---

4. "I'll be glad when I'm old enough to shave," said Mark. "Maybe in two or three years I can begin."

"Don't be in a rush to grow older," said his big brother. "Shaving your face every day isn't fun. It's just something you must do to look neat."

---

5. "I can't eat this steak," exclaimed Victoria. "It's practically raw. Would you please have it cooked some more?" The waiter took the steak into the kitchen. In a few minutes he returned with Victoria's food. "This tastes much better," said Victoria. "Thank you. I like my meat well done."

UNIT 15

			T	F	I
1.	(A)	The teacher was surprised to see the bees.	☐	☐	☐
	(B)	Many pupils were treated for bee stings.	☐	☐	☐
	(C)	Many pupils were frightened by the bees.	☐	☐	☐
	(D)	The truck had tipped over near the school.	☐	☐	☐

			T	F	I
2.	(A)	The dog was in the living room.	☐	☐	☐
	(B)	The dog is not allowed in the house.	☐	☐	☐
	(C)	Father punished the dog for being on the couch.	☐	☐	☐
	(D)	The dog is the family pet.	☐	☐	☐

			T	F	I
3.	(A)	Mrs. Kern was eating when she heard the woodpecker.	☐	☐	☐
	(B)	Woodpeckers get food from trees.	☐	☐	☐
	(C)	Mrs. Kern heard the bird early in the morning.	☐	☐	☐
	(D)	Mrs. Kern looked out the back door to see the bird.	☐	☐	☐

			T	F	I
4.	(A)	Mark's brother shaves every day.	☐	☐	☐
	(B)	Mark isn't old enough to shave.	☐	☐	☐
	(C)	Mark doesn't want to shave.	☐	☐	☐
	(D)	Mark thinks he'll be shaving in a few years.	☐	☐	☐

			T	F	I
5.	(A)	Victoria left without eating her steak.	☐	☐	☐
	(B)	Victoria wanted her steak cooked longer.	☐	☐	☐
	(C)	The waiter returned Victoria's steak to the kitchen.	☐	☐	☐
	(D)	Victoria said her steak was too well done.	☐	☐	☐

1. "How is your uncle?" asked Joe. "I heard that he was in the hospital."

   "Yes, he was in the hospital," said Ralph, "but he's fine now. My uncle was in the hospital because he hurt his back when he fell off a ladder. Yesterday he hired someone to finish painting his house."

---

2. "Nicole, please spell *jealous*. Again, the word is *jealous*," said Mr. Wang.

   Nicole closed her eyes, thought about certain spelling patterns, and then began, "j, e, a. . . ."

   After Nicole finished, several classmates cheered.

---

3. "Come over to my house Saturday morning. We can play with my new computer," said Robert. "My brother will be home, and the three of us can play."

   "I can come in the afternoon," said Tom, "but on Saturday mornings I watch the wildlife shows on television."

---

4. "What's your opinion of the new statue in the park?" asked Linda. "I can't even tell what it's supposed to be."

   "It's supposed to be an arrow shooting toward the sky," said Cindy. "There's a sign on the statue that tells about it."

---

5. "Where are Cathy and Rita?" asked Mother. "I'll bet they're in the school workshop again. Those girls never seem to get tired of building things."

   Cathy and Rita were in the workshop making a surprise for Mother. The surprise was a wooden chest that Mother could use for storing clothes.

UNIT 16

		T	F	I
1.	(A) Ralph's uncle was in a hospital.	☐	☐	☐
	(B) Joe had heard that Ralph's uncle wasn't hurt.	☐	☐	☐
	(C) Ralph's uncle still had a sore back.	☐	☐	☐
	(D) Ralph's uncle had been hurt while painting his house.	☐	☐	☐

		T	F	I
2.	(A) Mr. Wang said each word only once.	☐	☐	☐
	(B) Nicole paid attention to spelling patterns.	☐	☐	☐
	(C) Nicole was taking part in a spelling bee.	☐	☐	☐
	(D) Nicole spelled *jealous* correctly.	☐	☐	☐

		T	F	I
3.	(A) Tom usually watches TV on Saturday mornings.	☐	☐	☐
	(B) Robert likes his new computer.	☐	☐	☐
	(C) On Saturday, there are wildlife shows on television.	☐	☐	☐
	(D) Robert's brother is never home on weekends.	☐	☐	☐

		T	F	I
4.	(A) The statue has been in the park for a long time.	☐	☐	☐
	(B) The statue looks exactly like a real arrow.	☐	☐	☐
	(C) Cindy had read the sign on the statue.	☐	☐	☐
	(D) Linda had seen the statue.	☐	☐	☐

		T	F	I
5.	(A) Cathy and Rita like to build things.	☐	☐	☐
	(B) Mother knew what the girls were making.	☐	☐	☐
	(C) The girls built the chest at home.	☐	☐	☐
	(D) The girls are very good at building things.	☐	☐	☐

1.   Louis had a temperature of 101 degrees. He had a headache and an upset stomach. "You'd better go home," said Mr. Baker. "You're too sick to stay in school. Don't worry about the math test. I'll give it to you when you're well enough to come back to school."

_____

2.   "Be sure to buckle your safety belt," said Mother. "In case of an accident, wearing a safety belt may prevent you from getting hurt." Jean buckled her safety belt. So did Mother. Then, Mother started the car and they began their trip to the zoo.

_____

3.   "I can't find my baseball glove," complained Jane. "I left it in the closet, but it's not there. I must use my own glove if I'm going to play my best." That afternoon, just before her baseball game, Jane said, "I feel that I'm going to win for sure."

_____

4.   "What a thrill I had yesterday!" said Bonnie. "I went to a concert and heard my favorite singer. She was terrific!"

"That must have been fun," said Julia. "I saw my favorite singer once, and I even got his autograph. I hope I get to see him again soon."

_____

5.   "Lani, will you choose some fruits while I get the bread and meats?" Lani's father asked.

"Okay, Dad," Lani answered as she took off for the produce area. In a few minutes, Lani came back to her father who was already in the check-out line. She was carrying six huge bunches of grapes, four apples, and a bunch of bananas.

UNIT 17

		T	F	I
1.	(A) Louis won't have to take the math test.	☐	☐	☐
	(B) Louis went home because he had an accident.	☐	☐	☐
	(C) Mr. Baker is a teacher.	☐	☐	☐
	(D) Louis didn't feel well.	☐	☐	☐

		T	F	I
2.	(A) Both Mother and Jean wore safety belts.	☐	☐	☐
	(B) Jean told Mother to buckle her safety belt.	☐	☐	☐
	(C) Jean and Mother were going to the zoo.	☐	☐	☐
	(D) Mother doesn't think safety belts are necessary.	☐	☐	☐

		T	F	I
3.	(A) Jane found her baseball glove.	☐	☐	☐
	(B) Jane had left her glove in the closet.	☐	☐	☐
	(C) Jane decided not to play baseball.	☐	☐	☐
	(D) Jane wanted her own glove.	☐	☐	☐

		T	F	I
4.	(A) Julia once got a singer's autograph.	☐	☐	☐
	(B) Julia and Bonnie have the same favorite singer.	☐	☐	☐
	(C) Bonnie saw her favorite singer in a movie.	☐	☐	☐
	(D) Julia's favorite singer is still popular.	☐	☐	☐

		T	F	I
5.	(A) Lani went to the dairy section.	☐	☐	☐
	(B) Lani and her father were grocery shopping.	☐	☐	☐
	(C) Lani especially liked grapes.	☐	☐	☐
	(D) Lani reached the check-out line first.	☐	☐	☐

1. "Look at the sky," said Marion. "I wonder if it's going to rain."

"I hope not," replied Lois. "My parents are having a party this afternoon in our backyard. If it rains, they'll have the party in the house and I won't be able to watch television."

---

2. On Thursday, Dick was going to have his picture taken for the school newspaper. Dick had worked one hundred hours at the hospital. He was going to receive an award for donating his time. "One thing I must do before Thursday," thought Dick, "is go to the barber."

---

3. "May I borrow your large suitcase?" asked Mrs. Barry. "I have a suitcase, but it's too small for what I want to pack."

"Surely," said Mrs. Lopez. "I don't need it now, and it's a large suitcase. Most of the time I only need to use my smaller one."

---

4. "Let's see," said Juan. "I have a hoe, a shovel, a rake, and six different kinds of seeds. I guess I'm ready to begin." The day before, Juan had noticed how bare part of the community garden looked. Now he was going to do something about it.

---

5. Mika felt her two skate blades cutting smoothly across the ice. She was about to try a jump she'd never completed before, but she *knew* she could do it. The contest was coming up tomorrow—she had to do it!

UNIT 18

		T	F	I
1.	(A) Lois wanted it to rain.	☐	☐	☐
	(B) The party was supposed to be outdoors.	☐	☐	☐
	(C) Lois was not going to the party.	☐	☐	☐
	(D) The party was planned for the next day.	☐	☐	☐

		T	F	I
2.	(A) Dick wanted to look good in the picture.	☐	☐	☐
	(B) Dick earned a good deal of money at the hospital.	☐	☐	☐
	(C) Dick likes to help people.	☐	☐	☐
	(D) Dick's picture was to be in a magazine.	☐	☐	☐

		T	F	I
3.	(A) Mrs. Lopez has a large suitcase.	☐	☐	☐
	(B) Mrs. Barry is going on a trip.	☐	☐	☐
	(C) Mrs. Lopez has more than one suitcase.	☐	☐	☐
	(D) Mrs. Barry doesn't have a suitcase.	☐	☐	☐

		T	F	I
4.	(A) Juan couldn't find a tool to dig with.	☐	☐	☐
	(B) Juan was going to plant a garden.	☐	☐	☐
	(C) Juan's community doesn't have a garden.	☐	☐	☐
	(D) Juan had three different tools.	☐	☐	☐

		T	F	I
5.	(A) Mika was ice-skating.	☐	☐	☐
	(B) Today was the last day before the contest.	☐	☐	☐
	(C) Mika lacked faith in herself.	☐	☐	☐
	(D) Mika wanted to do the jump in the contest.	☐	☐	☐

1. "Can you read this map?" asked Bill. "I want to drive from my town to Maple City, but I can't decide which is the best route."

"Let me see the map," said Mr. Green. "I've been driving a truck for seven years, and I ought to be able to find the best route."

2. Many tourists come to Linda's town during the summer. They come because there are so many things to enjoy. There are a wonderful beach, an outdoor amusement park for children, museums, and historical buildings. There is something for all members of a family to enjoy. Linda likes the amusement park best.

3. Carla twitched her nose. "What is that scent I smell?" she asked. "I know I've smelled that odor before, but I can't think of what it is."

"The odor you smell is from the lamb I'm cooking," said Mother. "You recognize it because I cooked it once last year."

4. Cathy found a kitten. It was cold and dirty. Cathy took the kitten home and gave it a bath and some food. The next day, Cathy took the kitten to the park. A little girl saw the kitten and yelled, "Oh! There's Fluffy! I wondered what had happened to her." Cathy looked very unhappy.

5. "Boy, am I lucky! I just found a four-leaf clover," exclaimed Bobby. "I'll bet I do well on my arithmetic test today."

"You don't really believe that a four-leaf clover brings good luck, do you?" asked Jim. "You'll get a good mark on the test only if you've studied."

UNIT 19

		T	F	I
1.	(A) Mr. Green often uses a map when he drives a truck.	☐	☐	☐
	(B) Bill lives in Maple City.	☐	☐	☐
	(C) Bill was going to Maple City by bus.	☐	☐	☐
	(D) Bill had difficulty reading the map.	☐	☐	☐

		T	F	I
2.	(A) Linda likes the beach better than anything else.	☐	☐	☐
	(B) Adults as well as children enjoy Linda's town.	☐	☐	☐
	(C) Linda is not an adult.	☐	☐	☐
	(D) People flock to Linda's town in the winter.	☐	☐	☐

		T	F	I
3.	(A) Carla smelled the lamb being cooked.	☐	☐	☐
	(B) Carla hadn't eaten lamb often.	☐	☐	☐
	(C) Mother had never cooked lamb before.	☐	☐	☐
	(D) Carla's sister was cooking supper.	☐	☐	☐

		T	F	I
4.	(A) Cathy bought the kitten at a pet store.	☐	☐	☐
	(B) When Cathy went to the park, she took the kitten.	☐	☐	☐
	(C) Cathy found a dirty kitten.	☐	☐	☐
	(D) The kitten belonged to the little girl.	☐	☐	☐

		T	F	I
5.	(A) Bobby was glad he had found a four-leaf clover.	☐	☐	☐
	(B) Jim doesn't believe that four-leaf clovers bring good luck.	☐	☐	☐
	(C) Bobby was to take a test.	☐	☐	☐
	(D) Jim told Bobby he didn't have to study.	☐	☐	☐

"Where are Cathy and Rita?" asked Mother. "I'll bet they're in the school workshop again. Those girls never seem to get tired of building things."

Cathy and Rita were in the workshop making a surprise for Mother. The surprise was a wooden chest that Mother could use for storing clothes.

A. Exercising Your Skill

The paragraphs above tell you that Mother is going to be surprised by the wooden chest that Cathy and Rita are making for her. Can you think of times when you or other people have felt surprised? On your paper, add to the following sentences.

1. Sometimes people are surprised by noises, gifts, and _____ .

2. When people are surprised, they often jump, put their hands to their faces, and _____ .

Now write two sentences on your paper telling about a time when you were surprised. Describe what the surprise was and why you felt the way you did.

B. Expanding Your Skill

Compare the sentences you completed and the ones you wrote about yourself with your classmates' sentences. Add any new ideas that you like to your sentences. Choose one word or phrase from among your sentences, write it, and then write three or four examples of it. For example, next to the word *noises* you might write: *thunderclap*, *door slamming*, *telephone ringing in the middle of the night.*

C. Exploring Language

On your paper, write and finish the sentences below by telling why each person or animal might be surprised.

1. Karen gasped, "Yikes!" when _____ .
2. Miguel almost jumped out of his seat when _____ .
3. "Wow!" Lian exclaimed as she saw _____ .
4. The puppy yelped and ran into the house when _____ .
5. "Oh, no!" exclaimed Ms. Nicholson when _____ .
6. "I don't believe it!" said Fletch as _____ .

D. Expressing Yourself

Choose one of these activities.

1. Choose a partner. Then make up a skit in which you give an unexpected award to your partner. When receiving the award, your partner should use words, voice tones, and physical actions that show how surprised he or she is to receive the award. But the partner must not directly *say* that he or she is surprised.

2. From an old magazine, cut out a picture of someone who looks surprised. Paste the picture on paper. Then exchange pictures with a classmate. Write a paragraph in which you make up the reason or reasons why the person in the picture you now have looks surprised.

3. Imagine that you are giving a surprise birthday party for your best friend. Make up an attractive invitation, writing the name of the person the surprise party is for, where the party is, and what the date and time are. Then make a list of all the things you would need to make or buy for the party, such as food, decorations, or favors. Finally, pretend that you take a picture of your friend on the day of the party just as all the party guests call out "Surprise!" Draw a picture of the friend's face, showing how he or she would look at that very moment.

1. A telegram arrived for Mrs. Garcia. Mrs. Garcia had never received a telegram before, so she was very nervous. "I wonder if it's bad news," she thought. Mrs. Garcia opened the telegram and read it. "Wonderful!" she shouted. "I've just won first prize in the cooking contest I entered."

---

2. "I like it when you sleep over at my house because we always have a lot of fun," said Ralph. "The only thing I don't like is that you snore. You woke me up three times last night."

"I know that I snore," admitted Billy, "but I can't do anything to stop it."

---

3. Lou marked another X on the calendar. "Only five more days till school vacation, Mickie," he said. "Then we go to visit Uncle Cal for two weeks. You'll like him, Mickie. He tells great stories, and he has all sorts of animals on his farm. I can hardly wait!"

---

4. "I don't want to argue with you," said Rita. "I'm the captain of the softball team, and you're not going to pitch. You're going to play first base."

Maria went over to play first base. "Just wait until I'm captain," shouted Maria. "Then I'll play wherever I want to."

---

5. Mr. Jefferson parked his car in front of his house. That night there was a terrible storm. Lightning struck a tree in the front yard, and the tree fell on top of his car. The next morning, when Mr. Jefferson saw his car, he said, "I'm glad I wasn't in my car when the tree fell on it."

UNIT 20

			T	F	I
1.	(A)	The telegram made Mrs. Garcia nervous.	☐	☐	☐
	(B)	Mrs. Garcia knew the telegram would contain good news.	☐	☐	☐
	(C)	Mrs. Garcia is an excellent cook.	☐	☐	☐
	(D)	Mrs. Garcia had received many telegrams.	☐	☐	☐

			T	F	I
2.	(A)	Ralph and Billy have good times together.	☐	☐	☐
	(B)	Billy and Ralph slept in the same room.	☐	☐	☐
	(C)	Billy doesn't believe that he snores.	☐	☐	☐
	(D)	Billy and Ralph are good friends.	☐	☐	☐

			T	F	I
3.	(A)	Lou likes Uncle Cal's stories.	☐	☐	☐
	(B)	Lou had visited Uncle Cal before.	☐	☐	☐
	(C)	Lou didn't know when vacation started.	☐	☐	☐
	(D)	Uncle Cal lives on a farm.	☐	☐	☐

			T	F	I
4.	(A)	Maria wanted to pitch.	☐	☐	☐
	(B)	Rita was going to play first base.	☐	☐	☐
	(C)	Rita was captain of the team.	☐	☐	☐
	(D)	Maria did what Rita told her to do.	☐	☐	☐

			T	F	I
5.	(A)	Mr. Jefferson's car was struck by lightning.	☐	☐	☐
	(B)	The car was very badly damaged.	☐	☐	☐
	(C)	Mr. Jefferson had parked his car in the garage.	☐	☐	☐
	(D)	Mr. Jefferson's car was struck at night.	☐	☐	☐

1.   Julia looked at the scarf on the counter. "What's the price of that scarf?" she asked the clerk. "It will go perfectly with my new jacket." The clerk told Julia that the scarf cost five dollars. Julia said, "I'll be back for the scarf on Friday, after I get my allowance."

---

2.   "I thought a factory was going to be built beside the river," said Jean. "The last time I visited you, the builders were about ready to begin."

"It was decided not to build the factory there because it might pollute the river," said Tony. "They built the factory in the country instead."

---

3.   "I get great pleasure from watching the children play," said Grandfather. "They certainly like to play in the pool."

"They sure do," agreed Grandmother. "I think I'll buy them ice cream when they're through playing. Children always seem to like ice cream. Don't worry, I'll get you an ice cream, too."

---

4.   The hedges around the apartment house were getting tall and uneven. "I must get the hedges trimmed," said Mr. French, the superintendent. Mr. French hired a gardener. When the gardener had finished, the hedges looked beautiful.

"You must trim hedges more than once a year to have them look nice," said the gardener to Mr. French.

---

5.   "Throw the anchor overboard," called Aunt Helen. "This looks like a good spot to fish." Rosa threw the anchor into the water. Soon they were fishing.

"Wow!" yelled Rosa. "I think I've caught a big fish." Rosa pulled in her fish line. At the end of the line was a rubber boot.

UNIT 21

			T	F	I
1.	(A)	Julia had a new jacket.	☐	☐	☐
	(B)	Julia decided she didn't like the scarf.	☐	☐	☐
	(C)	Julia didn't have five dollars.	☐	☐	☐
	(D)	Julia told the clerk that she would return.	☐	☐	☐

			T	F	I
2.	(A)	The factory was built in a city.	☐	☐	☐
	(B)	Jean had visited Tony before.	☐	☐	☐
	(C)	Originally, the factory was to be by a river.	☐	☐	☐
	(D)	Jean and Tony don't live in the same town.	☐	☐	☐

			T	F	I
3.	(A)	Grandfather had fun watching the children.	☐	☐	☐
	(B)	Grandfather likes to eat ice cream.	☐	☐	☐
	(C)	The children were playing in a pool.	☐	☐	☐
	(D)	Grandfather was going to buy the ice cream.	☐	☐	☐

			T	F	I
4.	(A)	The hedges around the apartment house had been trimmed only once a year.	☐	☐	☐
	(B)	Mr. French trimmed the hedges himself.	☐	☐	☐
	(C)	The gardener did a good job.	☐	☐	☐
	(D)	Mr. French wanted the hedges removed.	☐	☐	☐

			T	F	I
5.	(A)	The anchor was too heavy for Rosa to lift.	☐	☐	☐
	(B)	Rosa pulled a boot out of the water.	☐	☐	☐
	(C)	Aunt Helen picked the fishing spot.	☐	☐	☐
	(D)	Aunt Helen thought she had caught a fish.	☐	☐	☐

1. "Don't walk barefoot near the pool," advised Joe. "That's where Gina dropped a bottle of juice."

"Thanks for the warning," said Barbara. Just then Gina came out of the pool office with a broom and a dustpan. It wouldn't be long before Barbara could go near the pool.

---

2. Uncle Jack put on his robe and slippers and came downstairs. He was happy to be visiting Jane and her family. Jane cooked her uncle pancakes for breakfast. "These are great pancakes," said Uncle Jack. "I'm not a good cook, so at home I usually eat cold cereal for breakfast."

---

3. James noticed that Bob had a scar on his hand. "How did you get that scar?" asked James. "Did you have an accident?"

"Yes," answered Bob. "I slipped climbing a fence and cut my hand on a nail. My doctor, however, says that the scar will fade away in time."

---

4. Toshio's fingers felt stiff from writing so long, but now Mr. Faraday was reading the last test question.

"Name three states that are in the southwestern part of the United States," he read.

Toshio started writing right away, a broad smile on his face.

---

5. The leak in the garage roof was getting worse. Every time it rained, more and more water came through it. "It's quite a job, but I guess I'm going to have to repair the garage roof," said Father. He went into the house to telephone his friend, George, who owed him a favor.

UNIT 22

		T	F	I
1.	(A) The bottle had broken when Gina dropped it.	☐	☐	☐
	(B) Joe told Barbara to jump into the pool.	☐	☐	☐
	(C) Gina was coming to clean near the pool.	☐	☐	☐
	(D) Gina had dropped the bottle near the pool.	☐	☐	☐

		T	F	I
2.	(A) Jane cooked breakfast for her uncle.	☐	☐	☐
	(B) At home, Uncle Jack often eats pancakes for breakfast.	☐	☐	☐
	(C) Uncle Jack thinks Jane is a good cook.	☐	☐	☐
	(D) Uncle Jack liked Jane's pancakes.	☐	☐	☐

		T	F	I
3.	(A) Bob had cut his hand in his house.	☐	☐	☐
	(B) When he had cut his hand, Bob had gone to a doctor.	☐	☐	☐
	(C) James asked Bob about his scar.	☐	☐	☐
	(D) Bob will always have the scar.	☐	☐	☐

		T	F	I
4.	(A) The test had been going on for a while.	☐	☐	☐
	(B) Mr. Faraday had lost his voice.	☐	☐	☐
	(C) Toshio knew the answer to the last question.	☐	☐	☐
	(D) The test was on math.	☐	☐	☐

		T	F	I
5.	(A) Father didn't care if the roof leaked.	☐	☐	☐
	(B) The garage roof had begun leaking only recently.	☐	☐	☐
	(C) Father decided to fix the garage roof.	☐	☐	☐
	(D) Father wanted George to help him fix the roof.	☐	☐	☐

UNIT 23

1.   "The plant that my aunt gave me is dying in the hallway," said Ashley. "Maybe I should move it to the kitchen window." A few weeks later, Ashley said, "Now the plant is growing well. It just needed a lot of sunshine."

---

2.   The doctor looked at the red spots on Rita's legs. "Have you been walking in the woods?" asked the doctor. "You have poison ivy. You can get poison ivy just by touching the leaves of the plants." Rita admitted that she had been in the woods.

---

3.   "I'm going to inspect your bedroom later," warned Father. "If it isn't neat and orderly, you're not going on the picnic with us."

Sam was upset, but he began cleaning up his room. Sam loves going on picnics. He loves eating the food, playing games, and running races. Before long, his bedroom was neat.

---

4.   "Don't go out on that limb," warned Judy. "It's too weak to hold you." Her cat, naturally, didn't pay any attention. It kept crawling out on the limb. Suddenly, there was a loud crack! The limb broke and the cat tumbled to the ground. Immediately, the cat jumped up and ran away.

---

5.   Luis looked at the roller coaster. "I'm not going on that ride," he exclaimed. "It's huge! I'll bet it goes faster than a car."

Carlos laughed. "It does go fast, but it's fun. Come on," said Carlos. "Let's take a ride on the roller coaster." Luis didn't change his mind.

UNIT 23

			T	F	I
1.	(A)	Not much sunshine comes into Ashley's hallway.	☐	☐	☐
	(B)	The plant grew well after it was moved.	☐	☐	☐
	(C)	Ashley had bought the plant in a flower store.	☐	☐	☐
	(D)	The plant was growing well in the hallway.	☐	☐	☐

			T	F	I
2.	(A)	Rita said that she had been in the woods.	☐	☐	☐
	(B)	Rita's legs hadn't been covered when she was in the woods.	☐	☐	☐
	(C)	Rita didn't see a doctor about the red spots.	☐	☐	☐
	(D)	The doctor knew what had caused the red spots.	☐	☐	☐

			T	F	I
3.	(A)	Sam doesn't like running races.	☐	☐	☐
	(B)	Sam doesn't like cleaning his room.	☐	☐	☐
	(C)	Sam's bedroom was not very neat at first.	☐	☐	☐
	(D)	Sam didn't clean up his bedroom.	☐	☐	☐

			T	F	I
4.	(A)	The cat didn't fall a great distance.	☐	☐	☐
	(B)	The cat always does what Judy says.	☐	☐	☐
	(C)	The cat fell from a garage roof.	☐	☐	☐
	(D)	After it fell, the cat was able to run.	☐	☐	☐

			T	F	I
5.	(A)	Carlos likes riding on roller coasters.	☐	☐	☐
	(B)	Luis finally went on the roller coaster.	☐	☐	☐
	(C)	Carlos wanted Luis to ride on the roller coaster.	☐	☐	☐
	(D)	The roller coaster doesn't really go fast.	☐	☐	☐

1.   Jason had been invited to a costume party. Jason's father said he could take things from the old trunk in the attic to use for his costume. Jason picked out a tall black hat and a long black cape. Then he asked his younger brother if he could borrow his toy rabbit.

_____

2.   The skirt that Marsha bought was exactly what she wanted. When she tried it on at home, however, the skirt was too long. "Mother, what can I do?" said Marsha. "I love the skirt, but it's too long." Marsha's mother told her not to worry. Mother said that she would shorten the skirt.

_____

3.   "These mosquitoes are killing me," complained Robert. "They haven't stopped biting us since we got here."

   "You're right," agreed Carlos. "Maybe we shouldn't put up our tent here near the river. Let's set up camp on that hill over there. We can always walk back to the river to fish if we want to."

_____

4.   "What a victory!" exclaimed Lois. "We were behind by six runs, but we still won. It was a terrific baseball game."

   "It really was," agreed Maria, "and you played wonderfully. We would have lost if you hadn't hit that home run." Lois smiled. She was glad that she had played so well.

_____

5.   "How do you like my new radio?" asked Jim. "It gets many stations, and they all come in loud and clear. You should get one like it."

   "It does have a nice sound," said Linda, "and it certainly is good-looking, but I don't think I could carry it."

UNIT 24

			T	F	I
1.	(A)	No one had invited Jason to the party.	☐	☐	☐
	(B)	Jason was going as a magician.	☐	☐	☐
	(C)	Jason's father would not let him open the old trunk.	☐	☐	☐
	(D)	Jason borrowed a toy from his brother.	☐	☐	☐

			T	F	I
2.	(A)	Marsha wanted the skirt to be shorter.	☐	☐	☐
	(B)	Mother said that she would fix the skirt.	☐	☐	☐
	(C)	Marsha had gotten the skirt as a gift.	☐	☐	☐
	(D)	Marsha hadn't tried on the skirt at the store.	☐	☐	☐

			T	F	I
3.	(A)	There were fewer mosquitoes on the hill.	☐	☐	☐
	(B)	Carlos didn't mind the mosquitoes.	☐	☐	☐
	(C)	Robert was bitten by many mosquitoes.	☐	☐	☐
	(D)	The boys were going to camp in a tent.	☐	☐	☐

			T	F	I
4.	(A)	Lois' team had been ahead throughout the whole game.	☐	☐	☐
	(B)	Lois had gotten an important hit in the game.	☐	☐	☐
	(C)	Lois had enjoyed the baseball game.	☐	☐	☐
	(D)	Lois didn't think she had played well.	☐	☐	☐

			T	F	I
5.	(A)	Jim had trouble hearing some stations.	☐	☐	☐
	(B)	Linda liked the looks of the radio.	☐	☐	☐
	(C)	Jim's radio was very large.	☐	☐	☐
	(D)	Jim had had his radio for a long time.	☐	☐	☐

1. "The kitchen floor is so clean and polished that I can see my reflection in it," said Alex. "Did you use something special to get it looking so good?"

"No," replied his uncle. "I did it the same way I always do it. It shines because I just finished cleaning it."

2. On Saturday, the weather was warm and sunny. Cindy looked out her bedroom window and smiled. Today was the day of the big parade. Cindy opened her closet and took out her band uniform. She was glad that her mother had remembered to have it cleaned and pressed.

3. Bobby took a bite of the pumpkin pie. "This pie tastes very good," he said, "but the crust is too hard. I think it was cooked too long."

"What do you know about cooking pies?" asked Helen. "You've never cooked any pies in your life! All you do is eat them."

4. "You should take better care of yourself," advised Mrs. Lyons. "If you don't eat better and get more rest, you're going to ruin your health."

"You're probably right," said Ralph, "but I like hot dogs, and I like watching TV. I look at TV every night and still feel fine in the morning."

5. "Are you ready to walk home with me?" asked Carla. "It's getting late, and our parents will be looking for us."

"Yes, I'm ready to go," said Barbara. "I only wish we had brought our umbrellas or raincoats. It certainly looks as if it's going to rain."

UNIT 25

			T	F	I
1.	(A)	Alex's uncle used a special cleaner on the floor.	☐	☐	☐
	(B)	Alex thought the floor looked very good.	☐	☐	☐
	(C)	Alex helped his uncle clean the floor.	☐	☐	☐
	(D)	After a while, the floor won't shine so brightly.	☐	☐	☐

			T	F	I
2.	(A)	It was a good day for a parade.	☐	☐	☐
	(B)	Cindy was going to march in the parade.	☐	☐	☐
	(C)	The big parade was on a Saturday.	☐	☐	☐
	(D)	Cindy went to the cleaners to get her uniform.	☐	☐	☐

			T	F	I
3.	(A)	Helen knows how to cook pies.	☐	☐	☐
	(B)	Bobby said something good about the pie.	☐	☐	☐
	(C)	Helen thought that Bobby was an excellent cook.	☐	☐	☐
	(D)	Bobby didn't taste the pumpkin pie.	☐	☐	☐

			T	F	I
4.	(A)	Mrs. Lyons thinks that Ralph sleeps too much.	☐	☐	☐
	(B)	Ralph watches TV at night.	☐	☐	☐
	(C)	Ralph eats a great many hot dogs.	☐	☐	☐
	(D)	Ralph always feels tired in the morning.	☐	☐	☐

			T	F	I
5.	(A)	Barbara and Carla were going to walk home together.	☐	☐	☐
	(B)	Carla and Barbara were going to take a bus home.	☐	☐	☐
	(C)	Carla was going to have to wait for Barbara.	☐	☐	☐
	(D)	Barbara was afraid it was going to rain.	☐	☐	☐

Julia looked at the scarf on the counter. "What's the price of that scarf?" she asked the clerk. "It will go perfectly with my new jacket." The clerk told Julia that the scarf cost five dollars. Julia said, "I'll be back for the scarf on Friday, after I get my allowance."

A. Exercising Your Skill

In the passage above, Julia is looking at a scarf in a store. You might guess that it is a department store, because that is a kind of store where scarves would probably be sold. What other kinds of stores or shops can you think of? List as many as you can. You might want to start with the following: department store, supermarket, video store.

B. Expanding Your Skill

Choose one of the types of stores you listed in Part A. Write it as a heading on your paper. Then, name as many things as you can think of that might be found or sold in that type of store. The list for *Department Store* might begin like this:

<u>Department Store</u>
counters
clerks
jackets
jewelry

Cover the heading of your list. Ask your classmates to guess the heading after they read your list. Try to guess the headings on your classmates' lists.

Choose one of the things you wrote under the headings for Part A. Write three or four sentences that describe the thing, but don't name it. That way, your sentences can serve as a kind of riddle. Then read your sentences to a classmate and see if he or she can guess what you are describing.

C. Exploring Language

Read the following paragraphs. On your paper, write one or two sentences telling where the character is, how you think he or she feels, and why.

1.   Inez walked up and down the rows of books. The computer index had indicated that the book she was looking for should be in this aisle. "Oh, no!" exclaimed Inez. "The book is out, and my report is due tomorrow!"

    Inez is at _____ .
    She feels _____ because _____ .

2.   Tovi walked down the long, unfamiliar hall. "The first day," he thought, "is always kind of scary. That's what Gran told me." Then he spotted a sign that said "New Students—Report to Room 101."

    Tovi is at _____ .
    Tovi feels _____ because _____ .

D. Expressing Yourself

Choose one of these activities.

1. Choose one of the stories above. Write another passage that tells about what might have happened next or later and what the character said. Give clues to the location and the character's feelings, but don't name them directly. See if a classmate can guess where the character is and how she or he feels.

2. Play a riddle game with a partner. Think of clues about different places in your city or town. Tell riddles such as the following:

    I am a large place with benches, swings, and lots of grass.
    People have picnics by my river. I am _____ .

Take turns making up and answering riddles.

Specific Skill Series

Teacher's Manual

Richard A. Boning

Fifth Edition

SRA/McGraw-Hill

A Division of The McGraw·Hill Companies

Send all inquiries to:
SRA/McGraw-Hill
8787 Orion Place
Columbus, OH 43240-4027

ISBN 0-02-688009-1

9 IPC 02 01

TABLE OF CONTENTS

STRUCTURE

The new *Specific Skill Series* is a nonconsumable program designed to develop nine crucial reading skills: *Working Within Words, Following Directions, Using the Context, Locating the Answer, Getting the Facts, Getting the Main Idea, Drawing Conclusions, Detecting the Sequence*, and *Identifying Inferences*.

Each skill is developed through a series of books that spans ten levels (Picture Level, Preparatory Level, A, B, C, D, E, F, G, H). The Picture Level books are for pupils who have not acquired a basic sight vocabulary. The Preparatory Level books are for pupils who have developed a basic sight vocabulary but are not yet ready for books on the first-grade reading level. The A books are suitable for pupils on the first reading level. Books B, C, D, E, F, G, H are appropriate for pupils who can read material on levels two through eight, respectively.

The *Specific Skill Series* gives students specific and concentrated experiences in reading for different purposes. It provides practice material for pupils on ten different levels. Each reading skill has certain distinctive characteristics. Thus it is that practice in any single one helps only to a limited degree in improving the others. For example, reading for the main idea, while extremely important in itself, does not necessarily improve one's skill in following directions. Subtle techniques, specific to each skill, provide the rationale for the development of the series.

CONTENT

The material of the *Specific Skill Series* is, first, largely informative and factual. It is also fascinatingly unusual, attracting and holding the student's interest. It provides an amazing fund of singular information. The passages themselves are sufficiently brief to hold pupils with the most restricted attention span, yet diverse enough to appeal to students of varying ages, interests, and abilities. By avoiding condescending juvenility, the series appeals to older students as well as younger.

THE NEW EDITION

The fifth edition of the *Specific Skill Series* maintains the quality and focus that has distinguished this program for more than 25 years. A key element central to the program's success has been the unique nature of the reading selections. Nonfiction pieces about current topics have been designed to stimulate the interest of students, motivating them to use the comprehension strategies they have learned to further their reading. To keep this important aspect of the program intact, a percentage of the reading selections have been replaced in order to ensure the continued relevance of the subject material.

In addition, a significant percentage of the artwork in the program has been replaced to give the books a contemporary look. The cover photographs are designed to appeal to readers of all ages.

All answer keys can be used with previous editions of the *Specific Skill Series.* In addition, the **reproducible blackline worksheets** and a reduced version of the **Class Record Sheet** chart are incorporated into the back of this Teacher's Manual for further convenience and affordability.

GENERAL INFORMATION

The application and general use of the *Specific Skill Series* will, of course, vary with the teacher's philosophy, the class makeup, and the specific classroom situation. There are many approaches that prove effective.

A. Placement

To assure that students get maximum benefit from each skill in the series, the *Specific Skill Placement Tests* are recommended. See page 5.

Standardized reading tests are also helpful in placing pupils at their proper levels. However, since such tests typically reflect a frustration score, it is advisable to place students at a level somewhat below the one indicated for them. An informal inventory can be used in determining pupil placement. If any doubt exists as to which level (letter) is appropriate, it is always best to begin with materials of lesser difficulty. Advancement to a higher level is always preferable to retrogression.

The actual test score on the first unit or two of any book is a very good indicator as to the appropriateness of the material. A score of less than 80% on these units indicates that the material is too difficult. It is important that a student meet with success at the outset.

B. Group/Individualized Approach

The wider the reading range within an individual class, the greater is the need for an individualized approach. When the reading range within a group is more narrow and the areas of need are more nearly identical, a group or whole-class approach is suggested.

Many teachers find that pairing of pupils of nearly identical skills is effective. (The more nearly identical in skill the students are, the more beneficial this activity.) Each member of the pair should complete a unit first and record answers individually. Then the two may compare their answers, discuss them, and record their joint conclusions on a third worksheet. They should be prepared to justify their answers to the teacher and the class.

C. Book Use

The *Specific Skill Series* should not be used merely for pupils who need remedial assistance. The major purpose of the series is to increase proficiency in *all* of the nine areas for *all* pupils. Both average and advanced students will find challenge in working in the same skill areas on higher levels.

Obviously, the first skill introduced should be the one most needed. If the individual or class is equally deficient in all nine areas, it may be best to start with the more literal skills, such as *Getting the Facts*.

The *Specific Skill Series* is more effective if a single skill is stressed over a period of time than if a number of skills are practiced simultaneously. Intensive work in one skill area is more productive than mixed or occasional use.

The number and length of sessions will vary considerably. Many factors must be taken into account. Short, frequent practice sessions are much more effective than sustained ones. A minimum of one short practice period every other day and a maximum of two brief periods every day are suggested.

D. Placement Tests

Specific Skill Series Placement Tests, which enable the teacher to place pupils at their appropriate levels in each skill, are available. The test book contains three tests: Primary (Pre-1–3 reading levels), Intermediate (4–6), and Advanced (7–8). Each test consists of representative units from the skill books themselves.

INTRODUCING THE SERIES IN THE CLASSROOM

For students to function most effectively in using the *Specific Skill Series,* it is necessary that procedures be introduced clearly and in detail.

Pupils must be made aware that—

A. One reads for different purposes, and there are specific skills and goals involved for each purpose. These should be discussed and analyzed at length, especially in relation to each other, before starting.

B. Each of the nine strands involves a *different* reading skill. The teacher should discuss and analyze the specific skill involved before proceeding with the book dealing with that skill. (How is this skill different from others? What is most important in developing this skill?)

C. The *Specific Skill Series* exercises provide practice and are *not* to be construed as tests. This is important. The books are designed to allow the student to improve a past record—not to compete with the achievements of peers. The uniform number of questions within each unit will encourage each pupil to gauge individual progress through the series. The teacher should make the students aware that the individual interest, knowledge, and background that one brings to each unit will influence both achievement and rate of progress. Fluctuation of scores is bound to result and should cause neither discouragement nor alarm.

D. There is no time limit for completion of a unit, a book, or the entire series. Pupils may proceed at their own pace. The primary concerns are accuracy and depth of understanding, not speed.

E. The books themselves should *not* be written in; blackline reproducible student worksheet masters for all skills on all levels are available in a perforated booklet. Masters for all skills on one level are included in the individual answer booklet for that level. It must be emphasized to students that answers are to be recorded on worksheets *in capital letters, vertically*.

WORKING WITH THE SERIES

Actual procedures of use and work should be clear to all students.

A. It is often worthwhile for students themselves to predict how well they will do on any given unit. This increases student enthusiasm and heightens personal involvement and the quality of performance. Such predictions become increasingly accurate as pupils proceed in any specific skill area, thus adding even more to the students' sense of achievement and identification.

B. Pupils' individual and group reactions to units, books, and the entire series should be elicited and discussed informally. Their comments concerning content, believability, and personal experiences, for instance, add substantially to class interest and knowledge.

C. No matter whether an individual (or partner) approach or a larger group approach is used, it is essential for the pupils to know how well they are doing. For this reason it is recommended that the units be scored as soon as they have been completed. The more immediate the scoring, the more effective the results.

The readers should not return to any story until their answers have been recorded and scored. Then a discussion of their responses will have considerable value. Each possible answer may be discussed in terms of its acceptability. This requires the readers to justify their choices.

D. Frequent rereading of the passages will prove extremely beneficial, especially when errors have occurred. This will bring students to a close reexamination of their original responses and help them avoid repetitions of the same kind of erroneous thinking. They will profit much from such self-analysis and correction.

E. Students should look upon their own errors not as mistakes but as opportunities for increasing their understanding and improving their reading as well as for raising their scores. They should be encouraged to ask questions concerning their errors so that they will realize the source of their own difficulty.

USING THE LANGUAGE ACTIVITY PAGES

The eight Language Activity Pages (LAPs) in each *Specific Skill* book integrate the book's particular skill into the student's general language development. Two-page sets of these activities appear one-quarter, one-half, and three-quarters of the way through, and at the end of each book (following units 6, 12, 19, and 25 in 25-unit books; following units 12, 24, 38, and 50 in 50-unit books). LAPs provide a variation on the multiple-choice format by giving students opportunities to use their own language and imaginations in both individual and group activities.

Each two-page set of LAP pages extends the students' proficiency in the skill into related language areas: further **reading** (newspapers, research sources . . .), **speaking** and **listening** (storytelling, drama, interviews, oral presentations . . .), **writing** (journals, biographies, news stories, reviews, scripts, reports . . .), and critical **thinking** (analyzing, synthesizing, comparing, classifying, evaluating . . .). In some cases the activities are tied in with one or more preceding units; otherwise they are independent of any particular unit.

Every LAP set has four sections, each broadening the application of the skill further into the students' general language development:

A. **Exercising Your Skill** generally takes the student the first step from recognition (multiple-choice) to recall (supplying answers from one's own mind).

B. **Expanding Your Skill** generally asks the student to apply the skill in other contexts.

C. **Exploring Language** generally asks the student to generate words and ideas by using the skill.

D. **Expressing Yourself** allows the student to use the skill in creative or critical language activities, such as writing a dramatic scene or organizing information for a TV newscast.

Utilizing the LAPs is limited only by the teacher's creative imagination. Here are a few suggestions: (1) Students who finish the units rapidly may do LAP activities for enrichment. (2) The activities may serve as a motivating device, arousing interest in the skill and showing its importance outside the classroom. (3) Relevant activities may be integrated with other subjects, such as social studies or science. Of course, different students or groups may do different activities. (Some activities in a set may depend on the completion of previous ones.) Creative teachers may find in the LAPs ideas for further activities of their own design.

LAP activities are not intended to be "marked" on any objective progress scale. Most activities are, in varying degrees, open-ended (thus there is no answer key). Teachers are free to evaluate student performance to any extent or in any form they judge appropriate.

As with other pages in *Specific Skill* books, students must be cautioned against writing on the LAP pages. Answer blanks have been shaded or kept short and tightly spaced to discourage writing-in. Students are to use their own paper for written activities (there are no reproducible answer blanks for LAPs).

SUGGESTED TEACHING TECHNIQUES

WORKING WITHIN WORDS

Working Within Words is designed to assist students in putting sounds to work in attacking words. Putting both sounds and syllables to work is essential if pupils are to become independent readers. One cannot be expected to understand and react to written ideas before identifying the printed words meant to convey those ideas. *Working Within Words* will help develop these word identification skills. Some of the units are designed to develop understanding of sound-symbol associations. Others are geared to give the reader many opportunities for immediate application of newly developed understandings and skills in realistic, functional settings.

The units are of two types: concept builders and functional exercises. The concept units are aimed at developing the understandings that underlie successful word identification experiences. The reader's attention is focused on the common patterns and parts of words. Each generalization is built step-by-step on the structure of previously formed concepts.

The functional exercises either follow the concept units or are contained within them. They provide the reader with many immediate and repeated experiences with words involving particular patterns or principles. The sentence settings are typical of the material at the level indicated by the letter on the cover. In many cases the choices offered are new words. Consequently, *Working Within Words* provides the opportunity for the reader to put sounds to work.

The *Working Within Words* books center on different word elements as the series progresses, yet there is reinforcement throughout. The more elementary books focus on such elements as consonants, consonant substitution, blends, phonograms, and vowel sounds. As the level of difficulty increases, the emphasis shifts to syllabication, prefixes, suffixes, and roots.

Teachers will find that listening drills are of great value. Prior to encountering any word element in *Working Within Words,* it is essential that auditory practice takes place. Success on the auditory level makes for success on the visual level.

Minimal direction is required, since the books in the *Working Within Words* strand offer patterned practice. Attention must be drawn, however, to the answer choices. In the concept units only two or three answer choices are offered. In the units that provide application of understandings, four or nine answer choices are offered. This provides more experiences with words of a particular pattern. In units that offer an F choice, the F stands for NONE. This means that none of the choices fits the contextual setting, that none makes sense in that particular setting.

In units 19, 20, and 21 of Book C and units 4, 5, and 6 of Book D the vowel is missing from one of the words in the sentence. Choices for the vowel sounds are given below the sentence. The reader first decides what the missing word is and then attempts to hear the vowel sound and select the letter indicating the correct answer.

A unit-by-unit list of concepts developed on each level is found on page 64 of the book for that level.

FOLLOWING DIRECTIONS

Proficiency in reading and following directions is basic for success in every school subject and in many nonacademic activities as well. Without the ability to follow directions, all other techniques and skills become difficult, if not impossible.

The *Following Directions* segment of the **Specific Skill Series** focuses attention on four types of directions.

First are the *testing* and *drilling* directions, commonly found in textbooks and workbooks. These provide a check on information presented or a skill taught.

The second type of direction (often found in science books, etc.) involves *experimentation*. Such material may require an answer to a problem, or provide the reader with an example or practical application of a principle.

The third type of direction involves the bringing together of parts or ingredients to form a whole (as with a cake or model airplane). Such directions are primarily concerned with *assembling,* and deal with segments and the order and manner in which they form a whole. Here, unlike directions involving experiments, the purpose is to make or create, rather than to solve a problem or demonstrate a principle.

Directions that explain how to do something (play a game, row a boat, paint a picture, etc.) constitute the fourth type. They can well be identified as *performing* directions. These accent the steps or sequences in learning to do something new, and the focus is on performance rather than end product.

Error Patterns: In all exercises, the first question has to do with the main point or purpose of the directions. Errors on the first question indicate that more attention must be drawn to the central thought of the directions. This is the only type of question on the Picture Level and Preparatory Level.

To do the last question in the testing and drilling kind of directions, the reader must have visualized the complete and correct response at the very outset. Errors on the last question indicate that more effort must be made to picture the correct response.

Errors on other questions generally reflect a lack of attention to detail and consequently require more focus on this.

General Instructions: Pupils should be made aware that—

A. There are many and varied situations in which the ability to follow directions is of crucial importance.

B. The reading of directional material requires a very precise and concentrated approach, involving a slower pace than does general reading. A single word may be all-important.

C. Words that show order and/or sequence are particularly important, especially in following directions requiring assembling, creating, performing, etc.

D. Practical experience in writing clear directions of their own will benefit them in following the directions of others.

E. The more extensively they practice following directions from any source (newspapers, magazines, manuals, etc.) the more facility they will acquire.

F. All the information *above* the heavy line in *Following Directions* (levels A–H) is to be studied carefully, even though none of it requires written response. (Questions requiring written responses are always *below* the heavy line.)

G. In the testing and drilling exercises, a sample is included immediately following the directions. This is merely to aid the reader in visualizing a correct response. It need not be marked. If the books are to remain non-consumable, of course, the sample above the heavy line *must not* be marked. *None of the pages in this book should be marked in any way by the pupils.*

H. The use of an incorrect symbol constitutes an error, just as does a correct symbol for the wrong answer.

I. The same idea can be expressed in different words. As the exercises advance in level, there are more inferential questions about the directions. Examples of this must be reviewed with the students.

J. In the Picture Level book, students examine the picture to determine if the direction is being followed correctly. In the Preparatory Level book, students examine both pictures to determine which picture is correctly following the direction.

USING THE CONTEXT

A thorough understanding of context and its concept often enables a reader to grasp the meanings of words, and thus of ideas. When the context is clear, specific meanings often emerge. Pupils should have at least some concept of context before beginning any work in the series.

The exercises in *Using the Context* have been developed primarily to improve silent reading comprehension. In order to complete these exercises successfully, the reader must relate the whole to the part and the part to the whole. This requires judgment and insight into the interrelationship of ideas. The reader's attention is also directed to language patterns, word form, precise usage, and grammatical correctness. Skill is developed in word recognition. *Using the Context* places a premium on precise thinking.

Correct answers are understandably more obvious at the earlier levels. The readers are asked to choose from words that are markedly dissimilar in form and meaning. (On the Picture Level, the readers choose the illustration that completes the sentence.) The selection of the correct answer requires more refined thinking as the books become more difficult. The alternate choices thus tend to fall into more diverse patterns. The major error patterns are—

A. *Nonpertinent choice:* The selection of an irrelevant word indicates a lack of understanding or little concern for meaning. Frequent errors of this type suggest a review of the recommended steps or a reconsideration of the appropriateness of the material.

B. *Restricted contextual choice:* The selection of a word that fits into a single sentence, but that fails to fit the total context, is a common error. This error pattern indicates a need to relate words to lengthier units.

C. *Imprecise choice:* The selection of a word that is either too inclusive or too specific is an example of this type of error. Such errors call attention to the need for emphasizing precise word usage.

D. *Ungrammatical choice:* The selection of a word that is grammatically incorrect is another error pattern. Such choices suggest a lack of sensitivity to language patterns and/or word function.

E. *Confused form choice:* The selection of a word that is visually similar to a correct answer, yet incorrect, indicates a need for more attention to visual discrimination.

There are many pupil activities that will prove helpful:

A. Each student should read a short selection completely. When missing words are encountered, the word "blank" should be substituted until the selection is finished. In this way the reader's attention is focused on the general content of the passage rather than on specific isolated words.

B. After reading the entire passage, the pupil should attempt to determine the most appropriate choices. If they are not immediately obvious, *each* of the possible choices should be tried before making a decision.

C. If a doubt remains about the correctness of choice, the pupil should reread the entire selection, substituting the words chosen before writing the letter of the correct answer on the worksheet.

D. Blocking off answer choices may also prove helpful. When this is done, pupils may be asked to write their own answers without benefit of any choices. (This technique proves more effective if the pupils use a book at least one reading level below their own.)

LOCATING THE ANSWER

This series has one clear-cut and fundamental purpose—to develop skill in finding answers. This ability requires clear understanding of questions, a grasp of phrase and sentence units, and power to discriminate between pertinent and irrelevant ideas. The *questions* in *Locating the Answer* are therefore of critical importance. Teacher questions and discussion concerning these will enable the student to develop and improve. Especially valuable are questions that focus attention on the *first word*.

At earlier levels the answer to the question is often worded much the same as the question itself. (On the Picture Level, the pupils are to determine which picture answers the question.) As the books increase in difficulty, there is proportionately less correspondence between the phrasing of the question and the phrasing of the answer. The reader must also select the appropriate answer from a wider range of sentences. At the upper levels the material does not always supply the answer. This "not indicated" factor and other features place a heavier demand upon the reader at each successive reading level.

The following suggestions will prove helpful:

A. Since the reader must *know the question* before seeking an answer, each question must be thoroughly understood before the answer is attempted. Any uncertainty whatsoever as to the question results in repeated references to it, which are unnecessary and highly undesirable.

B. Work on *question patterns* will aid the reader in understanding and retaining the question. Pupils should be made to realize that certain kinds of questions call for specific kinds of responses. The answer to a *when* question, for example, would involve an aspect of time.

C. Experiences should be provided to give readers practice in identifying and classifying phrases. Students must be taught to group phrases into the basic *who, what, when, where, why,* and *how* categories so that they can grasp the function of phrases in sentence meaning.

D. *Changing the word order* of the question is beneficial in that it clarifies what is asked for and implants it more firmly in the student's mind.

E. *Word substitution* in the questions is valuable in furthering understanding. Practice in this area will free the student from the limits of one word and focus attention on the concept of the question.

F. *Discussion of the key words* of questions is of immense help in locating answers. This again centers attention on the basic requirement of the question.

G. Using their own or other textbooks, students should practice *framing their own questions*. These questions should be presented to the class orally to give them practice in locating answers. *Any* practice in locating answers to *any* questions is valuable.

H. *Signal words* (words that alert the reader to what will follow) should be explained, and pupils should practice looking for these when searching for answers.

GETTING THE FACTS

Getting the Facts has been written to develop skill in recalling factual information *from a single reading*. Students must realize that there can be no "turning back" for an answer. The material is structured to prevent this: the story appears on one side of the page, the questions on the reverse. Readers must absorb as much as possible from one reading. The very realization that they may not return to the story will help them gain skill in *Getting the Facts*.

Getting the Facts varies in content. It contains stories about mysteries and unexplained happenings, remarkable people, and odd customs. It was the author's intention to include stories that would stretch the imagination, spark new hobbies, promote admiration for outstanding achievements, and develop a sense of wonder about our world. Interest ratings were obtained from junior and senior high students as well as elementary school pupils. The stories included in *Getting the Facts* are those to which the readers reacted most favorably. Only those stories that proved popular with students through a range of age and grade levels are included.

Before the student begins these exercises, several factors should be stressed:

A. When attempting to recall details, the student will read at a rate somewhat slower than when reading for the central thought. This should be no cause for concern.

B. The student must make specific mental notes, especially when encountering a date, a name, an event, or a descriptive word. This mental note-taking should become a habit.

C. The pupil must make a concentrated effort to visualize the text and to retain this visual image.

D. Reading for details is closely related to following directions, and both skills require precise recall.

GETTING THE MAIN IDEA

Identifying the central and most important idea of any passage is perhaps the most important and basic of all reading techniques. It is the primary study skill. Of course, in order to identify a central idea, the student must first understand what a main idea really is. As pupils mature, their concepts of the main idea will broaden and come more sharply into focus. They will increasingly come to realize the value of this skill.

The following suggestions may be of help in developing the skill of getting the main idea:

A. Topic Words: The meaning of *topic words*—words that indicate the substance of a passage—should be thoroughly explained. Pupils may be asked to locate topic words from any brief passages. Questions should concern the topic and require a very brief answer. It will prove effective for the teacher to read the passage aloud and accent the topic word (or the pronoun referring to it) each time it is encountered. Topic words are essential in determining the topic and what is being said about the topic. On the Picture Level, the pupils should be encouraged to reexamine the picture for the clues that are the basis for the main idea.

B. Key Question Words: The study of the first word of a question aids immeasurably. Pupils should realize that questions often begin with the words *why, where, when, how, who,* and *what.* Complete understanding of such words is basic to a complete understanding of *all* aspects of the question:

1. If most of a paragraph gives *reasons,* the pupils must know that the questions will often begin with *why.*

2. If a paragraph focuses on *location* or *position,* the question may begin with *where.*

3. If a paragraph is mostly concerned with *time,* the question may start with *when.*

4. If most of a paragraph explains the *way* or *method,* the question may begin with *how.*

5. If a paragraph centers on *people* or a *particular person,* the question will most often start with *who.*

6. If the word *what* is used at the beginning of key phrases, it may signify different things: *that which, how much, how,* or *anything that.* (Because of its many uses, *what* is of little value as an aid in

understanding questions, and the main idea is dependent on other words.)

C. Place Clues: Recognizing and analyzing paragraph structure is of great help. Students should learn to expect that the main idea is most often stated in the first and/or last sentence. They should also realize that it is not *always* found in the first/last sentence, and indeed, that it may not be stated at all. They should practice determining the location of the main idea within the paragraph.

D. Space Clues: Students should realize that the amount of space devoted to a thought or idea within the paragraph is important—that the main idea is not necessarily limited to a single sentence, though it may be *stated* in one sentence. If the thought they have selected as an answer is found, however, only in a word or phrase, it is almost certainly *not* the main idea. Repeated practice in ascertaining how much of the paragraph relates to a particular point is extremely valuable.

E. Turnabout Clues: The ability to reword a statement as a question can be very helpful. If pupils think that the main idea is stated in one particular sentence, they should change that sentence into a question. Then, of course, they must ask themselves if the paragraph answers the question they have formed.

F. General and Specific Ideas: The ability to distinguish between general and specific ideas is, of course, an overall skill of tremendous value. It is especially valuable in locating the main idea of a passage. Students must understand that some words are more general and all-inclusive than others. For example, the realization that *penny* and *nickel* are specific examples of the more inclusive general term *money* is essential. Practice with such word clusters is valuable. There should be many experiences provided in comparing sentences to determine which embody specific ideas, and which general.

Correcting Errors:

1. If pupils have chosen an answer naming characters not even mentioned in the passage, it is worthwhile to reread just the names contained in the passage.

2. If pupils have chosen an answer that is either in direct opposition to the central thought or not pertinent at all, they should be encouraged to tell the story in their own words.

3. If pupils select a detail or a subsidiary idea, they should be encouraged to find that idea in the story and to see how many sentences talk about it.

4. On the Picture Level, the pupils should be encouraged to reexamine the picture for the clues that are the basis for the main idea.

DRAWING CONCLUSIONS

Drawing Conclusions is designed to help develop the all-important ability to interpret and draw conclusions logically. The series will aid students in looking beyond the word itself—to go beyond mere factual recall. The reader is asked to choose the correct conclusion *based only on the information presented*.

The questions in the *Drawing Conclusions* series do not contain direct references: thus the answers do not use the same words as the questions. In the Picture Level book, the readers examine the picture for the correct answer. The books at the Preparatory, A, and B levels contain primarily indirect references; that is, the answers are found in the paragraph but with slightly different wording. Some easy conclusions are also included. In such cases the answers are not contained directly in the paragraph, but they can be determined without difficulty. As the books advance in challenge, there are more difficult conclusions, involving less evident relationships. The conclusions are also more dependent upon qualifying words such as *mostly, all, some, only*.

In *Drawing Conclusions* the student is asked to:
- A. find an *example* or *illustration*
- B. note a *contrast*
- C. *generalize*
- D. recognize *cause and effect* relationships
- E. detect a *mood*
- F. see an *analogy*
- G. identify *time and place* relationships
- H. make a *comparison*
- I. anticipate an *outcome*

Needless to say, the students should be thoroughly familiar with the ideas and principles each of these concepts embodies.

It is important that the teacher ask pupils to find, in the paragraph, the specific information that is relevant to the tentative conclusion. Then the conclusion must be tested against the information provided. When the emphasis is placed on finding evidence to prove answers and when the pupils put themselves in roles of detectives, not only does their ability to draw conclusions rapidly improve, but also they have fun.

A conclusion is a judgment, and, as such, it must be supported by the strongest evidence possible. In *Drawing Conclusions* the correct answer is the one that is either certain or nearly so, depending, of course, on the information provided and the choices offered.

Some alternate answer choices may be true. Pupils must know that the correct answer not only must be true but must be *supported by evidence from the paragraph*. The clue may involve a single word, phrase, or sentence. In some cases the entire paragraph itself must be considered supportive evidence.

DETECTING THE SEQUENCE

Detecting the Sequence has been designed to help improve students' skills in identifying the sequence of events within a reading selection. In this series, the variety of questions help develop students' understanding of multiple ways of expressing time relationships. Questions are text-dependent rather than picture-dependent.

Students should be reminded to note key time-relation words and expressions as they read. Those they already know, such as *while, before,* and *after,* should be reviewed for meaning. Those that may be new or denote more complex relationships, such as *since* and *meanwhile,* need to be made clear—as do expressions such as *even as this was occurring.* . . . Special note should be made of reversed time order in sentences such as *The fire started after the train arrived,* where the second-mentioned action (the train's arrival) happens before the first-mentioned one. On the intermediate level, the function of the past perfect tense should be explained, as in *Juliette Low thought about the Girl Guides she **had** led in London.* The use of *had* as an auxiliary verb signals an event that took place further in the past than another event mentioned: Juliette Low did the leading before she did the thinking.

A helpful activity is to have students make a chart of the various time relationships and to fill in all the words or expressions they can think of under each heading. A basic chart can have three headings: **Earlier Time, Same Time, Later Time.** On higher levels other headings can be added, such as **From Earlier Time to Now.**

Detecting the Sequence helps develop sequence skills through three general types of questions: (1) those that focus directly on when an event happened; (2) those that focus on which of several events happened first (or last) among the events mentioned; and (3) those that focus on whether a particular event happened before, at the same time as, or after another. The teacher should make clear to students that a question reading "Which happened first (last)?" means "Which happened before (after) any of the *other answer choices*?" (not "Which happened first [last] in the entire reading selection?").

Answering questions in *Detecting the Sequence* involves more than just reading for facts. Most questions require pupils to establish the time relationships between two separately stated ideas by utilizing time clues in the text (except on Picture Level).

In doing each unit on all levels above Picture, students should first read the selection carefully. At the end of each statement they should try to form a picture in their minds so that they will clearly understand what happened first, second, and so forth. As they read, students should look for key words that serve as sequence clues, such as *then, before, since, finally, later, while, when,* and *now.* After finishing the selection, students should review it mentally. Without looking at the selection, they should be able to recall the sequence in which events occurred. If they cannot do this, they should reread the selection. Students should then answer the questions on their worksheets. In answering, students may look at the selection as often as necessary.

Each unit in the Picture Level book consists of two pictures illustrating a sequence of events. The students are to examine each picture and determine which event happened first.

Each unit in the Preparatory Level book consists of a picture, a short story, and one question. The answer to the question, "What happened first?" is found in the short story. The purpose of the picture is to arouse interest in the unit, *not* to provide the answer to the question.

IDENTIFYING INFERENCES

Identifying Inferences is designed to develop one of the most difficult interpretive skills—to arrive at a *probable* conclusion from a limited amount of information. *Identifying Inferences* requires the readers to *read between the lines.* They must utilize previously acquired knowledge and past experiences in order to fully comprehend the message of the text.

In *Identifying Inferences,* the exercises on Picture Level through Level B require the reader to determine if statements following the exercises are inferences. The exercises of Levels C through H require the reader to determine if the statements are true statements, false statements, or inferences. The difficulty of the exercises increases at each higher level because of the concepts involved, the vocabulary, and the experiential background required for comprehension.

The difference between a *conclusion* and an *inference,* as presented in this series, is that a conclusion is a logical deduction based upon conclusive evidence, while an inference is an "educated guess" based upon evidence that is less than conclusive. Read this example:

> Captain Fujihara quickly parked his fire truck, grabbed his helmet, and rushed into the house at 615 Oak Street.

You can *conclude* that Captain Fujihara knows how to drive because that ability was required to park the fire truck. You can *infer* that there is a fire at 615 Oak Street because he grabbed his helmet and rushed into that house. This is an inference because firefighters do rush to people's homes. It is an inference because there may be another reason for Captain Fujihara's rushing to the house. He may live there and be late for supper. Thus an inference is supported by evidence, but the evidence is not necessarily conclusive.

Answer Keys

WORKING WITHIN WORDS

ANSWER KEY — PICTURE LEVEL

← ————————————— UNITS ————————————— →

	1	2	3	4	5	6	7	8	9	10	11	12	13	14	15	16	17	18	19	20	21	22	23	24	25	
1	3	4	1	2	3	4	2	4	1	2	3	1	3	2	4	1	3	1	4	2	1	2	4	4	3	1
2	2	1	4	3	1	1	3	3	2	4	1	4	2	3	3	4	1	3	2	4	2	3	1	3	2	2
3	1	2	3	4	4	2	1	2	4	3	2	3	4	1	1	2	4	2	1	3	4	4	3	1	4	3
4	4	3	2	1	2	3	4	1	3	1	4	2	1	4	2	3	2	4	3	1	3	1	2	2	1	4

	26	27	28	29	30	31	32	33	34	35	36	37	38	39	40	41	42	43	44	45	46	47	48	49	50	
1	2	1	4	3	2	1	4	2	4	2	1	4	3	4	3	2	1	4	3	2	4	4	1	2	3	1
2	4	3	2	1	4	3	1	4	3	1	4	2	1	2	1	4	2	3	4	3	1	2	3	4	1	2
3	1	4	3	2	1	4	2	3	2	4	2	3	4	1	2	3	4	1	2	1	3	1	2	3	2	3
4	3	2	1	4	3	2	3	1	1	3	3	1	2	3	4	1	3	2	1	4	2	3	4	1	4	4

WORKING WITHIN WORDS

ANSWER KEY — PREPARATORY LEVEL

← ————————————— UNITS ————————————— →

	1	2	3	4	5	6	7	8	9	10	11	12	13	14	15	16	17	18	19	20	21	22	23	24	25	
1	3	2	1	4	2	3	2	4	3	1	2	1	2	3	4	2	3	4	1	3	2	3	1	4	2	1
2	2	1	3	2	1	4	1	2	4	2	3	4	4	2	1	4	2	3	4	1	4	4	2	3	1	2
3	4	4	2	1	4	1	3	1	2	4	1	3	1	4	2	3	1	2	3	4	1	2	4	1	3	3
4	1	3	4	3	3	2	4	3	1	3	4	2	3	1	3	1	4	1	2	2	3	1	3	2	4	4

	26	27	28	29	30	31	32	33	34	35	36	37	38	39	40	41	42	43	44	45	46	47	48	49	50	
1	1	3	2	2	4	3	1	2	3	1	4	2	3	1	4	2	3	2	1	4	3	2	1	4	3	1
2	4	4	1	4	3	2	4	3	1	4	2	4	1	3	1	4	1	1	3	2	4	3	4	1	2	2
3	2	2	3	1	2	1	3	4	4	2	1	3	4	2	2	3	4	3	4	1	2	1	3	2	4	3
4	3	1	4	3	1	4	2	1	2	3	3	1	2	4	3	1	2	4	2	3	1	4	2	3	1	4

UNITS	1	2	3	4	5	6	7	8	9	10	11	12	13	14	15	16	17	18	19	20	21	22	23	24	25	
1	2	2	9	9	8	9	1	4	7	4	3	2	1	4	2	4	6	8	8	7	4	5	7	4	3	1
2	8	8	5	1	4	1	7	6	5	8	7	5	4	6	3	8	8	5	9	8	3	1	1	8	9	2
3	9	4	2	8	6	4	6	1	4	2	2	9	8	7	1	9	3	3	3	4	5	9	8	9	1	3
4	6	7	8	3	2	8	2	3	6	7	5	8	6	9	5	3	7	7	2	9	7	3	6	7	6	4
5	1	1	6	5	3	2	4	8	1	6	8	4	5	8	4	5	4	2	5	2	6	4	3	3	7	5
6	5	3	7	7	9	7	5	7	3	1	1	1	2	5	6	6	1	1	4	1	1	2	5	1	8	6

UNITS	26	27	28	29	30	31	32	33	34	35	36	37	38	39	40	41	42	43	44	45	46	47	48	49	50	
1	8	2	6	3	B	A	B	B	B	A	B	B	A	B	A	B	A	B	A	B	A	A	A	A	A	1
2	1	6	3	1	A	A	A	A	B	C	A	A	B	B	B	A	A	B	A	A	B	B	B	B	A	2
3	9	1	7	5	B	B	A	B	A	A	B	A	A	A	B	A	A	A	B	B	B	B	A	A	B	3
4	4	4	1	4	A	A	A	B	A	A	A	B	B	A	A	B	B	B	A	B	B	B	B	B	A	4
5	3	7	5	2	A	B	A	B	A	A	B	B	B	A	B	A	B	A	B	A	A	A	B	A	B	5
6	6	3	9	6	B	A	B	B	B	C	C	A	A	A	B	A	B	A	A	B	B	A	A	A	A	6

WORKING WITHIN WORDS

UNITS

	1	2	3	4	5	6	7	8	9	10	11	12	13	14	15	16	17	18	19	20	21	22	23	24	25	
1	5	1	4	6	8	B	C	A	B	A	A	C	B	B	3	3	8	7	8	7	3	1	5	A	B	**1**
2	4	7	3	5	1	C	A	C	C	C	B	B	C	C	6	5	7	6	7	3	4	7	2	B	A	**2**
3	9	5	9	7	9	A	C	C	B	B	A	B	B	C	4	6	3	9	1	5	1	4	8	B	A	**3**
4	2	3	5	9	3	C	C	C	B	C	C	B	A	A	9	4	1	2	3	8	8	8	3	A	B	**4**
5	8	6	6	8	5	C	C	C	A	B	B	B	B	A	8	2	2	1	4	9	6	3	4	A	A	**5**
6	7	2	7	2	7	C	B	B	C	A	B	B	A	C	5	9	4	8	9	6	2	9	6	B	C	**6**
7	1	4	2	1	4	B	A	A	B	C	A	C	C	A	1	7	5	5	6	2	9	2	7	A	A	**7**

WORKING WITHIN WORDS

UNITS

	26	27	28	29	30	31	32	33	34	35	36	37	38	39	40	41	42	43	44	45	46	47	48	49	50	
1	C	A	A	C	4	C	B	A	4	B	B	B	C	6	A	B	6	C	A	A	6	A	A	B	A	**1**
2	A	C	A	B	1	C	B	B	7	C	A	C	A	9	C	A	7	B	C	B	1	B	B	B	A	**2**
3	A	C	C	C	2	B	A	B	1	A	B	C	C	5	B	B	1	C	A	B	2	B	A	A	B	**3**
4	B	A	C	C	9	A	A	B	2	A	B	A	B	2	C	B	2	A	B	B	3	B	B	A	A	**4**
5	A	C	A	A	8	C	A	A	9	C	B	A	A	3	C	B	4	C	C	B	7	B	B	A	A	**5**
6	C	C	C	C	7	C	A	B	3	A	A	A	A	7	A	A	9	A	C	B	4	A	B	B	A	**6**
7	A	B	A	A	3	C	A	B	5	B	A	A	A	8	B	B	8	C	B	A	9	A	A	A	B	**7**

WORKING WITHIN WORDS

ANSWER KEY — BOOK C

UNITS

	1	2	3	4	5	6	7	8	9	10	11	12	13	14	15	16	17	18	19	20	21	22	23	24	25	
1	C	B	E	D	D	E	C	C	A	D	B	C	E	C	E	E	C	C	C	B	D	A	C	C	C	1
2	A	C	D	C	F	F	D	E	A	E	B	F	D	D	E	B	D	A	D	F	C	C	B	D	D	2
3	A	A	F	F	F	C	F	F	B	D	C	E	B	C	D	A	E	D	F	C	F	E	A	B	E	3
4	B	B	C	F	E	D	B	D	A	F	B	B	A	D	C	F	F	E	B	E	D	B	B	F	E	4
5	C	A	B	E	C	C	F	D	B	E	A	F	F	D	F	E	D	B	E	E	E	A	A	E	A	5
6	A	B	F	E	B	F	E	B	C	F	A	C	A	D	B	B	A	A	E	D	F	B	A	A	F	6
7	C	B	E	D	D	B	F	F	A	C	B	A	C	E	B	E	F	B	D	D	A	B	E	C	E	7
8	B	A	C	E	D	E	E	A	A	B	B	C	D	B	C	B	D	A	D	D	C	A	A	D	F	8
9	B	A	B	D	B	F	E	F	C	C	C	F	F	B	F	F	B	C	E	C	B	A	C	B	F	9
10	B	A	E	E	D	D	E	D	B	E	A	D	E	F	A	F	C	F	B	D	B	E	F	F	F	10

WORKING WITHIN WORDS

ANSWER KEY — BOOK C

UNITS

	26	27	28	29	30	31	32	33	34	35	36	37	38	39	40	41	42	43	44	45	46	47	48	49	50	
1	A	B	E	B	B	B	B	A	A	A	C	B	C	C	E	B	B	C	A	E	B	E	B	B	B	1
2	C	D	C	C	B	C	A	C	B	B	B	A	A	C	A	C	A	B	B	B	C	C	A	A	C	2
3	C	E	F	B	A	B	C	C	A	C	A	C	A	C	F	B	B	B	C	D	C	C	A	A	D	3
4	C	A	B	A	C	A	B	E	A	A	C	A	A	B	C	C	A	E	A	D	D	E	C	B	E	4
5	B	D	F	C	A	B	A	A	B	B	C	B	B	B	A	A	B	D	B	A	E	A	A	C	E	5
6	A	B	C	C	A	A	C	F	C	C	A	A	C	C	B	B	A	B	C	C	A	E	B	B	D	6
7	E	B	D	A	A	A	B	F	A	C	A	C	A	A	C	C	A	A	B	C	C	C	A	A	B	7
8	F	A	A	C	A	B	B	C	C	A	C	B	B	E	B	C	B	E	A	C	B	A	B	C	C	8
9	F	F	F	B	B	A	B	F	A	C	A	A	C	D	C	A	A	B	A	C	C	B	A	A	F	9
10	B	A	A	B	A	C	C	C	A	B	B	B	A	F	C	B	A	B	C	D	A	F	C	B	C	10

UNITS

	1	2	3	4	5	6	7	8	9	10	11	12	13	14	15	16	17	18	19	20	21	22	23	24	25	
1	A	A	B	A	C	F	A	E	E	A	C	D	C	B	D	C	B	B	B	D	A	C	C	C	B	1
2	C	B	C	C	B	A	C	D	D	B	B	A	B	A	A	B	C	B	A	B	A	B	B	B	A	2
3	A	B	B	C	C	D	B	E	B	D	B	D	E	B	D	C	A	B	C	D	B	B	A	A	C	3
4	B	C	A	C	B	F	E	D	C	F	C	B	A	C	E	B	A	B	C	B	A	B	B	A	C	4
5	C	B	A	D	E	D	E	E	E	A	B	E	D	C	E	A	B	C	A	D	B	B	B	A	B	5
6	B	B	A	D	C	B	D	F	C	B	C	D	C	B	D	C	C	C	B	D	C	B	B	A	B	6
7	B	A	A	F	D	D	C	E	D	E	F	E	B	B	D	B	A	B	C	C	A	B	A	C	C	7
8	C	B	B	F	F	F	B	D	E	C	A	A	B	C	E	A	B	C	A	E	C	B	C	B	B	8
9	A	A	A	C	F	D	F	A	C	E	D	C	C	B	D	C	A	A	B	E	A	B	A	B	B	9
10	C	B	B	F	D	C	A	E	B	E	D	C	B	C	E	B	B	C	B	D	C	A	A	A	A	10

UNITS

	26	27	28	29	30	31	32	33	34	35	36	37	38	39	40	41	42	43	44	45	46	47	48	49	50	
1	B	D	D	E	B	B	B	B	E	B	B	C	C	B	C	A	A	B	B	A	A	A	C	A	E	1
2	D	E	E	B	A	C	F	C	B	A	B	C	A	C	C	C	E	B	C	C	D	D	C	A	A	2
3	E	B	E	C	A	B	A	C	E	B	A	D	B	B	C	B	B	A	A	C	A	C	C	A	B	3
4	F	F	D	A	A	B	B	A	A	B	B	B	C	A	C	C	A	B	B	A	A	E	C	D	D	4
5	A	F	B	B	A	A	A	E	B	C	C	A	C	E	B	A	A	A	C	A	A	C	A	A	D	5
6	E	F	C	A	B	C	E	B	A	A	C	C	B	C	B	C	A	C	A	A	B	E	D	D	A	6
7	C	A	B	A	B	A	B	B	B	A	A	D	C	A	C	C	B	C	A	B	A	B	A	B	B	7
8	E	D	F	D	A	C	D	A	E	C	B	D	B	C	B	C	E	B	A	B	A	C	E	B	C	8
9	C	C	A	C	C	B	B	C	C	C	B	B	B	C	B	B	E	D	B	B	A	C	B	A	F	9
10	F	E	C	F	B	A	A	A	E	C	C	C	A	A	A	A	D	A	C	B	F	D	D	D	D	10

UNITS	1	2	3	4	5	6	7	8	9	10	11	12	13	14	15	16	17	18	19	20	21	22	23	24	25	
1	B	B	A	E	F	B	C	B	C	C	C	A	B	C	B	B	B	A	A	B	E	F	B	B	C	1
2	C	C	F	D	E	C	D	B	C	C	A	F	A	A	C	C	B	B	A	A	B	B	A	A	A	2
3	E	B	D	E	B	C	E	A	C	C	B	B	C	B	A	B	B	A	C	C	A	C	C	B	A	3
4	E	E	E	A	C	B	B	B	B	B	B	A	B	A	C	B	C	B	C	A	B	E	C	A	D	4
5	A	B	F	F	D	C	A	B	C	C	A	C	B	A	A	B	C	A	B	B	B	C	B	C	F	5
6	A	B	A	C	C	A	F	C	B	C	F	B	B	B	B	B	C	A	C	B	A	E	C	C	E	6
7	E	D	C	E	A	B	B	A	C	C	B	A	C	B	A	C	A	C	C	B	A	F	B	C	A	7
8	A	E	B	D	B	B	F	B	A	A	D	A	C	A	A	B	C	A	C	C	E	D	C	A	F	8
9	C	E	E	F	D	A	A	B	B	A	C	A	A	C	A	C	A	A	A	B	D	D	A	A	C	9
10	B	D	C	B	B	C	A	C	A	A	E	E	C	A	B	C	C	B	C	C	E	D	C	B	A	10

WORKING WITHIN WORDS

ANSWER KEY — BOOK E

UNITS	26	27	28	29	30	31	32	33	34	35	36	37	38	39	40	41	42	43	44	45	46	47	48	49	50	
1	B	D	C	A	A	C	A	A	B	B	B	B	A	C	A	B	C	B	B	A	B	B	C	B	C	1
2	B	C	B	C	B	B	A	C	C	C	C	B	B	A	A	A	A	A	C	C	C	C	A	B	C	2
3	C	C	C	B	B	F	C	A	B	C	A	A	A	C	C	A	B	C	C	B	B	A	C	B	B	3
4	B	B	A	A	B	E	B	C	C	C	C	B	A	C	A	B	B	A	A	C	A	B	B	A	B	4
5	C	B	A	C	B	B	A	A	C	C	A	C	A	C	B	A	C	C	A	C	A	C	C	C	B	5
6	B	A	B	B	A	D	B	B	B	B	A	A	B	A	A	C	C	C	A	A	C	B	A	C	C	6
7	A	E	A	A	A	E	A	B	C	B	A	A	B	C	B	B	A	B	B	A	A	A	A	B	C	7
8	C	C	A	A	B	D	C	C	C	C	B	B	A	C	B	A	B	C	B	B	A	A	B	A	C	8
9	B	C	C	B	A	B	A	C	C	C	C	C	B	A	C	C	A	A	A	C	B	C	B	B	A	9
10	A	E	A	A	B	C	B	B	A	B	A	B	A	B	B	B	C	B	C	A	B	A	A	B	B	10

WORKING WITHIN WORDS

UNITS

	1	2	3	4	5	6	7	8	9	10	11	12	13	14	15	16	17	18	19	20	21	22	23	24	25	
1	B	A	A	A	A	B	A	A	A	A	A	A	B	A	B	B	B	A	A	C	C	B	C	D	A	1
2	A	B	B	A	A	A	B	A	A	A	B	C	C	B	A	A	C	B	A	B	C	A	B	B	A	2
3	B	C	B	A	B	B	A	A	A	A	A	A	A	B	B	B	A	A	B	C	A	A	C	C	A	3
4	C	A	C	A	B	C	A	A	B	C	C	B	B	B	B	A	B	B	C	C	C	B	A	D	B	4
5	B	C	A	A	B	B	B	A	B	C	B	B	A	B	B	B	C	A	B	A	A	A	A	E	A	5
6	B	B	A	B	B	A	A	B	A	A	A	A	B	A	A	B	A	A	B	B	B	A	C	C	C	6
7	A	B	B	B	C	C	B	A	A	A	A	C	C	A	B	A	B	B	B	B	A	C	C	A	A	7
8	B	C	C	B	A	B	B	B	A	C	A	A	B	B	A	B	C	B	B	A	C	C	A	C	B	8
9	A	B	A	A	C	A	A	C	A	B	C	B	B	A	B	B	B	B	A	A	B	A	B	E	A	9
10	A	B	C	A	C	B	C	A	B	B	B	B	B	B	B	A	B	A	C	C	A	A	A	F	C	10

WORKING WITHIN WORDS

UNITS

	26	27	28	29	30	31	32	33	34	35	36	37	38	39	40	41	42	43	44	45	46	47	48	49	50	
1	B	A	A	A	B	A	A	B	B	B	A	B	A	B	B	B	B	B	B	B	C	C	C	C	A	1
2	B	A	B	A	B	A	B	A	A	A	A	A	B	A	B	A	C	B	B	B	C	A	A	A	B	2
3	A	A	A	B	B	B	B	A	A	C	B	B	B	A	B	A	B	B	B	B	A	A	A	B	B	3
4	B	A	B	B	A	B	C	A	A	A	A	A	B	B	C	C	C	C	B	A	C	C	C	C	B	4
5	A	B	C	B	A	A	C	A	B	B	B	A	B	C	B	B	A	B	A	B	A	A	A	C	B	5
6	B	A	B	A	A	A	B	B	A	A	A	B	A	B	B	B	C	A	C	C	A	B	B	B	A	6
7	A	B	B	B	A	A	B	A	B	B	B	B	B	C	A	A	A	C	C	B	B	B	B	C	A	7
8	C	A	C	C	B	A	B	C	C	C	A	B	B	A	C	A	A	A	B	B	A	A	B	A	A	8
9	A	C	A	A	B	C	B	B	A	A	C	C	C	A	A	A	B	B	B	C	A	C	B	B	A	9
10	A	A	A	A	A	A	B	B	B	A	A	A	A	A	A	A	C	A	A	B	B	B	A	A	B	10

WORKING WITHIN WORDS

UNITS

	1	2	3	4	5	6	7	8	9	10	11	12	13	14	15	16	17	18	19	20	21	22	23	24	25	
1	C	B	B	C	C	B	C	B	B	C	B	C	B	C	B	B	B	B	B	C	A	B	A	A	B	1
2	B	A	C	B	A	C	B	A	C	A	B	B	B	A	B	A	B	A	C	A	A	C	C	C	C	2
3	C	C	B	B	C	B	B	C	B	C	C	A	C	C	A	A	B	A	B	B	C	A	A	B	B	3
4	B	A	A	C	A	A	A	C	A	B	B	B	A	A	B	B	C	C	C	C	A	B	B	A	C	4
5	B	A	C	C	A	C	C	C	C	A	C	B	A	A	A	B	A	A	B	B	C	B	B	B	B	5
6	B	B	C	C	B	A	B	B	A	B	A	B	A	C	B	B	B	B	B	C	A	A	C	A	A	6
7	C	C	B	B	A	B	C	C	B	A	B	A	C	C	B	C	C	C	B	B	C	B	B	B	C	7
8	B	A	B	A	C	A	A	C	C	C	C	A	C	A	C	C	B	B	C	B	C	B	C	B	B	8
9	C	B	B	C	B	C	C	A	B	A	A	B	A	A	A	C	A	A	A	C	B	B	C	B	B	9
10	B	A	B	C	B	A	B	C	A	C	A	B	A	B	B	B	B	C	C	A	A	B	A	A	A	10

WORKING WITHIN WORDS

UNITS

	26	27	28	29	30	31	32	33	34	35	36	37	38	39	40	41	42	43	44	45	46	47	48	49	50	
1	C	C	A	C	B	A	C	C	B	B	B	A	C	A	B	B	B	A	C	C	C	A	B	C	B	1
2	A	B	B	A	A	C	C	B	C	B	C	A	A	B	B	B	C	A	C	B	B	A	A	B	C	2
3	A	A	B	C	C	B	C	C	A	A	C	B	C	A	B	C	A	B	B	A	A	B	A	C	B	3
4	A	B	A	C	C	B	B	B	B	A	A	C	B	A	A	C	B	C	B	A	A	A	C	A	A	4
5	C	B	A	C	A	A	A	A	C	A	A	A	A	C	C	A	C	A	C	B	C	A	A	B	B	5
6	C	B	C	C	C	A	C	A	C	C	C	B	A	B	C	B	C	B	C	B	B	B	A	B	C	6
7	B	A	C	C	B	B	B	C	A	B	B	C	C	B	A	C	B	B	A	A	A	C	C	C	B	7
8	B	B	B	A	A	B	A	A	B	B	B	A	A	A	C	A	A	C	B	C	B	C	B	A	C	8
9	B	A	C	C	B	C	C	C	A	B	A	B	B	C	C	B	C	A	A	B	C	B	A	B	A	9
10	A	B	C	A	B	A	A	A	A	C	B	A	A	B	A	A	B	A	A	A	A	B	B	A	B	10

UNITS

	1	2	3	4	5	6	7	8	9	10	11	12	13	14	15	16	17	18	19	20	21	22	23	24	25	
1	B	A	B	C	B	C	C	B	B	A	B	A	B	C	A	C	C	A	A	B	A	B	C	C	A	1
2	C	C	B	C	C	A	B	A	C	B	C	B	A	A	B	A	B	C	C	B	C	A	C	A	B	2
3	A	B	C	C	A	B	C	C	A	B	A	B	C	A	C	A	A	B	B	C	B	C	A	C	C	3
4	B	C	C	C	C	B	C	B	B	C	C	C	A	B	A	B	B	C	B	B	C	A	B	C	B	4
5	A	C	C	B	A	A	B	B	A	B	B	C	B	C	A	B	B	B	B	B	A	C	C	B	C	5
6	C	A	B	C	B	C	A	C	A	C	C	C	B	C	B	B	A	B	B	B	B	B	B	B	A	6
7	C	B	A	C	B	A	B	C	B	C	A	C	B	B	B	C	B	A	A	B	C	A	A	C	B	7
8	C	C	C	B	A	C	C	A	B	C	C	A	A	A	B	B	C	B	C	B	C	B	C	A	C	8
9	C	B	B	C	C	C	B	B	B	C	A	B	B	A	B	C	B	C	B	B	C	C	B	A	A	9
10	B	C	C	C	C	C	C	B	C	C	A	B	B	B	B	C	B	C	A	B	B	A	C	B	C	10

WORKING WITHIN WORDS

ANSWER KEY — BOOK H

UNITS

	26	27	28	29	30	31	32	33	34	35	36	37	38	39	40	41	42	43	44	45	46	47	48	49	50	
1	C	B	A	B	A	C	C	C	B	B	A	B	A	C	A	A	A	C	B	C	A	C	C	C	C	1
2	C	A	A	C	B	C	A	A	C	C	A	C	A	C	A	B	C	B	C	A	B	A	B	A	C	2
3	B	C	C	A	B	A	B	C	B	C	B	B	B	B	A	C	C	A	C	B	B	C	C	A	A	3
4	A	B	B	B	C	C	C	B	B	A	C	A	B	C	C	A	B	B	B	A	A	B	B	A	B	4
5	B	C	C	B	A	A	A	C	C	B	A	B	A	A	C	B	A	A	C	A	C	C	A	C	C	5
6	C	B	A	A	C	B	C	A	B	A	C	B	C	B	A	A	A	B	A	B	C	C	C	B	B	6
7	C	B	B	B	A	C	A	B	C	B	A	B	B	A	A	C	B	C	C	C	A	A	C	A	C	7
8	C	B	B	C	B	A	A	C	B	C	B	A	C	C	A	C	A	B	B	B	C	B	A	C	A	8
9	A	C	C	B	C	C	A	A	C	A	A	A	C	A	C	B	C	A	C	A	B	B	B	C	B	9
10	C	B	C	A	B	A	C	A	A	A	B	A	A	C	A	A	B	C	A	C	A	A	C	A	B	10

FOLLOWING DIRECTIONS

◄──────────────────────── UNITS ────────────────────────►

	1	2	3	4	5	6	7	8	9	10	11	12	13	14	15	16	17	18	19	20	21	22	23	24	25	
1	B	A	B	B	A	B	A	A	A	B	B	A	B	A	B	B	A	B	A	A	B	B	A	B	A	1

	26	27	28	29	30	31	32	33	34	35	36	37	38	39	40	41	42	43	44	45	46	47	48	49	50	
1	B	A	B	B	A	A	B	A	B	A	A	B	A	A	B	B	A	B	A	A	B	A	B	B	A	1

FOLLOWING DIRECTIONS

◄──────────────────────── UNITS ────────────────────────►

	1	2	3	4	5	6	7	8	9	10	11	12	13	14	15	16	17	18	19	20	21	22	23	24	25	
1	A	B	B	A	A	B	A	B	B	A	B	B	A	A	B	A	B	B	A	B	A	A	A	B	B	1

	26	27	28	29	30	31	32	33	34	35	36	37	38	39	40	41	42	43	44	45	46	47	48	49	50	
1	A	B	A	B	B	B	A	B	A	A	B	B	A	B	A	B	B	A	A	B	A	B	A	B	B	1

FOLLOWING DIRECTIONS

◄──────────────────────── UNITS ────────────────────────►

	1	2	3	4	5	6	7	8	9	10	11	12	13	14	15	16	17	18	19	20	21	22	23	24	25	
1	B	A	B	B	B	C	C	B	A	B	A	B	B	C	B	A	B	A	B	A	A	C	A	A	B	1
2	A	B	B	A	C	B	A	B	B	A	B	B	A	A	B	A	C	B	A	C	B	A	C	C	A	2
3	A	B	B	B	A	A	B	B	B	A	B	B	B	A	B	B	A	B	A	B	A	A	A	A	B	3

	26	27	28	29	30	31	32	33	34	35	36	37	38	39	40	41	42	43	44	45	46	47	48	49	50	
1	B	B	C	A	B	A	B	A	A	B	B	C	B	B	B	A	C	C	A	B	A	A	C	C	A	1
2	A	A	A	C	A	C	C	A	C	B	A	C	C	A	B	C	C	A	B	A	A	B	C	C	C	2
3	A	B	A	A	B	B	A	B	B	A	A	A	B	A	A	B	B	A	A	B	B	A	A	B	B	3

— 30 —

FOLLOWING DIRECTIONS

UNITS

	1	2	3	4	5	6	7	8	9	10	11	12	13	14	15	16	17	18	19	20	21	22	23	24	25	
1	C	B	C	A	B	A	B	A	B	A	A	B	A	B	C	A	A	C	B	C	A	A	A	B	C	1
2	A	A	A	A	B	A	A	C	A	B	B	A	A	A	B	C	A	B	B	A	A	B	B	A	C	2
3	A	B	A	A	B	A	A	B	B	B	A	A	B	A	A	A	B	B	B	B	B	A	A	A	B	3

	26	27	28	29	30	31	32	33	34	35	36	37	38	39	40	41	42	43	44	45	46	47	48	49	50	
1	A	A	A	A	A	A	A	A	A	C	C	A	A	A	B	B	A	A	C	A	A	A	A	B	C	1
2	A	C	B	A	B	C	B	B	A	C	C	B	B	A	C	B	B	A	C	B	A	B	A	C	B	2
3	A	A	A	B	B	A	B	A	A	B	B	A	B	A	B	A	B	C	B	A	A	A	A	A	B	3

FOLLOWING DIRECTIONS

UNITS

	1	2	3	4	5	6	7	8	9	10	11	12	13	14	15	16	17	18	19	20	21	22	23	24	25	
1	A	C	C	B	A	A	A	B	A	B	B	C	A	B	A	A	B	B	B	C	B	C	A	A	B	1
2	A	B	C	B	B	A	C	C	C	A	B	A	B	A	A	C	B	B	C	C	C	C	B	A	A	2
3	A	B	A	A	B	B	A	B	A	B	A	B	A	B	C	B	B	A	B	B	B	C	B	B	A	3
4	C	B	C	B	A	B	B	B	A	A	A	C	B	A	B	A	A	B	C	B	B	C	A	A	A	4

	26	27	28	29	30	31	32	33	34	35	36	37	38	39	40	41	42	43	44	45	46	47	48	49	50	
1	A	A	C	C	B	A	B	B	B	A	B	C	A	B	B	B	C	A	B	C	C	A	C	B	B	1
2	B	A	C	C	B	A	B	A	A	B	C	B	B	B	C	A	A	A	C	A	A	B	C	A	A	2
3	C	A	B	A	A	B	C	B	C	B	B	C	B	C	A	C	B	B	A	B	C	B	B	B	B	3
4	A	B	B	B	C	A	B	A	B	B	A	A	A	C	B	A	A	A	B	B	A	C	C	C	4

FOLLOWING DIRECTIONS

UNITS

	1	2	3	4	5	6	7	8	9	10	11	12	13	14	15	16	17	18	19	20	21	22	23	24	25	
1	B	B	B	C	A	C	A	C	C	B	C	B	B	A	C	B	C	C	A	C	B	B	C	B	B	1
2	C	C	A	C	B	C	C	C	A	A	B	A	B	A	B	B	A	A	A	C	A	A	B	A	B	2
3	A	B	B	A	A	B	A	A	C	B	B	B	B	B	A	C	A	A	C	C	A	B	A	C	B	C	3
4	B	B	B	B	A	A	B	A	B	B	B	C	A	A	A	A	A	B	C	B	A	A	B	A	A	4

	26	27	28	29	30	31	32	33	34	35	36	37	38	39	40	41	42	43	44	45	46	47	48	49	50	
1	A	B	A	A	C	B	B	B	B	B	B	B	B	B	C	C	C	B	A	C	B	C	A	C	A	1
2	B	B	A	A	A	C	B	A	B	B	B	B	B	A	B	A	B	A	B	B	A	B	C	B	A	2
3	A	B	A	A	B	C	B	A	B	B	B	A	A	A	B	A	C	B	A	C	B	A	C	A	C	3
4	B	B	A	B	A	A	A	A	A	B	B	A	B	B	B	A	A	B	A	B	B	A	A	B	B	4

FOLLOWING DIRECTIONS

UNITS

	1	2	3	4	5	6	7	8	9	10	11	12	13	14	15	16	17	18	19	20	21	22	23	24	25	
1	C	D	D	C	A	B	C	C	C	D	B	D	C	D	B	A	D	C	B	C	B	A	C	D	D	B	1
2	C	D	B	A	D	D	B	C	B	D	B	B	D	B	A	B	D	A	C	A	D	A	D	C	A	2
3	C	D	A	C	A	B	D	B	C	C	C	A	D	C	C	D	A	A	D	D	C	D	D	A	C	3
4	C	A	B	C	D	D	D	B	B	C	C	A	D	C	C	B	B	D	D	B	C	D	B	C	D	4

	26	27	28	29	30	31	32	33	34	35	36	37	38	39	40	41	42	43	44	45	46	47	48	49	50	
1	C	C	C	C	C	C	C	D	C	D	C	D	C	C	C	C	C	B	C	D	A	B	B	B	C	1
2	D	A	A	C	B	A	D	D	D	A	C	C	C	A	A	C	C	D	C	C	A	D	C	D	D	2
3	A	C	B	C	A	D	D	A	A	B	C	D	C	A	A	D	A	C	D	A	A	C	C	A	D	3
4	A	A	C	D	C	A	A	C	C	B	B	A	B	D	D	D	C	C	A	B	B	A	C	D	C	4

FOLLOWING DIRECTIONS

UNITS

	1	2	3	4	5	6	7	8	9	10	11	12	13	14	15	16	17	18	19	20	21	22	23	24	25	
1	D	A	D	A	A	D	A	D	A	A	A	B	A	B	D	D	D	C	D	A	D	B	D	D	D	1
2	A	D	B	D	B	D	C	A	D	D	C	C	D	B	A	A	C	A	B	B	A	A	B	C	B	2
3	C	A	B	A	B	A	A	A	D	D	B	B	B	B	C	B	C	C	D	D	C	A	A	B	C	3
4	D	D	B	C	B	D	C	C	C	B	B	B	C	B	A	C	A	B	D	D	D	A	C	C	D	4

	26	27	28	29	30	31	32	33	34	35	36	37	38	39	40	41	42	43	44	45	46	47	48	49	50	
1	A	C	B	B	C	B	D	A	C	A	B	C	B	D	D	D	D	C	A	A	A	C	C	B	C	1
2	C	C	D	A	A	D	C	D	B	D	D	D	C	B	B	A	B	B	A	B	D	B	A	C	A	2
3	D	A	A	D	B	C	A	D	D	B	C	C	D	C	C	C	C	D	C	B	D	B	B	A	B	3
4	D	B	A	A	D	B	C	A	C	A	A	D	A	D	D	A	D	C	C	B	B	C	A	D	B	4

FOLLOWING DIRECTIONS

UNITS

	1	2	3	4	5	6	7	8	9	10	11	12	13	14	15	16	17	18	19	20	21	22	23	24	25	
1	D	B	B	B	C	D	C	C	C	B	C	B	C	D	B	D	B	A	B	D	D	D	D	D	C	1
2	A	D	B	C	D	A	B	A	A	D	C	C	D	B	C	C	B	B	C	A	A	B	C	A	A	2
3	D	B	A	B	D	A	C	B	C	A	B	A	B	C	B	C	B	C	C	C	B	B	B	D	C	3
4	D	D	A	A	C	D	A	B	B	D	B	B	C	B	B	C	B	A	B	C	A	A	A	B	C	4

	26	27	28	29	30	31	32	33	34	35	36	37	38	39	40	41	42	43	44	45	46	47	48	49	50	
1	D	C	B	C	B	B	B	B	D	C	D	D	C	D	C	D	D	D	C	D	C	B	C	B	D	1
2	B	C	C	A	C	A	C	D	D	A	D	C	C	A	C	C	B	C	A	B	D	A	A	C	D	2
3	C	C	B	A	D	D	B	D	A	C	A	A	B	A	A	A	D	C	C	D	B	C	B	D	B	3
4	A	D	B	B	C	D	B	C	D	C	D	B	C	A	A	C	C	A	B	A	D	B	A	A	D	4

FOLLOWING DIRECTIONS

	1	2	3	4	5	6	7	8	9	10	11	12	13	14	15	16	17	18	19	20	21	22	23	24	25	
1	D	B	C	D	C	A	B	C	B	B	B	C	B	A	A	B	C	C	C	B	B	D	A	B	B	1
2	A	C	B	C	B	D	C	B	C	D	A	D	A	C	C	C	B	C	B	C	C	C	B	C	C	2
3	A	B	A	B	A	A	A	A	D	B	D	D	C	B	B	B	C	C	C	A	A	B	B	A	D	3
4	D	A	C	C	D	D	C	B	C	C	C	C	B	C	C	D	A	D	B	C	B	A	C	C	C	4

	26	27	28	29	30	31	32	33	34	35	36	37	38	39	40	41	42	43	44	45	46	47	48	49	50	
1	A	C	C	B	B	C	D	A	C	D	D	C	B	C	C	C	C	C	C	B	B	B	B	C	C	1
2	B	C	A	C	C	A	C	C	B	C	B	B	C	B	A	B	B	B	B	C	D	B	D	A	B	2
3	C	A	B	A	A	B	B	B	C	C	C	C	A	B	B	A	A	C	C	D	B	A	A	C	A	3
4	B	C	C	C	B	B	A	C	A	A	B	D	C	C	C	C	C	B	A	C	D	A	D	B	C	4

USING THE CONTEXT

	1	2	3	4	5	6	7	8	9	10	11	12	13	14	15	16	17	18	19	20	21	22	23	24	25	
1	2	1	3	4	2	1	4	3	2	1	4	2	3	1	2	4	3	2	1	2	4	3	1	2	4	1
2	4	3	2	3	4	3	2	1	4	2	3	3	4	3	4	1	2	3	4	1	2	1	4	3	2	2
3	3	2	4	1	3	2	1	4	1	4	2	1	1	2	3	2	4	1	3	4	3	4	2	4	1	3
4	1	4	1	2	1	4	3	2	3	3	1	4	2	4	1	3	1	4	2	3	1	2	3	1	3	4

	26	27	28	29	30	31	32	33	34	35	36	37	38	39	40	41	42	43	44	45	46	47	48	49	50	
1	3	1	2	4	3	1	2	4	3	4	2	3	1	4	2	1	3	1	1	3	2	4	1	3	2	1
2	1	3	4	2	4	4	1	1	2	2	4	1	3	3	1	4	4	3	2	4	3	1	2	1	4	2
3	2	4	1	3	1	2	3	2	4	1	3	2	4	2	3	2	1	4	3	2	4	3	4	2	3	3
4	4	2	3	1	2	3	4	3	1	3	1	4	2	1	4	3	2	2	4	1	1	2	3	4	1	4

USING THE CONTEXT

	1	2	3	4	5	6	7	8	9	10	11	12	13	14	15	16	17	18	19	20	21	22	23	24	25	
1	B	B	B	C	B	B	C	C	C	A	B	C	A	A	B	A	C	C	B	A	B	B	C	B	B	1
2	A	C	C	B	A	C	B	A	A	B	A	A	C	C	C	C	C	A	C	B	C	C	B	C	C	2
3	C	A	B	B	C	B	B	C	B	B	B	C	C	C	A	B	B	B	A	B	B	B	A	C	B	3
4	A	A	A	A	B	A	A	B	C	C	C	B	B	A	C	B	B	A	C	C	B	A	B	A	C	4
5	B	C	C	C	C	C	B	A	B	C	B	A	C	B	C	C	B	C	B	A	A	B	B	B	B	5
6	C	A	A	C	A	A	C	B	C	A	C	B	A	C	A	B	A	B	A	B	C	C	C	C	A	6
7	A	B	A	A	C	C	B	C	B	C	A	A	B	A	C	B	C	C	C	C	C	B	A	B	C	7
8	C	A	C	B	A	B	C	B	A	B	C	C	C	B	B	A	B	A	C	A	B	C	C	A	B	8
9	B	C	B	A	A	C	A	A	C	A	A	B	A	C	C	C	C	C	B	C	C	A	B	C	B	9
10	A	B	C	C	C	A	B	C	C	C	C	C	B	B	C	C	A	B	C	B	A	B	C	B	C	10

USING THE CONTEXT

UNITS

	1	2	3	4	5	6	7	8	9	10	11	12	13	14	15	16	17	18	19	20	21	22	23	24	25	
1	A	A	B	C	B	B	A	C	B	B	A	C	B	C	B	B	B	A	B	B	B	C	B	B	C	1
2	C	C	B	A	B	B	C	A	A	A	B	A	C	A	B	A	B	B	A	A	A	C	B	B	B	2
3	B	C	A	C	B	C	A	B	A	A	B	B	A	A	C	B	C	B	C	B	C	A	C	C	A	3
4	A	A	B	B	A	B	B	A	B	B	C	B	C	B	C	C	B	C	B	C	A	C	A	B	C	4
5	C	C	C	A	C	A	A	C	C	A	A	A	B	A	A	A	C	A	C	A	B	A	C	C	B	5
6	C	B	A	A	B	B	C	C	C	A	C	B	C	A	A	C	A	A	C	B	C	B	A	A	B	6
7	A	B	A	B	C	A	B	A	A	C	B	A	B	B	C	A	B	A	B	B	C	A	B	B	A	7
8	C	A	B	C	A	C	A	A	B	A	B	C	A	C	B	B	B	B	C	C	B	B	B	A	C	8
9	B	A	A	A	C	B	B	C	B	B	A	C	C	A	A	C	C	B	A	C	A	C	A	C	B	9
10	A	C	C	C	C	A	A	A	A	A	B	C	A	C	C	A	C	B	C	C	C	A	C	B	A	10

USING THE CONTEXT

UNITS

	1	2	3	4	5	6	7	8	9	10	11	12	13	14	15	16	17	18	19	20	21	22	23	24	25	
1	A	A	C	B	B	A	A	A	C	C	B	B	B	C	A	A	C	A	B	A	B	B	B	B	C	1
2	C	B	A	B	B	B	C	C	B	A	C	A	C	A	C	B	A	A	B	A	B	B	A	B	C	2
3	B	A	A	A	B	C	C	B	A	B	C	C	B	A	A	C	B	B	A	C	A	B	C	A	A	3
4	B	A	C	C	A	A	B	B	B	C	A	B	A	A	B	A	B	C	B	A	C	C	B	C	A	4
5	B	A	C	A	A	A	A	B	C	C	B	B	B	B	B	C	B	C	C	A	A	B	C	A	B	5
6	B	C	B	A	B	A	B	A	B	C	A	C	B	C	A	C	A	B	C	A	B	C	A	B	B	6
7	B	B	A	C	A	B	B	A	B	A	B	B	C	C	A	C	A	C	A	A	A	A	A	A	C	7
8	C	C	A	B	A	C	A	C	C	B	B	A	A	C	A	B	C	A	C	C	A	B	B	C	A	8
9	A	A	B	C	B	B	B	A	A	C	C	B	C	B	C	C	C	B	A	C	A	B	C	B	B	9
10	A	A	C	C	B	C	B	C	B	B	A	C	A	B	A	B	A	C	C	A	B	B	A	A	C	10

USING THE CONTEXT

ANSWER KEY — BOOK C

UNITS

	1	2	3	4	5	6	7	8	9	10	11	12
1	C	C	B	C	D	C	C	C	C	C	B	A
2	B	A	A	D	C	D	B	B	A	B	A	A
3	A	D	C	A	B	D	B	A	C	D	A	D
4	B	D	D	C	C	A	B	D	C	D	D	B
5	B	B	C	D	A	D	C	D	B	D	A	A
6	D	A	B	D	D	B	C	A	D	D	C	B
7	D	C	B	D	C	B	B	D	D	B	B	B
8	B	D	D	A	B	B	B	D	C	D	B	B
9	A	B	C	C	B	A	D	B	D	D	C	B
10	A	A	D	D	B	B	C	D	C	B	D	C
11	D	C	D	A	B	A	C	D	D	A	D	C
12	A	B	C	A	A	C	B	A	B	C	D	D
13	D	A	C	A	A	B	C	C	A	C	B	C
14	C	A	A	B	A	C	D	D	A	A	A	B
15	D	B	B	C	B	B	C	C	C	A	A	B
16	A	D	A	D	A	A	B	D	A	C	C	A
17	C	C	C	C	D	A	B	C	C	A	A	C
18	B	A	A	C	B	A	A	B	B	C	D	A
19	C	C	D	B	C	B	B	D	D	C	C	B
20	D	A	A	C	D	B	B	D	D	B	C	A

USING THE CONTEXT

ANSWER KEY — BOOK C

UNITS

	13	14	15	16	17	18	19	20	21	22	23	24	25	
1	C	A	A	A	B	A	B	B	B	A	C	C	B	1
2	D	C	B	A	A	C	D	C	C	B	C	C	A	2
3	C	D	C	C	B	C	D	C	C	B	D	B	B	3
4	A	B	B	B	A	B	D	A	B	A	D	A	A	4
5	D	D	B	B	B	B	B	A	B	A	A	A	D	5
6	C	D	A	A	A	C	C	C	D	C	B	A	B	6
7	C	D	A	B	D	C	D	C	D	D	A	B	C	7
8	D	C	A	B	A	D	A	A	A	C	A	D	A	8
9	C	B	A	D	D	A	B	C	A	A	C	C	D	9
10	C	B	C	D	D	A	B	A	B	B	C	C	D	10
11	C	B	D	A	D	B	C	A	D	C	A	A	D	11
12	B	D	C	B	C	B	C	B	B	A	B	B	C	12
13	D	C	C	B	B	D	C	B	C	C	C	B	C	13
14	B	B	B	A	B	C	C	A	A	C	D	C	A	14
15	D	C	C	C	C	B	B	C	B	B	A	A	D	15
16	D	A	C	B	A	D	D	B	A	A	C	B	A	16
17	B	C	A	A	A	D	D	A	B	B	D	D	A	17
18	C	D	C	C	A	C	B	A	A	C	A	D	D	18
19	C	D	A	C	A	C	C	A	A	B	B	B	D	19
20	D	B	A	B	B	A	C	A	C	B	A	D	A	20

USING THE CONTEXT

ANSWER KEY — BOOK D

— UNITS —

	13	14	15	16	17	18	19	20	21	22	23	24	25
1	C	A	A	D	B	B	B	B	B	A	B	A	B
2	D	A	B	B	A	B	A	C	C	B	B	B	A
3	A	C	C	C	A	D	B	C	D	D	B	D	C
4	B	B	D	B	B	A	C	C	A	A	C	A	C
5	B	B	D	B	A	B	B	B	D	B	C	A	B
6	A	C	B	C	D	D	C	D	C	C	A	B	A
7	A	B	A	B	D	A	B	B	B	B	A	B	B
8	C	B	C	C	A	D	B	A	A	D	B	B	D
9	D	B	D	D	B	D	A	C	C	B	C	B	C
10	A	C	D	D	A	D	B	C	D	A	B	C	B
11	D	A	B	B	B	C	B	A	C	B	C	C	B
12	C	B	C	A	B	B	A	A	B	A	B	A	A
13	A	C	D	B	A	B	D	B	C	B	B	C	C
14	A	D	B	D	B	D	C	C	C	D	B	A	D
15	C	A	D	A	C	C	D	D	D	A	C	C	B
16	B	D	A	A	C	B	A	B	B	B	B	B	A
17	B	C	C	A	B	A	C	A	C	B	A	D	C
18	A	D	D	A	C	A	B	C	A	C	B	A	D
19	D	B	C	D	C	C	B	B	B	A	B	B	B
20	A	C	A	B	B	B	A	B	A	A	A	A	A

USING THE CONTEXT

ANSWER KEY — BOOK D

— UNITS —

	1	2	3	4	5	6	7	8	9	10	11	12
1	C	D	D	A	B	C	A	B	D	B	B	B
2	B	C	A	C	A	D	C	C	B	C	C	C
3	A	B	A	A	C	B	B	A	B	A	B	C
4	C	B	D	A	D	C	A	B	D	B	B	D
5	B	B	A	B	D	C	B	D	D	B	A	C
6	D	A	B	D	B	A	A	A	B	C	A	A
7	D	C	B	A	D	A	A	C	C	D	B	C
8	C	B	C	D	C	B	C	B	C	A	D	B
9	D	D	D	C	D	C	B	D	D	B	C	C
10	C	A	B	D	C	A	A	A	C	C	C	D
11	C	B	C	B	A	C	B	D	D	B	B	B
12	B	C	C	C	C	A	C	A	B	A	B	D
13	C	C	A	D	D	A	C	D	B	C	C	B
14	C	B	B	B	B	A	A	B	B	C	D	D
15	A	B	B	A	A	B	B	C	C	D	A	B
16	C	D	A	B	B	A	D	B	D	D	A	D
17	A	C	C	C	B	A	B	D	C	A	B	D
18	C	B	B	D	B	D	A	B	D	A	A	D
19	C	A	B	D	C	B	D	A	B	A	C	C
20	A	B	C	C	D	C	A	D	A	A	C	D

UNITS (13–25)

Q	13	14	15	16	17	18	19	20	21	22	23	24	25
1	D	C	B	C	C	A	B	C	D	A	A	C	B
2	B	B	D	D	A	D	A	D	A	B	C	A	C
3	B	D	B	B	B	B	D	B	A	D	D	C	C
4	B	B	A	C	D	C	D	A	B	A	B	B	B
5	D	B	C	A	D	D	B	B	C	C	D	B	C
6	B	A	D	D	B	C	D	A	A	B	C	D	C
7	C	A	D	D	A	B	C	C	B	B	C	D	C
8	D	B	D	A	B	D	B	B	C	C	D	C	D
9	C	C	B	B	B	B	B	B	D	D	C	C	B
10	C	C	C	A	A	B	C	C	C	B	C	B	A
11	C	B	C	C	B	D	D	D	D	D	C	D	D
12	D	D	A	D	C	C	B	C	C	C	C	C	A
13	B	C	C	D	C	D	D	B	B	B	D	B	C
14	C	B	B	A	D	C	A	C	A	C	B	B	A
15	D	A	B	C	C	D	C	C	D	B	D	D	C
16	B	D	A	B	A	B	D	B	B	B	B	B	B
17	C	B	D	D	A	C	A	B	A	B	D	D	A
18	D	C	B	D	C	D	A	A	A	D	C	C	B
19	D	C	D	A	B	D	C	C	C	C	B	B	B
20	D	B	C	A	C	A	B	B	B	C	C	C	D

USING THE CONTEXT

ANSWER KEY — BOOK E

UNITS (1–12)

Q	1	2	3	4	5	6	7	8	9	10	11	12
1	B	B	B	B	B	C	B	D	B	C	B	D
2	C	B	D	D	C	D	D	A	B	A	A	D
3	A	C	B	B	C	D	B	C	C	C	B	A
4	A	B	A	B	C	A	B	A	B	B	D	B
5	A	C	A	C	D	D	B	D	D	C	D	B
6	B	D	C	A	C	A	D	C	A	C	D	B
7	C	D	C	B	A	B	C	B	C	D	D	B
8	D	B	D	B	B	D	D	C	D	B	D	C
9	B	D	A	C	C	A	C	B	D	D	A	D
10	D	A	B	A	C	B	A	A	C	C	A	A
11	D	B	D	B	D	B	B	B	C	C	C	B
12	D	D	B	C	C	A	C	A	D	D	B	C
13	A	D	D	B	B	C	C	C	C	B	A	C
14	C	C	B	A	B	B	A	C	B	A	D	B
15	C	D	C	C	D	A	D	C	D	C	C	D
16	B	C	B	B	B	A	B	A	C	B	D	B
17	B	D	C	D	D	B	B	C	D	B	A	A
18	B	C	B	C	B	D	C	B	C	A	B	B
19	B	B	B	B	D	C	D	B	D	B	A	B
20	D	D	C	A	B	C	C	D	D	D	C	B

USING THE CONTEXT

ANSWER KEY — BOOK F

UNITS 13–25

Q \ Unit	13	14	15	16	17	18	19	20	21	22	23	24	25
1	A	D	C	C	D	A	C	B	A	A	B	D	A
2	B	B	C	D	A	B	C	B	B	D	D	B	C
3	C	B	D	A	B	C	B	B	A	A	D	C	A
4	C	C	B	C	A	D	C	B	B	A	B	A	C
5	C	D	C	D	B	C	A	A	D	C	D	D	A
6	D	D	C	D	B	B	A	B	A	A	D	D	C
7	C	C	C	B	C	D	B	C	B	C	D	D	C
8	B	B	B	A	D	C	C	D	B	A	C	A	C
9	C	C	C	B	C	C	D	C	C	C	C	B	D
10	B	D	D	C	A	C	A	B	A	A	B	C	B
11	C	A	D	D	C	B	A	A	C	D	B	B	B
12	B	B	B	B	B	B	B	C	D	B	D	C	B
13	C	B	B	A	D	D	C	D	D	C	B	D	C
14	B	B	C	D	C	D	D	B	B	A	C	B	D
15	A	D	A	B	A	D	B	D	A	A	B	A	B
16	A	B	A	C	B	D	A	C	B	B	D	A	D
17	D	C	A	A	B	A	C	B	C	C	B	D	A
18	C	B	B	C	C	C	B	A	B	B	A	A	D
19	D	A	B	A	C	A	C	A	D	C	B	B	B
20	B	C	C	D	A	A	A	B	C	C	A	A	C

USING THE CONTEXT

ANSWER KEY — BOOK F

UNITS 1–12

Q \ Unit	1	2	3	4	5	6	7	8	9	10	11	12
1	C	A	C	C	C	D	C	D	A	D	C	C
2	D	A	D	A	C	B	B	A	D	D	A	B
3	A	D	D	D	A	A	D	A	C	C	A	A
4	A	D	D	C	A	D	C	D	C	B	B	C
5	D	C	D	D	A	A	B	B	A	C	C	C
6	C	B	D	A	D	C	C	C	A	C	B	B
7	D	B	B	A	B	B	B	B	B	D	C	A
8	C	C	C	D	A	D	B	D	C	C	B	D
9	A	C	A	D	C	C	D	D	B	C	C	D
10	B	D	B	B	A	A	A	C	C	D	B	A
11	B	B	D	C	C	D	C	B	C	A	D	C
12	B	D	D	D	D	C	B	C	B	B	C	D
13	B	D	D	C	C	B	C	D	B	D	D	D
14	B	C	B	A	B	C	B	B	A	B	C	B
15	A	D	A	C	D	A	C	B	A	C	C	A
16	C	C	A	A	B	C	D	A	D	D	B	C
17	B	B	D	B	B	A	A	B	C	D	C	C
18	C	A	C	A	C	B	C	D	D	A	B	D
19	C	D	D	C	B	D	B	D	B	B	B	C
20	B	C	B	D	B	D	B	C	B	C	C	D

— 40 —

USING THE CONTEXT

ANSWER KEY — BOOK G

← UNITS →

	1	2	3	4	5	6	7	8	9	10	11	12
1	C	C	C	C	B	B	D	D	C	A	D	A
2	B	B	A	D	C	A	C	D	B	B	D	D
3	C	A	B	A	C	D	C	D	A	A	A	D
4	D	B	C	A	B	C	B	C	A	B	A	D
5	D	D	D	B	B	C	D	B	D	C	B	B
6	B	A	C	C	A	A	C	D	A	D	B	C
7	B	C	D	B	C	D	D	C	B	A	D	A
8	B	C	D	B	A	B	B	D	C	A	D	A
9	D	D	A	C	D	B	B	C	B	D	D	C
10	D	B	C	D	C	D	A	C	B	C	D	B
11	C	C	A	B	B	A	C	A	C	A	A	A
12	C	C	A	B	A	C	A	B	D	C	C	B
13	C	D	B	B	B	A	A	D	C	B	C	A
14	D	D	C	C	A	D	A	B	B	C	B	B
15	B	B	B	D	D	C	D	A	A	B	D	A
16	B	B	A	B	D	C	D	B	D	C	D	D
17	C	A	A	D	A	A	D	A	C	C	C	C
18	A	D	A	D	B	D	D	D	C	D	B	D
19	B	B	D	B	D	A	B	C	B	C	A	C
20	C	C	C	D	A	B	B	B	C	C	A	B

USING THE CONTEXT

ANSWER KEY — BOOK G

← UNITS →

	13	14	15	16	17	18	19	20	21	22	23	24	25
1	A	B	C	D	D	A	C	C	C	B	B	C	C
2	C	C	C	C	C	D	C	D	B	A	C	A	C
3	B	B	A	D	C	D	B	D	B	B	C	B	A
4	C	C	D	D	C	A	C	D	D	B	B	B	D
5	B	B	D	C	B	B	C	C	C	B	C	A	D
6	D	C	A	B	D	A	C	B	B	C	A	C	C
7	D	D	D	D	D	A	D	C	B	A	D	A	D
8	D	D	D	D	C	C	C	C	A	B	C	B	D
9	D	C	B	A	C	D	C	C	A	A	D	A	C
10	C	A	B	B	B	D	B	B	B	B	A	D	A
11	A	B	C	D	D	B	A	D	A	C	D	B	D
12	C	A	B	C	B	A	C	D	B	D	D	C	D
13	C	B	A	D	D	C	C	D	A	C	A	B	D
14	B	B	C	B	B	C	D	D	C	B	C	A	A
15	B	C	C	C	C	B	B	C	B	C	A	D	C
16	D	C	A	A	D	C	B	B	D	D	B	C	A
17	C	C	C	B	A	B	B	C	B	C	B	C	A
18	C	A	B	C	B	B	C	B	B	C	A	D	A
19	D	A	A	B	B	B	D	C	D	D	A	A	B
20	C	A	D	D	D	D	D	D	C	A	A	C	C

USING THE CONTEXT

ANSWER KEY — BOOK H

— UNITS —

	1	2	3	4	5	6	7	8	9	10	11	12
1	C	C	C	D	B	B	C	B	B	B	A	B
2	B	B	D	C	D	C	C	B	B	C	D	D
3	A	B	B	B	C	B	C	B	A	C	D	B
4	B	C	C	B	C	C	B	A	C	C	D	C
5	B	B	B	B	D	A	C	C	B	B	B	B
6	D	C	C	C	B	D	C	C	B	B	C	D
7	B	B	C	C	C	B	C	C	C	C	C	B
8	C	A	C	B	B	C	D	C	B	D	C	C
9	C	D	C	D	C	C	D	C	C	C	D	C
10	B	D	B	B	C	A	B	B	C	B	C	C
11	B	B	D	C	B	B	A	B	B	A	C	B
12	C	A	A	C	B	B	D	C	C	C	A	D
13	B	C	C	B	B	D	A	A	B	B	B	B
14	D	C	A	A	C	A	B	B	D	C	D	A
15	C	A	C	D	B	D	A	C	C	B	C	B
16	A	C	D	D	B	D	B	C	D	D	D	C
17	B	B	B	D	B	C	B	D	D	D	D	C
18	D	A	D	D	A	B	D	C	C	C	C	C
19	D	B	B	C	D	D	C	D	C	B	A	B
20	B	B	B	B	C	D	D	D	C	C	B	B

USING THE CONTEXT

ANSWER KEY — BOOK H

— UNITS —

	13	14	15	16	17	18	19	20	21	22	23	24	25
1	C	D	D	B	B	D	B	D	B	C	B	A	B
2	A	B	D	C	B	C	C	B	C	C	C	C	D
3	D	C	D	B	C	B	C	D	C	C	C	B	B
4	C	D	D	D	C	D	C	C	B	C	B	B	B
5	C	D	B	B	D	C	D	C	B	D	C	C	C
6	B	C	D	B	C	A	C	B	C	B	B	C	C
7	D	C	B	D	C	B	D	C	B	C	B	C	C
8	C	B	C	C	B	A	A	B	D	B	C	A	D
9	B	B	D	D	D	B	D	B	C	D	D	B	D
10	D	C	C	B	D	B	D	B	C	C	A	B	B
11	D	B	B	B	A	B	B	D	C	D	C	B	B
12	C	B	C	C	B	D	D	D	D	C	A	C	C
13	C	C	C	C	C	D	C	C	C	D	D	B	B
14	B	B	B	C	C	D	C	D	C	B	D	C	B
15	B	C	B	C	C	D	B	C	D	C	C	C	C
16	D	C	C	D	B	B	D	C	D	B	C	C	B
17	D	C	B	C	D	C	D	B	C	D	C	C	D
18	B	C	C	B	B	C	C	B	C	D	C	D	B
19	B	A	B	B	D	B	D	A	B	C	B	C	B
20	C	C	D	C	C	B	C	A	B	C	A	C	C

LOCATING THE ANSWER

UNITS

	1	2	3	4	5	6	7	8	9	10	11	12	13	14	15	16	17	18	19	20	21	22	23	24	25	
1	C	B	A	B	C	A	A	B	C	B	A	B	C	A	B	C	B	A	C	B	A	B	C	B	B	1
2	A	C	C	A	B	B	C	C	A	A	B	C	B	C	A	A	C	C	B	A	B	C	A	A	C	2
3	B	A	B	C	A	C	B	A	B	C	C	A	A	B	C	B	A	B	A	C	C	A	B	C	A	3

LOCATING THE ANSWER

UNITS

	1	2	3	4	5	6	7	8	9	10	11	12	13	14	15	16	17	18	19	20	21	22	23	24	25	
1	B	A	B	B	B	A	A	B	B	A	B	B	A	B	A	B	B	A	B	B	A	B	A	B	B	1
2	A	B	B	A	B	B	A	A	B	B	A	B	B	A	A	A	B	B	A	A	B	B	B	B	A	2

LOCATING THE ANSWER

UNITS

	1	2	3	4	5	6	7	8	9	10	11	12	13	14	15	16	17	18	19	20	21	22	23	24	25	
1	C	B	C	B	A	C	B	B	B	C	B	B	B	C	C	C	A	A	B	B	B	A	B	C	A	1
2	A	C	A	A	C	A	C	A	A	B	B	C	B	C	A	B	B	B	C	A	C	B	B	B	A	2
3	C	A	A	B	C	B	A	C	B	A	C	B	C	B	A	A	B	C	B	A	C	C	C	A	A	3
4	A	A	C	A	C	A	B	B	C	B	B	C	A	B	B	C	C	C	B	C	B	A	C	A	B	4
5	C	B	B	B	C	B	B	B	A	B	B	C	B	A	C	C	B	C	A	A	A	B	C	C	A	5

LOCATING THE ANSWER

ANSWER KEY — BOOK B

UNITS

	1	2	3	4	5	6	7	8	9	10	11	12	13	14	15	16	17	18	19	20	21	22	23	24	25	
1	B	B	C	B	B	C	C	B	A	B	A	C	C	A	A	A	A	B	B	B	B	A	C	C	C	1
2	D	E	E	D	E	F	D	F	D	D	D	D	D	E	F	E	E	F	E	E	F	F	F	E	F	2
3	I	G	H	I	H	I	I	H	H	H	G	H	H	I	H	G	H	I	H	I	G	I	H	G		3
4	L	K	K	J	K	L	K	J	L	L	K	K	L	L	J	L	K	K	J	K	J	L	L	K	L	4
5	O	M	N	M	M	M	N	N	N	O	M	O	N	O	O	O	M	N	N	N	M	M	O	N		5
6	Q	Q	Q	P	R	P	Q	P	Q	R	R	Q	Q	P	R	Q	P	Q	R	Q	P	Q	R	R	Q	6
7	T	T	S	T	U	U	T	T	U	U	U	U	T	T	U	T	S	T	U	T	U	T	U	T	S	7
8	W	V	V	W	V	W	X	W	X	V	V	X	W	W	W	W	W	V	W	W	V	X	V	V	W	8

LOCATING THE ANSWER

ANSWER KEY — BOOK C

UNITS

	1	2	3	4	5	6	7	8	9	10	11	12	13	14	15	16	17	18	19	20	21	22	23	24	25	
1	A	B	B	A	A	A	B	B	A	C	B	C	A	E	A	C	B	B	B	B	C	A	A	B	A	1
2	H	D	D	D	D	D	D	D	E	E	D	F	D	G	C	F	F	E	E	C	E	D	D	D	E	2
3	L	F	E	E	G	F	F	E	F	F	F	F	H	F	H	G	G	I	G	H	F	G	E	E	F	H	3
4	M	I	G	F	H	I	H	G	I	H	H	I	J	J	H	K	K	H	I	G	H	J	G	G	K	4
5	N	L	J	I	I	K	J	J	L	J	K	L	K	K	I	L	L	K	K	I	K	L	K	J	M	5
6	P	M	M	L	K	M	N	M	N	M	N	M	N	O	K	M	N	M	L	M	L	P	L	L	O	6
7	R	N	N	N	M	O	P	N	P	P	O	P	P	R	N	O	P	O	N	N	M	R	P	M	Q	7
8	S	P	Q	R	O	Q	R	P	R	R	S	R	S	T	R	T	R	R	P	S	O	S	Q	O	R	8
9	V	R	R	S	Q	R	U	R	V	V	V	T	U	W	T	U	T	V	R	T	Q	V	S	Q	U	9
10	Z	U	U	Y	T	V	W	T	X	X	W	U	W	Z	W	W	Y	X	S	U	Y	X	X	U	W	10

— 44 —

LOCATING THE ANSWER

UNITS

	1	2	3	4	5	6	7	8	9	10	11	12	13	14	15	16	17	18	19	20	21	22	23	24	25	
1	B	B	D	B	A	C	B	B	C	C	A	B	B	A	D	B	B	B	C	C	B	D	A	A	A	1
2	F	C	G	G	B	E	E	E	E	F	B	C	C	B	E	E	G	C	D	D	D	G	D	C	E	2
3	K	F	I	H	F	F	H	I	J	K	G	E	E	D	G	K	I	F	H	F	F	H	E	E	F	3
4	L	G	K	J	G	I	J	J	L	L	I	I	H	H	H	L	M	I	J	H	J	K	I	G	G	4
5	N	L	M	K	I	J	N	K	P	N	M	K	K	K	O	N	N	K	J	K	M	K	J	K		5
6	O	P	O	P	K	N	P	L	Q	O	N	O	L	L	M	Q	P	P	M	M	P	Q	L	N	M	6
7	R	R	Q	S	N	R	R	N	S	P	P	Q	O	N	Q	R	S	Q	O	N	R	S	N	O	P	7
8	T	U	S	U	S	T	S	P	V	R	T	T	Q	S	U	S	T	U	R	S	T	T	S	R	R	8
9	U	W	T	X	U	V	W	R	X	U	U	U	U	V	W	W	W	V	V	S	W	U	V	W	T	U	9
10	X	X	W	Z	Y	X	Z	V	Z	W	Y	Z	X	Z	Z	Y	Y	Y	Z	Y	Y	Z	X	Z	Z	10

LOCATING THE ANSWER

UNITS

	1	2	3	4	5	6	7	8	9	10	11	12	13	14	15	16	17	18	19	20	21	22	23	24	25	
1	2	3	4	2	1	1	1	1	2	3	5	1	3	1	1	5	1	2	2	2	2	1	2	3	3	1
2	6	5	8	5	8	7	7	5	5	6	8	7	7	7	6	9	6	8	7	4	6	6	7	4	5	2
3	7	8	11	11	10	11	10	9	10	9	11	10	9	9	7	11	8	9	12	11	10	9	8	7	10	3
4	14	11	16	15	13	12	12	14	12	12	15	14	10	12	10	17	14	13	14	12	13	11	11	11	12	4
5	16	15	17	17	17	17	15	16	18	17	20	15	14	16	14	21	16	15	17	18	16	15	16	15	16	5
6	18	18	23	21	19	18	19	18	20	21	24	17	16	17	20	26	20	19	20	20	18	20	21	19	19	6
7	22	24	24	24	23	25	22	21	22	23	27	22	23	20	23	28	23	25	26	24	24	25	23	21	21	7
8	26	26	29	26	26	30	23	23	27	26	31	26	24	22	27	34	30	27	28	27	27	29	27	24	24	8
9	27	32	34	34	30	34	29	27	31	28	36	29	28	29	30	37	31	34	32	34	31	30	28	28	32	9
10	30	35	40	38	37	36	32	36	38	35	42	34	32	36	33	41	36	37	36	36	34	31	33	33	34	10

LOCATING THE ANSWER

UNITS

	1	2	3	4	5	6	7	8	9	10	11	12	13	14	15	16	17	18	19	20	21	22	23	24	25	
1	3	2	2	2	1	1	1	2	3	2	1	2	5	3	2	1	2	3	3	3	3	2	1	3	5	1
2	5	7	8	6	8	5	5	6	8	5	7	9	6	8	6	6	7	6	6	4	5	8	6	10	7	2
3	8	8	9	11	12	12	11	12	9	11	8	12	9	10	10	10	11	7	9	9	9	10	9	11	8	3
4	13	15	15	12	15	15	13	15	15	13	15	15	14	13	13	15	12	13	14	14	10	11	12	13	13	4
5	16	18	21	18	18	19	15	17	19	17	16	19	15	17	19	18	17	18	19	17	13	17	18	19	18	5
6	20	19	24	22	22	21	20	22	23	18	18	22	18	19	23	19	18	19	22	20	16	19	25	22	19	6
7	24	21	25	25	29	23	21	26	26	21	24	27	24	28	26	24	20	22	29	22	18	23	28	23	21	7
8	27	27	29	32	34	28	26	29	29	25	27	30	26	29	34	26	24	24	30	25	22	26	31	28	24	8
9	29	28	33	34	36	35	31	31	30	29	28	31	28	33	36	28	27	31	31	28	29	28	36	36	27	9
10	30	32	36	36	41	39	33	36	32	32	32	35	31	35	38	32	30	34	38	33	31	31	40	39	32	10

LOCATING THE ANSWER

UNITS

	1	2	3	4	5	6	7	8	9	10	11	12	13	14	15	16	17	18	19	20	21	22	23	24	25	
1	2	5	6	5	2	2	3	1	2	7	5	4	4	4	3	2	2	4	2	3	4	2	5	1	2	1
2	8	8	10	11	5	5	4	5	9	8	8	5	13	11	6	6	6	10	7	11	8	8	9	5	3	2
3	15	11	11	13	10	6	10	9	14	12	10	9	17	13	9	7	7	11	8	15	9	13	12	10	7	3
4	18	12	14	20	13	8	12	12	17	13	16	12	18	15	13	16	8	13	10	20	11	16	15	11	10	4
5	21	15	19	24	17	13	15	13	27	14	18	14	22	17	14	18	16	15	11	21	13	20	16	16	13	5
6	22	24	20	26	19	14	20	19	28	21	20	19	26	21	18	20	19	20	16	22	16	22	20	22	19	6
7	27	27	23	28	25	15	24	21	33	24	25	21	29	22	23	22	21	31	20	28	21	23	24	23	25	7
8	30	30	26	30	27	19	25	30	35	26	34	25	35	29	31	28	27	32	23	34	24	28	27	28	26	8
9	33	31	27	32	34	22	31	31	37	31	39	31	39	34	34	29	30	33	28	37	28	35	30	30	35	9
10	35	33	31	36	37	29	36	35	38	33	41	38	40	36	39	31	37	40	33	39	29	36	34	32	38	10

LOCATING THE ANSWER

ANSWER KEY — BOOK H

UNITS

	1	2	3	4	5	6	7	8	9	10	11	12	13	14	15	16	17	18	19	20	21	22	23	24	25	
1	2	1	3	3	3	4	1	3	1	3	1	1	1	4	2	2	3	2	4	3	4	2	1	3	1	1
2	7	7	6	5	11	6	6	8	6	7	9	6	5	9	7	7	6	8	5	10	7	9	4	5	5	2
3	12	9	10	10	15	12	9	10	11	13	11	10	7	12	10	12	8	9	10	12	9	12	6	9	11	3
4	14	10	15	16	21	14	12	12	14	16	16	16	9	16	17	16	12	16	11	16	11	17	10	12	15	4
5	19	15	17	18	23	18	15	13	18	20	19	18	14	20	20	22	17	17	14	23	15	22	13	18	20	5
6	22	19	23	25	28	23	19	19	22	25	23	25	16	24	22	28	24	22	17	27	22	27	17	20	23	6
7	25	20	29	27	33	26	26	23	25	28	26	27	25	26	26	31	29	29	26	32	25	33	21	23	26	7
8	31	31	31	33	34	32	31	29	28	31	32	30	29	31	30	36	30	31	31	34	27	37	25	34	34	8
9	36	38	37	34	38	35	35	30	32	35	35	32	33	37	35	39	33	38	34	38	34	38	30	39	37	9
10	39	42	40	39	41	38	39	41	37	39	41	39	38	38	38	40	36	42	42	42	40	41	38	42	42	10

GETTING THE FACTS

ANSWER KEY — PICTURE LEVEL

UNITS

	1	2	3	4	5	6	7	8	9	10	11	12	13	14	15	16	17	18	19	20	21	22	23	24	25	
1	A	B	B	A	A	B	B	A	B	A	A	B	B	A	B	A	B	A	B	B	A	B	A	A	B	1
2	B	B	A	A	B	B	A	B	B	A	B	B	A	B	A	B	A	B	A	A	B	B	B	B	B	2
3	A	A	B	B	B	A	B	A	B	B	A	A	B	B	A	B	B	B	A	B	A	B	B	A	B	3

GETTING THE FACTS

UNITS	1	2	3	4	5	6	7	8	9	10	11	12	13	14	15	16	17	18	19	20	21	22	23	24	25	
1	A	A	B	B	B	B	A	A	B	A	B	B	A	A	B	A	B	B	A	B	A	B	B	A	B	1
2	B	B	B	B	A	B	A	B	A	B	B	A	B	B	A	A	A	B	B	A	B	A	B	B	A	2
3	B	A	A	A	B	A	B	A	A	B	B	B	A	B	B	B	B	A	A	B	B	B	A	A	B	3

GETTING THE FACTS

UNITS	1	2	3	4	5	6	7	8	9	10	11	12	13	14	15	16	17	18	19	20	21	22	23	24	25	
1	B	A	C	C	B	A	C	C	C	C	C	B	B	C	B	A	C	B	C	B	B	C	B	C	C	1
2	C	A	C	C	C	C	B	B	B	A	B	B	C	C	C	B	B	B	A	B	B	A	C	C	A	2
3	A	C	C	A	A	A	A	C	A	B	A	A	B	B	A	C	A	C	B	A	A	B	A	B	C	3
4	A	B	A	C	A	A	C	A	B	C	C	B	A	B	A	C	C	A	C	A	C	B	B	C	C	4
5	B	A	A	C	C	C	B	B	C	C	B	C	B	B	B	A	A	C	A	B	A	C	C	A	B	5

GETTING THE FACTS

UNITS	1	2	3	4	5	6	7	8	9	10	11	12	13	14	15	16	17	18	19	20	21	22	23	24	25	
1	C	B	C	C	B	C	A	A	A	A	C	B	C	C	C	C	A	C	A	B	A	C	C	C	B	1
2	C	C	C	C	C	C	A	C	C	A	B	B	B	B	C	B	A	B	C	C	C	B	A	B	A	2
3	C	B	B	A	B	C	B	A	B	B	B	C	A	A	A	C	C	A	A	B	A	A	A	A	C	3
4	B	B	A	B	C	B	A	B	B	A	A	B	B	B	C	A	A	C	C	B	C	C	B	C	B	4
5	A	A	B	C	B	A	B	B	B	B	B	C	C	A	C	A	B	C	A	B	B	A	A	A	C	5

GETTING THE FACTS

UNITS

	1	2	3	4	5	6	7	8	9	10	11	12	13	14	15	16	17	18	19	20	21	22	23	24	25	
1	A	B	C	B	B	B	B	A	B	C	B	C	B	C	B	B	C	B	B	C	C	C	C	B	B	**1**
2	B	A	A	A	A	C	B	B	B	A	A	B	C	C	A	B	B	C	C	B	B	A	B	A	C	**2**
3	C	B	C	C	A	C	A	C	A	C	C	B	A	B	B	A	B	C	B	B	B	C	B	C	A	**3**
4	A	A	B	B	B	B	B	A	A	A	B	B	C	C	C	C	B	A	A	A	A	C	B	B	B	**4**
5	A	B	B	A	C	A	C	B	A	B	B	C	C	B	A	B	C	B	C	B	A	C	C	B	C	**5**
6	B	C	A	C	C	A	A	C	B	B	A	A	B	A	B	B	A	A	B	A	C	B	A	B	C	**6**
7	A	A	C	B	B	B	B	B	C	C	B	A	A	A	A	B	A	C	A	C	B	C	A	C	B	**7**
8	B	B	B	A	A	C	A	B	B	A	B	C	B	C	A	A	C	C	B	C	B	C	A	B	A	**8**

GETTING THE FACTS

UNITS

	1	2	3	4	5	6	7	8	9	10	11	12	13	14	15	16	17	18	19	20	21	22	23	24	25	
1	B	A	C	A	C	C	B	C	A	C	B	C	B	B	A	C	B	B	B	C	B	B	C	B	A	**1**
2	A	B	B	B	A	B	C	A	C	A	B	A	A	C	C	C	C	A	A	B	C	C	C	B	B	**2**
3	C	B	A	A	C	C	C	B	B	C	A	C	C	B	B	A	B	C	C	A	B	A	B	A	A	**3**
4	B	C	B	B	C	A	A	B	C	B	C	C	C	C	A	A	A	A	B	B	A	C	B	B	C	**4**
5	C	A	C	C	B	B	C	C	B	B	B	C	C	C	A	B	A	C	C	A	C	B	A	A	A	**5**
6	C	A	A	B	C	A	A	C	A	B	C	A	C	C	A	A	A	C	B	C	B	B	B	C	C	**6**
7	B	B	A	B	A	B	A	A	B	A	A	C	B	B	A	A	C	C	C	B	A	A	C	C	B	**7**
8	C	A	A	A	C	A	C	B	C	B	A	B	A	C	B	C	C	A	A	A	C	A	A	C	B	**8**
9	A	A	B	C	B	B	C	C	C	C	C	C	C	B	A	B	A	A	C	B	B	C	A	B	A	**9**
10	B	B	C	B	A	A	B	A	B	B	B	B	A	B	B	B	C	B	C	A	A	C	B	A	C	**10**

GETTING THE FACTS

UNITS	1	2	3	4	5	6	7	8	9	10	11	12	13	14	15	16	17	18	19	20	21	22	23	24	25	
1	C	C	C	C	B	A	B	C	D	A	C	C	A	D	C	D	D	D	C	D	B	C	A	B	C	1
2	D	D	A	B	C	C	C	D	D	A	D	A	A	C	C	D	A	D	C	D	B	D	B	B	B	2
3	A	B	D	A	D	D	C	B	B	C	D	D	D	D	B	C	C	B	C	D	A	D	D	D	D	3
4	C	D	C	D	A	C	D	D	A	D	D	D	D	A	A	B	D	D	B	C	C	C	C	D	D	4
5	D	A	D	C	C	C	A	C	D	C	C	C	B	D	D	D	B	C	A	D	C	C	D	C	A	5
6	D	B	D	A	D	B	C	D	D	B	D	B	C	C	A	C	C	D	D	A	D	D	C	D	D	6
7	C	D	B	D	D	D	C	C	C	A	A	D	D	D	D	D	A	C	A	D	B	A	B	B	C	7
8	B	C	C	C	C	A	D	D	D	D	B	A	A	B	C	A	D	D	D	A	D	B	D	C	B	8
9	D	B	D	D	B	D	A	D	C	C	C	D	D	C	D	D	C	B	C	C	D	C	D	D	D	9
10	D	A	A	D	D	D	D	C	B	D	C	D	D	D	B	B	D	D	D	D	C	D	D	C	D	10

GETTING THE FACTS

UNITS	1	2	3	4	5	6	7	8	9	10	11	12	13	14	15	16	17	18	19	20	21	22	23	24	25	
1	D	B	D	D	D	D	C	D	D	C	C	D	C	B	A	B	C	C	C	D	C	B	B	C	C	1
2	A	D	A	A	C	A	B	D	A	D	A	C	D	C	C	D	B	D	B	B	D	D	A	D	B	2
3	B	A	A	B	D	B	A	C	B	B	D	A	B	A	A	A	D	A	C	C	B	C	D	D	A	3
4	C	A	B	C	A	D	A	D	D	A	B	D	A	C	D	D	A	D	D	D	A	C	C	C	C	4
5	B	D	A	C	B	C	D	A	B	D	C	D	B	D	D	C	C	C	A	D	D	D	B	B	C	5
6	D	A	B	D	D	B	B	D	B	B	D	C	B	C	C	A	B	C	B	A	C	B	C	D	A	6
7	C	B	D	B	A	D	B	D	B	C	B	B	C	A	A	D	C	D	C	A	D	D	D	D	C	7
8	A	A	A	D	D	D	B	B	D	D	A	D	A	B	D	C	B	B	A	C	A	A	B	C	D	8
9	D	B	B	C	C	B	D	B	C	A	B	A	A	D	A	D	D	D	B	D	D	D	A	A	D	9
10	D	A	D	D	D	B	A	D	C	C	C	D	D	B	B	D	B	C	D	C	D	D	A	D	B	10

GETTING THE FACTS

UNITS

	1	2	3	4	5	6	7	8	9	10	11	12	13	14	15	16	17	18	19	20	21	22	23	24	25	
1	D	B	D	C	C	C	B	D	B	C	D	A	A	D	A	A	C	A	B	A	C	A	B	C	D	1
2	A	D	C	D	D	D	C	C	C	C	D	C	B	D	D	C	D	D	D	A	C	D	D	D	C	2
3	C	C	A	B	A	B	A	A	D	A	B	D	C	A	D	C	B	D	B	A	A	B	C	B	B	3
4	B	D	D	D	B	B	C	D	A	B	A	C	B	C	D	A	C	C	D	D	D	D	A	D	D	4
5	D	B	C	C	D	A	B	C	D	B	D	B	D	D	C	B	A	B	C	B	A	C	D	D	A	5
6	C	A	B	A	D	A	D	B	B	C	B	C	C	B	B	C	D	C	C	D	C	C	C	A	C	6
7	A	D	C	D	C	D	C	C	C	D	C	D	D	C	A	C	C	B	D	C	D	D	B	C	B	7
8	D	B	B	B	C	C	A	D	C	D	C	B	B	B	B	D	D	D	D	B	C	D	B	D	C	8
9	B	C	B	D	D	D	D	A	A	B	B	A	C	B	C	B	B	A	C	D	D	C	D	D	D	9
10	D	D	D	B	B	D	C	D	D	C	D	D	D	C	D	D	C	C	D	D	D	C	D	C	A	10

GETTING THE FACTS

UNITS

	1	2	3	4	5	6	7	8	9	10	11	12	13	14	15	16	17	18	19	20	21	22	23	24	25	
1	C	C	C	C	D	D	D	D	B	B	D	C	D	B	C	C	C	D	B	C	B	B	A	C	C	1
2	B	B	D	B	A	C	C	C	D	D	D	D	C	D	D	B	B	C	D	D	C	C	D	D	B	2
3	C	D	B	D	B	B	B	B	C	C	C	B	B	D	C	A	D	D	D	A	C	D	B	B	A	3
4	A	C	C	C	D	A	D	D	A	B	A	A	A	C	B	D	C	D	C	B	B	B	C	A	A	4
5	D	A	D	B	C	A	C	A	D	D	B	D	A	D	A	C	B	C	A	C	B	A	D	D	B	5
6	B	D	B	D	B	D	B	B	C	C	C	C	D	A	D	B	C	A	D	D	A	D	A	C	C	6
7	A	D	C	C	C	C	D	C	B	C	D	D	D	C	B	D	D	B	C	A	D	C	C	B	D	7
8	C	B	D	B	C	D	C	D	A	D	B	B	C	B	D	D	C	C	B	D	C	D	D	D	B	8
9	D	D	C	C	D	B	D	D	D	B	D	A	B	A	A	C	B	D	D	B	A	C	C	C	D	9
10	C	C	B	D	B	D	B	A	D	C	A	D	C	D	D	B	D	D	C	C	C	D	B	D	C	10

GETTING THE MAIN IDEA

ANSWER KEY — PICTURE LEVEL

← —————————————————————— UNITS —————————————————————— →

	1	2	3	4	5	6	7	8	9	10	11	12	13	14	15	16	17	18	19	20	21	22	23	24	25	
1	B	B	A	B	A	B	A	A	B	B	A	B	B	A	B	A	A	B	A	B	A	B	B	B	A	1

	26	27	28	29	30	31	32	33	34	35	36	37	38	39	40	41	42	43	44	45	46	47	48	49	50	
1	B	A	B	B	B	A	B	A	B	B	A	A	B	A	B	B	B	A	B	A	A	B	A	B	A	1

GETTING THE MAIN IDEA

ANSWER KEY — PREPARATORY LEVEL

← —————————————————————— UNITS —————————————————————— →

	1	2	3	4	5	6	7	8	9	10	11	12	13	14	15	16	17	18	19	20	21	22	23	24	25	
1	B	B	A	B	A	B	B	A	A	B	B	B	B	B	A	B	B	A	A	B	B	A	B	A	A	1

	26	27	28	29	30	31	32	33	34	35	36	37	38	39	40	41	42	43	44	45	46	47	48	49	50	
1	A	B	A	B	B	A	B	A	A	B	A	B	B	A	B	B	A	A	B	A	B	B	A	B	B	1

GETTING THE MAIN IDEA

ANSWER KEY — BOOK A

← —————————————————————— UNITS —————————————————————— →

	1	2	3	4	5	6	7	8	9	10	11	12	13	14	15	16	17	18	19	20	21	22	23	24	25	
1	C	B	C	B	C	C	B	B	B	C	B	C	A	C	A	B	C	B	B	A	C	A	B	C	B	1

	26	27	28	29	30	31	32	33	34	35	36	37	38	39	40	41	42	43	44	45	46	47	48	49	50	
1	C	B	C	C	A	A	A	C	A	A	A	B	C	A	A	B	C	A	A	A	B	B	C	A	A	1

GETTING THE MAIN IDEA

ANSWER KEY — BOOK B

← —————————————————————— UNITS —————————————————————— →

	1	2	3	4	5	6	7	8	9	10	11	12	13	14	15	16	17	18	19	20	21	22	23	24	25	
1	A	C	A	B	C	A	B	A	A	B	B	B	C	B	C	A	B	B	B	B	A	A	B	B	A	1
2	C	C	B	B	B	A	B	B	C	C	B	A	B	A	C	B	C	C	B	B	B	C	C	C	B	2
3	B	B	B	B	C	C	B	C	B	C	B	C	B	B	B	B	B	C	C	C	C	B	B	C	C	3
4	A	A	C	C	B	B	C	A	B	B	B	C	C	A	C	C	A	C	B	C	A	C	A	B	C	4

GETTING THE MAIN IDEA

UNITS

	1	2	3	4	5	6	7	8	9	10	11	12	13	14	15	16	17	18	19	20	21	22	23	24	25	
1	A	B	A	B	B	B	A	B	B	A	A	B	C	C	C	B	B	B	B	A	B	B	A	C	A	1
2	A	A	A	C	C	B	C	A	A	C	A	B	B	B	C	A	C	B	B	C	C	C	C	C	B	2
3	B	C	A	A	A	B	A	A	C	A	A	A	B	B	C	A	B	C	C	A	B	B	A	B	C	3
4	A	A	A	C	B	A	A	A	C	A	C	A	A	A	B	B	C	C	A	B	B	A	A	A	B	4
5	C	B	C	A	A	C	B	B	C	A	B	B	C	A	A	C	C	C	C	C	B	C	C	B	C	5

GETTING THE MAIN IDEA

UNITS

	1	2	3	4	5	6	7	8	9	10	11	12	13	14	15	16	17	18	19	20	21	22	23	24	25	
1	C	B	C	B	B	B	C	A	C	A	A	C	C	A	A	B	C	B	A	C	C	B	B	C	B	1
2	B	B	A	B	C	C	B	C	B	C	A	C	A	A	C	A	C	C	B	A	C	A	C	C	A	2
3	B	C	C	B	C	B	C	B	A	B	C	C	C	B	A	C	B	A	B	A	C	A	C	C	B	3
4	B	C	C	B	A	C	B	B	C	B	C	B	A	A	C	C	B	B	C	A	C	C	B	B	C	4
5	B	A	C	C	A	B	A	C	B	C	A	B	C	B	B	C	B	C	C	B	A	C	B	B	B	5

GETTING THE MAIN IDEA

UNITS

	1	2	3	4	5	6	7	8	9	10	11	12	13	14	15	16	17	18	19	20	21	22	23	24	25	
1	A	D	B	B	A	D	B	D	B	D	D	D	B	C	A	D	C	C	D	D	B	B	D	A	D	1
2	C	B	A	B	B	C	D	C	C	B	B	B	B	C	B	B	A	A	B	B	C	B	D	D	D	2
3	D	C	D	A	D	C	A	C	C	C	B	A	C	A	C	B	B	C	C	D	D	C	D	A	D	3
4	B	D	C	A	D	A	D	B	B	C	D	D	C	D	D	A	A	D	A	B	D	C	A	B	B	4
5	B	D	A	C	B	B	A	B	C	C	A	C	A	D	C	B	D	C	C	A	D	B	D	C	C	5

GETTING THE MAIN IDEA

UNITS

	1	2	3	4	5	6	7	8	9	10	11	12	13	14	15	16	17	18	19	20	21	22	23	24	25	
1	D	C	C	C	C	C	D	D	B	C	C	C	D	B	C	B	B	C	C	C	D	C	C	D	C	1
2	B	D	C	B	D	B	B	B	D	C	D	D	D	C	C	D	C	B	C	D	D	C	C	B	C	2
3	A	B	B	C	B	B	D	C	B	C	A	D	D	B	C	D	C	C	D	D	D	C	D	A	D	3
4	C	A	C	D	C	C	C	A	C	D	D	A	D	C	C	D	C	A	C	D	A	D	C	D	A	4
5	D	D	C	D	C	D	C	A	C	C	B	B	B	D	B	B	B	C	A	D	A	B	B	C	C	5

GETTING THE MAIN IDEA

	UNITS																									
	1	2	3	4	5	6	7	8	9	10	11	12	13	14	15	16	17	18	19	20	21	22	23	24	25	
1	D	D	C	C	B	B	A	B	B	D	A	D	D	D	B	D	C	A	D	B	B	C	D	D	B	1
2	A	B	D	C	B	B	A	C	D	A	C	B	B	B	B	C	C	C	D	B	A	B	D	A	D	2
3	D	C	C	C	C	B	D	B	C	C	A	C	B	C	B	C	B	A	D	B	C	A	B	B	C	3
4	C	B	B	C	A	C	C	A	B	B	C	C	D	B	A	B	A	C	C	D	C	C	D	D	A	4
5	A	D	D	A	A	C	D	B	A	C	C	B	A	A	A	D	D	C	A	A	C	C	D	C	C	5

GETTING THE MAIN IDEA

	UNITS																									
	1	2	3	4	5	6	7	8	9	10	11	12	13	14	15	16	17	18	19	20	21	22	23	24	25	
1	A	C	C	B	C	C	A	B	B	B	B	C	D	D	C	A	B	B	C	C	A	A	A	B	C	1
2	B	B	C	C	B	B	D	C	C	B	C	B	A	A	D	C	A	D	B	C	B	C	C	C	B	2
3	D	C	A	A	A	C	C	A	B	A	B	B	C	B	C	C	D	B	D	B	D	D	D	B	C	3
4	C	B	C	A	B	D	B	A	B	B	A	D	A	C	B	A	D	C	C	A	A	B	A	B	D	4
5	B	B	C	B	B	A	C	C	A	A	A	A	D	D	C	C	C	A	D	A	A	D	B	A	C	5

DRAWING CONCLUSIONS

UNITS

	1	2	3	4	5	6	7	8	9	10	11	12	13	14	15	16	17	18	19	20	21	22	23	24	25	
1	B	A	B	B	A	B	A	A	B	B	A	B	A	B	B	A	B	A	B	A	A	B	B	A	B	1

	26	27	28	29	30	31	32	33	34	35	36	37	38	39	40	41	42	43	44	45	46	47	48	49	50	
1	B	A	A	B	B	B	A	B	B	A	A	B	A	B	A	B	B	A	A	B	A	B	B	B	B	1

DRAWING CONCLUSIONS

UNITS

	1	2	3	4	5	6	7	8	9	10	11	12	13	14	15	16	17	18	19	20	21	22	23	24	25	
1	B	B	B	B	A	B	A	A	B	A	B	B	B	A	B	B	B	B	A	B	A	A	B	A	B	1

	26	27	28	29	30	31	32	33	34	35	36	37	38	39	40	41	42	43	44	45	46	47	48	49	50	
1	A	B	A	A	B	A	B	B	A	B	B	A	B	A	A	B	B	A	B	B	A	B	A	A	B	1

DRAWING CONCLUSIONS

UNITS

	1	2	3	4	5	6	7	8	9	10	11	12	13	14	15	16	17	18	19	20	21	22	23	24	25	
1	C	A	A	A	A	C	A	C	A	A	A	C	C	B	C	A	A	B	C	C	B	B	C	A	C	1

	26	27	28	29	30	31	32	33	34	35	36	37	38	39	40	41	42	43	44	45	46	47	48	49	50	
1	B	C	C	A	A	C	A	A	C	B	C	C	C	A	C	C	C	A	C	B	A	C	C	A	A	1

DRAWING CONCLUSIONS

UNITS

	1	2	3	4	5	6	7	8	9	10	11	12	13	14	15	16	17	18	19	20	21	22	23	24	25	
1	C	C	B	C	B	C	B	B	B	B	B	C	B	C	C	A	C	A	B	B	B	C	B	C	B	1
2	B	B	C	B	C	C	A	C	B	C	C	A	B	A	B	C	B	A	C	A	C	A	A	A	C	2
3	A	B	B	A	B	A	B	B	C	B	B	B	A	B	B	A	A	C	A	A	C	B	A	C	C	3
4	B	A	A	B	A	C	A	B	B	C	C	B	A	A	B	B	C	B	B	B	B	A	B	B	A	4

DRAWING CONCLUSIONS

ANSWER KEY — BOOK C

	UNITS																									
	1	2	3	4	5	6	7	8	9	10	11	12	13	14	15	16	17	18	19	20	21	22	23	24	25	
1	B	A	C	C	B	A	B	C	C	B	A	A	C	B	B	B	C	B	A	C	B	C	A	B	C	1
2	B	A	B	C	B	B	A	A	A	A	B	B	A	A	B	A	C	C	B	B	C	C	A	A	C	2
3	C	B	C	C	C	B	B	A	B	C	C	C	C	B	A	B	C	B	A	C	B	A	C	B	C	3
4	A	C	A	C	A	A	B	B	B	C	B	C	B	C	C	B	B	C	B	C	B	C	C	A	C	4
5	B	B	B	C	C	A	A	C	B	A	C	B	A	B	C	B	C	B	B	A	C	C	B	B	A	5

DRAWING CONCLUSIONS

ANSWER KEY — BOOK D

	UNITS																									
	1	2	3	4	5	6	7	8	9	10	11	12	13	14	15	16	17	18	19	20	21	22	23	24	25	
1	C	C	B	A	A	B	A	A	A	A	C	B	C	B	C	C	B	C	B	C	B	C	A	B	A	1
2	B	B	B	C	C	B	C	B	B	C	C	C	B	C	A	C	C	C	C	B	B	B	A	C	B	2
3	C	A	B	C	B	C	B	B	B	C	B	C	C	C	B	C	B	C	B	C	B	C	B	C	A	3
4	C	B	C	A	B	B	B	C	C	B	C	C	C	C	C	C	B	B	C	A	C	C	B	B	C	4
5	A	B	B	B	B	B	B	B	C	C	B	B	C	B	B	A	B	C	C	C	B	B	B	C	C	5

— 57 —

	1	2	3	4	5	6	7	8	9	10	11	12	13	14	15	16	17	18	19	20	21	22	23	24	25	
1	D	B	B	B	B	A	A	D	C	D	C	C	D	B	D	B	C	B	D	C	B	B	D	C	C	**1**
2	D	D	B	A	B	B	A	A	C	B	C	B	C	B	C	C	C	D	C	D	C	B	D	C	C	**2**
3	C	B	A	C	B	A	A	C	C	C	A	B	C	D	B	B	A	C	C	D	B	C	C	D	D	**3**
4	A	B	B	B	D	D	B	A	A	C	C	B	A	C	C	C	C	D	A	A	C	C	A	C	B	**4**
5	C	D	B	B	C	C	C	C	B	B	A	C	B	C	B	A	D	D	B	C	A	B	B	C	B	**5**

	1	2	3	4	5	6	7	8	9	10	11	12	13	14	15	16	17	18	19	20	21	22	23	24	25	
1	C	D	C	B	C	D	C	B	B	C	B	C	C	C	A	D	C	C	A	D	B	D	C	B	B	**1**
2	B	D	B	B	A	B	B	D	D	B	C	D	A	A	D	B	D	A	B	B	A	C	C	C	D	**2**
3	B	C	C	B	A	C	A	A	A	C	D	B	B	D	B	C	C	D	C	C	D	B	B	B	C	**3**
4	D	A	B	C	A	C	B	B	C	C	A	D	C	C	C	B	D	C	B	D	C	C	C	C	D	**4**
5	D	B	B	D	A	A	B	D	B	A	D	B	D	C	D	C	C	B	B	D	D	A	D	B	A	**5**

DRAWING CONCLUSIONS

UNITS

	1	2	3	4	5	6	7	8	9	10	11	12	13	14	15	16	17	18	19	20	21	22	23	24	25	
1	B	B	C	D	A	B	A	A	C	C	B	B	C	C	C	C	D	C	B	C	D	D	C	B	D	1
2	D	C	C	C	C	A	A	B	A	D	C	C	C	B	C	C	A	C	B	C	A	B	B	C	C	2
3	B	D	A	C	A	B	D	C	C	B	D	D	C	D	C	D	B	B	B	D	D	B	D	C	D	3
4	B	A	A	A	A	B	C	D	D	D	D	A	D	B	B	C	D	B	C	C	C	C	A	D	C	4
5	C	C	C	C	C	D	C	A	B	A	A	A	C	B	C	A	A	B	B	C	A	C	C	C	B	5

DRAWING CONCLUSIONS

UNITS

	1	2	3	4	5	6	7	8	9	10	11	12	13	14	15	16	17	18	19	20	21	22	23	24	25	
1	D	B	B	B	C	C	B	D	B	C	C	C	A	C	D	B	A	D	B	B	B	C	B	C	B	1
2	D	B	D	C	A	B	D	D	C	D	C	C	B	D	A	C	D	C	A	A	D	B	B	B	C	2
3	B	C	C	C	C	A	B	C	C	D	C	B	B	C	C	B	D	D	B	B	B	C	A	B	B	3
4	A	C	B	C	C	B	A	C	C	C	C	C	D	B	B	B	C	D	D	D	B	C	C	D	B	4
5	C	A	C	A	C	A	B	C	B	B	D	B	B	B	B	D	B	A	C	C	C	B	D	B	B	5

— 59 —

DETECTING THE SEQUENCE

UNITS

1	2	3	4	5	6	7	8	9	10	11	12	13	14	15	16	17	18	19	20	21	22	23	24	25
B	A	B	B	B	A	B	A	B	B	B	B	A	B	B	B	A	A	B	A	B	B	B	A	A

DETECTING THE SEQUENCE

UNITS

1	2	3	4	5	6	7	8	9	10	11	12	13	14	15	16	17	18	19	20	21	22	23	24	25
B	A	B	B	A	B	A	B	B	A	A	B	A	B	B	A	B	A	A	B	B	A	B	B	A

DETECTING THE SEQUENCE

UNITS

1	2	3	4	5	6	7	8	9	10	11	12	13	14	15	16	17	18	19	20	21	22	23	24	25
T	F	F	F	T	F	T	T	T	T	F	F	T	T	T	F	T	T	T	F	T	T	T	T	F

DETECTING THE SEQUENCE

UNITS

1	2	3	4	5	6	7	8	9	10	11	12	13	14	15	16	17	18	19	20	21	22	23	24	25
C	A	B	C	B	A	C	B	A	C	B	C	C	B	C	A	A	B	B	C	A	B	C	A	A

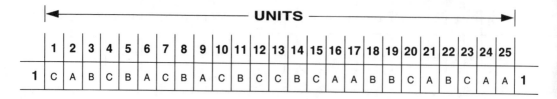

DETECTING THE SEQUENCE

UNITS

	1	2	3	4	5	6	7	8	9	10	11	12	13	14	15	16	17	18	19	20	21	22	23	24	25	
1	F	F	T	T	F	T	F	T	T	F	T	T	F	F	T	T	T	T	F	F	F	F	F	F	T	1

DETECTING THE SEQUENCE

UNITS

	1	2	3	4	5	6	7	8	9	10	11	12	13	14	15	16	17	18	19	20	21	22	23	24	25	
1	C	B	A	C	B	A	B	B	C	C	B	A	C	A	C	B	B	B	C	C	C	B	B	B	A	1
2	B	A	C	A	C	C	B	A	B	B	C	B	C	B	C	C	A	A	A	B	B	A	C	B	C	2

	26	27	28	29	30	31	32	33	34	35	36	37	38	39	40	41	42	43	44	45	46	47	48	49	50	
1	B	C	C	C	A	A	C	B	C	C	C	A	C	B	B	B	B	C	A	C	C	B	B	B	C	1
2	B	A	A	A	C	B	A	C	A	A	A	B	A	A	C	C	B	B	B	B	A	C	A	A	B	2

DETECTING THE SEQUENCE

UNITS

	1	2	3	4	5	6	7	8	9	10	11	12	13	14	15	16	17	18	19	20	21	22	23	24	25	
1	T	F	T	F	F	F	F	T	F	F	T	T	T	T	F	F	F	T	F	T	F	T	T	T	F	1

DETECTING THE SEQUENCE

← —————————————————— UNITS —————————————————— →

	1	2	3	4	5	6	7	8	9	10	11	12	13	14	15	16	17	18	19	20	21	22	23	24	25	
1	C	A	B	B	B	B	B	C	B	C	C	B	C	B	B	B	B	C	C	A	B	B	C	B	B	1
2	A	A	B	C	A	B	A	A	C	B	C	B	A	B	A	C	C	B	B	B	A	C	B	B	A	2
3	A	C	C	A	B	B	A	B	C	B	B	C	B	A	C	A	C	A	B	C	B	A	C	B	C	3
4	B	B	A	A	A	C	B	C	C	A	C	B	A	C	B	C	A	A	A	C	C	B	A	A	C	4

DETECTING THE SEQUENCE

← —————————————————— UNITS —————————————————— →

	1	2	3	4	5	6	7	8	9	10	11	12	13	14	15	16	17	18	19	20	21	22	23	24	25	
1	F	F	T	T	T	F	T	T	T	F	T	T	T	T	T	F	T	F	T	T	F	F	T	F	F	1
2	T	F	T	T	F	F	F	T	T	T	F	F	T	T	T	T	F	F	F	F	F	F	F	T	T	2

DETECTING THE SEQUENCE

← —————————————————— UNITS —————————————————— →

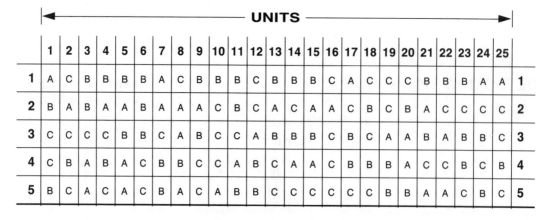

	1	2	3	4	5	6	7	8	9	10	11	12	13	14	15	16	17	18	19	20	21	22	23	24	25	
1	A	C	B	B	B	B	A	C	B	B	B	C	B	B	B	C	A	C	C	C	B	B	B	A	A	1
2	B	A	B	A	A	B	A	A	A	C	B	C	A	C	A	A	C	B	C	B	A	C	C	C	C	2
3	C	C	C	C	B	B	C	A	B	C	C	A	B	B	B	C	B	C	A	A	B	A	B	B	C	3
4	C	B	A	B	A	C	B	B	C	C	A	B	C	A	A	C	B	B	B	A	C	C	B	C	B	4
5	B	C	A	C	A	C	B	A	C	A	B	B	C	C	C	C	C	C	B	B	A	A	C	B	C	5

DETECTING THE SEQUENCE

UNITS

	1	2	3	4	5	6	7	8	9	10	11	12	13	14	15	16	17	18	19	20	21	22	23	24	25	
1	T	F	T	T	T	T	F	T	T	F	F	F	T	F	F	T	T	F	F	T	T	F	T	T	F	1
2	F	T	T	F	F	F	F	F	F	F	F	F	F	T	F	T	F	T	T	F	F	F	T	F	F	2

DETECTING THE SEQUENCE

UNITS

	1	2	3	4	5	6	7	8	9	10	11	12	13	14	15	16	17	18	19	20	21	22	23	24	25	
1	C	A	C	D	A	D	C	B	A	D	A	D	B	D	C	D	C	D	C	D	B	D	D	D	C	1
2	D	B	A	B	C	A	B	C	B	C	D	A	A	A	D	D	A	A	D	B	A	B	A	A	D	2
3	B	C	D	A	A	B	C	C	B	A	A	D	C	B	A	A	B	B	B	A	B	C	D	B	A	3
4	A	D	B	D	D	D	D	B	D	B	C	B	B	C	B	C	D	D	A	C	C	A	B	D	B	4
5	C	C	D	C	B	B	D	A	C	D	B	A	D	A	C	A	B	A	C	D	D	D	D	B	B	5

DETECTING THE SEQUENCE

UNITS

	1	2	3	4	5	6	7	8	9	10	11	12	13	14	15	16	17	18	19	20	21	22	23	24	25	
1	F	T	T	T	F	T	T	F	F	F	T	T	T	T	F	F	T	F	F	F	T	T	F	F	T	1
2	F	F	F	F	T	F	F	F	T	F	T	T	T	F	T	F	T	T	F	F	F	F	F	T	F	2

DETECTING THE SEQUENCE

UNITS

	1	2	3	4	5	6	7	8	9	10	11	12	13	14	15	16	17	18	19	20	21	22	23	24	25	
1	B	B	C	B	D	B	D	C	A	C	B	B	A	C	B	D	A	B	D	B	B	A	D	B	C	1
2	C	A	B	D	A	B	B	B	C	A	C	A	C	B	C	C	C	D	C	A	C	C	B	D	B	2
3	B	B	A	C	C	B	D	A	B	B	A	D	B	C	B	A	B	A	A	D	A	C	C	D	A	3
4	A	C	D	A	B	A	A	D	D	A	D	B	D	A	A	A	A	C	D	D	C	D	D	A	D	4
5	D	A	B	B	A	D	C	A	A	C	C	D	B	D	C	B	D	B	C	B	D	B	C	B	B	5

DETECTING THE SEQUENCE

UNITS

	1	2	3	4	5	6	7	8	9	10	11	12	13	14	15	16	17	18	19	20	21	22	23	24	25	
1	T	F	F	T	T	F	T	F	T	T	F	T	T	T	F	F	T	F	F	T	F	F	F	T	F	1
2	F	T	T	F	T	F	F	T	F	T	T	T	T	F	T	F	F	F	T	T	F	F	F	F	T	2
3	F	F	T	F	T	T	F	T	F	T	F	F	F	F	T	F	F	F	F	T	T	T	F	T	T	3

DETECTING THE SEQUENCE

UNITS

	1	2	3	4	5	6	7	8	9	10	11	12	13	14	15	16	17	18	19	20	21	22	23	24	25	
1	A	A	C	D	D	A	C	A	B	B	B	B	D	C	D	D	C	D	D	B	C	C	C	B	A	1
2	B	C	D	C	C	B	B	C	A	D	C	A	B	C	B	C	B	C	C	D	C	B	B	C	B	2
3	D	B	C	A	B	C	B	B	B	D	B	C	B	C	C	D	D	C	A	A	C	C	B	C	C	3
4	D	B	A	B	A	B	B	D	A	B	C	D	A	A	D	B	D	D	A	B	D	A	C	B	A	4
5	A	C	B	B	B	C	A	B	A	C	A	C	C	B	A	C	A	B	D	C	C	B	D	B	D	5

DETECTING THE SEQUENCE

ANSWER KEY — BOOK H
(For Pre-1990 Editions)

UNITS

	1	2	3	4	5	6	7	8	9	10	11	12	13	14	15	16	17	18	19	20	21	22	23	24	25	
1	T	T	T	F	F	F	T	T	F	F	T	T	T	T	T	T	T	F	T	T	T	F	T	T	T	1
2	F	F	T	F	F	F	T	T	T	T	T	F	F	F	T	T	T	F	F	F	T	T	F	T	T	2
3	F	T	T	F	T	F	T	F	F	T	F	F	T	T	T	T	T	F	T	F	F	F	T	T	T	3

DETECTING THE SEQUENCE

ANSWER KEY — BOOK H
(For Current Edition)

UNITS

	1	2	3	4	5	6	7	8	9	10	11	12	13	14	15	16	17	18	19	20	21	22	23	24	25	
1	C	B	C	D	C	C	B	B	C	B	C	C	A	A	A	B	C	B	B	B	B	D	B	C	D	1
2	D	C	B	C	B	A	A	C	D	B	C	C	D	A	B	A	A	D	C	A	B	C	B	D	B	2
3	B	A	C	A	A	D	C	B	B	A	B	A	D	C	A	C	B	B	C	C	B	C	D	B	D	3
4	D	D	D	C	C	D	C	B	C	C	D	D	C	B	A	A	B	C	B	C	A	A	C	A	C	4
5	A	B	B	D	B	C	A	A	A	B	D	D	B	B	C	D	A	C	C	D	C	C	A	B	B	5

IDENTIFYING INFERENCES

ANSWER KEY — PICTURE LEVEL

UNITS

	1	2	3	4	5	6	7	8	9	10	11	12	13	14	15	16	17	18	19	20	21	22	23	24	25	
1	B	A	B	B	A	B	A	A	B	B	B	A	B	A	B	B	B	A	B	A	A	B	A	A	B	1

	26	27	28	29	30	31	32	33	34	35	36	37	38	39	40	41	42	43	44	45	46	47	48	49	50	
1	B	A	A	B	B	A	B	B	A	B	A	A	B	B	A	B	B	A	B	A	B	B	A	B	B	1

IDENTIFYING INFERENCES

UNITS

1	2	3	4	5	6	7	8	9	10	11	12	13	14	15	16	17	18	19	20	21	22	23	24	25
B	B	A	B	A	B	A	B	B	A	A	B	A	B	B	B	A	B	A	A	B	A	B	B	A

26	27	28	29	30	31	32	33	34	35	36	37	38	39	40	41	42	43	44	45	46	47	48	49	50
B	A	A	B	A	B	B	A	B	B	B	A	B	A	A	B	A	B	B	B	A	B	A	A	B

IDENTIFYING INFERENCES

UNITS

1	2	3	4	5	6	7	8	9	10	11	12	13	14	15	16	17	18	19	20	21	22	23	24	25
C	B	B	A	C	B	A	C	C	A	B	C	C	B	A	C	B	C	B	A	B	C	B	C	A

26	27	28	29	30	31	32	33	34	35	36	37	38	39	40	41	42	43	44	45	46	47	48	49	50
B	B	A	C	B	A	C	C	B	A	C	B	B	A	A	C	B	C	C	B	A	C	B	C	A

IDENTIFYING INFERENCES

UNITS

	1	2	3	4	5	6	7	8	9	10	11	12	13	14	15	16	17	18	19	20	21	22	23	24	25	
1	C	B	C	B	C	B	A	B	C	C	C	A	C	C	A	C	B	A	C	B	A	B	C	B	A	1
2	A	B	C	A	B	A	C	C	A	B	B	C	B	A	B	A	A	C	C	A	C	C	B	A	C	2
3	B	C	B	C	C	C	B	B	C	B	B	B	C	B	C	B	C	B	A	C	C	B	B	C	B	3
4	C	A	A	B	A	C	C	B	A	A	A	C	B	B	B	C	B	C	C	B	A	A	C	B	A	4

UNITS

		1	2	3	4	5	6	7	8	9	10	11	12	13	
1	A	F	I	F	F	F	T	F	F	F	F	F	T	T	A
	B	T	F	I	I	I	I	T	T	F	I	I	I	I	B
	C	I	T	T	T	F	T	I	F	I	F	F	F	F	C
2	A	T	T	F	T	F	T	F	T	T	F	F	T	I	A
	B	F	F	I	I	T	I	F	I	I	F	F	I	F	B
	C	I	I	T	F	I	I	T	F	F	I	T	I	I	C
3	A	I	F	I	I	I	I	F	I	I	I	F	I	F	A
	B	F	T	I	F	F	F	T	F	T	T	T	T	I	B
	C	T	I	F	F	F	F	I	I	F	F	I	F	T	C
4	A	F	F	T	T	I	T	T	F	F	T	I	T	T	A
	B	T	F	I	I	I	I	I	F	T	T	I	T	T	B
	C	C	T	F	F	F	F	T	I	F	I	F	F	I	C
5	A	F	I	T	T	F	F	F	F	I	I	I	F	T	A
	B	F	T	T	I	I	T	T	F	T	T	T	F	I	B
	C	I	T	F	T	T	I	I	T	I	I	F	T	F	C

IDENTIFYING INFERENCES

ANSWER KEY — BOOK C

UNITS

		14	15	16	17	18	19	20	21	22	23	24	25	
1	A	T	T	T	I	F	T	T	F	I	T	T	T	A
	B	T	F	F	T	F	F	F	T	T	I	T	I	B
	C	I	I	I	I	T	T	T	I	T	F	I	F	C
2	A	I	I	I	T	I	T	F	I	F	F	F	T	A
	B	T	I	F	T	T	I	F	F	I	I	I	F	B
	C	F	T	I	F	F	F	T	I	T	T	T	I	C
3	A	T	F	T	F	T	I	I	F	T	T	F	I	A
	B	T	F	I	I	F	I	F	I	F	F	F	F	B
	C	I	I	F	T	F	T	T	T	T	T	I	T	C
4	A	F	T	F	F	T	F	F	F	I	I	I	F	A
	B	T	F	T	T	I	F	F	I	T	F	F	T	B
	C	I	I	T	I	F	T	I	F	F	I	T	I	C
5	A	F	T	T	T	F	I	I	F	I	F	T	T	A
	B	I	I	I	I	T	F	T	I	I	I	F	F	B
	C	T	I	I	T	I	T	I	T	T	T	I	T	C

IDENTIFYING INFERENCES

ANSWER KEY — BOOK D

UNITS

Unit		1	2	3	4	5	6	7	8	9	10	11	12	13	
1	A	F	T	T	T	T	T	T	F	T	T	T	F	F	A
	B	F	I	F	F	F	F	F	F	T	F	I	F	T	B
	C	I	—	I	I	I	I	—	T	—	—	F	—	T	C
	D	T	T	T	F	F	T	F	I	F	T	T	F	T	D
2	A	A	T	F	F	I	F	T	T	I	—	T	F	T	A
	B	I	F	I	F	—	—	I	F	F	F	F	F	F	B
	C	T	T	T	F	F	T	T	F	T	I	I	F	I	C
	D	T	F	F	T	I	T	F	I	T	T	F	F	T	D
3	A	I	T	I	T	T	I	F	I	F	F	T	T	T	A
	B	T	F	T	F	F	F	F	T	F	T	F	F	F	B
	C	T	F	F	T	T	F	I	F	T	T	F	F	F	C
	D	T	F	I	I	F	T	T	I	T	T	T	I	I	D
4	A	T	F	F	F	T	I	F	I	F	F	I	T	I	A
	B	I	F	F	F	F	F	F	T	I	I	T	F	T	B
	C	T	T	T	I	T	T	T	F	F	F	F	T	F	C
	D	F	F	F	F	F	—	I	T	T	T	F	T	T	D
5	A	F	I	F	F	T	F	F	T	I	I	F	T	T	A
	B	F	F	F	T	F	T	F	F	T	F	T	F	F	B
	C	I	T	I	—	I	—	F	F	F	T	—	T	I	C
	D	T	—	T	T	I	F	T	I	T	F	T	—	F	D

IDENTIFYING INFERENCES

ANSWER KEY — BOOK D

UNITS

Unit		14	15	16	17	18	19	20	21	22	23	24	25	
1	A	T	T	T	F	F	T	T	T	F	I	I	F	A
	B	F	F	F	F	T	F	F	F	F	T	I	T	B
	C	I	T	F	—	T	I	—	F	—	F	F	F	C
	D	T	I	I	T	F	F	F	T	T	F	F	I	D
2	A	A	F	F	T	I	T	F	F	T	—	F	T	A
	B	F	F	T	F	F	I	—	T	F	I	F	I	B
	C	I	F	F	T	F	F	F	C	T	F	F	T	C
	D	T	I	T	F	F	I	T	I	T	T	I	F	D
3	A	A	I	T	T	T	T	T	T	F	I	F	I	A
	B	T	I	I	I	T	I	I	I	F	I	F	T	B
	C	F	T	F	F	T	F	F	C	T	T	T	F	C
	D	I	I	T	T	F	T	T	F	T	F	T	F	D
4	A	I	—	T	T	F	F	T	I	T	I	F	F	A
	B	T	T	—	F	—	T	F	F	F	I	T	T	B
	C	F	F	I	F	F	T	T	T	—	F	T	I	C
	D	T	T	F	I	T	I	T	D	F	T	F	F	D
5	A	F	I	T	F	T	T	F	F	F	T	F	T	A
	B	B	T	F	T	T	—	T	T	F	F	T	F	B
	C	T	T	F	—	F	F	T	T	T	—	—	F	C
	D	T	F	T	F	I	F	F	D	I	T	F	T	D

IDENTIFYING INFERENCES

ANSWER KEY — BOOK E

UNITS 14–25

		14	15	16	17	18	19	20	21	22	23	24	25	
1	A	T	I	I	I	I	T	I	T	T	I	I	T	A
	B	T	I	F	F	F	F	F	F	F	F	F	T	B
	C	F	T	F	I	I	F	T	F	I	F	I	I	C
	D	I	F	T	I	F	T	T	I	I	I	I	T	D
2	A	I	I	I	I	I	I	I	I	I	I	I	I	A
	B	F	F	I	I	F	F	F	F	F	I	I	F	B
	C	T	T	T	F	T	T	T	I	T	T	I	F	C
	D	I	T	T	F	F	T	F	I	I	I	I	T	D
3	A	I	I	I	I	T	I	T	I	I	T	T	F	A
	B	F	T	I	I	I	F	F	F	F	I	I	I	B
	C	T	I	F	F	F	T	I	I	T	I	T	I	C
	D	I	F	T	I	F	I	F	T	F	F	I	T	D
4	A	A	F	T	T	F	F	F	I	I	I	F	T	A
	B	B	T	I	I	T	F	T	F	F	T	T	I	B
	C	C	I	F	F	I	I	I	I	I	F	I	F	C
	D	D	F	I	I	F	I	T	I	I	I	I	D	D
5	A	A	T	F	I	F	I	F	I	I	F	T	T	A
	B	B	F	I	I	F	F	T	T	F	F	F	I	B
	C	C	T	T	F	F	I	F	I	T	T	T	I	C
	D	D	I	T	F	I	T	T	I	I	I	T	F	D

IDENTIFYING INFERENCES

ANSWER KEY — BOOK E

UNITS 1–13

		1	2	3	4	5	6	7	8	9	10	11	12	13	
1	A	T	T	F	T	I	I	I	T	T	T	T	T	T	A
	B	F	F	T	T	I	F	F	I	I	F	F	F	I	B
	C	I	I	I	F	F	T	F	I	F	T	T	T	T	C
	D	I	I	F	I	F	T	I	I	F	T	I	I	I	D
2	A	A	F	F	T	T	I	I	I	F	T	I	F	I	A
	B	B	I	I	F	F	I	I	I	F	F	I	F	F	B
	C	C	T	F	I	I	T	T	I	F	I	F	T	I	C
	D	D	I	T	I	F	I	I	F	F	T	T	I	F	D
3	A	A	T	I	T	T	I	I	F	T	F	I	F	T	A
	B	B	I	I	F	T	T	I	I	T	F	I	T	I	B
	C	C	I	F	I	I	T	T	F	I	I	T	F	F	C
	D	D	F	T	F	F	F	I	F	F	T	F	I	F	D
4	A	A	T	T	T	F	I	I	I	F	F	T	I	F	A
	B	B	I	F	I	I	F	T	T	I	F	F	F	I	B
	C	C	I	I	I	T	T	I	I	F	I	I	F	F	C
	D	D	F	I	I	F	I	I	T	I	I	F	I	T	D
5	A	A	T	T	T	F	T	I	T	T	F	I	I	T	A
	B	B	T	F	I	F	F	I	T	F	T	F	F	F	B
	C	C	F	I	I	I	T	T	F	I	I	I	T	I	C
	D	D	I	I	I	I	I	I	F	I	I	I	T	I	D

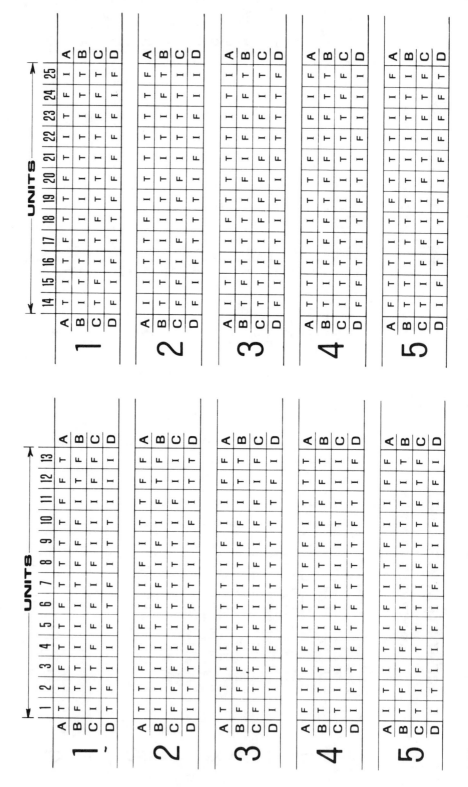

IDENTIFYING INFERENCES

ANSWER KEY — BOOK G

UNITS 14–25

IDENTIFYING INFERENCES

ANSWER KEY — BOOK G

UNITS 1–13

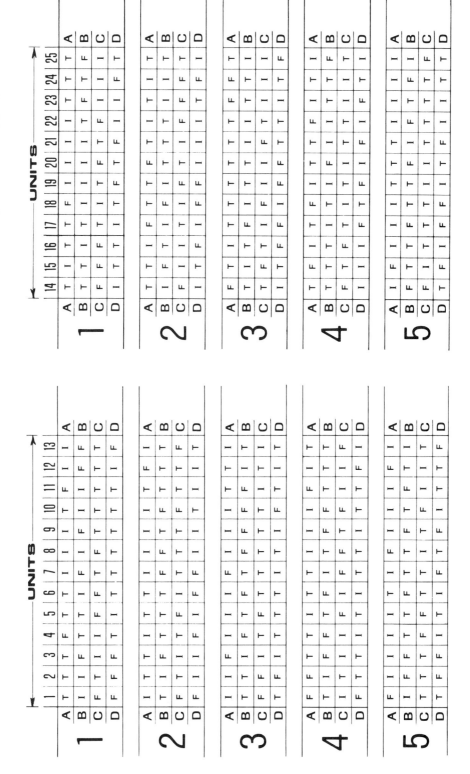

IDENTIFYING INFERENCES

ANSWER KEY — BOOK H

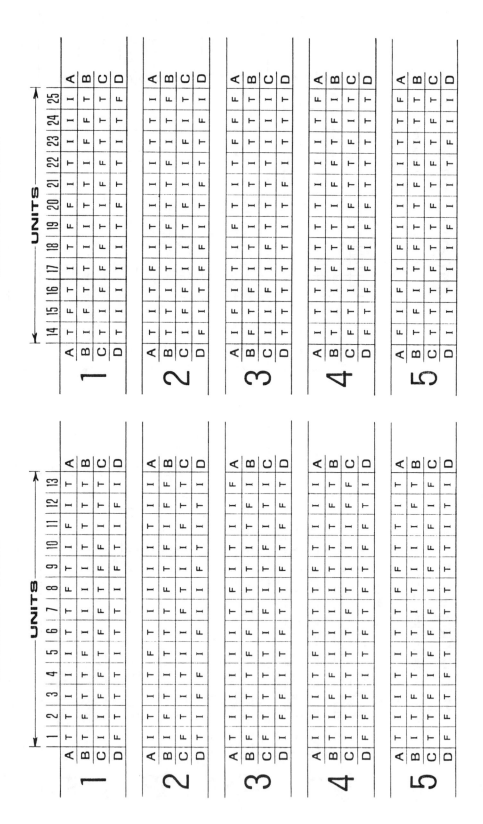

Reproducible Blackline Worksheets

WORKSHEET

Form 1

Detecting the Sequence—Picture Level–A

NAME _____

BOOK _____

UNITS

1	2	3	4	5	6	7	8	9	10	11	12	13	14	15	16	17	18	19	20	21	22	23	24	25

1

1

Locating the Answer—Preparatory Level

NAME _____ BOOK _____

UNITS

	1	2	3	4	5	6	7	8	9	10	11	12	13	14	15	16	17	18	19	20	21	22	23	24	25	
1																										1
2																										2
TOTAL																										TOTAL

WORKSHEET

Locating the Answer—Picture Level
Getting the Facts—Picture Level–Preparatory Level

NAME _____

BOOK _____

UNITS

	1	2	3	4	5	6	7	8	9	10	11	12	13	14	15	16	17	18	19	20	21	22	23	24	25	
1																										1
2																										2
3																										3
TOTAL																										TOTAL

Getting the Main Idea—B
Drawing Conclusions—B

Detecting the Sequence—C
Identifying Inferences—B

NAME _____

BOOK _____

	1	2	3	4	5	6	7	8	9	10	11	12	13	14	15	16	17	18	19	20	21	22	23	24	25	
1																										1
2																										2
3																										3
4																										4
TOTAL																										TOTAL

← UNITS →

WORKSHEET

Form 5

Locating the Answer—A
Getting the Facts—A–B
Detecting the Sequence—D–H

Getting the Main Idea—C–H
Drawing Conclusions—C–H

NAME _____

BOOK _____

← UNITS →

	1	2	3	4	5	6	7	8	9	10	11	12	13	14	15	16	17	18	19	20	21	22	23	24	25	
1																										1
2																										2
3																										3
4																										4
5																										5
TOTAL																										TOTAL

WORKSHEET

Form 6

Locating the Answer—B

Getting the Facts—C

NAME _____

BOOK _____

← UNITS →

	1	2	3	4	5	6	7	8	9	10	11	12	13	14	15	16	17	18	19	20	21	22	23	24	25	
1																										1
2																										2
3																										3
4																										4
5																										5
6																										6
7																										7
8																										8
TOTAL																										TOTAL

Using the Context—Prep-B   Locating the Answer—C–H
Getting the Facts—D–H

NAME _____ BOOK _____

UNITS

	1	2	3	4	5	6	7	8	9	10	11	12	13	14	15	16	17	18	19	20	21	22	23	24	25	
1																										1
2																										2
3																										3
4																										4
5																										5
6																										6
7																										7
8																										8
9																										9
10																										10
TOTAL																										TOTAL

Using the Context—C–H

NAME _____ BOOK _____

	◄──────				UNITS				──────►		
	1	**2**	**3**	**4**	**5**	**6**	**7**	**8**	**9**	**10**	**11**	**12**
1													**1**
2													**2**
3													**3**
4													**4**
5													**5**
6													**6**
7													**7**
8													**8**
9													**9**
10													**10**
11													**11**
12													**12**
13													**13**
14													**14**
15													**15**
16													**16**
17													**17**
18													**18**
19													**19**
20													**20**
TOTAL													**TOTAL**

Using the Context—C–H

NAME _____ BOOK _____

	13	14	15	16	17	18	19	20	21	22	23	24	25	
UNITS														
1														**1**
2														**2**
3														**3**
4														**4**
5														**5**
6														**6**
7														**7**
8														**8**
9														**9**
10														**10**
11														**11**
12														**12**
13														**13**
14														**14**
15														**15**
16														**16**
17														**17**
18														**18**
19														**19**
20														**20**
TOTAL														**TOTAL**

Identifying Inferences—C

NAME _____

		1	2	3	4	5	6	7	8	9	10	11	12	13		
1	A														A	
	B														B	
	C														C	
	TOTAL														TOTAL	
2	A														A	
	B														B	
	C														C	
	TOTAL														TOTAL	
3	A														A	
	B														B	
	C														C	
	TOTAL														TOTAL	
4	A														A	
	B														B	
	C														C	
	TOTAL														TOTAL	
5	A														A	
	B														B	
	C														C	
	TOTAL														TOTAL	
UNIT TOTAL															UNIT TOTAL	

UNITS

Identifying Inferences—C

NAME _____

		14	15	16	17	18	19	20	21	22	23	24	25		
1	A														A
	B														B
	C														C
	TOTAL														TOTAL
2	A														A
	B														B
	C														C
	TOTAL														TOTAL
3	A														A
	B														B
	C														C
	TOTAL														TOTAL
4	A														A
	B														B
	C														C
	TOTAL														TOTAL
5	A														A
	B														B
	C														C
	TOTAL														TOTAL
UNIT TOTAL															UNIT TOTAL

UNITS

Identifying Inferences—D–H

NAME _____ BOOK _____

← ——————————— **UNITS** ——————————— →

		1	2	3	4	5	6	7	8	9	10	11	12	13		
1	A															A
	B															B
	C															C
	D															D
	TOTAL															TOTAL
2	A															A
	B															B
	C															C
	D															D
	TOTAL															TOTAL
3	A															A
	B															B
	C															C
	D															D
	TOTAL															TOTAL
4	A															A
	B															B
	C															C
	D															D
	TOTAL															TOTAL
5	A															A
	B															B
	C															C
	D															D
	TOTAL															TOTAL
	UNIT TOTAL															UNIT TOTAL

Identifying Inferences—D–H

NAME _____ BOOK _____

← ——————— **UNITS** ——————— →

		14	15	16	17	18	19	20	21	22	23	24	25		
1	A													A	
	B													B	
	C													C	
	D													D	
	TOTAL													TOTAL	
2	A													A	
	B													B	
	C													C	
	D													D	
	TOTAL													TOTAL	
3	A													A	
	B													B	
	C													C	
	D													D	
	TOTAL													TOTAL	
4	A													A	
	B													B	
	C													C	
	D													D	
	TOTAL													TOTAL	
5	A													A	
	B													B	
	C													C	
	D													D	
	TOTAL													TOTAL	
UNIT TOTAL														UNIT TOTAL	

Following Directions—Picture Level–Preparatory Level
Getting the Main Idea—Picture Level–A
Drawing Conclusions—Picture Level–A
Identifying Inferences—Picture Level–A

NAME _____ BOOK _____

UNITS

1	2	3	4	5	6	7	8	9	10	11	12	13	14	15	16	17	18	19	20	21	22	23	24	25

1

1

26	27	28	29	30	31	32	33	34	35	36	37	38	39	40	41	42	43	44	45	46	47	48	49	50

1

1

Detecting the Sequence—B

NAME _____

← UNITS →

	1	2	3	4	5	6	7	8	9	10	11	12	13	14	15	16	17	18	19	20	21	22	23	24	25
1																									
2																									
TOTAL																									

	26	27	28	29	30	31	32	33	34	35	36	37	38	39	40	41	42	43	44	45	46	47	48	49	50
1																									
2																									
TOTAL																									

Following Directions—A-B

NAME _____

BOOK _____

UNITS

	1	2	3	4	5	6	7	8	9	10	11	12	13	14	15	16	17	18	19	20	21	22	23	24	25	
1																										1
2																										2
3																										3
TOTAL																										TOTAL

	26	27	28	29	30	31	32	33	34	35	36	37	38	39	40	41	42	43	44	45	46	47	48	49	50	
1																										1
2																										2
3																										3
TOTAL																										TOTAL

Working Within Words—Picture Level–Preparatory Level
Using the Context—Picture Level
Following Directions—C–H

NAME _____

BOOK _____

UNITS

	1	2	3	4	5	6	7	8	9	10	11	12	13	14	15	16	17	18	19	20	21	22	23	24	25	
1																										1
2																										2
3																										3
4																										4
TOTAL																										TOTAL

	26	27	28	29	30	31	32	33	34	35	36	37	38	39	40	41	42	43	44	45	46	47	48	49	50	
1																										1
2																										2
3																										3
4																										4
TOTAL																										TOTAL

WORKSHEET

Working Within Words—A

NAME _____

UNITS

	1	2	3	4	5	6	7	8	9	10	11	12	13	14	15	16	17	18	19	20	21	22	23	24	25	
1																										1
2																										2
3																										3
4																										4
5																										5
6																										6
TOTAL																										TOTAL

Working Within Words—A

NAME _____

UNITS

	26	27	28	29	30	31	32	33	34	35	36	37	38	39	40	41	42	43	44	45	46	47	48	49	50	
1																										1
2																										2
3																										3
4																										4
5																										5
6																										6
TOTAL																										TOTAL

Working Within Words—B

NAME _____

	1	2	3	4	5	6	7	8	9	10	11	12	13	14	15	16	17	18	19	20	21	22	23	24	25	
1																										1
2																										2
3																										3
4																										4
5																										5
6																										6
7																										7
TOTAL																										TOTAL

UNITS

Working Within Words—B

NAME

UNITS

	26	27	28	29	30	31	32	33	34	35	36	37	38	39	40	41	42	43	44	45	46	47	48	49	50	
1																										1
2																										2
3																										3
4																										4
5																										5
6																										6
7																										7
TOTAL																										TOTAL

Working Within Words—C–H

NAME _____

BOOK _____

UNITS

	1	2	3	4	5	6	7	8	9	10	11	12	13	14	15	16	17	18	19	20	21	22	23	24	25	
1																										1
2																										2
3																										3
4																										4
5																										5
6																										6
7																										7
8																										8
9																										9
10																										10
TOTAL																										TOTAL

Working Within Words—C–H

NAME _____

BOOK _____

UNITS

	26	27	28	29	30	31	32	33	34	35	36	37	38	39	40	41	42	43	44	45	46	47	48	49	50	
1																										1
2																										2
3																										3
4																										4
5																										5
6																										6
7																										7
8																										8
9																										9
10																										10
TOTAL																										TOTAL

SPECIFIC SKILL SERIES
CLASS RECORD SHEET

NAME		DETECTING THE SEQUENCE		DRAWING CONCLUSIONS		FOLLOWING DIRECTIONS		GETTING THE FACTS		GETTING THE MAIN IDEA		IDENTIFYING INFERENCES		LOCATING THE ANSWER		USING THE CONTEXT		WORKING WITHIN WORDS	
Last,	First	Letter	Average	Letter	Average	Letter	Average	Letter	Average	Letter	Average	Letter	Average	Letter	Average	Letter	Average	Letter	Average

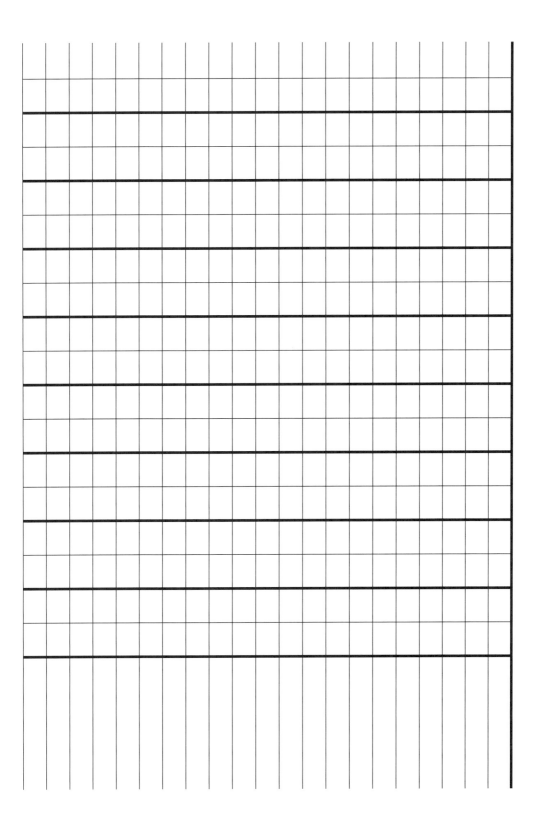

NOTES

NOTES

NOTES

NOTES